Mastering
MICROWAVE COOKERY

Marcia Cone and Thelma Snyder

Photographs by Michael Geiger

ILLUSTRATED BY GLENN WOLFF

SIMON AND SCHUSTER • NEW YORK

Copyright © 1986 by Marcia Cone and Thelma Snyder
All rights reserved
including the right of reproduction
in whole or in part in any form
Published by Simon and Schuster
A Division of Simon & Schuster, Inc.
Simon & Schuster Building
Rockefeller Center
1230 Avenue of the Americas
New York, New York 10020
SIMON AND SCHUSTER and colophon are registered trademarks
of Simon & Schuster, Inc.
Designed by Eve Kirch
Manufactured in the United States of America

3 5 7 9 10 8 6 4 2

Library of Congress Cataloging-in-Publication Data

Cone, Marcia.
Mastering microwave cookery.
Includes index.
1. Microwave cookery.   I. Snyder, Thelma.
II. Title.
TX832.C66   1986   641.5′882   86-10068

ISBN: 978-1-4516-6723-3

ACKNOWLEDGMENTS

Only when you author a book, do you find out how many other names deserve to be on the cover. One is Dave, who was there when Thelma needed him and who took over in her absence. It was Larry and Marie who always made room for Marcia. In this solitary business, the support of friends is beyond measure— you know who you are.

Beyond that, we'd like to thank Verle Blaha, whose knowledge of microwave ovens is surpassed only by his ability to explain them, and Marcia's college professor Karen Jamesen, who continues to take an interest in her work long after graduation. It was Harold McGee's well-researched *On Food and Cooking—The Science and Lore of the Kitchen* that clarified certain cooking principles for us.

The tremendous editorial efforts of Jane Low, Margery Tippie, Carol Siegel, and Kathy Guthmuller are appreciated, as are the artistic skills of designer Eve Kirch and illustrator Glenn Wolff. It was photographer Michael Geiger who captured the recipes in color and brought them to life.

And finally, we'd like to thank Barney Karpfinger, our literary agent, who suggested that we propose this book in the first place, and Carole Lalli, our editor at Simon & Schuster, who believed in it and helped shape it.

To our parents, who gave us the background
to attempt such a project
and the encouragement to carry it out

CONTENTS

Introduction 11
How to Use This Book 12

1. MICROWAVES—YOU KNOW MORE THAN YOU THINK 15
Campfires, Chili con Carne, and a Big Hug—A Lesson in Physics 17
Cooking with Sunlight—Basic Principles 20

2. RULES OF THUMB 41
Reheating Doneness 43   Rules of Thumb for Cooking Times 51
At-a-Glance Cooking Charts 55   Recipe Conversion 77

3. HOW TO CHOOSE UTENSILS 79
Specifics to Look for When You're in the Store 82   Cooking Utensils Inventory 83
Special Equipment 84

4. APPETIZERS AND SNACKS 87

5. SOUPS 115

6. EGGS AND CHEESE 139

CONTENTS

7. SAUCES, GRAVIES, AND SALAD DRESSINGS 167

8. PASTA, RICE, AND GRAINS 189

9. FISH AND SEAFOOD 209
Buying and Storing Fish and Seafood 212   Defrosting Frozen Fish and Seafood 213

10. MEAT 251
Buying and Using Meat 254   Defrosting Frozen Meat 256

11. POULTRY 335
Buying and Storing Fresh Poultry 338   Defrosting Frozen Poultry 339

12. VEGETABLES 389

13. FRUITS, FRUIT SAUCES, JELLIES, AND JAMS 485

14. CAKES, BREADS, AND MUFFINS 503

15. PIES, PUDDINGS, AND OTHER DESSERTS 537

16. CANDIES AND CONFECTIONS 583

17. MEAL PLANNING 601

18. TIPS 605

Index 611

INTRODUCTION

This book is about microwave cooking. It is also about coping with less leisure time than ever, about understanding a new method of cooking, and about being open to change.

The best part about this introduction is that you really don't have to read it to begin cooking—now isn't that a relief? Yet, if you have raised any of the following three questions, we have some answers for you. Otherwise, why not skip to page 12 for a brief overview of "How to Use This Book" and then jump right into the cooking? Here are the questions:

Will I make many mistakes when I start? Nothing can turn a good cook into a bad cook faster than the microwave oven.

New microwave owners who already are good cooks often dive into a recipe relying on a lifetime of conventional cooking knowledge. They may not have read the accompanying microwave manual or cookbook, or the instructions may not have been clear. The fault lies somewhere between the writer and the reader. That first attempt can make or break a potential microwave enthusiast, and as often as not a disenchanted cook is born. The microwave now falls into ill favor and is relegated to the tasks of boiling water and reheating leftovers.

Making mistakes is a fact of life. Based on our own experience, you can expect them. But don't let them make you feel inadequate. We came to microwave cooking through the love of good food, not the attraction of a high-tech appliance. Because of this, we have had to stumble through the rubbery chickens and reheated Styrofoam rolls to achieve the results we wanted. We came out on the other side, sometimes red-faced but wiser, and we can pride ourselves on recipes that don't sacrifice flavor to satisfy time. If it's not as good or better in the microwave, you won't find it here. And to help you in the beginning stages, look for the recipes with this symbol: ☼. They're the confidence-building recipes to spur you along.

How long will it take to learn about microwave cooking? One new microwave owner told us, "I've spent all my life learning how to cook, and now they've changed the rules."

Do you remember how frustrating it was to learn your first foreign language? It took hours of practice to put a subject, an object, and a verb into some sort of sensible order. The whole thing seemed hopeless until you were put to the test and through some happy circumstances you found yourself getting ready to go to Europe. Once there, while others were reduced to ridiculous gestures and pidgin English, you could order a *café au lait avec sucre* and actually get it. It took time to cultivate your new language, but speed and accuracy in an unknown land were the happy results.

We still have some trouble with foreign languages, so rest assured that microwave cooking is easier. You'll begin haltingly at first, as we all did, but progress from one day to the next can be exciting enough to spur you on. In summary: A little effort goes a long way.

Will people think less of my cooking abilities because I use the microwave? Why tell them? We like to bring out various dishes and surprise people later by telling them which was cooked in the microwave. "You mean that flaky piecrust came out of the microwave?" they'll say. One bite is worth a thousand words of explanation.

We have been told that serious cooks don't cook in the microwave. Our answer to that is that microwave cooks are just as serious, but busy. We describe this in the introduction to the Cakes, Breads, and Muffins chapter; leisurely afternoons once spent making special desserts were replaced by carpools and trips to the cleaners, not to mention full-time work. Conventional cooking is a luxury.

The microwave need not take love, fun, or quality out of cooking. There is nothing more satisfying than preparing a fragrant tomato sauce from scratch, or more loving than setting a homemade soup on the table. Neither of these pleasures need be banished by the microwave—if anything, they are now available to more people.

Our hope is that through this book you'll become comfortable with microwave cooking. We want to teach you how to cook as well as what to cook. We want you to be able to orchestrate a meal, as well as defrost the large casserole that you made last Tuesday.

When it comes to the technical parts, we'll present them in analogies that were fun for us to write, and hopefully more enjoyable for you to read and understand than some of the explanations you've heard before. All that we ask is that you approach this subject with a childlike curiosity. Quiet all the critical voices in your head that say "You'll never master this." You will! Leave all your preconceived notions outside your kitchen door and get ready to explore the wonderful eating in store for you with, of all things, the microwave!

How to Use This Book

Order and simplification are the first steps toward the mastery of a subject. The actual enemy is the unknown.
—Thomas Mann

Our goal in this book was to bring order and simplicity to microwave cooking. If you have the time, the best way to approach this book is to read Chapter 1, the microwave basics chapter, which lays the groundwork. But we admit, a bit reluctantly, that we often don't read cookbook introductions or basics because of our excitement to get into the recipes.

With that in mind, here is the least time-consuming approach to the book:

Chapter 2, "Rules of Thumb." You'll probably want to refer to this chapter when baking a potato, reheating or defrosting a casserole, doubling a recipe, or cooking any simple food (eggs, chops, vegetables, and so forth). "Rules of Thumb" is based on and sums up the basic microwave principles we discuss at length in Chapter 1, but here we rely on cooking charts, word pictures, and line drawings to convey most of our information quickly.

The Recipes. If you live strictly for sustenance, you can make any one of our recipes at random. The microwave cooking principles are in there but not trumpeted. Even if no principles are digested, you will be well fed. Go for the ☼ symbol indicating those recipes that are easily and successfully prepared—we call them confidence builders.

When you feel you've got more time, read the "teaching" recipes, which are always marked with a ✺ symbol. These are the recipes that make the microwave principles come alive. Recipes that use similar principles follow each teaching recipe.

1

MICROWAVES—
YOU KNOW
MORE THAN
YOU THINK

There is so much mystery surrounding microwaves and how they cook, and yet microwaves are not so different from energy forms that you already know. Sunlight, household electricity, CB radio waves, police radar, and microwaves are all identical in their fundamental nature. All are electrical and magnetic forms of energy that travel in waves (cycles) at the speed of light. Some cycle faster per second than others, and these can be measured on something called an "electromagnetic spectrum" (see page 18).

Campfires, Chili con Carne, and a Big Hug—A Lesson in Physics

Imagine that you are at the site of an open campfire with two friends. Each of you has brought a pot of chili to heat for dinner. One of you places a rock beside the flames to get it hot, and puts the chili pot on top of the hot rock. One suspends a pot of chili above the flames. The other finds space to hang a pot of chili beside the open flames. Do you know that all three chilies are cooking by different methods of heat transference?

The chili on the heated stone is being cooked by *conduction*, and can be likened to the way you cook on top of the stove, through direct conduction of heat from your stove heating element to the food in the pan. The chili that is suspended above the fire is being cooked by *convection*, or the hot air that rises from the flames. This is similar to the way that you cook in your conventional oven—the hot air heats the dish and the food. The chili that is being held to the side of the flames is not being cooked by rising hot air, or heat conduction, but by *radiation*, or the electromagnetic waves given off by the fire.

If you were to document the cooking techniques and times for the cooking of the three chilies—in effect, write three recipes—all would be different. Some would take more or less time; some would require more or less stirring. Likewise, trying to compare cooking times and techniques of oven cooking to cooking on top of the stove or cooking in the

ELECTROMAGNETIC SPECTRUM

Frequency	Use
0	Direct Current
50	Electrical Power
60	Electrical Power
400	Electrical Power Aircraft
20 000	Marine Weather
500 000	Marine Emergency and Call
830 000	AM Broadcasting WCCO
54 000 000	TV Broadcasting Channel 2
100 000 000	FM Radio
216 000 000	TV Channel 13
806 000 000	TV UHF Channel 69
2 450 000 000	**Microwave Ovens**
3 000 000 000	Marine Radar
10 000 000 000	Police Radar for Speed
22 235 000 000	Water Vapor Line
300 000 000 000	Upper Limit of Communication
1 000 000 000 000	Infrared Heat
423 000 000 000 000	Red
483 000 000 000 000	Orange
525 000 000 000 000	Yellow
576 000 000 000 000	Green
639 000 000 000 000	Blue
682 000 000 000 000	Indigo
732 000 000 000 000	Violet
1 000 000 000 000 000	Ultraviolet
1 000 000 000 000 000 000	X Rays
100 000 000 000 000 000 000	Gamma Rays

microwave doesn't always work. In other words, comparison of microwave cooking to the cooking you already know is limited.

Oh, and by the way—you don't need to be afraid of the term "radiation." By *Webster's* primary definition, radiation is "the emission and diffusion of rays of heat, light, electricity or sound." In fact, do you know that when you hug your spouse, child, or friend you are radiating 3,200 million cycles (megahertz), which can also be expressed as 3.2 terahertz. That is a much higher frequency than a microwave oven! The number was arrived at by determining the radiation frequency given off by the body at 92.8° Fahrenheit, and it falls into the infrared band on the electromagnetic spectrum.

Only when the frequencies reach the stage known as "ionizing" do the wavelengths become short enough and the frequency high enough to disrupt cell structure, which is true of X rays. It is a law of physics that a lower frequency won't cause this—and if you are concerned, think about it the next time you hug your mate.

Why Are Microwaves Better for Cooking Than Other Waves?

If the basic properties of all these types of electrical and magnetic waves are the same, couldn't we use almost any frequency, even CB radio bands or light, to cook food? Well, in fact we could, but the particular frequency of 2,450 million cycles (megahertz) with a 4½-inch wavelength has the best depth of penetration (¾ to 2 inches), coupling (or linking of energy), and rate of absorption by food than any other wavelength. And so the Federal Communications Commission has legally set aside this frequency for use in microwave ovens.

How Does Relating Microwaves to Sunlight Help Me Cook?

So far we have established that to compare conventional oven cooking with microwave cooking (or top-of-the-stove cooking, for that matter) is to compare apples, oranges, and grapes. But to compare sunlight to microwaves is to compare oranges to oranges.

"But how will knowing about sunlight help me to cook my Aunt Mary's casserole?" you ask. Understanding microwaves through the analogy of sunlight will tell you why you choose a glass casserole over metal, why stirring may be necessary, and why the casserole may have to stand before being served. While it won't tell you at what power or how long to cook the casserole—because that is related more to the properties of the food itself and how it should be treated—with each basic recipe, we give you reasons why we chose certain power settings and cooking times (see also "Demystification of Power and Cooking Times," page 20).

Based on all we have said, there are no easy rules for converting conventional recipes to microwave recipes, but Chapter 2, "Rules of Thumb," will give you some general guidelines. Also, you may find a recipe similar to Aunt Mary's casserole in this book, with similar ingredients and amounts, and follow those times and power settings.

> ### Demystification of Power and Cooking Times
>
> We are often asked something like, "If I have a recipe that cooks at 350°F for 35 minutes, how do I do that in the microwave?"
>
> There are no direct conversions, but here are some guidelines. A cooking temperature in a conventional oven, or a power setting in a microwave, is determined by the makeup of the food to be cooked. The more delicate the food, the lower the temperature or power.
>
> #### Description of Power Settings
>
> We have chosen to cook with four microwave powers:
>
> HIGH or full power (this is the effective cooking wattage or output listed in your oven manual)
> MEDIUM, which may be 50 to 70 percent of full power on your oven
> DEFROST, which may be 30 to 50 percent of full power
> LOW, which will be 10 to 20 percent of full power or the lowest power setting on your oven.
>
> (MEDIUM-HIGH will be 70 to 80 percent of full power, and is given as an option but not a standard, because it is less commonly found on older ovens.)
>
> We call the powers by name in the recipes, rather than percentage or number, because the percentages can vary on each oven as the manufacturers adjust for the amount of cooking wattage in their particular ovens. Without getting too technical, we think that if you can boil water, you can decide where these powers fall on your oven dial, even if the names are different. Follow this test:
>
> *Simple Oven Test:* Run the water from your kitchen faucet until it is cold, about 62°F (17°C). (If your water seems too warm, cool it down with an ice cube, removing the cube before the test. It is important that the water be close to this temperature to start.) Pour 1 cup cold tap water into a 1-cup glass measure. Make sure that you use fresh tap water with each test and cool down the glass measure to room temperature each time.

Cooking with Sunlight— Basic Principles

What you know about sunlight will help you to understand your microwave oven: Sunlight warms us through a glass window on a winter day. Sunlight is converted to heat on our skin, causing us to tan or turn red.

Cooking from the Outside to the Inside

When you are out in the sun for an hour, what part of you gets warm first—your skin or your internal organs? Let's put it another way. Imagine that you are eating an ice cream bar

1. HIGH power—Heat water on HIGH power for 2½ to 3 minutes. If the water boils within this time range, your oven is probably between 600 and 650 watts, and for HIGH power recipes, it will put you in the middle of the cooking time ranges. If it hasn't boiled in this time, your oven will be on the longer side of the cooking times; if the water has boiled much before 2½ minutes, you will be cooking for the shorter times on HIGH.
2. MEDIUM power—Heat water on MEDIUM power. If the water boils within 5 to 6 minutes, you know that you have chosen the right power, even though the name might not be MEDIUM. If it boils a minute or more before the range, choose a slightly lower power setting or decrease the cooking time. If it begins to boil a minute or more after the range, choose a *slightly* higher power if you have it.
3. DEFROST power—Heat water on DEFROST power for 8 to 10 minutes, and look at the description for MEDIUM power, adjusting upward or downward on your oven.
4. LOW power is only critical in raising yeast dough, and you'll find a specific test there (see page 530).

Cooking Times

There is always a range of cooking times given because everyone owns a different oven; HIGH power is anywhere between 500 and 750 watts in cooking output. This makes it confusing for all of us.

Rather than a number etched in stone, think of the cooking times as a guideline. Begin with the lowest times until you feel that you know your oven well enough to find the proper timing. Think of it as a movie review of one to four stars. In judging your oven you may not always agree with us on the high or low end, but we will always be consistent, so you'll know how to grade your own oven.

Doneness. The reason we have spent so much time on the doneness charts is that cooking times don't mean anything unless you know what you're looking for in the doneness of a product. If you use cooking times and doneness appearance in conjunction, you really can't go wrong.

---

outdoors on the sunniest day in August. Which will melt first—the outside or the inside? The outside, of course. The sun is converted to heat as soon as it hits the surface of the ice cream—just as microwaves are converted to heat the instant they are absorbed by the food. The 4½-inch wavelength penetrates ¾ to 2 inches into the surface of the food.

Water molecules are very good absorbers of microwaves; sugar and fat are better, salts even better. That's why foods high in fat and sugar will cook relatively faster than foods made primarily of water. Salt water boils faster than plain water, and meats or vegetables salted directly on their surfaces may overcook or develop dark spots.

Food molecules vibrate at 2,450 million times per second, which corresponds to the frequency on the electromagnetic spectrum. As you can imagine, this vibration creates a great deal of friction, which results in heat. It's just as if you were to rub your hands together 2,450 million times per second. The heat has to go somewhere, and by conduction it moves inside, layer by layer.

So why did people first say that microwaves cook food from the inside out? The first ovens were designed with a wavelength that cycled less often, 915 million cycles per second, and was longer in length, 12 inches, having a much deeper penetration into the food. That would be fine for large pieces of food, but the first foods to be tested were small items such as rolls and hot dogs. To the first observers, it may have appeared that the food was cooking as quickly on the inside as the outside and so they deduced that the microwaves were cooking from inside out. This was never the case.

Fact: Microwaves cook the food from the outside to the inside.

Energy Is Converted to Heat on the Food Surface Before Cooking Begins

When you eat an ice cream cone that the sun has melted, you aren't eating sunlight, are you? Of course not. The sunlight has already been converted to heat, and that is what melts the food.

Microwaves are also converted to heat the moment they contact the food. As with sunlight on the ice cream, the microwaves begin the heat conduction process on the surface of the food. This is also the reason that the air in a microwave oven doesn't get hot. All the heating takes place on the surface of the food first.

Fact: Microwaves are changed to heat the moment they come in contact with the food—the air is not heated.

Stirring—A Way to Even Up Cooking

We've already learned that foods cook from the outside to the inside. In that case, if you wanted to soften a frozen quart of ice cream, is there anything that you could do *mechanically* to speed up that softening process?

You could stir. When you saw the outside of the ice cream beginning to melt, you could stir those softened parts on the outside into the colder center and vice versa. The same thing can be done with ice cream, or any stirrable food, in the microwave oven.

Stirring is part of conventional cooking, too. When you're heating a soup or sauce on top of the stove, you'll stir to move the food over the bottom of the pan so that the heat building up on the bottom will be evenly distributed. In the microwave oven, the heat is building up on all of the outside surfaces, not just the bottom. Less stirring is generally required in microwave cooking than cooking on top of the stove. *There are certain occasions when stirring is critical at a particular time for the best cooking.* This is true of certain sauces or recipes made with eggs. Please heed those directions and otherwise stir when generally indicated.

If you want an example of how stirring will even up cooking, scramble two eggs in the microwave. Beat two eggs in a bowl and pour them into a glass custard cup about 3 inches in diameter. After just 35 seconds on HIGH power, you'll be able to see how the eggs are cooking approximately ¾ inch from the outside surfaces. If you continue to cook them without stirring, the outer edges will become overcooked. Ah, but if you stir once, you will have perfect eggs!

Fact: Stirring redistributes heat from the outer layers of the foods to the inner layers. It is critical to stir all sauces, puddings, quiche fillings, and egg-based dishes exactly where indicated. Stirrable foods such as vegetables, stews, and casseroles will cook more quickly and evenly when stirred.

Food Arrangement

We have already said that foods begin cooking around the outside of the dish first. For this reason foods that can't be stirred should be arranged with the thicker pieces, such as stalks of broccoli or the thicker portion of chicken legs, to the outside. The end result will be more even cooking.

Fact: Arrange foods with the thicker (longer cooking) portions to the outside, for more even cooking.

Rearrangement

Accompanying the above rule, foods cannot always be arranged as ideally as possible, so they need to be repositioned or shifted around so that all get an equal amount of energy.

Fact: When indicated, rearrange individual dishes, or food items in a dish, so that all receive an equal amount of energy.

Turning Over

The best way to get a good tan is to turn over in the sun at least once, so that both front and back receive an equal amount of sun.

In a microwave oven, large, high pieces of meat such as turkey, beef, pork, lamb, and some chops and chicken pieces, which can't be stirred, are turned over for the same reason.

In some cases, the hot liquid in the bottom of the dish will transfer additional heat to the surface of food sitting in it, causing it to cook faster. Turning over adjusts for this also.

Fact: As you turn over to get a more even tan, turn larger pieces of food over to cook more evenly.

Rotating Dishes

Have you ever noticed that the sunlight you receive in May is stronger than in August? That is because the position of the sun in relation to the earth in May causes the sun's rays to hit the earth's surface at a more direct angle.

We will use this as a loose translation of how microwave ovens cook in what is known as a cooking pattern. Each oven is designed with a different method of transmitting the microwaves. Some ovens have a stirrer blade in the top that resembles a metal ceiling fan. As a ceiling fan moves air, this stirrer blade moves the microwaves because it is made of a reflective metal—plastic would not accomplish the same thing. Some ovens have antennas that direct the energy as they move. And there are more systems.

Each manufacturer designs that stirrer blade or antenna differently in conjunction with the oven cavity to achieve the best cooking pattern. You have heard of May-December marriages, a marriage of two ages that don't seem to mesh. Some ovens are May-August microwave ovens with fast cooking areas, often called "hot spots," and slower cooking areas, called "cold spots."

Microwave oven designs are improving all the time, but because microwave ovens have been on the consumer market for almost twenty years, there are still some ovens that cook unevenly. If you have an oven that cooks unevenly you will have noticed faster cooking areas on bacon strips, or on a food that can't be stirred, such as a cake. Some ovens have a carousel or rotating plate in the bottom of the oven to move the food through the energy, and thus aid in even cooking.

If you find that your oven doesn't heat evenly, we recommend that you rotate the dish where indicated. Rotating means turning a dish in a circular fashion, clockwise or counterclockwise, to reposition it in the oven. It is done with foods where stirring is impossible for the redistribution of heat: examples are cake, bread, and certain casseroles.

We write our recipes keeping in mind that some people may have to rotate their food. That way everyone will be able to reproduce the recipes. If you find it unnecessary to rotate dishes in your oven, just ignore those instructions.

Fact: If you have a May-August oven with fast and slow cooking areas, rotate those foods that can't be stirred, rearranged, or turned over.

Starting Temperature

Take that ice cream bar again. In fact, take two. One that has been frozen solid in the back of your freezer and one that is not quite as cold in the front. If you put both out into the sun, which one will begin to melt first?

The one that wasn't as cold. Sunlight has to raise the food temperature to a certain degree before it melts. The colder the food is to begin with the longer this process will take. In microwave cooking, two foods of identical amounts, character, and density (mass per volume) will cook at different rates of speed if their starting temperatures are different. This is something to keep in mind when preparing a recipe.

Fact: Two identical foods will cook at dif-

ferent speeds if their starting temperatures are different. The colder food cooks more slowly; the warmer food cooks faster.

If you have just walked into the house from a trip to the grocery store that ended in a few more stops before you got home, the once refrigerated and frozen foods are now warmer. If you went to cook them in the microwave at this point, you would have to reduce the cooking time. A microwave recipe assumes that you are cooking the food from its normal storage temperature. If not, as with the warmed-up groceries, you may find overcooking to be a problem.

Likewise, a food such as condensed soup or chicken broth that is normally stored at room temperature will take longer to heat up if you're taking it from an open can that has been in the refrigerator.

Fact: Recipes are written assuming that foods are being taken from their normal storage state: refrigerated, frozen, or room temperature. Time adjustments should be made if this is changed.

Is It Helpful to Know Your Oven's Cooking Pattern?

Some people feel that it is. We would agree, in some cases. A poor cooking pattern or an oven that cooks unevenly can always be corrected in stirrable foods by doing nothing more than stirring. Cakes, custards and casseroles, or any food that can't be stirred, will be more sensitive to an oven's uneven cooking pattern. In these cases, it can be helpful to know where the oven might be cooking a little bit faster, so that you can rotate more often. If your oven cooks evenly, you can eliminate rotating entirely.

So while the test we give below is not foolproof or exhaustive (most oven manufacturers test many types of food that cover many heights within the oven), we have found it helpful.

To Test: In the supermarket's refrigerated case you'll find a 15-ounce package of piecrusts with two 9-inch piecrusts inside. We have found these most satisfactory to test because of the high fat content that is uniformly mixed throughout the dough. It is the fat that quickly absorbs microwaves in a short time. The uniform refrigerated temperature and thickness of the dough are also important in standardizing the results.

Remove one of the refrigerated crusts from the cellophane wrapper and open it onto a piece of wax paper. Place paper and dough in the microwave. Cook on HIGH for 7 minutes.

The top of the dough will give you an indication of whether the oven is cooking evenly. An even-cooking oven will produce an evenly colored pie dough, with no outstanding brown spots. Now turn the cooked dough over. Because of the heat that builds up between the dough and the oven shelf, more brown spots will be visible, even on the dough that appeared evenly cooked on top. These brown spots indicate the "hot spots" or the places an oven seems to cook the fastest. Don't panic if you see quite a few of them! A high-fat pie dough will exaggerate them more than most foods. Just be aware of those particularly fast cooking areas.

Unless you have real problems with recipes that can't be stirred, don't dash out to buy all sorts of gadgets that supposedly help the food cook more evenly. The only time you will need help is with cakes, and that will just be a matter of a couple of rotations.

> ### Starting Temperature and Storage Temperature... One and the Same
>
> Have you ever asked yourself: "How did I overcook my fish when I followed the instructions?" or "Why did it take so long to cook those vegetables?" If you keep your onions in the refrigerator, or leave your fish on the kitchen counter for 20 minutes before you cook, the starting temperature could be the reason why.
>
> Look at the storage temperatures below. We're not asking you to change the way you store or cook foods, just make adjustments in your cooking times for any differences.
>
> *Frozen:*
> Packaged vegetables and fruit
>
> *Refrigerated temperature foods (42°F):*
> Fresh meat, poultry, and fish
> Fresh greens and most vegetables
> Leeks, scallions
> Summer squash
> Eggs
> Milk
> Cheese
> Butter
>
> *Room temperature:*
> Garlic, onions
> Tomatoes
> Potatoes, sweet potatoes,
>   root vegetables,
>   winter squash
> Tomato paste, canned tomatoes
> Dry beans
> Canned broth

Surface Area of Food

Cooking in the wok was developed because, historically, parts of China had little wood available for fuel. Food had to be cooked as quickly as possible to conserve this fuel, and one of the shortcuts was to cut the food up into small pieces, to expose as much surface area as possible to the heat.

The more surfaces exposed in microwave cooking, the quicker it will cook. One whole carrot will take less time to cook in the microwave if the carrot is cut in half. It will take even less time when it is thinly sliced or grated. This applies to any foods that can be cut into pieces.

When a food is cut into pieces, it is important to make those pieces as equal in size as possible to ensure even cooking.

Fact: Wok cooking teaches us that the more surface area exposed on a food by cutting it into pieces, the quicker it will cook.

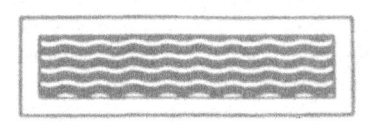

Dishes Get Hot from Heat Conduction from the Food, Not from Microwave Energy

Did you ever sit near your living-room window on a cold winter day and find that you were warmed by the radiant heat of the sun? If you reached out to touch the glass, you would find that it was cool. The sunlight was being absorbed by you or the window seat, and very little was being absorbed by the window.

This is what happens in a microwave oven. The microwaves pass through the cooking dish to heat the food. If the dish becomes hot, it is because the heat is being conducted to it from the food that it touches. This is particularly evident when you heat a cup of coffee. The cup may become warm, but the handle, which has no contact with the food, remains cool.

Here are two other reasons that a dish may become hot: (1) if a dish is designed to absorb heat (see Browning Dishes, page 85, or Simmerpots, page 86), or (2) if a ceramic, often handmade, dish contains metal flecks in the clay or glaze, it may link microwaves (coupling) to produce heat.

Sometimes food seems to cool off more quickly from a microwave oven than from a conventional oven. Because there is no hot air in the oven to keep the dish warm, certain foods will cool off more quickly. Other foods, such as potatoes, stews, and foods that hold heat well will remain hot long after they have stopped cooking. It will be helpful to tent the larger roasts and poultry with foil during standing time to retain as much heat as possible. For more, see Standing Time, page 35.

Fact: Microwave energy doesn't heat the cooking dishes, but hot foods will transfer heat to the sides of the dishes that they touch, although not the handles.

Covers

If you wanted to go out in the sun but remain cool, how would you dress? Probably by wearing as little as possible, or if you had to wear more clothes, they would be very loose.

In microwave cooking, coverings retain heat and moisture, too. The tighter the cover the more heat and steam retained, which causes the food to cook faster and the surface to remain moister. A tight lid or plastic wrap will accomplish just this. Wax paper, on the other hand, is a loose covering and will only partially retain steam for faster, more even cooking without making the surface wet. No covering will allow moisture to evaporate. Paper towels will soak up some of the moisture on the surface and keep it driest of all. Before applying a cover, decide whether steaming will enhance the final outcome of the food.

Fact: Covers retain moisture and heat in microwave cooking for steaming and for quicker and sometimes more even cooking.

Covers

The primary purpose of a cover is to retain moisture. This adds steam heat to the microwave vibration of molecules so that the total cooking speeds up and causes certain foods to cook more evenly.

Before you cover, you must ask yourself: Will steam heat enhance this food? If the answer is yes, how much steam is beneficial, a little or a lot?

We indicate one of the following terms in our recipes. If no term is indicated, as with sautéing onions or garlic, you can cover or not cover, as you wish.

Cover tightly means to cover with a casserole lid or plastic wrap that has been folded back on one corner. Even a plate that fits the casserole is good for this. Foods that would normally be steamed, boiled, or braised are best cooked with this cover.

It is best to turn back a corner of the plastic wrap to keep the wrap from splitting as steam builds up. This will enable you to use the plastic wrap over again if you need to stir halfway through cooking. When more stirring or checking is involved, as with stews, soups, or pasta sauces, we recommend a lid. Always open a tight cover away from you to prevent steam burns. *Foods that benefit: vegetables, fruits, casseroles, stews, less tender cuts of meat, thick pieces of fish, some shellfish, and soups.*

Cover with wax paper means to lay the wax paper loosely on top of a dish. If your oven has a turntable, you may need to tuck the wax paper under the dish to keep it secure.

Wax paper aids in the speed and evenness of cooking by keeping in some steam and protects the oven from spatters. Because wax paper can't be formed to fit the dish, it allows quite a bit of steam to escape, which keeps the food from becoming too soggy. *Foods that benefit: chicken parts, pork chops, individual plates of food to be reheated.*

Cover with paper towel means to lay a paper towel on top of the food in the dish. This, like wax paper, should be tucked under the dish when your oven has a rotating turntable. It tends to fall off the dish, otherwise.

Paper towels absorb extra fat or moisture that comes as a result of cooking certain foods. Choose unrecycled paper towels. Recycled paper towels may have metal flecks that could spark, particularly when drying seeds or refreshing potato chips. *Foods that benefit: bacon strips cooked to be dry, some fish fillets and scallops (which exude water), rolls to be reheated (to keep bread surface dry while still retaining some moisture).*

Cook uncovered applies where a drier cooked surface is desired, or when a liquid needs to be evaporated. *Foods that benefit: Mushrooms, roast beef, turkey, cakes, and pastry crusts.*

Metal

What would happen if you were to try to make tea outdoors, using the radiant energy of the sun, but you chose to put the water and tea bags into a shiny metal container, with a shiny metal lid. Would the water get hot? No.

The shiny metal would reflect the sunlight and the water would not get hot, ever.

Metal also reflects microwaves, making it a good material to contain the microwaves in the oven walls. That is why microwave ovens have a metal or painted metal interior, and a metal bottom below a glass or ceramic shelf. But metal as a cooking utensil would slow down or stop microwave cooking completely, making it very inefficient.

The real question about metal usage comes from some microwave oven manufacturers who feel that if an oven is operated empty (with no food to absorb the energy) or if metal is used in the oven, microwaves could be reflected back to the magnetron tube, causing it to heat up and become damaged. It has been proven that this is not a real threat, but it is always best to check your oven warranty first and make sure you are covered.

Fact: Shiny metal reflects sunlight. Metal also reflects microwaves and is not a good material for microwave dishes.

The Browning Equation: What Will Brown and Why?

Protein (amines) + Sugar + Heat = Brown

When heat is added to the proteins and sugars found in animal or plant foods, a chemical reaction or "association" occurs that is known as browning. That is why a piecrust takes on a golden appearance in the oven, or a roast beef browns. It is this same reaction that gives a fried egg a brown edge if it is cooked on too high a heat.

In microwave cooking, the only heat generated is on the surface of the food. Often the food's surface cools down considerably by the evaporation of steam, which acts the way perspiration does in cooling off your skin. The process doesn't help browning much though; browning requires high heat.

The only way to make browning possible in the microwave is to increase the surface heat of the food sufficiently, so that browning can occur. This happens in these instances:

1. *Sufficient cooking time:* A roast beef will begin to brown after 10 to 15 minutes on HIGH power because more heat builds up on the surface than can be cooled off by evaporation.
2. *High enough fat content:* In a roast beef,

(Continued)

the fat of the marbled meat melts and bubbles up to the surface during cooking. Because fat can get up to almost 400°F (where water boils away at 212°F), it can raise the surface temperature of the meat. That is also why bacon browns so well in a short time. It is very fatty and gets hot quickly.

3. *Adding a hot surface to the food:* A browning dish reaches almost 560°F when heated, a temperature high enough to cause an association between protein and sugar. (For more, see Browning Dishes, page 85.) This will brown bread products (pizzas, grilled sandwiches, or scones) that wouldn't brown any other way.

4. *Increased sugar:* Bacon also has sugar added during the curing process that can associate with the protein under high heat to enhance browning. The same thing will happen to a meat that has been glazed during cooking with a mixture that contains sugar. Sugar alone won't do it, it only helps to brown with the protein and heat already present.

Adjusting the Browning Equation

Based on what we know about sugar, fats, and surface temperature, we can adjust the browning equation with a few well-placed marinades, fats, coatings, or a browning dish.

Only in the case of cakes, breads, and fish, where there is too much moisture evaporating during cooking, does it become impossible to get a natural brown color. The only way that it can be corrected is with the addition of dark ingredients, such as chocolate, or a brown dish coating that sticks to the surface of the cake. Here are some corrections for the browning equation:

Hamburgers—browning grill adds dry heat; soy sauce and Kitchen Bouquet add coloring

Poultry—marinade adds more sugar, as do honey glaze, sugar-fruit glaze; dipping skinned chicken in butter or oil and coating with crumbs (adds fat and starch), Shake 'n Bake (has browning agent)

Fish/Shellfish—paprika (coloring), mayonnaise (thick coating containing egg protein and fat to raise temperature)

Pastry Crust—cooked on HIGH will be lightly golden because of high fat

Pizza, Tortillas—browning grill

Breads/Cakes—make with darker grains or chocolate, toasted nut or coconut coatings; upside-down cakes with brown sugar toppings

Sandwiches—browning grill, or toast bread first

When Is the Conventional Oven Good to Use?

Anytime that you want a browned-crisp coating on a casserole or cheese-topped dish, or anytime that you want crisping, where the browning grill isn't appropriate. An example of this is the crisping that results when a chicken or turkey is popped into a preheated conventional oven at 500°F for approximately 5 to 15 minutes.

Ribs or chicken wings can be crisped up nicely under the broiler for 5 to 10 minutes at the end of cooking.

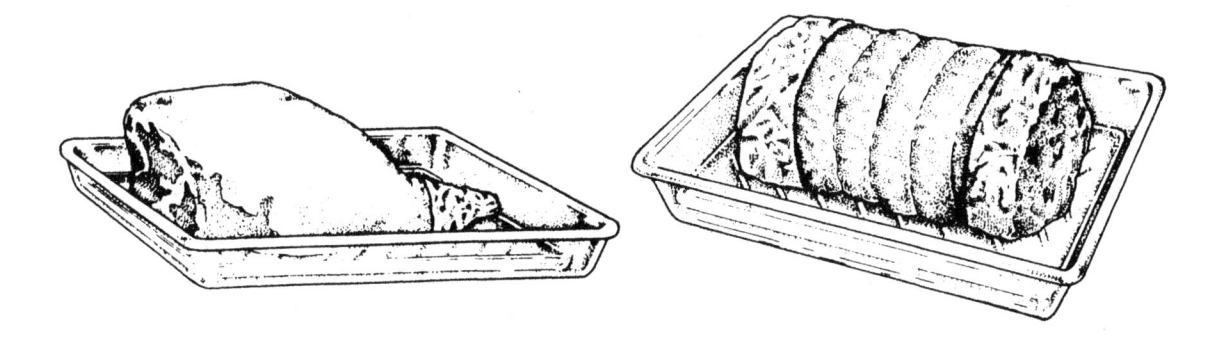

Metal as a Shield

Shiny metal reflects sunlight. If you have ever seen someone with a metal nose shield, or someone holding a metal reflector to direct the rays to their face, you have observed this in action.

Metal reflects microwaves from whatever food it covers. This can be an advantage to keep thinner legs or wings on a turkey from overcooking. Foil can be wrapped around these parts, halfway through cooking, so that the whole turkey will be cooked evenly. The ends of roasts and the corners of brownies baked in a square dish can be protected with metal foil in the same way.

Fact: The way that a metal shield keeps your nose from getting sunburned, is the way that metal protects the protruding areas of food it covers from overcooking.

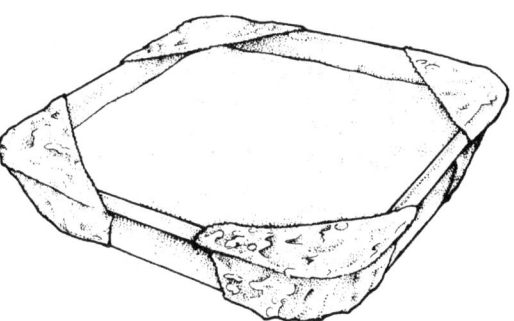

Sparking and Arcing

A browning dish is a specially designed dish with metal strips in it that cause microwaves to couple or link, which produces an electrical current. On top of that, the dish is treated with a metal coating that is resistant to the electrical current, causing this area to heat up. We liken it to toaster coils, which get hot because they are also resistant to the electricity that runs through them.

Coupling is used to advantage in a browning dish, but what would happen if you had a metal twistie, made of high-resistance steel, whose ends were twisted to the space of 1 and 2 inches apart (about half a wavelength)? The microwaves would be coupled and the steel twistie would get hot and burst into flames.

Dishes with metal trim, although circular, also couple microwaves which may cause the trim to discolor or break off. Foil ends that are not smoothly wrapped over an area when food is shielded will do the same thing. Dish trims are usually gold or silver, which are low-resistance metals, as is aluminum foil. In other words, there may be sparking from the coupled waves, but there will be no heat. And oddly enough, with dishes having metal trim, sparking may not even occur if there is enough food on the plate to absorb the microwaves. But why take chances?

Metal TV trays, no more than ¾ inch in depth, with a substantial volume of food in them, will not arc. The food will absorb the microwave energy and there are no "antennalike" areas to link the microwaves. Arcing only occurs if the metal tray is placed next to the metal walls and you create the possibility of coupling the energy. It should be noted, though, that the food in a metal tray will take longer to cook because the microwaves can only heat it from the top.

Fact: To avoid arcing or sparking, avoid dishes that have metal trim, metal skewers that touch, a metal twistie on a plastic bag, or metal foil not folded smoothly over a dish corner. Place metal TV trays in the center of the oven.

The Volume Principle: Add More Food—Add More Cooking Time

The Volume Principle is probably one of the most difficult principles to explain. The best way to discuss it might be to imagine that there are only 100 microwaves in the oven at a time (this is too simplistic, but bear with us). If one baked potato is placed in the oven, all 100 waves go to that potato and it cooks in 4 minutes. If two potatoes are put in the oven, the 100 waves are now divided 50-50 between the potatoes. The potatoes take 8 minutes. Add two more and you increase the cooking time again, but not by double.

This is where a microwave oven is not at all like a conventional oven. There is no residual heat built up in the oven by long periods of cooking which causes ten baked potatoes to cook in the same time as one.

Fact: The more food you add to the oven, the more time it will take to cook.

The Volume Principle

The Volume Principle refers to raw food items, such as corn on the cob or bacon, not recipes (for Doubling Recipes, see next page). So when you want to increase the number of potatoes from one to four, how do you quickly determine the cooking time?

Step 1: Determine the cooking time for one food item, be it a whole vegetable, a strip of bacon, a chicken cutlet.

Step 2: To cook two of that food item, double the cooking time.

Step 3: To increase the food items by more than two, start by doubling for the second item (Step 2), but for each additional food item beyond two, add only half the cooking time of the first food item.

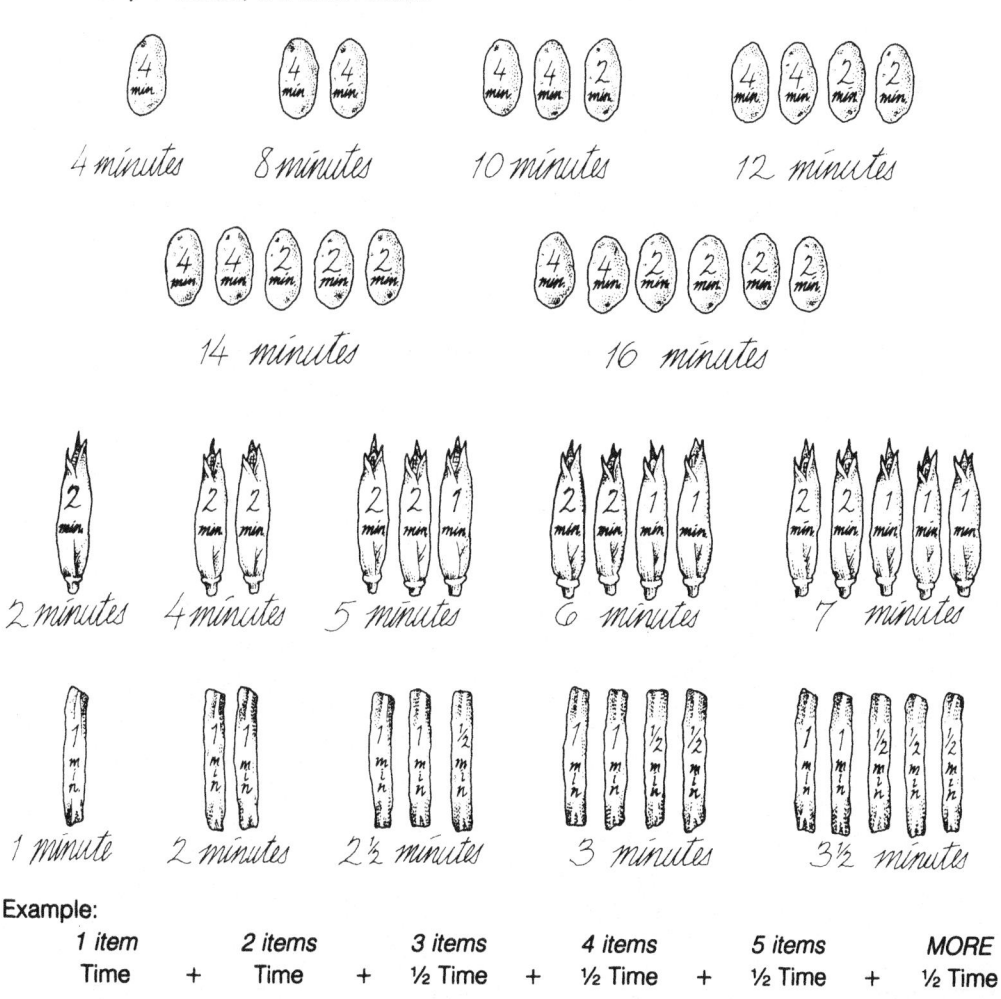

4 minutes — 8 minutes — 10 minutes — 12 minutes

14 minutes — 16 minutes

2 minutes — 4 minutes — 5 minutes — 6 minutes — 7 minutes

1 minute — 2 minutes — 2½ minutes — 3 minutes — 3½ minutes

Example:

1 item	2 items	3 items	4 items	5 items	MORE
Time +	Time +	½ Time +	½ Time +	½ Time +	½ Time

Doubling Recipes = Time and a Half

When doubling casserole recipes, soups, stews, or vegetables, double ingredients and add half the original cooking time. This only applies to recipes, not individual foods, which are covered by the Volume Principle on the previous page. Cakes, pies, bar cookies, lasagna, and breads are exceptions to this rule, because they do not double well.

Examples:

One power setting and time in a soup, casserole, or vegetable:

2 cups vegetables — 6 minutes

4 cups vegetables — 9 minutes

Time + ½ Time = 1½ Time

Two power settings and times in a stew (HIGH to MEDIUM):

casserole — 30 minutes
high 10 minutes
med. 20 minutes
─────────────
30 minutes

double casserole — 45 minutes
high 15 minutes
med. 30 minutes
─────────────
45 minutes

(Time #1 + ½ Time #1) + (Time #2 + ½ Time #2) = 1½ Time #1 + 1½ Time #2

NOTE: When doubling stews, double all ingredients except the liquid, which is only increased by half the original amount.

Cutting Recipe in Half

When reducing a recipe by half the ingredients, cut the cooking time in half. A smaller dish must be used to keep the ingredients from spreading out too much and overcooking.

Exceptions to this are cakes, pies, bar cookies, and breads.
Example:

Original Recipe
2 quart casserole
10 minutes

One half Original Recipe
1 quart casserole
5 minutes

Time − ½ Time = ½ Time

Standing Time

How many times have you been out in the sun for a few hours, gone indoors thinking you were only slightly pink and found later that your skin felt as if it were on fire?

You had misjudged your condition based on appearances because full color often doesn't show up until some time later. For our purposes we'll call the time after exposure standing time.

In the time since you had left the sun, your body temperature was raised by the heat you absorbed and you felt it more intensely on your skin.

When it comes to microwave cooking, people often misjudge the doneness of the food because they haven't factored in the standing time, which is the time that the food continues to cook without any microwave energy.

Often we call for covering the food during standing time to hold in the heat. We talk about tenting a food with aluminum foil (a reflective material) for the best results.

Somewhere the idea got started that standing time is necessary to let the microwaves out of the food. This is not true! There are no microwaves in the food, just as there is no sunlight in your body after you have spent a day in the sun.

Fact: Just as your skin becomes darker after you have left the sun, most foods continue to cook for a period of time without any microwave energy. The food can stand inside or outside of the oven during this time.

Standing Time

After the microwave cooking time is completed, almost all foods require a standing time to finish cooking through.

Where is the best place for standing? Standing can be done in the oven—if it is turned off, of course—or outside of the oven on the kitchen counter. The important factor is that it stand on a flat, solid surface to help insulate the heat within the food to complete its cooking job.

Why is pastry different? The guiding principle here is that we are aiming for a dry crust, not a soggy one. That is why we tell you to let it stand on a cooling rack so that moisture can escape.

How is standing time determined? The foods with the longer standing times have one or more of these properties:

1. large weight in relation to size
2. large foods, not cut into pieces
3. a long cooking time

Here are some examples:

Food	Cooking Time	Standing Time
10- to 16-pound turkey	1¼ to 2 hours	15 to 20 minutes
3-pound roast beef	18 to 21 minutes	5 to 10 minutes
Acorn squash	6 to 8 minutes	5 minutes
1 pound fish	2½ to 5 minutes	2 minutes
1 pound carrots, thinly sliced	4 to 5 minutes	1 minute
1 egg	35 seconds to 1 minute	1 minute

NOTE: If the standing time is very little—in other words, no longer than it would take to get from the oven to the table—we may not mention any standing time.

In most cases we ask you to keep the food covered on a flat surface while standing, so that all the heat will be directed back into the food. In the case of the larger cuts of meat (roasts and turkeys), we ask you to tent the food as shown here.

Safety

Microwave oven safety is something many people talk about but few seem to understand. Let us quote someone who knows. Dr. James A. Van Allen, discoverer of the radiation belts around the earth, said this:

> [In my judgment, the likelihood] of microwave oven hazard is about the same as the likelihood of getting a skin tan from moonlight.
>
> There is not a shred of scientific evidence that microwaves at such low intensities as from a microwave oven have any effect whatever on human health— even for indefinitely prolonged exposures. I am personally prepared to sit on top of my microwave oven for a solid year while it is in full operation, with no apprehension for my safety.

Is it safe to open the oven door to stir the food? If you are in a room and you turn the light off, the light is gone. It doesn't stay for one second beyond the moment you have turned it off. Continuing the analogy of light, if you open the microwave oven door, even before the timer is finished running, the door latch disengages the power that produces the microwaves. The microwaves are cut off immediately and not one second later. There are no residual microwaves in the oven.

Is there a problem for pacemaker wearers? In 1974, a team of medical doctors, headed by Dr. Nicholas P.D. Smyth, presented an article about pacemakers and outside interference that appeared in the *Journal of the American Medical Association*. To paraphrase, they discussed the problems of older fixed rate or constant pacemakers which, as their name implies, fired constantly, sometimes competitively with the heart. The new demand pacemaker was designed to be sensitive to the heart rate by monitoring the R wave.

"The solution of one problem, however, often creates new ones," they said. It was soon apparent that such pacemakers could sense electromagnetic potentials other than the intrinsic myocardial potentials. These extraneous signals are collectively referred to as "electromagnetic interference (EMI)." These signals from such sources as automobile ignition systems and small electric motors were able to produce, in a few cases, unwanted and potentially dangerous inhibition of the pulse generator. "Other sources were weapon detectors, high-energy radio, television, and leaky microwave ovens."

At the same time they said, "Government agencies perform a useful function in controlling EMI emissions in microwave ovens." They went on to say, "It is our belief that the action of environmental EMI on the patient with an implanted demand pacemaker does not at this time constitute an important clinical problem."

That was 1974. Second and third generation pacemakers are now encased in reflective metal shells to shield them from any unwanted interference. Those original demand pacemakers, which must be replaced every few years, are now obsolete.

Do you need to test your microwave oven for leakage? As of October 6, 1971, all microwave oven manufacturers had to comply with the government's strict standards as stated in the Health and Safety Act.

Microwave ovens need only be checked by an appliance serviceman after the oven has been repaired, or if the oven has been damaged.

The Ring Rule

This is an important rule that we refer to often in the recipes. It combines the Arrangement rule (page 23), the Dish Shape rule (page 81), and also the Dish Depth rule (page 82). From these rules we learn that by arranging the food with the center open and the thicker portions to the outside, the food cooks more evenly. We also learn that the circle is the best shape for cooking.

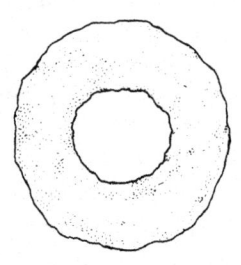

The sum of these two is a cooking arrangement in the shape of a doughnut or ring. This ring shape is the best possible way to cook foods in the microwave, because microwave energy is hitting the food from an inner and outer surface area for more even cooking.

This ring shape also shortens cooking time, because there are more surface areas exposed. An example of this can be shown with two 1½-pound meat loaves. When one is formed into a standard loaf it takes between 13 to 18 minutes on HIGH power. When that identical meat loaf is cooked in a Bundt dish it takes between 8 and 13 minutes on HIGH power.

The Ring Rule can be tailored to cake batters, quick breads, potatoes, or fish rolls placed in a ring—or anything that couldn't otherwise be stirred but can be arranged in a circle. Individual items should be placed with one inch between them. Often these foods don't require rearranging during cooking, and not only that, we have been pleasantly surprised at how artistic the final presentation can be.

To feed the eye as well as the palate, we often garnish the center of the dish with fresh herbs, flower blossoms, or sautéed vegetables, depending on the food we're serving.

Fact: When foods can be arranged in a ring with an open center, the food cooks more evenly, cooks more quickly, and can be presented more attractively.

Rings—Combining Foods That Can't Be Stirred into One Dish

We've explained the Ring Rule on page 38, where we stated that the highest concentration of microwave energy is found around the outside. The circle or ring is the best shape for cooking. Therefore more than one food can be combined in the same dish by placing the thicker, denser, or longer-cooking foods on the outside.

How do you know what foods should be placed on the outside? You can judge them by looking at their individual cooking times. Here are two ways to apply this:

Example 1: Stuffed Cabbage

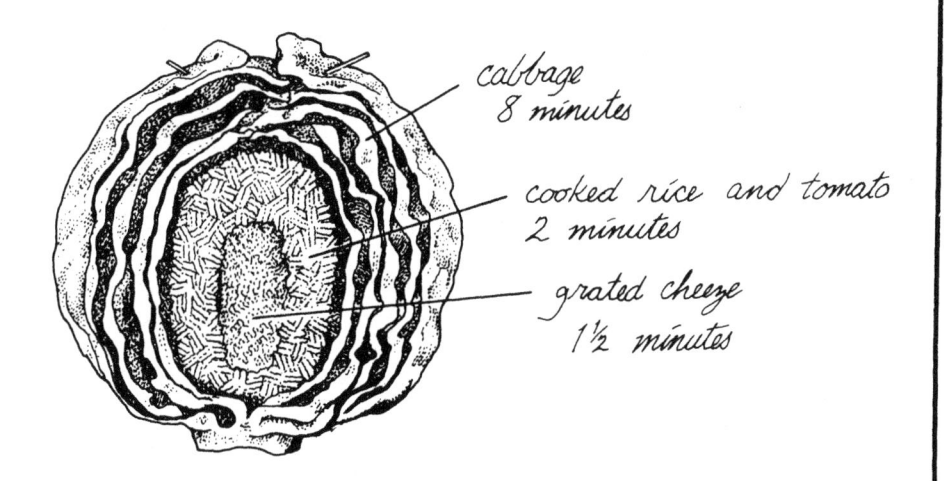

cabbage 8 minutes

cooked rice and tomato 2 minutes

grated cheese 1½ minutes

Example 2: Lightly Breaded Ham and Cheese Rollups (page 105)

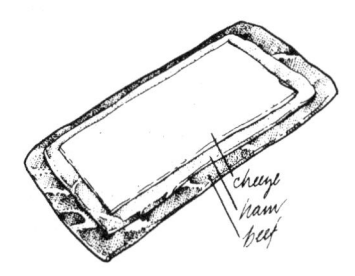

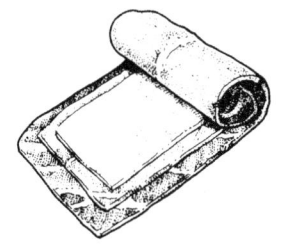

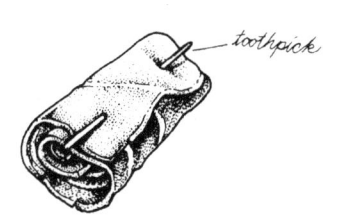

cheese / ham / beef

toothpick

RULES OF THUMB

We know the first thing that a microwave owner learns how to do is to reheat. That's the way we started. Not long afterward comes the cooking of simple foods, and if confidence continues to build the process may even culminate in the conversion of a favorite recipe from conventional methods to microwave. We based the organization of this chapter on these steps.

You begin with time ranges for reheating different foods, and learn to gauge the doneness of each by sensing the heat on the outside of the dish with your thumb or fingers.

The "Rules of Thumb" for cooking times teaches you how to quickly determine the cooking times of certain foods by first measuring them with your thumb.

The "At-a-Glance" cooking charts are a further expansion that gives you times for many foods, along with ways to vary the flavors with different cooking liquids, herb coatings, and glazes. Even a food simply cooked can be different each time it's made. After that, we hope that you will go on to converting your own recipes based on the guidelines at the end of this chapter.

The Rules of Thumb are just what they say—quick guidelines that get you off on the right track but give you enough freedom to cook the food according to your tastes.

Reheating Doneness

How can you determine how much time it will take to reheat something all the way through? There is no pat answer, but there are simple guidelines.

How hot is hot enough? Because reheating times can vary according to type, amount, and the starting temperature of the food (room, refrigerated, or frozen), we have divided foods into various categories and call for them to be heated to one of two donenesses.

1. *Warm to the touch* is slightly warmer than the sensation of baby's milk dripped on your wrist, but we have you feel it with your

fingers. It applies to reheating breads only.

2. *The Macungie (pronounced Ma-kun-jee) Rule* is a measure of time that your hand can be held on the bottom or top of a hot *covered* plate or casserole. This time is counted out in "1 Macungie, 2 Macungie" and so on, and each is basically the measure of a second.

Why Macungie? We always remember our fathers heating the barbecue grill until they could hold their hand over the coals for no longer than "1 Mississippi, 2 Mississippi, 3 Mississippi." At this point they knew that the fire was hot enough.

When we were driving through Macungie, Pennsylvania, on our way to a work assignment, we immediately took to that name, discovering that "Macungie" was one of those words that could be chewed between your teeth, like saltwater taffy or tobacco, giving a lot of satisfaction with no cavities or nasty side effects. "Macungie" was also a good length of measure. When we call for a doneness of "2 Macungie," hold your hand on the part of the dish indicated, and count "1 Macungie, 2 Macungie" and see if the dish is hot enough to force you to pull away your hand. If it is, you have experienced the Macungie Rule.

Casseroles are defined as any stirrable dish such as appetizer dips, vegetables, meat and/or vegetables in a sauce, chili, stews, etc.

REFRIGERATED CASSEROLES REHEATING DONENESS

Cover refrigerated casserole with lid or plastic wrap. Heat *on* HIGH *until the sides feel "2 Macungie," stir;* HIGH *until top or bottom feels "3 Macungie"; stir once in the middle.**

Guidelines for specific times follow below.

NOTE: The top cover and the dish bottom may be different temperatures—go with the hotter surface.

*If there is much cheese or beans in the casserole, heat it entirely on MEDIUM *or stir the cheese in at the end, after heating.*

SPECIFICS—REFRIGERATED CASSEROLES

Amount	Reheating Procedure
1 cup	Cover tightly. HIGH 2 minutes until sides are *2 Macungie*; stir. HIGH 1 minute, or until hottest surface, bottom or top, is *3 Macungie*.
2 cups	Cover tightly. HIGH 3 minutes, or until sides are *2 Macungie*; stir. HIGH 1 minute, or until bottom or top is *3 Macungie*.
4 cups	Cover tightly. HIGH 5 minutes, or until sides are *2 Macungie*; stir. HIGH 1 to 3 minutes, or until bottom or top is *3 Macungie*.
6 to 8 cups	Cover tightly. HIGH 5 minutes, or until sides are *2 Macungie*; stir. Cover again. HIGH 4 to 6 minutes, or until bottom or top is *3 Macungie*.

FROZEN CASSEROLES REHEATING DONENESS

Start with the container in which the casserole was frozen; cover tightly. Heat *on* HIGH *5 minutes;* MEDIUM *5 to 15 minutes until defrosted and can be stirred to break up and remove to another casserole.**

Follow reheating procedure for Refrigerated Casseroles.

SPECIFICS—FROZEN CASSEROLES

2 cups	Cover tightly. HIGH 5 minutes; then MEDIUM 5 minutes; stir and remove. HIGH 3 minutes, or until sides are *2 Macungie*; stir. HIGH 4 minutes, or until top or bottom is *3 Macungie*.
4 cups	Cover tightly. HIGH 5 minutes; then MEDIUM 5 minutes; stir and remove. HIGH 5 minutes, or until sides are *2 Macungie*; stir. HIGH 3 to 7 minutes, or until bottom or top is *3 Macungie*.
6 to 8 cups	Cover tightly. HIGH 5 minutes, then on MEDIUM 10 to 15 minutes; stir and remove. Cover again. HIGH 5 minutes, or until sides are *2 Macungie*; stir. HIGH 15 to 20 minutes, or until top or bottom is *3 Macungie*, stirring every 5 minutes.

*Final reheating should be done in a larger casserole than is normally used for storing, one that is not a soft plastic so as to not be affected by heating food.

REFRIGERATED LAYERED CASSEROLES REHEATING DONENESS

Cover tightly. Heat *on* HIGH *5 minutes, rotate;* MEDIUM *until hottest surface, top or bottom center, feels "3 Macungie."*

Layered Casseroles: Any casserole like a lasagna that can't be stirred because it is layered or arranged.

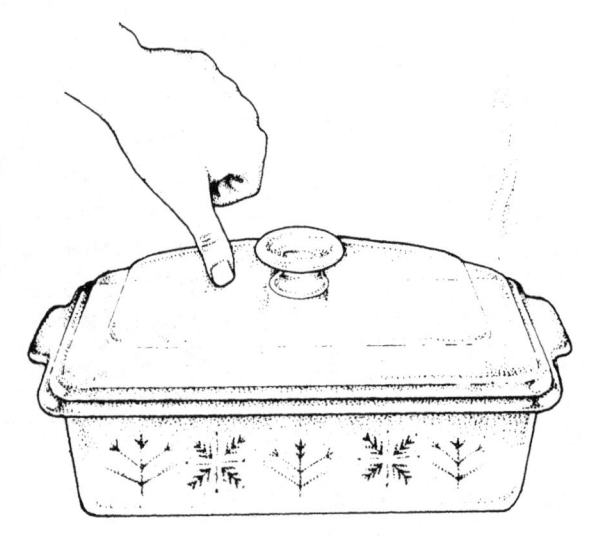

SPECIFICS—REFRIGERATED LAYERED CASSEROLES

Amount	Reheating Procedure
1-quart rectangular	Cover tightly. HIGH 5 minutes; then MEDIUM 12 to 15 minutes, or until top or bottom feels *3 Macungie*, rotating once.
2-quart rectangular	Cover tightly. HIGH 5 minutes; then MEDIUM 15 to 17 minutes, or until top or bottom is *3 Macungie*, rotating once.

FROZEN LAYERED CASSEROLES REHEATING DONENESS

Cover tightly. Heat *on* HIGH *5 to 10 minutes, rotate;* MEDIUM *until hottest surface, top or bottom center, feels "3 Macungie."*

SPECIFICS—FROZEN LAYERED CASSEROLES

1-quart rectangular	Cover tightly. HIGH 5 minutes; then MEDIUM 10 to 15 minutes, or until top or bottom is *3 Macungie*, rotating and covering corners with foil if necessary.
2-quart rectangular	Cover tightly. HIGH 10 minutes, then on MEDIUM 30 to 40 minutes, or until top or bottom is *3 Macungie*, rotating and covering corners with foil if necessary.

REFRIGERATED, ROOM TEMPERATURE, AND FROZEN SOUPS AND SAUCES REHEATING DONENESS

Cover tightly. Heat *on* HIGH *until sides are "2 Macungie," stir;* HIGH *until hottest surface top or bottom, is "3 Macungie"; stirring once.*

Soups and Sauces: Any soup or sauce. If it is a cream soup, do not bring to a boil.

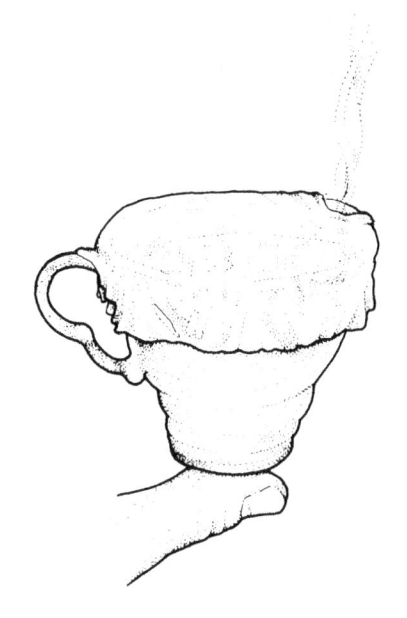

SPECIFICS—REFRIGERATED AND ROOM TEMPERATURE SOUPS AND SAUCES

Amount	Reheating Procedure
1 cup	Cover tightly. *Refrigerated* is HIGH 2 to 2½ minutes or until top or bottom is *3 Macungie*. *Room temperature* is HIGH 1 to 1½ minutes.
2 cups	Cover tightly. *Refrigerated or Room temperature* is HIGH 5 to 6 minutes, or until bottom or top is *3 Macungie*, stirring once.
4 cups	Cover tightly. *Refrigerated or Room temperature* is HIGH 7 to 8 minutes, or until top or bottom is *3 Macungie*, stirring once.

SPECIFICS—FROZEN SOUPS AND SAUCES

Amount	Reheating Procedure
1 cup	Cover tightly. HIGH 5 minutes, or until top or bottom is *3 Macungie*, stirring once.
2 cups	Cover tightly. HIGH 10 minutes, or until top or bottom is *3 Macungie*, stirring after 5 minutes.
4 cups	Cover tightly. HIGH 15 minutes, or until top or bottom is *3 Macungie*, stirring every 5 minutes.

ROOM TEMPERATURE INDIVIDUAL PLATES REHEATING DONENESS

Cover with plastic wrap. Heat *on* HIGH *until top is* "*3 Macungie.*"

Individual Plates: Defined as a plate of food containing a serving of meat and two vegetables. Place less dense vegetables to the center of the dish.

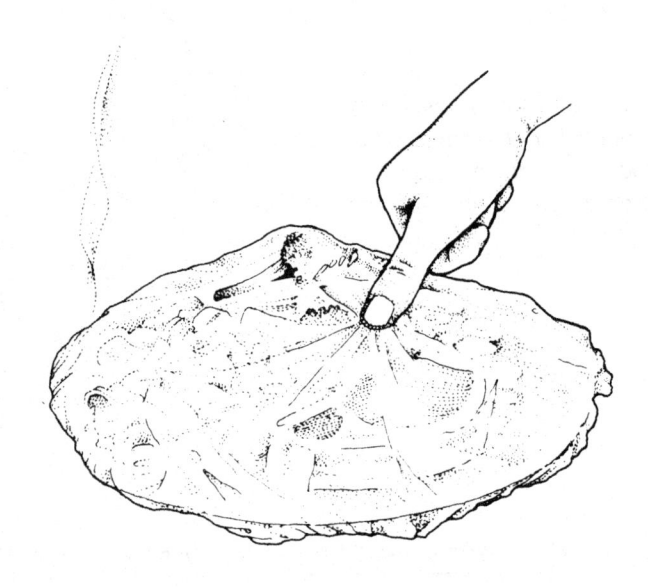

SPECIFICS—ROOM TEMPERATURE PLATES

Amount	Reheating Procedure
1 plate	Cover with plastic wrap. HIGH 1½ minutes, or until top is *3 Macungie*.
2 plates	Cover with plastic wrap. HIGH 3 minutes, or until top is *3 Macungie*.

REFRIGERATED INDIVIDUAL PLATES REHEATING DONENESS

Cover with plastic wrap. Heat *on* MEDIUM-HIGH *until top is* "*3 Macungie.*"

SPECIFICS—REFRIGERATED PLATES

1 plate	Cover with plastic wrap. MEDIUM-HIGH 3 minutes, or until top is *3 Macungie*.
2 plates	Cover with plastic wrap. MEDIUM-HIGH 5 minutes, or until top is *3 Macungie*.

REFRIGERATED SLICED MEATS REHEATING DONENESS

Cover with plastic wrap. Heat *on* MEDIUM-HIGH *until top is "3 Macungie."*

Plates of Sliced or Cubed Meat: Slices or cubes of beef, pork, veal, poultry, ribs, or meat loaf, and recipes made with thin slices of tender meat or pork or beef ribs.

SPECIFICS—REFRIGERATED SLICED MEATS

Amount	Reheating Procedure
1 serving (4 ounces) 2 skewers	Cover with plastic wrap. MEDIUM-HIGH 2 minutes, or until top is *3 Macungie.*
2 servings (8 ounces) 4 skewers	Cover with plastic wrap. MEDIUM-HIGH 3 minutes, or until top is *3 Macungie.*
2 servings ribs (about 2 pounds)	Cover with wax paper. MEDIUM 6 to 10 minutes, or until top is *3 Macungie.*

REFRIGERATED RICE AND NOODLES REHEATING DONENESS

Cover with plastic wrap. Heat *on* HIGH *until top is "3 Macungie."*

SPECIFICS—REFRIGERATED RICE OR NOODLES

1 cup cooked rice or noodles	Cover tightly. HIGH 1 minute, or until top is *3 Macungie*; stir.
2 cups cooked rice or noodles	Cover tightly. HIGH 2 minutes, or until top is *3 Macungie*; stir.
4 cups cooked rice or noodles	Cover tightly. HIGH 3 minutes, or until top is *3 Macungie*; stir after 2 minutes.

BREAD REHEATING DONENESS

NOTE: Bread should be reheated until it is warm to the thumb, because breads are more delicate and porous than meats or vegetables.

SPECIFICS—VARIOUS BREAD PRODUCTS

1 bagel 2 slices of bread 1 large or 2 small muffins or biscuits 1 Danish 1 6-inch pita	Wrap in paper towel. If room temperature: HIGH 10 to 15 seconds. If frozen: HIGH 35 to 45 seconds, or until warm to the thumb.
1 loaf of Italian bread	Wrap in paper towel. If room temperature: HIGH 35 to 45 seconds. If frozen: HIGH 1 minute, or until warm to the thumb.

Bread Reheating Doneness (*continued*)

Flour Tortillas 1 tortilla	Wrap in dampened paper towel. HIGH 10 seconds, or until warm to the thumb.
2 tortillas	Same as above. HIGH 20 seconds, or until warm to the thumb.
6 to 8 tortillas	Same as above. HIGH 1 minute, or until warm to the thumb.

MISCELLANEOUS REHEATING OR DEFROSTING DONENESS

Everything else we haven't discussed that may need reheating or defrosting.

1 fast-food big burger or ½ steak sandwich, room temperature	Wrap in paper towel or box. HIGH 15 to 30 seconds, or until warm to the thumb.
1 fast-food French fries, room temperature	In box. No cover. HIGH 15 to 30 seconds, or until warm to the thumb.
1 8-ounce baby bottle, refrigerated	Remove nipple. MEDIUM 30 seconds to 1 minute. Replace nipple and shake. Test on wrist.
4-ounce baby food jar	Remove from jar. HIGH 15 seconds; or until warm, stirring once.
Frozen Juice Concentrate	
1 10-ounce can	Remove lid. DEFROST 2 to 4 minutes, or until outside is warm to the thumb but inside is icy.
1 16-ounce can	Remove lid. DEFROST 6 to 8 minutes, or until outside is warm to the thumb but inside is icy.
Frozen Fruit	
1 cup	DEFROST 2½ minutes; stand 5 minutes.
2 cups	DEFROST 5 minutes; stand 5 minutes.
Hot Beverages	
1 cup	HIGH 1 to 2 minutes.
2 cups	HIGH 3 to 4 minutes.
3 cups	HIGH 4 to 5 minutes.

Rules of Thumb for Cooking Times

With some foods cooking times can easily be determined by measuring the food thickness or length. We will choose an arbitrary length—the thumb—which we will say is 2½ inches in length. The figures below and on the next few pages refer to the chart on page 52.

POTATOES

Size	Doneness	Cooking Procedure
1 potato		
1 thumblength long and half that wide—small round potato (if potato is thinner, reduce time by 30 seconds): fig. 1	Until potato, when squeezed firmly with fingers, gives slightly on the surface	Prick skin. Cook on HIGH 2½ to 5 minutes. Stand 5 minutes.
1½ thumblengths long and half that wide—medium round potato (if potato is thinner, reduce time by 1 minute): fig. 2	Same as above	Prick skin. Cook on HIGH 3 to 6 minutes. Stand 5 minutes.
2 thumblengths long and half that wide—large round potato (if potato is thinner, reduce time by 1½ minutes): fig. 3	Same as above	Prick skin. Cook on HIGH 4 to 7 minutes. Stand 5 minutes.

CAULIFLOWER

Size	Doneness	Cooking Procedure
1 whole head cauliflower, leaves removed		
1 thumblength from bottom edge to center (small): fig. 4	Can be pierced easily with fork	Wrap in plastic wrap, or place in casserole with 2 to 4 tablespoons water, covered with plastic wrap. Cook HIGH 6 minutes. Stand 3 minutes.

Rules of Thumb

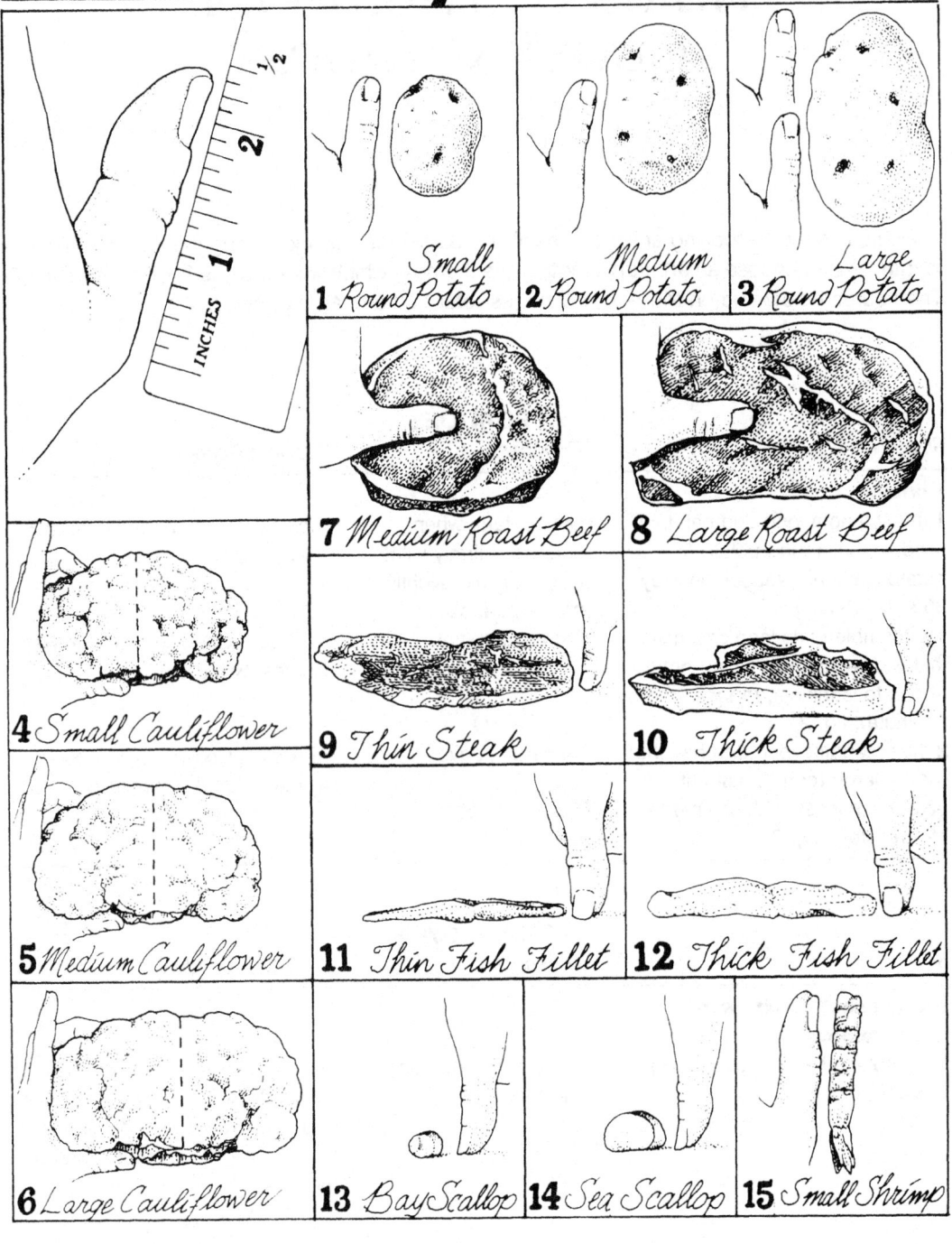

1 Small Round Potato
2 Medium Round Potato
3 Large Round Potato
4 Small Cauliflower
5 Medium Cauliflower
6 Large Cauliflower
7 Medium Roast Beef
8 Large Roast Beef
9 Thin Steak
10 Thick Steak
11 Thin Fish Fillet
12 Thick Fish Fillet
13 Bay Scallop
14 Sea Scallop
15 Small Shrimp

Cauliflower (*continued*)

Size	Doneness	Cooking Procedure
1¼ thumblengths from bottom edge to center (medium): fig. 5	Same as above	Cover as above. Cook HIGH 7 minutes. Stand 3 minutes.
1½ thumblengths from bottom edge to center (large): fig. 6	Same as above	Cover as above. Cook HIGH 8 to 10 minutes. Stand 3 minutes.

MEAT

Size	Doneness	Cooking Procedure
Roast beef		
1 thumblength reaches within ½ inch of center (place your thumb along center of roast, with thumbnail pointing to center): fig. 7	Rare (115°F) Medium (120°F) Well (145°F)	HIGH 5 minutes; then on MEDIUM 7 to 9 minutes per pound 8 to 11 minutes per pound 10 to 14 minutes per pound Turn over once, halfway through cooking time.
1 thumblength reaches within 1 inch of the center: fig. 8	Rare (120°F) Medium (125°F) Well (145°F)	HIGH 10 minutes; then on MEDIUM 7 to 9 minutes per pound 8 to 11 minutes per pound 10 to 14 minutes per pound Turn over once, halfway through cooking time.

NOTES: Let all roasts stand, tented with foil, for 10 minutes. Roasts with smaller diameters are cooked to lower temperatures because the heat travels faster to the center during standing time.

Size	Doneness	Cooking Procedure
Steaks/chops		
½ thumblength thick (1 inch thick): fig. 9		Place on preheated browning grill (HIGH 5 to 9 minutes).
	Rare	Cook HIGH 1 minute per side.
	Medium	Cook HIGH 2 minutes per side.
	Well	Cook HIGH 2 minutes; turn over and cook 3 to 5 minutes more.
¾ thumblength thick (1 to 2 inches): fig. 10		Place on preheated browning grill.
	Rare	Cook HIGH 2 minutes per side.
	Medium	Cook HIGH 2½ minutes; turn over and cook 3½ to 4½ minutes more.
	Well	Cook HIGH 3 minutes; turn over and cook 4 to 5 minutes more.

Meat (continued)

Size	Doneness	Cooking Procedure
Hamburgers/sausage patties		Place on preheated browning grill (HIGH 5 to 8 minutes).
1 to 2 (¼ thumblength thick)	Rare	Cook HIGH ½ minute per side.
	Medium	Cook HIGH ½ minute; turn over and cook 1 minute more.
	Well	Cook HIGH 1 minute; turn over and cook 1½ to 3 minutes more.
4 (¼ thumblength thick)	Rare	Cook HIGH 1 minute per side.
	Medium	Cook HIGH 1 minute; turn over and cook 1½ to 2 minutes more.
	Well	Cook HIGH 1½ minutes; turn over and cook 2 to 4 minutes more.

FISH AND SEAFOOD

Thickness	Doneness	Cooking Procedure
Fish fillets		
¼ thumblength thick Thin fillets: fig. 11	Flakes under pressure when pressed	Fold under thinner edges (see illustration on page 215). Cover with paper towel. Cook HIGH 2½ to 5 minutes per pound.
Almost ½ thumblength Thick fillets: fig. 12	Same as above	Cover tightly. Cook MEDIUM 9 to 11 minutes per pound, turning over once.
Scallops		
¼ thumblength in diameter Bay: fig. 13	Same as above	Cover with paper towel. Cook MEDIUM 3½ to 5 minutes per pound; stirring once.
½ thumblength or more in diameter Sea: fig. 14	Same as above	Cover with paper towel. Cook MEDIUM 4 to 6½ minutes per pound, stirring once.
Shrimp		
Less than 1 thumblength—small shrimp (don't measure tail): fig. 15	Shrimp turns opaque	Cover tightly. Cook HIGH 2 to 3 minutes per pound, stirring once.
1 to 1½ thumblengths—medium shrimp (don't measure tail)	Same as above	Cover tightly. Cook HIGH 2½ to 3½ minutes per pound, stirring once.

At-a-Glance Cooking Charts

EGG COOKING CHART

Name/Amount	Cooking Procedure	Variation
Poached Eggs		
1 egg	Heat 1 tablespoon water and ¼ teaspoon vinegar to boiling in custard cup. Add egg. Pierce yolk membrane. Cover tightly. Cook MEDIUM 45 seconds to 1½ minutes. Stand, covered, 1 minute.	Substitute 1 teaspoon butter for water and vinegar.
2 eggs	Same as above, but double ingredients and custard cups. Cover tightly. Cook on MEDIUM 1 to 1¾ minutes. Stand, covered, 1½ minutes.	Substitute 2 teaspoons butter for water and vinegar.
Scrambled Eggs		
1 egg, beaten	Place in custard cup. Cook HIGH 35 seconds to 1 minute; stir after 15 seconds.	Add 1 teaspoon water, milk, cream, or club soda for lighter eggs. *No acid.*
2 eggs, beaten	Place in 8-ounce dish. Cook HIGH 1 to 2 minutes; stir after 30 seconds.	Add 2 teaspoons of above.
6 eggs, beaten	Place in 9-inch pie plate or 1½-quart casserole. Cook HIGH 3 to 5 minutes; stir twice.	Add 3 tablespoons of above.
8 eggs, beaten	Place in 9-inch pie plate or 1½-quart casserole. Cook HIGH 3½ to 6 minutes; stir twice.	Same as above.

Hard-Cooked Eggs

NOTE: Hard-cooked eggs are never cooked in their shells in the microwave. Too much steam would build up underneath the shell to burst it. For 2 or more eggs allow at least 1-inch space between egg cups and rearrange once.

1 egg	Break egg in 5- or 6-ounce custard cup. Puncture yolk membrane. Cover tightly. Cook MEDIUM 2 to 2½ minutes, to set whites. Stand, covered, 1 minute.
2 eggs	MEDIUM 4 to 5 minutes. Stand 1 minute.
4 eggs	MEDIUM 6 to 7 minutes. Stand 1 minute.

CEREAL, PASTA, AND RICE COOKING CHART

Name/Amount	Cooking Procedure
Cereal (Farina or Cream of Wheat) or Oatmeal 1 serving	In 16-ounce cereal bowl, 3 tablespoons cereal, or ⅓ cup oatmeal plus ¾ cup water and pinch of salt. Cook HIGH 2 minutes; stir. Cook HIGH 1½ to 2½ minutes more; stir.
2 servings	Double ingredients above in two separate cereal bowls. Cook both bowls on HIGH 4 minutes; stir. Cook HIGH 3 to 5 minutes more, stirring once.
4 servings	In 3-quart casserole, ¾ cup fine cereal or 1⅓ cups oatmeal plus 3 cups water and ½ teaspoon salt. Cook HIGH 4 minutes; stir. Cook 5 to 8 minutes more, stirring once.
Instant Cereal or Oatmeal 1 serving	In 16-ounce cereal bowl, 3 tablespoons cereal or ⅓ cup oatmeal plus ¾ cup water. Cook HIGH 1½ minutes, stir. Cook HIGH 1 to 2½ minutes, stirring every 30 seconds.
2 servings	Double ingredients above, dividing between two separate bowls. Cook HIGH 2 minutes; stir. Cook HIGH 1 to 4 minutes, stirring every 30 seconds.
Grits or Polenta 4 to 6 servings	In 3-quart casserole, 1 cup grits or polenta (coarse cornmeal), plus 3½ cups water, and ½ teaspoon salt. Cover tightly. Cook HIGH 5 minutes; stir. Re-cover; cook 4 to 7 minutes, stirring once.
Long-Grain Rice 4 servings	In 3-quart casserole, 1 cup rice plus 1¾ cups water and ½ teaspoon salt. Cover tightly. Cook HIGH 4 to 7 minutes to boil; MEDIUM 10 minutes, or until liquid is absorbed. Stand, covered, 5 minutes.
Basmati Rice 4 servings	Same as above, but after water comes to a boil; cook MEDIUM 6 to 10 minutes, until liquid is absorbed. Stand, covered, 5 minutes.
Brown Rice 4 servings	In 3-quart casserole, 1 cup rice plus 2⅓ cups water, ½ teaspoon salt. Cover tightly. Cook HIGH 6 to 10 minutes to boil; MEDIUM 25 to 30 minutes, or until liquid is absorbed. Stand, covered, 5 minutes.

Instant Rice

Combine rice and water in amounts indicated on package. Place in appropriate casserole. Cover tightly. Cook HIGH 3 to 8 minutes; or until water boils. Stand, covered, 5 minutes.

Macaroni Noodles

NOTE: Because this method for cooking macaroni is no faster or better than on top of the stove, it is only recommended if you are on board a boat or in a trailer where a traditional range isn't available.

2 cups, dry (4 cups cooked) — Pour 4 cups water into 4-quart casserole. Cover tightly. Cook HIGH 8 to 12 minutes, or until boiling. Stir in macaroni and cover again. Cook HIGH 2 to 4 minutes to boil again; stir. Cover again. Cook MEDIUM 3 to 5 minutes, or until noodles are tender. Stand, covered, 2 minutes. Drain.

FISH AND SEAFOOD COOKING CHART

Name/Amount	Cooking Procedure	Variation
Thin Fillets (½ inch thick)		
4-ounce fillet	Place in custard cup, folding thinner ends underneath thicker center in envelope fashion. Add 1 teaspoon lemon juice. Cover with paper towel. Cook HIGH 1 to 3 minutes.	Liquid: lime or orange juice, herb vinegar, dry white wine, or butter.
1 pound	Fold thinner ends of fillets under thicker center to form individual envelopes. Place seam side down in ring around outside of 9- to 12-inch round plate (or 2-quart rectangular). Add 1 tablespoon lemon juice. Cover with paper towel. Cook HIGH 2½ to 5 minutes. Stand, covered, 2 minutes.	
Thick Fillets (¾ to 1 inch thick)		
6-ounce fillet	Place in individual baking dish. Add 2 teaspoons lemon juice. Cover tightly. Cook MEDIUM 3 to 4 minutes. Stand, covered, 1 minute.	Same.
1 pound	Sprinkle with 1 to 2 tablespoons liquid (2 tablespoons for rich fish, page 216). If it has skin, place skin-side down in 2-quart shallow dish. Cover tightly. Cook MEDIUM 9 to 11 minutes; turn over once. (In 500 watt oven cook HIGH 5 to 8 minutes; turn once.) Stand, covered, 5 minutes.	

Name/Amount	Cooking Procedure	Variation
Steaks (1 inch thick)		
4-ounce steak	Melt 1 tablespoon butter, optional, in small baking dish. Add fish and 1 teaspoon lemon juice. Cover tightly. Cook MEDIUM 3 to 7 minutes, turning over after 1½ minutes. Stand, covered, 2 minutes.	Same.
1-pound steak	Melt 3 tablespoons butter, optional, in 2-quart shallow baking dish. Place fish in circle around outside of dish and add 2 tablespoons lemon juice. Cover tightly. Cook MEDIUM 7 to 9 minutes; turning over once. Stand, covered, 5 minutes.	
Whole Fish		
3 pounds	Place in 3-quart rectangular dish. Add 2 tablespoons lemon juice. Cover tightly. Cook MEDIUM 20 to 25 minutes (7 to 8 minutes per pound); turn over once. Stand, covered, 5 minutes.	Same.
4 trout (6 to 8 ounces *each*)	Place in 3-quart rectangular dish. Add 2 tablespoons lemon juice. Cover tightly. Cook MEDIUM 12 to 18 minutes. Stand, covered, 5 minutes.	
Scallops		
1 pound bay (small scallops)	Arrange in ring on outside of 9-inch pie plate. Add 2 tablespoons lemon juice, coating scallops on all sides. Cover with paper towel. Cover tightly. Cook MEDIUM 3½ to 5 minutes. Stand, covered, 2 minutes.	Same.
1 pound sea (large scallops)	Same as above. Cook MEDIUM 4 to 6½ minutes. Stand, covered, 2 minutes.	
Lobster Tails		
4 (6 ounces *each*)	With sharp scissors, cut through underside of tails. Place, cut-side up, on 10-inch round dish, with thinner end of tail toward center. Sprinkle tails with 2 tablespoons lemon juice. Cover tightly. Cook MEDIUM 12 to 15 minutes, rotating dish once. Stand, covered, 5 minutes.	Same.
Shrimp		
1 pound small (shelled or unshelled)	Place in 9-inch pie plate, pushing shrimp toward outside, leaving center open. Add 2	Same.

	tablespoons lemon juice. Cook HIGH 2½ to 6½ minutes, stirring once. Stand, covered, 2 to 3 minutes.
Mussels 1 pound, well cleaned	Place mussels in 12-inch round shallow dish or 3-quart casserole, pushing to outer edge and leaving center open. Cover tightly. Cook HIGH 2½ to 4 minutes, or until mussels open and pull away from shells, rotating dish if necessary.
Clams 1 dozen	Place clams in 10-inch round shallow dish or 2-quart casserole, pushing to outer edge and leaving center open. Cover tightly. Cook HIGH 3 to 5 minutes, or until clams open.

MEAT COOKING CHART

Name/Amount	Cooking Procedure
Ground Beef 1 pound	Place meat in heavy-duty plastic colander, sitting in bowl; or 1-quart casserole. Cook HIGH 5 to 8 minutes, stirring once.
Tender Beef Roasts Rolled Rump or Eye of Round 5-inch diameter *or less*	On roasting rack in 2-quart rectangular dish, place fat side down. Cook, uncovered, HIGH 5 minutes; then *Rare:* MEDIUM 7 to 9 minutes per pound or 115°F; *Medium-Rare:* MEDIUM 8 to 11 minutes per pound or 120°F; *Medium:* MEDIUM 9 to 12 minutes per pound or 130°F; *Well:* MEDIUM 10 to 14 minutes per pound or 145°F; turning over halfway through cooking time. Salt and pepper. Tent loosely with foil. Stand 5 to 10 minutes.
5-inch diameter *or more*	Same dish as above. Place fat side down and cook, uncovered HIGH 10 minutes; then *Rare:* MEDIUM 7 to 9 minutes per pound or 120°F; *Medium-Rare:* MEDIUM 8 to 11 minutes per pound or 125°F; *Medium:* MEDIUM 9 to 12 minutes per pound or 130°F; *Well:* MEDIUM 10 to 14 minutes per pound or 145°F; turning over halfway through total cooking time. Salt and pepper. Tent loosely with foil. Stand 5 to 10 minutes.
Rib Roasts and over 5-pound Rolled Roasts	In 2- to 3-quart dish, follow procedure above for over 5-inch diameter roasts. After turning over; cover bone end of rib roasts and ends of rolled roasts smoothly with foil (see page 257).

Name/Amount	Cooking Procedure

Beef Tenderloin

Fold under thin tip end. On roasting rack in 2-quart rectangular dish, cook, uncovered, HIGH 5 minutes per pound; then *Rare:* MEDIUM 6 to 8 minutes per pound or 115°F.; *Medium-Rare:* MEDIUM 8 to 11 minutes per pound or 120°F; *Medium:* MEDIUM 9 to 12 minutes per pound or 130°F; *Well:* MEDIUM 10 to 14 minutes per pound or 145°F. Cover ends with foil and turn over halfway through total cooking time. Salt and pepper. Tent loosely with foil. Stand 5 to 10 minutes.

Tender Steaks
Sirloin, Porterhouse, Tenderloin, Shell, Strip, Club, London Broil (1 to 4 steaks)
   1 inch thick or less

Preheat microwave browning dish according to manufacturer's instructions (HIGH 5 to 9 minutes). Slash fat around outside. Press steak onto hot dish. Cook, uncovered, HIGH—*Rare: 1 minute each side; Medium-Rare: 1½ minutes each side; Medium: 2 minutes each side; Well: 2 minutes; turn over 3 to 5 minutes more.*

   1½ to 2 inches thick

Cook HIGH—*Rare: 2 minutes each side; Medium-Rare: 2 minutes; turn over, then 3 to 4 minutes; Medium: 2½ minutes; turn over 3½ to 4½ minutes more; Well: 3 minutes; turn over, then 4 to 5 minutes.*

Lamb Chops
1 to 4 chops

Preheat microwave browning dish according to manufacturer's instructions (HIGH 5 to 9 minutes). Press chops onto hot dish. Cook, uncovered, HIGH 1 minute each side.
   Variation: Serve with Melted Butters (page 183), or Mint Sauce (page 276).

Leg of Lamb, Shank of Leg, Lamb Shoulder

Rub with oil, minced garlic, salt, and pepper. Cover 2 inches of bone or thin end of leg smoothly with foil. On microwave roasting rack in 2-quart rectangular dish, fat-side down. No cover.

3 pounds or less

Rare: HIGH 5 minutes. MEDIUM 7 to 9 minutes per pound or 120°F; turning over halfway through total cooking time. *Medium:* HIGH 5 minutes. MEDIUM 8 to 10 minutes per pound or 135°F, turning over halfway through total cooking time. *Well:* HIGH 5 minutes. MEDIUM 9 to 12 minutes per pound or 140°F, turning over halfway through total cooking time. Tent loosely with foil. Stand 10 to 15 minutes.

more than 3 pounds

Same dish as above. *Rare:* HIGH 10 minutes. MEDIUM 8 to 9 minutes per pound or 120°F, turning over halfway through total cooking time. *Medium:* HIGH 10 minutes. MEDIUM 8 to 10 minutes per pound or 135°F, turning over halfway through total cooking time. *Well:* HIGH 10 minutes. MEDIUM 11 to 12 minutes per pound or 140°F, turning over halfway through total cooking time. Tent loosely with foil. Stand 10 minutes.

Bacon
(timing will vary with thickness) — On roasting rack or paper-lined plate. Cover with paper towel. HIGH

1 strip	45 to 50 seconds.
2 strips	1¾ to 2¼ minutes. Stand briefly.
3 strips	2¼ to 3 minutes.
4 strips	2½ to 3¼ minutes.
6 strips	3¼ to 4 minutes.
8 strips*	4 to 5 minutes. Let stand 2 to 3 minutes.

NOTE: To separate frozen bacon strips, place a 1-pound package of bacon in the oven and heat on HIGH for 30 seconds.

Fresh Sausage Patties

1 to 2 patties	On paper-lined plate. Cover with paper towel. Cook HIGH 1 minute; turn over and cook 2 to 3 minutes more.
8 to 12 patties (1 pound) Large browning dish or small browning dish in two batches	Preheat microwave browning dish on HIGH 5 to 8 minutes. Press patties down on dish. Cook, uncovered, on HIGH 1½ minutes; turn over and cook 2½ to 3½ minutes more.
8 to 12 patties (1 pound) on roasting rack	Place on microwave roasting rack. Cover with paper towel. Cook HIGH 4 minutes; turn over and rearrange, cooking 2 to 4 minutes more.

Precooked Sausage Links

1 pound, browning dish	Preheat microwave browning dish on HIGH 5 to 8 minutes. Add links. Cook HIGH 1 minute; turn over and cook 1 to 2 minutes more.
1 pound, roasting rack	Follow Sausage Patties instructions above.

Fresh Sausage,
Casing removed (Italian, bulk)

1 pound	Break up in 2-quart casserole. Cook HIGH 5 minutes; drain and break up. Continue cooking 3 to 5 minutes more.

*Cooking more than 8 strips in the microwave is inefficient.

Name/Amount	Cooking Procedure

Large or Small Fresh Sausage in Casing (Italian, Bratwurst, French Veal)

1 pound — Preheat microwave browning dish on HIGH 5 to 8 minutes. Add sausage. Cook, uncovered, HIGH 2 minutes; turn over 2 to 4 minutes more.

Smoked or Cured Sausage (Frankfurters, Bratwurst, or Kielbasa)

Pierce casing with fork. On suitable microwaveproof dish. Cover with wax paper.

	(¾ to 1 inch thick)	(1½ to 2 inches thick)
1 link	HIGH 30 to 40 seconds.	40 to 50 seconds.
2 links	HIGH 1 to 1¼ minutes.	1¼ to 1½ minutes.
3 links	HIGH 1¼ to 1½ minutes.	1½ to 2 minutes.
4 links	HIGH 1½ to 2 minutes.	2 to 2½ minutes.

Frankfurters in Buns

Wrap in paper towel. Follow times above.

Large Smoked Sausage (Bratwurst or Kielbasa)

On suitable microwaveproof dish. Cover with wax paper. Cook HIGH 4 to 5 minutes per pound.

Fresh Ham or Pork Roast (With bone or boneless)

5 pounds or less — In 2-quart casserole with lid; fat-side down. Cover tightly. Cook HIGH 5 minutes; MEDIUM 11 to 12 minutes per pound to 165°F, turning over halfway through total cooking time. Stand, covered, 10 minutes.

more than 5 pounds — Same dish as above. Cover tightly. Cook HIGH 10 minutes; MEDIUM 12 to 13 minutes per pound to 165°F, turning over halfway through total cooking time. Stand, covered, 10 to 15 minutes.

Pork Tenderloin

In 2- to 3-quart casserole with lid. Cover tightly. Cook on HIGH 5 minutes; MEDIUM 11 to 12 minutes per pound to 165°F, covering ends with foil and turning over halfway through total cooking time. Tent loosely with foil. Stand, covered, 10 to 15 minutes.

Crown Roast of Pork

On microwave roasting rack in 2-quart rectangular dish; bone-side down. Cover tightly. Cook HIGH 10 minutes; cook MEDIUM 12 to 13 minutes per pound to 165°F, turning over halfway through total cooking time and stuffing as desired. Stand, covered, 10 minutes. Garnish.

Fresh Pork Chops

Dip in egg and coat with homemade fine bread-crumb coating or dip in packaged coating. Place on microwave roasting rack or plate. Cover with paper towel.

1 chop	Cook HIGH 1 minute; turn and cook MEDIUM 3 minutes.
2 chops	Cook HIGH 2 minutes; turn and cook MEDIUM 6 minutes.
3 chops	Cook HIGH 3 minutes; turn and cook MEDIUM 6 minutes.

Pork Spareribs

Meaty-side down, meatiest ends to outside in 3-quart dish. Cover with wax paper. Cook HIGH 5 minutes; rearrange. Cook MEDIUM 20 minutes per pound, turning over once. Uncover last 10 minutes and brush with barbecue sauce.

Fully Cooked Canned Ham

Add ¼ cup water to suitable microwave dish. Cover tightly. Cook HIGH 5 minutes. Cook MEDIUM 5 to 8 minutes per pound or to 125°F; turn over once halfway through total cooking time. Glaze if desired during last 5 minutes, cooking uncovered. Stand 10 minutes.

Fully Cooked Ham with Bone

Add ¼ cup water to suitable dish. Cover bone with foil. Cover dish tightly. Cook HIGH 5 minutes; then cook MEDIUM 10 to 12 minutes per pound or to 125°F; turn over halfway through total cooking time and remove foil. Glaze if desired during last 5 minutes, cooking uncovered. Stand 10 minutes.

Uncooked Smoked Ham with Bone

Same as above but cook HIGH 5 minutes, then MEDIUM 11 to 13 minutes per pound or 125°F. Glaze if desired during last 5 minutes, cooking uncovered. Stand 10 minutes.

Fully Cooked Boneless Ham

Same as above but cook HIGH 5 minutes, then MEDIUM 12 to 15 minutes per pound or 125°F. Glaze if desired during last 5 minutes, cooking uncovered. Stand 10 minutes.

Name/Amount	Cooking Procedure
Fully Cooked Ham Steaks	Cover tightly in microwaveproof dish. Cook until bottom dish or top lid is *3 Macungie* to touch. (For more, see the Macungie Rule, page 44.)
1 small steak (½ pound)	Cook MEDIUM 3 to 4 minutes, turning over once.
2 steaks (1 pound)	Cook MEDIUM 6 to 8 minutes, turning over once.
4 steaks	Cook MEDIUM 12 to 15 minutes, turning over once.
Fully Cooked Picnic or Canadian-Style Bacon or Tongue	Add ½ cup water to suitable dish. Cover tightly. Cook HIGH 5 minutes, then MEDIUM 10 to 12 minutes per pound or to 125°F, turning over halfway through total cooking. Glaze if desired during last 5 minutes, cooking uncovered. Stand 5 minutes. *Variation*: Substitute fruit juice for water. Glaze last 10 minutes.
Canadian Bacon Slices (¼ inch thick)	In suitable microwave dish cover with wax paper. Cook MEDIUM
1 slice	45 to 50 seconds.
2 slices	1¾ to 2¼ minutes.
3 slices	2¼ to 3 minutes.
4 slices	3¼ to 4 minutes.

POULTRY COOKING CHART

Name/Amount	Cooking Procedure	Variations
Whole Chicken 2 to 6 pounds	Truss. Salt and pepper. Breast side down in 2- to 3-quart rectangular dish. Cook, uncovered, HIGH 6 to 9 minutes per pound; turn over halfway through cooking. Stand, covered with foil, 5 to 10 minutes.	Glaze (pages 347–48) before cooking; *or* Stuff (pages 349–50) before cooking; *or*

6 to 8 pounds	Truss. Salt and pepper. Breast side down in 3-quart rectangular baking dish. Cook, uncovered, HIGH 10 minutes. Cook MEDIUM 10 minutes per pound, turning over halfway through cooking. Stand, tented with foil, 10 minutes.	Crisp at end of cooking in 500°F oven 5 to 10 minutes.

Chicken Parts
(1 serving equals 8 to 9 ounces—½ breast or 1 thigh plus 1 leg, no wings)

1 serving	In small microwaveproof plate. Cover with wax paper. Cook HIGH 4 to 7 minutes.	Glaze (pages 347–48) before cooking. No cover; *or*
2 servings	Same dish as above. Cook HIGH 8 to 14 minutes.	Remove skin. Dip pieces in 1 beaten egg, seasoned bread crumbs, sprinkled with paprika. Cover with paper towel; *or*
3 servings	In 10-inch pie plate, place meaty areas outside. Cover with wax paper. Cook HIGH 12 to 18 minutes.	Shake in prepared coating mix. Cover with paper towel; *or*
4 to 5 servings	Same dish as above. Cook HIGH 16 to 24 minutes; turn over once. Let stand, covered, 5 minutes.	Remove skin. Brush with Sweet and Sour Marinade (page 352) before cooking.

Chicken Breasts

1 (about 1 pound) Makes 2 cups cubed chicken	Rub with juice of ½ lemon. Insert 2 sprigs or leaves fresh herbs, or ¼ teaspoon dried between skin and meat. In small microwaveproof plate, place breast side up. Cover tightly. Cook HIGH 6 to 8 minutes.	Eliminate herbs. Glaze (pages 347–48) before cooking. No cover; *or* Remove skin.
2 (about 2 pounds) Makes 4 cups cubed chicken	Double lemon juice and herbs above. Place breast-side down, with meaty portions along outside of pie plate. Cover tightly. Cook HIGH 13 to 17 minutes, turning over and rearranging once halfway through cooking.	Eliminate herbs. Dip pieces in 1 beaten egg, then in seasoned bread crumbs, sprinkled with paprika. Cover with paper towel.

Name/Amount	Cooking Procedure	Variations
Boneless Chicken Breasts 2 (about 1 pound)	In 10-inch pie plate with 1 tablespoon lemon juice. Salt and pepper. Cover with wax paper. Cook HIGH 6 to 8 minutes, turning over after 4 minutes.	Substitute white wine or dry vermouth for lemon juice.
Turkey 12 to 16 pounds*	Truss. Breast side down in 3-quart rectangular dish. Brush with ¼ cup melted butter. Cook, uncovered, MEDIUM-HIGH 9 minutes per pound, turning once and draining fat halfway through cooking. Stand, tented with foil, 10 to 15 minutes. (If no MEDIUM-HIGH setting, cook HIGH 10 minutes, then MEDIUM 10 to 12 minutes per pound. Crisp at end of cooking in 500°F oven 5 to 10 minutes.	Same as above.
Turkey Breast 5 to 6 pounds	Breast side down in 2-quart rectangular dish. Cook, uncovered, HIGH 7 minutes per pound. Turn over. Cook MEDIUM 8 to 9 minutes per pound. Stand, tented with foil, 10 minutes.	Glaze (pages 347–48) before cooking; or crisp at end of cooking in 500°F oven 5 to 10 minutes.
Cornish Game Hens 1 to 1½ pounds *each*	Remove giblets. Breast-side down in cooking dish. Baste with melted better. Cook, uncovered, HIGH 8 minutes per pound, turning over once. Stand, covered with foil, 5 minutes.	Glaze (pages 347–48) before cooking; or stuff with ½ cup stuffing (349–51); or crisp at end of cooking in 500°F oven for 5 minutes.
Duck and Goose 5 to 6 pounds	Remove fat from neck and cavity. Remove giblets. Truss. Prick skin. Place breast side down on microwaveproof roasting rack in 2-quart rectangular dish. Cook, uncovered, HIGH 6 to 7 minutes per pound, turning over once and draining juices. Transfer to metal roasting rack in same dish. Crisp in 500°F conventional oven for 10 minutes. Let stand, tented with foil, 5 to 15 minutes.	

*Cook larger turkeys in conventional oven.

Chicken Livers

½ to 1½ pounds	Rinse in cold water; pat dry. In 9-inch pie plate with 1 tablespoon butter. Cover with wax paper. Cook MEDIUM 9 to 11 minutes per pound, stirring twice. Salt and pepper. Stand, covered, 2 to 5 minutes.	Substitute water for butter.

VEGETABLE COOKING CHART

Serve vegetables with any of the toppings suggested in the chapter on vegetables.

Name/Amount	Cooking Procedure
Frozen Vegetables Vacuum-Sealed	
10 ounces (2 cups) frozen vegetables in butter or cream sauce, or no sauce	Cut huge X on one side of pouch. Place cut-side down in 1-quart casserole or serving dish. Cook HIGH 3 to 7 minutes. Look at *cream* sauce after 2 minutes. If it appears to be overcooking on the corners, pour vegetables and sauce into bowl and stir. Cover tightly, and continue to cook.
High-Water-Content Vegetables	
10 ounces (2 cups) frozen asparagus, eggplant, zucchini	Place in 1-quart casserole or serving dish. Cover tightly. Cook HIGH 2 minutes; stir. Cover again. Cook HIGH 2 to 5 minutes more.
Medium-Water-Content Vegetables	
10 ounces (2 cups) frozen broccoli; Brussels sprouts; carrots; cauliflower; corn; okra	Place in 1-quart casserole or serving dish. Add 2 tablespoons water. Cover tightly. Cook HIGH 2 minutes; stir. Cover again and cook HIGH 2 to 6 minutes more.
16 to 18 ounces (4 cups) frozen vegetables	Add 2 tablespoons water in casserole twice as high as vegetables. Cover tightly. Cook HIGH 6 to 8 minutes, stirring once.
Low-Water-Content Vegetables	
10 ounces (2 cups) frozen lima beans; black-eyed peas; beans: green, wax, French-style or Italian cut beans	Place in 1-quart casserole or serving dish. Add ¼ cup water. Cover tightly. Cook HIGH 3 minutes; stir. Cover again and cook HIGH 1 to 5 minutes more. NOTE: If these seem to overcook and get hard on HIGH power, cook MEDIUM 5 minutes; stir and cook 5 to 6 minutes more.
Canned Vegetables	
16 ounces canned vegetables	Drain liquid, reserving 2 tablespoons in 1-quart casserole or serving dish. Add vegetables. Cover with wax paper. Cook HIGH 2 to 3 minutes, stirring once.

Name/Amount	Cooking Procedure
(canned vegetables continued) 16 ounces canned baked beans	Place in 1-quart casserole or serving dish. Cover with wax paper. Cook MEDIUM 3 to 5 minutes, stirring once.

DRY AND FRESH VEGETABLES COOKING CHART

Vegetables are listed under the following categories: cabbage family, edible pods and seeds, fruit, greens, legumes or dried beans, mushrooms, onions, potatoes, root vegetables, squash, and stalk vegetables.

Vegetable/Amount	Cooking Procedure	Variation
CABBAGE FAMILY **Bok Choy** 2 pounds, stalks cut into ⅛-inch pieces and leaves chopped into ½-inch strips	In 3-quart casserole with ¼ cup water. Cover tightly. Cook HIGH 4 to 5 minutes, stirring once.	Add 2 tablespoons soy sauce.
Brussels Sprouts 1 pound whole, trimmed, with X cut into bottom of each stem	In 1½-quart casserole with ¼ cup water. Cover tightly. Cook HIGH 4 to 8 minutes, stirring once. Stand, covered, 3 minutes.	Substitute chicken or vegetable broth or 2 tablespoons butter for ¼ cup water.
Cabbage, Red or Green 1 pound, cut into 4 wedges (savoy wedges same time) 1 pound, shredded (4 to 5 cups)	In 2-quart rectangle with ¼ cup water. Cover tightly. Cook HIGH 12 to 15 minutes; rearrange once. Stand, covered, 2 minutes. In 1½-quart casserole with ¼ cup water. Cover tightly. Cook HIGH 7 to 13 minutes, stirring once. Stand, covered, 3 minutes.	Same as above.
Cabbage, Savoy 1 pound, shredded	In 3-quart casserole with ¼ cup water. Cover tightly. Cook HIGH 7 to 13 minutes, stirring once. Stand, covered, 3 minutes.	Same as above.
Cauliflower 1 pound, whole, trimmed and core removed	In 1½-quart casserole with 2 tablespoons water. Cover tightly. Cook HIGH 6 to 9 minutes. Stand, covered, 3 minutes.	Substitute chicken or vegetable broth for water.

1 pound, core removed and broken into flowerets (2 cups)	In 1½-quart casserole with ¼ cup water. Cover tightly. Cook HIGH 4 to 7 minutes, stirring once. Stand, covered, 3 minutes.	Same as above or 2 tablespoons butter for water.

Kohlrabi

2 pounds (4 to 5 medium), peeled, halved and cut into ¼-inch cubes or ⅛-inch slices	In 2-quart casserole with ¼ cup water. Cover tightly. Cook HIGH 8 to 12 minutes, stirring once. Stand, covered, 2 to 3 minutes.	Same as above.

EDIBLE PODS AND SEEDS

Beans, Broad, Fava, or Lima

1 cup, shelled and rinsed	In 1-quart casserole with ¼ cup water. Cover tightly. Cook HIGH 3 to 5 minutes to boil; stir. Cook MEDIUM 4 to 8 minutes, stirring once. Stand, covered, 2 to 3 minutes.	Substitute chicken, beef, or vegetable broth for water.
2 cups, shelled and rinsed	In 1½-quart casserole with ½ cup water. Cover tightly. Cook HIGH 5 to 7 minutes to boil; stir. Cook MEDIUM 5 to 10 minutes, stirring once. Stand, covered, 2 to 3 minutes.	

Beans, Green or Wax

1 pound whole, trimmed	In 2-quart casserole with ½ cup water. Cover tightly. Cook HIGH 5 to 13 minutes, stirring twice (5 minutes is tender crisp). Stand, covered, 3 to 5 minutes.	Substitute vegetable or chicken broth or chopped tomatoes.
1 pound, cut into 2-inch pieces	In 2-quart casserole with ⅓ cup water. Cover tightly. Cook HIGH 5 to 11 minutes, stirring twice (5 minutes is tender crisp). Stand, covered, 3 to 5 minutes.	Same as above.

Corn on the Cob

1 medium ear	Leave in husk or wrap husked ear in wax paper. Place in oven. Cook HIGH 3 to 6 minutes, turning over once. Stand, wrapped, 1 to 2 minutes.
2 medium ears, husked	Same as above. Cook HIGH 4 to 9 minutes, turning over once. Stand, wrapped, 1 to 2 minutes.
3 or 4 medium ears, husked	In a 2-quart rectangular dish with ¼ cup water. Cover tightly. Cook HIGH 6 to 16 minutes, turning over every 4 minutes. Stand, covered, 1 to 2 minutes.

Name/Amount	Cooking Procedure	Variation
Corn Kernels (Fresh) 1½ cups fresh kernels	In 1½-quart casserole with 2 tablespoons water. Cover tightly. Cook HIGH 4 to 7 minutes, stirring once.	Substitute 2 tablespoons chicken or vegetable broth or 2 tablespoons butter.
Peas, Green 2 cups (2 pounds), shelled	In 1½-quart casserole with ¼ cup water. Cover tightly. Cook HIGH 4 to 7 minutes, stirring once.	Same as above.
Peas, Snow or Sugar Snap ¼ pound	In a small casserole or pie plate with 2 tablespoons water. Cover tightly. Cook HIGH 1 to 4 minutes, stirring once.	Substitute 2 tablespoons broth or butter.

FRUIT
Eggplant

1 medium eggplant (1 pound), skin pierced	Place in oven. Cook HIGH 5 to 7 minutes, turning over once. Cook until collapsed and very soft inside.	
2 medium eggplants (1 pound *each*), skin pierced	Same as above. Cook HIGH 10 to 14 minutes, turning over once.	
Peppers, Parboiled 6 whole, stem and seeds removed	Place cut-side down in 2-quart rectangular dish with 2 tablespoons liquid. Cover tightly. Cook HIGH 5 to 6 minutes, turning over once, until partially cooked but still retain crispness and shape.	
Tomatoes 4 (about 2 pounds), peeled and quartered	Place in 2-quart casserole. Cover tightly. Cook HIGH 2½ to 5 minutes, stirring once.	

GREENS

NOTE: If greens have just been washed and are wet, add no liquid. If they have been drying awhile, add ¼ cup water.

Beet Tops

2 pounds, washed but not dried	In 3-quart casserole. Cover tightly. Cook HIGH 7 to 8 minutes, stirring once.	

Collard or Turnip
2 pounds, washed, but not dried, leaves coarsely chopped | In 3-quart casserole. Cover tightly. Cook HIGH 10 to 15 minutes, stirring every 10 minutes. | Add 2 slices bacon, cut up.

Dandelion Leaves (Young)
2 pounds, washed but not dried, trimmed | In 3-quart casserole. Cover tightly. Cook HIGH 7 to 10 minutes, stirring once.

Kale
2 pounds, washed, but not dried, coarsely chopped | In 3-quart casserole. Cover tightly. Cook HIGH 15 to 20 minutes, stirring every 5 minutes. | Same as above.

Mustard
2 pounds, washed, but not dried, stems removed, and leaves coarsely chopped | In 3-quart casserole. Cover tightly. Cook HIGH 15 to 20 minutes, stirring every 5 minutes. | Add 2 slices bacon, cut up.

Spinach or Sorrel
2 pounds, washed but not dried, trimmed | In 3-quart casserole. Cover tightly. Cook HIGH 7 to 10 minutes, stirring once.

Swiss Chard
2 pounds, washed, but not dried, stems removed, and leaves cut into ½-inch strips | In 3-quart casserole. Cover tightly. Cook HIGH 7 to 10 minutes, stirring once.

LEGUMES OR DRIED BEANS
NOTE: 2 cups dry presoaked beans will yield 5 cups when cooked.

Black, Kidney, Navy, or Pinto Beans, or Black-eyed Peas
2 cups, presoaked and drained | In 4-quart casserole with 3 cups water. Cover tightly. Cook HIGH 10 to 15 minutes to boil; stir. Cook MEDIUM 30 to 45 minutes, stirring after 15 minutes. Stand, covered, 5 minutes.

Chick-Peas
2 cups, presoaked and drained | In 4-quart casserole with 3½ cups water. Cover tightly. Cook HIGH 10 to 15 minutes to boil; stir. Cook MEDIUM 30 to 45 minutes, stirring every 10 minutes. Stand, covered, 5 minutes.

Name/Amount	Cooking Procedure	Variation
Split Peas (Green or Yellow) or Lentils		
2 cups, presoaked and drained	In 4-quart casserole with 3 cups water. Cover tightly. Cook HIGH 10 to 15 minutes to boil; stir. Cook MEDIUM 30 to 45 minutes, stirring every 10 to 15 minutes. Stand, covered, 5 minutes.	
MUSHROOMS		
½ pound whole, trimmed	In 1-quart casserole. Cook, uncovered, HIGH 2 to 4 minutes, stirring once.	
1 pound whole, trimmed	In 1-quart casserole. Cook, uncovered, HIGH 3 to 6½ minutes, stirring after 2 minutes.	
3 ounces (½ cup), sliced	In pie plate. 1 tablespoon butter. Cook, uncovered, HIGH 1 to 3 minutes, stirring after 1 minute.	Substitute 1 tablespoon wine, or chicken broth.
½ pound, sliced	In 1-quart casserole with 2 tablespoons butter. Cook, uncovered, HIGH 2 to 4 minutes, stirring after 1 minute.	
1 pound, sliced	In 1½-quart casserole with 2 tablespoons butter. Cook, uncovered, HIGH 3 to 6 minutes, stirring after 2 minutes.	
ONIONS		
Leeks		
2 pounds, roots and ends trimmed, leaving 1½ inches dark green stalk. Cut in quarters with 2 right-angle slices down to white base of stalk.	In 2-quart rectangular dish with ¼ cup water. Cover tightly. Cook HIGH 7 to 12 minutes, rearranging once.	Substitute white wine, any broth, or 2 tablespoons butter.
Onions, Pearl or Small White		
1 pound, peeled	In 1- to 1½-quart casserole with 2 tablespoons water. Cover tightly. Cook HIGH 6 to 8 minutes, stirring once.	Same as above.
Onions, White or Yellow		
1 pound, peeled (4, quartered, or 16 small)	In a 1½-quart casserole with 2 tablespoons water. Cover tightly. Cook HIGH 7 to 8 minutes, stirring and turning over once.	Substitute vermouth, Madeira, dry sherry, any broth, or butter
4 medium-size onions, peeled and sliced	In 2-quart casserole with 2 tablespoons water. Cover tightly. Cook HIGH 6 to 8 minutes, stirring once.	

Scallions or Green Onions

1 pound, trimmed	In 2-quart rectangular dish with 2 tablespoons water. Cover tightly. Cook HIGH 6 to 10 minutes, rearranging stalks once.	Substitute 2 tablespoons lemon juice plus 2 teaspoons sugar.

POTATOES
Baking Potatoes, Russet/Idaho, Sweet Potatoes

1 medium, pierced	Place on paper towel in oven. Cook HIGH 3 to 5 minutes, turning over once. Wrap in terrycloth towel. Stand, 5 to 10 minutes for white potatoes, 3 for sweet potatoes.
2 medium, pierced	Place on paper towel with 1-inch space between them. Cook HIGH 5 to 9 minutes, turning over once. Stand 5 to 10 minutes for potatoes, 3 for sweet potatoes.
4 medium, pierced	Place on paper towel in a circle with 1-inch space between them. Cook HIGH 10 to 13 minutes, turning over once. Stand 5 to 10 minutes for potatoes, 3 for sweet potatoes.

New or Long White (Boiling)

4 medium or 1 to 1½ pounds new, peeled* and sliced, cubed or quartered	In 2-quart casserole with ¼ cup water. Cover tightly. Cook HIGH 7 to 10 minutes, stirring once. Stand, covered, 3 minutes
6 medium or 1½ to 2 pounds new, peeled* and sliced, cubed or quartered	In 2-quart casserole with ¼ cup water. Cover tightly. Cook HIGH 9 to 12 minutes, stirring twice. Stand, covered, 3 minutes.

ROOT VEGETABLES
Beets

1 pound, 2-inch diameter whole, trimmed, leaving 1-inch stem†	In 1½-quart casserole with ½ cup water. Cover tightly. Cook HIGH 15 to 20 minutes, stirring every 5 minutes. Stand, covered, 3 to 5 minutes. Slip off skins and slice.

Carrots

12 ounces, cut into 2-inch chunks or spears	In 1-quart casserole plus 2 tablespoons water. Cover tightly. Cook HIGH 6 to 8 minutes, stirring once. Stand, covered, 3 minutes.	Substitute 2 tablespoons orange juice, chicken or vegetable broth, or butter.

*Peeling is optional.
†Prevents too much bleeding into cooking liquid.

Name/Amount	Cooking Procedure	Variation
(carrots continued)		
2 cups, cut into ¼-inch slices	In 1-quart casserole plus 2 tablespoons water. Cover tightly. Cook HIGH 4 to 8 minutes, stirring once. Stand, covered, 3 minutes.	
12 ounces baby whole, trimmed	In 1-quart casserole with 2 tablespoons water. Cover tightly. Cook HIGH 6 to 8 minutes, stirring once. Stand, covered, 3 minutes.	Same as above.
Jerusalem Artichokes (Sun Chokes)		
1 pound, scrubbed (peel if desired), cut into ¼-inch slices	In 2-quart casserole with ¼ cup water. Cover tightly. Cook HIGH 6 to 9 minutes, stirring once. Stand, covered, 3 to 5 minutes.	
Jicama		
1 pound, peeled and cut into ½-inch cubes or ¼-inch strips	In 2-quart casserole with ¼ cup water. Cover tightly. Cook HIGH 8 to 10 minutes, stirring once. Stand, covered, 3 to 5 minutes.	
Parsnips/Salsify		
1 pound (4 medium), cut up	In 1-quart casserole with ¼ cup water. Cover tightly. Cook HIGH 5 to 7 minutes, stirring once. Stand, covered, 3 minutes.	
Rutabagas		
1½ pounds, peeled and cut into ½-inch cubes	In 2-quart casserole with ¼ cup water. Cover tightly. Cook HIGH 10 to 14 minutes, stirring every 3 minutes. Stand, covered, 3 minutes.	
Turnips		
1½ pounds (4 medium), cut into ¼-inch slices	In 1-quart casserole with ¼ cup water. Cover tightly. Cook HIGH 9 to 11 minutes, stirring once. Stand, covered, 3 minutes.	
1½ pounds (4 medium), cut into ½-inch cubes	In 1-quart casserole with ¼ cup water. Cover tightly. Cook HIGH 12 to 14 minutes, stirring once. Stand, covered, 3 minutes.	
SQUASH, SUMMER (THIN SKINNED)		
Crookneck (Yellow) or Straightneck Squash		
1 medium (about ½ pound), cut into ¼-inch slices	In 2-quart casserole. Cover tightly. Cook HIGH 2 to 5 minutes, stirring after 1 minute.	

Pattypan (Immature) or Scalloped Squash

4 cups, cut into ¾-inch cubes or ½-inch slices	In 1½-quart casserole with 2 tablespoons water. Cook HIGH 6 to 10 minutes, stirring after 3 minutes.	Substitute 2 tablespoons butter.

Zucchini

1 medium (about ½ pound), cut into ¼-inch slices	In 2-quart casserole. Cover tightly. Cook HIGH 2 to 5 minutes, stirring after 1 minute.

SQUASH, WINTER (THICK SKINNED)

Acorn

1 (1½ pounds) whole, pierced	Place on paper towel in oven. Cook HIGH 8 to 11½ minutes, turning over after 5 minutes. Stand 5 to 10 minutes.
2 (1½ pounds each) whole, pierced	Place on paper towel in oven. Cook HIGH 12 to 16 minutes, turning over after 8 minutes. Stand 5 to 10 minutes.

Butternut or Hubbard

2 pounds, cut lengthwise in half and widthwise into quarters, seeded	In 2-quart rectangular dish, cut side up. Cover tightly. Cook HIGH 12 to 18 minutes; rearrange every 4 minutes.

Pattypan (Mature)

1 (½ pound) whole, with top cut off and seeds removed	Cover tops tightly with plastic wrap. Place on paper towel. Cook HIGH 2 to 4½ minutes. Stand, covered, 3 minutes.
2 (½ pound each) whole, with tops cut off and seeds removed	Same preparation as above. Cook HIGH 3 to 5 minutes. Stand, covered, 3 minutes.

Pumpkin (Cooking Variety)

1 (4 to 5 pounds), halved (For a larger pumpkin, cook half at a time)	Cover cut sides with plastic wrap. Place on paper towel in oven. Cook HIGH 16 to 24 minutes; rearrange every 4 minutes. Remove seeds.

Spaghetti Squash

1 pound, whole	Place on paper towel in oven. Cook HIGH 6 to 10 minutes, turning over after 3 minutes. Stand 5 minutes. Cut open, remove seeds, and separate flesh into spaghetti strings with fork.	Serve with meat sauce, fresh parsley and Parmesan, or 1 cup cubed tofu and tomato sauce.

Name/Amount	Cooking Procedure	Variation
STALK VEGETABLES		
Asparagus		
1 pound, ends snapped	In 2-quart rectangular dish with ¼ cup water. Place tips toward center of dish. Cover tightly. Cook HIGH 4 to 9 minutes, rearranging once. Stand, covered, 3 minutes.	Substitute vegetable or chicken broth or 2 tablespoons butter.
1 pound, ends snapped and spears cut into 1-inch pieces	In 2-quart casserole with ¼ cup water. Cover tightly. Cook HIGH 3 to 7 minutes. Stand, covered, 2 minutes.	
Broccoli		
1 pound, trimmed, cut into spears, peeling lower 2 inches of stalks, if desired	In 2-quart rectangular dish or casserole with ¼ cup water. Arrange stalks to outside. Cover tightly. Cook HIGH 6 to 10 minutes, rearranging once. Stand, covered, 3 minutes.	Same as above.
1 pound, 4 inches of stalk removed, remainder cut into flowerets	In 2-quart casserole with ¼ cup water. Cover tightly. Cook HIGH 5 to 8 minutes, stirring once. Stand, covered, 3 minutes.	
Celery		
6 to 8 medium ribs	In 2-quart rectangular dish with ¼ cup water. Place thick ends toward outside. Cover tightly. Cook HIGH 5 to 9 minutes, rearranging once. Stand, covered, 3 minutes.	Same as above.
6 to 8 medium ribs, sliced	In 1½-quart casserole with 2 tablespoons water. Cover tightly. Cook HIGH 3 to 6 minutes, stirring once. Stand, covered, 3 minutes.	
Fennel		
2 heads, thin leafy tops cut off, stalks halved lengthwise and cut into ½-inch pieces	In 2-quart rectangular dish with ¼ cup water. Thicker pieces outside. Cover tightly. Cook HIGH 7 to 9 minutes; reposition once.	Same as above.
Swiss Chard Stalks		
2 cups, cut into ½-inch pieces	In 1-quart casserole with 2 tablespoons water. Cover tightly. Cook HIGH 2 to 5 minutes, stirring once.	

Recipe Conversion

We tried to come up with a simple, surefire way to convert your conventional recipes. We really did! But just when we thought we had all the bases covered, we'd come across a conventional recipe that would defy all the rules.

We came to the conclusion that there is no surefire method for conversion, and the only suggestion to be trusted is "to find a microwave recipe that is similar to your conventional one." If you can't find a similar recipe, there must be a reason why, and it could be that the recipe may not work as well in the microwave. We don't want to discourage you from experimenting, but we do want to squash hopes of finding a quick, pat method.

Having said that, here is what you can do if you find a microwave recipe that is similar to yours. First, read the recipe basics, which will indicate what the important techniques are in the recipe. Specifically look at the following factors and adapt your recipe accordingly:

1. *Dish size.* Compare the yield of your recipe to the similar microwave recipe and choose an appropriate dish size.
2. *Power settings and timings.* If the recipe uses two power settings, look at the "or until" that follows the cooking time to give you an indication of what you are looking for in each step.
3. *Special techniques.* Stirring, rotating, or turning over are a few. These will aid evenness of cooking.
4. *Type of lid or cover.* A tight cover, such as a lid or plastic wrap, will keep in steam and moisture; a paper towel covering will absorb moisture and keep the surface dry.
5. *Amount of liquid.* You will probably have to reduce the liquid in your recipe by a quarter of the amount, but look at the microwave recipe to make sure. In other words, if your recipe calls for 1 cup, reduce that to ¾ cup.
6. *Amount of fat for sautéing.* Fat for sautéing in microwave cooking is added for flavor, rather than to keep any food from sticking. It can be cut in half or eliminated.
7. *Cooking steps.* Try to parallel the cooking steps in the microwave recipe. If ingredients are added in stages, it is because they cook best that way.
8. *Doneness.* Check for early doneness, based on the basic information given about the recipe. Don't overcook! Remember that if a standing time is called for, this will be a time for cooking to continue.

3

HOW TO CHOOSE UTENSILS

Dish Materials

Have you ever brewed tea with the radiant energy of the sun? You can do this by placing tea bags into cold water in a glass pitcher and setting it in the sun. The sunlight passes through the glass to heat the water. In a few hours the tea is brewed. Therefore glass is a good material for maximum heating.

Because microwaves have a lower frequency and longer wavelength than sunlight (see chart, page 18) they will pass through clear and colored glass, plastic, and paper. Dishes that withstand temperatures of up to 450°F are important to withstand the temperatures of hot food. Certain plastics, polysulfones, or heat-set polyesters, are best for cooking and reheating; other plastics, if not indicated for microwave use, should be restricted to reheating only because the heat from the food, particularly a high-fat or -sugar food, will melt or warp the plastic that it touches.

Avoid dishes with metal trim.

Fact: Choose glass, ceramic, paper, and plastic dishes for cooking in the microwave.

Dish Shape

When you're out in the hot sun, which parts of your body are going to get more sunburned than the others?

Knees, noses, and knuckles will probably receive the most sun. That's because knees (if you're sitting) and knuckles expose more angles for the sun's rays to hit. To contrast this, your arms will get more evenly tanned because they are rounded and smooth.

This happens to the food in the corners of square and rectangular dishes. The food in corners absorbs microwave energy from more angles and cooks more quickly. That's why the best shapes for microwave cooking are round, oval, or Bundt-shaped dishes. If a square or rectangular dish is necessary to cook brownies or a casserole, metal foil placed over the corners will shield the food and keep it from overcooking.

Fact: Food in the corners of dishes tends to overcook first, in the way that your knees and nose redden more in the sun. Choose rounded, oval, or Bundt-shaped dishes for cooking.

Dish Depth

Back to those ice cream bars again. Take twelve ice cream bars. In one dish make two rows of three ice cream bars, one row on top of the other. In another long rectangular dish lay the other six bars side by side. Place them in the hot sun. Which six bars will melt more quickly? The bars in the dish where they could be laid out flat, exposing more of their surface area to the sun.

The same is true of casserole surface areas in the microwave. The more surface areas you expose, the faster a food will cook. This is not always good. A stew, tomato sauce, or soup in a shallow, wide dish will boil over. A cake that calls for a 9-inch round dish will cook too quickly if placed in a 10-inch round dish. The Basics sections in the category you're cooking will tell you whether the dish size is important, and so will the recipes.

When cooking a liquid, such as soup or sauce, choose a casserole that is twice as high as the food in it. That way stirring will be easier and boilover eliminated.

Fact: Follow Basics and recipe instructions for choosing the proper dish for the food you're cooking.

Specifics to Look for When You're in the Store

- "Suitable for Microwave" seal somewhere on it. Especially with plastic dishes. If glass, the dishes should be heatproof, so that they can endure the heat of the food and not crack. If you're unsure, check according to the test on page 85.
- No metal trim, which will spark or arc as it reflects microwave energy. For more, see sparking and arcing, page 32.
- Round or oval dishes.
- Straight sides, instead of sides that angle down and inward, are more desirable for even cooking and stirring.
- Protruding handles that won't get hot from the heat of the foods in the dish.
- Nesting dishes, particularly nice for storage without waste.
- Casseroles with lids for recipes requiring

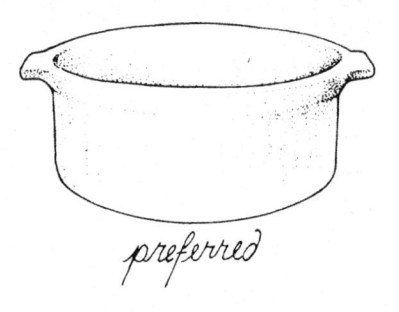

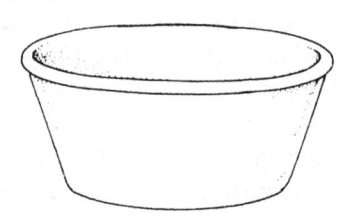

preferred

much stirring, such as stews, soups, or pasta sauces. Glass lids are much more durable for this task than plastic wrap. A clear glass casserole is much easier to see into to check for boiling.

Cooking Utensils Inventory

Our choices include utensils designed mainly for four to six servings, as well as dishes that are suitable for single servings.

Necessary

Type	Common Uses
4-cup glass measure 2-cup glass measure	For measuring and melting, making cream sauces, heating broth cubes
six 4-ounce custard cups (If you can find 10-ounce custard cups with lids the applications will be even greater.)	Cooking eggs, melting butter, single-serving meat loaves, fish rolls, egg custards, or turning 2-quart glass dish into a Bundt dish. Great for cooking and freezing individual servings, baby food
1- and 2-quart glass casseroles with lids*	Four-serving casseroles, soups, sauces, shellfish, vegetables
4-quart glass casserole with lid*	Longer cooking soups and tomato sauces that may boil up, stews
Hard plastic freezer containers	Good for storing and defrosting
8½-inch round cake dish and/or 9-inch pie plate	Layer cakes, rolled fish fillets, pies, shellfish
2-quart rectangular (12- x -8-inch) or oval baking dish	Chicken cutlets, fish fillets, pork chops, asparagus, pasta casseroles
Roasting rack (fits 2- or 3-quart rectangular dishes)	Pork and beef roasts when making gravy from juices, turkey
12-inch diameter circular dish	Perfect for many main dishes that can be placed in a ring; hors d'oeuvres
Cereal bowl	Handy for melting chocolate, sautéing nuts in butter
Small wire whisk	Excellent for smooth sauces

*Lids make peeking, stirring, and re-covering food so much easier than plastic wrap.

Nice to Have

Clay simmerpot with glazed interior on bottom (page 86)	Tougher cuts of meat, stewed chicken, and stews (often makes these more tender), foods that benefit from longer, slower cooking
3-quart rectangular (13- × -9-inch) or oval baking dish (won't fit into all ovens so measure oven interior before buying)	Pork and beef roasts, turkey, pork chops, whole fish, and some casseroles
Larger self-contained roasting rack (10½- × -11-inch)	For roasts, bacon, dry-coated chicken cutlets, breaded mushrooms and other vegetables
Heavy duty Ziploc bags	Freezing, storing, and reheating right in bag
13- × -9-inch browning dish (again, measure oven and go with smaller size if necessary)	Grilled meats, pizzas and toasted sandwiches
Conventional or microwave thermometer	Meat cookery
Heavy-duty plastic mixing spoons with hooks on handles	Nice to stir and leave in cooking dish; hooks keep from falling in
Heavy-duty paperboard cooking dishes	For freezing and reheating leftovers

Special Equipment

Temperature Probe

A temperature probe is not a utensil that you buy for your oven. It either comes with your oven, or it doesn't. The name has often been misleading to new owners who think that the word *temperature* has something to do with heat in the oven. It doesn't. *It measures the internal temperature of the food only.* An accessory that you can purchase is called a "microwave meat thermometer." It operates in the same way but has no connection with the oven.

A temperature probe is a metal spike with a cord. The cord is plugged into the inside of the oven, the point of the metal spike is inserted in the center of the food to be cooked, and it is the ½-to 1-inch tip that measures the temperature. Once the temperature probe is plugged in, you are cooking to the internal temperature of the food, and this replaces cooking time. When the food has reached the temperature that you set it for, the oven will signal or give some other indication.

In cooking roasts, we often give both a cooking time and an end temperature, so that you can use your probe. We don't recommend temperature probes for poultry because of the many bones, and irregular shape of the bird that may cause a higher and inaccurate reading before the meat is done.

The art of cooking with a temperature probe

happens to be personal preference. Some owners find that their probes may indicate that the food is done, when in fact it really isn't. This could be because the metal probe conducts heat faster than the food molecules around it. Nevertheless, if you like cooking with a probe in your conventional oven, you will probably be more inclined to use it in your microwave oven than someone who doesn't.

Are Your Dishes Microwaveproof? Here's a Test

We call for cooking dishes that are "microwaveproof." We've already mentioned that glass, paper, and plastics are good dish materials and that metals have a limited use.

What if you have just purchased a beautiful handmade ceramic casserole dish with no information on it?

Here is a simple test to see if it is suitable for the microwave:

1. Pour half a cup of tap water into a glass measure or bowl.
2. Place the dish to be tested beside the water dish in the oven.
3. Turn the oven on HIGH power for 1 minute.

If the water has become hot and your ceramic dish remains cool, your dish will be fine for microwave cooking.

If, on the other hand, the ceramic becomes warm, the dish is absorbing some microwave energy and this will increase the overall cooking time. The dish may also eventually crack from heating up and cooling down too quickly.

Browning Dishes

If a dish is placed in the oven with no food, it will absorb some of the microwave energy ... an insignificant amount if it is glass, paper, or plastic but it will absorb some nonetheless.

Browning dishes, although they look to be made of ceramic, have a center that is specially treated with metal strips or an area dimensioned to the length of about half a microwave wavelength. When heated alone, without any food, this treatment causes the microwaves to be "coupled" or linked, which produces an electrical current.

The dish also has a special tin oxide coating. Once the waves are "coupled," this tin oxide coating provides high resistance to the electrical current. The net result is a hot surface (560°F) to brown foods that would not normally brown in the microwave. Be assured that the handles of the dish will remain cool because they are not treated the way the center is.

When we call for a browning dish, we will specify the size if necessary. We never call for a browning dish with a lid, because we feel a cover for steaming will defeat the purpose of having a hot, dry cooking surface.

Fact: A specially designed dish becomes hot in the microwave because it contains metal strips dimensioned to "couple" or link microwave wavelengths into producing an electrical current, along with a high-resistance coating to this electrical current, that gets hot. The dish is good for searing small food items that won't normally brown.

Simmerpots

We don't know for sure, but we think that Attila the Hun was probably one of the first great promoters of simmerpots.

He probably didn't have his own "pot" per se—he didn't stay in one place long enough to accumulate much. But while he was busy ravaging the German countryside, he might have gathered some of that rich clay and wrapped it around a freshly killed fowl. Hours later, after throwing it into a pit of hot coals, Attila, or one of his underlings, could have broken open the clay (which plucked out the feathers, too) to find a lovely steamed chicken.

Now, pots are made of a special porous clay which absorbs water when it is soaked and releases it in the form of steam during cooking. This added moisture helps to tenderize the food and make it juicier.

We prefer pots with glazed interiors on the bottom because they won't absorb too much liquid and they are much easier to clean after cooking.

Instructions on your pot will say something like: "Soak the pot and lid in cold water for at least 30 minutes or overnight. After you have cooked with the simmerpot once, the pot and lid need only be soaked for 10 to 15 minutes in cold water prior to cooking."

After this soaking, the water is drained from the pot but not wiped dry. With this additional liquid in the pot, most recipes calling for the simmerpot will call for slightly less liquid.

Two general rules can be followed for adapting recipes to microwave simmerpot cooking:

1. Reduce liquid by ½ cup for *our* standard microwave stew recipes calling for approximately 1 pound stew meat and 2 cups vegetables. Also reduce liquid by ½ cup for whole meats or chickens.
2. For stews and whole meats, cooking begins at 5 minutes per pound on HIGH. Soups begin at up to 15 minutes on HIGH to bring to a boil. It is the water in the pot that is also absorbing energy and so slowing down the heating process in both cases.

And remember: Use potholders! The water in the pot is being heated along with the food and it can become very hot.

APPETIZERS AND SNACKS

Trying to group these recipes was like attempting to categorize a rush-hour crowd on the New York subway. There seemed to be no common denominator other than destination—in the case of these recipes, the stomach.

As American snacking became the rule and not the exception, cookbook writers expanded their first chapters to include not only premeal treats, but foods that could be consumed at any hour of the day. I'm not complaining because I'm all for snacking. Our only lament is that we would prefer to consider snacking as more than something just to replace a meal that has slipped by unnoticed, taking more time to enjoy it.

In India, a place where Eastern hospitality blends with British social graces, I found the best environment for convivial snacking. The home where I stayed in Delhi had two customary teatimes a day. If someone came to visit at a non-teatime, that called for additional tea. If we were visiting, even with a local merchant, we were offered yet more tea, and all the accompanying nuts and savories.

Informal snacking was part of traveling on foot, too, as one jostled past the hundreds of street stands that lined every main thoroughfare; within arm's reach was a panoply of colors and aromas that were hard to resist. Train travel seemed designed with socializing in mind. At every stop, men, women, and boys peddled food from cigar-type boxes that hung around their necks to the awaiting passengers.

Every snacktime was filled with melodious conversation as Indians spoke English with their musical lilt. Stories were shared between slurps of tea and mouthfuls of food. I found the most important part of serving food became the grace with which it was served. Simple food was embellished by kindness, and the less effort and strain the host exhibited, the more comfortable the guests were made to feel.

In this country, eating is often the only time we allow ourselves to relax. Real enjoyment of ourselves or of our guests often depends on whether we're rested or exhausted by the food's preparation; so it was with convenience and ease in mind that we collected the grab-bag of edibles, from pork to popcorn, that follows. With them we try to give advanced preparation and reheating suggestions where appropriate, along with many variations. A chopped egg filling can be dressed up with caviar, or dressed down for Monday's lunch. Marinated vegetables change to accommodate the seasonal produce. Sweet and sour chicken wings, depending on the climate, may be served hot or cold.

But when I'm ready to relax, I'll usually choose the Spicy Hot Popcorn or Spicy Nuts and a perfectly brewed cup of Earl Grey tea. Each crunchy nugget, washed down with a flowery billow of tea, will be a balm for both body and soul, and a transport to a time when snacking was lovely—and planned.

—MARCIA

WON TONS WITH SCALLOP STUFFING IN BASIL BUTTER

MAKES ABOUT 36 (16 WILL SERVE 4)   BEGIN 25 MINUTES BEFORE SERVING
COOKING TIME: 10 TO 15 MINUTES

East meets West when traditional Chinese morsels are served in Italian ravioli fashion. Mushrooms and scallops bond in a naturally light filling that is complemented by a rousing basil butter.

We thought that, as long as you're making these, why not have extra to freeze and bring out someday as a main course for two? If you have children at home they will enjoy helping you fill and fold them.

9 tablespoons butter	⅛ teaspoon pepper
1 scallion, sliced	4 quarts water, plus 1 tablespoon
1 tablespoon all-purpose flour	1 teaspoon cornstarch
8 ounces scallops, finely chopped	36 won ton skins (see Note)
8 ounces mushrooms, finely minced	¼ cup chopped fresh basil, plus some whole leaves
¼ teaspoon salt	Freshly grated Parmesan cheese

In a 1-quart casserole combine 1 tablespoon butter and the scallion. Cook on HIGH for 1 minute, or until the scallion is slightly tender. Stir in the flour to form a paste. Add scallops, mushrooms, salt, and pepper; stir to mix well. Cook, uncovered, on HIGH for 4 minutes to form a moist paste, stirring halfway through cooking.

Bring the 4 quarts water to a boil in a stockpot on top of the stove.

To prepare won tons: In a small bowl stir the cornstarch with 1 tablespoon water until smooth. Place a heaping teaspoon of scallop mixture in the center of a won ton skin. Brush the edges of the skin lightly with the cornstarch mixture. Fold in half, with points touching to form a triangle. Press firmly around the edges to seal. Leave as a triangle, or brush the edges with more cornstarch and fold again into a won ton shape as directed on the won ton package. Repeat with the other skins.

When the water comes to a boil, drop in 16 filled won tons. Boil for 5 to 6 minutes, until cooked through.

Meanwhile, in a 4-cup glass measure combine the remaining 8 tablespoons butter and the chopped basil. Cook on HIGH for 1 to 2 minutes, or until the butter is melted. Remove cooked won tons from the stockpot with a slotted spoon; arrange 4 on each serving plate. Spoon the basil butter on top, sprinkle with Parmesan cheese, and garnish each plate with a basil leaf or 2.

NOTE: Won ton skins can be purchased at most Oriental grocery stores. To freeze the remaining uncooked won tons, place one layer of won tons in a plastic container or baking dish lined with foil; top the layer with wax paper. Continue to layer won tons this way. Place the lid on top or seal tightly with foil, pressing out as much air as possible. Freeze for up to 2 months. Won tons can be boiled from their frozen state; just add a few minutes to the cooking time.

✹ BASIC MARINATED VEGETABLES

MAKES 4 SERVINGS BEGIN 1½ HOURS BEFORE SERVING
COOKING TIME: 12 TO 15 MINUTES

What we're doing in this recipe is blanching small amounts of vegetables to tender-crisp, using the marinade in place of water. The marinade flavors the vegetables and itself is flavored each time a vegetable is added. For this reason, the vegetables are added according to flavor strength so the stronger vegetables won't overpower the marinade. All the vegetables, except the mushrooms, are covered tightly with a lid or plastic wrap to retain steam for more even and faster cooking; mushrooms will turn very dark if they absorb too much liquid.

Because we have suggested eight vegetables from which to choose, this recipe will accommodate itself to any season. In the summer, vegetables prepared this way travel well in covered jelly jars to picnic sites as well as to evening outdoor concerts—they have the class and elegance to accompany Bach.

Marinade:
- 3 tablespoons olive oil
- 2 tablespoons lemon juice
- 1 tablespoon chopped fresh parsley
- ¼ teaspoon salt
- ⅛ teaspoon pepper

Vegetables (choose 4):
- 12 ounces quartered mushrooms
- ½ pound (2 small or 1 medium) zucchini, cut into ¼-inch-thick slices
- ½ pound whole green snap beans, ends removed
- 2 red, green, or yellow bell peppers, cut into ¼-inch lengths
- 2 large or 3 medium carrots, cut into 2-inch sticks
- 1 small (½ pound) eggplant, cut into 2-inch sticks
- 4 celery ribs, cut into 2-inch sticks
- Lettuce leaves

Combine the marinade ingredients in a 1-quart microwaveproof casserole or 4-cup glass measure.

If cooking mushrooms, add them to the marinade first. Cook, uncovered, on HIGH 2 minutes, stirring halfway through cooking. Reserving the liquid, transfer the mushrooms with a slotted spoon to a 2-quart dish.

Cook the other 3 vegetables of your choice, one at a time, in the order that they are listed and according to the timetable below, covering tightly. They should be tender-crisp. After each vegetable is cooked, transfer to the 2-quart dish for refrigeration, reserving the marinade for each remaining vegetable.

Zucchini	HIGH	2 minutes	Stir Halfway
Green snap beans	HIGH	3 minutes	Stir halfway
Peppers	HIGH	2 minutes	Stir halfway
Carrots	HIGH	3 minutes	Stir halfway
Eggplant	HIGH	3 minutes	Stir halfway
Celery	HIGH	3 minutes	Stir halfway

Pour the warm marinade over the cooked vegetables. Cover and chill for at least 1 hour. When ready to serve, bring to room temperature for fullest flavor. Arrange attractively on a large platter lined with lettuce leaves.

NOTE: Vegetables can be refrigerated for up to 4 days.

VARIATIONS:

Marinated Vegetables with Crunch: Just before serving, sprinkle 4 teaspoons pine nuts or sesame seeds on the platter of arranged vegetables. It's amazing how a simple touch like this can set a dish off and make it especially nice for company.

Marinated Vegetables aux Fines Herbes: Add 1 tablespoon chopped fresh basil or 1 teaspoon dried to the marinade before cooking green beans and peppers; add 1 tablespoon chopped fresh dill or 1 teaspoon dried to the marinade before cooking eggplant; or add 1 sprig tarragon or 1 teaspoon dried to the marinade before cooking any of the vegetables. Any of these will bring a nice aromatic lift to the basic marinade.

Marinated Vegetables with Creamy Mustard Sauce: Add 1 tablespoon Dijon or rough country mustard with seeds to the marinade ingredients before cooking the vegetables. After the vegetables have been cooked, chill the remaining marinade separately. When the marinade is chilled, add ½ cup plain yogurt and 1 tablespoon additional mustard; mix well. Serve as a vegetable dressing or dipping sauce. The rough mustard in this sauce will sharpen your taste buds.

Reheating or Crisping Appetizer Basics:

1. Most appetizers reheat well on MEDIUM-HIGH power.
2. Deep-fried foods such as fried clams or onion rings won't come out crispy in the microwave, but we can't think of a quicker, simpler way to get them hot. Place 1 cup on a plate lined with a paper towel. Heat on HIGH for 35 seconds.
3. Maybe you never thought about the microwave for anything other than making foods hot, but as you can see from the following examples, it's perfect for bringing foods to "room temp," too. Some foods are best served at room temperature, where their full flavors burst forth in a way they couldn't under the chill of the refrigerator.

- To warm cheese, place ½ pound unwrapped cheese in the microwave. Heat on MEDIUM for 45 seconds to 1 minute, or until the chill is gone.
- To bring 4 cups refrigerated vegetables to room temperature, heat on MEDIUM for 3 to 4 minutes, stirring once.
- To bring 3 cups chopped liver to room temperature, heat on MEDIUM for 2 to 3 minutes.
- To bring 2 cups Appetizer Eggplant Dip to room temperature, heat on MEDIUM for 2 to 3 minutes.

4. Stale crackers or chips that won't last a humid week in August can be made dry and crunchy again in the microwave. To refresh 8 to 10 crackers or pretzels, 12 potato chips, or 1 cup popcorn, place them on paper plates or a paper towel (this absorbs moisture). Heat on MEDIUM-HIGH for 1½ minutes. Let stand for 2 minutes before serving.

EGG PINWHEELS

MAKES 48   BEGIN 1 HOUR BEFORE SERVING

---

12 slices of fresh, firm white or whole-wheat bread
½ recipe (1¼ cups) any of the Hard-Cooked Egg Spreads (page 148)

Watercress sprigs or radish tops, plus chopped watercress for garnish (optional)
Paprika (optional)

Remove the crusts from the bread and place each slice between 2 sheets of wax paper. Roll each out to make a thin 4- × -4½-inch rectangle. Remove the wax paper.

Place 1½ tablespoons of egg spread in the upper half of each rectangle, spreading to within ½ inch of the edge. Lay a few sprigs of watercress or radish tops down the middle. Starting with the filled side, roll in jelly-roll fashion to form a finger-shaped roll; seal the edges with slight pressure.

Slice each roll into 4 pinwheels. Sprinkle paprika or chopped watercress on top of cut edge.

NOTE: The filling can be made in advance, but roll it in the bread right before serving so it doesn't dry out.

CHOPPED LIVER WITH BRANDY

MAKES 8 TO 10 SERVINGS   BEGIN 6½ HOURS BEFORE SERVING
COOKING TIME: 12 MINUTES

Although this may be a poor man's pâté, we couldn't just call it chopped liver and let it go at that. Chicken livers glow when they are given a bit of brandy but should be refrigerated for several hours to mellow once brandy has been added. After that has been accomplished, a once-lowly mixture becomes regal when placed in the palm of a water cracker or bagel.

- 1 tablespoon margarine or butter
- 2 medium onions, coarsely chopped
- 1 pound chicken livers
- 2 tablespoons chopped fresh parsley
- 1 tablespoon brandy
- ¼ teaspoon salt
- ⅛ teaspoon pepper
- 1 egg, hard-cooked (page 55), chopped
- Fresh chives, chopped

In a 2-quart casserole combine the margarine and onions. Cook on HIGH for 2 minutes, or until the onions are tender.

Stir in the remaining ingredients except the hard-cooked egg and chives. Cover tightly and cook on MEDIUM for 10 minutes, or until the livers are slightly firm and no longer pink, stirring halfway through cooking. Let stand, covered, for 5 minutes.

Place the liver mixture in a food processor or blender, a few tablespoons at first, and grind until fine. If using a blender, you may have to transfer this ground mixture to a separate bowl before adding more.) Place the livers in a mixing bowl and stir in the hard-cooked egg.

Pack the mixture into a 3-cup crock (or pack into 3 little flowerpots so you can place them in various sections of the room for easy service). Chill thoroughly, about 6 hours. Garnish with chopped chives and serve with crackers or thin slices of toast.

VARIATIONS:

Nutty Chopped Liver Spread: Add ¼ cup coarsely chopped nuts to the pureed liver mixture along with the egg. Garnish with an additional 2 tablespoons chopped nuts.

Deviled Chopped Liver: Add 2 teaspoons dry mustard, ¼ teaspoon grated nutmeg, and

3 to 4 drops hot pepper sauce to the pureed liver mixture along with the egg. Chopped liver was never so lively—hot pepper sauce really adds a welcome zip!

Chopped Liver and Anchovy Spread: Add 3 or 4 anchovy fillets, chopped, and 2 tablespoons capers to the pureed liver mixture along with the egg. If you're an anchovy lover, try this one.

ITALIAN BASIL, PEPPERS, AND ONIONS

MAKES ABOUT 2½ CUPS   BEGIN 30 MINUTES BEFORE SERVING
COOKING TIME: ABOUT 10 MINUTES

In this most colorful and refreshing vegetable dish, fresh basil and other herbs are added at the end to accentuate the garden-picked flavor.

If both red and green bell peppers are available, their presence will add a dash of color, with the red pepper imparting a slightly sweeter taste. Serve on toast rounds or Flavored Pita Triangles (page 97) or as a topping for Italian Sand Dollars (page 96)—or serve as a side dish for steak, lamb, or shish kebab. We like it especially well at room temperature, but you can also serve it hot.

- 2 tablespoons olive oil
- 2 cups thinly sliced onions
- 2 garlic cloves, minced
- 2 large red and green bell peppers, quartered
- ½ cup chopped fresh basil
- ¼ teaspoon dried oregano
- ¼ teaspoon dried thyme

In a 2-quart casserole combine the olive oil, onions, garlic, and peppers. Cover tightly and cook on HIGH for 8 to 10 minutes, or until the vegetables are very tender, stirring after 4 minutes. Stir in the basil, oregano, and thyme.

Cover again, and cook on HIGH for 1 minute. Serve at room temperature or hot.

NOTE: Keeps 1 week in the refrigerator.

ITALIAN SAND DOLLARS WITH CHEDDAR-ONION TOPPING

MAKES 8 TO 9 FOUR-INCH ROUNDS   BEGIN 1½ HOURS BEFORE SERVING
COOKING TIME: 5 TO 9 MINUTES

What could be easier than pastry cooked on disposable wax paper? This method also produces the driest and flakiest pastry crust imaginable, and one that, in appearance, reminds us of a sand dollar. A touch of Parmesan cheese adds a subtle richness to the crust.

- 1 cup all-purpose flour
- 2 tablespoons grated Parmesan cheese
- 7 tablespoons butter
- 1 egg, beaten
- 2 cups thinly sliced onions
- ⅛ teaspoon salt
- ⅛ teaspoon pepper
- ½ cup shredded sharp cheddar cheese

In a large mixing or food processor bowl, or on a countertop, combine the flour and Parmesan cheese, mixing well. With your fingertips, food processor blade, or pastry blender, and working quickly, cut 5 tablespoons butter into the flour until the particles are pea-size. Stir in the egg with a fork. Form the dough into a ball; be careful not to overwork, or the dough will become tough. Flatten into a square about ½ inch thick; this will make rolling out easier. Wrap the dough in plastic and chill for at least 1 hour or overnight.

Meanwhile, combine the remaining 2 tablespoons butter and the onions in a 1-quart casserole. Cook on HIGH for 3 to 5 minutes, or until the onions are tender, stirring once. Stir in the salt and pepper.

Roll the dough out into an 11½-inch square that is approximately ⅛ inch thick. Press the bottom of a 1-pound coffee can on top of the dough, counting out 8 or 9 circles. Trace each cup outline with a knife and cut pastry rounds.

Line the microwave oven with a double thickness of wax paper. Place all pastry rounds on top of the paper in a circle, leaving a small space between them. Cook, uncovered, on HIGH for 3 to 7 minutes, or until the pastry appears opaque and dry and the butter starts to bead or bubble up on the pastry, repositioning the rounds if necessary.

Slide the paper and pastry onto a cooling rack. When cooled, transfer as many that will fit onto a 10½-inch-square or 12-inch-round microwave-proof serving tray, positioning circles around the outer edge and leaving the center open.

Sprinkle each pastry wheel with 1 tablespoon grated cheddar cheese, then 1 tablespoon of the onion mixture. Cook on HIGH for 1½ to 2 minutes, until the cheese is melted. Let stand for 2 minutes before serving.

NOTE: The pastry can be cooked a day ahead and wrapped in foil to store at room temperature. The topping can be added right before serving to heat through.

VARIATION:

Sand Dollars with Italian Basil, Peppers, and Onions: Make the pastry dough as described above and refrigerate. Meanwhile, prepare Italian Basil, Peppers, and Onions (see preceding recipe). Roll out the pastry wheels. Substituting mozzarella cheese for sharp cheddar, top each wheel with 1 tablespoon of the cheese and 1 tablespoon of the vegetable mixture.

FLAVORED PITA TRIANGLES

MAKES 8   BEGIN 10 MINUTES BEFORE SERVING
COOKING TIME: 3 TO 5 MINUTES

Here is a simple snack that can also be served with a salad at lunchtime. The finely grated hard cheese cooked on HIGH will make the bread slightly crisp, but don't overcook, or the pita bread will become tough. Serve plain or with the Appetizer Eggplant Dip on page 100. The nice thing is that, if the pitas become cold, they are easily reheated right in a wicker serving basket.

- ¼ cup butter
- 1 garlic clove, finely chopped, or ¼ teaspoon powdered
- 2 whole pita breads, each about 4½ inches in diameter
- ½ teaspoon dried oregano
- 1 tablespoon grated Parmesan cheese

In a 1-cup glass measure or small bowl combine the butter and garlic. Cook on HIGH for 1 to 2 minutes, or until the butter is melted. Set aside.

Cut each pita round into quarters. Fold each quarter back and separate into two, making 16 triangles in all.

Brush the inside of the pita triangles with the melted garlic butter. Sprinkle with oregano and cheese. Place all the triangles on a large roasting rack or 2 paper plates. Cook, uncovered, on HIGH for 2 to 3 minutes, or until the cheese is just melted.

VARIATIONS:

Sesame-Topped Pitas: Sprinkle 2 tablespoons toasted sesame seeds (see page 609) over all the pita triangles before cooking.

Vegetable-Topped Pitas: Eliminate the butter and garlic. Top each pita triangle with 1 tablespoon grated mozzarella cheese and 1 tablespoon Italian Basil, Peppers, and Onions (see page 95). Place in a single layer on a microwaveproof serving tray or 2 paper plates. Cook, uncovered, on HIGH for ½ to 2 minutes, or until the cheese is melted. Serve hot.

☀ MUSHROOM PÂTÉ

MAKES ABOUT 1 CUP BEGIN 1½ HOURS BEFORE SERVING
COOKING TIME: 6 TO 7 MINUTES

This nutmeg-sparked pâté will please vegetarians and meat eaters alike. It is also a great way to utilize leftover mushroom stems; a food processor will make quick work of them and leave you with a finer-textured pâté. The mixture is cooked uncovered so that the alcohol will evaporate and the moisture from the mushrooms is released for thickening.

- 2 tablespoons butter
- ¼ cup thinly sliced scallions
- 2 tablespoons all-purpose flour
- 2 tablespoons heavy cream or plain yogurt
- 8 ounces fresh mushrooms, finely chopped
- 2 tablespoons dry vermouth or sherry
- ¼ teaspoon salt
- ¼ teaspoon pepper
- ¼ teaspoon freshly grated nutmeg
- ¼ cup chopped hazelnuts, walnuts, almonds, or pecans
- 2 tablespoons chopped fresh scallion greens or chives

In a 1-quart casserole combine the butter and scallions. Cook on HIGH for 2 minutes, or until the scallions are tender. Stir in the flour to make a smooth paste.

Stir in the remaining ingredients except the nuts and chopped scallions or chives; mix well. Cook, uncovered, on HIGH for 4 to 5 minutes, stirring after 2 minutes or until mushrooms cook down and darken slightly and flavors are well blended.

Fold in the chopped nuts. Pack the mixture into a crock or other serving dish and chill. Garnish with chives or scallion tops.

NOTE: Keeps 1 week in the refrigerator.

GINGER-STUFFED SNOW PEA PODS

MAKES ABOUT 24 BEGIN 30 TO 40 MINUTES BEFORE SERVING
COOKING TIME: 1 MINUTE

These stuffed pods are very attractive arranged in a fan around New Potato Appetizers (page 101).

- ¼ pound snow peas
- 1 tablespoon water
- 4 ounces whipped cream cheese
- 1 recipe Pickled Ginger (recipe follows)

Wash and remove the strings from the snow peas. In a 9-inch plate combine the snow peas and water. Cover tightly and cook on HIGH for 1 minute. Chill

With a sharp knife, split each pod open carefully on the straight side, leaving small peas intact and being careful not to break the pod. Spread some cream cheese on the inside of each pod. Insert 3 ginger slices into each pod and close. Chill until serving time.

VARIATIONS:

Salmon-Stuffed Pea Pods: Substitute 2 ounces smoked salmon, thinly sliced and cut into ¼-inch squares, for the ginger. Place 2 to 3 squares of salmon on top of the cream cheese inside each pod. Close the pods and chill again.

Cream Cheese and Chive-Stuffed Pea Pods: Eliminate the ginger. Combine ¼ cup chopped chives with the cream cheese. Fill the pea pods, close, and chill again.

Cream Cheese and Herb-Stuffed Pea Pods: Eliminate the ginger. Combine ¼ cup chopped assorted fresh herbs with the cream cheese. Fill the pea pods, close, and chill again.

Cream Cheese and Anchovy Pea Pods: Eliminate the ginger. Combine ¼ cup chopped anchovies with the cream cheese. Fill the pea pods, close, and chill again.

PICKLED GINGER

MAKES ABOUT ¼ CUP   BEGIN 30 MINUTES BEFORE SERVING
COOKING TIME: 3 TO 4 MINUTES

We first tasted this in a Japanese sushi bar as a palate cleanser between our courses of raw fish. It formed a small mountain of explosive flavor on our wooden tray, and our taste buds responded immediately. Fresh ginger that is not too woody is paramount for achieving the proper texture.

Although this recipe was designed for Ginger-Stuffed Pea Pods (see preceding recipe), it can also be served with cooked fish or on a salad platter.

---

2 **ounces fresh ginger, peeled**	½ **teaspoon granulated sugar**
2 **tablespoons rice vinegar or distilled white vinegar**	

Quarter each piece of ginger lengthwise, then slice each quarter paper thin. In a small dish combine the ginger, vinegar, and sugar. Cover tightly and cook on HIGH for 3 to 4 minutes, or until the ginger is soft, stirring once.

Chill before serving.

NOTE: Keeps about 2 weeks in a tightly covered jar in the refrigerator. If it appears dry, it can be refreshed with a few drops of water.

SPICY NUTS

MAKES 1 CUP   BEGIN 10 MINUTES BEFORE SERVING
COOKING TIME: 5 TO 7 MINUTES

There is no better way to make guests feel welcome than to place before them a warm delicacy straight from the oven. These nuts can be that gesture, without making the guests also feel they have caused you any trouble.

- 2 tablespoons butter
- 2 tablespoons Worcestershire sauce
- 1 teaspoon hot pepper sauce
- ½ teaspoon salt
- ¼ teaspoon ground cinnamon
- Pinch of garlic powder
- Pinch of ground cloves
- 1 cup shelled whole pecans, almonds, walnuts, or hazelnuts

Place the butter in a 2-quart rectangular dish. Cook on HIGH for 30 seconds to 1 minute, or until melted. Stir in the remaining ingredients except the nuts.

Stir in the nuts, coating well. Cook, uncovered, on HIGH for 4 to 6 minutes, or until heated through, stirring halfway through cooking.

NOTE: Keeps in a tightly sealed jar at room temperature for about 1 month.

APPETIZER EGGPLANT DIP

MAKES 2 CUPS   BEGIN 45 MINUTES BEFORE SERVING
COOKING TIME: 5 TO 7 MINUTES

Spoon into a bowl for dipping with celery sticks, rice crackers, or Flavored Pita Triangles (page 97).

- 1 medium eggplant
- 3 tablespoons olive or other oil
- 2 tablespoons lime or lemon juice
- 1 tablespoon soy sauce
- 1 tablespoon finely chopped fresh ginger
- 1 garlic clove, minced
- 1 teaspoon granulated sugar
- ¼ teaspoon pepper
- ¼ cup pine nuts or toasted sesame seeds (page 609)

Prick the eggplant in a few places with a stainless-steel fork. Place on a paper towel or plate in the microwave oven. Cook, uncovered, on HIGH for 5 to 7 minutes, or until the eggplant is tender and collapses. Let it cool in the refrigerator for 30 minutes.

Cut the eggplant in half lengthwise and scoop out the flesh. Place in a blender, food processor, or electric mixer bowl. Add the remaining ingredients except the nuts. Puree or mix until smooth. Stir in the nuts.

NEW POTATO APPETIZERS

MAKES 24 BEGIN 20 TO 25 MINUTES BEFORE SERVING
COOKING TIME: 12 TO 14 MINUTES

The microwave has turned the hour potato into a 4-minute miracle. New potatoes not only look good on a dinner plate, but add an imaginative touch to an appetizer table. Small potatoes of equal size will be the key to even cooking and ease of serving. Lay all the toppings out and let your guests be as inventive as they wish.

12 small new potatoes, about 2 inches in diameter

Toppings:
  Sour cream or plain yogurt
  Small bowls of cooked bacon pieces (See Bacon, page 61)
  Chopped fresh chives and/or other fresh herbs
  Caviar
  Capers
  Chopped anchovies
  Selection of herb butters (page 183)

Garnishes:
  Fresh dill
  Fresh chives cut into thin strands
  Radishes carved into roses
  Nasturtium blossoms

Pierce the potatoes with a fork and place them in a ring on a piece of paper towel in the microwave oven. Cook on HIGH for 12 to 14 minutes, or until done (see page 450), repositioning if necessary. Let the potatoes stand for 5 minutes.

Cut the potatoes in half. With a teaspoon or melon baller, scoop out about ½ teaspoon of potato. (Chill and save these chunks to add to a salad later.) Place the hollowed-out potatoes on a serving platter surrounded by a selection of toppings, or fill and serve to your guests. The potatoes can be served hot, at room temperature, or chilled. Garnish the platter with any or all of the suggested items.

PITA PIZZAS

MAKES 24 BEGIN 15 TO 20 MINUTES BEFORE SERVING
COOKING TIME: 8 TO 12 MINUTES

Pita halves are heated half a batch at a time, on a rack or paper plates to keep the bread from getting soggy, so that the second round comes warm from the oven just as you are finishing the first. A great snack for kids.

- 1 cup Basic "Batch" Tomato Sauce (page 178), or canned
- 4 pita breads, each 6 inches in diameter, halved horizontally to form 8 rounds
- 1 teaspoon dried oregano
- 4 ounces grated mozzarella cheese

Spoon 2 tablespoons tomato sauce on the inside of each pita half and spread to within ½ inch of the outer edge. Sprinkle each with oregano and mozzarella.

Place 4 pita rounds on a large roasting rack or paper plates and put in the microwave oven. Cook, uncovered, on MEDIUM for 4 to 6 minutes, or until the cheese is melted and bread heated through, rotating halfway through cooking. Repeat with the remaining 4 pita halves. Quarter each cooked pita with a sharp scissor or knife and serve hot.

VARIATIONS:

Sausage Pita Pizzas: Arrange ½ pound cooked Italian sausage, thinly sliced, on top of the tomato sauce before adding the cheese.

Mushroom Pita Pizzas: Arrange ¼ pound fresh mushrooms, sliced, or a 4-ounce can, drained, on top of the tomato sauce before adding the cheese.

Kid's Single Serving Snack: Cut only 1 pita bread in half, horizontally. Top each half with 2 tablespoons tomato sauce as directed. Sprinkle each with 1 tablespoon mozzarella cheese and a pinch of dried oregano. Place the pita halves on a paper plate. Cook on MEDIUM for 1 to 1½ minutes. A quick snack for hungry adults, too!

Melted Cheese Crackers Basics:

1. A 12-inch round serving platter provides the largest surface area and allows the crackers or chips to be arranged in rings for the most even melting of the cheese.

2. The cheese is then melted on MEDIUM power so that the protein does not cook too quickly, which causes it to turn rubbery. Also, the slower cooking allows the crackers in the

inner circle to cook in about the same time as those in the outer circle.
3. Crackers or toasted bread, as opposed to soft bread, will stay crisp and not become soggy when cheese is heated on top. If large quantities of these crackers are needed, it is best to cook them in batches. This is still practical because of the short amount of cooking time they take.

Fancy Melted Cheese and Crackers

Here are some cheese-and-cracker combinations for you to try. Place any 24 crackers topped with 8 ounces grated cheese on a 12-inch round platter and cook on MEDIUM for 2½ to 3 minutes.

Danish Cheese Rounds: Melba toast rounds with cream Havarti cheese, sprinkled with ¼ cup chopped walnuts before melting the cheese.

Melted Bacon-Cheddar Snacks: Saltine or water biscuits with sharp cheddar cheese, sprinkled with ¼ cup crumbled, cooked bacon (see page 61) before melting the cheese.

Pecan-Cheese Ritz: Ritz crackers with mild cheddar cheese, sprinkled with ¼ cup chopped pecans or almonds before melting the cheese.

Alsatian Cheese Ryes: Rye crackers spread lightly with Dijon or brown mustard and sprinkled with grated Swiss cheese. Top with ¼ cup chopped cooked ham, if desired, before melting the cheese.

Italian Cheese Snacks: Melba toast or thinly sliced toasted French bread with mozzarella cheese and sprinkled with ¼ cup chopped pepperoni, olives, capers, or pine nuts before melting the cheese.

Deutsch Melted Cheese and Sausage: Rye crackers with Muenster cheese and topped with thin slices of cooked smoked sausage before melting the cheese. Serve with a variety of mustards for dipping.

✹ CHEESE NACHOS

MAKES 24   BEGIN 5 TO 10 MINUTES BEFORE SERVING
COOKING TIME: 3 TO 4 MINUTES

A 12-inch flat basket, lined with a napkin, also works well, and makes a colorful presentation.

---

24 taco chips
8 ounces Monterey Jack cheese, shredded

¼ cup olive slices or jalapeño rings
1 recipe Salsa Cruda (page 185)

Place the chips on a 12-inch round or oval microwaveproof serving platter. Sprinkle the cheese and olives evenly over the chips and cook on MEDIUM for 2½ to 3½ minutes, or until the cheese melts. Let stand for 1 minute before serving. Dip into the salsa.

VARIATION:

Nachos Grandes: After placing the chips on the platter, divide ½ cup chile con carne or refried beans among the crackers. Continue with the basic recipe.

CHILE CON QUESO

MAKES ABOUT 2 CUPS   BEGIN 25 MINUTES BEFORE SERVING
COOKING TIME: 10 TO 16 MINUTES

A goopy, soul-satisfying cheese dip that people of all ages love to scoop up with chips. We found that it is also good spooned over burritos. You may determine the amount of fiery peppers to add.

The tomatoes must be cooked uncovered to evaporate some juices that would otherwise curdle the cheese.

- 1 tablespoon vegetable oil
- 1 medium onion, chopped
- 2 medium tomatoes, peeled and chopped, or 1 cup undrained, canned
- 4 mild Anaheim chilies, peeled and cut into thin strips, or 1 4-ounce can chopped chilies
- 1 or more jalapeño pepper, peeled and chopped
- ¾ pound Monterey Jack, Muenster, or mild cheddar cheese, cut into ½-inch cubes

In a 1-quart casserole combine the oil and onion. Cook on HIGH for 2 to 3 minutes, or until tender. Stir in the tomatoes and peppers. Cook, uncovered, on HIGH for 3 to 5 minutes to cook down and blend the flavors, stirring once. Stir in the cheese. Cook on MEDIUM for 5 to 8 minutes, or until the cheese is melted, stirring twice.

NOTE: If the cheese becomes too cool for dipping, heat on MEDIUM for 1 to 3 minutes, stirring once.

✺ LIGHTLY BREADED HAM AND CHEESE ROLLUPS

MAKES 20 SERVINGS   BEGIN 15 MINUTES BEFORE SERVING
COOKING TIME: 8 TO 10 MINUTES

Quick and delicious—always a hit. Try these combinations: Westphalian ham and Emmentaler cheese, prosciutto with Fontina, or Black Forest ham with goat cheese.

8 thin 6-×-4-inch slices of cooked ham	1 4-inch sour pickle, cut into lengthwise quarters
4 slices of Muenster cheese, trimmed to fit on ham	1 egg, beaten
	1 tablespoon vegetable oil
	¼ cup fine dry bread crumbs

On top of each slice of ham, place a piece of cheese, and top with another piece of ham. About ½ inch from one narrow end of the ham, place a pickle spear. Roll from the pickle end, jelly-roll style, and press the ends down to secure.

Combine the egg and oil in a cereal bowl. Place the bread crumbs in another cereal bowl. Dip each roll into the egg mixture, then into the bread crumbs, turning to coat completely in both. Position the rollups around the outer rim of a 10-inch round microwaveproof plate, leaving the center open. Cook, uncovered, on MEDIUM for 8 to 10 minutes, or until the rolls feel warm to the touch and a little cheese starts to ooze out. (The rolls are cooked on MEDIUM because of the cheese, and cooked uncovered to keep a dry crust.)

Spacing 5 toothpicks evenly along the roll, pressing them in about every ½ inch, cut between the toothpicks. Slice between the toothpicks to make 5 servings from each roll.

Serve with a variety of mustards.

VARIATIONS:

Smoked Turkey and Cheese Rolls: Substitute smoked turkey slices for the ham.

Spicy Ham and Cheese Rolls: Substitute 4 hot pepper rings, cut up, for the pickle.

Olive Ham and Cheese Rolls: Substitute 5 or 6 olives for each pickle quarter.

Double Cheese and Ham Rolls: Combine 1 tablespoon grated Parmesan cheese with bread crumbs. For a spicier coating mix, add a pinch of cayenne pepper.

Popcorn Basics

1. Popcorn is best cooked in small amounts in a sandwich-size brown paper bag. No recycled bags please that could contain metal flecks. The sandwich bag is gently folded down at the top. No scrunching, please. This can cause too much heat to build up. We have tried popcorn in all sorts of popping utensils and we keep coming back to the good old paper bag for the driest, most voluminous popcorn ever—in or out of the microwave! The paper bag helps absorb moisture that would toughen the popped corn, as would happen with a bowl or microwave popper.
2. Popcorn is cooked in the bag with no butter or oil. Microwaves are attracted to moisture, and there is enough moisture present in *fresh* popcorn to cook it. (Because no additional moisture is added, the moisture present in popcorn is critical. That is why you must be careful to keep popcorn fresh, in a tightly sealed jar.)

   Oil used to pop corn on top of the conventional stove or in a conventional electric popper will reach almost 400°F before it begins to smoke or break down—which is why it is perfect for raising the temperature of the popcorn high enough to pop. By adding oil in the microwave, you only lure the microwaves from their prime target and end up with hot oil and poorly popped corn. (Only a microwave popcorn manufacturer can evenly and lightly coat the kernels so this doesn't happen.)
3. The popcorn is done when popping slows down to about 2 seconds in between pops. If the popcorn hasn't popped within 3 minutes, take it out of the oven. Either the popcorn is too old or the oven wattage is not high enough to pop it. If your oven is 500 watts or less, don't even attempt popcorn.

✺ 3-MINUTE POPCORN

MAKES 2 CUPS   BEGIN 5 MINUTES BEFORE SERVING
COOKING TIME: 3 MINUTES

Nothing goes with movies or home video viewing like popcorn. And nothing is easier than popping corn in a brown bag in the microwave, yet this apparently simple process raises more questions among consumers and more eyebrows among the experts than any other procedure we discuss in our schools. If you follow our instructions carefully, you can't go wrong.

The Spicy Hot variation (see below) was a suggestion of a friend of ours who has a catering business. She often sets out baskets of herbed popcorn as guests arrive for a meal. She has many variations, but this version is the most popular and would be good for an outdoor tea accompanied by other savories. Just make sure to have plenty of ice-cold drinks on hand to assuage this feisty but pleasing appetizer.

Place ⅓ cup popping corn in a brown sandwich-size paper bag. Gently fold down the top of the bag twice, to close lightly but firmly. Cook on HIGH for 2½ to 3 minutes, or until popping begins to slow down but is not completely stopped, watching closely the last minute. Serve with salt, straight from the bag, or in a bowl with melted butter.

VARIATION:

Spicy Hot Popcorn: Place 2 tablespoons butter in a 1-cup glass measure. Cook on HIGH for 35 to 45 seconds, or until melted. Stir in ⅛ teaspoon cayenne pepper and 3 to 4 drops hot pepper sauce. Pour the freshly cooked popcorn into a bowl and drizzle the butter on top. Stir until well coated, then serve.

BASIC GRANOLA

MAKES ABOUT 6 CUPS   BEGIN 15 MINUTES BEFORE SERVING
COOKING TIME: 6 TO 9 MINUTES

Serve this as a cereal with milk or with yogurt or use as a crust for a fruit pie (pages 546–48).

- 2 cups rolled oats
- ½ cup sunflower or pumpkin seeds
- ½ cup coarsely chopped walnuts or almonds
- ½ cup shredded coconut
- ½ cup wheat germ
- ¼ cup vegetable oil
- ¼ cup brown sugar
- ¼ cup honey or molasses
- 1 teaspoon vanilla

In a 2-quart rectangular baking dish combine all the ingredients, mixing together well. Cook on HIGH for 3 minutes; stir. Cook on HIGH for 3 to 6 minutes more, or until the oatmeal is slightly crisp and the flavors have blended. Let cool in its dish. Store in a tightly covered jar.

VARIATIONS:

Cinnamon Granola: Add 1 teaspoon ground cinnamon.

Granola with Dried Fruit: Stir 1 cup raisins, coarsely chopped dried apricots, pineapple, apples, or peaches into the cooked granola.

Granola with Chocolate Chips: Stir 1 cup mini-chocolate chips into the cooked granola.

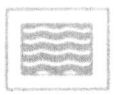

☼ SAUSAGE WITH SWEET AND SOUR SAUCE

MAKES 6 TO 8 SERVINGS BEGIN 15 MINUTES BEFORE SERVING
COOKING TIME: 5 TO 9 MINUTES

- 1 pound smoked sausage (frankfurters, kielbasa, chorizo), cut into ¼-inch slices
- ¼ cup apricot preserves (see Note)
- ¼ cup catsup
- 2 tablespoons dry red wine
- 2 tablespoons red wine vinegar
- 1 tablespoon honey

Place the sausages around the outside rim of a 10-inch circular microwaveproof serving platter, leaving the center open. Cook, uncovered, on HIGH for 2 to 4 minutes, until heated through.

Meanwhile, in a 1-quart serving casserole combine the remaining ingredients. Cook, uncovered, on HIGH for 3 to 5 minutes, or until boiling, stirring halfway through cooking. Serve by placing the sauce in the center of the platter and serving the sausage on toothpicks, or you can stir the sausage back into the sauce.

NOTE: Low-sugar preserves work well.

VARIATIONS:

Substitute grape or currant jelly for the apricot preserves.

ORIENTAL CHICKEN WINGS

MAKES 7 TO 10 PIECES BEGIN AT LEAST 2 HOURS AND 20 MINUTES BEFORE SERVING
COOKING TIME: 10 TO 11 MINUTES

Sweet and sour, with a hint of garlic—those are the flavors that permeate these chicken wings. A combination of high surface heat (due to the fatty skin) and the honey and soy sauce will help the chicken wings to brown during cooking, even though the cooking time is short and the meat is light colored. The sesame seeds add an element of crunch to simulate crispiness, which, without any dry heat, the microwave can't provide here. You'll be pleased with the succulent results and the ease with which this appetizer or snack—or even main course—is prepared.

- 2 tablespoons soy sauce
- 1 tablespoon honey
- 1 tablespoon vinegar
- 1 teaspoon finely chopped fresh ginger, or ½ teaspoon ground
- 1 tablespoon vegetable oil
- 1 garlic clove, minced
- 2 or 3 drops hot pepper sauce
- 1 pound chicken wings
- 2 tablespoons sesame seeds

In a 9-inch pie plate combine the soy sauce, honey, vinegar, ginger, oil, garlic, and hot pepper sauce.

Cut off and discard the chicken wing tips. Cut the wings at the joints. Add the wings to the marinade. Refrigerate for 2 hours or overnight, turning over two or three times.

Drain the marinade and reserve. To keep the wings dry while cooking, place them on a roasting rack in a 2-quart dish or around the outer rim of a 10-inch round microwaveproof platter. Sprinkle with 1 tablespoon sesame seeds. Cook, uncovered, on HIGH for 5 minutes. Turn the wings over and brush with the reserved marinade, then sprinkle with the remaining sesame seeds. Cook, uncovered, on HIGH for 5 to 6 minutes, or until the meat is no longer pink. Let stand for 5 minutes.

VARIATION:

Chilled Sweet and Sour Chicken Wings: Chill the cooked chicken. Prepare Sweet and Sour Apricot Sauce (page 182). Serve the wings with the sauce for dipping. Great for picnics!

YUMMY GOLDEN BARBECUED RIBS

MAKES ABOUT 20 RIBS   BEGIN COOKING 40 TO 45 MINUTES BEFORE SERVING
COOKING TIME: 38 TO 45 MINUTES

The ribs in this recipe will brown because of high surface heat (due to the fatty meat), the sugar in the preserves, and the fact that the meat is already dark colored. The recipe was designed for succulent pork ribs—beef ribs just don't work out as well. We found this dish good for casual entertaining, but have a cache of napkins stashed nearby.

2½ to 3 pounds pork spareribs, cut into individual ribs
½ cup apricot preserves

2 tablespoons Dijon-type mustard
2 tablespoons lemon juice

Place the ribs in a 2-quart baking dish. Cover tightly and cook on HIGH for 5 minutes. Reposition the ribs and cover again. Cook on MEDIUM for 25 to 30 minutes, or until the ribs are tender and cooked through, rearranging once if necessary.

Meanwhile, combine the remaining ingredients in a small bowl, stirring well to blend. Drain the ribs and place on a bacon rack, if available, in a 2-quart baking dish. Brush half of the sauce on the ribs. Cook, uncovered, on HIGH for 4 to 5 minutes. Turn the ribs over and reposition them by placing less-cooked ones near the outside edges. Brush on the remaining sauce. Cook, uncovered, on HIGH for 4 to 5 minutes, or until the sauce has cooked on. Let stand for 5 minutes before serving.

NOTE: Ribs can be cooked to the final brushing of the sauce and then refrigerated. To reheat, cook, uncovered, on HIGH for 6 to 10 minutes, rearranging once.

CHILLED STEAMED MUSSELS WITH HERB SAUCE

MAKES 4 TO 6 SERVINGS BEGIN 1½ HOURS BEFORE SERVING, FOR CLEANING AND CHILLING
COOKING TIME: 3 TO 5 MINUTES

- 1 pound mussels, washed and cleaned
- 2 tablespoons white wine or lemon juice
- 1 recipe Chilled Fresh Herb Sauce (page 176)

Place the mussels around the outer rim of a 12-inch round microwaveproof cooking dish. Cover tightly and cook on HIGH for 2½ to 4½ minutes, or until all the shells have opened and the flesh plumps and pulls away from the shell; rotate the dish once halfway through cooking. Chill the mussels in their broth for 1 hour.

To serve, drain the liquid from the mussels. Remove the top half of the mussel shell. Serve each mussel with a dab of herb sauce on top.

VARIATION:

Mussels with Tartar Sauce: Serve with Tartar Sauce (page 246).

Dishes for Heating and Serving Appetizers

Appetizers lend themselves to creative presentations almost more than any other category of foods. You can pull out your loveliest serving platter or choose an unlikely container, such as a flowerpot, to achieve the effect that you want.

Before cooking in any container, check it with the microwave test on page 85. Here are some suggestions for serving:

- Flowerpot crocks for pâté
- 6-inch metal pails for shrimp on long skewers or popcorn
- Hollowed-out red cabbage or pattypan squash for dips
- Antique scoops for spiced nuts
- Wooden mushroom baskets, lined with lettuce, for marinated vegetables

Garnish with fresh clover, nasturtium buds, violets, or honeysuckle flowers, all of which are edible.

APPETIZERS AND SNACKS

✺ CLAMS CASINO

MAKES 6 TO 8 SERVINGS   BEGIN 20 MINUTES BEFORE SERVING (DEPENDING ON HOW LONG IT TAKES YOU TO OPEN CLAMS)
COOKING TIME: 10 TO 13 MINUTES

Get a good clam knife for this recipe or have your fish store open the clams for you. Once clams are open, the remaining steps are a cinch. Shellfish in their shells are usually cooked on HIGH, *but here, because their top shells have been removed, the clams are cooked on* MEDIUM *to prevent them from cooking too quickly and getting tough. The same* MEDIUM *power that is so good for the clams, however, is too slow for the bacon. It would never cook in the same amount of time—which is why it is partially cooked before being added to the clams. The wax paper cover has a multiple purpose—it keeps some of the steam in to cook the clams, protects against bacon splatter, and yet is light enough to keep the bacon from getting soggy.*

You can skillfully serve a large party on a clam appetizer, without seeming repetitive, by making a batch of each of the variations. Our tastes lean toward the spicy Clams Salsa, but do decide for yourself.

---

6 slices of bacon	2 tablespoons lemon juice
24 littleneck clams	2 tablespoons finely chopped fresh parsley
¼ cup finely chopped scallions	
¼ cup finely chopped green peppers	Lemon wedges (optional)

Place the bacon on a bacon rack and cover with a paper towel or place between paper towels on a plate. Cook on HIGH for 2½ to 3 minutes, or until partially cooked but still limp. Set aside. Cut the bacon into quarters.

Open the clams and detach from both shells. Place each clam on a shell half and discard the other shells. Position the clams around the outer rim of a 12-inch round microwaveproof serving dish or tray.

Spoon the scallions evenly over each clam. Sprinkle with green pepper, lemon juice, and parsley. Top each clam with a piece of bacon, then cover with wax paper. Cook on MEDIUM for 8 to 10 minutes, or until the clams and bacon are cooked. Let stand, covered, for 2 minutes before serving. Serve with lemon wedges, if desired.

VARIATIONS:
Low-Calorie Clams on the Half Shell: Omit the bacon from the basic recipe.

Clams Casino with Garlic and Herbs: Substitute 2 teaspoons finely chopped garlic for the green pepper.

Clams Salsa: Substitute chopped cilantro (coriander) for the parsley. Substitute 2 tablespoons chopped jalapeño pepper for the green pepper, and lime juice for lemon juice. Add ¼ cup finely chopped fresh tomato to the top, before adding the bacon. This, as we say, is our favorite!

HOT CRAB DIP

MAKES ABOUT 2 CUPS   BEGIN 10 MINUTES BEFORE SERVING
COOKING TIME: 2 TO 4 MINUTES

- 8 ounces fresh, canned, or frozen crabmeat, cooked
- 8 ounces whipped cream cheese
- 1 tablespoon dry sherry or dry vermouth
- 1 teaspoon lemon juice
- ⅛ teaspoon cayenne pepper

In a 1-quart casserole combine all the ingredients. Cook on HIGH for 2 to 4 minutes, or until heated through, stirring halfway through cooking. Transfer to a dish for dipping. Best served with crackers.

CRAB-STUFFED MUSHROOMS

MAKES 24   BEGIN 15 MINUTES BEFORE SERVING
COOKING TIME: 3 TO 5 MINUTES

Delicious as a first course for 8.

- 1 recipe Hot Crab Dip (recipe above)
- 24 large mushroom caps
- ¼ cup finely chopped nuts (optional)

Divide the crab dip between the 24 mushroom caps. Arrange around the outer rim of a 12-inch round microwaveproof platter.

Cook on HIGH for 3 to 5 minutes, or until the stuffing and mushrooms are hot. Sprinkle with the nuts, if desired.

☼ BRANDIED SHRIMP

MAKES 10 SERVINGS   BEGIN 15 TO 20 MINUTES BEFORE SERVING
COOKING TIME: 3 TO 4 MINUTES

- 2 tablespoons butter
- 2 garlic cloves, minced
- ½ teaspoon red pepper flakes
- 1 tablespoon brandy
- 1 tablespoon lemon juice
- 1 pound shelled large shrimp
- Lemon wedges

In a 9-inch round dish combine the butter and garlic. Cook on HIGH for 35 to 45 seconds, or until the butter is melted. Stir in the remaining ingredients, except the lemon wedges. Cover tightly and cook on HIGH for 3 to 4 minutes, or until the shrimp are pink and cooked, stirring once after 3 minutes. Let stand, covered, for 2 to 3 minutes. Serve on toothpicks and with lemon wedges.

VARIATIONS:

Herbed Shrimp: Eliminate the brandy. Add 3 tablespoons fresh herbs, or 3 teaspoons dried, to the shrimp before cooking. A combination of parsley, chives, and tarragon is nice.

Fresh Basil Shrimp: Sprinkle the shrimp with 3 tablespoons chopped fresh basil before serving.

Brandied Shrimp with Mushrooms: During standing time, cook ½ pound button mushrooms, page 72, and stir into shrimp to serve. As a main course, it makes 2 to 3 servings.

Dilled Shrimp: Sprinkle the shrimp with 3 tablespoons chopped fresh dill before serving.

5

SOUPS

When I was growing up, soup was not only nourishment, it was a way of earmarking events. I knew that when my German mother served a thick *Tomatencremesuppe*, cream of tomato soup, that Fastnacht or Shrove Wednesday was fast approaching. When the scent of her *Gulaschsuppe* filtered into my bedroom, I knew that company would be coming for a late evening supper.

A birthday or a special dinner for in-laws called for *Pilzcremesuppe*, or cream of mushroom soup. A bowl of *Griesssuppe* in the morning meant that I was sick enough to stay home from school. *Griess*, or cereal, cooks up into a hearty, viscous soup that slides down so easily. Its recuperative powers were well known in our house. Mother thought that had we eaten our liver dumpling soup, *Griesssuppe* might have been rendered unnecessary, but secretly I looked forward to those *Griesssuppe* days when I could read in bed and be comforted with a hot bowl of my thick cereal remedy.

Soup making still accompanies events in my home, although I find its greatest service to be restorative. There is something about soup that makes us all feel healthier, once we've sipped a bowl. I know nothing like it to lift my spirits on a damp winter day, or calm me before I drift off to sleep.

This book gave me the opportunity to put down some of those recipes I grew to love as a child, in a form pleasing to mothers with less time than my own mother had. The selection includes these soups with their decidedly Old World flavor, as well as the newer, lighter soups we enjoy now, too. Fresh Hot Tomato Soup, Sweet Spanish Almond and Greek Lemon Soups, and a dessert-type brew we call Lida's Peach-Brandy Soup are among those in the lighter vein.

Though we have so little time these days, perhaps we can still give our children vivid pictures of homemade soups for their scrapbook of memories.

—THELMA

Broth or Stock Basics:

1. It is important to choose a large (4-quart) casserole for stocks because of the large amount of liquid that could boil over during the hour's cooking.
2. All ingredients for the stock/broth are combined at one time so the liquid will receive its fullest flavor. Only with the fish stock, with its shorter cooking time, do vegetables need to be sautéed first.
3. All stocks are cooked on HIGH first to bring them to a boil and then on MEDIUM to develop flavor. Use of a tight cover, lid, or plastic wrap is important to aid in this simmering process.
4. Even though the cooking period is long, the stock needs to be stirred only once, between power changes. That is because stirring is unnecessary—and, frankly, a nuisance. There is no possibility of sticking or burning, and everything will be cooked through to the center, by conduction of heat, over this long period of time.
5. Standing time continues to develop more flavor.

✸ CHICKEN BROTH OR STOCK

MAKES 4½ TO 5 CUPS   BEGIN 1¾ HOURS BEFORE SERVING
COOKING TIME: 1¼ HOURS

A basic chicken broth such as this works well in the microwave, saving about an hour of cooking time. If you make this with a whole chicken you'll be left with lovely moist meat for salad and nice little scraps for kitty's dinner. Serve the stock as a plain broth or with cooked rice, noodles, egg drops, won tons, julienned chicken, thinly sliced vegetables, or fresh herbs.

---

3 pounds chicken, cut-up parts or backs, necks, and wings	¼ cup coarsely chopped fresh parsley, or 2 tablespoons dried
1 leek, sliced	4 peppercorns
1 onion, sliced	2 whole cloves
1 celery rib with leaves, sliced	1 teaspoon salt (optional)
1 carrot, sliced	1 bay leaf, crushed
	5 cups water

In a 4-quart casserole combine all the ingredients. Cover tightly and cook on HIGH for 15 to 20 minutes, or until boiling. Uncover and turn the chicken pieces over. Cover again and cook on MEDIUM for 1 hour. Let stand, covered, for 10 minutes.

Strain, reserving meat for another use, if desired. Refrigerate the stock for up to 1 week or freeze for up to 2 months.

✹ MOCK BROWN BROTH OR STOCK

MAKES ABOUT 5 CUPS   BEGIN 1½ HOURS BEFORE SERVING
COOKING TIME: 1 HOUR

We prefer to make brown stocks with bones that have been conventionally roasted first before we put them in our large stockpot on top of the stove. If we are in a hurry or don't wish to take all this time (which is more often than not), we find that this shortcut stock made with ground beef is very acceptable.

1½ pounds lean ground beef	1 teaspoon salt (optional)
2 onions, thinly sliced	4 peppercorns
2 carrots, sliced	3 sprigs fresh thyme, or ½ teaspoon dried
1 leek, trimmed, white part sliced	
1 celery rib with leaves	2 whole cloves
¼ cup chopped fresh parsley with stems	1 bay leaf, crushed
	5 cups water
1 tablespoon dry sherry (optional)	

In a 4-quart casserole combine all the ingredients. Cover tightly and cook on HIGH for 10 to 15 minutes, or until boiling; stir and skim if necessary. Cover again and cook on MEDIUM for 45 minutes to develop flavor. Let stand, covered, for 10 minutes. Strain for use in gravies or soups.

✹ VEGETABLE BROTH OR STOCK

MAKES 4 CUPS   BEGIN 1½ HOURS BEFORE SERVING
COOKING TIME: 1 HOUR

A vegetarian broth that makes a nice base for vegetable, noodle, or rice soup.

2 tablespoons butter or margarine	½ teaspoon salt (optional)
2 carrots, thinly sliced	¼ teaspoon pepper
2 onions or 4 leeks, thinly sliced	1 bay leaf, crushed
2 celery ribs with leaves, thinly sliced	3 sprigs of fresh thyme, or ½ teaspoon dried
¼ cup chopped fresh parsley with stems	5 cups water

In a 4-quart casserole combine all the ingredients. Cover tightly and cook on HIGH for 15 to 20 minutes, or until boiling; stir. Cover again and cook on MEDIUM for 45 minutes to develop the flavor. Let stand, covered, for 10 minutes. Strain.

VARIATION:

Vegetable Soup: Add to the broth 2 cups tender-crisp cooked vegetables (thinly sliced green beans, celery, and/or spinach; see the vegetable cooking charts in Chapter 2). Season with freshly grated nutmeg.

FISH BROTH OR STOCK

MAKES 3 CUPS   BEGIN 40 TO 50 MINUTES BEFORE SERVING
COOKING TIME: 23 TO 30 MINUTES

This is the simplest and quickest of stocks to make. Keeping that in mind, when you go to the fish store, ask for heads and any available fish bones. They are usually given freely or for a nominal fee.

Another way to approach this is to buy an inexpensive fish such as whiting; you should be able to buy two small whole cleaned fish for almost nothing. Avoid oily fish for this purpose, though, or your stock will become too strong in flavor.

This is an excellent soup base for vegetable or fish soup and also for fish sauces (see pages 244–46).

- 1 cup coarsely chopped onion
- 2 leeks, trimmed, white stalks sliced
- 1 celery rib with leaves, chopped
- 1 carrot, chopped
- 1 tablespoon lemon juice
- 6 sprigs fresh parsley, or 1 tablespoon dried
- ½ teaspoon dried thyme
- ½ teaspoon salt (optional)
- ¼ teaspoon pepper
- 3 cups water
- ½ cup dry white wine
- 1 pound bones and trimmings from lean fish (no gills)

In a 3-quart casserole combine the first 9 ingredients. Cover tightly and cook on HIGH for 5 minutes. Stir in remaining ingredients. Cover again and cook on HIGH for 8 to 10 minutes, or until boiling. Cover again and cook on MEDIUM for 10 to 15 minutes to develop the flavor. Let stand, covered, for 10 minutes. Strain.

CATCH OF THE DAY SOUP

MAKES 4 SERVINGS BEGIN 25 TO 30 MINUTES BEFORE SERVING
COOKING TIME: 12 TO 18 MINUTES

Serve with chunks of crusty bread.

- 3 cups Fish Broth or Stock (previous recipe)
- 1½ pounds lean fish fillets or steaks, skin removed, cut into 1-inch cubes
- ¼ cup chopped fresh parsley
- Salt and pepper
- ½ teaspoon red pepper flakes (optional)

In a 3-quart casserole combine all the ingredients. Cover tightly and cook on HIGH for 12 to 18 minutes, or until the fish turns opaque and flakes when pressed with a fork. Let stand, covered, for 5 to 10 minutes before serving.

VARIATION:

Simple Shellfish Soup: Substitute 1½ pounds scallops or shelled shrimp, or a combination of the two, for the fish. Serve each bowl with a heaping spoonful of Aioli (page 175), Salsa Cruda (page 185), or Cumin Salsa (page 186).

CORN SOUP WITH JALAPEÑO SALSA

MAKES 4 TO 6 SERVINGS BEGIN 20 TO 25 MINUTES BEFORE SERVING
COOKING TIME: 15 TO 20 MINUTES

- 2 tablespoons butter
- 1 medium onion, chopped
- 2 tablespoons all-purpose flour
- 2 cups fresh or frozen corn kernels
- 1 cup Chicken Broth or Stock (page 118)
- 2 cups milk
- 2 teaspoons chopped fresh parsley
- ¼ teaspoon black pepper
- ⅛ teaspoon cayenne pepper (optional)
- 1 recipe Warm Jalapeño Salsa (page 187)

In a 3-quart casserole combine the butter and onion. Cook on HIGH for 1 to 2 minutes, or until the onion is tender. Stir in the flour to form a paste. Stir in the corn and broth. Cover tightly and cook on HIGH for 8 to 10 minutes, or until the corn is tender. Stir in the remaining ingredients except salsa. Cover again and cook on HIGH for 6 to 8 minutes, or until heated through. Spoon a heaping teaspoonful of salsa into each bowl of soup.

VARIATION:

Cream Corn Soup: Puree the cooked corn and broth mixture in a blender or food processor, reserving some corn kernels for garnish. Omit the salsa. Garnish with corn kernels and chopped fresh cilantro (coriander) or crumbled bacon.

WHOLESOME CEREAL SOUP
(GRIESSSUPPE)

MAKES 4 SERVINGS   BEGIN 15 TO 20 MINUTES BEFORE SERVING
COOKING TIME: 11 TO 19 MINUTES

This is a soup that was our convenience food when I was a child growing up in a German-American home. It was dished out when we needed a quick meal, when mother hadn't restocked the refrigerator, or even when we weren't feeling well. By stirring in yogurt or cheese, this soup will qualify as a meatless main dish.

Here frequent stirring is needed to prevent lumping; cooking uncovered makes this process easier. Cooking uncovered lets the liquid evaporate and the soup thicken.

- 2 **tablespoons butter or margarine**
- 2 **tablespoons chopped onion or scallions**
- 1 **cup farina or wheat cereal**
- 4 **cups Beef, Chicken, or Vegetable Broth or Stock, (page 119)**
- **Salt and pepper**

In a 3-quart casserole combine the butter and onion. Cook on HIGH 2 to 4 minutes or until the onion is tender. Stir in the cereal to coat. Pour in the broth and salt and pepper; stir.

Cook, on HIGH for 9 to 15 minutes, or until thickened, stirring every 2 to 3 minutes.

Let stand for 3 minutes before serving.

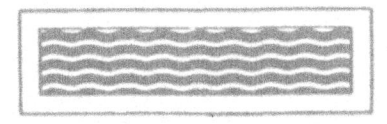

VARIATIONS:

Cereal Soup with Herbs: Stir in 2 tablespoons chopped fresh herbs at the end of cooking.

Cereal Soup with Chives: Garnish with 2 tablespoons chopped chives before serving.

Cereal Soup with Egg: Stir a lightly beaten egg into each serving at the end of cooking. Let stand for 3 minutes and the egg will cook slightly.

Cereal Soup with Yogurt (or Sour Cream): Spoon ¼ cup plain yogurt (or sour cream) on the top of each serving.

Cereal Soup with Cheese: Top each serving with 2 tablespoons grated cheese.

SINGLE SERVING: In a 4-cup glass measure combine 1 teaspoon each butter and chopped scallion. Cook on HIGH for 35 seconds to 1 minute or until the scallion is tender. Stir in the cereal to coat; then add the broth. Cook, uncovered, for 3 to 4 minutes, or until thickened, stirring twice. When no one else is at home or when I want a hearty breakfast, this is what I make for myself.

Vegetable Soup Basics:*

1. If onions or garlic are present in the soup they should always be sautéed first to release the flavor and for proper tenderness.
2. The main vegetable—be it potato, carrot, beet, asparagus, broccoli, or cauliflower—is always cooked to tender first before a large quantity of liquid is added. Too much liquid will slow down the cooking, and it is also easier to puree the vegetables alone, without the extra volume of liquid.
3. The vegetables to liquid ratio is approximately 2 to 1.
4. A large (3-quart) casserole makes it easier to stir and prevents boilovers.
5. These soups are cooked on HIGH because not as much time is needed to develop flavor as in a stock, and there are no delicate ingredients to toughen on HIGH power. Care should be taken not to boil a soup to which cream or yogurt has been added, for these could separate.
6. Because you want to retain as much liquid as possible, a tight cover is necessary to cook the vegetables and heat the broth. Because of the frequent stirring, it is best that this cover be a glass lid, easy to take off and put back on, rather than plastic wrap.
7. Standing time is very short so we don't mention it.

*This applies to vegetables other than tomatoes or mushrooms.

POTATO SOUP FOR ALL SEASONS

MAKES 4 TO 6 SERVINGS   BEGIN 30 TO 40 MINUTES BEFORE SERVING
COOKING TIME: 18 TO 25 MINUTES

This is a creamy potato soup upon which eight other soups can be based, according to the season and the vegetables available. We have left the potato skins on for added nutrition, but they can be removed if a lighter-colored soup is desired. Because the potatoes will be the thickener in this soup and are a dense vegetable, they need to be cooked longer than the other vegetables.

- 2 tablespoons butter
- 1 garlic clove, minced
- 1 medium onion, chopped
- 2 cups grated potatoes (about 2 medium)
- 3½ cups grated or thinly sliced zucchini
- 3 tablespoons fresh dill, or 2 teaspoons dried
- 2 cups Chicken Broth or Stock (page 118)
- 1 cup half and half, heavy cream, plain yogurt, sour cream, or sour cream and evaporated milk combined
- ¼ teaspoon pepper
- Salt

In a 3-quart casserole combine the butter, garlic, and onion. Cook on HIGH for 2 to 3 minutes, or until the onion is tender. Add the potatoes, cover again, and cook on HIGH for 6 to 8 minutes, or until the potatoes are tender; stir once.

Stir in 3 cups of the zucchini and add the dill. Cover again and cook on HIGH for 4 to 6 minutes, or until the zucchini is tender, stirring once. Place the mixture in a blender or food processor to puree. Return to the casserole.

Stir in the broth. Cover again and cook on HIGH for 6 to 8 minutes, or until boiling, stirring once. Stir in the cream to blend. Add pepper, and salt to taste. Serve warm or chilled, garnished with remaining ½ cup zucchini.

VARIATIONS:

Curried Potato-Zucchini Soup: Add 1 tablespoon curry powder with the butter.

Potato-Watercress Soup: Add 3 cups chopped fresh watercress to the soup in place of the zucchini, and add 1 tablespoon lemon juice to the broth. Garnish with ½ cup chopped fresh watercress.

Potato-Parsley Soup: Add 3 cups chopped fresh parsley to the soup in place of the zucchini. Stir in ½ teaspoon grated nutmeg at the end of cooking. Garnish with ½ cup chopped fresh parsley.

Potato-Scallion Soup: Add 3 cups thinly sliced scallions to the soup in place of the zucchini. Substitute chopped fresh basil for the dill. Garnish with ½ cup chopped scallions. This makes a mild-flavored onion soup.

Tomato-Potato Soup: Add 3 cups fresh or canned tomatoes, sliced and seeded, to the soup in place of the zucchini. Substitute chopped fresh basil or parsley for the dill. Garnish with ½ cup chopped tomato.

Spinach-Potato Soup: Add 3 cups thinly sliced spinach to the soup in place of the zucchini. Substitute chopped fresh parsley for the dill. Add ¼ teaspoon grated nutmeg at the end of cooking.

Potato-Sorrel Soup: Add 3 cups thinly sliced sorrel leaves to the soup in place of the zucchini. Substitute chopped fresh parsley for the dill. After pureeing, add sour cream. Add ¼ teaspoon dried thyme leaves at the end of cooking. Garnish with ½ cup chopped chives or scallions.

Carrot-Potato Soup: Substitute 3 cups grated carrots to the soup for the zucchini, but add with the potatoes. Cover tightly and cook the potatoes and carrots on HIGH for 10 to 14 minutes, or until tender. Substitute chopped fresh parsley for the dill.

COUNTRY POTATO-LEEK SOUP

MAKES 4 TO 6 SERVINGS   BEGIN 30 TO 40 MINUTES BEFORE SERVING
COOKING TIME: 19 TO 27 MINUTES

When the potato skins are removed, this is a classic vichyssoise.

- 2 tablespoons butter
- 1 garlic clove, minced
- 1 medium onion, chopped
- 3 cups thinly sliced leeks
- 2 cups grated potatoes (about 2 medium)
- 2 tablespoons fresh dill, or 2 teaspoons dried
- 2 cups Chicken Broth or Stock (page 118)
- 1 cup heavy cream or sour cream
- ½ cup chopped fresh chives

In a 3-quart casserole combine the butter, garlic, onion, and leeks. Cover tightly and cook on HIGH for 3 to 5 minutes, or until the vegetables are almost tender. Add the potatoes, re-cover, and cook on HIGH for 10 to 14 minutes, or until all the vegetables are tender, stirring once. Stir in the dill. Place the mixture in a blender or food processor to puree. Return to the casserole.

Stir in the broth, cover again, and cook on HIGH for 6 to 8 minutes, or until boiling, stirring once. Stir in the cream to blend. Serve warm or chilled, garnished with chives.

ORANGE-FLAVORED CARROT SOUP

MAKES 4 TO 6 SERVINGS   BEGIN 30 TO 40 MINUTES BEFORE SERVING
COOKING TIME: 18 TO 27 MINUTES

- 2 tablespoons butter
- 1 cup chopped onion
- 4 cups grated carrots (about 1 pound)
- 1 cup orange juice
- 2 cups Chicken Broth or Stock (page 118)
- 1 teaspoon dried thyme
- ½ teaspoon salt
- ¼ teaspoon pepper
- Plain yogurt (optional)

In a 3-quart casserole combine the butter and onion. Cook on HIGH for 2 to 3 minutes, or until the onion is tender. Add the carrots and orange juice. Cover tightly and cook on HIGH for 10 to 14 minutes, or until the carrots are tender, stirring once.

Leave the mixture as is for a textured soup, or puree in a blender or food processor and return to the casserole. Add the broth, thyme, salt, and pepper. Cover again and cook on HIGH for 6 to 10 minutes, stirring once. Let stand, covered, for 5 minutes.

Serve with a dollop of yogurt, if desired.

VICTORY GARDEN BEET SOUP

MAKES 4 SERVINGS   BEGIN 45 MINUTES TO 1 HOUR BEFORE SERVING (A FOOD PROCESSOR QUICKENS)
COOKING TIME: 26 to 34 MINUTES

Here is a light, flavorful soup that calls for chicken broth rather than the more traditional beef broth. We concocted this soup when both beets and zucchini were in abundance in our garden.

- 2 tablespoons butter
- ½ cup chopped onion
- 1 pound beets, peeled and grated or cut into ¼-inch cubes
- 1 cup grated zucchini
- ¼ cup orange juice
- 1 tablespoon lemon juice
- ⅛ teaspoon pepper
- Pinch of salt
- 2 cups Chicken Broth or Stock (page 118)
- 1 cup plain yogurt or sour cream
- 2 tablespoons finely snipped fresh chives or scallion tops

In a 3-quart casserole combine the butter and onion. Cook on HIGH for 2 to 3 minutes, or until the onion is tender. Add the beets. Cover tightly and cook on HIGH for 12 to 16 minutes, or until the beets are tender, stirring twice.

Add the zucchini, orange and lemon juice, pepper, and salt. Pour in the broth. Cover again and cook on HIGH for 12 to 15 minutes, or until boiling, stirring once. Let stand, covered, for 5 minutes. Serve hot or cold, ladled into bowls or cups, topped with a dollop of yogurt or sour cream and sprinkled with chopped chives.

CREAMY BROCCOLI SOUP

MAKES 4 TO 6 SERVINGS   BEGIN 25 TO 30 MINUTES BEFORE SERVING
COOKING TIME: 15 TO 22 MINUTES

- 2 tablespoons butter or margarine
- 1 onion, finely chopped
- 2 cups trimmed and coarsely chopped broccoli (about 1 bunch), plus 6 small flowerets
- 2 cups Chicken Broth or Stock (page 118)
- ½ teaspoon salt
- ¼ teaspoon black pepper
- Pinch of cayenne pepper
- Sour cream or plain yogurt (optional)

In a 2-quart casserole combine the butter and onion. Cook on HIGH for 1 to 2 minutes, or until the onion is tender. Add the broccoli. Cover tightly and cook on HIGH for 8 to 10 minutes, or until the broccoli is tender, stirring once. Place the mixture in a food processor or blender to puree. Return to the casserole.

Stir in the broth, salt, and peppers. Cover again and cook on HIGH 6 to 10 minutes, or until hot, stirring once. Garnish with the broccoli flowerets and a dollop of sour cream or plain yogurt, if desired.

VARIATIONS:

Cauliflower Soup: Substitute cauliflower for the broccoli.

Cream of Broccoli or Cauliflower Soup: Substitute 1 cup cream or plain yogurt for 1 cup chicken broth. Serve hot or cold. If served hot, after the addition of yogurt cover tightly and cook the pureed soup on HIGH for *only* 4 to 6 minutes, or until hot. Do not boil. If served cold, no cooking is necessary after pureeing. The yogurt will add a slightly zesty flavor.

Creamy Broccoli or Cauliflower Cheese Soup: Substitute 1 cup cream or plain yogurt for 1 cup chicken broth. For a spicy soup, add ½ teaspoon dry mustard, ¼ teaspoon grated nutmeg, and 2 tablespoons dry sherry (optional). After adding yogurt, cover tightly and cook on HIGH for *only* 4 to 6 minutes, or until hot. Do not boil. Before serving, stir in ½ cup grated cheddar cheese until melted.

CREAM OF ASPARAGUS SOUP

MAKES 6 SERVINGS   BEGIN 25 TO 30 MINUTES BEFORE SERVING
COOKING TIME: 15 TO 19 MINUTES

Cream of asparagus soup heralds the advent of spring with its soft green color and enticing taste. It utilizes the stems of the asparagus, while the majority of the tips are saved for a salad.

1½ tablespoons butter	2 cups Chicken Broth or Stock (page 118)
¼ cup chopped shallots or scallions	1 cup half and half or plain yogurt
1 pound asparagus stalks, cut into ½-inch pieces	¼ teaspoon salt
	Pepper

In a 3-quart casserole combine the butter and shallots. Cook on HIGH for 2 minutes, or until the shallots are tender. Set 6 asparagus tips in small dish and cover tightly. Cook on HIGH for 1 minute and set aside for garnish; reserve remainder for another use. Stir the asparagus stalks into the casserole. Cover tightly and cook on HIGH for 5 to 7 minutes, or until the asparagus is tender, stirring once. Place in a blender or food processor to puree. Return to the casserole.

Stir in the chicken broth, half and half, salt, and pepper to taste. Cover again and cook on HIGH for 8 to 10 minutes, or until the soup is hot but not boiling, stirring once. Pour into bowls and garnish with the asparagus tips.

NOTE: Asparagus tips can be added to Carryover Vegetable Stir-Shake (page 480) or Mixed Wok-Style Vegetables (page 481).

CREAMY DILLED PUMPKIN SOUP

MAKES 4 TO 6 SERVINGS   BEGIN 30 MINUTES BEFORE SERVING
COOKING TIME: 24 MINUTES

One big advantage of making soup in the microwave is that while it is cooking you are free to go on to other activities. Constant stirring is not necessary. For something different, you might want to serve this soup in a hollowed-out pumpkin bowl.

---

2 tablespoons butter	3 cups fresh or canned pumpkin, cooked and mashed
½ cup chopped onion	

2 cups Chicken Broth or Stock (page 118)
½ cup white wine
1 cup half and half or evaporated skimmed milk
½ teaspoon grated nutmeg
½ teaspoon dried thyme
⅛ teaspoon cayenne pepper
Freshly snipped dill

In a 3-quart casserole combine the butter and onion. Cook on HIGH for 2 minutes, or until the onion is tender. Stir in the pumpkin, chicken broth, and wine. Cover again and cook on HIGH for 2 minutes; stir. Cook on MEDIUM for 15 minutes to develop the flavor, stirring every 5 minutes.

Stir in the remaining ingredients except dill. Cover again and cook on MEDIUM for 5 minutes, or until heated through; stir. Let stand, covered, for 5 minutes before serving. Garnish with dill.

VARIATION:

Creamy Dilled Squash Soup: Substitute mashed cooked winter squash for the pumpkin. Nice to make in the winter when there is squash left over from the holidays.

Tomato or Mushroom Soup Basics:

1. Tomatoes and mushrooms give off a lot of liquid when heated, and so should be cooked uncovered first, to evaporate some of this liquid. The exception to this is if there are other vegetables in the soup that need the steaming effect of a cover to cook completely.
2. As with other vegetable soups, if tomatoes and mushrooms are the basic vegetables, they are cooked first before adding the remaining liquid. The additional liquid would only slow down the cooking of these vegetables if added in the beginning.
3. Both tomato and mushroom soups need to be thickened with either tomato paste or flour. Flour will provide more thickening than tomato paste. Allow a 2 to 3 ratio of flour to tomato paste if you want to make that substitution in the tomato soups.

Reheating One Serving of Soup

To reheat an 8- to 10-ounce serving of refrigerated soup: Pour into a bowl and cover with wax paper. Cook on HIGH for 2 to 4 minutes, or until heated through, stirring once. If the soup has cheese or yogurt in it, cook instead on MEDIUM for 3 to 5 minutes, stirring once.

❋ FRESH HOT TOMATO SOUP

MAKES 4 SERVINGS   BEGIN 35 TO 40 MINUTES BEFORE SERVING
COOKING TIME: 23 TO 32 MINUTES

When tomatoes ripen in my garden, I go through predictable tomato stages—first getting my fill of pure, sliced tomatoes, then moving on to tomato salads with fresh basil and stuffed tomatoes. I know winter is around the corner when I start in on pasta sauces and soups for freezing. This soup is tremendously flavorful and so easy to vary for single servings.

- 2 tablespoons butter
- 2 medium onions, chopped
- 2 celery ribs, thinly sliced
- 2 pounds tomatoes, peeled, seeded, and coarsely chopped, or 2 cups undrained canned
- 1 teaspoon sugar
- 3 sprigs fresh thyme, or ½ teaspoon dried
- 1 bay leaf, broken in half
- 2 cups Chicken Broth or Stock (page 118)
- 2 tablespoons tomato paste
- ½ teaspoon salt
- ¼ teaspoon pepper
- Sour cream, plain yogurt, or Parmesan cheese with chopped fresh chives or scallion greens

In a 2-quart casserole combine the butter, onions, and celery. Cook on HIGH for 5 to 7 minutes, or until the onions and celery are almost tender, stirring once. Stir in the tomatoes, sugar, thyme, and bay leaf. Cover tightly and cook on HIGH for 12 to 15 minutes, or until the tomatoes break up, stirring once. Remove the bay leaf.

Place the mixture in a blender or food processor to puree. Return to the casserole. Add the chicken broth, tomato paste, salt, and pepper. Cover tightly and cook on HIGH for 6 to 10 minutes, or until heated through, stirring once.

Serve topped with sour cream, yogurt, or Parmesan cheese and chopped chives.

VARIATIONS:

Sherried Tomato Soup: Stir in 2 tablespoons dry sherry with the chicken broth.

Spicy Tomato Soup: Stir in ½ teaspoon each cayenne pepper and Worcestershire sauce with the chicken broth.

Curried Tomato Soup: Stir in 1 teaspoon curry powder with the chicken broth.

Dilled Tomato Soup: Stir in 1 tablespoon chopped fresh dill with the chicken broth. Serve warm or cold.

Tomato-Rice Soup: Stir in 1 cup cooked rice with the chicken broth.

Cream of Tomato Soup: Substitute 1½ cups half and half or milk for the chicken broth.

Serve warm or chilled. If serving chilled, eliminate the final heating.

SINGLE SERVING: For variation, stir in 2 teaspoons dry sherry or brandy, ¼ teaspoon curry powder, ½ teaspoon chopped fresh dill, or ½ cup cooked rice before reheating. See page 129 for reheating instructions.

☀ CHILLED CREAM OF TOMATO-BASIL SOUP

MAKES 6 SERVINGS   BEGIN 30 MINUTES TO 1 HOUR BEFORE SERVING TO CHILL
COOKING TIME: 17 TO 25 MINUTES

August heat brings tomatoes and basil to their peak, giving us the tools to make this delicious soup. But it is for that August heat that we add cooling yogurt and serve this rich and creamy soup chilled.

- 2 tablespoons butter
- 1 garlic clove, minced
- 1 cup thinly sliced onions
- 3 pounds ripe tomatoes, peeled, seeded, and chopped
- 3 tablespoons tomato paste
- 2 cups Chicken Broth or Stock (page 118)
- ½ teaspoon sugar
- Salt and pepper
- ¼ cup finely chopped fresh basil
- 1 cup plain yogurt, sour cream, or crème fraîche, plus additional for garnish
- 1 teaspoon grated orange rind (optional)

In a 2-quart casserole combine the butter, garlic, and onions. Cook on HIGH for 2 to 3 minutes, or until the onions are tender. Stir in the tomatoes and tomato paste. Cook on HIGH 5 to 8 minutes, or until boiling, stirring twice. Place the mixture in a blender or food processor to puree. Return to the casserole.

Add the broth, sugar, and salt and pepper to taste. Cover tightly and cook on HIGH for 10 to 14 minutes, or until just boiling, stirring once. Stir in the basil and yogurt or sour cream to blend. Chill.

To serve, ladle into soup bowls or cups and top with a dollop of yogurt, sour cream, or crème fraîche and grated orange rind, if desired.

QUICK TOMATO SOUP

MAKES 6 SERVINGS   BEGIN 15 MINUTES BEFORE SERVING
COOKING TIME: 11 TO 14 MINUTES

- 2 tablespoons butter or margarine
- 1 medium onion, finely chopped
- 1 quart tomato juice
- 1 cup Chicken Broth or Stock (page 118) or water
- 2 tablespoons tomato paste
- 1 tablespoon lemon juice
- ½ teaspoon sugar
- ½ teaspoon dried thyme
- ¼ teaspoon pepper
- Salt

In a 2-quart casserole combine the butter and onion. Cook on HIGH for 1 to 2 minutes, or until the onion is tender. Stir in the remaining ingredients. Cover tightly and cook on HIGH for 10 to 12 minutes, or until heated through, stirring once. Serve warm or chilled.

VARIATIONS:
Quick Gingered Tomato-Orange Soup: Substitute 1 cup orange juice for the chicken broth or water. Add ½ teaspoon powdered ginger. Serve warm or chilled with a thin slice of orange.

Quick Chilled Cream of Tomato Soup: Eliminate the broth or water and chill the cooked soup. Before serving, stir in 1 cup heavy cream, plain yogurt, or sour cream. Serve chilled, topped with plain yogurt or sour cream and a thin slice of lemon.

☀ MUSHROOM SOUP

MAKES 4 SERVINGS   BEGIN 15 TO 20 MINUTES BEFORE SERVING
COOKING TIME: 9 TO 19 MINUTES

Anyone who loves the fresh taste of mushrooms will love this soup.

- 2 tablespoons butter
- 1 medium onion, minced
- 1 pound fresh mushrooms, sliced
- 2 tablespoons all-purpose flour
- 2 tablespoons dry sherry, vermouth, or Madeira
- 2 cups Chicken Broth or Stock (page 118)
- Salt and pepper

In a 2-quart casserole combine the butter and onion. Cook on HIGH for 1 to 3 minutes, or until the onion is tender. Stir in the mushrooms. Cook on HIGH for 3 to 6 minutes, stirring once.

Stir in the flour until smooth. Stir in the sherry and broth. Cover tightly and cook on HIGH for 5 to 10 minutes or until heated through, stirring once or twice. Add salt and pepper to taste.

VARIATION:

Cream of Mushroom Soup: Stir in ½ cup heavy cream, plain yogurt, or sour cream at the end of cooking. Cook on HIGH for 1 to 3 minutes more, if necessary, to heat through.

✹ CHEDDAR CHEESE SOUP

MAKES 4 SERVINGS   BEGIN 20 TO 25 MINUTES BEFORE SERVING
COOKING TIME: 10 TO 12 MINUTES

This is a hearty, heady soup that warms and revives after skiing, shoveling snow, or taking a brisk walk. We even sipped on it this summer after a chilly morning spent tubing down the Esopus River in upstate New York.

Cheese soups and fondues are similar in that flour is used as a thickener in both and both are made with an alcoholic beverage, wine or beer, as a base. In the soup, however, the cheese and flour are melted together first before the alcohol is added so that the small amount of cheese has a chance to melt, while in fondue the liquid is heated first before the cheese is added because the liquid is in smaller proportion. As is true of any recipe containing reasonably large amounts of alcohol, the soup is cooked uncovered in the end so that the alcohol can evaporate during cooking; and as is true of any recipe containing soft cheese, MEDIUM power and frequent stirring are necessary so the cheese melts evenly and doesn't become tough or rubbery.

---

1 tablespoon butter
1 garlic clove, minced
1 tablespoon all-purpose flour
1½ cups grated cheddar cheese
2 cups dry white wine
¼ teaspoon salt
⅛ teaspoon cayenne pepper
Freshly ground black pepper to taste
Pinch of grated nutmeg

In a 2-quart casserole combine the butter and garlic. Cook on HIGH for 1 minute, or until the garlic is tender. Stir in the flour and 1 cup cheese, blending well. Cover tightly and cook on MEDIUM for 2 to 3 minutes, until the cheese is melted; stir.

Add the remaining ingredients, except the nutmeg. Cook, uncovered, on MEDIUM for 7 to 8 minutes, or until boiling, stirring every 2 minutes. Let stand for 5 minutes.

To serve, sprinkle 2 tablespoons of grated cheese on top of each cup with some freshly ground pepper and grated nutmeg. Good with crusty French or Italian bread.

VARIATIONS:

Cheddar-Beer Soup: Substitute flat beer for the wine.

Cheddar-Mustard Soup: Substitute Chicken Broth or Stock (page 118) for the wine. Add 1 tablespoon Dijon mustard.

Basics for Soups Best Cooked on Medium Power:

1. Some soups after being brought to a boil are best cooked on MEDIUM power either to (a) cook longer for flavor development, as in Manhattan Clam Chowder or Austrian Goulash Soup, or to (b) prevent sensitive ingredients from overcooking as in the Greek Lemon or Sweet Spanish Almond Soups.
2. Frequent stirring is not critical because the power has been reduced sufficiently so that conduction of heat to the center is slower and more even.
3. If the soup is being simmered a long time to develop flavor, a tight cover in the form of a lid or plastic wrap aids in this process.

MANHATTAN CLAM CHOWDER

MAKES 8 TO 10 SERVINGS   BEGIN 1½ TO 2 HOURS BEFORE SERVING
COOKING TIME: 1 TO 1¼ HOURS

This chowder is always better the following day when it has had time to develop more flavor. But because it is a favorite, we usually have a small cupful on the day it is made.

Even though one could cook this soup entirely on HIGH, the flavor is improved by cooking it longer on MEDIUM power. Consequently, you don't save much time in the kitchen, but there is a savings when it comes to cleanup. It takes only one casserole to cook both clams and soup, and the same one is appropriate for serving and refrigerator storage.

1½ dozen chowder clams	1 cup thinly sliced carrots
2 tablespoons water, plus more if necessary	1 cup thinly sliced celery
	½ cup coarsely chopped green pepper
2 cups tomato juice	2 cups diced, peeled potatoes
4 tablespoons butter	2 cups fresh or undrained canned tomatoes, peeled and chopped
1½ cups chopped onions	

1 tablespoon chopped fresh basil, or 1 teaspoon dried	1 bay leaf
½ teaspoon dried thyme	Salt
¼ teaspoon pepper	½ cup chopped fresh parsley

Wash the clams well. In a 3-quart casserole combine the clams and water. Cover tightly and cook on HIGH for 10 to 15 minutes, or until the clams have opened, stirring once after 5 minutes. Remove the clams from the casserole and set them aside.

Strain the cooking liquid into a 2-quart glass measure; there will be approximately 3 cups. Add the tomato juice and additional water to the cooking liquid to make 6 cups. Set aside.

In the same casserole, combine the butter, onions, carrots, celery, and green pepper. Cover tightly and cook on HIGH for 10 minutes, stirring after 5 minutes. Add the potatoes, tomatoes, basil, thyme, pepper, bay leaf, and clam-tomato juices. Cover again and cook on HIGH for 15 to 20 minutes, or until boiling; stir.

Meanwhile, remove the clams from their shells and chop coarsely. Add the clams. Cook on MEDIUM for 30 minutes to develop the flavor, stirring once and adding salt to taste. Remove and discard the bay leaf, sprinkle the soup with parsley, and serve.

SWEET SPANISH ALMOND SOUP

MAKES 4 TO 6 SERVINGS   BEGIN 20 TO 25 MINUTES BEFORE SERVING
COOKING TIME: 12 TO 17 MINUTES

3 tablespoons butter	½ cup heavy cream, half and half, or evaporated milk
1 medium Spanish onion, chopped	1 tablespoon honey
1 cup ground blanched almonds	1 tablespoon almond-flavored liqueur
2 cups Chicken Broth or Stock (page 118)	¼ teaspoon grated nutmeg, plus additional for garnish

In a 2-quart casserole combine the butter and onion. Cook on HIGH for 3 minutes, or until the onion is tender. Stir in the almonds and broth. Cover tightly and cook on HIGH for 6 to 10 minutes, or until boiling. Stir in the remaining ingredients, except garnish. Cover again and cook on MEDIUM for 3 to 4 minutes, or until heated through. Do not boil. Serve in bowls garnished with grated nutmeg.

GREEK LEMON SOUP

MAKES 4 TO 6 SERVINGS   BEGIN 30 TO 45 MINUTES BEFORE SERVING TIME
COOKING TIME: 21 TO 32 MINUTES

Be sure you don't let the soup boil after the eggs are added; they will become rubbery if this happens.

- 4 cups Chicken Broth or Stock (page 118)
- ¼ cup long-grain rice
- 2 eggs, well beaten
- Juice of 1 lemon
- 1 tablespoon chopped fresh dill, or 1 teaspoon dried
- 1 tablespoon chopped fresh parsley
- Freshly ground pepper
- Thin lemon slices

Place the chicken broth in a 2-quart casserole. Cover tightly and cook on HIGH for 6 to 10 minutes, or until boiling, stirring once.

Add the rice, cover again, and cook on MEDIUM for 12 to 18 minutes, or until the rice is tender. Remove from the oven. Slowly pour ½ cup rice-and-broth into the eggs, beating constantly. Slowly pour the egg mixture back into the soup casserole, beating constantly. Cook on MEDIUM for 3 to 4 minutes, or until heated through but not boiling, stirring after 2 minutes. Stir in the lemon juice.

To serve, sprinkle with dill, parsley, and pepper to taste. Garnish with very thin slices of lemon.

AUSTRIAN GOULASH SOUP

MAKES 4 TO 6 SERVINGS   BEGIN 1¼ HOURS BEFORE SERVING
COOKING TIME: 49 TO 63 MINUTES

We ate several versions of this soup in Austria and Germany. This version comes closest to the one we liked best. Serve in cups as a first course or in bowls, for lunch, with slabs of pumpernickel.

- 2 tablespoons oil or butter
- 1 garlic clove, minced
- 2 cups chopped onions
- 2 tablespoons all-purpose flour
- 1 pound beef chuck, cut into ½-inch cubes
- 1 cup green pepper, cut into ½-inch cubes
- 1½ tablespoons tomato paste
- 2 cups beef broth or stock (see Mock Brown Broth or Stock, page 119)

2 teaspoons paprika	½ teaspoon salt
¼ teaspoon cayenne pepper	¼ teaspoon black pepper
½ teaspoon caraway seeds	

In a 3-quart casserole combine the oil, garlic, and onions. Cook on HIGH for 1 to 3 minutes, or until the onions are tender. Stir in the flour to make a smooth paste. Stir in the meat. Cover tightly and cook on HIGH for 10 minutes, or until meat has almost lost all of its pink color. Stir once.

Stir in the remaining ingredients. Cover again and cook on HIGH for 8 to 10 minutes, or until boiling; stir. Cover again and cook on MEDIUM for 30 to 40 minutes, or until the meat is tender and the soup is flavorful, stirring twice. Let stand, covered, for 10 minutes.

MÜNCHNER LIVER DUMPLING SOUP

MAKES 6 TO 8 SERVINGS   BEGIN 25 TO 35 MINUTES BEFORE SERVING
COOKING TIME: 13 TO 20 MINUTES

We have served this to people who claimed they did not like liver but, in spite of that, loved this soup. Maybe that's because the liver here can almost be described as "airy," bobbing to the surface in floating islands, lightly seasoned with parsley and nutmeg. We first had this in Munich or "München."

1 pound beef or calf liver	½ teaspoon salt
1 cup dry bread crumbs	¼ teaspoon pepper
1 egg, slightly beaten	⅛ teaspoon grated nutmeg
¼ cup finely chopped fresh parsley	4 cups beef broth or stock (see Mock Brown Broth or Stock, page 119)
2 tablespoons all-purpose flour	
2 tablespoons finely chopped scallions	

Remove the outer membrane of the liver and discard. Cut the liver into large chunks. Grind, using finest blade of a food grinder, or chop fine in a food processor. In a medium-size bowl combine the chopped liver with the remaining ingredients, except the broth.

Pour the broth into a 3-quart casserole.

Cover tightly and cook on HIGH for 8 to 10 minutes, or until boiling. Dip 2 serving teaspoons into the hot broth, then, with one of the spoons, scoop out a heaping teaspoon of liver mixture. Drop the mixture into the broth, pushing it off with the other spoon. Dip the spoons again and continue making dumplings and dropping them into the broth until all the liver mixture is gone. Cover the casserole tightly and cook on HIGH for 5 to 10 minutes, or until the dumplings are set and cooked through. Let stand, covered, for 5 minutes. Serve in bowls and sprinkle with fresh parsley.

VARIATION:

Chicken Liver Dumpling Soup: Substitute chicken livers for the beef liver. Substitute Chicken Broth or Stock (page 118) for the beef broth, adding 1 tablespoon dry sherry or vermouth with the broth.

LIDA'S PEACH-BRANDY SOUP

MAKES 4 SERVINGS BEGIN 10 TO 15 MINUTES BEFORE SERVING
COOKING TIME: 7 MINUTES

It was a tossup as to whether this soup would go into the dessert chapter or with the soups. We could eat it for lunch with yogurt stirred in or make a particularly dramatic dessert by adding flamed sugar cubes.

The microwave retains the flavor of the fresh peaches—they taste as if they were just plucked from the orchard.

- 4 ripe peaches, peeled, thinly sliced, and chopped, or 2 cups drained canned
- ¼ cup granulated sugar
- ½ cup dry white wine
- 2 tablespoons Triple Sec
- ½ teaspoon grated lemon rind
- ½ teaspoon ground cinnamon
- ½ cup whipped cream
- 4 sugar cubes (optional)
- 2 tablespoons brandy for flaming (optional)

In a 2-quart glass casserole combine the peaches, sugar, wine, Triple Sec, lemon rind, and cinnamon. Cook on HIGH for 6 minutes, or until boiling and the wine scent is faint, stirring once.

When the soup is hot, pour into 4 bowls, garnishing each with a dollop of whipped cream. If you wish, add a sugar cube on top. Heat the brandy on HIGH for 20 seconds in a 1-cup glass measure. Ignite and pour a little of it directly on each sugar cube. Serve the soup immediately.

VARIATION:

Peach Soup with Yogurt: Eliminate the cream, brandy, and sugar cubes. Stir ¼ cup plain yogurt into each serving of the soup.

6

EGGS AND CHEESE

Eggs are treated as their recipe names generally imply, with gentleness. Think of "once over easy," "coddled" (which means to treat tenderly or pamper), and "soufflé" (which comes from the French word meaning "a murmuring or blowing sound"). If cooked too fervently or beaten too hard, eggs become tough and the antithesis of those tranquil things we are trying to turn them into.

The rule of thumb for cheese cookery is also to "handle with kid gloves." And since cheese and eggs often go together, as they do here in Ricotta Cheese Timbales and Cheese Soufflé, the two make a good match. Gentle treatment translates to mean, in microwave cooking language, MEDIUM power and stir often, if possible.

Since eggs are most commonly served in the mornings, it shouldn't be hard to remember to treat your eggs as you would treat your stomach—gently. If you do, you'll produce puffy omelets and other egg dishes that you wouldn't have had the time or inclination to try before.

—THELMA

Buying and Storing Eggs

- The freshness of an egg is important and can be determined when the egg is cracked onto a plate and the yolk sits up above a gelatinous white that immediately surrounds it. This will give you the most volume in your cakes and soufflés, and will prevent "popping"* of an egg during poaching. For poaching, the fresher the egg the better.
- Look for eggs that have a slightly dull sheen to the shell. The color of the shell is of very little importance.
- When we call for eggs, we are asking for a grade Large egg, and cooking times are designed for this size.

*Popping describes the sound that steam makes bursting through the egg membrane.

- Eggs should be stored at refrigerator temperature, and all of our cooking times are based on this. If your eggs have been out on the kitchen counter awhile before cooking, you may have to reduce the cooking time called for in the recipes.
- Having said that, in beating egg whites, the greatest volume can be achieved when the eggs have reached room temperature. The bowl, aluminum or nonplastic, and beaters should be very clean and free from grease. If any part of the yolk, which contains fat, falls into the white, it will inhibit the egg white structure.

Poached Egg Basics:

1. One of the most important steps in poaching eggs is to boil the water or—in the case of shirred eggs—melt the butter beforehand. The hot liquid can then coat the eggs to begin the cooking on all surfaces evenly and continue to conduct heat to the centers. Vinegar in the water causes the outside of the egg white to coagulate quicker.
2. Puncturing the yolk membrane lightly before cooking prevents possible steam buildup in the yolk that could cause it to burst.
3. Placing the eggs in a circle with space 1 inch between cooking dishes will give all the eggs equal exposure to microwave energy. Depending on your oven, some eggs may appear to be cooking faster than others. These should be repositioned with the eggs that aren't cooking as quickly, partway through cooking.
4. Eggs should be cooked on MEDIUM power so that the protein does not cook too quickly and toughen, as it would on HIGH.
5. Egg yolks contain more fat than whites and therefore will attract more microwave energy, cooking more quickly. Covering the eggs holds in steam to even up this cooking process between yolk and white.
6. *Doneness:* Eggs should *not* be cooked until completely set; the setting of the whites will take place during standing. To achieve a poached egg with a yolk that still runs, look for these clues in the egg white. When taken from the oven, the cooked white should be firm and opaque around the outside, while around the yolk a thin line of clear uncooked white will remain. This will set during standing time. Remove any eggs that appear done and continue to cook the others.

   Underdone: Most of the white will still appear transparent, not opaque. Return the eggs to the oven and continue to cook on MEDIUM for 15 to 20 seconds at a time. After a few times cooking these eggs, you will know what cooking times are best for your oven.

   Overdone: An overcooked poached egg will have a firm yolk and white. It may not be suitable for your original plans, but it can stand in as a perfectly good hard-cooked egg. Chop up for garnish or for Hard-Cooked Egg Salad.

✹ POACHED EGGS

MAKES 4 SERVINGS   BEGIN 8 TO 10 MINUTES BEFORE SERVING
COOKING TIME: 3½ TO 6½ MINUTES

Poached eggs are cooked in boiling water with a touch of vinegar added; this helps coagulate the whites. They are so easy to prepare, and can be summoned up for occasions other than breakfast. (See "Adding an Egg for a Complete Protein to Vegetable Dishes," page 147). Serve them plain or as described in the recipes that follow.

| 8 tablespoons water | 1 teaspoon white vinegar | 4 eggs |

In each of four 5- to 6-ounce custard cups combine 2 tablespoons water and ¼ teaspoon vinegar. Cook on HIGH for 1 to 3 minutes, or until the water boils.

Break 1 egg into each dish; puncture each yolk lightly with a toothpick or fork. Cover tightly and place the cups in a circle in the oven with at least 1 inch between them. (See Note.) Cook on MEDIUM for 2½ to 3½ minutes, or until almost set, repositioning the dishes once if necessary and removing the eggs as they are done. Let stand, covered, 2 to 3 minutes before serving.

NOTE: By placing individual poached eggs (or timbales) on a microwaveproof tray, you will make it easy to rotate them during cooking and to transfer them from the oven to the table.

VARIATION:

Square Eggs: Square eggs fit best on square toast. Substitute four clean 3-inch-square glass ashtrays for the custard cups, then proceed with the basic recipe.

EGGS BENEDICT

MAKES 4 SERVINGS   BEGIN 10 TO 15 MINUTES BEFORE SERVING
COOKING TIME: 6¾ TO 10½ MINUTES WITH BACON; 4½ TO 9½ MINUTES WITH HAM

4 slices of Canadian bacon or ham	1 teaspoon white vinegar
2 English muffins	4 eggs
8 tablespoons water	1 recipe Hollandaise Sauce (page 174)

Place the Canadian bacon or ham slices on a microwaveproof plate. Cover with wax paper and cook on MEDIUM for 3¼ to 4 minutes for Canadian bacon, 1 to 3 minutes for cooked ham. Meanwhile, split and toast the English muffins.

Poach the eggs according to the directions on page 143, using 2 tablespoons water and ¼ teaspoon vinegar per egg. While the eggs are cooking, place a slice of bacon or ham on each English muffin half. During the standing time of the eggs, make the hollandaise sauce. Place the poached eggs on the bacon or ham slices; pour the sauce on top. Serve immediately.

VARIATION:

Poached Eggs with Cheese on Muffins: While eggs are cooking, place the bacon or ham slices on the toasted English muffin halves; set the muffins on microwaveproof plates. Place the poached eggs on top of the meat; top each egg with a slice of American cheese. Cook on MEDIUM for 30 seconds to 1 minute to melt the cheese.

POACHED EGGS MORNAY

MAKES 4 SERVINGS   BEGIN 8 TO 10 MINUTES BEFORE SERVING
COOKING TIME: 3½ TO 5½ MINUTES

- 8 tablespoons water
- 1 teaspoon white vinegar
- 4 eggs
- 4 slices of bread
- 4 teaspoons butter
- 4 slices of smoked turkey
- 1 recipe Mornay Sauce (page 171)

Poach the eggs according to the directions on page 143, using 2 tablespoons water and ¼ teaspoon vinegar per egg. While the eggs are cooking, toast and butter the bread. Place 1 slice of smoked turkey on each slice of toast.

During the standing time of the eggs, make the Mornay sauce. Place the eggs on top of the turkey; pour the sauce on top. Serve immediately.

VARIATION:

Poached Eggs with Mustard Sauce: Eliminate the smoked turkey from the recipe. While the eggs are cooking, toast and butter the bread. During standing time of the eggs, make Mustard Sauce (page 171). Place the poached eggs on the toast; pour the sauce on top.

POACHED EGGS WITH ASPARAGUS AND HOLLANDAISE

MAKES 4 SERVINGS   BEGIN 15 MINUTES BEFORE SERVING
COOKING TIME: 5½ TO 10½ MINUTES

- **4 asparagus spears, trimmed**
- **9 tablespoons water**
- **1 teaspoon white vinegar**
- **4 eggs**
- **4 slices of bread**
- **4 teaspoons butter**
- **1 recipe Hollandaise Sauce (page 174)**

Place the asparagus with 1 tablespoon water in a small casserole. Cover tightly and cook on HIGH for 2 to 4 minutes, or until tender. Set aside.

Poach the eggs according to the directions on page 143, using 2 tablespoons water and ¼ teaspoon vinegar per egg. While the eggs are cooking, toast and butter the bread; place 1 asparagus spear on each slice of toast.

During standing time of the eggs, make the hollandaise sauce. Place the poached eggs on top of the asparagus; pour the sauce on top. Serve immediately.

HUEVOS RANCHEROS

MAKES 4 SERVINGS   BEGIN 18 TO 25 MINUTES BEFORE SERVING
COOKING TIME: 4 TO 7 MINUTES

- **8 tablespoons water**
- **1 teaspoon white vinegar**
- **4 eggs**
- **4 flour tortillas**
- **1 recipe Salsa Ranchera (page 146)**

Poach the eggs according to the directions on page 143, using 2 tablespoons water and ¼ teaspoon vinegar per egg. While the eggs are standing, wrap the tortillas in dampened paper toweling; place in the microwave and heat on HIGH for 30 seconds, or until warm to the thumb. At the same time, reheat the salsa, if necessary, on HIGH for 1 to 3 minutes.

Place 1 poached egg on top of each tortilla. Spoon the salsa over the eggs and serve immediately.

SALSA RANCHERA

MAKES ABOUT 2 CUPS
COOKING TIME: 10 TO 15 MINUTES

- 2 tablespoons oil
- 1 garlic clove, minced
- 1 medium onion, chopped
- 2 cups tomatoes, peeled, seeded, and coarsely chopped, or 2 cups undrained canned
- 1 or 2 serrano or jalapeño peppers (jalapeño are hotter), seeded and chopped

In a 2-quart casserole combine the oil, garlic, and onion. Cook on HIGH for 2 to 3 minutes, or until the onion is tender. Add the remaining ingredients. Cook on HIGH for 8 to 12 minutes, or until heated through and flavors are blended, stirring once or twice.

SHIRRED EGGS

MAKES 4 SERVINGS   BEGIN 8 TO 10 MINUTES BEFORE SERVING
COOKING TIME: 3 TO 5 MINUTES

Shirred eggs are simply poached eggs that are cooked in hot, melted butter instead of water. What you get are buttery poached eggs that don't need to be drained. Serve them as is or substitute them in any recipe calling for poached eggs.

4 teaspoons butter   4 eggs

Place 1 teaspoon butter in each of four 5- to 6-ounce custard cups. Cook on HIGH for 35 seconds to 1 minute to melt.

Break 1 egg into each dish; puncture each yolk lightly with a toothpick or fork. Cover tightly and place the cups in a circle in the oven with at least 1 inch between them. Cook on MEDIUM for 2½ to 3½ minutes, or until almost set, repositioning the dishes once if necessary and removing the eggs as they are done. Let stand, covered, for 2 to 3 minutes.

VARIATIONS:

Shirred Eggs with Herbs: Sprinkle the eggs with 1 tablespoon chopped fresh herbs before serving. (If adding dried herbs, reduce to 1 teaspoon and add with the butter.)

Shirred Eggs with Cheese: Sprinkle each egg with 1 tablespoon grated Swiss or Gruyère cheese at the end of cooking before standing. Cover again and let stand to melt the cheese and set the eggs.

Shirred Eggs with Mushrooms: Prepare ½ pound Sautéed Mushrooms (page 439). During standing time of the eggs, reheat the mushrooms on HIGH for 1 to 2 minutes. Serve the eggs over the mushrooms and sprinkle with chopped fresh parsley.

Adding an Egg for a Complete Protein to Vegetable Dishes

- Place a poached egg on top of each serving of Vegetarian Chili (page 436).
- Place a poached egg on top of each of the Fragrant Whole Tomatoes (page 422).
- Stir a chopped poached egg into Sautéed Light or Sautéed Rich Greens (pages 428 and 429).
- Serve a poached egg on top of each serving of Lentil or Pea Puree (page 435).

Hard-Cooked Egg Basics:

1. Hard-cooked eggs are never cooked in their shells because of the steam that will build up and shatter the shell as it tries to escape. This is also the reason why the yolk membrane must be pierced, to prevent the steam buildup in the egg.
2. Because the eggs are not cooked in their shells, they will take on the shape of the cooking dish rather than the egg shell.
3. As with poached eggs, the hard-cooked eggs should be placed in a circle with 1 inch of space between them, so that all surfaces receive an equal amount of microwave energy.
4. No additional cooking liquid is needed to add flavor or even up the cooking, as with poached or shirred eggs. Doneness in hard-cooked eggs is not as precise as it is in soft-cooked eggs. A tight cover will retain steam to even up the cooking between yolk and white.
5. Hard-cooked eggs must be cooked on MEDIUM power, so that the whites don't cook too quickly and become tough.
6. *Doneness:* Unlike poached eggs, hard-cooked eggs should be cooked to the point where their whites are completely set. Standing time will allow the yolk to set completely to hard-cooked doneness.

✸ HARD-COOKED EGGS

MAKES 6 SERVINGS   BEGIN ABOUT 10 MINUTES BEFORE SERVING
COOKING TIME: 5 TO 8 MINUTES

These are suitable for any recipe that calls for chopped hard-cooked eggs, as in a salad filling or for garnishing a plate.

6 eggs

Break each egg into a 5- or 6-ounce custard cup. Puncture each yolk with a toothpick or fork. Cover tightly and place the dishes in a circle in the oven with at least 1 inch between them. Cook on MEDIUM for 5 to 8 minutes, or until the egg whites are set, repositioning the dishes after 3 minutes for more even cooking. Let stand for 2 minutes.

HARD-COOKED EGG SPREAD

MAKES ABOUT 2½ CUPS   BEGIN 1 HOUR BEFORE SERVING TIME

This is a chameleon among appetizers, for it can blend into so many snacking situations. It is delicious with crackers, and it can be dressed up with caviar or quickly whipped into a packed-lunch sandwich. If you keep the ingredients on hand and chilled, this spread can be made at a moment's notice.

- 6 eggs, hard-cooked (recipe above)
- ½ cup Mayonnaise (page 175)
- 2 tablespoons chopped fresh chives
- 1 tablespoon lemon juice
- ¼ teaspoon salt
- ⅛ teaspoon pepper

Finely chop the eggs in a food processor or by hand. Combine in a small bowl with the remaining ingredients. Chill.

VARIATIONS:

Hard-Cooked Egg–Mock Truffle Spread: Add ½ cup coarsely chopped black olives to the basic recipe. In appearance, you might find that the olives resemble truffles.

Hard-Cooked Egg–Nut Spread: Add ½ cup coarsely chopped nuts to the basic recipe. This addition gives texture and body to a spread on bread.

Deviled Egg Spread: Add ¼ teaspoon dry mustard, ¼ teaspoon Worcestershire sauce, and 3 or 4 drops hot pepper sauce to the basic recipe. Sprinkle with paprika as a garnish. Great if you like zip! A good sandwich filling.

Mock Caviar Egg Spread: Add 4 anchovy fillets, chopped, to the basic recipe. Anchovies add to eggs what caviar does—a salty punch but at a fraction of the cost. This is one of our favorites!

Elegant Egg Mound: Mold the basic recipe into a mound on a small serving platter and chill. Spread the mound evenly with 1 cup sour cream or plain yogurt. Cover the sour cream with 6 ounces of caviar. Serve with crackers accompanied by ice-cold vodka, champagne, or sparkling water.

Individual Egg Salad Sandwich Filling:

Hard-cook 1 egg according to the chart on page 55. Combine the chopped egg with 2 teaspoons mayonnaise or plain yogurt, a generous dash of dry mustard, salt, and pepper in a custard cup. Makes a quick 1-serving sandwich filling.

Scrambled Eggs Basics:

1. The size and shape of the dish is important when scrambling eggs. A round dish is necessary for more even cooking around all outside edges. If the dish is too small, the eggs will cook up and over the dish. If the dish is too large, the eggs will spread out too thinly in the dish and thus overcook.
2. Butter adds flavor to scrambled eggs, but it isn't necessary to prevent sticking. The addition of liquid to eggs makes them fluffier.
3. Scrambled eggs may be cooked on HIGH because the yolks and whites are beaten together before cooking. Also, unlike timbales or egg custards, scrambled eggs can be stirred during cooking to redistribute the higher heat that builds up on the outer edges.
4. The outer edges, which cook more quickly than the center, must be stirred at least twice during cooking, to transfer the less-cooked areas to the outside rim, where they will cook faster.
5. Scrambled eggs don't really need a cover—and it is much easier to stir them when there isn't a cover to contend with.
6. *Doneness:* Scrambled eggs should be moist and glistening, but not quite set when you pull them from the oven. The final stirring will redistribute the heat once more to

finish cooking. No standing time is necessary.

Underdone: Eggs will still be runny. They should be stirred and cooked at 30-second intervals.

Overdone: Overcooking will make eggs tough, rubbery, and sometimes cause them to take on a greenish tinge. There's nothing that can be done with them at this point, so make sure that you stir where directed and cook only until moist.

✹ SCRAMBLED EGGS

MAKES 4 SERVINGS   BEGIN 5 MINUTES BEFORE SERVING
COOKING TIME: 3 TO 4 MINUTES

Someone once told us that they didn't like the way scrambled eggs came out of the microwave, because they were too fluffy! They are—and that's why we like them. They have more volume and require less stirring than conventionally cooked eggs.

By mastering the techniques in this recipe, you'll be able to produce the scrambled egg variations that follow and create more of your own.

| 1 tablespoon butter or margarine | 2 tablespoons milk, cream, water, or |
| 4 eggs | club soda (see Note) |

Place the butter in a 1-quart round casserole. Cook on HIGH for 35 to 45 seconds, or until melted. Add the remaining ingredients, beating well with a wire whisk or fork. Cook on HIGH for 1½ minutes; stir the cooked outer edges of each egg to the center, letting the less-cooked portions flow to the outside. Cook on HIGH for 1 minute more, or until almost set but still moist, stirring once. Stir again at the end of cooking.

NOTE: Club soda makes nice, light, airy eggs.

VARIATIONS:

Scrambled Eggs with Cheese: Stir in ½ cup grated cheese at the end of cooking. The cheese will melt when stirred into the eggs.

Curried Scrambled Eggs: Add 1 teaspoon curry powder to the eggs before cooking.

Scrambled Eggs and Meat: Add ½ to ¾ cup of cubed cooked ham, beef, or pork to the egg mixture before cooking.

Omelet Basics:

1. A 9-inch round pie plate is even more important to the cooking of an omelet than it is to scrambled eggs, because an omelet can't be stirred as often and needs to take on the shape of the round dish.
2. Butter, melted in the dish before cooking, will add flavor and help the omelet to slide out of the dish more easily for serving.
3. Omelets are cooked on HIGH power because the eggs and yolks are beaten together before cooking, and unlike certain other egg dishes such as timbales or egg custards, they can be stirred once during cooking to redistribute heat.
4. A wax paper cover will help the eggs to cook more evenly by retaining some steam, yet it avoids the sogginess that would occur with a tight cover.
5. The stirring that is called for in the basic omelet is a gentle moving of cooked sections from outside to center, without breaking them up. This will keep the top of the finished omelet flat and smooth.
6. *Doneness:* A finished omelet will be set throughout, but the top of the center will still appear moist. No standing time is necessary before adding the fillings and/or folding the omelet.

Underdone: The omelet will be set on the outside, but when the moistness in the center is checked with a knife, it will still be wet to the bottom of the dish. Cover and continue to cook at 30-second intervals.

Overdone: Overdoneness generally occurs if too large a dish is used or if the omelet isn't covered. The omelet will be solid, with the outside rim beginning to toughen and shrink away from the plate. Trim those tougher outer edges and the omelet can still be served successfully. Why not try adding Rose Sauce (page 172) or Mornay Sauce (page 171), warming it over the omelet on MEDIUM power.

✹ BASIC OMELET

MAKES 1 TO 2 SERVINGS   BEGIN 5 TO 8 MINUTES BEFORE SERVING
COOKING TIME: 3 TO 4 MINUTES

An omelet in the microwave will not become browned on the bottom, but it will cook quickly and can be folded with no effort. As in conventional cooking, the secret to cooking an omelet in the microwave is choosing the correct dish.

1 tablespoon butter	**¼ teaspoon salt**
3 eggs	**Dash of pepper**
1 tablespoon water or milk	**Chopped fresh herbs (optional)**

Place the butter in a 9-inch pie plate. Cook on HIGH for 35 seconds to 1 minute to melt. In a small bowl combine the eggs, water or milk, salt, and pepper.

Pour the eggs into the plate with the butter. Cover with wax paper and cook on HIGH for 1½ minutes; gently move the cooked outer edges of the omelet to the center, letting the uncooked portions flow to the outside. Cover again and cook on HIGH for 1 to 2 minutes more, or until the center is set but still moist. Spoon the desired filling down the center. Loosen the edges of the omelet with a spatula and fold or, with 2 forks, roll the omelet over the filling. Slide the omelet onto a serving plate. Garnish with herbs, if desired.

Fillings for Omelets

- ¼ cup shredded cheddar, Swiss, mozzarella, Muenster, or Monterey Jack cheese. Serve with Salsa Ranchera (page 146), if desired.
- 1 tablespoon chopped fresh herbs.
- ¼ cup crumbled, cooked bacon (page 61).
- ¼ cup Ground Beef Chili (page 321) or Vegetarian Chili (page 436).

Or add ½ cup of the following to the center of any cooked omelet:

- Italian Basil, Peppers, and Onions (page 95)
- Hot Crab Dip (page 112)
- Ratatouille (page 421)
- Sautéed Spinach (page 428)
- Braised Scallions (page 448)
- Sesame Sautéed Asparagus (page 476)
- Sautéed Summer Squash (page 469)
- Leftover meat or vegetables
- Sautéed Mushrooms (page 439)

Puffy Omelet Basics:

1. Salt is not added to beaten egg whites because, although it will strengthen proteins, it reduces elasticity, which you want for volume.
2. Cream of tartar, on the other hand, is a weak acid and is a necessary addition to egg whites to chemically neutralize the proteins so that they will coagulate into a foam.
3. As in the basic omelet, the 9-inch pie plate is the most desirable size dish for the eggs to cook properly.
4. Butter, melted in the dish before cooking, will add flavor and help the omelet to slide out of the dish more easily for serving.
5. It is especially important to smooth the surface of the puffy omelet in the dish before cooking, so that all areas cook evenly and a nice flat surface will form.
6. As with the basic omelet, puffy omelets are cooked on HIGH power unless they contain cheese. In that case, the omelet should be cooked on a lower power to prevent the cheese from toughening.
7. Puffy omelets are cooked uncovered because you want to produce a nice dry

surface, with no excess moisture. Also, omelets often rise above the dish and push off the cover.
8. Stirring is necessary only in the ricotta cheese omelet. Since cheese is higher in fat, those areas containing more cheese will become hot, and stirring redistributes this heat.
9. Standing time is not necessary before serving an omelet, or adding fillings.
10. For doneness, see Soufflé Basics, page 154.

☀ PUFFY OMELET

MAKES 1 TO 2 SERVINGS   BEGIN 10 MINUTES BEFORE SERVING
COOKING TIME: 2 TO 3½ MINUTES

This omelet is a sheer delight to make and eat. It puffs up like a small soufflé in under 3 minutes, and needs no stirring or special attention. We highly recommend this when you want to treat yourself but don't want to spend much time at it.

1 tablespoon butter	**⅛ teaspoon cream of tartar**
3 eggs, separated	**1 tablespoon water**

Place the butter in a 9-inch pie plate. Cook on HIGH for 35 seconds to 1 minute, or until melted. Combine the egg whites and cream of tartar in a medium mixing bowl, beating until stiff but not dry. In a small bowl combine the egg yolks and water, stirring until thick and lemon-colored. Gently fold the yolks into the whites.

Pour the egg mixture into the pie plate with melted butter and spread smoothly with a spatula. Cook on HIGH for 1½ to 2½ minutes, or until set. Spoon on a filling (page 152), if desired, or serve plain. Score the omelet down the center with a knife. Fold and slide the omelet onto a serving plate.

VARIATIONS:

Dessert Omelet: Add 1 tablespoon sugar to the yolks before beating. Make the omelet as directed in the basic recipe. Pour ¼ cup apricot preserves, raspberry jam, strawberry jam, or peach preserves into a 1-cup glass measure. Cook on HIGH for 45 seconds to melt. Pour into the center of the cooked omelet, and roll or fold the omelet over the filling. Sprinkle with 1 tablespoon confectioners' sugar. Cut into 1-inch slices and sprinkle with slivered almonds or other nuts. This is delicious served hot or cold, and is nice when you feel like having a spur-of-the-moment dessert for dinner.

Dessert Omelet with Brandy: Add 1 tablespoon brandy to the jam before heating in the Dessert Omelet variation above.

Dessert Omelet with Berries: Spoon ¼ cup fresh berries over the Dessert Omelet variation above.

PUFFY RICOTTA CHEESE OMELET

MAKES 1 TO 2 SERVINGS BEGIN 20 MINUTES BEFORE SERVING
COOKING TIME: 6 TO 7½ MINUTES

A deliciously rich omelet that needs no additional filling to be satisfying.

- 1 tablespoon butter
- 2 eggs, separated
- ½ cup ricotta or small-curd cottage cheese
- 2 tablespoons milk
- 2 tablespoons chopped fresh basil (see Note), chives, or scallions
- Salt and pepper to taste
- ⅛ teaspoon cream of tartar

Place the butter in a 9-inch pie plate. Cook on HIGH for 35 seconds to 1 minute to melt. In a medium bowl combine the egg yolks, ricotta cheese, milk, herbs, and salt and pepper, stirring to blend. In a small bowl combine the egg whites and cream of tartar, beating until stiff but not dry. Fold the egg whites into the yolk mixture.

Pour the egg mixture into the pie plate, spreading smoothly with a spatula. Cook on MEDIUM for 2½ minutes; gently move the cooked outer edges to the center, letting the less-cooked portions flow to the outside. Cook on MEDIUM for 3 to 4 minutes more, or until set.

Fold the omelet in half and slide onto a serving plate.

NOTE: Basil is preferred when using ricotta cheese.

VARIATIONS:

Puffy Ricotta Cheese Omelet with Herbs: Sprinkle 1 tablespoon chopped fresh herbs over the omelet before serving.

Puffy Ricotta Cheese Omelet with Rose Sauce: Spoon Rose Sauce (page 172) down the center of the cooked folded omelet before serving.

Soufflé Basics:

1. It is necessary to establish a thickened white sauce base before adding the eggs. Any addition of salt should be made here and not to the whites.
2. Cream of tartar, a weak acid, is added to egg whites to chemically neutralize the proteins so that they will coagulate into a foam.
3. A straight-sided casserole or soufflé dish is necessary if the soufflé is to rise properly. Do not butter the dish before adding the soufflé mixture—it is not necessary.

4. It is important to smooth the top of the soufflé mixture so it will rise evenly—but do it delicately.
5. Soufflés are cooked on DEFROST to enable the beaten egg whites, which are lifting the white sauce and cheese, to rise slowly and surely to form the delicate, characteristic soufflé structure. A higher power will cause the soufflé to rise too quickly, tighten up, and then fall.
6. Soufflés are cooked uncovered to keep the surface as dry as possible and to let them rise above the dish.
7. Because this is such a porous structure, and one that cooks so slowly, no standing time is needed.
8. *Doneness:* Although a puffy omelet and a soufflé rise to different heights, they both rise and swell like breathing organisms, extending themselves over the tops of their cooking dishes. The structures will be light and voluminous, and when touched, lightly, the dry top surface will stick to the finger and reveal a dry interior below. When cut open for serving, the deep center of the soufflé will still be moist—almost wet—but not runny.

Underdone: The surface will still appear wet in spots, and may not have risen up over the dish. If it hasn't risen above the dish, it still has a way to go. If the soufflé or omelet has risen but still appears moist on top, rotate the dish one-quarter turn and continue to cook at 30-second intervals for the omelet and 1- to 2-minute intervals for the soufflé.

Overdone: If cooked on too high a power, the soufflé or puffy omelet will not rise to its full height but will begin to collapse on itself and shrink up, weeping out liquid. If cooked too long, the basic puffy omelet will also begin to collapse on itself. The texture in both cases will become like that of Styrofoam—tough and almost brittle.

☀ NEW YANKEE CHEESE SOUFFLÉ

MAKES 4 SERVINGS   BEGIN 45 MINUTES BEFORE SERVING
COOKING TIME: 23 TO 29 MINUTES

Soufflés are one dish that strike fear into the hearts of cooks, yet they are so impressive we all want to try a hand at them. The biggest apprehension is that a soufflé might never reach the table with the glory it manifests in the oven. Microwave cooks will be happy to know that a soufflé is not affected by opening the oven door, because the structure is not dependent upon hot air to hold it aloft.

We could compare this soufflé to one made by an old Yankee neighbor in Connecticut on the top of the range in a steamer. It still had a dry but uncrusty surface, yet was very light, with a moist center.

A microwave soufflé is a new twist to a delicious old-fashioned meal. Serve with Pureed Tomato Sauce (page 179), Mornay Sauce (page 171), or Rose Sauce (page 172).

¼ cup butter	½ teaspoon dry mustard
¼ cup finely chopped onion	½ teaspoon salt
¼ cup all-purpose flour	⅛ teaspoon pepper
1 cup half and half or evaporated milk	4 eggs, separated
1 cup grated cheddar, Gruyère, or Swiss cheese	⅛ teaspoon cream of tartar

In a 1-quart casserole combine the butter and onion. Cook on HIGH for 2 to 3 minutes, or until the onion is tender. Stir in the flour to blend, then stir in the half and half. Cook on HIGH for 1½ minutes; stir. Cook for 1 to 2 minutes more, or until thickened; stir again. Stir in the cheese, mustard, salt, pepper, and egg yolks.

In a medium bowl combine the egg whites and cream of tartar, beating until stiff but not dry. Fold the whites into the cheese mixture. Pour into a 1½-quart soufflé dish, spreading the top evenly with a spatula. Cook on DEFROST for 10 minutes; rotate the dish. Cook on DEFROST for 8 to 12 minutes more, or until the top is dry.

Egg Custard and Timbale Basics:

1. Timbales are custards made with eggs, or eggs and cheese. Because of these delicate ingredients, in a conventional oven timbales are cooked in a pan of water to slow down cooking. To accomplish this same end in the microwave, timbales are cooked on MEDIUM power.
2. Buttering and coating the custard dishes with either bread crumbs, nuts, or some other mixture gives them a brown crust and makes unmolding easier.
3. The timbales are cooked uncovered to let excess moisture evaporate; this will help them to solidify and form a dry surface. Because the egg whites and yolks are beaten together before they are cooked, it is not necessary to cover tightly as in poached eggs.
4. Placing the timbales in a circle, 1 inch apart, will give all eggs equal exposure to microwave energy. Depending on your oven, some timbales may appear to be cooking faster than others. These should be repositioned with those that aren't cooking as quickly, partway through cooking.
5. *Doneness:* As the timbales approach doneness, the custard will not jiggle when the cup is picked up and shaken slightly. A knife inserted about ½ inch from the center may have some butter on it, but will come out clean of custard. Cheese timbales will have a center, with a diameter no longer than the length of the thumb from middle knuckle to end, that appears uncooked. The size of this area is the thing that's important, not the appearance.

During standing time, the timbales will solidify and begin to pull away from the sides of the cups.

Underdone: The timbales will have begun to solidify, but a knife will not come out clean when inserted about ½ inch from the center. Continue to cook those that are not done by adding 30 seconds to 1 minute at a time, depending on how many are left.

Overdone: When cooked on HIGH power or cooked too long, the timbales will begin to constrict and pull away from the sides, leaving a lot of water that has wept out of the structure. The timbales (or custards) will be very tough.

✸ SHIMMERING CARROT TIMBALES

MAKES 4 SERVINGS   BEGIN 50 MINUTES TO 1 HOUR BEFORE SERVING
COOKING TIME: 14 TO 20 MINUTES

Timbales are individual egg custards that can hold either cheese, vegetables, or meat leftovers in their structure. When unmolded they appear as shimmering clouds on your plate. Each rich bite will melt on your tongue. Try them for lunch or brunch, for they are a meal in themselves, with the addition of just a light salad.

3 tablespoons butter	¼ teaspoon salt
¼ cup fine dry bread crumbs or finely chopped nuts	Pinch of black pepper
1½ cups finely grated carrots	½ cup grated Gruyère or Swiss cheese
2 tablespoons finely chopped onion	3 eggs, beaten
2 tablespoons orange juice	¾ cup half and half
2 tablespoons chopped fresh parsley, or 1 teaspoon dried	Shimmering Orange Sauce (page 159)

Divide 1 tablespoon butter between four 5- or 6-ounce custard cups and butter the insides well. Divide the bread crumbs or nuts between the custard cups, sprinkling to coat the buttered insides. Set aside.

In a 2-quart casserole combine the remaining 2 tablespoons butter, carrots, onion, and orange juice. Cover tightly and cook on HIGH for 6 to 8 minutes, or until tender, stirring after 4 minutes. Stir in the parsley, salt, pepper, and cheese. Stir in the eggs and half and half, blending well.

Pour the mixture into the prepared custard cups, dividing evenly. Place the cups in a circle in the oven with 1 inch between them. Cook, uncovered, on MEDIUM for 8 to 12 minutes, or until the custards are firm and a knife inserted close to the center comes out clean, rearranging custards if necessary after 5 minutes. Let stand, covered, for 5 minutes.

The custards unmold easily when a knife is inserted between the custard and cup. Invert a small serving plate on top of each cup and turn over quickly to release the timbales. Spoon the orange sauce over the timbales and serve immediately.

NOTE: For an attractive presentation use straight-sided oval ramekins. After unmolding, cut on the diagonal from top to bottom and place both pieces on individual serving plates. Spoon around timbale.

VARIATIONS:

Sugar-Coated Carrot Timbales: After coating the custard cups with crumbs, divide 2 teaspoons brown sugar between the cups, sprinkling on the bottom of each. Proceed with the basic recipe. This makes a nice brown topping, and adds sweetness as well.

Zucchini Timbales: Substitute 3 tablespoons fine dry bread crumbs mixed with 1 tablespoon grated Parmesan cheese for ¼ cup bread crumbs. Eliminate the carrots. Cook the remaining butter, onion, and orange juice on HIGH for 1½ to 2 minutes, or until the onion is tender. Substitute 1 tablespoon chopped fresh basil or dill (½ teaspoon dried) for the parsley. Add 1½ cups grated unpeeled zucchini with the cheese. Proceed with the basic recipe. Serve with Pureed Tomato Sauce (page 179). The zucchini cooks to tender-crisp right in the custard.

Green and Red Pepper Timbales: Substitute 3 tablespoons fine dry bread crumbs mixed with 1 tablespoon chopped fresh parsley for ¼ cup bread crumbs. Substitute 1½ cups coarsely chopped mixed red and green bell peppers for the carrots. Cover the pepper-onion mixture tightly and cook on HIGH for 3 to 4 minutes, or until the vegetables are tender, stirring after 2 minutes. Substitute 1 tablespoon chopped fresh cilantro (coriander) for the parsley. Substitute a pinch of cayenne pepper for black pepper. Substitute Monterey Jack cheese for the Gruyère. Proceed with the basic recipe. Serve with Salsa Ranchera (page 146), if desired.

Asparagus Timbales: Substitute ¼ cup finely chopped walnuts for the bread crumbs. Substitute 1½ cups coarsely chopped asparagus spears for the carrots and 1 teaspoon lemon juice for the 2 tablespoons orange juice. Cover the asparagus-onion mixture tightly and cook on HIGH for 4 to 6 minutes, or until the vegetables are tender, stirring after 2 minutes. Substitute Muenster cheese for the Gruyère. Proceed with the basic recipe. Serve with Hollandaise Sauce (page 174), if desired.

Broccoli Timbales: Substitute 1½ cups coarsely chopped broccoli for the carrots and 1 teaspoon lemon juice for the 2 tablespoons orange juice. Cover the broccoli-onion mixture tightly and cook on HIGH for 4 to 6 minutes, or until the vegetables are tender, stirring after 2 minutes. Substitute Muenster cheese for the Gruyère. Proceed with the basic recipe.

Chicken Timbales: Eliminate the carrots. Substitute 1 teaspoon lemon juice for the 2 tablespoons orange juice. Combine the remaining butter, onion, and lemon juice. Cover tightly and cook on HIGH for 1½ to 2 minutes, or until the onion is tender. Stir in 1½ cups coarsely chopped cooked chicken. Substitute Muenster cheese for the Gruyère. Proceed with the basic recipe. Serve with Mushroom Sauce (page 172), if desired.

Ham Timbales: Eliminate the carrots. Substitute 1 teaspoon lemon juice for the 2 tablespoons orange juice. Combine the remaining butter, onion, and lemon juice. Cover tightly and cook on HIGH for 1½ to 2 minutes, or until the onion is tender. Stir in 1½ cups coarsely chopped cooked ham. Substitute cheddar cheese for the Gruyère. Proceed with the basic recipe.

SHIMMERING ORANGE SAUCE

MAKES ABOUT ½ CUP
COOKING TIME: 4 TO 6 MINUTES

2 tablespoons orange juice
1 teaspoon cornstarch
1 cup beef broth (see Mock Brown Broth or Stock, page 119)
1 tablespoon grated orange rind (optional)

In a 2-cup glass measure combine the orange juice and cornstarch. Stir in the beef broth. Cook on HIGH for 4 to 6 minutes, or until the mixture is thickened and reduced to between ½ and ¾ cup. Stir in the orange rind, if desired. Spoon the sauce on top of each timbale.

PESTO-COATED RICOTTA CHEESE TIMBALES

MAKES 4 SERVINGS   BEGIN 30 MINUTES BEFORE SERVING
COOKING TIME: 8 TO 12 MINUTES

Here's another type of timbale, displaying the more pronounced flavors of basil, Parmesan, and ricotta cheese. They're very easy to make and a welcome change for dinner when served with a salad or hot vegetable dish.

Pesto:
2 tablespoons pine nuts
1 small garlic clove
1 cup packed fresh basil leaves
½ cup grated Parmesan cheese
¼ cup olive oil

Ricotta Filling:
1 cup ricotta cheese
½ cup grated mozzarella or Muenster cheese
½ teaspoon salt
¼ teaspoon pepper
2 eggs, beaten

In a food processor or blender grind the pesto ingredients in the order that they are listed to form a thick paste. Divide the pesto between four 5- or 6-ounce custard cups, using a spoon to press the pesto three-quarters of the way up the sides of the cups. Set aside.

In a medium bowl combine the ricotta filling ingredients, stirring well to mix. Spoon the filling into the pesto-lined cups, dividing evenly. Place the cups in the oven in a circle with at least 1 inch between them. Cook, uncovered, on MEDIUM for 8 to 12 minutes, or until a knife inserted close to the center comes out clean, rearranging custards if necessary after 5 minutes. Let stand for 5 minutes before turning out.

MUSHROOM–COTTAGE CHEESE TIMBALES

MAKES 4 SERVINGS   BEGIN 30 MINUTES BEFORE SERVING
COOKING TIME: 12 TO 16 MINUTES

- 1 tablespoon butter
- 2 tablespoons finely chopped scallions
- 1½ cups finely chopped fresh mushrooms
- 1 teaspoon lemon juice
- 2 tablespoons fine dry bread crumbs
- 1 cup cottage cheese
- 2 eggs, beaten
- ½ cup grated Muenster or Monterey Jack cheese
- ½ teaspoon salt
- ¼ teaspoon black pepper
- 1 tablespoon chopped fresh parsley
- Dash of cayenne pepper

In a 9-inch pie plate combine the butter, scallions, and mushrooms. Cook, uncovered, on HIGH for 4 minutes, or until the mushrooms are tender and the moisture has evaporated, stirring once. Stir in the lemon juice and bread crumbs, mixing well. Divide the mixture between four 5- to 6-ounce custard cups, using a spoon to press the mixture three-quarters of the way up the sides of the cups.

In a medium bowl combine the remaining ingredients. Spoon into the mushroom-lined cups. Place the cups in the oven in a circle with at least 1 inch between them. Cook, uncovered, on MEDIUM for 8 to 12 minutes, or until a knife inserted close to the center comes out clean, rearranging the custards if necessary after 5 minutes. Let stand for 5 minutes.

Wok-Style Vegetables over Pasta, page 482

Glazed Pork Butt with Poached Winter Fruits, page 313

Brandied Shrimp with Mushrooms, page 113

Steak au Poivre with New Red Potatoes and Radishes, page 280

Green Chili with Black Beans, page 298

Chilled Individual Coho Salmon with Three Sauces, page 231

Petite Stuffed Cabbages, page 405

Poached Pear on Pear-Shaped Shell, page 552

Cheese Melting or Softening Basics:

1. Cheese is stored at refrigerator temperature and cooking times are determined accordingly.
2. A general rule is that cheese in recipes should be heated on MEDIUM power, unless it is a hard cheese such as Parmesan or Romano. At this setting, the cheese will melt more evenly and the protein structure won't tighten quickly the way it would on HIGH power.
3. Grated cheese will melt more quickly than cubed.
4. When possible, cheese should be stirred often, for more even heating and melting. This ensures that no one area will heat too quickly.
5. For fondue or a melted cheese dish, liquid is heated on HIGH before stirring in the cheese.
6. If cheese can't be stirred, as on crackers or as in the recipe for Breaded Warm Cheese with Salad, individual items or dishes should be arranged in a circle around the outer rim of a round plate, or oven, leaving the center open. This will bring about the most even heating.
7. When refrigerated cheese is brought to room temperature, it should not be covered. Covering it may cause the outside surface to get too warm and begin to melt. For example, to bring ½ pound refrigerated cheese to room temperature, unwrap and cook on MEDIUM for 45 seconds to 1 minute, or until no longer chilled on the surface.

❋ VERMONT FONDUE

MAKES 4 TO 6 SERVINGS   BEGIN COOKING 15 TO 20 MINUTES BEFORE SERVING
COOKING TIME: 11 TO 17 MINUTES

When it's time to unclamp snowy ski boots, our minds turn to the libations and hot food that are sure to follow. This is one of our favorite snacks because it requires a minimum of concentration to prepare, is rich and filling, and stretches to accommodate a crowd if enough dippers are provided.

The fondue is cooked uncovered to evaporate alcohol (but not flavor) and, by doing this, thickens the flour mixture to the consistency of a thin white sauce. For more information see Cheddar Cheese Soup (page 133).

Serve with skewered crusty bread or apple slices.

---

2 **tablespoons butter**	1 **tablespoon prepared mustard**
1 **garlic clove, minced**	1 **pound sharp cheddar cheese,**
2 **tablespoons all-purpose flour**	**grated or cut into ½-inch cubes**
¾ **cup flat beer**	2 **to 3 drops of hot pepper sauce**

In a 1-quart microwaveproof crock combine the butter and garlic. Cook on HIGH for 1 to 2 minutes, or until the garlic is tender. Stir in the flour until smooth. Add the beer. Cook on HIGH for 2 to 4 minutes, or until boiling and slightly thickened, stirring once.

Add the mustard and cheese. Cook on MEDIUM for 8 to 11 minutes, or until the cheese is melted and smooth, stirring every 2 minutes. Stir in the hot pepper sauce.

VARIATIONS:

French Fondue: Eliminate the garlic, but melt the butter as directed. Substitute white wine for beer and Gruyère or Swiss cheese for the cheddar.

Rarebit Sandwiches: Top 4 to 6 toasted bread slices with tomato slices. Pour Vermont Fondue or the French Fondue variation above on top. Garnish with 8 to 12 crisp bacon strips (see page 61).

FONDUE WITH BLANCHED VEGETABLES

MAKES 4 TO 6 SERVINGS   BEGIN 1 HOUR BEFORE SERVING
COOKING TIME: 3 TO 6 MINUTES

- 2 **cups trimmed whole green beans**
- 2 **cups carrots, cut into 2-inch sticks**
- 2 **cups broccoli flowerets**
- 3 **tablespoons water**
- 1 **recipe Vermont Fondue (page 161)**
  Celery, cut into sticks
  Scallions
  Green peppers, sliced

Before preparing the fondue, blanch the green beans, carrots, and broccoli: In a 1-quart casserole cook each of the 3 vegetables separately with 1 tablespoon water each. Cover tightly and cook each one on HIGH for 1 to 2 minutes, or until tender-crisp. Chill the vegetables.

Prepare the fondue. Dip in the blanched vegetables. Add the uncooked celery sticks, scallions, and green peppers to the vegetable selection.

☀ BREADED WARM CHEESE WITH SALAD

MAKES 4 SERVINGS   BEGIN 10 MINUTES BEFORE SERVING
COOKING TIME: 1 TO 3 MINUTES

We love cheese prepared in this way. With the oil coating it becomes lightly browned, and it makes a delicious first course when served with lettuce or with marinated vegetables. A soft, dense cheese lends itself best to this type of presentation.

4 ounces goat cheese (feta, Montrachet, Bûcheron, Caprino) or mozzarella
1 tablespoon olive oil
¼ cup fine dry bread crumbs
1 head of lettuce (romaine, Boston, Bibb, redleaf, watercress, or a combination)

Dressing:
3 tablespoons olive oil
1 tablespoon red wine vinegar
⅛ teaspoon dry mustard
⅛ teaspoon salt
Freshly ground pepper

Garnish (optional):
Apple wedges,
toasted pine nuts, or
fresh blossoms (nasturtium, clover, violet, or chive)

Cut the cheese into 1-ounce serving pieces according to its shape (log cheese would be cut into 4 rounds; rectangles, into 4 ½-inch-thick rectangles).

Pour 1 tablespoon olive oil into a custard cup. Place the bread crumbs in a cereal bowl. Dip each side of a single piece of cheese into the oil, then into the bread crumbs to coat evenly on all sides. Place the coated cheese around the outside rim of a small microwave-proof plate. Set aside.

Wash and dry the lettuce and place in a large bowl.

Combine the dressing ingredients in a small bowl.

Just before serving the cheese and salad, toss the salad greens with the dressing. Divide the greens between 4 salad plates, leaving a place for the heated cheese.

Heat the cheese, uncovered, on MEDIUM for 1 to 2½ minutes, until top of the cheese and bottom of the dish feel warm to the touch, and a tiny bit of cheese starts to ooze from the coating. Place the heated cheese on salad plates. Garnish, if desired, with apple wedges, 1 tablespoon toasted pine nuts, or blossoms.

NOTE: *To Double:* Since this is a nice company dish, double the ingredients and place on a large plate. Heat the cheese on MEDIUM for 3 to 5 minutes.

VARIATIONS:

Breaded Warm Cheese with Marinated Vegetables: Substitute Marinated Vegetables (page 91) for the salad greens and dressing.

Spiced Breaded Warm Cheese with Salad: Add 1 tablespoon finely chopped fresh herbs or 1 teaspoon freshly ground black pepper to the bread crumbs. Adds a nice zip.

Appetizer Breaded Warm Cheese: Eliminate the salad greens and dressing. Cut the cheese into ½-ounce pieces. Coat as directed. Cook on MEDIUM for 40 seconds to 1 minute 40 seconds, or until done. Serve with toothpicks.

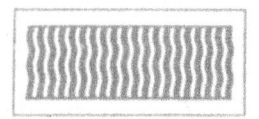

CHEESE RACLETTE

MAKES 4 SERVINGS   BEGIN ABOUT 20 MINUTES BEFORE SERVING
COOKING TIME: 4 TO 8 MINUTES

Raclette comes from the French verb racler *meaning "to scrape." In the mountains of the upper Rhône valley, and in northern Italy, cheese is heated outdoors on a stone set by a charcoal fire. As the cut surface of the cheese begins to curl and soften, it is scraped off with a long knife and placed on a plate with hot potatoes in their skins, small pickled onions, and cornichons, or small pickles. If you can't go to France, why not heat up some raclette* toute de suite *in a microwave and at least dream of the simple mountain life?*

- **4 boiling potatoes**
- **8 ounces Raclette, Gruyère, or Monterey Jack cheese cut in ¼-inch slices**
- **8 small dill pickles**
- **1 loaf of crusty bread, cut in chunks**

Cook the potatoes according to the instructions for boiling potatoes (page 73).

Meanwhile, divide the cheese slices between four 4- to 6-inch round custard cups (for easier dipping and scraping) or microwaveproof plates. Cook on MEDIUM for 4 to 8 minutes, or until the color becomes light and the cheese is soft but not runny, rearranging the dishes after 3 minutes. Eat the cheese with slices of warm potato, slices of pickle, and chunks of crusty bread.

VARIATION:

Raclette with Apples and Pears: Substitute sliced apples and pears for the potatoes and pickles. In some areas of France it is served this way.

OPEN-FACE TOASTED CHEESE SANDWICH

MAKES 1 SANDWICH   BEGIN 5 MINUTES BEFORE SERVING
COOKING TIME: 35 TO 40 SECONDS

The bread for this sandwich will not toast in the microwave because there is no dry heat in the oven; you will have to use a conventional toaster. It is best to place this toasted bread on top of a paper towel to keep the bottom from getting soggy as it heats. The second piece of toast is added to the sandwich after the cheese melts, to prevent it from becoming soggy.

1 slice of bread	2 slices of cheddar, Swiss, or other cheese

Toast the bread in a conventional toaster. Place 1 piece of toast on a paper towel-lined microwaveproof plate. Top with the cheese slices. Cook on MEDIUM for 35 to 45 seconds, or until the cheese is melted.

VARIATIONS:

Open-Face Toasted Cheese–Tomato Sandwich: Top the cheese with sliced tomato before cooking.

Open-Face Toasted Ham-and-Cheese Sandwich: Place 1 slice of ham on the toast before adding the cheese. Cook on MEDIUM for 45 seconds to 1 minute, or until the cheese is melted.

More Ham and Cheese Sandwiches

When making a melted ham and cheese sandwich between 2 slices of toast, the sandwich can be heated on HIGH because the cheese is protected by both top and bottom slices of bread.

Here is the way to heat these sandwiches quickly in the microwave. Place 1 or 2 slices each of boiled ham and cheese on each slice of toasted bread. Top with another slice of toast. Wrap each sandwich lightly in a paper towel and heat as follows on HIGH:

1 sandwich	20 to 30 seconds
2 sandwiches	45 seconds to 1 minute
4 sandwiches	1¼ to 1½ minutes

To make the same melted ham and cheese sandwich on a hard or Kaiser roll, place 1 or 2 slices each of boiled ham and cheese between the sliced roll. Wrap each sandwich lightly in a paper towel and heat as follows on HIGH:

1 roll	30 to 40 seconds
2 rolls	45 seconds to 1 minute
4 rolls	1¼ to 1½ minutes

BROWNING DISH CHEESE SANDWICH

MAKES 4   BEGIN 8 MINUTES BEFORE SERVING
COOKING TIME: 3½ TO 5½ MINUTES

This is a rather unconventional way to use the browning dish in that once the dish is heated, all the cooking is done outside of the oven. The bread will toast and cheese melt just from the heat given off from the browning dish, which will keep them crisp. After all our trial runs, we felt that this was the best method.

- **8 slices of bread**
- **8 slices of cheddar, Swiss, or other cheese**
- **¼ cup butter, softened (see Note)**

Preheat the large browning dish in the microwave oven according to the manufacturer's directions for toasted sandwiches (on HIGH between 3 and 5 minutes). Meanwhile, make 4 cheese sandwiches with 2 slices of cheese between 2 slices of bread. Spread the butter on the outside of each sandwich, on both slices of bread. Place the sandwiches on the preheated dish, pressing them against the dish's surface. After the sandwiches have stood on the hot dish for 15 to 20 seconds, turn them over, pressing the other sides against the dish. Let the sandwiches stand for 20 to 25 seconds on the dish before serving.

NOTE: Butter can be softened in the microwave by heating on MEDIUM for 30 seconds.

7

SAUCES, GRAVIES, AND SALAD DRESSINGS

Two things were true of sauces in the past. They were designed to mask food of a lesser quality and they were often very rich in cream and butter. Today we enjoy an unprecedented array of fresh foods, making "coverups" unnecessary. And the trend toward lighter cooking has caused us to look for lighter sauces. You'll find these in our lower-calorie recipes for Green Tomato Salsa, Salsa Cruda, and Oriental Dressing.

All things being equal, it is still a fine-flavored sauce that transforms an excellent dish into an exceptional one. I love to analyze a particularly good sauce and unravel its mysteries, and often I get the chance when my husband Dave and I try out a new restaurant. Long after we've paid the bill and driven away, Dave, who believes that there is only so much that can be said about food, will turn to me and say, "Honey, can we talk about something else?"

One thing that makes this sauce analysis both difficult and delightful for me now is the whole slew of new ingredients available in our local markets. Our inventory of sauces in this country is bulging with the flavors of Mexico, Indonesia, and India—and even regional parts of America are contributing. Our sauce collection—and note that it incorporates sauces that are not prepared in the microwave—includes more than one salsa, a spicy peanut sauce from Indonesia, fresh tomato sauces from Italy, and the more classical hollandaise and a basic white sauce, along with our innovative Rose and Mushroom Sauces. If we have counted correctly, you'll be able to choosefrom over sixty savory and sweet sauces in this chapter and throughout the book.

—THELMA

Successful Sauce Secrets

The two biggest questions that people have about cooked sauces are: How do I keep them from lumping? And how do I thicken them properly? Two important answers for the microwave are: Remember to stir where indicated—this will prevent lumping; and choose a large enough casserole to facilitate stirring and prevent boilovers. Boiling is what causes the starches to swell for thickening and lets moisture evaporate. To do this properly, the casserole should be twice the height of the sauce to contain the bubbles.

We think you'll agree with us that the extra few minutes sauces take to make will be worth the trouble to raise your meal from prosaic to absolutely provocative.

Flour- or Cornstarch-Thickened Sauce or Gravy Basics:

1. Flour and butter are most often kept in 1 to 1 proportions for a proper blend in the sauce.
2. The ratio of flour to water is generally 1½ to 2 tablespoons flour per cup of liquid. Cornstarch has more thickening power; it will thicken well when 1 tablespoon per cup of liquid is added. Make sure that you have formed a smooth paste before adding milk or water.
3. Because there are no delicate ingredients in a basic white sauce or gravy and because starches in flour and cornstarch swell to their greatest at boiling temperatures, this type of sauce is cooked quickly on HIGH to reach that point for optimum thickening.
4. Again, because there are no delicate ingredients, two stirrings through the entire cooking process will be adequate to keep the sauce smooth and redistribute the heat.
5. This kind of sauce should be cooked uncovered so it can thicken properly.
6. If egg yolks are added to a sauce of this type, some of the hot sauce should be added to them first, before returning that mixture to the sauce. This will gradually raise the temperature of the eggs to prevent curdling. The sauce can then be heated on HIGH power until boiling and thickened.
7. *Doneness:* When the sauce is bubbling and has reached the desired thickness, it is time to remove it from the oven. There will be no standing time.

   Underdone: The sauce is not yet boiling and it hasn't thickened properly. Continue to add 1 minute at a time until you are satisfied with the thickness, stirring every 30 seconds.

   Lumpy: Did you blend the flour well into the melted butter? Did you stir as indicated, and remember that a whisk is best? To correct, pass sauce through a medium to fine sieve.

   Too thin or too thick: Too thick, just add

a little more liquid. Too thin, overboiling can cause sauces to become thin again. Make a paste of 1 tablespoon flour with 1 tablespoon cold water or softened butter. Stir into the sauce and continue to cook on HIGH until thickened, stirring every 30 seconds.

✹ WHITE SAUCE

MAKES ABOUT 1 CUP BEGIN 10 MINUTES BEFORE SERVING
COOKING TIME: 5 TO 6 MINUTES

A white sauce is practically impossible to ruin, if the melted butter and flour are blended first into a smooth paste. After that it is just a matter of stirring and watching for the proper thickness.

We find this the best thickness for a white sauce, especially when including additional ingredients as below. For a thicker sauce, see the Variations.

---

2 tablespoons butter or margarine	⅛ teaspoon pepper
2 tablespoons all-purpose flour	1 cup milk
¼ teaspoon salt	

Place the butter in a 4-cup glass measure. Cook on HIGH for 35 to 45 seconds, or until melted. Stir in the flour, salt, and pepper to form a smooth paste. Pour in the milk, mixing with a wire whisk while pouring to blend. Cook on HIGH for 4 to 5 minutes, or until boiling and thickened, stirring every 2 minutes to ensure smoothness.

VARIATIONS:

Thin White Sauce: Reduce the flour and butter to 1 tablespoon each.

Thicker White Sauce: Increase both the flour and butter to 3 or 4 tablespoons each.

Curry Sauce: Add 1 teaspoon curry powder with the salt and pepper.

Mustard Sauce: Add ½ teaspoon dry mustard or 2 tablespoons Dijon or country-style mustard with salt and pepper.

Herb Sauce: Stir 2 tablespoons freshly chopped herbs into the sauce at the end of cooking time.

Mornay Sauce: Stir ½ cup shredded or grated cheese into the sauce at the end of cooking time, making sure the sauce is completely thickened before adding the cheese. Stir until melted.

Sherry Cream Sauce: Reduce the flour to 1 tablespoon; the butter remains the same for flavor. Add 2 tablespoons dry sherry, Marsala, or dry vermouth with the milk.

ROSE SAUCE

MAKES 1½ CUPS   BEGIN 10 MINUTES BEFORE SERVING
COOKING TIME: 6 TO 8 MINUTES

We found this subtle sauce pleasing over thin strands of pasta or chicken cutlets.

- 2 tablespoons butter
- 1 tablespoon all-purpose flour
- 1 cup Chicken Broth or Stock (page 118)
- 1 tablespoon white wine
- 2 tablespoons tomato paste
- Salt
- ¼ teaspoon pepper
- ½ to 1 cup light cream

Place the butter in a 2-cup glass measure. Cook on HIGH for 35 seconds to 1 minute to melt. Stir in the flour to make a smooth paste. Stir in the broth and wine. Cook on HIGH for 3 minutes, stirring well. Stir in the tomato paste. Cook for 2 to 3 minutes, or until boiling and thickened, stirring after 1 minute. Add the salt and pepper to taste. Stir in the cream. Cook on HIGH for 1 minute, right before serving.

VARIATION:

Herb Rose Sauce: Stir in 1 tablespoon chopped fresh parsley, basil, or tarragon, or 1 teaspoon dried, with the salt and pepper.

MUSHROOM SAUCE

MAKES 1½ CUPS   BEGIN 10 MINUTES BEFORE SERVING
COOKING TIME: 5½ TO 9 MINUTES

Serve with grilled meats, meat loaf, timbales, eggs, or over pasta.

- 2 tablespoons butter
- 1 tablespoon all-purpose flour
- 1 cup beef broth (see Mock Brown Broth or Stock, page 119)
- 1 teaspoon lemon juice
- ¼ pound fresh mushrooms, sliced

Place the butter in a 1-quart casserole. Cook on HIGH for 35 seconds to 1 minute to melt. Stir in the flour to make a smooth paste. Stir in the broth and lemon juice. Cook on HIGH for 3 to 5 minutes, or until slightly thickened, stirring once. Stir in the mushrooms. Cook on HIGH for 2 to 3 minutes, or until the mushrooms are heated through.

VARIATIONS:

Sherried Mushroom Sauce: Add 2 tablespoons sherry with the broth.

Herbed Mushroom Sauce: Add ¼ cup chopped fresh herbs at the end of cooking.

Rosy Mushroom Sauce: Add 1 tablespoon tomato paste with the broth.

PAN DRIPPINGS GRAVY

MAKES 1 CUP   BEGIN 10 MINUTES BEFORE SERVING
COOKING TIME: 5 TO 8 MINUTES

Some folks prefer a thicker gravy, and this can be done with the flour increased to 2 tablespoons.

- 2 tablespoons fat from drippings, or melted butter
- 1½ tablespoons all-purpose flour
- 1 cup broth or broth and defatted juices (see Broths and Stocks, pages 118–20)
- 1 tablespoon dry vermouth (optional)
- Salt and pepper

In a 1-quart casserole combine the fat and flour to make a paste. Stir in the broth and vermouth. Cook on HIGH for 5 to 8 minutes, or until thickened, stirring 2 to 3 times with a wire whisk. Salt and pepper to taste.

Cooked Egg Emulsion Basics:

1. Butter is melted, then cooled slightly, before adding egg yolks, so as not to coagulate the yolks too quickly.
2. The sauce is cooked uncovered so moisture can be evaporated to thicken the sauce.
3. The egg yolk–thickened sauce must be cooked on MEDIUM to keep the eggs from coagulating as they would on HIGH. What is accomplished on top of the conventional stove by using a double boiler is done here by lowering the power.
4. Vigorous stirring is critical to a good hollandaise sauce because it helps to redistribute the heat that builds up faster on the outside of the dish. After the first minute of cooking, the sauce should be stirred every 30 seconds.
5. There is no standing time with this sauce.
6. *Doneness:* Hollandaise sauce is finished when it appears very thick, dropping like mayonnaise from a spoon after being stirred. It may appear slightly lumpy when taken from the oven the final time, but should smooth with rapid stirring.

   Underdone: The sauce will be runny, not

thick. Continue to cook on MEDIUM at 30-second intervals, stirring in between each.

Overdone: If sauce has curdled, in a separate small bowl combine 1 egg yolk and a pinch of dry mustard (a good emulsifier). Add a small amount of curdled sauce to the yolk, and then return this to the remaining sauce, stirring rapidly with a whisk until the sauce becomes smooth. The amount of lemon juice or acid in the recipe enables any curdling of egg proteins to be reversible with the slow addition of the egg yolk. Very tiny flecks of coagulated egg may remain; a suggestion here is to add 1 tablespoon fresh chopped thyme or 1 teaspoon dried to mask the texture.

✳ HOLLANDAISE SAUCE

MAKES ABOUT ⅔ CUP   BEGIN 5 MINUTES BEFORE SERVING
COOKING TIME: 3 TO 4 MINUTES

If the thought of making a hollandaise sauce is enough to make you run out of the kitchen, we understand. Any egg yolk–thickened sauce or emulsion needs more attention than any other sauce. That is why the butter should be melted but not hot and why the sauce should be cooked on MEDIUM power with frequent stirring to prevent the egg yolk mixture from curdling.

But rest assured that we have a cure for any curdled hollandaise sauce (see above), one that works every time!

| ½ cup unsalted butter | ¼ teaspoon salt |
| 1 tablespoon lemon juice | 4 egg yolks |

Place the butter in a 1-quart casserole. Cook on HIGH for 1 to 2 minutes, or until melted. Add the lemon juice and salt, stirring with a wire whisk to cool the butter slightly.

Add the egg yolks to the butter, stirring to blend. Cook on MEDIUM for 30 seconds; stir well to mix. Cook on MEDIUM for 30 seconds more and stir. Cook on MEDIUM for 30 seconds more, or until thickened. Stir the sauce well with the whisk until smooth.

VARIATIONS:

Béarnaise Sauce: Add 2 tablespoons chopped scallions, 2 tablespoons chopped fresh tarragon or 2 teaspoons dried, and 2 tablespoons dry white wine to the melted butter with the lemon juice.

Maltaise Sauce: Add 2 to 3 tablespoons orange juice and 1 teaspoon grated orange rind to the cooked sauce.

MAYONNAISE

MAKES ABOUT 1 CUP   BEGIN 5 MINUTES BEFORE SERVING

---

1 large egg
½ teaspoon salt
¼ teaspoon dry mustard

1 tablespoon lemon juice or vinegar
1 cup vegetable oil

Blender or processor method: Combine the egg, salt, and dry mustard in the container of a blender or processor; process to mix. Pour in the lemon juice or vinegar and process quickly. If using a blender, add a few drops of oil at a time before blending; with a processor, add the oil by droplets while the processor is running. Continue adding just a few drops of oil at a time until an emulsion has formed, then add the oil, 1 tablespoon at a time and in gradually larger amounts, processing each time, until the mixture is thick and creamy.

By hand: Follow the same procedure, using a medium bowl and wire whisk. Again add the oil in a few droplets, beating between each addition until an emulsion has formed, then add the remaining oil in slightly larger amounts, beating in between additions.

VARIATION:

Herbed Mayonnaise: Stir in ¼ cup chopped fresh parsley, basil, chives, dill, or a mixture, or 1½ tablespoons dried herbs, to the finished mayonnaise.

AIOLI

MAKES ABOUT 1 CUP   BEGIN 15 TO 20 MINUTES BEFORE SERVING
COOKING TIME: 3 TO 4 MINUTES

A baked potato adds texture and thickness to this luscious garlicky mayonnaise, which is delicious with fish.

---

1 medium baking potato
1 large egg yolk
2 to 3 garlic cloves, minced
1 tablespoon lemon juice

¼ teaspoon salt
1 cup olive and vegetable oil, combined

Pierce the potato. Place on a paper towel in the microwave oven. Cook on HIGH for 3 to 4 minutes, or until tender, turning over once.

Let stand for 5 minutes. When cooled, peel and add as directed.

Food processor method: (Don't use a

blender.) Place the peeled potato in a processor and puree until smooth; do not overprocess or it will become gummy. Add the egg yolk, garlic, lemon juice, and salt; process to blend. Add the oil very slowly while the processor is running. Continue processing until the mixture is thick and creamy.

By hand: In a medium bowl rice or mash very well the peeled potato. Beat with an electric mixer until smooth. Add the egg yolk, garlic, lemon juice, and salt; beat until thickened and smooth. Add the oil very slowly while beating with the mixer. Continue the process until the mixture is thick and creamy.

Serve immediately. If the mixture separates after standing, just stir the oil back into it.

The Problem of Separated Mayonnaise

Mayonnaise will separate if the oil is not added slowly enough, or if the mayonnaise is beaten too hard and long after the emulsion forms, causing it to break down.

If the emulsion separates, remove the curdled mixture from the blender or processor to another bowl. Spoon off any excess oil at the top (if you saw an emulsion form, but then saw it separate with overbeating, follow the hand method).

Processor or blender: Combine 1 egg yolk and a pinch of dry mustard (a good emulsifier) in the processor bowl and blend. Add the curdled mayonnaise to the egg yolk a teaspoon at a time, processing in between, until an emulsion forms. Add increasingly larger spoonfuls and process until all the curdled sauce has been added to the now smooth mayonnaise.

By hand: Follow the same procedure, combining the yolk and dry mustard in another medium bowl; beat well in between each addition of curdled sauce.

CHILLED FRESH HERB SAUCE

MAKES ABOUT 1 CUP   BEGIN 5 MINUTES BEFORE SERVING

½ cup plain yogurt
½ cup Mayonnaise (page 175)
2 tablespoons lemon juice

2 tablespoons chopped fresh parsley
1 tablespoon chopped fresh chives
1 tablespoon chopped fresh tarragon

In a small bowl combine all the ingredients. Stir to mix well. Serve with any cold fish.

VARIATIONS:

Chilled Horseradish-Dill Sauce: Substitute ¼ cup prepared horseradish and 2 tablespoons chopped fresh dill for the herbs.

Chilled Dill-Mustard Sauce: Substitute ¼ cup chopped fresh dill and 1 tablespoon Dijon mustard for the herbs.

WHIPPED HERB CREAM

MAKES ABOUT 1 CUP   BEGIN 5 MINUTES BEFORE SERVING

Delicious over warm or chilled lean fish, or cucumber slices.

---

1 cup heavy cream
1 teaspoon grated lemon rind

¼ cup chopped fresh herbs

In a small bowl whip the heavy cream. Fold in the lemon rind and herbs. Serve cold.

VARIATION:

Whipped Herb Cream Sauce with Horseradish: Substitute 2 tablespoons prepared horseradish for the herbs.

GREEN SAUCE

MAKES 1½ CUPS   BEGIN 8 MINUTES BEFORE SERVING
COOKING TIME: 1 MINUTE

Dab on cold poached fish or serve with shrimp or fish mousse; also delicious with cold chicken or veal or on sliced tomatoes as a salad.

---

1 cup spinach leaves
¼ cup chopped fresh parsley
2 tablespoons chopped fresh chives or scallions

½ cup Mayonnaise (page 175)
½ cup plain yogurt

Wash the leaves and lightly shake dry, leaving some water on the leaves. Place the spinach in a 1-quart casserole. Cover tightly and cook on HIGH for 1 minute, to blanch. Drain well. Remove to a food processor or blender; add the remaining ingredients. Puree until smooth. Chill and serve.

Tomato Sauce Basics:

1. It is important to choose a large (at least 2-quart) casserole for cooking tomato sauces to make stirring easier and to keep splattering to a minimum.
2. Tomatoes will thicken if cooked uncovered so that the excess moisture evaporates, and should be cooked until the proper thickness is reached. Standing time will continue the evaporation process slightly.
3. Tomatoes can be cooked on HIGH because they are not a delicate food and evaporation is quickened in this way.
4. Frequent stirring is necessary to redistribute heat when working with a large amount of tomatoes.
5. *Doneness:* A tomato sauce is done when it is the proper consistency and flavor, something each of us must judge for ourselves, depending on how we plan to serve the sauce. This timing for thickening will vary with the type of tomatoes you've cooked and the amount of liquid in them.

    Underdone: If after the specified cooking time (uncovered, of course), the tomato sauce has not reached the desired thickness, either continue to cook or stir in 1 to 2 tablespoons tomato paste and cook for a few more minutes.

✸ BASIC "BATCH" TOMATO SAUCE

MAKES 2 CUPS   BEGIN 20 TO 40 MINUTES BEFORE SERVING
COOKING TIME: 12 TO 16 MINUTES

A pure, almost unadulterated sauce, that is best when made with fresh tomatoes but also very good when made with canned plum tomatoes. It is good over pasta or on pizza.

In late August we harvest our own tomatoes, as well as purchase a bushel or two from the farmers' market. We have an assembly line of peeler, seeder, food processor operator, and cooker peopled by all family members. In 4 to 6 hours we have a year's supply of tomato sauce.

2 pounds red ripe tomatoes, peeled, seeded, and coarsely chopped, or 2 cups undrained canned

2 tablespoons butter or olive oil
½ teaspoon salt
¼ teaspoon pepper

In a 2-quart casserole combine all the ingredients. Cook, uncovered, on HIGH for 12 to 16 minutes, or until the tomatoes have cooked down and thickened, stirring four times. Let stand for 5 minutes before serving.

VARIATIONS:

Tomato-Basil Sauce: Stir in 1 tablespoon chopped fresh basil or 1 teaspoon dried at the end of cooking. Let stand for 5 minutes.

Italian Tomato Sauce: Combine 2 minced garlic cloves with the olive oil in the casserole before adding the other ingredients. Cook on HIGH for 35 seconds, or until tender. Stir in the remaining ingredients plus ¼ teaspoon optional red pepper flakes. Follow the basic recipe. Stir in 1 teaspoon dried oregano at the end of cooking. Let stand for 5 minutes.

Parsley-Cheese Tomato Sauce: Combine 2 minced garlic cloves with the oil in the casserole before adding the other ingredients. Cook on HIGH for 35 seconds, or until tender. Stir in 2 tablespoons chopped fresh parsley or 2 teaspoons dried with the remaining ingredients. Follow the basic recipe. Stir in ¼ cup grated Parmesan cheese and 1 tablespoon chopped fresh basil at the end of cooking. Let stand for 5 minutes.

PUREED TOMATO SAUCE

MAKES ABOUT 2 CUPS   BEGIN 25 TO 45 MINUTES BEFORE SERVING
COOKING TIME: 14 TO 27 MINUTES

This sauce is for people who don't like chunky tomato sauce, and who want a richer flavor that added herbs bring. The sauce can also be made in season and frozen.

- 2 tablespoons olive or vegetable oil, or butter
- ½ cup chopped onion, or 2 garlic cloves, minced
- 2 pounds tomatoes, stems removed, quartered, or 2 cups undrained canned, coarsely chopped
- 3 tablespoons tomato paste
- 2 tablespoons chopped fresh parsley, or 2 teaspoons dried
- ½ teaspoon sugar
- ½ teaspoon dried thyme
- 1 teaspoon fresh oregano leaves, or ½ teaspoon dried
- ½ teaspoon salt
- ¼ teaspoon black pepper
- ⅛ teaspoon cayenne pepper (optional)

In a 2-quart casserole combine the oil and onion. Cook on HIGH for 2 to 5 minutes, or until the onion is tender, stirring once. Add the tomatoes. Cook on HIGH for 8 to 12 minutes, or until the tomatoes are very tender and can be passed through a strainer, stirring twice.

Puree the tomato mixture and return to the casserole. Add the remaining ingredients; stir. Cook on HIGH for 4 to 10 minutes, or until the sauce is slightly thickened. Let stand for 5 minutes before serving.

VARIATIONS:

Spicy Pureed Tomato Sauce: Add ¼ teaspoon crushed hot pepper flakes with the seasonings.

Tomato and Meat Sauce: At the end of cooking, cook ½ pound ground meat by placing it in a separate casserole. Cook on HIGH for 2 to 5 minutes, stirring once. Drain and break up the meat. Add the meat to the sauce. Cook, uncovered, on HIGH for 5 minutes more before serving.

Adding meat to chilled or frozen sauce: If the sauce has been refrigerated, add the cooked meat as directed and cook, uncovered, on HIGH for 10 minutes, stirring once.

If the sauce has been frozen, cook the sauce alone, uncovered, on HIGH for 10 to 15 minutes, stirring often to break up the ice crystals. After the ice crystals are melted, add the meat. Cook on HIGH for 5 to 10 minutes, or until heated through.

TOMATO-MEAT SAUCE

MAKES 5 CUPS   BEGIN ABOUT 30 TO 40 MINUTES BEFORE SERVING
COOKING TIME: 18 TO 28 MINUTES

A tight cover is necessary for this sauce since it contains so many additional vegetables.

- 1 tablespoon olive oil
- 2 garlic cloves, minced
- 1 medium onion, chopped
- 1 large celery rib, finely chopped
- 1 pound lean ground beef
- 1 28-ounce can plum tomatoes with juices, chopped
- ¼ cup tomato paste
- ¼ cup chopped fresh parsley
- 1 tablespoon chopped fresh basil, or 1 teaspoon dried
- 1 teaspoon chopped fresh oregano, or ½ teaspoon dried
- 1 teaspoon sugar
- 1 teaspoon salt
- ¼ teaspoon pepper
- ¼ teaspoon hot pepper flakes (optional)

In a 3-quart casserole combine the oil, garlic, onion, and celery. Cover tightly and cook on HIGH for 3 to 5 minutes, or until the vegetables are tender-crisp, stirring once. Stir in the ground beef, spreading evenly in the dish. Cover again and cook on HIGH for 5 to 8 minutes, or until still slightly pink, stirring once to break up the pieces. Drain the fat from the meat and vegetables.

Add the remaining ingredients. Cover tightly and cook on HIGH for 10 to 15 minutes, or until the flavors are developed, stirring after 5 minutes. Let stand, covered, for 5 minutes. Serve over pasta or use in meat lasagna.

VARIATIONS:

Tomato-Sausage Sauce: Substitute 1 pound sweet or hot Italian sausage, casing removed and sausage broken up, for the ground beef.

Tomato-Meat Sauce with Mushrooms: Add ¼ pound mushrooms, sliced, during last 5 minutes of cooking.

BLAZING BARBECUE SAUCE

MAKES 1¾ CUPS   BEGIN 15 MINUTES BEFORE SERVING
COOKING TIME: 7 TO 10 MINUTES

This sauce can be used to make barbecued beef (see page 309) or as a marinade for ribs, steaks, chops or chicken.

2 tablespoons butter	3 tablespoons cider vinegar
1 garlic clove, minced	2 tablespoons prepared mustard
2 tablespoons chopped onion	2 tablespoons soy sauce
¼ cup brown sugar	2 tablespoons lemon juice
1 cup catsup	1 tablespoon Worcestershire sauce
½ cup water	2 to 3 drops hot pepper sauce

In a 4-cup glass measure combine the butter, garlic, and onion. Cook on HIGH for 2 to 3 minutes, or until tender. Stir in the remaining ingredients. Cook on HIGH for 5 to 7 minutes, or until boiling, stirring after 2 minutes.

VARIATION:

Barbecue Sauce with Chili: Add 1 tablespoon chili powder to the sauce.

☀ SWEET AND SOUR APRICOT SAUCE

MAKES 1 CUP   BEGIN ABOUT 5 MINUTES BEFORE SERVING
COOKING TIME: 4 TO 5 MINUTES

This sauce is delicious when served with roast pork, Oriental dishes, breaded vegetables, sausages, spareribs, or meatballs.

Because of the high sugar content of the sauce, it is very important to stir after the first 2 minutes of cooking time.

- 1 cup apricot preserves
- 2 teaspoons soy sauce
- 1 tablespoon vinegar
- 1 tablespoon lemon or lime juice
- Dash of hot pepper sauce

Combine all the ingredients in a 2-cup glass measure. Cook on HIGH for 2 minutes; stir. Cook on HIGH for 2 to 3 minutes more, or until boiling. Stir and serve warm or chilled.

VARIATIONS:

Floridian Sweet and Sour Apricot Sauce: Add 2 tablespoons thinly sliced orange rind with the other ingredients.

Sweet and Sour Apricot Sauce with Ginger: Add 1 teaspoon grated fresh ginger with the other ingredients.

Sweet and Sour Orange Sauce: Substitute orange marmalade for the apricot preserves.

PEANUT SATAY SAUCE

MAKES 1½ CUPS   BEGIN ABOUT 10 TO 15 MINUTES BEFORE SERVING
COOKING TIME: 4 TO 9 MINUTES

This peanut sauce is found everywhere in Indonesia and Malaysia and is served over the dish it is named for, satay, which is skewered meat, chicken, fish, or vegetables. The thick rich sauce is spicy yet slightly sweet, and we love to keep it around as a dip for apples or toasted cubes of bread.

- 1 tablespoon sesame, peanut, or vegetable oil
- 1 garlic clove, minced
- 1 medium onion, finely chopped
- ⅔ cup water
- ½ cup chunky peanut butter
- 3 tablespoons soy sauce
- 2 tablespoons brown sugar
- 2 tablespoons catsup
- ¼ teaspoon red pepper flakes
- 1 tablespoon lime or lemon juice

In a 4-cup glass measure or bowl combine the oil, garlic, and onion. Cook on HIGH for 2 to 4 minutes, or until the onion is tender. Stir in the water. Cook on HIGH for 2 to 5 minutes, or until the water is boiling. Stir in the remaining ingredients. Serve.

MELTED BUTTERS

MAKES ABOUT ½ CUP BEGIN 5 MINUTES BEFORE SERVING
COOKING TIME: 1 TO 1½ MINUTES

There are so many uses for melted and softened butters, plain or flavored. They are delicious over hot vegetables, on fish, and stirred into pasta, rice, or noodles.

½ cup butter

Place the butter in a 1-cup glass measure. Cover with wax paper and cook on HIGH for 1 to 1½ minutes to melt.

VARIATIONS:

Garlic Butter: Add 2 minced garlic cloves to the butter before melting. Cook until the garlic is tender.

Shallot-Garlic Butter: Add 2 minced garlic cloves, 2 tablespoons finely chopped shallots, and 2 tablespoons finely chopped fresh parsley to the butter before melting.

Lemon or Lime Butter: Add 2 tablespoons lemon or lime juice to the melted butter.

Orange or Tangerine Butter: Add ¼ cup orange or tangerine juice to the melted butter. Try over sweet potatoes, sprinkled with a little brown sugar.

Basil or Parsley Butter: Add ¼ cup chopped fresh basil or parsley to the melted butter.

Dill or Tarragon Butter: Add 2 tablespoons chopped fresh tarragon or dill, or 2 teaspoons dried, to the melted butter.

Chive Butter: Add 2 tablespoons to ¼ cup chopped fresh chives to the melted butter.

Mustard Butter: Add 1 tablespoon prepared Dijon mustard to the melted butter; stir to blend.

SOFTENED BUTTER

MAKES ABOUT ½ CUP   BEGIN ABOUT 1 HOUR BEFORE SERVING
COOKING TIME: ½ MINUTE

Serve with bread or fish, or stirred into noodles.

½ cup butter	Any of the Melted Butters additions (page 183)

Place the butter in a small microwaveproof bowl. Heat on DEFROST for 30 seconds, or until soft. With a whisk or electric mixer beat in one of the additions for any melted butter. Refrigerate.

NOTE: To mold the butter, if desired: Spoon the chilled butter onto wax paper to form a strip down the middle. Roll the paper around the butter to form a 1-inch-diameter log. If you wish, roll the butter log in ¼ cup finely chopped fresh chives or parsley. Chill for at least 1 hour. Slice and serve pats on individual plates.

ORIENTAL DRESSING

MAKES ABOUT ¾ CUP   BEGIN 5 MINUTES BEFORE SERVING

Here's an effortless way to liven the flavor in leftover chilled vegetables or fish fillets. Allow 1 tablespoon per serving. In the summer, keep this in the refrigerator in a jar for a tasty but low-calorie salad dressing. It will last about a month.

¼ cup soy sauce 1 tablespoon sesame, walnut, or vegetable oil 2 tablespoons rice or wine vinegar	2 tablespoons orange juice 2 teaspoons sugar 1 garlic clove, minced

Combine all the ingredients in a 1-cup jar with a lid. Shake well and chill.

VARIATIONS:

Ginger Dressing: Add 2 teaspoons grated fresh ginger to the dressing.

Mustard Dressing: Add 1 teaspoon dry mustard to the dressing.

Extra Zippy Oriental Dressing: Add 2 teaspoons grated fresh ginger and 1 teaspoon dry mustard to the dressing. For those whose palates enjoy extra stimulation.

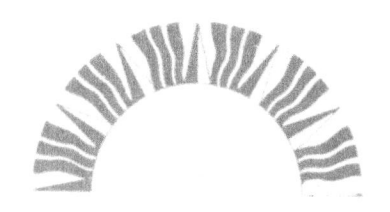

HERB VINAIGRETTE

MAKES ABOUT 1 CUP   BEGIN 5 MINUTES BEFORE SERVING

- ½ cup olive oil
- ¼ cup red wine vinegar
- 1 tablespoon Dijon mustard
- ½ teaspoon salt
- ¼ teaspoon freshly ground pepper
- 3 tablespoons chopped fresh parsley, chives, or dill

Combine all the ingredients in a small bowl and mix or shake together well.

VARIATIONS:

Basil Vinaigrette: Substitute 3 tablespoons chopped fresh basil for the fresh herbs.

Anchovy Vinaigrette: Add 1 tablespoon chopped anchovy fillets to the basic dressing.

Caper Vinaigrette: Add 2 tablespoons drained capers to the basic recipe.

SALSA CRUDA

MAKES ABOUT 2 CUPS   BEGIN 5 TO 10 MINUTES BEFORE SERVING

This is wonderful when served with chili or tacos.

- 2 medium tomatoes
- 1 medium onion
- 2 jalapeño peppers
- 1 tablespoon lemon or lime juice
- 1 tablespoon water
- 1 tablespoon chopped cilantro (coriander)
- ½ teaspoon salt

Combine all the ingredients in a food processor, or finely chop by hand.

CUMIN SALSA

MAKES ABOUT 2 CUPS   BEGIN 5 TO 10 MINUTES BEFORE SERVING

Add a West Coast touch to cold poached fish or chicken.

- 2 cups coarsely chopped ripe tomatoes
- 1 tablespoon chopped fresh cilantro (coriander)
- 1 tablespoon lime juice
- 1 or 2 tablespoons chopped seeded jalapeño peppers
- 2 tablespoons thinly sliced scallions
- 2 teaspoons whole cuminseed, or ½ teaspoon ground
- ½ teaspoon salt

Combine all the ingredients together in a bowl or food processor, making sure not to overprocess. Serve cold.

To Peel Tomatoes

Place 4 cups water in a 2-quart casserole. Cover tightly and heat on HIGH for 7 to 10 minutes, until boiling. Plunge the tomatoes into the water for 30 seconds, to loosen the skins.

GREEN TOMATO SALSA

MAKES ABOUT 2 CUPS   BEGIN 5 MINUTES BEFORE SERVING

A good way to utilize unripe tomatoes at the end of the season, or substitute with tomatillas.

- 10 green plum tomatoes or tomatillas, or 5 medium green tomatoes
- 2 jalapeño peppers
- 1 small onion
- 1 garlic clove
- 2 tablespoons chopped fresh cilantro (coriander)
- 1 tablespoon vegetable oil
- Salt and pepper

Combine all the ingredients in a blender or food processor.

WARM JALAPEÑO SALSA

MAKES ABOUT ½ CUP   BEGIN 10 MINUTES BEFORE SERVING
COOKING TIME: 5 TO 7 MINUTES

- 1 tablespoon vegetable oil
- 1 medium onion, chopped
- 2 medium tomatoes, peeled, seeded, and chopped
- 1 jalapeño pepper, seeded and chopped
- ½ teaspoon salt

Combine the oil and onion in a 2-quart casserole. Cook on HIGH for 1 to 2 minutes, or until the onion is tender. Stir in the remaining ingredients. Cook on HIGH for 4 to 5 minutes, or until heated, stirring once.

✸ CRANBERRY SAUCE

MAKES 2 CUPS
COOKING TIME: 4 TO 7 MINUTES

This sauce is cooked covered with wax paper, which prevents spatters without causing a boilover the way a tight cover would. Serve it hot or cold with beef, game, or poultry or chilled to dress up a cottage cheese salad.

- 1 pound fresh or frozen cranberries
- 1 cup sugar
- ¼ cup water

Combine all the ingredients in a 2-quart casserole. Cover with wax paper and cook on HIGH for 4 to 7 minutes, or until the berries have popped, stirring after 2 minutes. Serve hot or cold.

NOTE: For more about sauces see Berry Sauce Basics, page 497.

VARIATIONS:

Orange-Cranberry Sauce: Substitute ¼ cup orange juice for the water. Add 1 tablespoon grated orange rind.

Pineapple-Cranberry Sauce: Substitute ¼ cup pineapple juice for the water. Stir in ½ cup drained, crushed pineapple at the end of cooking time.

Cranberry Sauce with Spirits: Substitute ¼ cup orange-flavored liqueur for the water. Add 1 tablespoon grated orange rind.

Cranberry Sauce with Cassis: Substitute ¼ cup cassis for the water.

Cranberry Sauce with Raspberry Vinegar: Eliminate the water. Add 2 tablespoons raspberry vinegar. This is a wonderfully tart sauce that is perfect for game, pork, sausage, or duck. For Quick Raspberry Vinegar, see page 366.

8

PASTA, RICE, AND GRAINS

"They had best *not* stir the rice, though it sticks to the pot," wrote Miguel de Cervantes in his classic novel *Don Quixote*. Cervantes doesn't tell us why one shouldn't stir the rice, but what he claimed for sixteenth-century rice cookery is true in twentieth-century microwave cooking as well, although not to avoid sticking.

Because stirring is such an important principle in microwave cooking for redistributing heat, we had always felt that rice must be stirred, too. But then again we had never tried cooking rice without stirring. One time the inevitable happened—we forgot to stir. When disaster seemed imminent, we found instead a better-textured rice and a new rice method. Now we don't stir. Incidents like this keep us humble.

I find that half the fun of eating rice is in the shopping. Now, I'm not talking about buying boxes of white rice in supermarkets, but instead sniffing out tiny markets in Philadelphia that sell specialty rice. This means adventures to the Indian market for basmati rice, or to a purveyor who is even closer to me, a little Armenian market whose bread is baked a few blocks away in an old church. I always enjoy peeking into the back room to see if the shop owner's grandmother is sipping her Turkish coffee and if there is a backgammon game in progress.

It is down to the Italian market for the Arborio rice for risotto. This is not the store for people with fear of small spaces. The skinny aisle is blanketed on the right wall by shelves of Italian imports piled to the ceiling, and on the left by a line of amiable customers. Queuing up is a pleasure here, for there is so much to choose from it takes time to decide which cheese to stir into the risotto this time. The proprietors, who are brothers, try to help by offering slivers of cheese to those waiting in line.

Brown rice is a specialty of a "country store" in the city where regional American rice and dry beans are scooped from bins propped up on the floor.

It always amazes me how so many different nationalities can have the same affinity for rice but for different reasons. The creamy yellow rice with saffron from Italy only vaguely resembles a brown rice dish from Bengal state in India. Yet these distinct treatments gave us so many ideas to draw from when compiling a rice and pasta chapter. We can skip around the world from Italian Risotto to East Indian Rice to Stuffed Grape Leaves and back home to a more familiar long-grain Rice Pilaf.

In this book, we have kept the pasta cookery to a minimum, for outside of lasagna (and macaroni in a pinch), pasta is much better when it bubbles freely in a large pasta pot on top of the stove.

But let us not forget the grains: fine-grain cereal, oatmeal, cornmeal grits, and polenta. Although these may seem plebian, southerners have elevated grits to the company of steak in a spicy New Orleans dish called Grillades (page 286). To northern Italians, sliced golden corn polenta with Fontina cheese is now an exquisite first course.

And on top of it all, none of these dishes are diminished in the least by reheating. Rice and grains, which are so easy to store at home, will always supply you with a satisfying meal.

—MARCIA

Cooked Cereal Basics:

1. In cooking cereal and/or oatmeal in the microwave, there is no need to heat the water before adding them.
2. The casserole should be twice as high as the cereal and water mixture to prevent any boilovers. For individual servings, make sure that the bowl is at least a deep 16-ounce bowl (a 1-quart casserole would be even better).
3. When cooking cereal, no cover is necessary for any amount. In fact, it may cause a boilover!
4. Stirring twice during cooking is important to eliminate lumps and speed cooking by redistributing heat.
5. Standing time is not necessary because the water is already absorbed by the end of cooking.
6. *Doneness:* The finished cereal should be thick, but not pasty, yet stirrable, with all the liquid absorbed. The longer you cook it, the thicker it will get. The cereal will be smooth, too, if you have stirred twice as indicated in the instructions.

✹ HOT CEREAL

MAKES 4 SERVINGS   BEGIN ABOUT 10 MINUTES BEFORE SERVING
COOKING TIME: 8 TO 10 MINUTES

Before serving, add brown sugar, honey, maple syrup, chopped dried fruits or raisins, milk or yogurt.

| ½ teaspoon salt (optional) | ¾ cup fine-milled cereal (farina or |
| 3 cups water | Cream of Wheat) or 1⅓ cups oatmeal |

In a 3-quart casserole combine all the ingredients. Cook on HIGH for 4 minutes; stir. Cook on HIGH for 4 to 6 minutes more, or until all the liquid is absorbed, stirring once again.

Cooked Grits and Polenta Basics:

1. In cooking grits or polenta in the microwave, there is no need to heat the water before adding the cereal.
2. The casserole should be twice as high as the cereal and water mixture to prevent any boilovers. For individual servings, the bowl should be 16 ounces, but boilovers are less likely with grits than with cereal or oatmeal.
3. No cover is necessary for cooking individual servings, but we find that a cover when making 4 to 6 servings is helpful in keeping the surface moist. Without a cover on this larger amount, a dry surface will form, probably because of the fine grain and the fact that less water is called for than with cereal.
4. Stirring twice during cooking is important to eliminate lumps and speed cooking by redistributing heat.
5. Standing time is not necessary because the water is already absorbed by the end of cooking.
6. For doneness, see Cooked Cereal Basics, page 192.

GRITS

MAKES 4 TO 6 SERVINGS   BEGIN ABOUT 15 MINUTES BEFORE SERVING
COOKING TIME: 9 TO 11 MINUTES

Grits are cooked in the same way that fine-milled cereal is cooked, but the former are very versatile and can be incorporated into other recipes when cooked in this amount. White grits are a familiar item on southern menus when served for breakfast or for dinner with meat and gravy. Serve with eggs, milk, and maple syrup, or as a side dish with poultry, sausages, or pot roast and gravy.

½ teaspoon salt (optional)
3½ cups water

1 cup hominy grits

In a 3-quart casserole combine all the ingredients. Cover tightly and cook on HIGH for 5 minutes; stir. Cover again and cook on HIGH for 4 to 7 minutes, or until all the water is absorbed, stirring again.

VARIATIONS:

Grits Cooked in Broth: Combine 2 tablespoons butter and 1 onion, chopped, in a 3-quart casserole. Cook on HIGH for 1½ to 2½ minutes, or until the onion is tender. Add grits and salt. Substitute 3½ cups beef broth (see Mock Brown Broth or Stock, page 119) for the water. Follow the basic recipe. Serve with Grillades (page 286), or any beef and gravy.

Grits in a Mold: Spoon the cooked grits into a 4-cup mold. Let stand for 10 minutes. Unmold on a serving platter, surrounded with meats or gravy.

Individual Grits Molds: Spoon the cooked grits into 6 or 8 custard cups. Let stand for 10 minutes. Unmold onto individual serving plates. Sprinkle with grated cheese or fresh herbs.

GRITS AND CHEDDAR CASSEROLE

MAKES 4 TO 6 MAIN-DISH SERVINGS; 8 TO 12 SIDE-DISH SERVINGS
BEGIN 30 TO 45 MINUTES BEFORE SERVING, INCLUDING GRITS
COOKING TIME: 15 TO 20 MINUTES

This can be served as a main dish with a mixed green salad, or as a side dish. We find it an especially nice offering on a brunch table served with bacon, Canadian bacon, or sausages.

- 2 tablespoons butter
- 2 medium onions, finely chopped
- 1 recipe Grits (page 193)
- 2½ cups grated sharp cheddar cheese
- 3 eggs, beaten
- Dash or two of hot red pepper sauce

In a 2-quart casserole combine the butter and onions. Cook on HIGH for 3 to 5 minutes, or until the onions are tender. Stir in the cooked grits and 2 cups cheese until the cheese is melted. Stir in the eggs and hot red pepper sauce. Cook on MEDIUM for 12 to 14 minutes, or until heated through and set. Sprinkle with the remaining ½ cup cheese. Cook on MEDIUM for 1 to 3 minutes, or until the cheese is melted. Let stand for 10 minutes before serving, to set completely and cool slightly.

VARIATIONS:

Picante Grits and Cheese Casserole: Add ¼ cup chopped canned hot peppers, drained, or 1 or 2 chopped fresh jalapeño peppers along with the onions.

Grits and Cheese Casserole with Bacon: Add ½ cup chopped cooked bacon (see page 61) with eggs.

POLENTA

MAKES 4 TO 6 SERVINGS   BEGIN ABOUT 15 MINUTES BEFORE SERVING
COOKING TIME: 9 TO 12 MINUTES

Polenta, from northern Italy, can best be described as a steaming corn cereal when heated; when cooled it solidifies into a corn slab that has the texture of moist bread and can be sliced. Serve with tomato sauce or melted butter with chopped fresh basil or sage as a first course, or as a side dish with fowl or grilled Italian sausages and tomato sauce.

1 cup coarse yellow cornmeal	1 tablespoon olive oil
½ teaspoon salt (optional)	3½ cups water

In a 3-quart casserole combine all the ingredients. Cover tightly and cook on HIGH for 5 minutes; stir. Cover again and cook on HIGH for 4 to 7 minutes, or until all the water is absorbed, stirring once again.

VARIATION:

Cheese Polenta: Follow the basic recipe. Stir ⅓ cup grated Parmesan cheese and ¼ cup unsalted butter into the cooked polenta to melt.

Glossary of Terms for Rice

Brown rice has the outer layer or hull removed but is still covered by a bran layer, containing the B vitamins and giving it a characteristic brown color.

Polished rice is first hulled and then the bran and the fatty layer underneath are removed. In this process the B vitamins and a small portion of the rice's protein are lost. Generally, polished rice has vitamins added to the outside in a solution which will unfortunately be partially lost if the rice is rinsed before cooking, or cooked in too much water that is later discarded. Carolina rice is a long-grain polished rice.

Converted rice is partially cooked or steamed before milling, which helps to loosen the hull but also causes the B vitamins in the bran to permeate the rice kernel before the bran is removed. Converted long-grain rice may take slightly longer to cook than Carolina rice.

Basmati rice is grown in the northern part of India and in Pakistan. It is a long grain with a low proportion of waxy starch, which causes it to be dry and flaky when cooked. It is generally converted before milling. We would recommend rinsing it off before cooking. The aroma and flavor of this rice hint at the fragrant scents found in the Indian bazaars.

Arborio rice is a starchy, short-grained rice with a round kernel. It is often cooked by the slow-braising method for a dish called "risotto," and the round kernel seems to help it keep the al dente doneness that is so desired in this dish.

Wild rice is no longer wild and is but a distant cousin to rice. This grain native to the northern United States and parts of Canada has a nutty roasted flavor, which is accounted for by a fermenting and heating (browning) process. The extra care given it also boosts it into the high-price range. But for that you also get a higher proportion of protein as compared to regular rice.

Rice Basics:

1. In conventional cooking, water is generally brought to a boil before rice is added. In the microwave, rice and water are combined before cooking, because microwaves seem to be attracted to the water first and not the rice. The water comes to a boil, and then each grain of rice begins to absorb it and cooking begins. There is no possibility of the rice burning or sticking to the dish because the water gets hot before it conducts heat to the dish.
2. A large casserole, twice the height of the rice and water, is necessary so that boiling water won't froth over the top. A glass casserole makes it easier to judge the boiling.
3. A tight cover is necessary to keep in all the moisture for absorption by the rice. Because of this tight seal and little evaporation, less water is needed for cooking rice than is called for conventionally.
4. Rice is first cooked on HIGH power to bring the water to a boil. Once the water has boiled, the power is turned down to MEDIUM to lower the temperature of the water and slow the water absorption by the rice. This is true for all rice. Only the timing varies, depending on the type of rice.
5. We found that a better, drier, less gummy rice is produced if there is no stirring during cooking. Stirring tends to break the outside of the rice and cause it to be gummy.
6. Standing time is necessary to allow the final absorption of water.
7. *Doneness:* The rice will appear dry on the surface at the end of cooking, but if stirred, there will be a little unabsorbed liquid below the rice on the bottom of the dish. This will be absorbed during standing time.

    Underdone: The rice will not cook completely if there is not enough water or if the cover is not tight enough. If the rice appears hard, even though the liquid has been absorbed, add an additional ½ cup hot water. Continue to cook on MEDIUM power until the water is absorbed.

    Overdone: When the rice is overcooked, the grains will burst. This will happen if: 1) the rice has been cooked too long (until every bit of liquid is absorbed before the standing time); 2) the rice has been cooked on HIGH power for the full time; or 3) the proper amount of liquid hasn't been added. It is still edible, just serve with a sauce.

✸ LONG-GRAIN RICE

MAKES 4 SERVINGS (3 CUPS)   BEGIN 25 MINUTES BEFORE SERVING
COOKING TIME: 14 TO 17 MINUTES

People always ask, "Would you cook rice in the microwave?" There are two answers to this: If you need your microwave to cook another part of the meal, then it makes sense to cook the rice on top of the stove. On the other hand, there is nothing like the microwave to turn out perfect rice without burning or sticking. Often, the rest of the meal can be cooked during the rice's standing time. Even if the rice stands covered for 10 minutes, it will remain hot.

1¾ cups water
½ teaspoon salt (optional)

1 cup raw long-grain or converted rice

In a 3-quart casserole combine the water and salt, if desired. Stir in the rice. Cover tightly and cook on HIGH for 4 to 7 minutes, or until the liquid begins to boil. Reduce the power to MEDIUM; cook for 10 minutes, or until most of the liquid is absorbed and the rice is tender. Let stand, covered, for 5 minutes.

NOTES: *To Double:* Double all the ingredients in a 4-quart casserole. Cover tightly and cook on HIGH for 7 to 10 minutes, or until boiling. Cook on MEDIUM for 12 to 14 minutes, or until the liquid is absorbed.

To Reheat: Cover tightly and cook on HIGH for 1 to 6 minutes, depending on the amount of rice being heated, stirring every minute to ensure even heating.

VARIATIONS:

Long-Grain Rice with Almonds: During standing time, melt 2 tablespoons butter in a small dish on HIGH for 35 seconds to 1 minute. Stir in ¼ cup slivered almonds. Stir the butter and almonds into the rice at the end of standing time.

Long-Grain Rice with Almonds and Currants: During standing time, melt 2 tablespoons butter in a 1-cup glass measure on HIGH for 35 seconds to 1 minute. Stir in ¼ cup *each* slivered almonds and currants or coarsely chopped raisins. Stir the butter, nuts, and currants into the rice at the end of standing time.

Long-Grain Rice with Mushrooms: During standing time, prepare Sautéed Mushrooms (page 439). Stir the mushrooms into the rice at the end of standing time.

Long-Grain Oriental Rice: During standing time, prepare Oriental Dressing (page 184). Stir the dressing into the rice at the end of standing time.

Long-Grain Rice with Japanese Vegetables: During standing time, prepare Japanese Vegetables (page 478). Stir the vegetables into the rice at the end of standing time. Pass extra sauce at the table.

Long-Grain Pineapple Rice: Substitute 1¾ cups pineapple juice for the water. Add ¼ teaspoon powdered ginger with the rice. Follow the basic recipe. During standing time, heat 1 cup crushed pineapple on HIGH for 1 to 2 minutes. Stir the pineapple into the rice after standing time. Good with pork or fowl.

Long-Grain Lemon Rice: Add 1 teaspoon grated lemon rind and 2 tablespoons lemon juice with the water. Follow the basic recipe. Garnish the cooked rice with chopped fresh parsley and thinly sliced lemons. Good with fish.

Creamy Rice Salad: Let the rice cool after standing time. Stir in 1 green or red pepper, thinly sliced, ¼ cup chopped fresh parsley, and ¼ cup thinly sliced scallions. Combine ¼ cup plain yogurt, ¼ cup Mayonnaise (page 175), and ½ teaspoon Dijon mustard in a small bowl. Stir into the rice. Serve chilled or at room temperature.

Rice Salad Vinaigrette: Combine ¼ cup salad oil, 2 tablespoons vinegar, ½ teaspoon Dijon mustard, ½ teaspoon salt, and ¼ teaspoon pepper in a small bowl. Stir into the warm rice. Let cool. Stir in ¼ cup chopped fresh parsley and ¼ cup thinly sliced scallions. Serve chilled or at room temperature.

Rice Salad with Meat: Prepare either rice salad variation above, adding ½ cup cubed cooked meat, poultry, or fish.

COOKING TWO SERVINGS OF RICE

When 4 servings is too much, reduce your preparation time with these instructions.

½ cup long-grain rice

¾ cup water

Combine ingredients in a 2-quart casserole. Cover tightly and cook on HIGH 3 to 5 minutes, or until boiling; then on MEDIUM 7 to 10 minutes, or until most of the water is absorbed. Stir and let stand, covered, 3 minutes.

BASMATI RICE

MAKES 4 SERVINGS (3 CUPS)   BEGIN 25 MINUTES BEFORE SERVING
COOKING TIME: 11 TO 18 MINUTES

Basmati is considered one of the best rices in the world. It produces a sweet, aromatic bouquet as it cooks, which is unlike any other rice. It is usually soaked in water for a half hour before cooking; we were pleased to find that this wasn't necessary for the microwave. You can find basmati rice in Middle Eastern and Indian specialty stores, and you'll discover that because of its thin white grain it takes less time to cook than long-grain rice.

1 cup basmati rice
1¾ cups water

½ teaspoon salt (optional)

Wash the rice well to remove any seeds or small stones.

In a 3-quart casserole combine the water and salt, if desired. Stir in the rice. Cover tightly and cook on HIGH for 4 to 7 minutes, or until the liquid is boiling; then cook on MEDIUM for 6 to 10 minutes more, or until most of the liquid is absorbed and the rice is tender. Let stand, covered, for 5 minutes.

VARIATIONS:

Follow any of the variations for Long-Grain Rice (page 196).

BROWN RICE

MAKES 4 SERVINGS (3 CUPS)   BEGIN 35 TO 45 MINUTES BEFORE SERVING
COOKING TIME: 31 TO 40 MINUTES

Brown rice, because of the outer bran coating, retains a light, pleasing crunchy texture when cooked.

2⅓ cups water	1 cup brown rice
½ teaspoon salt (optional)	

In a 3-quart casserole combine the water and salt, if desired. Stir in the rice. Cover tightly and cook on HIGH for 6 to 10 minutes, or until the water begins to boil; then cook on MEDIUM for 25 to 30 minutes, or until most of the liquid is absorbed. Let stand, covered, for 5 minutes.

VARIATIONS:

Brown Rice with Wok-Style Vegetables: During standing time, prepare Mixed Wok-Style Vegetables (page 481). Serve the vegetables over the rice.

Oriental Salad: After standing time, stir in ¼ cup sliced scallions and ¼ cup Oriental Dressing (page 184) into the cooked rice. Chill for 1 to 2 hours.

Brown Rice Salad with Marinated Vegetables: Prepare Marinated Vegetables (page 91). Chill. Prepare the basic recipe and chill. Stir the chilled vegetables into the rice and serve.

Fruited Brown Rice Salad: Chill the rice for at least 1 hour after cooking. Combine ¾ cup plain yogurt, ¼ cup brown sugar, and 1 tablespoon lime or lemon juice in a small bowl. Stir into the chilled rice. Fold 3 cups fresh berries or cubed fruit into the rice. Serves 4 to 6.

Raisin 'n Nut Brown Rice Salad: Substitute 1 cup chopped nuts and 1 cup raisins for the fresh fruit in the preceding variation.

WILD RICE

MAKES 6 SERVINGS   BEGIN 30 TO 40 MINUTES BEFORE SERVING
COOKING TIME: 25 TO 32 MINUTES

Wild rice is technically not rice. It is cooked in liquid to soften it, but the kernels do not absorb much water the way regular rice does. Rather, wild rice steams and the grains burst open in this tenderizing process.

⅔ cup wild rice	1½ cups water

In a 3-quart casserole combine the rice and water. Cover tightly and cook on HIGH for 5 to 7 minutes, or until boiling; stir. Cook, covered, on MEDIUM for 20 to 25 minutes, or until most of the rice has burst slightly. Let stand, covered, 5 minutes. Drain any excess water and serve.

EAST INDIAN RICE

MAKES 4 TO 6 SERVINGS   BEGIN 50 TO 55 MINUTES BEFORE SERVING
COOKING TIME: 34 TO 44 MINUTES

If exotic spice blends appeal to you, this is an absolutely delicious rice dish. Browning the garlic is important to the flavor, and stirring is necessary to break up the ginger.

- 2 tablespoons vegetable oil
- 3 garlic cloves, minced
- 2 tablespoons minced fresh ginger
- 1 teaspoon cuminseed
- ¼ teaspoon hot red pepper flakes
- 2¾ cups Chicken Broth (page 118), Vegetable Broth (page 119), or water
- 1 cup brown, long-grain, or converted rice
- ½ teaspoon ground cinnamon
- ½ teaspoon cilantro (coriander)
- ½ teaspoon grated nutmeg
- ½ teaspoon salt (optional)
- 2 tablespoons thinly sliced scallions
- ⅓ cup slivered almonds or coarsely chopped peanuts

In a 3-quart casserole combine the oil, garlic, ginger, cuminseed, and pepper flakes. Stir to coat with oil. Cook on HIGH for 3 to 4 minutes, or until the garlic is slightly brown, stirring after 1 minute.

Stir in the broth or water, rice, cinnamon, cilantro, nutmeg, and salt, if desired. Cover tightly and cook on HIGH for 6 to 10 minutes, or until the liquid is boiling; then cook on MEDIUM for 25 to 30 minutes, or until most of the liquid is absorbed. Let stand, covered, for 5 minutes. Sprinkle with the scallions and nuts before serving.

VARIATION:

East Indian Rice with Raisins: Add ½ cup raisins at the end of cooking, before standing time.

Moghul Rice with Ground Lamb: Add 1 pound cooked, drained ground lamb with the rice.

Pilaf and Risotto Basics:

1. The first step is to sauté the onion and/or garlic in butter until tender. This is to release the onion flavor and obtain the proper cooked texture. The rice is then stirred into the melted butter to coat the grains before adding broth.
2. The main difference between cooking risotto and cooking pilaf is that for risotto the broth is heated first before adding the rice to produce the desired al dente doneness.
3. In both risotto and pilaf, the rice is cooked in a large 3-quart casserole to prevent boilovers.
4. Since 1 cup long-grain or basmati rice takes 1¾ cups liquid, this allows you to substitute rices in pilaf, or go with a converted rice for risotto if Arborio rice is not available.
5. A tight cover is necessary to keep the liquid from evaporating, so that the rice can absorb it and cook properly.
6. Risotto and pilaf are cooked on HIGH power to bring the water to a boil, and then on MEDIUM to let the rice absorb the hot liquid slowly.
7. Standing time is important so that all of the last remaining liquid may be absorbed.
8. Many vegetables, meats, or seafoods may be added to risotto or pilaf. For the best texture, cook these additions separately from the rice and stir in right before serving.
9. *Doneness:* The rice will appear dry on the surface and will have absorbed most of the liquid, with just a small amount left at the bottom of the dish. In risotto, the liquid will be absorbed when the cheese is stirred in. Each grain will be tender but remain firm in shape and texture.

❋ RICE PILAF

MAKES 4 TO 6 SERVINGS   BEGIN 20 TO 25 MINUTES BEFORE SERVING
COOKING TIME: 13 TO 19 MINUTES

A pilaf has butter and onion added for flavoring, and possibly other additions to make it a main dish.

- 2 tablespoons butter
- 1 medium onion, finely chopped
- 1 cup long-grain, coverted, or basmati rice
- 1¾ cups Chicken Broth or Stock (page 118)
- 1 tablespoon chopped fresh parsley, or 1 teaspoon dried

In a 3-quart casserole combine the butter and onion. Cook on HIGH for 2 to 3 minutes, or until the onion is tender.

Stir in the rice, coating every grain. Stir in the broth. Cover tightly and cook on HIGH for 4 to 6 minutes, or until the liquid is boiling; then cook on MEDIUM for 7 to 10 minutes or until most of the liquid has been absorbed and the rice is tender. Stir in the parsley. Cover again and let stand for 5 minutes.

VARIATIONS:

Creamy Rice Pilaf: Stir in 1 cup sour cream with the parsley.

Rice Pilaf with Nuts: Stir in ½ cup chopped pine nuts, pistachios, or almonds with the parsley.

Saffron Rice Pilaf: Add ¼ teaspoon crushed saffron threads or ⅛ teaspoon powdered saffron with the rice.

Turmeric Rice Pilaf: Add ½ teaspoon powdered turmeric with the rice. This will add the saffron color but no saffron flavor. It is less expensive than saffron and complements a plate that has green vegetables or red sauce or vegetables.

Individual Rice Molds: At the end of standing time, spoon the cooked rice into 4 or 6 custard cups. Cover loosely with foil. Let stand for 5 minutes. Unmold onto a serving plate or platter. This is a simple way to make a serving of rice very attractive.

Mexican Rice: Substitute 1 8-ounce can Spanish- or California-style tomato sauce or tomato juice for 1 cup of broth. Add the remaining ¾ cup chicken broth.

Meat, Chicken, or Seafood Pilaf: During standing time, cover and heat 1 cup cooked and cut-up meat, chicken, or fish on HIGH for 1⅓ to 2 minutes, or until hot, stirring once. Stir into the rice and continue to let stand.

☼ RISOTTO

MAKES 4 TO 6 SERVINGS   BEGIN 25 TO 30 MINUTES BEFORE SERVING
COOKING TIME: 16 TO 21 MINUTES

Risotto is a shimmering Italian rice dish made with Arborio or short-grain rice. It is cooked until al dente, or with a slight bite, and the microwave method will be 15 minutes of carefree cooking, compared to the normal 45 minutes of constant stirring on top of the stove; the cheese melted into the butter provides the creamy coating.

3 tablespoons butter
1 garlic clove, minced
1 small onion, finely chopped
1¾ cups Chicken Broth or Stock (page 118)

1 cup Arborio, short-grain, or converted rice
¼ cup grated Parmesan cheese

In a 3-quart casserole combine the butter, garlic, and onion. Cook on HIGH for 2 to 3 minutes, or until the onion is tender. Set aside.

Pour the broth into a 2-cup glass measure. Cook uncovered on HIGH for 2 minutes, or until heated but not boiling.

Meanwhile, stir the rice into the onions and butter, coating every grain. Stir in the warm broth. Cover tightly and cook on HIGH for 4 to 6 minutes, or until boiling. Cook on MEDIUM for 8 to 10 minutes more, or until the rice swells and almost all the liquid is absorbed. Stir in the cheese. Cover again and let stand for 5 minutes.

VARIATIONS:

Risotto with Saffron: Add ¼ teaspoon crushed saffron threads or ⅛ teaspoon powdered saffron with the rice.

Risotto with Mushrooms: During standing time, combine ½ pound mushrooms, sliced, and 1 tablespoon butter in a 1-quart casserole. Cook, uncovered, on HIGH for 2 minutes, or until tender. Stir into the rice or spoon over the rice before serving.

Risotto with Asparagus: Add ¼ cup half and half or heavy cream to the cooked rice with the cheese. During standing time, combine 1 pound asparagus, cut into 1-inch pieces, with 2 tablespoons butter in a 1½-quart casserole. Cover tightly and cook on HIGH for 3 to 7 minutes, or until the asparagus is tender. Stir into the rice at the end of standing time. Serve with freshly ground black pepper.

Risotto with Zucchini: Add ¼ cup cream to the cooked rice with the cheese. During standing time, combine 1 pound medium zucchini, cut into ½-inch slices, with 2 tablespoons butter. (If using larger zucchini, quarter before slicing.) Cook, uncovered, on HIGH for 2 to 4 minutes. Stir into the rice at the end of standing time.

Risotto with Herbs: Add 2 tablespoons chopped fresh parsley and 1 tablespoon chopped fresh basil to the cooked rice with the cheese.

Risotto with Peas and Snow Peas: During standing time, prepare Peas and Snow Peas (page 412). Stir into the rice at the end of standing time.

Risotto with Scallops: During standing time, prepare Scallops with Sesame Seed Topping (page 239), eliminating the bread crumbs. Stir into the rice at the end of standing time.

STUFFED GRAPE LEAVES

MAKES 6 TO 8 SERVINGS   BEGIN ABOUT 1 HOUR BEFORE SERVING
COOKING TIME: 30 TO 40 MINUTES

We loved the taste of these dainty rolls swathed in light lemon sauce the first time we had them in a Greek restaurant a number of years ago. The labor in rolling each one becomes fun when we have the family helping out.

When stuffed grape leaves are cooked conventionally, the broken leaves are placed on the bottom of the cooking pan to prevent overcooking. For a similar reason, we have covered the tops of the stuffed rolls with these broken leaves to protect them from overcooking in the microwave.

- 1 1-pound jar grape leaves
- 3 cups beef broth (see Mock Brown Broth or Stock, page 119)
- 1½ pounds lean ground beef or lamb
- 1 cup long-grain rice
- 1 medium onion, finely chopped
- 2 tablespoons chopped fresh parsley, or 2 teaspoons dried
- 2 teaspoons dried thyme
- 1 teaspoon chopped fresh mint, or ½ teaspoon dried
- ¼ teaspoon pepper
- ⅛ teaspoon ground cinnamon

Wash the grape leaves well in cold water to remove as much salty brine as possible. Handle the leaves gently to prevent breaking.

In a large bowl combine 1 cup broth and the remaining ingredients, mixing well. Place a rounded tablespoon of meat and rice mixture in the center of each grape leaf. Fold the side edges over the meat and roll tightly toward the point of the leaf. Place seam-side down in a 3-quart rectangular dish, forming 2 layers. Pour the remaining 2 cups broth over the rolls. Cover the rolls evenly with any torn leaves. Cover the dish tightly and cook on HIGH for 10 minutes, then on MEDIUM for 20 to 30 minutes, or until the center rolls show that the meat is no longer pink and the rice is tender. Let stand for 5 to 10 minutes before serving. Remove the cover and broken leaves on top. Serve plain or with Avgolemono Sauce (recipe follows).

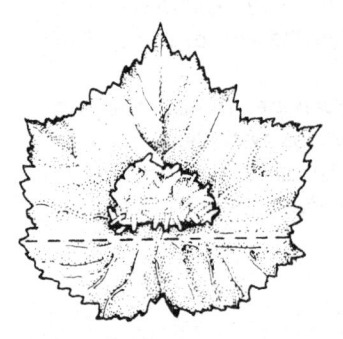

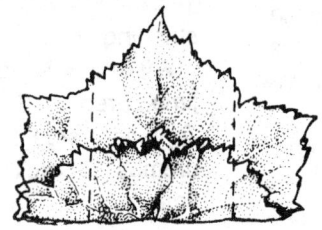

VARIATION:

Stuffed Grape Leaves in Tomato Sauce: Before starting to roll the leaves, prepare a tomato sauce: Combine 1 tablespoon olive oil, 1 minced garlic clove, and 1 onion, thinly sliced, in a 3-quart casserole. Cook on HIGH for 2 to 3 minutes, or until the onion is tender. Stir in a 28-ounce can of plum tomatoes with juices, chopped coarsely. Cook on HIGH for 5 minutes, stirring after 3 minutes.

Prepare the grape-leaf filling and roll as directed. Place the rolled grape leaves in the tomato sauce. Top with torn grape leaves as directed. Proceed with the basic recipe, eliminating the 2 cups of broth. This variation is our families' favorite way of eating this traditional Greek dish.

AVGOLEMONO SAUCE

MAKES 1½ CUPS

3 eggs, beaten
Juice of 1 lemon

Drained cooking broth (½ to 1 cup) from Stuffed Grape Leaves (page 203)

In a small bowl combine the eggs and lemon juice. Slowly beat the eggs into the warm broth.

Serve over the stuffed grape leaves.

SUBGUM CHINESE RICE

MAKES 4 SERVINGS BEGIN 15 MINUTES BEFORE SERVING
COOKING TIME: 6 TO 9½ MINUTES

This is one of our favorite ways to use up leftover rice, whether it's our own or take-home from the Chinese restaurant. The dish is good enough, though, to cook rice especially for it.

- 2 eggs
- 1 tablespoon water
- 1 tablespoon vegetable oil
- ¼ cup thinly sliced scallions
- 3 cups leftover cooked rice
- 2 tablespoons soy sauce
- ½ teaspoon sugar
- ½ cup diced leftover pork, ham, roast beef, or shrimp

In a small microwaveproof bowl combine the eggs and water, beating to blend well. Cook on HIGH for 1 to 1½ minutes, or until set, stirring after 1 minute. With a fork, break the eggs into small pieces. Set aside.

In a 2-quart casserole combine the oil and scallions. Cook on HIGH for 1 to 2 minutes.

Add the rice to the cooked scallion in oil, stirring well to coat. In a small dish combine the soy sauce and sugar. Pour over the rice. Add the diced meat and egg pieces to the rice. Cover tightly and cook on HIGH for 1 minute; stir. Cover again and cook on HIGH for 3 to 5 minutes, stirring each minute. Serve alone, with other meats and vegetables, or as a second course after a bowl of soup.

SINGLE SERVING: Combine 1 egg and 1 teaspoon water. Cook on HIGH for 35 seconds, stirring once during cooking. Break up with a fork. In a 1-quart casserole combine 1 teaspoon oil and 2 tablespoons scallion. Cook on HIGH for 1 minute, or until tender. Stir in 1 cup cooked rice. Combine 1 tablespoon soy sauce and ¼ teaspoon sugar; add to the rice. Add the cooked egg and 2 tablespoons to ¼ cup diced meat. Cover tightly and cook on HIGH for 1 to 3 minutes, stirring once.

Single Serving Vegetarian Rice: Substitute 8 ounces cubed, conventionally sautéed tofu for the egg and meat.

Lasagna Basics

1. This is the only pasta casserole that we recommend making with dry pasta. Normally pasta should be cooked first, but there is enough moisture between the tomato sauce and cheeses to steam the dry pasta.
2. The method of layering is very important because the dry noodles need to be surrounded by moisture-producing ingredients. This is why it is important that the top noodle layer be completely covered with sauce. A tight cover is also very important to hold that moisture in.
3. This casserole must be cooked on MEDIUM power for two reasons: (1) The casserole contains soft cheese, which will toughen on HIGH power; and (2) like rice, pasta should be cooked slowly by the heated liquid surrounding it.
4. A 2-quart dish is the largest size in which a rectangular layered casserole will cook evenly. Larger than that and the corners cook much faster than the center.
5. The casserole needs to be rotated twice, one-quarter turn each time, during cooking to ensure that all areas are cooking evenly.
6. Standing time is important to complete the cooking through to the center.

LASAGNA

MAKES 6 TO 8 SERVINGS   BEGIN 1 HOUR 15 MINUTES TO 1 HOUR 20 MINUTES BEFORE SERVING
COOKING TIME: 35 TO 40 MINUTES

Lasagna can be made in the microwave with uncooked noodles! If you don't have the Tomato-Meat Sauce prepared, you can still make the lasagna; a quick variation follows.

4½ cups Tomato-Meat Sauce (page 180)
8 ounces lasagna noodles
1 15-ounce container ricotta cheese
8 ounces mozzarella cheese, grated or thinly sliced
1 cup grated Parmesan cheese

Pour 1 cup tomato-meat sauce into a 2-quart rectangular baking dish, spreading evenly over the bottom. Top with the following ingredients in this order: one-third of the noodles, spread out in a single layer; half the ricotta; half the mozzarella; ⅓ cup Parmesan; 1 cup tomato-meat sauce.

Repeat the process one more time. Top the final layer of noodles with 1½ cups meat sauce. Sprinkle the top with the remaining ⅓ cup Parmesan.

Cover tightly and cook on MEDIUM for 35 to 40 minutes, or until the noodles are tender and the sauce is bubbling, rotating the casserole one-quarter turn twice. Let stand, covered, for 5 minutes.

NOTE: *To Reheat:* If the whole lasagna casserole is frozen after cooking, cover tightly with plastic wrap to reheat. Cook on HIGH for 10 minutes, then on MEDIUM for 30 to 40 minutes, or until the bottom of the dish feels warm or *3 Macungie*. If necessary, shield the corners with foil if they begin to overcook.

VARIATION:

Lasagna with Quick Meat Sauce: Place 1 pound ground beef in a 2-quart casserole, spreading out evenly. Cook on HIGH for 5 to 8 minutes, or until a slight pink color still remains, stirring once. Stir again and drain. Add 3 cups canned tomato sauce. Cover tightly and cook on HIGH for 5 to 8 minutes, or until heated, stirring once. Proceed with basic recipe.

MACARONI AND CHEESE

MAKES 4 SERVINGS   BEGIN 25 MINUTES BEFORE SERVING
COOKING TIME: 12 TO 13 MINUTES

A topping of buttered bread crumbs or crushed potato chips provides a brown, crisp appearance.

- **4 cups hot, elbow macaroni**
- **4 tablespoons butter or margarine**
- **2 cups grated mild cheddar or American cheese**
- **¾ cup milk**
- **½ teaspoon salt**
- **⅛ teaspoon pepper**
- **½ cup fine dry bread crumbs**

In a 3-quart casserole combine the macaroni and 2 tablespoons butter; stir until the butter is almost melted. Add the cheese, milk, salt, and pepper, stirring well to blend. Cover tightly and cook on MEDIUM for 12 minutes, or until the cheese is melted and the milk thickened, stirring every 4 minutes. Set aside

Place the remaining 2 tablespoons butter in a 1-cup glass measure. Cook on HIGH for 35 seconds to 1 minute to melt. Stir in the bread crumbs. Sprinkle on top of the macaroni. Let stand for 2 minutes.

VARIATIONS:

Macaroni and Cheese with Potato Chip Topping: Substitute ½ cup crushed potato chips for the bread crumbs and remaining 2 tablespoons butter.

Macaroni and Cheese with Zing: Add 2 dashes Tabasco to the milk before stirring into the macaroni.

Macaroni and Cheese with Ham: Add 1 cup chopped cooked ham to the macaroni with cheese. Serve with hot Basic "Batch" or Pureed Tomato Sauce (pages 178 or 179).

9

FISH AND SEAFOOD

Although my mother was an excellent cook and we lived in Connecticut, we rarely ate fresh fish. My father just didn't care for it, so consequently that area of my culinary education was left dormant.

It wasn't until my husband Dave and I moved to our first apartment at Point Lookout, Long Island, that I was introduced to fresh fish in the best way possible. It was through our landlady that I met a man who became both fish procurer and friend to us.

Nate was the most specialized fish man I knew because he would travel to the homes of his customers after he had made rounds to the stores. He kept his wares in a cooler in the trunk of his Chevy. When he opened the lid, they would shimmer like silver knives, catching the sun. Not only would he identify each one, but he'd show me how to fix them.

He was so concerned that his product be treated properly that he refused to sell squid to a novice like me. He insisted that I wouldn't enjoy them because I wouldn't be able to clean them properly the first time. I guess he had a reputation to protect. I had no choice but to follow my tutor's advice and continue experimenting with those fish that he brought to me.

Since then my education and appreciation for fish and seafood of all types, including squid, has broadened. I find I'm not the only one, as people all over the country flock to fish restaurants, purchase unusual species at the market, and support the volumes of fish- and seafood-only cookbooks in the bookstores.

As we began this chapter, we knew that there would be an abundance of recipes to offer you, but we had no idea we'd have to pull up short to keep them from swallowing up more than half the book. The speed with which this section's recipes were turned out in the microwave transformed the kitchen into a veritable fish factory. We just didn't want to stop—and the cats had the same sentiments.

Part of our enthusiasm stemmed from the fact that the cooking liquid left in the dish after each preparation was similar to a mild fish stock. We found that it lent itself to a wide selection of sauces, and there was no end of flavors that could be blended. We heated it with cream, jalapeño peppers, tomatoes, lime, and mustard. All turned out so successfully and yet so differently that... well, you can see our dilemma.

As we tested these recipes through the steamiest months of summer, we found that they could often be served hot or cold. A chilled fish dish brought out the second day was a refreshing treat on a hot August evening. Once again, we were amazed with their versatility.

We think you'll be as enthusiastic as we are with the collection of dishes found in this chapter.

—THELMA

Buying and Storing Fish and Seafood

Buying Fish

FRESH:
- Fish should smell fresh; there should be no strong fish odor. This is a sign of decomposition.
- Fish should have firm, elastic flesh that springs back when touched.
- There should be no visible texture to the flesh; smooth flesh indicates that the protein layers are tightly packed.
- Whole fish should have dark pink to bright red gills and clear, protruding eyes. Whole fish are best bought already dressed (gutted) because there will be less likelihood of decomposition.

FROZEN:
- Fish of very good quality can be purchased this way because often the fish are frozen directly from the ocean right on the commercial boats. Try not to buy fish that has been thawed and refrozen again. The flesh will be much dryer and the flavor blander. Avoid these telltale signs:
- Pink blood in the bottom of the package.
- An obvious texture to the fish flesh. This indicates a breakdown of collagen, which is the glue between the protein packets.
- Misshapen packages, which indicate that they may have been frozen.

Storing Fish

- First make sure that the fish is cleaned, with gills, internal organs, and all blood removed.
- Ideally, fish should be cooked and eaten immediately. If that is not possible, sprinkle lightly with lemon juice (the acid inhibits surface bacteria) and cover tightly with plastic wrap. Keep in the coldest part of your refrigerator (32°F to 35°F) for no more than two days.
- If you can't eat it within two days, freeze the fish. Rinse under cold water, then don't dry; allow a thin film of water to remain. Lay the fish in an open plastic bag in a single layer. Freeze. When fish are frozen solid, rinse once more and follow the same procedure until frozen again. Now you have "glazed" the fish. Seal the bags tightly. At 0°F, lean fish can be kept for six months; rich, or fattier, fish for three months.

Buying Shellfish

SCALLOPS:

Scallops are either small bay scallops or larger, firmer sea scallops. If fresh, they should have a sweet, not fishy, odor.

SHRIMP:

Fresh shrimp are greenish in color and should have a dry and firm shell.

CLAMS AND MUSSELS:

Clams should be tightly closed, or should close when you touch them, if they are still alive. Any that are open or cracked should be discarded. Mussels should be tightly closed if they are fresh.

Storing Shellfish

Keep in moistureproof wrap, to keep dry, and store in the coldest part of the refrigerator (32°F to 35°F) for no more than two days.

Defrosting Frozen Fish and Seafood

FISH AND LOBSTER:

- The melting away of ice from frozen fish is a process that should just begin in the microwave oven. Defrosting should never be completed in the microwave, or the fish will lose natural juices too quickly and become dry and tasteless.
- Frozen fish and lobster should be completely defrosted before actually cooking.
- Fish defrost in 6 minutes per pound on DEFROST power.
- Turn the fish over after half the defrosting time. The ice that melts in the bottom of the dish will begin to get warm and conduct heat to the surface of the fish it touches. (A microwave roasting rack, placed in a 2-quart rectangular dish, is recommended to keep fish from defrosting too quickly on one side. When the fish is placed on a rack, it is raised above any juices that are becoming very hot in the bottom of the dish. If you don't have a roasting rack, small microwaveproof plates can be inverted in a 2-quart dish as a good substitute.)
- If the frozen fish is wrapped in paper, which can't be removed, begin to defrost with the paper on and remove after half the defrosting time.

- If any thin edges appear to be cooking during defrosting, cover them smoothly with foil. This will reflect the microwave energy.
- The frozen fish should still have ice crystals after defrosting, and the edges should never feel warmer than room temperature. You won't be able to separate frozen fillets after defrosting, because they will still be frozen in the middle. All ice will dissolve when placed in cold water after defrosting for standing time. Let the fish stand for the following times:

Amount	Standing time
1 pound	5 minutes in cold water
1½ pounds	10 minutes in cold water
2 to 2½ pounds	15 minutes in cold water

Pat the fish dry before cooking.

SQUID:

- Squid defrosts in 6 minutes per pound on DEFROST power. Turn twice during defrosting, breaking up when possible.
- Remove the squid from its bag before defrosting and place on a roasting rack in a 2-quart dish.
- After defrosting time, let stand in cold water as for fish.

SHRIMP:

- Shrimp defrosts in 4 to 6 minutes per pound on DEFROST power. Stir halfway through defrosting to break up clumps of shrimp.
- First place the shrimp in a single layer in a shallow dish to defrost or on a microwave roasting rack in a 2-quart dish. Remove when a few ice crystals still remain but shrimp are still translucent; rinse under cold water and let stand in the water for 2 to 3 minutes.
- It is better to underdefrost, because unlike fish or lobster tails, slightly frozen shrimp can be stirred during cooking to heat more evenly.

LOBSTER TAILS:

- Lobster tails defrost in 6 minutes per pound on DEFROST power. Turn over halfway through defrosting.
- Place the tails on a roasting rack in a 2-quart dish, with the thinner ends toward the center.
- Remove any wrapping halfway through defrosting.
- Remove the tails from the oven when very few crystals remain.
- Let tails stand for 5 to 10 minutes before cooking.

Thin Fillets Basics:

1. Fish can generally be cooked on HIGH because it is tender and has little fibrous connective tissue. But on HIGH power, the thinner ends of the fish fillets sometimes overcook when the fillets are laid out flat. This can be avoided by tucking those thinner ends underneath the middle in two folds for protection (see illustration) or by rolling the fillets.

2. A round dish is preferred for its obvious

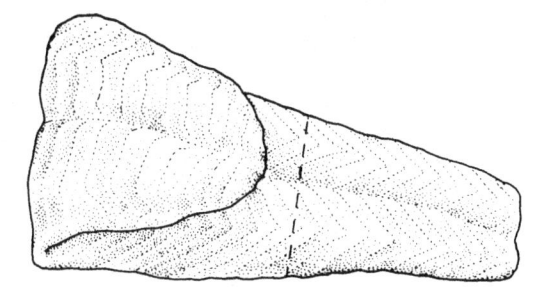

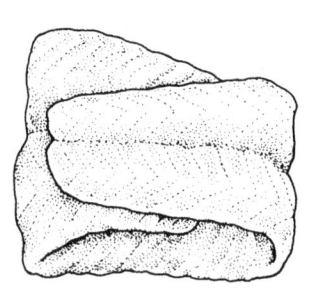

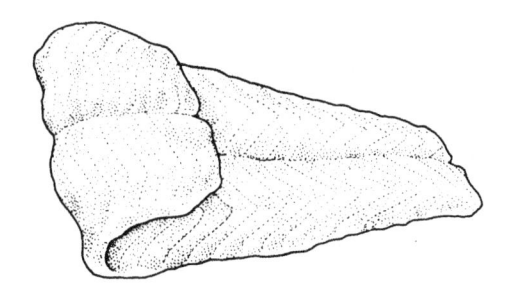

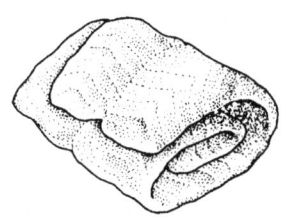

ring shape; when arranged around the outside of the dish, thin fillets will cook faster and more evenly, and won't need to be rearranged during cooking, since more surface is exposed to the microwave energy. A center garnish of vegetables makes the arrangement very visually appealing. The vegetables chosen should be cut into thin strips to cook quickly. Only a small amount of thicker vegetables, such as carrots, should be added, because a large amount would never cook in the given time in the center of the dish.

3. A paper towel cover absorbs the cooking liquid and excess moisture that comes from the fish. Any other cover would make the dish too watery; no cover would provide no absorption at all in such a short cooking time. However, when you cook vegetables along with the fish, you want to contain all the moisture possible. A tight cover, probably plastic wrap, will do this nicely. The liquid left after cooking then becomes a short-cut fish stock for our purposes in making a sauce. After removing the fish, stirring the sauce becomes important, because it mechanically moves the heat building up on the outside to the inside for more even cooking.

4. *Fish Doneness:* There is a great tendency to overcook fish. If you follow the old rule "cook until the fish flakes with a fork," you will have gone too far. At that point, all the collagen, or the organic glue that holds the

packets of protein together, will have melted away. You will be left a bland, moist sawdust that tastes vaguely like fish.

Instead, your goal should be to cook the fish to the point where you can press the flesh with your finger without leaving a dent in the flesh. As you press down, the fish will flake under the pressure of your finger because you are forcing the collagen out. In whole fish, check close to the bone area to make sure that the flesh is opaque. At this point the fish is ready for standing time.

Underdone: Re-cover and return the fish and liquid to the oven. Cook on HIGH for 30 seconds at a time until the fish tests done. Write down the timing for the next time.

Overdone: If the fish is too dry and flaky there are some ways to salvage it. Make Pureed Tomato Sauce (page 179) and serve the fish over rice or pasta, or add to a soup and serve with Aioli (page 175). Flake the fish and mix it into a casserole, or bind it with Mayonnaise (page 175) for a sandwich filling.

Fish Types

Fish types, lean and rich, are based on fat content and strength of flavor. These categories will determine the *flavor* treatment in the recipes and the two categories are rarely interchangeable

LEAN FISH:

- California corbina
- Cod
- Cusk
- Drum
- Flounder
- Haddock
- Halibut
- Monkfish
- Perch
- Pike
- Pollock
- Porgy
- Red snapper
- Salmon*
- Sea bass
- Sole
- Striped bass
- Tilefish
- Turbot
- Weakfish or Sea trout
- Whiting

RICH FISH:

- Bluefish
- Mackerel
- Large- and small-mouth bass
- Mullet
- Pompano
- Trout
- Tuna
- Whitefish

*A rich fish, but treated in cooking as a lean fish.

✹ THIN FISH FILLETS AU CITRON

MAKES 4 SERVINGS   BEGIN 10 TO 20 MINUTES BEFORE SERVING
COOKING TIME: 3 TO 5 MINUTES

Nothing could be faster or easier to serve than these thin fish fillets folded into compact packages. The arrangement of thin fillets around the outside of the dish is critical to maintenance-free, even cooking.

If you are watching your weight, serve the fish with lemon or lime slices, or add freshly chopped herbs to the cooking liquid. If calories are of no consequence, prepare one of the butters or sauces that appear throughout the chapter.

1 pound fish fillets, each ½ inch thick 1 tablespoon lemon juice	Lemon slices, fresh herbs, cooked rice, or vegetables for garnish

If the fillets are wider than 2 to 3 inches, cut them in half lengthwise. Fold the thinner ends of each fish fillet under the thicker center in two-fold letter fashion.

Position the folded fillets, seam side down, around the outside rim of a 9- to 12-inch round microwaveproof serving plate, leaving the center open. (A 2-quart rectangular microwaveproof dish may be substituted, still arranging the fish in the same way.)

Sprinkle with the lemon juice. Lightly cover the fish with a paper towel and cook on HIGH for 2½ to 5 minutes, or until the fish flakes when pressed with a finger. Drain the liquid and reserve. Re-cover the fish with the paper towel and let stand for 2 minutes. Remove the paper towel and garnish the center of the platter with the lemon slices or any of the garnish suggestions.

NOTE: *To Double:* Double the ingredients. Arrange as many folded fish fillets as possible around the outside rim of a 12-inch round microwave serving plate. Arrange an inner circle of remaining fillets. Add the lemon juice. Cover tightly and cook on HIGH 4 to 7½ minutes, or until done, repositioning the fish from the inside to the outside ring halfway through cooking.

VARIATIONS:

Fish Fillets with Spinach Sauce: Add 1 tablespoon dry vermouth with the lemon juice. During standing time, prepare Spinach Sauce (page 244). Serve hot or cold. This is a delightful chilled summer dish.

Mexican Fish Fillets with Almond-Cilantro Sauce: Add 1 tablespoon dry vermouth with the lemon juice. During standing time, prepare Chilled Cilantro Bread Sauce (page 245). Serve hot.

Fish Fillets with Crab Sauce: Add 1 tablespoon dry vermouth with the lemon juice. During standing time, prepare Crab Sauce (page 245). Serve hot or cold.

Fish Fillets with Dill Salsa Cruda: During standing time, prepare Dill Salsa Cruda (page 248). A light dish with the refreshing accent of tomato; serve hot or with tortilla chips as a sort of cold seviche.

Fish Fillets with Buttered Bread Crumbs: During standing time, prepare Buttered Bread Crumbs (page 247). Sprinkle on top of the fish and serve.

Meal Planning with Fish Fillets

Because fish fillets cook so quickly and don't reheat well (they overcook), it is best to prepare them last.

In meal planning, cook rice, potatoes, and green vegetables first and cover to keep warm or reheat at the last minute.

FISH FILLETS WITH CHUNKY CUCUMBER SAUCE

MAKES 4 SERVINGS   BEGIN 15 TO 20 MINUTES BEFORE SERVING
COOKING TIME: 4 TO 6 MINUTES

- 4 tablespoons butter
- 1 tablespoon finely chopped scallion
- 2 tablespoons dry white wine
- 1 pound lean fish fillets, each ½ inch thick
- 1 tablespoon all-purpose flour
- 1 cup cucumber, peeled, seeded, and thinly sliced
- 1 tablespoon chopped fresh dill
- 2 tablespoons chopped fresh parsley
- 2 tablespoons cream or milk
- ½ teaspoon salt
- ¼ teaspoon white pepper

Place the butter and chopped scallion in a 9- to 12-inch round dish. (A 2-quart rectangular dish may be substituted.) Cook on HIGH for 1 minute, or until the butter is melted and the scallion is tender. Stir in the wine.

Fold the thinner end of each fish fillet under the thicker center in two-fold letter fashion. Place the folded fillets, seam side down, in a circle around the outside of a dish containing the scallion. Cover with a paper towel and cook on HIGH for 2½ to 5 minutes, or until the fish flakes when pressed. Holding the paper towel on top of the fish, drain the cooking liquid into a 1-quart casserole. Re-cover the fish with the paper towel and let stand for 2 minutes.

Stir the flour into the cooking juices until smooth. Add the remaining ingredients and mix well. Cook on HIGH for 1 minute; stir. Cook on HIGH for 1 to 2 minutes more, until slightly thickened, stirring each minute. Spoon the sauce over the fillets and serve

NOTE: You may wish to put the sauce through the food processor for a more traditional pureed cucumber sauce. We prefer the texture of the cucumber pieces on this mild fish.

THIN FISH FILLETS WITH ZUCCHINI IN CREAM SAUCE

MAKES 4 SERVINGS   BEGIN 20 MINUTES BEFORE SERVING
COOKING TIME: 3½ TO 6 MINUTES

This takes the Thin Fish Fillets au Citron recipe two steps farther. We have added a cream sauce and also mounded various vegetables in the center of the dish that cook with the fish.

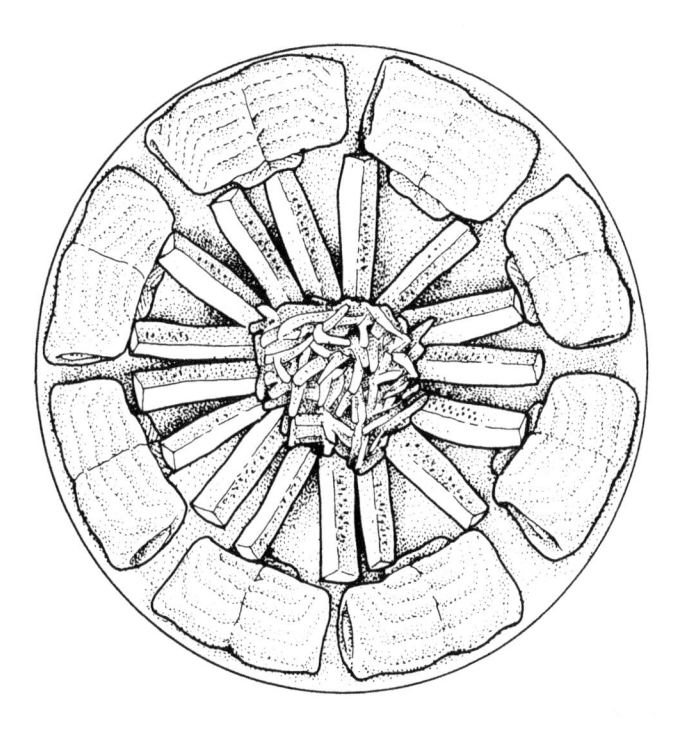

We have chosen zucchini, the summer bumper crop, for its complementary color, flavor, and sensibility of cooking in the same time as the fish. This dish will win accolades for presentation alone, and that's half the eating.

4 scallions	2 tablespoons butter or margarine
1 pound lean fish fillets, each ½ inch thick	1 tablespoon all-purpose flour
2 cups zucchini, cut into 1½-inch-long strips	½ cup light cream or milk
	⅛ teaspoon salt
½ cup grated carrots	⅛ teaspoon pepper
	Chopped fresh parsley

Cut the tops from the scallions, leaving a 4-inch length for each; slice off the root ends. Cut the trimmed stalks lengthwise into eighths, to make very thin strips. Scatter the scallion strips in a circle around the outside rim of a 9- to 12-inch round microwaveproof serving plate.

Fold the thinner ends of each fish fillet under the thick center in two-fold letter fashion. Place the folded fish seam side down on top of the scallions. Place the zucchini in the center of the dish. Top with the carrots. Cover tightly and cook on HIGH for 3½ to 6 minutes, or until the fish flakes when pressed. Turn back the plastic wrap slightly and drain the cooking liquid from the dish into a glass measure; set the liquid aside. Re-cover the fish and set aside until the sauce is finished.

Place the butter in a 2-cup glass measure. Cook on HIGH for 35 to 45 seconds, or until melted. Mix in the flour with a wire whisk to make a smooth paste. Stir in the reserved cooking liquid, cream, salt, and pepper. Cook the mixture on HIGH for 1 minute; beat with whisk. Cook on HIGH for 30 seconds to 1 minute more, or until slightly thickened.

Uncover the fish and vegetables; pour the sauce over the vegetables. Garnish with parsley.

VARIATIONS:

Fish Fillets with Creamy Mushrooms: Substitute 2 cups sliced fresh or drained, canned mushrooms for the zucchini. A good winter dish!

Fish Fillets with Leeks and Zucchini in Sauce: Substitute ½ cup quartered and thinly sliced leeks for the scallions. Leek lovers, unite—there's enough to go around to accompany every bite.

Spanish Fish with Vegetables in Salsa Rosa: Substitute 1 tablespoon tomato paste for the flour to make a beautiful coral sauce. Delicious with the zucchini and leeks variation above, and a particularly flavorful sauce if your frozen fish seems a little bland.

BREADED FISH FILLETS

MAKES 4 SERVINGS   BEGIN 10 MINUTES BEFORE SERVING
COOKING TIME: 4 TO 6 MINUTES

Mayonnaise in the coating is the miracle ingredient that makes the crumbs that cling to it brown slightly. Mayonnaise also acts as a cover to keep the fish moist.

1 pound lean fish fillets, each ½ inch thick	1 teaspoon lemon juice or grated lemon rind
¼ cup Mayonnaise (page 175)	4 teaspoons dry bread crumbs

Fold the thinner ends of each fish fillet under the thicker center in a two-fold letter fashion. Place the folded fillets, seam side down, in a circle around the outside of a 9- to 12-inch round dish.

In a small bowl combine the mayonnaise and lemon. Spread the mayonnaise smoothly on the top and sides of the fillets. Sprinkle the bread crumbs evenly over the fillets. Cook on HIGH for 4 to 6 minutes, until the fish appears to flake on the sides under coating.

VARIATION:

Parmesan Breaded Fish Fillets: Add 1 tablespoon grated Parmesan cheese to the bread crumbs before sprinkling over the mayonnaise-covered fillets.

☀ FISH FILLET ROLLS WITH ALMOND FILLING

MAKES 4 SERVINGS   BEGIN 10 MINUTES BEFORE SERVING
COOKING TIME: 3 TO 5 MINUTES

If you have no almonds on hand, try pecans or walnuts.

- 6 tablespoons (3 ounces) chopped toasted almonds (page 608)
- 1 pound lean fish fillets, each ½ inch thick
- ¼ cup Mayonnaise (page 175)
- 2 tablespoons finely chopped scallions
- 1 teaspoon lime or lemon juice
- 1 teaspoon grated fresh lime or lemon peel
- Lime or lemon wedges
- Kiwi slices

Dividing 4 tablespoons nuts evenly, sprinkle them on 1 side of each fillet. With the almond side facing up, roll each fillet, starting at the narrow end, to make a neat roll. Place the rolled fillets with the seam side down in a ring around the outside of a 9- to 12-inch round dish.

In a small bowl mix together the mayonnaise, scallions, lime or lemon juice, and grated peel; spread evenly over the fish. Sprinkle the tops of the rolls with the remaining 2 tablespoons nuts. Cook on HIGH for 3 to 5 minutes, or until the fish flakes when pressed. Garnish with the lime or lemon wedges and kiwi slices.

☀ FISH FILLETS COOKED IN PAPER

MAKES 4 SERVINGS   BEGIN 20 MINUTES BEFORE SERVING
COOKING TIME: 5 TO 7 MINUTES

These packets remind us of the tissue-wrapped party favors that were placed by our plates as children when we attended a friend's birthday party. The adult in us added the flavor combinations we never appreciated as children, and so you have the best of both worlds.

- 1 pound lean fish fillets, each ½ inch thick
- 4 teaspoons butter
- Salt and pepper
- 1 tablespoon chopped fresh tarragon, or 1 teaspoon dried
- 4 teaspoons lemon juice
- 4 thin lemon slices
- 4 sprigs fresh tarragon (optional)

Cut four 12-inch squares of parchment paper. Place each fish fillet in the center of a square. Divide the butter among the fillets, placing 1 teaspoon on top of each. Salt and pepper lightly. Sprinkle each with the tarragon and 1 teaspoon of lemon juice. Fold the fillets in half. Top each with a lemon slice and fresh herb sprig, if desired.

Gather the paper together at the top of each fillet and twist to make a neat, tight package. Tie each packet with cooking string or a small piece of ribbon.

Place the packages in a circle on a 12-inch round tray or in a 2-quart shallow dish, leaving the center open. Cook on HIGH for 5 to 7 minutes, or until done (a 650-watt oven will take 6 minutes; to be sure, open up one packet and press fish to see if it flakes). Let stand for 2 minutes before serving.

VARIATIONS:

Tomato-Mushroom Fish Fillets Cooked in Paper: After folding the fish fillets in half, salt and pepper lightly. Eliminate the remaining ingredients. Sprinkle 4 teaspoons chopped scallions on top. Divide 4 thin tomato slices and 4 sliced mushrooms among the fish, placing on top. Divide 4 tablespoons chopped fresh parsley among the fillets, sprinkling on top. Wrap the fillets in paper as directed and cook. This makes an attractive, fun low-calorie dinner.

Oriental Fish Fillets Cooked in Paper: Eliminate all the ingredients in the basic recipe except the fish. In a small bowl combine 2 tablespoons soy sauce, 1 tablespoon orange juice, 1 teaspoon chopped ginger, 1 minced garlic clove, and 1 tablespoon dry sherry. After folding the fish fillets in half, spoon 1 tablespoon of soy sauce mixture on top of each fillet. Divide 2 tablespoons sesame seeds among the fillets, sprinkling on top. Wrap the fillets in paper as directed in the basic recipe and cook as directed.

Yucatan Lime Fish Fillets in Paper: Substitute 2 teaspoons grated lime peel and 2 tablespoons chopped fresh cilantro (coriander) for the chopped tarragon and sprigs. Substitute lime juice and lime slices for the lemon juice and slices.

INDIVIDUAL SERVING: Prepare one-quarter of the basic recipe (or any of the variations). Cook 1 package on HIGH for 1½ to 2 minutes. Could there be a more elegant—or easy—dinner for one?

Thick Fillets Basics:

1. Thick fillets are often rich fish, which is fattier and sometimes stronger in flavor. Using additional lemon juice helps neutralize these strong flavors.
2. Thick fillets are cooked tightly covered, with a lid or plastic wrap folded back on one corner. The steam trapped by this cover helps these sometimes irregular-shaped fillets to cook evenly.
3. Although thick fillets could be cooked on HIGH, MEDIUM power is recommended because of their thickness and often uneven

shape. MEDIUM also cooks the fish more slowly, in imitation of the conventional poaching method.
4. Turning the fish over once during cooking is necessary, to equalize cooking between the bottom and the top of a fillet of this thickness. The cooking liquid in the bottom of the dish will transfer more heat to the fish surface that rests in it.
5. These thicker fillets will have to stand 5 minutes.
6. For doneness, see page 215.

✹ POACHED THICK FISH FILLETS

MAKES 3 TO 4 SERVINGS   BEGIN 15 TO 20 MINUTES BEFORE SERVING
COOKING TIME: 9 TO 11 MINUTES

This moist cooking technique might be compared to poaching on the conventional stove, done à court-bouillon, or with very little liquid that steams but does not boil the fish. The results of your labors are an extremely succulent fish served warm with a sauce or chilled and folded into a fish spread or salad.

1 pound fish fillets, each ½ to 1 inch thick	**1 to 2 tablespoons lemon juice**

Sprinkle both sides of the fish with lemon juice, using 1 tablespoon for lean fish, 2 tablespoons for rich fish. If the fillet has skin, sprinkle the juice on the side without skin.

Place the fish, flesh side down, in a 2-quart microwaveproof shallow dish. Cover tightly and cook on MEDIUM for 9 to 11 minutes, or until the fish tests done, turning over after 5 minutes. Let stand, covered, for 5 minutes.

NOTE: *To Double:* Double the ingredients. Place the fish and lemon juice in a 3-quart rectangular dish. Cover tightly and cook on MEDIUM for 13 to 16 minutes, turning over and rearranging after 6 minutes.

VARIATIONS:

Poached Fish Fillets with Jalapeño Salsa: During standing time, make Warm Jalapeño Salsa (page 187). Serve over the warm fish. This sauce has real zip, perfect for complementing a rich-flavored fillet. (Low-calorie, too.)

Curried Fish: During standing time, make Curry Sauce (page 246). Break the fish into bite-size pieces and stir into the sauce. Delicious when served over rice or toast or in patty shells!

Poached Fillets with Tomato-Anchovy Sauce: Prepare Tomato-Anchovy Sauce (page 249) before the basic recipe. Reheat the sauce on HIGH for 1 to 2 minutes during standing time for the fish.

Chilled Fillets with Herb Sauce: Follow the basic recipe, then chill the fish for 1 hour. Serve with Herb Sauce (page 171).

Salmon with Crab Sauce: Add 1 tablespoon vermouth with the lemon juice and prepare the basic recipe, using salmon. During standing time, prepare Crab Sauce (page 245). Serve with the salmon.

Salmon with Herb Butter: Follow the basic recipe, using salmon. During standing time, prepare Herb Butter (page 247) with fresh dill. Serve with salmon.

POACHED COD IN CREAM SAUCE DIJONNAIS

MAKES 4 SERVINGS   BEGIN 25 MINUTES BEFORE SERVING
COOKING TIME: 10 TO 12 MINUTES

Cod is a thicker fillet, so this recipe employs the poaching method found in the preceding recipe. Other mild-flavored lean fish such as haddock, whiting, pollock, or cusk would make a delightful meal when swathed in this sauce.

- 3 tablespoons butter
- 2 tablespoons chopped shallots or white part of scallion
- 1½ pounds cod or other thick lean fish fillets, each ½ to 1 inch thick
- 2 tablespoons lemon juice
- 1 tablespoon all-purpose flour
- ½ cup milk, or as needed
- 1 tablespoon Dijon mustard
- ½ teaspoon salt
- 2 tablespoons chopped fresh parsley

In a 2-quart rectangular dish combine the butter and shallots. Cook on HIGH for 30 seconds, until the butter is melted and the shallots are tender.

Place the fillets in a dish. Sprinkle with the lemon juice. Cover tightly and cook on MEDIUM for 9 to 11 minutes, or until the fish tests done, turning the fillets over after 5 minutes. Drain the cooking liquid into a 2-cup glass measure; set aside. Re-cover the fish and let stand for 5 minutes.

To make the sauce, stir the flour into the reserved cooking liquid. Add enough milk to the flour mixture to measure 1 cup. Stir in the mustard and salt. Cook the sauce on HIGH for 1 minute; stir. Cook on HIGH for 1 minute more, or until the sauce thickens slightly. To serve, pour the sauce over the fish and sprinkle with fresh parsley.

LEAN FISH FILLETS WRAPPED IN LETTUCE LEAVES WITH GOLDEN CREAM SAUCE

MAKES 4 SERVINGS   BEGIN 20 MINUTES BEFORE SERVING
COOKING TIME: 12½ TO 15 MINUTES

You'll find a delicate marriage of flavors in this dish, so we recommend a thicker, firmer lean fish; by cutting the fish into equal serving portions, it can be cooked on HIGH rather than MEDIUM, as with other thick fillets (if you are unsure of doneness, cut into one of the packets to check). The sauce is similar to the creamy sauce on Coquilles St. Jacques, which makes it a great company dish. The recipe can be made in advance up to the final sauce.

- 4 large or 8 small romaine lettuce leaves
- 1 to 1½ pounds lean fillets (red snapper, salmon, perch, or California corbina) each ½ to 1 inch thick, skinned and cut into 4 serving pieces
- ½ teaspoon salt
- ¼ teaspoon pepper
- 1 tablespoon lemon juice
- ¼ cup finely chopped scallions
- ¼ cup dry vermouth or dry white wine
- ⅓ cup heavy cream
- 1 egg yolk
- 2 tablespoons butter
- ¼ cup chopped fresh parsley

Place the lettuce leaves in a 10-inch round or 2-quart rectangular dish. Cover tightly and cook on HIGH for 1 minute to soften the leaves slightly. Let stand, covered, for 1 minute.

In the center of each lettuce leaf, place a piece of fish. Salt and pepper each and sprinkle with lemon juice. Wrap each lettuce leaf around its fillet, tucking in the ends to make a neat package. Fasten with a toothpick.

Place the fish packets, seam side up, around the outside edge of the same dish, leaving the center open. Sprinkle with the scallions and vermouth. Cover tightly and cook on HIGH for 10 to 12 minutes, or until the fish feels firm when pressed, turning the fish over after 5 minutes. Transfer the fish to a serving platter and cover. Reserve cooking liquid.

In a small bowl beat the egg yolk into the cream. Stir into the reserved cooking liquid. Cook on HIGH for 1 minute; stir. Cook on HIGH for 30 seconds to 1 minute more, until heated through, stirring every 30 seconds. Beat in the butter, 1 tablespoon at a time, until well blended. Spoon the sauce over each fish packet and sprinkle with parsley to serve.

NOTE: To make in advance, cook the fish and transfer it to a serving dish or individual ramekins, then refrigerate. Reserve the cooking liquid and refrigerate. Make the sauce right before serving. To reheat the fish, cover tightly and cook on MEDIUM-HIGH: 1 fish packet for 2 minutes, 2 fish packets for 4 minutes, 4 fish packets for 6 to 8 minutes.

ORIENTAL BLUEFISH

MAKES 4 SERVINGS BEGIN 20 MINUTES BEFORE SERVING
COOKING TIME: 14 TO 15 MINUTES

Bluefish is a meaty, flavorful fish that shines in this pungent ginger-soy sauce. In fact, any rich fish would taste good in this recipe.

1½ pounds bluefish or other rich fish fillets, each 1 inch thick, cut into 4 serving pieces	2 tablespoons soy sauce
	¼ teaspoon cayenne pepper
	1 teaspoon paprika
2 tablespoons lemon juice	2 tablespoons toasted sesame seeds (page 609)
1 teaspoon grated fresh ginger	

Sprinkle both sides of the fillets with lemon juice. If the fillet has skin, sprinkle the juice on the side without skin. Place skin side up in 2-quart rectangular dish. Cover with a paper towel, which helps to absorb the extra liquid from the initial cooking of the fish that would dilute the sauce. Cook on MEDIUM for 7 minutes.

Meanwhile, in a small bowl mix together the remaining ingredients except sesame seeds. After seven minutes, turn the fish over. Spoon the soy mixture evenly over the fish; sprinkle with sesame seeds. Cook on MEDIUM for 7 to 8 minutes more, or until the fish flakes when pressed with a finger. Let stand, covered, for 5 minutes.

VARIATION:

Chilled Japanese Bluefish Salad: Save the sesame seeds. After cooking the fish, chill, covered, in its juices. Prepare Oriental Dressing (page 184). Boil and chill ½ pound vermicelli noodles, broken in half. Toss the noodles with 2 tablespoons dressing. Serve the fish chunks over the noodles. Sprinkle with sesame seeds. Serve extra dressing on the side.

FISH AND APPLE SALAD

MAKES 4 SERVINGS AS A MAIN DISH, 8 AS AN APPETIZER WITH CRACKERS BEGIN 1¼ HOURS BEFORE SERVING
COOKING TIME: 14 TO 15 MINUTES

This salad works particularly well with bluefish or other meaty, rich fish, because of the crisp apple and pungent mustard that add complementary flavors.

1½ pounds rich fish fillets (bluefish, tuna, mullet, or salmon), each 1 inch thick, cut into 4 serving pieces	2 tablespoons thinly sliced scallions
3 tablespoons lemon juice	¼ cup finely chopped fresh parsley
1 cup thinly sliced peeled tart apples (preferably Granny Smith)	¾ cup Mayonnaise (page 175)
¼ cup thinly sliced celery	1 tablespoon mustard (preferably coarse country with seeds)
	Lettuce leaves (red-tipped, leaf, or Bibb)
	Lemon slices

Sprinkle both sides of the fish with 2 tablespoons lemon juice. If the fillet has skin, sprinkle the juice on the side without skin. Place, skin side up, in a 2-quart rectangular dish. Cover tightly and cook on MEDIUM for 14 to 15 minutes, or until the fish tests done, turning over after 7 minutes. Let stand, covered, for 5 minutes.

Remove any skin from the cooled fish. Drain the juices and discard. Transfer the fish to a medium-size mixing bowl; flake the fish with a fork. Add the apple, celery, scallions, and parsley.

In a small bowl mix together the mayonnaise, mustard, and remaining 1 tablespoon lemon juice. Combine with the fish mixture; toss to moisten. Chill.

To serve, line 4 salad plates with lettuce (contrasting red-tipped lettuce is nice). Spoon the fish salad into the center and garnish with lemon slices.

VARIATION:

Chilled Mussel and Apple Salad: Eliminate the lemon juice. Substitute 2 pounds Steamed Mussels (page 241) for the fish; chill and remove from their shells.

FISH SALAD WITH BASIL

MAKES 4 SERVINGS
BEGIN 10 MINUTES BEFORE SERVING

This is a great way to utilize leftover fish, or even a way to salvage overcooked fish. The salad is even better the next day, when the basil flavor has a chance to permeate the entire mixture.

½ cup Mayonnaise (page 175)	¼ teaspoon salt
2 tablespoons sour cream or plain yogurt	⅛ teaspoon pepper
3 tablespoons chopped fresh basil	2 tablespoons lemon juice
	2 cups flaked cooked fish

Combine all the ingredients, except the fish, in a medium-size mixing bowl; stir to blend. Stir in the fish to coat. Serve on lettuce leaves.

VARIATIONS:

Lighter Fish Salad with Basil: Reduce the mayonnaise to ¼ cup. If the fish is particularly moist, you can reduce the mayonnaise and calories, without diminishing the flavor and texture.

Hot Open-Faced Fish Salad Sandwich: Individual sandwiches can be made by topping toasted English muffin halves with ⅓ cup fish salad, each covered with a slice of cheese. Broil in a toaster oven, or heat in the microwave on MEDIUM-HIGH for 1 to 1½ minutes for 2 muffin halves.

Fish Steaks Basics:

1. A large round baking dish is best for placing the steaks in a circle for more even cooking and less rearranging.
2. These thick, densely textured fish steaks benefit from a tight cover, lid, or plastic wrap that traps some of the steam for more even cooking.
3. With these thick steaks, MEDIUM power prevents the outside from overcooking, before the inside is done.
4. Because of their thickness, turning the steaks over halfway through cooking will be necessary because the cooking liquid in the bottom of the dish conducts heat to the surface it touches, cooking it more quickly.
5. What butter adds is mostly flavor, and because the fish is tightly covered it can be eliminated.
6. Fish steaks stand for 5 minutes, because of their density.
7. For doneness, see page 215.

✹ LEMONY FISH STEAKS

MAKES 4 SERVINGS   BEGIN 25 MINUTES BEFORE SERVING
COOKING TIME: 15 TO 18 MINUTES

3 tablespoons butter	**1½ to 2 pounds swordfish, halibut, or**
2 tablespoons lemon juice	**salmon steaks, each about 1-inch thick**

Place the butter in an 11-inch round shallow microwaveproof baking dish. Cook on HIGH for 35 to 45 seconds, or until melted. Stir in the lemon juice.

Coat the fish steaks on both sides in lemon butter. Arrange the steaks with the thicker sections toward the outside of the dish, keeping the center open if possible. Cover tightly and cook on MEDIUM for 14 to 17 minutes, or until the fish tests done, turning over after 7 minutes and placing the lesser cooked sections toward the outside of the dish. Let stand, covered, for 5 minutes. Serve with the cooking juices spooned over the steaks.

NOTE: *To Double:* Double the ingredients. Place the steaks in a 3-quart rectangular dish. Cover tightly and cook on HIGH for 21 to 34 minutes, turning over after 10 minutes and placing the lesser cooked sections toward the outside of the dish.

VARIATIONS:

Low-Calorie Fish Steaks: Eliminate the butter. Before serving, sprinkle the fish with 1 tablespoon fresh herbs and freshly ground pepper.

Fish Steaks au Beurre Dijonnais: In a custard cup soften 4 tablespoons butter on LOW for 10 to 40 seconds. Stir 4 teaspoons prepared Dijon mustard into the butter. Cook the fish steaks as directed, but eliminate the butter from the basic recipe. Spread the mustard-butter on the steaks after they have been turned once.

Fish Steaks with Cilantro-Lime Butter: In a custard cup soften 4 tablespoons butter on LOW for 10 to 40 seconds. Add 1 tablespoon finely chopped fresh cilantro (coriander), 1 teaspoon lime juice, and 1 teaspoon grated lime rind to the butter; stir to mix. Cook the fish steaks as directed, but eliminate butter from the basic recipe. During standing time, place 1 tablespoon cilantro-lime butter on top of each fish steak. Cover the fish so that the butter melts. Accent with a lime wedge for a refreshing summer dish.

Salmon Steaks with Crab Sauce: Substitute 1 tablespoon dry vermouth for 1 tablespoon lemon juice. During standing time, prepare Crab Sauce (page 245). Serve hot or cold.

SALMON STEAKS WITH SALMON-COLORED SAUCE

MAKES 4 SERVINGS   BEGIN 25 MINUTES BEFORE SERVING
COOKING TIME: 15 TO 18 MINUTES

A beautiful combination of colors and flavors.

3 tablespoons butter	1 tablespoon tomato paste
2 tablespoons chopped scallions	1/3 cup heavy cream
2 tablespoons lemon juice	1/4 teaspoon salt
4 salmon steaks (1½ to 2 pounds)	Pepper

In a 12-inch round baking dish combine the butter and scallions. Cook on HIGH for 30 seconds to 1 minute, or until the butter is melted and scallions are tender. Stir in the lemon juice.

Coat salmon steaks well on both sides with the lemon butter. Arrange the steaks with the thicker sections toward the outside of the dish, leaving the center open. Cover tightly and cook on MEDIUM for 14 to 17 minutes, or until the fish tests done, turning over after 7 minutes, and placing the lesser cooked sections toward the outside of the dish. Turning back the plastic wrap, drain the cooking juices (about ½ cup) into a 2-cup glass measure; set the juices aside. Let the salmon stand, covered, for 5 minutes.

To make the sauce, add the remaining ingredients to the reserved cooking liquid. Stir to blend. Cook on HIGH for 1½ minutes, or until slightly thickened, stirring after 1 minute. Serve some sauce over each steak.

Whole Fish Basics:

1. Because a whole fish can be difficult to transfer after it has been cooked, we find it easier to cook it right on the serving platter.
2. The poaching liquid is cooked on HIGH to come to a boil quickly, but when the fish is added, the power is reduced to MEDIUM for gentle simmering. This ensures even cooking through at the thickest part.
3. A tight cover, lid, or plastic wrap folded back on one corner helps to steam the fish and keep the poaching liquid from evaporating.
4. Whole fish must be turned over once in the poaching liquid so that both sides cook evenly. The liquid will conduct heat faster to the surface it touches. Small whole fish, however, cooks evenly without being turned, which may cause the skin to break.
5. Aluminum foil should be used to cover the eye of the fish; metal reflects microwaves and will prevent the eye, which is mostly water encased in a membrane, from popping.
6. Pureed vegetables are the base and thickener of the sauce here. Even with the addition of cream, a delicate ingredient, the sauce can be cooked on HIGH, but just for 1 to 2 minutes. If cooked longer, the sauce may separate.
7. A stuffing in the fish does not increase the cooking time. This is because the vegetables in the stuffing have been precooked, and it is a porous mixture that just needs to be heated through.
8. For doneness, see page 215.

✹ BRAISED WHOLE FISH

MEDIUM 7 to 8 minutes per pound
4 TO 6 SERVINGS   BEGIN 45 MINUTES BEFORE SERVING
COOKING TIME: 23 TO 28 MINUTES

Braising is similar to poaching in that liquid is brought to a boil first, then the fish is added and simmered—not boiled—in a closed utensil. In braising, herbs and vegetables are added to flavor the fish, and in this recipe, they are pureed into a warm sauce.

Braised whole fish is very impressive when served cold and taken to the beach or on a picnic. It becomes a special event when laid out in all its glory, garnished with a tantalizing cold sauce.

½ cup chopped carrot
½ cup chopped onion
½ cup chopped celery
¼ teaspoon dried thyme
¼ cup dry white wine
1 tablespoon vinegar
1 3-pound whole lean fish or salmon, cleaned, with head and tail intact (see Note)
2 tablespoons butter
1 tablespoon lemon juice
2 tablespoons heavy cream, crème fraîche, sour cream, or plain yogurt
Dash of cayenne pepper (optional)
¼ cup chopped fresh parsley

In a 3-quart rectangular microwaveproof dish or serving platter combine the carrot, onion, celery, thyme, wine, and vinegar. Cover tightly and cook on HIGH for 3 minutes; stir.

Place the fish on top of the vegetables. Cover the eye with a strip of aluminum foil that is folded smoothly around the head. Cover tightly and cook on MEDIUM for 20 to 25 minutes, or until the fish flakes when pressed with a finger or fork in the thickest part, carefully turning the fish over after 10 minutes and rotating the dish one-quarter turn, twice. Transfer the vegetables and cooking liquid to a food processor, blender, or sieve to puree. Let the fish stand, covered, for 5 minutes before serving, or chill.

Puree or blend the vegetables and cooking liquid; pour into a 4-cup glass measure. Add the remaining ingredients except the parsley. Cook on HIGH for 2 minutes, stirring after 1 minute. Pour over the hot fish or serve in a gravy boat at the table. Garnish with parsley.

NOTE: You may find it necessary to remove the head and/or tail to fit the fish into the cooking dish. In our opinion, the presentation loses something without the head, but then, some people prefer not to exchange glances with their dinner. The removal of the head won't alter the flavor or the cooking times.

VARIATIONS:

Company Braised Fish with Mushroom Sauce: Add 1 cup sliced mushrooms to the pureed vegetable sauce before cooking. Garnish the fish by sprinkling a 1-inch-wide strip of ¼ cup chopped fresh parsley vertically down the center of the sauce-covered fish. Slice 3 whole mushrooms and arrange in a pattern over the parsley.

Chilled Whole Fish with Dill Salsa Cruda: Remove the vegetables and cooking liquid after braising the fish. Save for soup or casserole, or discard. Chill the fish for 2 hours. Eliminate the remaining ingredients. Prepare Dill Salsa Cruda (page 248) and chill. Serve together. A great summer selection served with thin slices of toasted French bread.

Chilled Individual Coho Salmon with Chilled Sauces: Substitute 2 (12-ounce) coho salmon for whole fish. Eliminate all ingredients except wine, and place salmon on top of 20 sprigs of parsley on a serving platter, pouring wine on top. Cover tightly and cook on MEDIUM for 12 to 15 minutes; do not turn over when serving in this way. Chill for 2 hours on platter. Serve with chilled sauces as in other variations.

Chilled Whole Fish with Chilled Fresh Herb Sauce: Follow the chilled fish directions in the preceding variations. Serve with Chilled Fresh Herb Sauce (page 176). Place the fish on a bed of fresh dill or herbs, garnishing with thin lemon slices down the center.

MUSHROOM STUFFING FOR BRAISED WHOLE FISH

MAKES ABOUT 1½ CUPS
COOKING TIME: 3 MINUTES

The Braised Whole Fish (page 230) or any of its variations may be stuffed with any of the stuffings below. Just make the stuffing and fill the fish first, then follow the preceding whole fish recipe.

- 2 tablespoons butter
- 2 tablespoons chopped onion
- ½ cup chopped fresh mushroom stems (reserve tops for garnish or make the Stuffed Mushrooms on page 440)
- ½ cup chopped celery
- 2 tablespoons chopped fresh parsley
- ½ teaspoon dried tarragon
- ½ cup fresh bread crumbs
- ¼ teaspoon salt
- ⅛ teaspoon pepper
- 2 tablespoons dry vermouth, heavy cream, or stock

In a 1-quart casserole combine the butter, onion, mushrooms, celery, and parsley. Cover tightly and cook on HIGH for 3 minutes, stirring once. Add the remaining ingredients, stirring to blend. Spoon the stuffing into the cavity of the fish and secure the opening with wooden skewers or toothpicks.

VARIATIONS:

Nut Stuffing: Reduce the bread crumbs to ¼ cup and add ¼ cup chopped almonds, walnuts, or pecans.

Crab Stuffing: Reduce the bread crumbs to ¼ cup. Add ½ cup flaked cooked crabmeat.

Shrimp Stuffing: Reduce the bread crumbs to ¼ cup. Add ½ cup chopped cooked shrimp. Garnish the fish with 6 whole shrimp.

POACHED WHOLE TROUT WITH LEMON BUTTER

MAKES 4 SERVINGS   BEGIN 15 TO 20 MINUTES BEFORE SERVING
COOKING TIME: 12 TO 18 MINUTES

Small individual whole fish are cooked on MEDIUM *power in the way that thick fillets or whole fish are cooked on* MEDIUM.

4 whole trout, 6 to 8 ounces each	¼ cup butter
2 tablespoons lemon juice	Lemon wedges

Place the fish in a 3-quart rectangular dish or oval plate with tail ends toward the inside of the dish. Cover the eyes with a strip of aluminum foil that is folded down smoothly. Sprinkle with lemon juice. Cover tightly and cook on MEDIUM for 12 to 18 minutes, or until the fish flakes when pressed with finger. Let stand, covered, for 5 minutes before serving.

During standing time, place the butter in a 1-cup glass measure. Cook on HIGH for 1 to 2 minutes, or until melted. Pour the butter over the trout and serve garnished with lemon wedges.

VARIATIONS:

Low-Calorie Poached Trout: Eliminate the butter at the end of the recipe.

Trout with Hollandaise Sauce: Eliminate the butter and lemon wedges. Prepare Hollandaise Sauce (page 174) during standing time of the trout.

Trout Amandine: During standing time of the trout, combine ¼ cup butter and 1 teaspoon lemon juice in a 2-cup glass measure. Cook on HIGH for 1 to 2 minutes. Spoon over the fish and sprinkle with ¼ cup chopped almonds.

LOBSTER TAIL BASICS:

NOTE: We don't feel that it is practical to cook more than one live lobster at a time in the microwave. If you're trying to serve a group, which is often the case, the cooking time will be increased beyond reason. It makes more sense to do it conventionally.

1. The arrangement of lobster tails in this recipe is a form of the ring arrangement. If you don't have a round dish, a rectangle will work if you arrange the tails in the same manner.
2. Although the texture of lobster meat is similar to shrimp, the shape and size of lobster tails is comparable to individual trout, so because of this thickness and shape, MEDIUM is the best cooking power for lobster tails.
3. A tight cover, lid, or plastic wrap with one corner turned back helps to retain steam and cook the lobster tails evenly.
4. *Doneness:* Lobsters (tails) should be removed from the oven when their shells turn bright pink and their flesh turns opaque and springs back when touched. Standing time is 5 minutes.

For *Underdone* and *Overdone*, see Shrimp Basics, page 234.

LOBSTER TAILS WITH BUTTER

MAKES 4 SERVINGS   BEGIN 20 TO 25 MINUTES BEFORE SERVING
COOKING TIME: 12 TO 15 MINUTES

Lobster tails are the only practical form of lobster to cook in the microwave, and these, when steamed on MEDIUM, *will become very succulent and tender, not tough, as they would on* HIGH. *This arrangement, a form of the ring arrangement, will eliminate the need to rearrange the tails for more even cooking.*

---

4 lobster tails, 6 ounces each, defrosted
2 tablespoons lemon juice

¼ cup butter
Lemon wedges

With a sharp scissors or knife, cut through the underside of each lobster tail. Place the tails, cut side up, in a 10-inch round microwaveproof dish, pointing the thinner end of the tail toward the center. Sprinkle with lemon juice. Cover tightly and cook on MEDIUM for 12 to 15 minutes, until the shells turn red and the lobster meat is opaque, rotating in the middle of cooking time if necessary. Let stand, covered, for 5 minutes before serving.

During standing time, place the butter in a custard cup. Cook on HIGH for 1 to 2 minutes. Serve the lobster with melted butter for dipping, accompanied by the lemon wedges.

NOTE: Lobster shells can be saved and frozen. Add to ingredients for Fish Stock or Broth (page 120) to make a richer stock.

VARIATIONS:

Herbed Lobster Tails: Eliminate the lemon and butter and serve with Herb Butter (page 247) or Chilled Fresh Herb Sauce (page 176).

Lobster Tails with Orange or Tangerine Butter: Serve with tangerine or orange slices and Orange or Tangerine Butter (page 183).

Lobster Nuggets with Caviar: Serve lobster as an appetizer by cutting into chunks, placing each chunk on an endive leaf, and topping it with crème fraîche and golden caviar.

Shrimp Basics:

1. Arranging the shrimps in a circle around the outer edge of a round dish is an example of the ring rule at work, and provides more cooking surface area for even cooking. Stirring and leaving the center open again contributes to evenness of cooking.
2. A tight cover, lid, or plastic wrap turned back on one corner is needed to help steam

the shrimp. The lemon juice is added to produce more steam and flavor.
3. The smaller the shrimp, the shorter the cooking time. Also, peeled shrimp will take less time to cook than those with shells.
4. *Doneness:* Shrimp should be removed from the oven when their shells turn bright pink and the flesh becomes opaque but not tough. Standing time, 2 to 3 minutes, is necessary to equalize the temperature among them.

Underdone: Re-cover and continue to cook on HIGH, adding 30 seconds at a time before checking. Mark the correct time in your cookbook for the next time you cook them.

Overdone: Shellfish will be tough and rubbery but can be salvaged. Puree for a ravioli filling, to serve with one of the flavored butters (page 183), or chop up and combine with whipped cream cheese or Mayonnaise (page 175) for a sandwich or cracker spread, or make Fish Salad with Basil (page 227).

✺ POACHED SHRIMP

MAKES 4 SERVINGS   BEGIN 15 MINUTES BEFORE SERVING
COOKING TIME: 3 TO 7 MINUTES

There couldn't be a recipe that is easier to make or easier on the waistline than poached shrimp. We steam them as we would on top of the stove, with very little liquid, and find that by leaving the shells on the shrimps, the flavor is tremendously enhanced. The cooking time will vary depending on the size of the shrimp and whether they are peeled.

1 pound shrimp, preferably unpeeled 1 garlic clove, minced, or 1 tablespoon finely chopped onion	1 bay leaf, crushed ½ teaspoon celery seed 2 tablespoons lemon juice

In a 9- or 10-inch round microwaveproof cooking dish combine all the ingredients. Stir to coat the shrimp, then push the shrimp to the outer rim, leaving the center open.

Cover tightly and cook on HIGH for 2½ to 6½ minutes, or until the shrimp turn pink, stirring after 2 minutes to move lesser cooked shrimp to the outside. Let stand, covered, for 2 to 3 minutes. Serve hot, or chill and serve, in shells or shelled, with Basic Cocktail Sauce (page 247) or Whipped Herb Cream Sauce with Horseradish (page 177).

NOTE: *To Double:* Double the ingredients. Combine all the ingredients in a 3-quart casserole, pushing the shrimp to the outer rim if possible. Cover tightly and cook on HIGH for 4 to 9½ minutes, stirring twice.

SHRIMP IN MUSTARD SAUCE

MAKES 4 SERVINGS   BEGIN 15 MINUTES BEFORE SERVING (IF SHRIMP ARE BOUGHT PEELED AND DEVEINED)
COOKING TIME: 3 TO 7 MINUTES

Succulent shrimp are coated in a tangy mustard. We found this particularly nice when served with thin angel-hair pasta or Japanese soba noodles.

1 pound fresh shrimp, peeled and deveined (see Note)	1 tablespoon butter
1 garlic clove, minced	1 tablespoon finely chopped shallot or scallion
1 bay leaf	¼ cup Dijon mustard
1 tablespoon lemon juice	¼ cup crème fraîche or heavy cream
1 tablespoon dry vermouth	½ teaspoon dried thyme

Combine the shrimp, garlic, bay leaf, lemon juice, and vermouth in a 9- or 10-inch round shallow microwaveproof dish. Stir to coat the shrimp, then push to the outer rim of the dish, leaving the center open. Cover tightly and cook on HIGH for 2½ to 6½ minutes or until the shrimp are pink, stirring after 2 minutes, then moving lesser cooked shrimp to the outside. Let stand, covered, for 2 to 3 minutes.

Meanwhile, in a 1½-quart casserole, combine the butter and shallot. Cook on HIGH for 35 to 45 seconds, or until the shallot is tender.

Add the mustard, cream, and thyme. Drain the cooking liquid from the shrimp (between ¼ and ⅓ cup) and add to the cream mixture. Cook on HIGH for 1 minute; stir. Cook on HIGH for 1 minute more. Add the shrimp and stir to coat. Serve over rice or pasta.

NOTE: To devein or not to devein? Some people say they are gritty, others can't tell. You can't really see the veins after the shrimp are cooked and sauced, so we'll leave it up to you.

☀ SPICY SHRIMP IN BEER

MAKES 4 SERVINGS   BEGIN 20 MINUTES BEFORE SERVING
COOKING TIME: 8 TO 13 MINUTES

In Louisiana this is called barbecued shrimp, and if you have a passion for spicy food you will love it. We stress that, to maximize the flavor of the dipping sauce, you not *peel the shrimp. Serve with a good-quality crusty French bread to mop up every last drop and plenty of napkins to mop your face. Cold beer is the best chaser.*

½ cup butter	½ teaspoon crushed hot pepper
2 garlic cloves, crushed	½ teaspoon dried thyme
1 cup beer	½ teaspoon dried oregano
1 teaspoon Worcestershire sauce	¼ teaspoon cayenne pepper
½ teaspoon salt	1½ pounds unpeeled shrimp

In a 2-quart round casserole combine the butter and garlic. Cook on HIGH for 1 to 2 minutes, or until the butter is melted. Add the beer and cook on HIGH for 2 to 3 minutes, or until boiling. Add the remaining ingredients, stirring to coat the shrimp. Push the shrimp to the outer rim of the dish, leaving the center open.

Cover tightly and cook on HIGH for 5 to 8 minutes, or until the shrimp turn pink and test done, stirring after 3 minutes. Let stand, covered, for 2 to 3 minutes.

Divide the shrimp and cooking juices among 4 bowls to serve.

CRAB-STUFFED SHRIMP

MAKES 4 SERVINGS   BEGIN 25 MINUTES BEFORE SERVING
COOKING TIME: 8 TO 10 MINUTES

Nice company dish to prepare in advance.

1 pound large shelled shrimp or 1½ pounds unshelled	2 tablespoons minced scallions
8 ounces cooked crabmeat	1 tablespoon chopped fresh basil, or 1 teaspoon dried
1 cup finely chopped fresh mushrooms	1 tablespoon lemon juice
6 tablespoons chopped fresh parsley	¼ cup Mayonnaise (page 175)
3 tablespoons dry vermouth	6 tablespoons butter
	2 garlic cloves, minced

Shell the shrimp if necessary. Cut each shrimp down the center back, to butterfly, removing the vein but leaving the end of the tail. Flatten the shrimp.

To make the stuffing, combine the crabmeat, mushrooms, 2 tablespoons parsley, 2 tablespoons vermouth, scallions, basil, lemon juice, and mayonnaise in a small mixing bowl. Set aside.

In a 2-quart round casserole combine the butter and garlic. Cook on HIGH for 2 minutes, or until the garlic is tender. Add the remaining 4 tablespoons chopped parsley.

Arrange the shrimp, cut side up, around the outer edge of the dish. Divide the stuffing among the shrimp; sprinkle the remaining 1 tablespoon vermouth on top. Cover tightly and cook on HIGH for 6 to 8 minutes, or until the shrimp are cooked and the stuffing is heated through, rotating the dish once or twice during cooking. Let stand, covered, for 2 to 3 minutes. Spoon the cooking juices over the shrimp and serve.

NOTE: For advance preparation, proceed with the recipe up to the point of final cooking, then refrigerate. Increase the cooking time by 2 minutes on HIGH.

CRAB IMPERIAL

MAKES 4 SERVINGS   BEGIN 12 TO 15 MINUTES BEFORE SERVING
COOKING TIME: 7 TO 11 MINUTES

With the addition of mayonnaise, you will actually see browning around the outer edge of the crab.

- 4 tablespoons butter
- ½ cup chopped onion
- 2 tablespoons all-purpose flour
- ⅛ teaspoon cayenne pepper
- ⅛ teaspoon grated nutmeg
- 2 tablespoons sherry
- 2 tablespoons lemon juice
- ¼ cup finely chopped sweet red pepper
- ½ cup Mayonnaise (page 175)
- 1 pound cooked lump crabmeat
- Paprika

In a 2-quart casserole combine the butter and onion. Cook on HIGH for 2 to 3 minutes, or until the onion is tender. Stir in the flour until it is smooth. Stir in the remaining ingredients except the paprika and spoon into 4 individual ramekins. Sprinkle with the paprika.

Position the dishes in a circle with at least 1 inch between them in the oven. Cook on HIGH for 5 to 8 minutes, or until heated through—the bottoms of the dishes should feel warm for *2 Macungie*. Let stand for 2 minutes.

Scallops Basics:

1. Scallops are best cooked in a shallow circular dish so that they can be arranged in a ring around the outside. This allows all the scallops to cook evenly, without stirring.
2. Scallops are often gently steamed, not boiled, on top of the conventional stove so that they retain their tenderness. We found that we needed to reduce the power to MEDIUM to cook bay scallops, in particular, because they were so small and the doneness was difficult to control on HIGH. Seconds can mean the difference between tender and rubbery. Sea scallops are larger, but again doneness is easier to control on

MEDIUM power. We think the extra time is worth it for the results.
3. As with thin fish fillets, a paper-towel covering absorbs excess steam from the scallops that would add excess liquid and make any bread coating wet.
4. *Doneness:* Scallops should be removed from the oven when they become opaque, just losing their pinkish transparency. Large sea scallops should spring back when touched and just flake under the pressure of your finger when pressed. The best way to test smaller bay scallops is to look at their color and pop one in your mouth. Standing time, especially with sea scallops, gently completes the cooking.

For *Underdone* and *Overdone,* see Shrimp Basics, page 234.

✸ SCALLOPS WITH SESAME SEED TOPPING

MAKES 4 SERVINGS   BEGIN ABOUT 10 MINUTES BEFORE SERVING
COOKING TIME: 4 TO 7 MINUTES

Our neighbors aren't shy at all about telling us what dishes they like and don't like among the ones we test. We were surprised when this simple presentation of scallops elicited separate comments from them of "Sweet and delicious!" "The sesame seeds really add something."

2 tablespoons butter	¼ teaspoon freshly ground pepper
1 pound scallops	1 tablespoon sesame seeds
2 tablespoons dry bread crumbs	Lemon wedges
¼ teaspoon salt, or to taste	

Place the butter in a 9-inch microwaveproof pie plate. Cook on HIGH for 30 to 45 seconds to melt.

Stir the scallops into the butter to coat the tops and bottoms well. Arrange the scallops in a ring around the outside of the dish. Sprinkle the tops with bread crumbs, salt, pepper, and sesame seeds. Cover with a paper towel, which helps to absorb excess moisture. If using bay scallops, cook on MEDIUM for 3½ to 5 minutes; if sea scallops, cook on MEDIUM for 4 to 6½ minutes, or until just opaque and resilient to the touch. Let stand, covered, for 2 minutes. Serve with lemon wedges.

NOTE: *To Double:* Double the ingredients. Place the scallops around the outside of a 2-quart rectangular dish, leaving the center open. Reserve bread crumb topping and add after final stirring. Cover with a paper towel. Cook on MEDIUM for 5 to 7½ minutes, stirring twice during cooking.

VARIATIONS:

Riviera-Style Scallops: Add 2 minced garlic cloves to the butter. Cook on HIGH for 35 seconds to 1 minute, or until the garlic is tender. Stir in the salt, pepper, and 2 tablespoons chopped fresh parsley. Add the scallops and turn to coat well. Eliminate the bread crumbs and sesame seeds. Cook as directed. This variation tastes like shrimp scampi, but is more refined when made with scallops.

Scallops in Dill Salsa Cruda: Eliminate the bread crumbs. During scallop standing time, prepare Dill Salsa Cruda (page 248). Serve with the scallops. Also serve chilled with chilled scallops on lettuce leaves. What a refreshing summer or Mexican-style dish!

SCALLOPS IN MUSTARD CREAM SAUCE

MAKES 4 SERVINGS   BEGIN 15 MINUTES BEFORE SERVING
COOKING TIME: 4 TO 7¼ MINUTES

The following recipe is a favorite of ours. The subtle flavor of creamy mustard enhances the delicate flavor of the scallops, besides which the sauce is easily cooked during the standing time. Delicious served on a bed of rice.

---

2 tablespoons butter	1 tablespoon prepared Dijon mustard or country-style mustard with seeds
1 pound scallops	
1 egg yolk	
½ cup heavy cream or half and half	Salt and pepper

Place the butter in a 9-inch pie plate. Cook on HIGH for 30 to 45 seconds, or until melted.

Stir the scallops into the butter to coat the tops and bottoms well. Arrange the scallops in a ring around the outside of the plate. Cover with a paper towel. If using bay scallops, cook on MEDIUM for 3½ to 5 minutes; if using sea scallops cook on MEDIUM for 4 to 6½ minutes, or until just opaque and tender. Drain the cooking juices (2 to 4 tablespoons) from the scallops and set aside. Let the scallops stand, covered, for 2 minutes.

Place the egg yolk in a 1½-quart casserole; beat lightly. Stir in the cream and mustard. Add the reserved scallop juice. Cook on HIGH for 1 to 1½ minutes, or until thickened, stirring after 1 minute. At this point the sauce should be thickened and almost boiling, but do not allow it to boil or it will curdle. If the sauce has not thickened, continue to cook at 30-second intervals, stirring each time, until thickened. Add salt and pepper to taste.

Place the cooked scallops in the sauce and stir to coat. Serve in individual ramekins.

VARIATIONS:

Scallops in Saffron Cream Sauce: Substitute 1 pinch of saffron threads for the mustard. Garnish with nasturtium flowers or slivered scallions.

Scallop Appetizers with Golden Caviar: Divide the saffron scallops in the above variation into 6 or 8 ramekins. Top each with a teaspoon of golden caviar.

Clams and Mussels Basics:

1. A wide, low round dish will be best for arranging these shellfish in a ring. If you don't have this size dish, choose a smaller, deeper dish and stir in the middle of cooking to move the less cooked clams or mussels to the outside, where they will cook faster.
2. No liquid is necessary because clams and mussels contain a lot of moisture inside their shells.
3. The purpose of cooking mussels on HIGH is to produce enough steam within the shells for them to pop open, exposing the succulent meat. Once opened, it is just a matter of seconds or a minute for the mollusks to finish cooking.

    The only time that clams are cooked on MEDIUM power is if their shells have been opened, as in Clams Casino (page 111).

4. A tight cover, lid, or plastic wrap turned back slightly keeps in all available moisture for steaming.
5. *Doneness:* Clams should be removed from the oven when their shells have opened. If one appears not to open, remove it and put it in another dish and continue to cook. This will prevent the others from overcooking as they are set aside. If clam does not open, discard it.

    Mussels should also be removed from the oven when their shells open, but the flesh should plump up and pull away from the shells. There is no standing time for either. Discard any mussels that haven't opened.

    For *Underdone* and *Overdone*, see Shrimp Basics, page 234.

✺ STEAMED CLAMS OR MUSSELS

MAKES 1 SERVING AS A MAIN COURSE; 2 AS A FIRST COURSE   BEGIN 10 MINUTES BEFORE SERVING
COOKING TIME: 3 TO 5 MINUTES

Mussels will open faster than clams because the muscles fastening them shut are smaller than the clams'. However, because mussels are often meatier and larger than clams, they may take a little longer to cook once the shell is opened. A glass cover and casserole will allow you to watch as they open up.

1 dozen clams or ¾ to 1 pound mussels, scrubbed well	¼ cup any of the Melted Butters (page 183) Lemon wedges (optional)

Arrange the clams or mussels around the outer rim of a 10- to 12-inch shallow round microwaveproof dish, leaving the center open. Cover tightly and cook on HIGH for 2½ to 5 minutes, or until all the shells have opened, rotating the dish once in the middle of cooking time if necessary. Serve with one of the melted butters or lemon wedges and the broth (or reserve the broth for a later soup).

NOTE: *To Double:* The most efficient way to double clams and mussels is in 2 separate batches. Put in another plate while people begin eating and you won't miss a beat.

MUSSELS STEAMED IN WINE

MAKES 4 TO 6 SERVINGS   BEGIN 20 MINUTES BEFORE SERVING
COOKING TIME: 11 TO 13 MINUTES

The added ingredients flavor the mollusks and cook into a type of light soup broth. Serve with crusty bread.

- 2 tablespoons butter
- 2 garlic cloves, minced
- 2 tablespoons chopped scallions
- ½ cup dry white wine
- 6 peppercorns
- 1 tablespoon chopped fresh basil, or 1 teaspoon dried
- ½ teaspoon red pepper flakes (optional)
- 3 pounds mussels, scrubbed clean
- ¼ cup chopped fresh parsley

In a 3-quart casserole combine the butter, garlic, and scallions. Cook on HIGH for 35 seconds to 1 minute to melt the butter. Stir in the wine, peppercorns, basil, and pepper flakes. Cover tightly and cook on HIGH for 5 minutes.

Add the mussels. Cover again and cook on HIGH for 5 to 7 minutes, until the mussels have opened, stirring after 3 minutes. Let stand, covered, for 2 minutes before serving. Serve in soup bowls with the broth. Sprinkle with the parsley.

Squid Basics:

The basic fact about cooking squid is that there is no basic microwave technique. In conventional cooking, it might be sautéed or fried, but in the microwave, squid is cooked in a sauce, according to what that sauce dictates.

The important point is not to overcook squid, so that it will remain tender, not rubbery.

SQUID IN TOMATO SAUCE

MAKES 4 SERVINGS   BEGIN 35 MINUTES BEFORE SERVING
COOKING TIME: 19 TO 23 MINUTES

Fragrant and fiery describes this dish. These tender morsels will win over the most skeptical eaters. Notice that the recipe is cooked uncovered because of the addition of tomatoes, which will water out and need as much evaporation as possible. Serve over rice or spaghetti.

- 1 tablespoon olive oil
- 2 garlic cloves, minced
- 1 cup fresh or drained canned tomatoes, peeled, seeded, and chopped
- ½ teaspoon dried thyme
- ½ teaspoon dried rosemary
- ¼ teaspoon hot pepper sauce, or more to taste
- ½ teaspoon salt
- ¼ teaspoon pepper
- 1½ pounds squid with tentacles, cleaned and dressed
- ¼ cup chopped fresh parsley

In a 3-quart casserole combine the oil and garlic. Cook on HIGH for 30 to 45 seconds, or until the garlic is tender but not brown. Add the remaining ingredients except the squid and parsley, stirring to blend. Cook on HIGH for 10 minutes, stirring once.

Meanwhile, rinse the squid well. Cut each squid crosswise into ¼-inch rounds. Slice the tentacles in half lengthwise. Add the squid to the sauce and stir. Cook on HIGH for 8 to 12 minutes, or until tender and opaque, stirring after 4 minutes. Sprinkle with parsley. Let stand for 5 minutes.

SQUID IN FRESH GINGER SAUCE

MAKES 4 SERVINGS   BEGIN 20 TO 25 MINUTES BEFORE SERVING
COOKING TIME: 8 TO 10 MINUTES

A deliciously different way to serve squid. This spicy concoction has become one of our favorite dishes. Serve over rice or thin noodles.

- 1 tablespoon finely chopped fresh ginger
- 1 medium onion, thinly sliced
- 2 garlic cloves, minced
- 1 tablespoon vegetable oil
- 2 tablespoons soy sauce
- 1 tablespoon vinegar
- 2 teaspoons cornstarch
- 1½ pounds squid, cleaned and dressed

In a 1½-quart casserole combine the ginger, onion, garlic, and vegetable oil. Cook on HIGH for 2 minutes, or until the onion is tender.

In a small bowl combine the soy sauce, vinegar, and cornstarch. Stir until there are no lumps. Add to the onion mixture.

Cut the squid crosswise into ¼-inch circles. Cut the tentacles in half lengthwise. Add the squid to the onion-soy mixture; stir to coat. Cover tightly and cook on HIGH for 6 to 8 minutes, or until the squid is tender and opaque, stirring after 4 minutes. Let stand, covered, for 5 minutes.

Sauces Made from the Cooking Liquid of Fish

When cooking basic recipes for 1- to 1½-pound thick skinned fillets, thin fillets, whole fish, or fish steaks, add 1 tablespoon dry vermouth to the fish before cooking. Reserve the cooking liquid—our short-cut fish stocks—and prepare one of the following four sauces.

SPINACH SAUCE

MAKES ABOUT 1½ CUPS
COOKING TIME: 5½ MINUTES

A sauce rich in iron that complements a mild-flavored lean fish.

⅓ to ½ cup cooking liquid from fish
1 cup (about ¼ pound) finely chopped cleaned spinach
1 cup sour cream, plain yogurt, or crème fraîche
2 tablespoons butter
Salt and pepper

Remove the fish from the cooking dish, letting the cooking liquid remain. Stir in the chopped spinach. Cover tightly and cook on HIGH for 4 minutes, stirring halfway through cooking. Stir in the sour cream. Cook, uncovered, on HIGH for 1 minute; stir. Cook on HIGH for 30 seconds more, or until heated through.

Break up the butter into 8 pieces and stir in 1 tablespoon at a time until melted. Salt and pepper to taste.

VARIATIONS:

Sorrel Sauce: Substitute 1 cup sorrel leaves for the spinach.

Watercress Sauce: Substitute 1 cup watercress for the spinach.

CRAB SAUCE

MAKES ABOUT 1 CUP
COOKING TIME: 5 TO 6 MINUTES

Tasty with lean thin fillets, salmon steaks, or whole fish.

- 2 tablespoons finely chopped shallots
- 1 tablespoon butter
- 2 tablespoons dry vermouth
- 4 ounces flaked cooked crabmeat
- 1/3 cup heavy cream
- 1/3 to 1/2 cup cooking liquid from fish
- Salt and pepper

In a 1-quart casserole combine the shallots and butter. Cook on HIGH for 1 minute to melt the butter. Add the vermouth. Cook on HIGH for 2 minutes. Stir in the remaining ingredients. Cook on HIGH for 2 to 3 minutes, stirring once.

CHILLED CILANTRO BREAD SAUCE

MAKES ABOUT 1/2 CUP

An easy-to-make Mexican sauce, thickened with bread and almonds, to complement cold lean fish or bluefish. Best served with lime wedges.

- 1/3 to 1/2 cup cooking liquid from fish
- 1 slice of white bread
- 1/2 cup almonds
- 3 canned serrano chilies
- 1/4 cup chopped fresh parsley
- 1/4 cup chopped fresh cilantro (coriander)
- 2 tablespoons lime juice
- 1/4 teaspoon salt
- 1/8 teaspoon pepper

Puree all the ingredients in a food processor or blender or through a fine sieve. Chill.

CURRY SAUCE

MAKES 1¼ TO 1¾ CUPS
COOKING TIME: ABOUT 3 MINUTES

A delicious spice blend. Break the cooked fish into bite-size chunks and add to this sauce. Serve over rice.

- 2 tablespoons butter
- 2 tablespoons finely chopped scallions
- 2 tablespoons curry powder
- ½ teaspoon ground cumin
- ½ teaspoon ground cinnamon
- ⅓ to ½ cup cooking liquid from fish
- 1 cup plain yogurt

In a 2-quart casserole combine the butter, scallions, curry powder, cumin, and cinnamon. Cook on HIGH for 40 seconds to 1 minute, until the butter is melted and the scallions are tender. Add the remaining ingredients. Cook on HIGH for 1 minute; stir. Cook on HIGH for 1 minute more, or until heated through.

TARTAR SAUCE

MAKES 1¼ CUPS

Serve with chilled or warm fish.

- 1 cup Mayonnaise (page 175)
- 1 egg, hard-cooked and finely chopped
- 1 teaspoon prepared mustard
- 2 tablespoons relish
- 2 tablespoons capers, finely chopped
- 1 tablespoon chopped fresh parsley
- 1 tablespoon snipped fresh chives
- 1 teaspoon lemon juice

In a small bowl combine all the ingredients well.

BASIC COCKTAIL SAUCE

MAKES 1 CUP

Serve with shrimp or any cold fish.

¾ cup catsup
¼ cup prepared horseradish

2 tablespoons fresh lemon juice
Dash hot red pepper sauce

In a small bowl combine all the ingredients well.

LEMON BUTTER

MAKES ENOUGH FOR 1½ POUNDS FISH
COOKING TIME: ABOUT 1 MINUTE

¼ cup butter

1 tablespoon lemon juice

Place the butter in a 1-cup glass measure. Cook on HIGH for 40 seconds to 1 minute to melt. Stir in the lemon juice.

VARIATIONS:

Herb Butter: Stir in 2 tablespoons chopped fresh herbs after melting butter.
Buttered Bread Crumbs: Add ¼ cup fine dry bread crumbs after the lemon juice.
Nut Butter: Add ¼ cup chopped nuts after the lemon juice.

INDIVIDUAL SERVING (4-OUNCES FISH): Place 1 tablespoon butter and 2 teaspoons lemon juice in a 1-cup glass measure. Cook on HIGH for 20 to 30 seconds to melt. To make variations, add 2 teaspoons chopped fresh herbs, 1 tablespoon fine dry bread crumbs, or 1 tablespoon chopped nuts respectively.

DILL SALSA CRUDA

MAKES 1½ CUPS
COOKING TIME: 2 TO 3 MINUTES

Salsa cruda means the sauce is just barely cooked, so look for tomatoes in season for peak sauce flavor. Dill and lime make this a special sauce for scallops, fish steaks, or lean fish. Try the jalapeño variation with rich fish fillets.

- 1 tablespoon olive oil
- 1 garlic clove, minced
- 1 scallion, finely chopped
- 1 pound ripe plum tomatoes, peeled, seeded, and coarsely chopped
- 2 tablespoons finely chopped fresh dill
- 1 tablespoon lime or lemon juice
- ¼ teaspoon salt
- ⅛ teaspoon pepper

In a 1½-quart casserole combine the oil, garlic, and scallion. Cook on HIGH for 30 to 40 seconds, or until the garlic and onion are tender. Add the remaining ingredients; stir. Cook on HIGH for 1 to 2 minutes, until just heated through but tomatoes hold their shape.

VARIATIONS:

Jalapeño Salsa: Eliminate the dill and add 1 or 2 jalapeño peppers, finely chopped, and 1 teaspoon chopped fresh cilantro (coriander) with the remaining ingredients. Flavor that makes your taste buds stand up and take notice!

Mint Salsa Cruda: Substitute fresh mint for the dill.

TOMATO-ANCHOVY SAUCE

MAKES 1 CUP
COOKING TIME: 7 MINUTES

Not overwhelming in anchovy flavor, but these little flat fish do add an extra zing to any rich fish.

- 1 medium onion, chopped
- 1 garlic clove, minced
- 1 tablespoon olive oil
- 1 cup fresh or drained canned tomatoes, peeled, seeded, and chopped
- 1 to 2 tablespoons minced, drained anchovy fillets
- 1/8 teaspoon freshly ground pepper
- 2 tablespoons chopped fresh parsley

In a 1-quart casserole combine the onion, garlic, and olive oil. Cook on HIGH for 2 minutes, or until the onion is tender. Stir in the remaining ingredients. Cook on HIGH for 5 minutes, until well heated, stirring once halfway through cooking.

10

MEAT

Bridget Gaffney came from potato-famined Ireland to well-heeled Newport, Rhode Island, and landed a job as a meat cook at one of the mansions. I understand that she had quite a reputation—for her tempting roasts and her temper. If she caught one of the butcher's delivery boys trying to slip her a poor cut of meat, she would lash out at him in a torrent of Gaelic brogue. Bridget Gaffney was my great-grandmother.

Bill Cone was known as one of the best barbecue cooks in our neighborhood. It was hard to keep his hobby a secret when, like the proverbial postman, he allowed not rain nor sleet nor snow to keep him from his self-appointed task—weekend roasts and chops seared on the outdoor grill. Dad trusted only one butcher in Pittsburgh for his meats and was a regular customer there. Dad was Bridget Gaffney's grandson, although he had no temper that I ever saw.

I wish that, in respect to specialties, I could say that I was my father's daughter, but over the years I had become neglectful about choosing good meat. If it were for someone else, that was another story. A client, for example, who needed meat to photograph would receive the best. I must say that it was the extensive testing for this book that showed me how important good-quality meat is to the final product. I also began to understand why those delivery boys probably deserved my great-grandmother's ire.

Now I go back to the place where I first shopped for meat as a food stylist, a meat market in a now renovated arcade at the Reading Train Terminal. The market supports many butchers, but my favorite has been there since 1906 advertising "Beautiful beef, lovely lamb and veal to die for." And even though I know less about meat than my great-grandmother or father knew, I know enough to go to someone who does.

As important as the quality of meat is to a successful recipe, so is proper cookery. Meat has been given a bad reputation in the microwave, and if meat is not treated properly, the reputation is well deserved. If meat is cooked on too high a power, or for too long, it can dry out and become tough from loss of fluid. Salting the surface of meat before cooking can also cause the meat to overcook and become tough.

To offset that fluid loss, it is often important to lower the cooking power after a few minutes. And when it comes to determining the cooking time, we have found that diameter or thickness of the meat is as important as the meat poundage.

Harold McGee in his book *On Food and Cooking* says, "[Microwave cooking]... is very effective in solubilizing collagen—why we don't know." Solubilizing collagen is what causes tough meats to become tender in cooking. Stews are an example of this type of meat, and while they don't cook long enough alone to develop the same browning flavor that accompanies conventional stews, more of the meat flavor is present. You'll find that the rich blend of spices and other ingredients that we add to the stew, highlights that flavor. Veal Stefado, Carbonnade a la Flamande, and any of the chilies are just some of our favorites that we would be proud to compare to any conventional stew.

As is true with meat cubes, smaller pieces of meat—hamburgers, steaks, and chops—won't brown in the short time they cook, unless given some help with a browning dish or, in the case of pork chops, a breaded coating. But when done properly the results are delicious, with less mess and cleanup than in conventional broiling. But if you want to see an example of natural browning, try the meat loaf. Even the crispy trails of meat mingled with fat are there.

And for what I'm sure would have satisfied my father, we have given instructions on how to shorten barbecuing time, by beginning the cooking process in the microwave. Who knows, maybe this shortened cooking time may boost barbecuing year-round into a national craze.

—MARCIA

Buying and Using Meat

Beef

- If there is much fat on the outside of large pieces of meat, it should be evenly trimmed on all sides but not removed. Fat will aid in flavoring and tenderizing the meat.
- When slicing a large piece of meat, before or after cooking, be sure to slice it across the grain. Think of meat as a piece of celery, which we also cut across the rib so that the long strings are easier to eat and digest. Meat will be tenderer when sliced across the grain.
- Meat wrapped in plastic or butcher's paper can be stored in its wrapping. Cubes and roasts are often wrapped in wax paper to prevent them from leaking. Because the paper is not a tight cover, the surface of the meat may become dark when exposed to air, but this will not harm the quality. A steak is often wrapped in absorbent paper that sticks to the surface to protect it from the air and keep it bright red in color.
- The smaller the piece of meat or the more surface area exposed, the less time the meat can be kept in the refrigerator at 30° to 40°F.

    Ground meat—one to two days
    Cube steaks and beef cubes—two days
    Large steaks and roasts—three to five days

If you find you haven't cooked the meat within this time, wrap it tightly in freezer paper to freeze. Later defrost according to the microwave instructions.
- Beef grain should be well marbled or streaked with white fat; avoid fat that is off-white or yellow. Transparent streaks of fat are probably not fat at all but gristle, which makes meat chewy. When in doubt, ask the butcher or meat man at your supermarket.
- More tender cuts of beef will have a finer grain and contain more fat throughout the grain. These cuts are generally cooked in a browning dish or cooked, uncovered, in the microwave.
- Less tender beef has less visible fat in the meat grain itself. These cuts are cooked with additional liquid and a cover to retain moisture. They are also generally cooked on a lower power setting, to keep them from getting tough.
- Buying a whole chuck roast is often the best bet for getting good-quality, equal size cubes for stews.

Lamb and Veal

The lighter the color the better the quality. Because lamb and veal are so young, little marbling is present. Baby spring lamb that is six to eight months old will be light pink and have blood in the bones. Veal will be pink or almost white. Milk-fed veal is the lightest in color and tenderest; grain-fed veal is slightly darker.

Pork and Ham

Pork and ham can be purchased in one of two categories: 1) fresh or 2) fully cooked. Curing or smoking flavors either category. If a pork or ham is not marked "fully cooked," assume that it is fresh and should be cooked as indicated below.

FRESH PORK AND HAM:

- Fresh pork includes chops, pork roasts, and ribs. Fresh hams can have a bone or can be boneless.
- Fresh pork should be lightly pink with a fine grain; ham should be rosy pink and firm to the touch.
- Fresh pork will have small flecks of white fat throughout the meat, but these will not be as noticeable as in beef.
- Fresh pork can be stored for three to five days in the refrigerator, if the package has been unopened.
- Fresh pork must be cooked completely through to a temperature of 165°F (which upon standing time will reach 170°F). Fresh hams are cooked to the same doneness to make sure that they are completely heated through.
- There has been some adverse publicity about cooking fresh pork in the microwave

because it was felt that the final temperature could not be evenly held throughout the meat. The aim in cooking fresh pork is to 1) kill trichinae and 2) improve flavor. If pork is cooked to 137°F and held long enough, all trichinae will be destroyed. The directions to cook pork until 170°F assure that the 137°F has been held long enough and also that the temperature is high enough to develop full flavor.* (If you have an old thermometer, it may read Pork = 180°F, which was the old standard.)

If pork is not covered in the microwave, the outside surface may cool off due to the evaporation of moisture. Cooling will allow the surface temperature to fluctuate below the desired 137°F. But if pork is covered tightly with a lid or plastic wrap to keep the heat and steam in, the surface temperature remains high.

Pork chops are covered with a breaded coating, to seal in heat, or cooked in a sauce with a cover to maintain the proper temperature. When these steps are followed, the pork temperature can be controlled.

FULLY COOKED HAM OR SAUSAGE:

- There is some marbling, but this is difficult to tell in fully cooked hams. These should be firm to the touch.
- Fully cooked hams can be kept refrigerated for seven days.
- Fully cooked ham can be eaten cold, and is cooked primarily to bring out its flavor, which improves with cooking. The goal of cooking is to heat the ham to 125°F (which upon standing reaches 130°F).

BACON:

- Bacon can be kept refrigerated for five to seven days, once the package has been opened. If unopened, check the usage date on the package.

Defrosting Frozen Meat

- Uncover frozen meat, sausages, and liver and remove all Styrofoam liners before defrosting or as soon as possible during defrosting, to prevent any buildup of heat under the packaging that may begin to cook meat.
- Leave bacon in its wrapping; it's easier to defrost that way and cooking is unlikely.
- Place frozen meat on a microwave roasting rack in a rectangular dish to raise it above the liquid that will come out in the defrosting process and begin to get hot. If no roasting rack is available, substitute a small microwaveproof dish, and invert it in the rectangular dish, placing the meat on top.
- Repackage fresh ground meat into 1- to 1½-pound packages of equal thickness before freezing so defrosting will be easier.
- Frozen packages of ground meat with thin edges need to be watched closely and broken in half partway through defrosting to rearrange thicker inside portions to the outside.

*National Live Stock and Meat Board.

DEFROSTING TIMES FOR VARIOUS MEATS
(Please read preceding specific information about defrosting first.)

Name	Power and Time	Amount	Standing Time
Bacon	DEFROST 6 minutes	per 1 pound	Stand 5 minutes
Ground Beef	DEFROST 4 to 7 minutes	per 1 pound	Stand 5 minutes
Bulk or Link Sausage	DEFROST 4 to 5 minutes	per 1 pound	Stand 5 minutes
Hamburgers, Sausage Patties, or Frankfurters	DEFROST 1 minute	1	Stand 5 minutes
	DEFROST 2 minutes	2	
	DEFROST 2½ minutes	3	
	DEFROST 3 minutes	4	
Beef Chunks	DEFROST 7 to 8 minutes	per 1 pound	Stand 5 minutes
Small Steaks and Chops	DEFROST 5 to 7 minutes	per 1 pound	Stand 5 minutes
Thick Large Steaks (1½ to 2 inches thick)	DEFROST 7 minutes	per 1 pound	Stand 5 minutes
Thin Large Steaks (under ¾ inch thick)	DEFROST 4 to 5 minutes	per 1 pound	Stand 5 minutes
Roasts (Beef, Pork, Lamb, and Veal)	MEDIUM 5 to 6 minutes; then DEFROST 5 to 6 minutes	per 1 pound	Stand 15 to 30 minutes
Beef Liver	DEFROST 7 to 8 minutes	per 1 pound	Stand 5 minutes
	DEFROST 5 to 6 minutes	per ½ pound	

- Ground beef, bulk sausage, and links should be turned over once during defrosting and broken into pieces, arranging the icier areas to the outside.
- Meat chunks should be broken up once or twice during defrosting, placing icier chunks to the outside.
- Steaks and chops should be turned over once during defrosting. If frozen steaks or chops are stacked when frozen, separate as soon as possible during defrosting.
- Roasts should be turned over twice during defrosting.
- If any edges or corners appear to be cooking, cover these smoothly with foil. This will reflect the microwave energy.
- After defrosting, meat should still have some ice crystals. The ice crystals will disappear during standing time.
- Standing time, after defrosting, is important. A large roast should stand 15 to 30 minutes. All other meat will stand 5 minutes to finish defrosting.

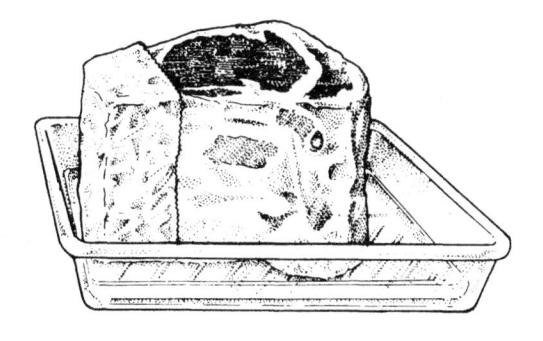

- *Meat Defrosting Doneness:* Meat should still be riddled with ice crystals, but the meat should be pliable, not solid. Cubes should *not* feel warm to the touch and if any do, they should be removed before the end of defrosting.

When steaks are pressed with your finger, upon removal from the microwave, the depression left by the finger should fill up with red juices. After standing time, a new depression made in the meat will not fill up with juices.

Ground meat will be pliable but still icy in the center. Patties, meatballs, or meat loaf can be formed while ice crystals still remain.

Tender-Cut Roast Beef Basics:

1. The diameter, along with the weight of the roast, determines the power setting and the cooking time, but we find the diameter to be the most critical factor, particularly when cooking to rare. Roasts begin on HIGH first to build up heat on the outside for better browning, and then are finished on MEDIUM power, for a juicier and more desirable end product.

    What varies between a small and a large roast is the amount of time each is cooked on HIGH. A small-diameter roast will cook for only 5 minutes on HIGH, and a larger roast, over 5 inches in diameter, is cooked for 10 minutes on HIGH.
2. A tender roast needs no additional liquid added to tenderize it.
3. A roasting rack will lift the meat above its juices, which contain fat and water that would attract the microwaves more to that area, causing overcooking.
4. A roast beef is very uniform in shape and does not need a cover to help it cook through evenly. Cooking the roast without a cover also keeps the surface drier.
5. Roasts should be salted at the end of cooking so that the salt placed on the raw surface of the meat doesn't absorb an excessive amount of microwaves, causing the meat to toughen.
6. A tender roast needs to be turned over halfway through the total cooking time, for the most even cooking.
7. A large roast may need to be shielded with foil on either end.
8. Loosely tenting the roast with foil will retain the heat that has built up in the roast during cooking and reflect it back into the roast for continued cooking.
9. *Doneness:* The best way to judge the doneness of a beef roast is by the time and the internal temperature indicated in the recipe for rare, medium, or well done. The microwave sensor or thermometer is inserted in the center of the roast. The outer surfaces of the roast will be predominantly brown, except for the outside center surface, which will still be quite red. Don't be misled by this. The reddish color will diminish as the roast stands and the internal temperature rises 10° to 15°F.

    Underdone: The first few times you cook a roast in the microwave you will do well to judge it by a microwave temperature probe or conventional meat thermometer, inserted outside of the oven.

    Overdone: An overdone roast will be too tough only if your meat wasn't of the best quality. The well-done meat can be thinly sliced and served with its flavorful juices over mashed potatoes.

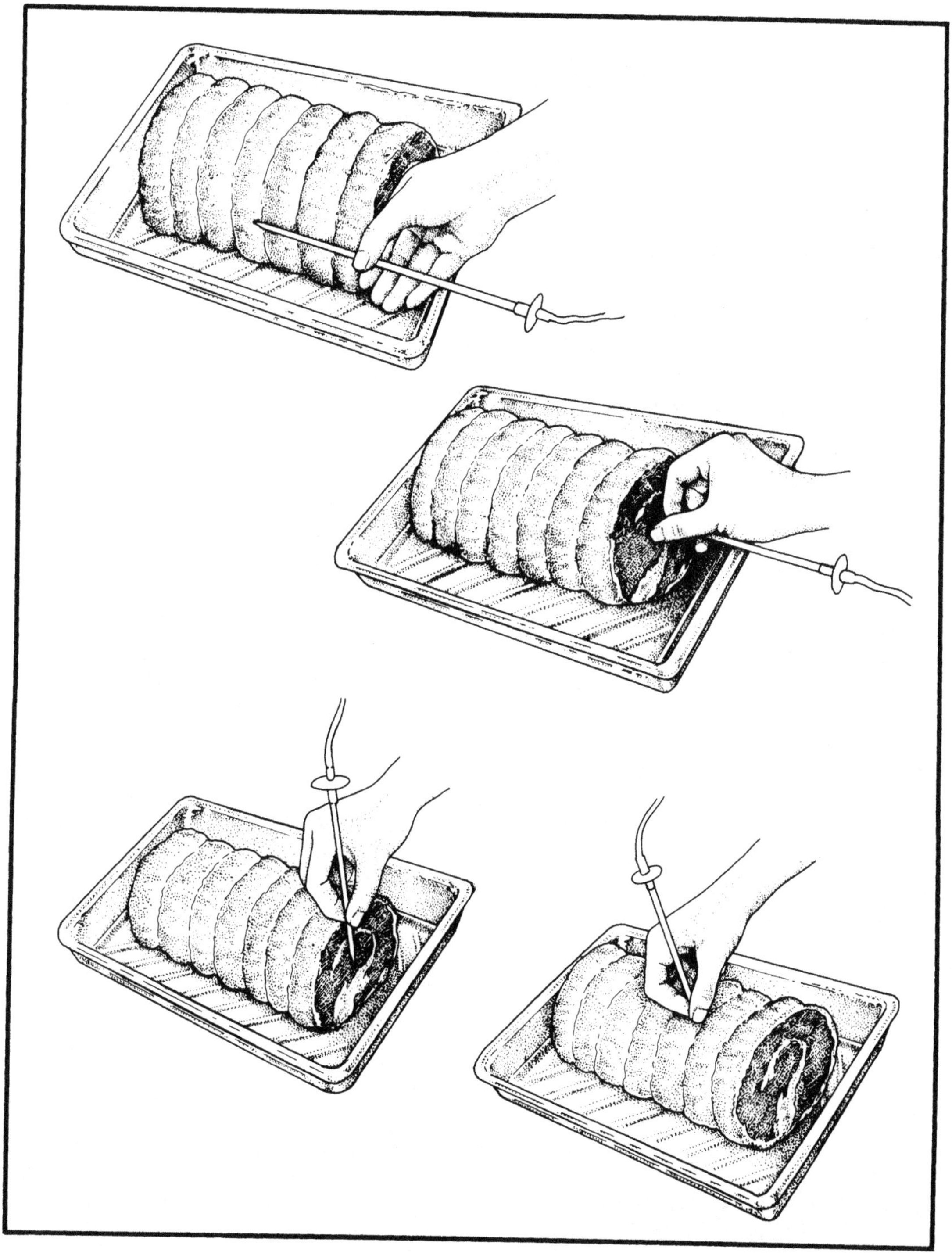

✺ TENDER ROAST BEEF

MAKES 4 TO 6 SERVINGS
BEGIN 20 MINUTES TO 1 HOUR AND 20 MINUTES BEFORE SERVING, DEPENDING ON SIZE OF ROAST
COOKING TIME: 12 TO 66 MINUTES

There is more to meat cookery than simply following instructions according to weight. The diameter has as much to do with how long to cook a roast as weight does. This is even more important in microwave cooking. We recommend that you choose roasts that are uniformly shaped, so that any shielding of the smaller ends with foil will be unnecessary.

---

1 3- to 4-pound beef roast (rolled rib, eye round, or sirloin roast), 5-inch diameter or less	**Salt and pepper**

Place the roast fat side down on a microwave roasting rack in a 2-quart rectangular dish.

Cook on HIGH for 5 minutes. Cook on MEDIUM for 7 to 9 minutes per pound for rare (115°F), 8 to 11 minutes per pound for medium-rare (120°F), 9 to 12 minutes per pound for medium (130°F), 10 to 14 minutes per pound for well-done (145°F), turning over halfway through the total cooking.

Let stand for 5 to 10 minutes. Salt and pepper before serving.

NOTE: For a different size roast, see the cooking chart on page 59.

VARIATIONS:

Roast Beef with Horseradish Cream: Prepare Horseradish Cream (page 273) during standing time.

Roast Beef with Cranberry Sauce: Prepare Cranberry Sauce with Quick Raspberry Vinegar (page 366) during standing time. Pass with the roast beef at the table.

Roast Beef au Jus: Before standing time transfer the finished roast to a serving platter. Tent with foil. Remove the rack from the dish. Remove any excess fat from the meat juices. Stir 1 cup beef broth (see Mock Brown Broth or Stock, page 119) into the meat juices. Cook, uncovered, on HIGH for 4 to 6 minutes, or until boiling, stirring once. Salt and pepper to taste.

Roast Beef with Gravy: Before standing time transfer the roast to a serving platter. Tent with foil. Remove the rack from the dish. Remove any excess fat from the meat juices. Blend 1½ tablespoons all-purpose flour into 2 tablespoons water. Stir the flour paste and 1 cup beef broth (see Mock Brown Broth or Stock, page 119) into the meat juices. Cook, uncovered, on HIGH for 4 to 6 minutes, or until thickened and boiling, stirring once. Season with salt and pepper to taste.

Roast Beef with Vermouth Gravy: Follow the Roast Beef with Gravy variation above, but add 2 tablespoons dry vermouth with beef broth.

Roast Beef with Buttered Red Wine Sauce: Before standing time transfer the roast to a serving platter. Tent with foil. Remove the rack from the dish. Remove any excess fat from the meat juices. Add ½ cup beef broth (see Mock Brown Broth or Stock, page 119) and ½ cup red wine to the meat juices. Cook on HIGH for 5 minutes, stirring after 3 minutes. Add ¼ cup unsalted butter. Cook on HIGH for 1½ to 2 minutes to melt the butter, stirring once. Stir in ¼ cup chopped fresh parsley. Spoon over the sliced beef. Delicious on a hot roast beef sandwich, too.

Company Roast Beef with Burgundy-Scallion Sauce: Before standing time transfer the finished roast to a serving platter. Tent with foil. Remove the rack from the dish. Remove any excess fat from the meat juices. Add ½ cup thinly sliced scallions, ¼ cup red Burgundy or other dry red wine, and 1 tablespoon red wine vinegar to the meat juices. Cook on HIGH for 5 minutes, stirring after 3 minutes. Stir in ¼ cup unsalted butter. Cook on HIGH for 1½ to 2 minutes, or until the butter is melted, stirring once. Serve over sliced beef.

Roast Beef au Jus Cognac Sauce: Follow the Burgundy-Scallion Sauce variation above, but substitute ¼ cup Cognac or Armagnac for wine.

Roast Beef Sandwiches: Prepare any of the au jus, gravy, or sauce variations above. For 2 sandwiches, thinly slice ½ pound chilled beef. Place 2 slices of white bread on each of 2 plates. Top with the meat and pour on the juices. Cover with wax paper. Heat on MEDIUM for 2 to 4 minutes, or until hot.

BEEF STRIP AND RED ONION SALAD

MAKES 4 SERVINGS   BEGIN 10 MINUTES BEFORE SERVING

Convert those beef leftovers into this tasty salad.

---

3 to 4 cups thinly sliced cooked beef (preferably rare), chilled 1 small red onion, thinly sliced ½ cup Herb Vinaigrette (page 185) Freshly ground pepper	Watercress, lettuce, or mixed greens Cornichons (small pickles) (optional)

In a medium bowl combine the chilled beef, onion, dressing, and pepper; toss well. Serve on watercress, lettuce, or greens. Garnish with cornichons, if desired.

VARIATIONS:

Beef Strip Salad with Peppers: Add 1 green and 1 sweet red pepper, cut into ¼-inch strips, with the onion.

Beef Strip Salad with Capers: Add 1 tablespoon drained capers with the onion.

Less Tender-Cut Roast Basics (Beef, Veal, Lamb):

1. Less tender-cut roasts are tougher cuts of meat with more connective tissue and need to be cooked slowly and with additional liquid to help them become tender during cooking. A 3- to 4-pound roast can be braised in about 1 cup broth or wine, which will, however, dissolve any salt added to the meat surface.
2. For the most flavor, less tender roasts should be marinated or cooked with vegetables.
3. The roast and liquid are first cooked on HIGH power to heat the liquid and the outside of the meat. The power is then turned down to MEDIUM to slowly simmer the meat until tender.
4. The less tender-cut roast is covered tightly to help steam and simmer it, along with the vegetables. A glass lid is best because it makes re-covering after turning over, adding ingredients and checking doneness easier.
5. The meat should be turned over halfway through cooking so that the heated liquid has a chance to cover both sides of the meat.
6. Standing time of about 10 minutes is important to complete the cooking of the meat. In this time, a gravy can be made or vegetables cooked for serving. A foil cover will keep the meat warm.
7. *Doneness:* A less tender roast should feel tender when a carving fork is inserted.

   Overdone: A less tender roast will become tough and dry around the outer edges if not cooked on MEDIUM power with the proper amount of liquid and a tight lid. If the roast is tough when done, slice it very thinly across the grain and serve it with a gravy, or chop it up for hash.

✸ BEEF POT ROAST

MAKES 6 TO 8 SERVINGS   BEGIN ABOUT 1½ HOURS BEFORE SERVING
COOKING TIME: 1 HOUR 2 MINUTES TO 1 HOUR 12 MINUTES

A veal roast can also be substituted for beef in this recipe; see the Veal Pot Roast variation below. This roast has a light gravy thickened primarily with vegetables.

- 1 3-pound beef rump or chuck roast
- ½ teaspoon salt
- ¼ teaspoon pepper
- 2 tablespoons butter
- 1 medium onion, finely chopped
- 1 celery rib, finely chopped
- 1 medium carrot, peeled and finely chopped
- 1 tablespoon all-purpose flour
- 1 sprig fresh thyme, or ½ teaspoon dried
- 1 cup beef broth (see Mock Brown Broth or Stock, page 119)

Rub the roast with salt and pepper.

In a 3-quart casserole with a lid combine the butter, onion, celery, and carrot. Cover tightly and cook on HIGH for 2 minutes. Sprinkle the vegetables evenly with the flour and stir to blend. Stir in the thyme and broth.

Add the meat. Cover tightly and cook on HIGH for 15 minutes. Cook on MEDIUM for 45 to 55 minutes, or until the meat is tender, turning the meat over halfway through the total cooking time. Transfer the meat to a serving platter. Cover with foil and let stand for 10 minutes.

Force the cooking liquid and vegetables through a sieve, or add to a food processor in 2 batches to puree; this will help to thicken the gravy. Return the strained juices and vegetables to casserole. Cook, uncovered, on HIGH for 4 to 6 minutes, or until boiling, stirring once.

Slice the roast and spoon the gravy over the slices.

VARIATIONS:

Beef Pot Roast with Tomato Sauce: Eliminate the celery and carrot. Substitute 2 tablespoons tomato paste for the flour.

Beef Pot Roast with Potatoes: Add 2 potatoes, quartered, when turning the roast after HIGH power. Remove with the meat when the other vegetables are pureed.

Beef Pot Roast with Red Wine: Substitute ½ cup red wine for half of the beef broth.

Beef Pot Roast in Ale: Substitute ½ cup ale or beer for half of the beef broth.

Beef Pot Roast with Tomatoes: Substitute 1 cup fresh or undrained canned tomatoes, peeled and chopped, with ½ teaspoon salt for the beef broth. Substitute 2 tablespoons tomato paste for the flour. Substitute 1 tablespoon fresh or ½ teaspoon dried basil for the thyme.

Beef Pot Roast with Cream Gravy: Reduce the beef broth to ½ cup. Add 1 cup light cream or half and half when cooking the gravy. Just bring to the boiling point.

Beef Pot Roast with Mushrooms: Add 1 pound mushrooms, sliced, to the gravy when cooking. Cook the gravy on HIGH for 7 to 10 minutes to cook the mushrooms, stirring twice. Sprinkle with 2 tablespoons chopped fresh parsley.

Veal Pot Roast: Substitute a rolled veal roast for the beef. Substitute Chicken Broth (page 118) for the beef broth. Follow the basic recipe or any of the variations above, using white wine for red wine.

Braised Lamb Shanks: Substitute 3 pounds lamb shanks or 3 to 4 individual shanks. Follow the veal roast variation above.

MARINATED POT ROAST

MAKES 6 TO 8 SERVINGS   BEGIN THE DAY BEFORE SERVING
COOKING TIME: 1¼ HOURS TO 1 HOUR 20 MINUTES

If time and planning allows, we feel that marinating is well worth the effort to add both flavor and tenderness to this meat. Piercing the meat with a fork will allow the marinade to penetrate. A veal or lamb roast can be substituted for the beef. See the last two variations below.

1 3- to 4-pound beef rump or bottom round roast	1 bay leaf
2 medium carrots, sliced	1 garlic clove, minced
1 medium onion, sliced	½ teaspoon salt
1 cup dry red wine	¼ teaspoon pepper
1 tablespoon brandy or vinegar	⅛ teaspoon dried rosemary

Pierce the meat with a fork in several places. In a 4-quart casserole with a lid combine the remaining ingredients. Add the meat. Cover and refrigerate. Let marinate for 6 to 14 hours, turning over a few times.

When ready, cover tightly and cook on HIGH for 15 minutes. Cook on MEDIUM for 60 to 65 minutes, or until tender, turning the meat over halfway through the total cooking time. Let stand, covered, for 10 minutes.

VARIATIONS:

Marinated Pot Roast with Vegetable Gravy: Transfer the roast to a serving platter. Cover with foil. Force the vegetables and cooking liquid through a sieve, or add to a food processor in 2 batches to puree. Blend 1 tablespoon all-purpose flour and ¼ cup beef broth (see Mock Brown Broth or Stock, page 119) in a small bowl until smooth. Stir into the pureed vegetable mixture. Cook, uncovered, on HIGH for 4 to 5 minutes, or until slightly thickened, stirring once to make smooth. Cut the beef into thin slices and spoon some of the gravy over the meat. Serve the rest in a gravy boat.

Marinated Pot Roast with Pearl Onions: During standing time, cook 1 pound pearl onions (page 72). Garnish the pot roast with the onions.

Marinated Pot Roast with Pearl Onions and Peas: During standing time, cook 1 pound pearl onions (page 72) and 2 pounds or 2 cups peas (page 70). Thinly slice the meat. To serve, spoon the peas into 6 lettuce-leaf cups and place them around the sliced meat. Spoon some onions between the lettuce cups.

Marinated Lamb Shoulder: Substitute a lamb shoulder for the beef.

Marinated Veal Roast with Vegetables: Substitute a rolled veal roast for the beef. Substitute dry white wine for red wine and Chicken Broth (page 118) for beef broth.

SAUERBRATEN

MAKES 6 TO 8 SERVINGS   BEGIN 3 TO 6 DAYS BEFORE SERVING
COOKING TIME: 1 HOUR 19 MINUTES TO 1 HOUR 26 MINUTES

Marinating the meat for slightly longer in red wine vinegar adds the sour flavor that is balanced by the sweet gingersnap cookies in the sauce; the gingersnaps also serve to thicken the sauce. The microwave can't cut down on the time necessary for marination, but it can make the cooking process go quickly. We think the flavor is worth the wait!

6 cloves	½ cup red wine vinegar
1 bay leaf	½ teaspoon salt
1 3- to 4-pound beef rump, bottom round, or large-diameter-cut roast	¼ teaspoon pepper
	8 gingersnap cookies, crushed (¾ to 1 cup)
2 medium carrots, sliced	
1 stalk celery, sliced	1 tablespoon all-purpose flour
1 medium onion, sliced	¼ cup beef broth (see Mock Brown Broth or Stock, page 119)
1 garlic clove, minced	
1 cup dry red wine or water	

Tie the cloves and bay leaf in a cheesecloth bag. Pierce the meat with a fork in several places and place it in a 3-quart rectangular casserole. Add the cheesecloth bag and the remaining ingredients, except the gingersnap cookies, flour, and beef broth. Cover and marinate for 3 to 6 days, turning over twice the first day and once every day after that.

After marinating discard the cheesecloth bag. Add the gingersnaps. Cover tightly and cook on HIGH for 15 minutes; stir the gravy. Cover again and cook on MEDIUM for 60 to 65 minutes, or until tender, turning the meat over halfway through the total cooking time. Let stand, covered, for 10 minutes.

Transfer the cooked roast to a serving platter. Cover with foil. Force the cooking liquid and vegetables through a sieve or add to a food processor in 2 batches to puree. In a small bowl combine the flour and beef broth to blend. Add to the pureed vegetable mixture. Cook, uncovered, on HIGH for 4 to 6 minutes, or until boiling, stirring once.

VARIATION:

Sauerbraten with Tomatoes: Add ½ cup fresh or undrained canned tomatoes, peeled, seeded, and chopped, with the gingersnaps.

Boiled Beef Basics:

1. A brisket is a less tender cut of meat that is best simmered in water with vegetables for flavoring. After bringing the water to a boil on HIGH, the power is turned down to MEDIUM to gently simmer the meat to doneness.
2. To keep the outer areas from drying out we cook these large briskets with more water than is suggested in other microwave cookbooks, which add about 15 minutes to the cooking time, but we prefer the results. Two cups water is called for with a 3- to 4-pound brisket.
3. All available steam is necessary to keep the meat tender and cook the vegetables. A tight cover, preferably a glass lid, that is easy to remove when the meat is turned over, is the choice. An oval 4-quart covered casserole is best.
4. The meat should be turned over twice

through cooking so that the heated liquid has a chance to cover both sides of the meat, adding flavor, moistness, and heat.
5. Standing time is important to complete the cooking of the meat. In this time a vegetable is cooked, if desired.
6. *Doneness:* It is tender yet holds its shape and doesn't fall apart to slice nicely.

✹ BOILED BEEF

MAKES 8 TO 10 SERVINGS   BEGIN ABOUT 1¼ HOURS BEFORE SERVING
COOKING TIME: 1 HOUR 12 MINUTES TO 1 HOUR 25 MINUTES

The final broth makes a good soup, which, with vegetables, noodles, or egg drops added to it, can become the first course.

- 1 3-pound lean first-cut fresh beef brisket or bottom round
- 2 cups water
- 1 onion, quartered
- 1 carrot, sliced
- 1 celery rib, sliced
- 3 whole cloves
- 4 whole peppercorns
- ½ teaspoon salt
- 2 sprigs fresh parsley, or 1 tablespoon dried
- 1 garlic clove, crushed
- 1 sprig fresh thyme, or ¼ teaspoon dried
- Country mustard with seeds
- Horseradish

Place the beef brisket in a 4-quart casserole with a lid. Pour water over the meat. Cover tightly and cook on HIGH for 12 to 15 minutes to bring to a rolling boil; turn the meat over. Cover again and cook on MEDIUM for 30 minutes; turn the meat over.

Add the remaining ingredients except the mustard and horseradish. Cover again and cook on MEDIUM for 30 to 40 minutes, or until the meat is fork tender and the vegetables are cooked. Let stand, covered, for 10 to 15 minutes. Strain the cooking liquid. Add the carrot and celery to the cooking liquid and serve as a first course broth. Discard the remaining onions and herbs. Thinly slice the meat and serve with mustard and horseradish. Goes well with pickled beets and boiled new potatoes (page 73) as accompaniments.

VARIATIONS:

Boiled Beef with Pasta in Broth: Remove the beef from the broth and strain the broth into a 1-quart casserole. Add ½ cup pastina or arroz. Cover tightly and cook on HIGH for 1 minute, or until the pasta is tender.

Boiled Beef with Egg Drop Broth: Remove the beef from the broth and strain the broth into a 1-quart casserole. Cover tightly and cook on HIGH for 4 to 8 minutes, or until boiling. Meanwhile, in a small dish combine 1 egg and 1 tablespoon all-purpose flour until smooth. Stir into the boiling soup.

Beef Boiled in Beer: Substitute beer for the water.

Boiled Beef with Beef-Onion Gravy: Remove the beef from the broth. In a 4-cup measure combine 2 tablespoons butter and 1 medium onion, chopped. Cook on HIGH for 2 to 3 minutes, or until the onion is tender. Stir in 3 tablespoons all-purpose flour to make a smooth paste. Stir in 2 cups beef broth, 1 tablespoon vinegar or lemon juice, salt, and pepper. Cook on HIGH for 6 to 8 minutes, or until boiling and slightly thickened, stirring after 5 minutes.

BASIC BOILED CORNED BEEF DINNER

MAKES 8 TO 10 SERVINGS   BEGIN ABOUT 1 ¾ HOURS BEFORE SERVING
COOKING TIME: 1 HOUR 12 MINUTES TO 1 HOUR 25 MINUTES

This corned beef dinner combines carrots, potatoes, and cabbage—all in the same dish. The carrots and potatoes are cooked with the meat but because cabbage takes a lot of room and tends to fall apart if cooked too long, that is best done during standing time. It will stretch to feed a crowd or give the family Reuben-sandwich and corned-beef-hash leftovers. See our leftover suggestions on the next few pages or serve corn beef, sliced, with Horseradish Cream (page 273) as a first course.

1 3- to-4 pound corned beef brisket	**1 medium head of cabbage, cut into 8 to 10 wedges**
2 cups water	**Mustard**
4 large carrots cut into 1 inch pieces	**Horseradish**
4 potatoes, peeled and quartered	

Rinse the corned beef well, since *corned beef is very salty if not rinsed.*

Place it into 4-quart casserole with a lid. Pour the water over the meat. Cover tightly and cook on HIGH for 12 to 15 minutes to bring to a rolling boil; turn the meat over. Cover again and cook on MEDIUM for 30 minutes; turn the meat over.

Add the carrots and potatoes. Cover again and cook on MEDIUM for 30 to 40 minutes or until the meat is fork tender and the vegetables are cooked. Let stand, covered, for 10 to 15 minutes.

Meanwhile, remove ¼ cup cooking liquid and pour into a 1½-quart casserole. Add the cabbage. Cover tightly and cook on HIGH for 12 to 15 minutes, or until tender.

After standing time, slice the beef diagonally across the grain into thin pieces. Place on a serving platter. Surround with the cooked vegetables. Spoon some of the cooking liquid over all. Serve with mustard and horseradish.

VARIATION:

Boiled Beef Dinner: Substitute a 3-pound lean first-cut fresh beef brisket for the corned beef.

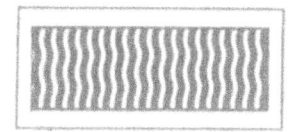

CORNED BEEF SALAD WITH HORSERADISH DRESSING

MAKES 4 SERVINGS

This is the first of three delicious ways to use leftover sliced corned beef.

- ⅓ cup Mayonnaise (page 175)
- ⅓ cup plain yogurt
- 2 tablespoons prepared horseradish
- 2 tablespoons chopped chives or scallions
- 1 pound Boiled Corned Beef (page 267) or Boiled Beef (page 266), thinly sliced and cut into bite-size pieces
- 1 green pepper, cut into ¼-inch strips, halved

In a medium bowl combine the mayonnaise, yogurt, horseradish, and chives. Toss with the corned beef and peppers.

GLAZED CORNED BEEF

MAKES 8 TO 10 SERVINGS   BEGIN ABOUT 1½ HOURS BEFORE SERVING
COOKING TIME: 1 HOUR 7 MINUTES TO 1¼ HOURS

We first had this at a buffet and thought it was perfect because it goes a long way when served with other things. Try Poached Winter Fruits (page 493) as an accompaniment.

- 1 3- to 4-pound corned beef brisket
- 2 cups water
- ½ cup apricot preserves
- 2 tablespoons Dijon mustard (whole-grain preferred)
- 2 tablespoons brown sugar
- ½ teaspoon ground ginger
- ½ teaspoon ground cinnamon

Rinse the corned beef well; place in a 4-quart casserole with a lid. Pour the water over the meat. Cover tightly and cook on HIGH for 12 to 15 minutes to bring to a rolling boil; turn the meat over. Cover again and cook on MEDIUM for 30 minutes; turn the meat over. Continue to cook on MEDIUM for 25 to 30 minutes. Let stand, covered, for 10 minutes.

Meanwhile, make the glaze by combining the remaining ingredients in a small bowl. Remove the beef from the liquid and place on a microwaveproof platter. Spread the glaze over the corned beef. Cook, uncovered, on HIGH for 5 minutes, basting with the juices twice. Let stand for 15 minutes before serving.

Slice the corned beef very thinly across the grain and serve warm or at room temperature.

VARIATION:

Glazed Boiled Beef: Substitute a 3-pound lean first-cut fresh beef brisket for the corned beef.

CORNED BEEF SANDWICHES

MAKES 2 SERVINGS
COOKING TIME: 2 TO 4 MINUTES

½ pound cooked corned beef, thinly sliced

4 slices of good rye or pumpernickel
Mustard

Place the corned beef slices on a plate, overlapping slightly, with the center open. Cover with plastic wrap and heat on MEDIUM-HIGH for 2 to 4 minutes, until heated through. Pile onto good rye or pumpernickel bread and serve with a variety of mustards.

REUBEN SANDWICHES

MAKES 1 TO 4 SERVINGS
COOKING TIME: 1 TO 2 MINUTES

One to four sandwiches will heat in about the same time on the browning dish. Just vary the ingredients according to the amount you desire.

Butter
2 to 8 slices of pumpernickel bread
Russian dressing (optional)

Cooked corned beef, thinly sliced
Sauerkraut (optional)
Swiss cheese, sliced

Preheat the microwave browning dish on HIGH for 4 or 5 minutes.

Meanwhile, butter 1 side of each bread slice; this side will be placed on the browner. Spread half of bread slices with the Russian dressing on the unbuttered side. Top 1 Russian dressing side of bread with the corned beef, sauerkraut, and Swiss cheese. Cover with the other slice of bread, buttered side out.

Place the sandwich or sandwiches onto the heated browning dish, pressing down with a metal spatula. Cook on HIGH for 30 seconds; turn over. Cook on HIGH for 30 seconds to 1½ minutes, or until the filling is heated through.

Roast Pork Loin or Fresh Ham Basics:

1. Pork loin roasts and fresh hams are *always* covered with a tight lid—vented plastic wrap is *not* tight enough here—to retain the most steam and give optimum uniformity in heating.
2. Pork is cooked with fat side down first to heat the fat well and let it baste the entire loin when it is turned over. Turning over aids in the even cooking and is necessary for any large piece of meat.
3. The pork roast is cooked on HIGH first to heat the entire surface well and build up heat, then on MEDIUM power for the remaining time so it remains juicy and doesn't get overcooked and dry on the outside.
4. It is best to temperature-test a pork roast for doneness with a microwave oven temperature probe or conventional oven thermometer, once the pork has been removed.
5. A pork roast has liquid poured over it before cooking and thus can be rubbed with a little salt.
6. The standing time for pork roasts is 10 to 15 minutes to let the internal temperature rise and equalize throughout the meat. Meat should still be covered with a lid or tented foil during this time.
7. *Doneness:* Meat should feel tender but firm when pierced with a knife. Meat will be light in color and the juices will be slightly pink. There should be no pink areas next to the bone.

    If measured with a conventional thermometer, the internal temperature upon removal from the oven will be 165°F after the thermometer has been inserted for at least 1 minute. This will rise to 170°F after standing time. The meat thermometer should be inserted into the meatiest section of the roast, not touching any fatty areas, or in the center of a boneless roast. When inserting the thermometer into a fresh ham with a bone, insert it into the meatiest area until it touches the bone, then withdraw the tip until it is in the meatiest area.

    Underdone: Pork may appear done on the outside, so the best way to check it is with a thermometer.

    Overdone: If the temperature has risen too high and the meat appears firm but dry, slice thinly across the grain and serve in gravy. Reheating the slices in gravy also helps to moisten.

✸ ROAST PORK LOIN OR FRESH HAM

HIGH *5 minutes, then* MEDIUM *11 to 12 minutes per pound*
MAKES 4 TO 6 SERVINGS   BEGIN ABOUT 1 HOUR BEFORE SERVING
COOKING TIME: 38 TO 41 MINUTES

A fresh pork roast in 1 hour? Not bad! And a roast that remains juicy yet golden brown because of the surface fat. Save those drippings and make one of the rich, smooth gravies that follow.

Serve with Applesauce (page 492) or Spicy Poached Pears (page 490). During standing time, cook vegetables if desired.

1 3-pound pork loin, roast, or fresh ham (see Note)	1 medium onion, chopped
½ teaspoon salt	½ cup Chicken Broth or Stock (page 118), white wine, or apple juice
⅛ teaspoon pepper	
1 sprig fresh thyme, or ¼ teaspoon dried	

Season the meat with salt and pepper. Place the meat, fat side down, in a 3-quart casserole with a lid. Add the thyme and onion. Pour the broth over the pork. Cover tightly and cook on HIGH for 5 minutes, then on MEDIUM for 16 minutes.

Turn the meat over. Cover tightly and cook on MEDIUM for 17 to 20 minutes, or until the meat is done and an inserted thermometer registers 165°F. Transfer the pork to a serving platter. Cover with foil. Let stand for about 10 minutes, until the internal temperature registers 170°F.

NOTE: For a larger size pork loin or ham, see the cooking chart on page 62.

VARIATIONS:

Pork Roast with Gravy: During standing time, strain the meat juices into a 4-cup glass measure; there will be between 1½ and 2 cups cooking juices with fat. Remove as much fat as possible. In a small bowl combine 3 tablespoons all-purpose flour with ¼ cup chicken broth to make a smooth paste. Stir the flour paste, another ¾ cup chicken broth, and an optional 1 tablespoon brandy into the meat juices. Cook, uncovered, on HIGH for 4 to 7 minutes, or until boiling and slightly thickened, stirring twice. Season with salt and pepper to taste. If you wish to thicken the gravy even more, remove ¼ cup gravy and combine with an additional 1 tablespoon flour. Stir back into the gravy and continue to cook, uncovered, on HIGH until thickened.

Pork Roast with Cream Gravy: Follow the Pork Roast with Gravy variation above. Reduce the chicken broth to ½ cup. Stir in ½ cup cream or crème fraîche to the gravy at the end, right before serving. Heat again, if desired, but do not boil. Serve with Brandied Apple Slices (page 494).

Marmalade-Glazed Pork Roast with Carrots: Instead of chopping the onion cut it into thin slices. Add 4 carrots, thinly sliced, with the onions. Spread ¼ cup marmalade over the top of the roast after it has been turned over. Cover and continue cooking. When the roast tests done, transfer to a serving platter. With a slotted spoon, transfer the carrots and onion to the same serving platter. Tent with foil. Follow the Pork Roast with Gravy variation above, substituting 1 tablespoon orange-flavored liqueur for the brandy. Serve with Sweet and Sour Orange Sauce (page 182), if desired. Marmalade delicately sweetens pork and carrots, and the extra sugar causes pork to brown even more.

Pork Roast with Mustard: In a small bowl combine ¼ cup prepared mustard, 2 tablespoons brown sugar, and 1 tablespoon soy sauce. Spread it on the pork after turning the pork over halfway through cooking. Prepare the Pork Roast with Gravy variation above, if desired. The mustard gives the gravy a nice flavor, and glazes the roast.

Oriental Pork Roast: Prepare Sweet and Sour Apricot Sauce (page 182); set aside. Begin cooking the pork. Prepare Oriental Dressing (page 184). Brush the sauce on the pork after turning the pork over halfway through cooking. Prepare Oriental Vegetable Kabobs (page 483) during standing time. Serve the pork with the sweet and sour sauce and vegetables.

Cold Roast Pork: Chill the pork and slice. Serve with Herbed Mayonnaise (page 175) or Green Peppercorn Sauce (page 272). Great for a buffet table.

GREEN PEPPERCORN SAUCE

MAKES 1 CUP

- ½ cup Mayonnaise (page 175)
- ½ cup plain yogurt
- 1 tablespoon green peppercorns, drained

In a small bowl combine all the ingredients.

PITA SANDWICHES WITH BEEF, LAMB, OR PORK

MAKES 4 TO 6 SERVINGS
COOKING TIME: 3 TO 7 MINUTES

Here is an excellent way to use meat leftovers.

- 1 tablespoon butter or margarine
- 1 garlic clove, minced
- 1 medium onion, thinly sliced
- 1 pound cooked meat, thinly sliced
- ¼ teaspoon dried oregano
- Salt and pepper
- 4 large pita bread rounds, halved
- 1 cup thinly sliced lettuce
- 1 tomato, thinly sliced
- Herb Yogurt Sauce (page 273) (optional)

In a 1-quart casserole combine the butter, garlic, and onion. Cook on HIGH for 2 to 4 minutes, or until the onion is tender. Stir in the sliced meat, oregano, and salt and pepper to taste. Cover with wax paper and cook on HIGH for 1 to 3 minutes, or until heated through, stirring once. Spoon into the pita pockets. Top with lettuce and tomato. Spoon some yogurt sauce on top, if desired.

HORSERADISH CREAM

MAKES 1 CUP

Serve with sliced beef.

- 1 cup heavy cream, whipped
- ¼ cup prepared horseradish

In a bowl fold the horseradish into the whipped cream and mix.

HERB YOGURT SAUCE

MAKES 1 CUP

Serve with beef or lamb.

- 1 cup plain yogurt
- 1 tablespoon lemon or lime juice
- ¼ cup chopped fresh dill or parsley
- ½ teaspoon crushed cuminseed, or ⅛ teaspoon ground

In a small bowl combine all ingredients.

FLOUR TORTILLAS WITH SLICED MEAT

MAKES 4 SERVINGS
COOKING TIME: 1 MINUTE

- 1 pound cooked beef, lamb or pork, thinly sliced
- 12 flour tortillas, heated (page 50)
- 1 recipe Green Tomato Salsa (page 186)
- 1 recipe Salsa Ranchera (page 146)
- 1 cup thinly sliced lettuce
- 2 tomatoes, thinly sliced
- 1 cup shredded Monterey Jack or cheddar cheese
- 1 cup sour cream

Set the ingredients out in individual dishes and let everyone help themselves to this delicious and fun meal. Enclose the meat in the warm tortilla and top with a sauce, lettuce, tomatoes, cheese and sour cream.

SHEPHERD'S PIE

MAKES 4 SERVINGS
COOKING TIME: 18 TO 28 MINUTES

- 3 tablespoons butter
- ½ cup coarsely chopped onion
- 1 tablespoon all-purpose flour
- 1 cup gravy or broth
- 2 cups coarsely chopped cooked beef or lamb
- ¼ cup chopped fresh parsley
- ¼ teaspoon dried thyme
- Dash of nutmeg
- Salt and pepper
- 3 cups mashed cooked potatoes
- 3 tablespoons fine dry bread crumbs

In a 2-quart casserole combine 1 tablespoon butter and the onion. Cook on HIGH for 2 to 5 minutes, or until the onion is tender. Stir in the flour to form a paste. Add the gravy, beef, parsley, thyme, nutmeg and salt and pepper to taste. Cover tightly and cook on HIGH for 5 to 7 minutes, or until the liquid is boiling, stirring after 3 minutes.

Place the remaining 2 tablespoons butter in a 1-cup glass measure. Cook on HIGH for 35 seconds to 1 minute, or until melted.

Meanwhile, spread the mashed potatoes on top of the meat mixture. Sprinkle with pepper and the bread crumbs. Drizzle with the melted butter. Cover with wax paper and cook on MEDIUM for 10 to 15 minutes, or until heated through to 2 Macungie on the bottom of the dish (see page 44).

VARIATIONS:

Shepherd's Pie with Mushrooms: Add ½ cup sliced mushrooms with the meat.

Shepherd's Pie with Sweet Potatoes: Substitute 3 cups mashed cooked sweet potatoes for the white potatoes. Good after the holidays.

Shepherd's Pie with Mint: When using lamb, add ½ teaspoon dried mint. Mint is a nice complement.

MARINATED PORK SALAD

MAKES 2 SERVINGS

We look forward to cold pork with which to make sandwiches, but here is an interesting alternative.

- 8 ounces cooked pork, thinly sliced and cut into ¼-inch strips, chilled
- ¼ cup Oriental Dressing (page 184)
- 1 cup rinsed bean sprouts
- 2 green onions, thinly sliced
- 1 sweet red pepper, cut into ¼-inch strips
- 1 green pepper, cut into ¼-inch strips
- 1 celery rib, thinly sliced

In a medium bowl combine the pork and dressing. Let marinate for 1 hour. Stir in the remaining ingredients and serve.

SWEET AND SOUR PORK

MAKES 4 SERVINGS
COOKING TIME: 3 TO 5 MINUTES

- 1 tablespoon vegetable oil
- 1 garlic clove, minced
- 4 scallions, cut into 1-inch pieces
- 1 8-ounce can unsweetened pineapple chunks
- 2 cups diced cooked pork
- 2 tablespoons brown sugar
- 2 tablespoons vinegar
- 1 tablespoon cornstarch

In a 2-quart casserole combine the oil, garlic, and scallions. Cook on HIGH for 1 minute.

Drain the pineapple chunks, reserving the liquid. Stir the pineapple chunks and pork into the garlic and scallions. In a small bowl stir the reserved pineapple juice, brown sugar, vinegar, and cornstarch until smooth. Stir into the pork mixture. Cook on HIGH for 2 to 4 minutes, or until heated through, stirring each minute.

ORIENTAL PORK AND BROCCOLI

MAKES 4 SERVINGS
COOKING TIME: 5 TO 6 MINUTES

- 1 tablespoon vegetable oil
- 4 scallions, thinly sliced
- 3 tablespoons water
- 4 teaspoons soy sauce
- 1 tablespoon sherry or dry vermouth
- 2 teaspoons cornstarch
- 2 cups cubed cooked pork
- 4 cups broccoli flowerets

In a 2-quart casserole combine the oil and scallions. Cook on HIGH for 1 minute.

In a small bowl combine the water, soy sauce, sherry, and cornstarch until well blended. Stir the soy mixture into the scallions. Stir in the pork cubes to coat well. Cook on HIGH for 2 minutes, or until hot and slightly thickened, stirring once. Stir in the broccoli. Cover tightly and cook on HIGH for 2 to 3 minutes more, stirring once.

Lamb Roast Basics:

1. Leg of lamb can be cooked without a cover, but because one end is thinner than the other, it needs to be covered with foil. Lamb roasts don't need shielding unless they are unevenly shaped.
2. Placing a lamb roast on a roasting rack, or inverted plates, will raise the lamb above the fat and juices so one side doesn't get quite so hot.
3. Lamb roasts are cooked on HIGH power first to build up heat on the surface and then turned down to MEDIUM to cook the lamb through evenly.
4. Lamb roasts, like any large pieces of meat, need to be turned over halfway through cooking to ensure that they cook evenly. Starting fat side down will help to baste the lamb evenly once the fat starts melting, and the lamb is turned over.
5. Standing time, under loosely tented foil, is important to reflect the heat inward toward the meat and raise the internal temperature.
6. *Doneness:* The front part of the leg will appear quite red when cooking to rare, but don't let this disturb you. Trust the reading on the thermometer and it will be perfect.

If using a microwave sensor, insert it from the end of the leg with the round bone, so that the tip is in the center of the meaty area, and does not touch the bone. If not using a sensor, but a conventional non-microwave thermometer at the end, follow the sensor instructions and wait for 1 minute to obtain an accurate reading.

When tented loosely with foil, the temperature of the roast will rise between 15 and 20 degrees during standing time, which is why we cook it to what appears very rare.

MINT SAUCE

MAKES 1 CUP
COOKING TIME: 1 TO 2 MINUTES

¼ cup water
3 tablespoons sugar

½ cup vinegar
⅓ cup chopped fresh mint leaves

In a 1-cup glass measure combine the water and sugar. Cook on HIGH for 1 to 2 minutes, or until boiling, stirring to dissolve the sugar. Add the vinegar and mint. Chill before serving.

✹ ROAST LEG OF LAMB

MAKES 6 SERVINGS   BEGIN ABOUT 40 MINUTES BEFORE SERVING
COOKING TIME: 26 TO 29 MINUTES

We have found that many people who have told us they did not care for lamb changed their minds when it was prepared for them to rare doneness in the microwave oven. For the best flavor and results, trim the fell and fat to a minimum, leaving just a few streaks for basting.
Serve with Mint Sauce (page 276) or Cumberland Sauce (page 278).

- **1 3-pound leg of lamb**
- **1 tablespoon vegetable oil**
- **1 garlic clove, minced**
- **½ teaspoon dried rosemary**
- **Salt and pepper**

Rub the leg with the oil and garlic. Sprinkle lightly with the rosemary, salt and pepper. Shield the thin leg end with foil, covering 2 inches of end. Place on a large microwave roasting rack with the fat side down in a 2-quart rectangular dish. Cook on HIGH for 5 minutes (if 3 pounds or under) or for 10 minutes (if over 3 pounds). Cook on MEDIUM for 7 to 9 minutes per pound for rare (120°F), 8 to 10 minutes per pound for medium (135°F), 9 to 12 minutes per pound for well (145°F), turning the lamb over halfway through total cooking time. Tent loosely with foil. Let stand for 10 minutes. Serve with its natural juices.

VARIATIONS:

Leg of Lamb with Gravy: During standing time, pour 1 cup beef broth (see Mock Brown Broth or Stock, page 119) into a 4-cup glass measure. In a small bowl blend 1½ tablespoons all-purpose flour into 1 tablespoon cold water. Add 2 tablespoons broth to the flour paste, stirring until smooth. Stir the paste back into the broth. After the lamb has stood 10 minutes, drain the juices into the broth. Cook, uncovered, on HIGH for 3 to 5 minutes, or until thickened. Add salt and pepper to taste.

Leg of Lamb with Garlic Cloves: Make 6 small deep slashes on the surface of the lamb. Insert 6 small peeled garlic cloves into the slashes.

Leg of Lamb with Peppercorn and Mustard Coating: In a small bowl combine 2 tablespoons prepared mustard, 2 tablespoons crushed black peppercorns, and 1 teaspoon soy sauce. Spread over the surface of the lamb. Eliminate the other seasonings and garlic.

Lamb Shoulder with Rosemary: Substitute boned, rolled lamb shoulder for leg of lamb.

CUMBERLAND SAUCE

MAKES 1¼ CUPS
COOKING TIME: 3 TO 5 MINUTES

- 1 cup port wine
- 1 tablespoon cornstarch
- 1 tablespoon brown sugar
- 1 teaspoon dry mustard
- ¼ teaspoon ground ginger
- ¼ cup red currant jelly
- 1 tablespoon grated orange rind
- ¼ cup orange juice
- 2 tablespoons lemon juice

In a 4-cup glass measure combine the wine, cornstarch, brown sugar, mustard, and ginger, stirring until smooth. Cook on HIGH for 2 minutes; stir. Add the remaining ingredients. Cook, uncovered, on HIGH for 1 to 3 minutes, until thickened, stirring once.

Tender-Cut Beefsteak Basics:

1. We have found that with this combined cooking of browning dish heat and microwave energy, the cooking time for a steak depends strictly on its thickness, not weight.
2. Because it is the heat of the browning dish that browns the surface of the steak, it is important to press the steak firmly against the hot dish with a *metal* spatula. We recommend the browning dish, because the steak cooks in such a short time that it wouldn't brown without it.
3. Steaks on the browning dish are cooked uncovered so the meat won't become steamed.
4. Turning over a steak is necessary to brown both sides on the hot surface of the browning dish.
5. Any food cooked on a browning dish is cooked on HIGH power because the dish as well as the food is absorbing energy.
6. A steak cooks very quickly because there is a combination of conduction, from the browning dish, and radiant energy, from the microwaves. There is no standing time to speak of.
7. Season the steak at the end so its surface won't toughen.
8. *Doneness:* We have found the best way to test for steak doneness is to make a small slit closest to the bone or thickest part and judge the meat by its internal color at the end of cooking. Because the steak cooks so quickly, there is not much heat built up inside to make standing time necessary, except when it is over 1½ inches thick. If this is the case, let steak stand 5 to 10 minutes.

✸ TENDER-CUT BEEFSTEAK

MAKES 4 SERVINGS   BEGIN ABOUT 15 MINUTES BEFORE SERVING
COOKING TIME: 4 TO 8 MINUTES

The only really acceptable way to microwave a tender cut of steak is on a browning dish that gets hot and sears the outer surface to brown; the steak, however, remains moist inside because it is so quickly cooked with microwave energy. The hot dish will enable you to make some delicious "au jus" accompaniments for the steak, including a "flambéed" one. Serve with baked potatoes (see page 73) or Long-Grain Rice (page 196). Cooking both before the steak, they will still be hot to serve with the steak. To serve any other vegetable with the steak, cook before the steak, also, but reheat at the end.

---

1   2- to 3-pound sirloin, porterhouse, tenderloin, strip, or London broil steak, 1½ to 2 inches thick (see Note)
     Salt and pepper

Preheat a large microwave browning dish according to the manufacturer's instructions for steak, or about 9 minutes on HIGH.

Meanwhile, slash the fat about ½ inch deep at 1-inch intervals, around outside of the steak. This will prevent curling of the steak. Place the steak down on the hot browning grill, pressing the meat against the grill with a metal spatula. Cook, uncovered: rare, on HIGH for 2 minutes, then turn over and cook for 2 minutes more; for medium-rare, on HIGH for 2 minutes, then turn over and cook for 3 to 4 minutes more; for medium, on HIGH for 2½ minutes, then turn over and cook for 3½ to 4½ minutes more; for well done, on HIGH for 3 minutes, then turn over and cook for 4 to 5 minutes more.

Salt and pepper the steak before serving.

NOTE: For a steak of a different thickness, see the cooking chart on page 60.

VARIATIONS:

Steak with Herb Butter: Prepare a softened herb butter (page 183). Spread over the top of the grilled steak.

Steak with Mustard Butter: Prepare softened Mustard Butter (page 183). Spread over the top of the grilled steak.

Steak with Garlic Butter: Prepare softened Garlic Butter (page 183). Spread on the top of the grilled steak.

London Broil with Mushroom Sauce: Prepare Mushroom Sauce (page 172). Cook the London broil according to the basic recipe and thinly slice across the grain. Reheat the mushroom sauce and pour over the steak slices.

Steak with Brandy Sauce: Transfer the grilled steak to a carving platter. Tent loosely with foil. Pour ½ cup beef broth (see Mock

Brown Broth or Stock, page 119), 2 tablespoons dry sherry or vermouth, and 2 tablespoons brandy onto the hot browning dish. Cook on HIGH for 2 minutes. To the hot sauce add 2 tablespoons chopped fresh parsley and 1 tablespoon chopped fresh chives and any meat juice from the cutting board. Thinly slice the steak across the grain. Pour the sauce over the slices.

London Broil with Caper Sauce: Transfer the grilled steak to a carving platter. Tent loosely with foil. To the hot dish add ½ cup beef broth (see Mock Brown Broth or Stock, page 119), ¼ cup finely chopped shallots or green scallions, 1 tablespoon Dijon mustard, and 2 tablespoons drained capers. Cook on HIGH for 2 minutes. Stir in 2 tablespoons chopped fresh parsley and any meat juice from the board. Slice the steak across the grain. Spoon the sauce over the steak.

To Double a Sauce: Double the sauce ingredients and cooking time. Pass the extra sauce at the table.

STEAK AU POIVRE

(Pepper Steak)

MAKES 4 TO 6 SERVINGS   BEGIN ABOUT 30 MINUTES BEFORE SERVING
COOKING TIME: 5 TO 9 MINUTES

If you have any of this steak left over, see the next page for some serving suggestions, and a recipe for cheese steak sandwiches.

¼ cup coarsely ground pepper	1 teaspoon Worcestershire sauce
1 2- to 3-pound London broil steak or 4 club steaks	1 teaspoon lemon juice
	Dash of hot pepper sauce
2 tablespoons butter	2 tablespoons Cognac
½ cup beef broth (see Mock Brown Broth or Stock, page 119)	2 tablespoons chopped fresh parsley

Preheat a large microwave browning dish according to the manufacturer's instructions for steak, or about 9 minutes on HIGH. Meanwhile, press the pepper into both sides of the steak with the heel of your hand.

Spread the butter on the hot dish. Press the steak onto the dish with a metal spatula. Cook uncovered as directed on page 279. If cooking four club steaks, reposition the steaks when you turn them over.

Transfer the steak to a serving platter. Tent loosely with foil. To the browning dish add the beef broth, Worcestershire sauce, lemon juice, and hot pepper sauce. Cook on HIGH for 1 minute. Immediately add Cognac and ignite. Let the flames die down; this burns off the raw alcohol flavor. Pour the sauce over the steak and sprinkle with parsley.

CHEESE STEAK SANDWICH

MAKES 1 SERVING
COOKING TIME: 1 TO 2 MINUTES

The type of cheese and toppings you choose is up to you. We like sharp cheddar and hot pepper rings, but other people prefer Monterey Jack cheese, topped with tomatoes and lettuce.

- 4 to 6 slices of cooked steak
- 1 hero sandwich roll, split and toasted
- 1 to 2 slices of any cheese

Toppings:
- Hot pepper rings
- Tomato slices
- Lettuce shreds
- Spirited Onion Rings (recipe below)

Place the steak in a single layer on bottom of the toasted roll. Top the steak with cheese. Wrap the sandwich in a paper towel. Place on a microwaveproof plate. Heat on MEDIUM for 1 to 2 minutes, or until the cheese has melted. Add any of the suggested toppings. Top with the upper part of the roll and serve.

NOTE: *To Double:* Double the ingredients and heat on MEDIUM for 2 to 4 minutes.

Have Leftover Beefsteak?

Serve cold thinly sliced steak on garlic toasts as an appetizer or snack with drinks. Also, one of our favorite ways to serve leftover steak is for brunch with eggs: Thinly slice the meat, then, to take the chill off it, place 5 to 6 ounces on a microwaveproof plate in the oven. Heat, uncovered, on MEDIUM-HIGH for 2 to 3 minutes. Watch it closely so that it doesn't cook.

SPIRITED ONION RINGS

MAKES 2 SERVINGS

- 2 tablespoons butter
- 2 large Spanish onions, sliced
- 1 tablespoon dry vermouth or other dry white wine
- ½ teaspoon salt
- ¼ teaspoon pepper

In a 1-quart casserole combine all the ingredients. Cook on HIGH for 3 to 5 minutes, or until very tender, stirring once. Serve on sandwiches or with steaks.

Less Tender-Cut Beefsteak Basics:

1. A less tender chuck steak is best cooked with additional liquid to tenderize it. About 1 cup liquid is good for braising a 2- to 3-pound steak.
2. A tight cover, such as plastic wrap turned back on one corner to vent steam, will retain the most moisture to help tenderize the steak.
3. It is best to bring the liquid to a boil first on HIGH power and then allow the steak to simmer in this liquid on MEDIUM power, so that it cooks slowly and doesn't toughen.
4. Turn the steak over for the most even cooking, to allow both sides of the steak to benefit from the tenderizing moisture and to flavor the hot liquid.
5. *Doneness:* The braised steak will be tender when a carving fork is inserted and there is little or no pink color apparent when sliced open. During standing time the heat is conducted to the center of the meat and continues to tenderize it.

✺ BRISKLY BRAISED CHUCK STEAK

MAKES 4 TO 6 SERVINGS   BEGIN 1¼ HOURS BEFORE SERVING
COOKING TIME: 47 TO 61 MINUTES

Serve with noodles or boiled potatoes (page 73), cooked during standing time.

- 1 tablespoon butter
- 1 garlic clove, minced
- 1 onion, sliced
- 1 tablespoon all-purpose flour
- 1 cup beef broth (see Mock Brown Broth or Stock, page 119)
- 1 2- to 3-pound chuck steak
- Salt and pepper

In a 3-quart rectangular dish combine the butter, garlic, and onion. Cook on HIGH for 2 to 3 minutes, or until tender. Stir in the flour until smooth. Stir in the beef broth. Add the meat. Cover tightly and cook on HIGH for 5 to 8 minutes, or until the liquid is boiling. Cook on MEDIUM for 20 minutes; turn the meat over. Cover again and cook on MEDIUM for 20 to 30 minutes or until tender. Add the salt and pepper to taste; the addition of salt will depend on the saltiness of the broth. Let stand, covered, for 5 to 10 minutes.

VARIATIONS:

Chuck Steak with Gravy: Transfer the braised steak to a serving platter and cover with foil. Into the meat juices stir 1 to 2 tablespoons tomato paste, or 1 tablespoon flour blended into ¼ cup broth, water, dry sherry, or vermouth. Cook on HIGH for 4 to 7 minutes, or until boiling and thickened, stirring once.

Chuck Steak with Sour Cream Gravy: Prepare the Chuck Steak with Gravy variation above. Stir 1 cup sour cream into the finished gravy. Cook on HIGH for 2 to 3 minutes until heated but not boiling, stirring twice. Stir in 2 tablespoons chopped fresh parsley. Serve over the steak.

Braised Chuck Steak with Carrots and Potatoes: When turning the meat over, add 2 carrots, cut into 1-inch pieces, and 2 potatoes, cut into eighths. Cover again.

Braised Chuck Steak with Tomatoes and Peppers: Substitute 2 tablespoons tomato paste for the flour. Substitute 1 cup fresh or undrained canned tomatoes, peeled, seeded, and chopped, for the beef broth. When turning the meat over, add 2 green peppers, sliced ¼ inch thick, and ½ teaspoon dried basil.

Braised Chuck Steak with Mushrooms: Transfer the braised meat to a serving platter and cover with foil. Add ½ pound mushrooms, sliced, and 2 tablespoons dry vermouth to the meat juices. Cook, uncovered, on HIGH 3 to 5 minutes, or until the mushrooms are heated through, stirring after 3 minutes. Serve over the steak.

Chuck Steak Braised in Red Wine: Substitute ½ cup red wine for half of the beef broth. Add ¼ teaspoon dried rosemary with the wine.

Tender Meat Strips Basics:

1. Make sure to cut the strips as equal in thickness as possible for the most even cooking. It is a lot easier to slice meat if it has been partially frozen for 30 to 40 minutes. (In fact it has been said of Count Stroganoff, that he discovered beef Stroganoff when his meat was frozen so solid it could only be cut into thin strips!)
2. Tender strips may be cooked on HIGH and require no liquid to tenderize them. Large amounts of liquids are added as a flavorful sauce. When these are added, MEDIUM power is called for, to develop the flavor of those sauces. In addition, recipes calling for thin strips of meat are best reheated on MEDIUM power so they don't toughen, stirring once or twice.
3. Tender strips gain the best flavor from a marinade or a rich or spicy sauce.
4. A 10-inch pie plate or 2-quart casserole is the right diameter dish to contain all the ingredients without spreading out the meat so thinly that it overcooks.
5. A tight cover is called for if there are vegetables to be cooked or simmered with the meat. In the case of the Stroganoff, the mushrooms will give off their own cooking liquid, and the cooking dish should be loosely covered so that the sauce can thicken.
6. Initial cooking of onions and other crisp vegetables are needed to develop flavor before adding the meat. If there are a large quantity of onions, they are arranged inside the ring of meat. This is because the microwave penetrates the outer meat ring, cooking the thicker meat and the thinner vegetables in the same amount of time.
7. Tender strips are stirred halfway through for the most even cooking.
8. Standing time is important if the recipe has been cooking for a long while on MEDIUM power.

STEAK TERIYAKI

MAKES 4 SERVINGS   BEGIN ABOUT 30 MINUTES BEFORE SERVING
COOKING TIME: 7 TO 12 MINUTES

This is a quick and easy meal that is best when served over rice. Cook the rice while the meat is marinating, and it will still be hot when it's time to serve.

- 3 tablespoons soy sauce
- 1 tablespoon lemon juice
- 1 tablespoon brown sugar
- 1 teaspoon cornstarch
- 1 pound round steak, sliced across the grain into ¼-inch-thick strips
- 1 tablespoon sesame or vegetable oil
- 1 garlic clove, minced
- 1 large Bermuda onion, thinly sliced
- 1 teaspoon chopped fresh ginger, or ¼ teaspoon ground
- 1 sweet red pepper, cut into ¼-inch strips
- 1 green pepper, cut into ¼-inch strips

In a medium bowl combine the soy sauce, lemon juice, sugar, and cornstarch, stirring until smooth. Stir in the beef strips. Let marinate for 15 to 20 minutes at room temperature.

In a 10-inch pie plate combine the oil, garlic, onion, and ginger. Cook on HIGH for 2 to 4 minutes, or until the onion is tender-crisp. Move the onion into the center of the dish, leaving about a 2-inch space around the outer rim. With a slotted spoon, remove the meat from the marinade and place it around the onions to fill space; reserve the marinade. Cover tightly and cook on HIGH for 3 minutes, or until almost all pink color is gone from the meat. Stir the onion and meat together.

Stir in the remaining marinade and pepper strips. Cover tightly and cook on HIGH for 2 to 4 minutes, or until no pink color remains in the meat and the peppers are tender-crisp; stir. Serve over rice.

VARIATIONS:

Beef Teriyaki with Tomatoes: At the end of cooking, add 2 ripe tomatoes, cut into eighths. Cover again and cook on HIGH for 1 to 2 minutes, or until the tomatoes are heated through but still hold their shape. This adds a nice color if only green peppers are available.

Beef Teriyaki with Snow Peas: Substitute ¼ pound snow peas, trimmed, for 1 pepper.

Spicy Beef Teriyaki: Add ¼ teaspoon red pepper flakes with peppers. We love it this way!

Beef Teriyaki with Broccoli Flowerets: Substitute 2 cups broccoli flowerets for the peppers.

Beef Teriyaki with Chinese Cabbage: Substitute 2 cups Chinese cabbage, sliced into ¼-inch strips, for the peppers.

BEEF STROGANOFF

MAKES 4 SERVINGS   BEGIN 40 TO 50 MINUTES BEFORE SERVING
COOKING TIME: 25 TO 34 MINUTES

Serve this over buttered noodles or over Long-Grain Rice (page 196), cooked before the meat and reheated during the Stroganoff standing time.

2 tablespoons butter	1 cup beef broth (see Mock Brown Broth or Stock, page 119)
1 medium onion, thinly sliced	½ teaspoon salt
1½ pounds boneless beef sirloin or fillet, cut across the grain into ¼-inch strips	¼ teaspoon pepper
	¼ cup dry white or red wine
3 tablespoons all-purpose flour	¾ pound fresh mushrooms, sliced
	1 cup sour cream

In a 2-quart casserole combine the butter and onion. Cook on HIGH for 2 to 4 minutes, or until the onion is tender. Meanwhile, in a medium bowl toss the meat strips with flour to coat. Stir the meat into the casserole. Cover with wax paper and cook on HIGH for 3 minutes, or until almost all pink color is gone.

Stir in the broth, salt, pepper, and wine. Cover tightly and cook on HIGH for 8 minutes, or until boiling. Stir in the mushrooms. Cover again, and cook on MEDIUM for 10 to 15 minutes, or until slightly thickened and the flavors have developed.

Stir in the sour cream. Cover again and cook on MEDIUM for 2 to 4 minutes to heat through. Let stand, covered, for 5 minutes.

GRILLADES

MAKES 4 SERVINGS   BEGIN 40 TO 50 MINUTES BEFORE SERVING
COOKING TIME: 26 TO 36 MINUTES

This is a spicy Creole specialty that is especially delicious over grits. Even if you don't like grits, this recipe could change your mind. Serve for lunch or as a different twist to brunch, along with strong chicory coffee. Prepare Grits (page 193) before or after the basic recipe. Either one will stay hot when covered.

- 1 tablespoon vegetable oil
- 1 garlic clove, minced
- 1 medium onion, finely chopped
- ½ cup finely chopped celery
- 1 pound beef round steak, cut across grain into ¼-inch strips
- 3 tablespoons all-purpose flour
- 1 cup fresh or undrained canned tomatoes, peeled and chopped
- 1 cup beef broth (see Mock Brown Broth or Stock, page 119)
- 1 green pepper, coarsely chopped
- ½ cup chopped fresh parsley, or 2 tablespoons dried
- ½ teaspoon cayenne pepper
- Pinch of salt

In a 2-quart casserole combine the oil, garlic, onion, and celery. Cover tightly and cook on HIGH for 2 to 4 minutes, or until the vegetables are tender. Meanwhile, in a medium bowl toss the meat strips with the flour to coat. Stir the meat into the onions and celery. Move the mixture to the outside rim of the casserole. Cover tightly and cook on HIGH for 4 minutes, or until only a slight pink color remains in meat, stirring after 2 minutes.

Add the remaining ingredients. Cover tightly and cook on HIGH for 5 to 8 minutes, or until the mixture is boiling; stir. Cover again and cook on MEDIUM for 15 to 20 minutes, or until the vegetables are tender and the flavor has developed. Let stand, covered, for 5 minutes.

Tender-Cut Chunks Basics (Beef, Lamb, Pork):

1. Tender-cut chunks of meat take just a short period of time to cook on HIGH power. They contain little connective tissue that will toughen.
2. Cubes should be cut to fairly equal size for even cooking.
3. No additional liquid is needed for cooking. A marinade is used for flavoring and some in coloring to help in the browning.
4. Arrangement on the skewer is very important, because the microwave energy will cook those pieces on the outside edges

first. That is why the meat should be placed on the outside, with faster-cooking vegetables in the middle. If only meat is used, the skewers are arranged in spoke fashion on a round plate with an open space in the center.
5. The number of skewers with no more than 6 chunks of meat on the skewer is important to overall evenness of cooking. Leaving a small space between the meat chunks will help all surface areas of the meat to cook.
6. Skewers that are not arranged in spoke fashion on a round plate, as the satay is, need to be rearranged more frequently for even cooking. The most microwave energy will be attracted to the meat on the outer ends of the skewers.
7. Skewers are ready to serve when they come out of the oven.
8. *Doneness:* Chunks should have no pink color remaining on the outside and be firm to the touch yet fork tender.

Underdone: If any pieces of meat look much redder than those on the outside, you may wish to rearrange them with the chunks on the end of the skewer.

Overdone: If skewers aren't rearranged or turned over as directed, the outer skewers may overcook. Grind up and substitute for ground beef in Picadillo (page 325).

✺ BEEF OR LAMB KABOBS

MAKES 4 SERVINGS AS A MAIN COURSE, 24 AS AN APPETIZER   BEGIN 15 MINUTES BEFORE SERVING
COOKING TIME: 6 TO 10 MINUTES

When cut into cubes and skewered, 1 pound of steak can be stretched into an ample meal for four. Cooking the skewered meat and vegetables at the same time makes for easy meal planning and preparation. If desired, cook Long-Grain Rice (page 196) and then cook the meat during the rice standing time. Arrange the kabobs over the rice to serve.

1 pound tender beef or lamb, cut into even 1-inch cubes	4 medium onions, cut into quarters

Skewer the meat and onions onto 8 wooden skewers, placing the meat on each end with the onions in the center and leaving space between all items on the skewers. Lay the long skewers widthwise across a 2-quart baking dish. Cook on HIGH for 6 to 10 minutes or until the meat reaches desired doneness, turning over and repositioning the skewers every 2 minutes, moving the less cooked kabobs to the outside ends.

NOTE: Onions will cook to tender-crisp. If you want them cooked more than that, cook them alone on HIGH for 1 to 2 minutes, or until tender-crisp, before skewering with the meat.

VARIATIONS:

Marinated Oriental Beef or Lamb Kabobs: Prepare Oriental Dressing (page 184). Marinate the meat-and-vegetable skewers in

½ cup dressing in the cooking dish for 30 minutes or overnight before cooking, reserving remaining ¼ cup dressing. Drain the marinade from the kabobs before cooking and reserve to brush on during cooking. Serve reserved ¼ cup dressing at the table.

Tomato-Marinated Kabobs: Combine ½ cup tomato juice, 1 tablespoon lemon juice, ¼ teaspoon dried rosemary, ¼ teaspoon salt, and ⅛ teaspoon black pepper in the cooking dish. Marinate the meat-and-vegetable skewers in the tomato marinade for 30 minutes or overnight before cooking. Drain the marinade from the dish and reserve. Brush the kabobs with the reserved marinade during cooking.

Lemon-Curry Marinade: Combine ¼ cup olive or vegetable oil, 2 tablespoons lime or lemon juice, and 1 teaspoon curry powder in the cooking dish. Marinate the meat-and-vegetable skewers in the lemon marinade for 30 minutes or overnight before cooking. Drain the marinade from the dish and reserve. Brush the kabobs with the reserved marinade during cooking.

Lamb and Zucchini Kabobs: Cut 1 small zucchini and 1 small yellow summer squash into 1-inch circles. Place in the center of the skewers, with the onions next and then the meat on the outer ends. Cook as directed in the basic recipe. Serve with Herb Yogurt Sauce (page 273) and pita bread.

Beef and Mushroom-Tomato Kabobs: Substitute ¼ pound whole mushrooms and 4 tomatoes, quartered, for the onions, placing quickest-cooking tomatoes in the center of the skewers, with the mushrooms next to them and then the meat on the outer ends. Cook as directed in the basic recipe.

BEEF, PORK, OR LAMB SATAY

MAKES 4 SERVINGS AS A MAIN COURSE, 24 AS AN APPETIZER   BEGIN AT LEAST 45 MINUTES BEFORE SERVING
COOKING TIME: 7 TO 12 MINUTES

Satay is the national dish of Indonesia, and it is cooked on wooden sticks there over open coals. The distinguishing characteristic of this dish is the spicy peanut sauce that is lavished over it.

---

1 tablespoon sesame or vegetable oil	1 pound lean boneless lamb, pork loin, or lean steak, cut into even 1-inch cubes
¼ cup soy sauce	
2 tablespoons orange juice, or 1 tablespoon lime or lemon juice	1 recipe Peanut Satay Sauce (page 182)
1 tablespoon brown sugar	Lime or lemon wedges
1 garlic clove, minced	

In a large bowl combine the oil, soy sauce, orange juice, brown sugar, and garlic. Stir in the meat. Let it marinate for 30 minutes or overnight.

Thread 2 pieces of meat on toothpicks or 5 to 6 pieces on larger wooden skewers. Arrange in spoke fashion on a 12-inch microwaveproof serving platter, leaving the center open. Cook, uncovered, on HIGH for 7 to 12 minutes, or until cooked to desired doneness, rearranging the less cooked ends to the outside if necessary. Reheat the peanut sauce and serve in the center of the plate for dipping, or spoon over the skewers. Garnish with lime or lemon wedges.

Less Tender Meat Cubes Basics (Beef, Veal, Lamb, Pork):

1. Before adding the meat, chopped garlic, onion, or other vegetables must be cooked slightly first for them to achieve the proper texture and release their full flavor.
2. Cooking the meat, coated with flour first, aids in browning, which will add to the flavor. The flour will later thicken the gravy also. If tomato paste is substituted for flour, it is added with the remaining ingredients later.
3. Ragouts, stews or daubes are usually made from less tender chunks of meat. Even though the beef is a tougher cut of meat, it should be of good quality and free of gristle. Go to a reliable butcher or buy a large chunk of meat and cube it yourself. This can make or break the stew.

   The meat requires more moisture and slower cooking to tenderize and develop flavor. Once the vegetables and liquid have been added and brought to a boil, the stews are cooked mainly on MEDIUM power to accomplish this. A clear glass casserole makes it easy to see if the liquid has boiled yet.
4. Stews are covered tightly to seal in the steam to tenderize the meat. A glass lid will make uncovering and re-covering for stirring easier.
5. Because stews are large in volume, it is critical to stir where indicated to achieve the most even cooking.
6. The basic meat-cube stew formula goes like this: 2 pounds meat cubes to 2 cups liquid, thickened by 3 tablespoons flour, ¼ cup tomato paste, or a combination of 2 tablespoons each tomato paste and flour. If a clay simmerpot which has been soaked in water is used, reduce cooking liquid by ½ cup. Whole vegetables are variables to be added with the liquid, or—in the case of potatoes, mushrooms, snow peas, and green beans—should be cooked separately and stirred into the stew right before serving. Sour cream or yogurt are also stirred in at the end of cooking so they don't curdle. For more, see the stew recipes and their variations.
7. Standing time is very important to heat through all the meat and vegetables. Stews should be covered during this time to keep the steam and heat inside.
8. Stews often taste better and become thicker the following day. Because they take a little longer to cook than most meals, try preparing them while you're cleaning up the kitchen after a meal. If you plan to freeze a stew with potatoes, it is best to omit the

potatoes and cook them the day you'll be eating them. The flavor and texture will be much better.

9. *Doneness:* The meat and vegetables should be fork tender and the sauce should be well blended in flavor.

If the meat is too tough: See point 3 above. To remedy, if you have a food processor, the meat can be ground or finely chopped at this point and blended with the remaining ingredients. The flavors will still be very good.

If the sauce is too thin: The sauce will thicken somewhat upon refrigeration if you plan to serve it the next day. If you would like to thicken it immediately, blend 1 tablespoon flour with 2 tablespoons cold water or broth. Stir into the stew. Cook, uncovered, on MEDIUM power until thickened, stirring once.

If the sauce is too thick: Add more broth or canned undrained tomatoes. Continue to cook, covered, on MEDIUM power to heat it through. Do not add wine at the end because the alcohol flavor will be too raw.

✺ BEEF RAGOUT

MAKES 4 TO 6 SERVINGS   BEGIN ABOUT 1½ HOURS BEFORE SERVING
COOKING TIME: 1 HOUR TO 1 HOUR 25 MINUTES

We often suggest stews for entertaining, because they are flavorful and taste better when made a day in advance, and need no knives with forks for a large group. To that, our more honest friends respond, "You're kidding! Stew is something I feed to the family when I'm clean out of imagination and money." So we decided to call stews "ragouts," which intimates more flavor and lifts them out of the commonplace, because the recipes that follow are uncommonly good!

2 tablespoons butter, margarine or vegetable oil	2 cups beef stock (see Mock Brown Broth or Stock, page 119)
1 garlic clove, minced	2 tablespoons tomato paste (optional, for richer gravy)
1 cup coarsely chopped onions	
2 pounds boneless beef chuck or rump, cut into even 1-inch cubes	½ teaspoon fresh thyme leaves, or a pinch of dried
3 tablespoons all-purpose flour	½ teaspoon salt
6 carrots, cut into 1-inch pieces	¼ teaspoon pepper

In a 3-quart casserole combine the butter or oil, garlic, and onions. Cook on HIGH for 3 to 5 minutes or until the onions are tender, stirring once.

Meanwhile, in a large bowl toss the meat cubes with flour to coat. Add the meat to the onions. Cover tightly and cook on HIGH for 10 minutes, or until little or no pink color remains, stirring after 5 minutes to move the less cooked pieces to the outside.

Stir in the remaining ingredients. Cover again and cook on HIGH for 7 to 10 minutes, or until the liquid is boiling; stir. Cover again and cook on MEDIUM for 40 to 60 minutes, or until the meat is tender, stirring once or twice. Let stand, covered, for 10 minutes. (If having potatoes or a vegetable, cook at this time if you plan to serve them with your stew.)

VARIATIONS:

Beef and Pork Ragout: Substitute 1 pound pork, cut into cubes, for 1 pound beef cubes. This combination gives an interesting flavor.

Brazilian Braised Beef with Coffee: Substitute 1 cup strong freshly brewed coffee for 1 cup broth. Coffee adds a rich flavor that most people won't detect as coffee.

Beef Ragout Blanc: Substitute 1 cup dry white wine for 1 cup broth.

New England Ragout with Turnips: Substitute 2 pounds turnips, cut into 2- x -½-inch strips, for carrots.

Beef Ragout with Sour Cream: At the end of cooking and before standing time, stir in 1 cup sour cream.

BOEUF BOURGUIGNON

MAKES 4 TO 6 SERVINGS   BEGIN ABOUT 1½ TO 1¾ HOURS BEFORE SERVING
COOKING TIME: 1 TO 1½ HOURS

As is done in the classic Beef Burgundy, the mushrooms and small onions are cooked separately at the end to retain their individual texture and buttery flavor. Serve with boiled potatoes (page 73), noodles, or rice and crusty French bread.

2 strips of thick bacon, cut into ½-inch pieces	1 cup Burgundy or Chianti wine
2 garlic cloves, minced	2 tablespoons tomato paste
1 cup coarsely chopped onions	1 teaspoon fresh thyme, or ¼ teaspoon dried
2 pounds boneless beef round or chuck, cut into even 1-inch cubes	½ teaspoon salt
3 tablespoons all-purpose flour	¼ teaspoon pepper
1 carrot, thinly sliced	1 pound small white onions
1 cup beef broth (see Mock Brown Broth or Stock, page 119)	2 tablespoons butter
	1 pound whole mushrooms, trimmed
	2 tablespoons chopped fresh parsley

In a 3-quart casserole combine the bacon, garlic, and chopped onions. Cook on HIGH for 3 to 5 minutes, or until the onions are tender, stirring once.

Meanwhile, in a large bowl toss the meat cubes with flour to coat. Add the meat to the onions. Cover tightly and cook on HIGH for 10 minutes, or until little or no pink color remains, stirring after 5 minutes to move the less cooked pieces to the outside.

Stir in all but the last 4 ingredients. Cover again and cook on HIGH for 7 to 10 minutes, or until boiling; stir. Cover again and cook on MEDIUM for 40 to 60 minutes, or until the meat is tender, stirring once or twice. Let stand, covered, for 10 minutes before serving.

During standing time, in a 1-quart casserole combine the small onions and butter. Cover tightly and cook on HIGH for 6 to 8 minutes, or until tender, stirring once. Add to stew.

Place the mushrooms in the same casserole. Cook, uncovered, on HIGH for 3 to 6½ minutes, or until tender, stirring after 2 minutes. Stir into the beef stew. Sprinkle with fresh parsley.

CARBONNADES A LA FLAMANDE

MAKES 4 TO 6 SERVINGS   BEGIN ABOUT 1¾ HOURS BEFORE SERVING
COOKING TIME: 1 HOUR 2 MINUTES TO 1 HOUR 28 MINUTES

A robust Belgian, or Flemish, beef stew well laced with onions and in a mouthwatering sweet and sour sauce. Serve with New Buttered Potatoes with Parsley (page 457) or buttered noodles.

- 2 tablespoons vegetable oil
- 2 garlic cloves, minced
- 3 cups thinly sliced onions
- 2 pounds boneless beef chuck or rump, cut into even 1-inch cubes
- 2 tablespoons all-purpose flour
- 1 cup beef broth (see Mock Brown Broth or Stock, page 119)
- 1 tablespoon brown sugar
- 1 tablespoon wine vinegar
- 1 tablespoon chopped fresh parsley, or 1 teaspoon dried
- ½ teaspoon salt
- ¼ teaspoon pepper
- ¼ teaspoon dried thyme

In a 3-quart casserole combine the oil, garlic, and onions. Cook on HIGH for 5 to 8 minutes, or until tender, stirring once.

Meanwhile, in a large bowl toss the meat cubes with flour to coat. Add the meat to the onions. Cover tightly and cook on HIGH for 10 minutes, or until little or no pink color remains, stirring after 5 minutes to move the less cooked pieces to the outside.

Stir in the remaining ingredients. Cover again and cook on HIGH for 7 to 10 minutes, or until boiling; stir. Cover again and cook on MEDIUM for 40 to 60 minutes, or until the meat is tender, stirring once or twice. Let stand, covered, for 10 minutes.

HUNGARIAN GOULASH

MAKES 4 TO 6 SERVINGS   BEGIN ABOUT 1½ HOURS BEFORE SERVING
COOKING TIME: 1 HOUR TO 1 HOUR 25 MINUTES

The distinguishing ingredient in this Hungarian beef stew is the paprika. If you are fortunate enough to be able to obtain real Hungarian paprika, the taste will be that much better. Serve the stew with spaetzle, Polenta (page 194), or buttered noodles and pumpernickel bread.

- 2 tablespoons butter or vegetable oil
- 2 garlic cloves, minced
- 2 cups chopped onions
- 2 pounds boneless beef round, pork, or veal, cut into even 1-inch cubes
- 2 tablespoons all-purpose flour
- 2 cups beef broth (see Mock Brown Broth or Stock, page 119)
- 2 tablespoons tomato paste
- 1 tablespoon paprika (preferably Hungarian)
- ½ teaspoon salt
- ¼ teaspoon pepper
- 2 teaspoons caraway seeds (optional)

In a 3-quart casserole combine the butter, garlic, and onions. Cook on HIGH for 3 to 5 minutes, or until the onions are tender, stirring once.

Meanwhile, in a large bowl toss the meat cubes with flour to coat. Add the meat to the onions. Cover tightly and cook on HIGH for 10 minutes, or until little or no pink color remains, stirring after 5 minutes to move the less cooked pieces to the outside.

Stir in the remaining ingredients. Cover again and cook on HIGH for 7 to 10 minutes, or until boiling; stir. Cover again and cook on MEDIUM for 40 to 60 minutes, or until the meat is tender, stirring once or twice. Let stand, covered, for 10 minutes.

VARIATIONS:

Goulash with Mushrooms: During standing time, cook 1 pound mushrooms, sliced (page 72). Stir into the goulash before serving.

Creamed Goulash: Pork or veal cubes are preferred. Reduce the beef broth to 1 cup. At the end of cooking and before standing time, stir in 1 cup sour cream.

Goulash with Sauerkraut: Pork or veal cubes are preferred. Reduce the beef broth to 1 cup. Add 1 pound rinsed sauerkraut with the meat. At the end of cooking and before standing time, stir in 1 cup sour cream. Serve with buttered noodles or spaetzle.

Goulash with Red and Green Peppers: During standing time, combine 1 sweet red and 1 green pepper, cut into strips, in a small microwaveproof dish. Cover tightly and cook on HIGH for 3 to 5 minutes. Garnish the stew with peppers before serving.

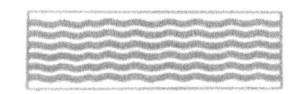

BEEF OR VEAL STEFADO

MAKES 4 TO 6 SERVINGS   BEGIN ABOUT 1½ HOURS BEFORE SERVING
COOKING TIME: 58 TO 81 MINUTES

This delicious Greek stew has a very appealing but subtle cinnamon flavor. Serve with Rice Pilaf (page 201), made before the stew and reheated, and with Flavored Pita Triangles (page 97) or pita bread.

- 2 tablespoons olive oil
- 2 garlic cloves, minced
- 2 pounds boneless beef chuck, rump, or veal shoulder, cut into even 1-inch cubes
- 1 cup beef broth (see Mock Brown Broth or Stock, page 119)
- ½ cup dry red wine
- ¼ cup tomato paste
- 1 tablespoon red wine vinegar
- ½ teaspoon dried oregano
- ½ teaspoon salt
- ¼ teaspoon pepper
- 1 3-inch piece of cinnamon stick
- 1½ pounds small white onions, peeled

In a 3-quart casserole combine the oil and garlic. Cook on HIGH for 35 seconds to 1 minute or until tender. Stir in the meat cubes.

Cover tightly, and cook uncovered on HIGH for 10 minutes, or until little or no pink color remains, stirring after 5 minutes to move the less cooked pieces to the outside.

Stir in the remaining ingredients. Cover again and cook on HIGH for 7 to 10 minutes, or until boiling; stir. Cook on MEDIUM for 40 to 60 minutes, or until the meat is tender, stirring once or twice. Let stand, covered, for 10 minutes. Remove cinnamon stick and serve.

VARIATIONS:

Stefado with Nuts: Stir in ½ cup coarsely chopped walnuts or pecans before serving.

Stefado with Feta Cheese: At the end of cooking, before standing time, stir in ¼ pound feta cheese, cubed. If the cheese doesn't melt during standing time, cover tightly and cook on MEDIUM for 3 to 5 minutes, stirring once until melted.

Stefado with Tomatoes: Add 1 cup fresh or undrained canned tomatoes, peeled, seeded, and chopped, with the broth.

☀ VEAL DAUBE

MAKES 4 TO 6 SERVINGS   BEGIN ABOUT 1½ HOURS BEFORE SERVING
COOKING TIME: 1 HOUR TO 1 HOUR 25 MINUTES

By any other name, this is a veal stew served over noodles, rice, or Polenta (page 194) and accompanied by crusty French bread. Veal chunks will melt in your mouth!

- 2 tablespoons butter
- 1 garlic clove, minced
- 1 cup chopped onions
- 2 pounds boneless veal shoulder, cut into even 1-inch cubes
- 3 tablespoons all-purpose flour
- 1 cup sliced carrots
- 1½ cups Chicken Broth or Stock (page 118)
- ½ cup dry white wine or Chicken Broth or Stock
- 2 tablespoons lemon juice
- 1 tablespoon chopped fresh parsley, or 1 teaspoon dried
- ½ teaspoon salt
- ¼ teaspoon pepper

In a 3-quart casserole combine the butter, garlic, and onions. Cook on HIGH for 3 to 5 minutes, or until the onions are tender, stirring once.

Meanwhile, in a large bowl toss the veal cubes with flour to coat. Add the veal to the onions. Cover tightly and cook on HIGH for 10 minutes, or until little or no pink color remains, stirring after 5 minutes to move the less cooked pieces to the outside.

Stir in the remaining ingredients. Cover again and cook on HIGH for 7 to 10 minutes, or until boiling; stir. Cover again and cook on MEDIUM for 40 to 60 minutes, or until the meat is tender, stirring once or twice. Let stand, covered, for 10 minutes.

VARIATIONS:

Daube aux Champignons: During standing time, cook 1 pound mushrooms, sliced (page 72). Stir the mushrooms into the stew before serving. Sprinkle with 2 tablespoons chopped fresh parsley to serve.

Veal Daube with Capers: Before serving, sprinkle with 2 tablespoons capers.

Creamy Veal Daube: At the end of cooking and before standing time, stir in ½ cup crème fraîche or sour cream. Sprinkle with 2 tablespoons chopped fresh parsley before serving.

Veal Daube with Red Wine: Substitute red wine for the white wine.

Scandinavian Veal Stew with Dill: At the end of cooking and before standing time, stir in ½ cup crème fraîche or sour cream and ¼ cup chopped fresh dill. Rich and very tasty!

Kentucky Veal Stew with Bourbon: Add 2 tablespoons bourbon with the broth.

Italian Veal Stew with Peppers: Substitute 1½ cups fresh or undrained canned tomatoes, peeled, seeded, and chopped, for the chicken broth. Substitute 1 tablespoon fresh basil or 1 teaspoon dried for the parsley. After the stew has cooked on MEDIUM for 20 minutes, add 2 green peppers, sliced into ½-inch strips, and ¼ teaspoon red pepper flakes (optional). Continue to cook on MEDIUM for the remaining 20 to 30 minutes, or until the meat is tender. Serve with garlic bread and pasta if desired.

LAMB RAGOUT

MAKES 6 SERVINGS   BEGIN 1½ HOURS BEFORE SERVING
COOKING TIME: 1 TO 1¼ HOURS

Serve with rice or Rice Pilaf (page 201), made before the stew and reheated during standing time.

- 2 tablespoons butter
- 1 garlic clove, minced
- 1 cup coarsely chopped onions
- 1 carrot, thinly sliced
- 1 celery rib, thinly sliced
- 2 pounds boneless lamb shoulder, cut into even 1-inch cubes
- 2 tablespoons all-purpose flour
- 2 tablespoons tomato paste
- 1½ cups Chicken Broth or Stock (page 118)
- ½ cup dry white wine
- ⅛ teaspoon dried thyme

In a 3-quart casserole combine the butter, garlic, onions, carrots, and celery. Cover tightly and cook on HIGH for 3 to 5 minutes, or until the vegetables are tender.

Meanwhile, in a large bowl toss the lamb cubes with flour to coat. Cover again and cook on HIGH for 10 minutes, or until little or no pink color remains, stirring after 5 minutes to move the less cooked pieces to the outside.

Stir in the remaining ingredients. Cover again and cook on HIGH for 7 to 10 minutes, or until boiling; stir. Cover again and cook on MEDIUM 40 to 60 minutes, or until the meat is tender, stirring once or twice. Let stand, covered, for 10 minutes.

VARIATIONS:

Lamb Ragout with Peas and Snow Peas: During standing time, cook Peas and Snow Peas (page 412). Stir into the stew right before serving.

Lamb Ragout with Sour Cream: At the end of cooking and before standing time, stir in ½ cup sour cream.

Lamb Ragout with Potatoes: During standing time, cook boiled potatoes, quartered (page 73). Stir into the stew.

Lamb Navarin: During standing time, cook 2 cups carrots, sliced (page 74) and ½ pound mushrooms, sliced (page 72) or ½ pound green beans, trimmed (page 69). Stir into the stew.

VEAL OR LAMB CURRY

MAKES 6 SERVINGS   BEGIN ABOUT 1½ HOURS BEFORE SERVING
COOKING TIME: 1 HOUR TO 1 HOUR 25 MINUTES

Serve with boiled potatoes (page 73), made during standing time, pita bread, and chutney if desired. Or serve with Rice Pilaf (page 201), made before the curry and reheated during standing time.

- 2 tablespoons vegetable oil
- 1 garlic clove, minced
- 1 medium onion, chopped
- 1 carrot, chopped
- 1 celery rib, chopped
- 2 pounds boneless lamb or veal shoulder, cut into even 1-inch cubes
- 2 tablespoons all-purpose flour
- 2 cups Chicken Broth or Stock (page 118)
- 1 tart apple, peeled, cored, and cut into ½-inch cubes (about 1 cup)
- 2 tablespoons tomato paste
- 1 tablespoon curry powder
- ½ teaspoon salt
- ¼ teaspoon pepper
- ½ cup plain yogurt or sour cream

In a 3-quart casserole combine the oil, garlic, onion, carrot, and celery. Cover tightly and cook on HIGH for 3 to 5 minutes, or until the vegetables are tender.

Meanwhile, in a large bowl toss the meat chunks with flour to coat. Add the meat to the vegetables. Cover again and cook on HIGH for 10 minutes, or until little or no pink color remains, stirring after 5 minutes to move the less cooked pieces to the outside.

Stir in the remaining ingredients, except yogurt. Cover again and cook on HIGH for 7 to 10 minutes, or until boiling; stir. Cover again and cook on MEDIUM for 40 to 60 minutes, or until the meat is tender, stirring once or twice. Stir in the yogurt or sour cream. Let stand, covered, for 10 minutes.

VARIATION:

Veal and Lamb Curry with Coconut: Substitute 1 cup canned coconut milk (found in Oriental grocery stores) for 1 cup broth. Sprinkle with ¼ cup grated unsweetened coconut before serving.

CHILI WITH CUBED BEEF

MAKES 6 SERVINGS   BEGIN ABOUT 1½ HOURS BEFORE SERVING
COOKING TIME: 58 TO 81 MINUTES

This chili has a deep mahogany-colored sauce that is thinner than most chilies you may have tried, but which is marvelous when sopped up with flour tortillas or when spooned over pinto beans or rice. The basic recipe has more intense flavor than the variation that you will find made with tomatoes and beans.

Serve in bowls and pass warmed flour tortillas and Green Tomato Salsa (page 186) or Salsa Ranchera (page 146), if desired. Spoon over cooked pinto beans or rice made before the chili and reheated later.

- 2 tablespoons shortening or vegetable oil
- 3 garlic cloves, minced
- 2 pounds boneless lean beef chuck, cut into even 1-inch cubes
- 2 tablespoons all-purpose flour
- 2 cups beef broth (see Mock Brown Broth or Stock, page 119)
- 2 to 3 tablespoons chili powder (preferably Mexican hot)
- 1 teaspoon cuminseed, or ¼ teaspoon powdered
- 1 teaspoon dried oregano
- ½ teaspoon salt
- ¼ teaspoon pepper

In a 3-quart casserole combine the shortening and garlic. Cook on HIGH for 35 seconds to 1 minute, or until tender.

Meanwhile, in a large bowl toss the meat cubes with flour to coat. Add the meat to the garlic. Cover tightly and cook on HIGH for 10 minutes, or until little or no pink color remains, stirring after 5 minutes to move the less cooked pieces to the outside.

Stir in the remaining ingredients. Cover again and cook on HIGH for 7 to 10 minutes, or until boiling; stir. Cover again and cook on MEDIUM for 40 to 60 minutes, or until the meat is tender, stirring once or twice. Let stand, covered, for 10 minutes.

VARIATIONS:

Cubed Beef Chili with Tomatoes: Substitute 1 cup fresh or undrained canned tomatoes, peeled and chopped, for 1 cup of the beef broth.

Cubed Beef Chili with Tomatoes and Beans: Substitute 1 cup fresh or undrained canned tomatoes, peeled and chopped, for 1 cup of the broth. Add 2 cups cooked or canned pinto beans with the remaining ingredients. This is the chili most Americans are used to.

Cubed Beef Chili with Beer: Substitute 1 cup beer for the broth.

Chili with Pork Cubes: Substitute 1 pound pork, cut into cubes, for the beef.

GREEN CHILI

MAKES 4 TO 6 SERVINGS   BEGIN ABOUT 1¼ HOURS BEFORE SERVING
COOKING TIME: 1 TO 1¼ HOURS

A Mexican stew with a light sauce having a mild green color and a pleasant hot flavor; serve it with warm tortillas and rice. It thickens and is even better when heated the next day for breakfast and with leftover flour tortillas.

2 tablespoons vegetable oil	2 serrano chilies, or hotter jalapeño peppers, seeded and chopped
2 garlic cloves, minced	1 teaspoon dried oregano
1 onion, coarsely chopped	1 teaspoon cuminseed
2 pounds trimmed boneless pork, cut into even 1-inch cubes	½ teaspoon salt
2 tablespoons all-purpose flour	⅛ teaspoon pepper
1 pound mild long green chilies, chopped, or 10 canned	Sour cream
2 cups Chicken Broth or Stock (page 118)	

In a 3-quart casserole combine the oil, garlic, and onion. Cook on HIGH for 3 to 5 minutes, or until tender, stirring once.

Meanwhile, in a large bowl toss the pork cubes with flour to coat. Stir the pork into the onion mixture. Cover tightly and cook on HIGH for 10 minutes, or until no pink color remains, stirring after 5 minutes to move the less cooked pieces to the outside.

Stir in the remaining ingredients except the sour cream. Cover again and cook on HIGH for 7 to 10 minutes or until boiling; stir. Cover again and cook on MEDIUM for 40 to 60 minutes, or until the flavors have developed. Pass the sour cream at the table.

SIMMERED BEEF ROLLS

MAKES 4 SERVINGS   BEGIN 1 TO 1¼ HOURS BEFORE SERVING
COOKING TIME: 38 TO 48 MINUTES

This was always considered a company meal when we were growing up. Serve on a bed of noodles and with the gravy.

1½ to 2 pounds boneless beef round, thinly sliced	1 cup fresh bread crumbs
½ teaspoon salt	1 egg, beaten
¼ teaspoon pepper	2 tablespoons chopped fresh parsley, or 1 tablespoon dried
¼ pound Fresh Sausage Patties, (page 319) or bulk sausage	1 tablespoon butter
2 tablespoons finely chopped onion, plus 1 medium onion, thinly sliced	1 garlic clove, minced
	1½ tablespoons all-purpose flour
	1 cup beef broth (see Mock Brown Broth or Stock, page 119)

Cut the beef into eight 4- × -5-inch squares. Pound the beef slices to about ¼ inch thickness. Lightly salt and pepper.

In a 2-quart rectangular dish or 3-quart casserole combine the sausage and chopped onion. Cook, uncovered, on HIGH for 3 to 5 minutes, or until the sausage is no longer pink, stirring once. Stir in the bread crumbs, egg, and parsley.

Spoon about 2 tablespoons sausage mixture onto the end of each beef square. Roll the beef and secure with string or toothpicks. Continue the procedure with the others. Set aside.

In the same dish in which you cooked the sausage, combine the butter, garlic, and sliced onion. Cook, uncovered, on HIGH for 2 to 3 minutes, or until the onion is tender. Stir in the flour to blend. Stir in the broth to blend. Cook on HIGH for 3 to 5 minutes, or until boiling, stirring once.

Add the meat rolls. Cover tightly and cook on HIGH for 5 minutes, then MEDIUM for 10 minutes. Turn the rolls over and reposition them to place the lesser cooked ones to the outside of the dish. Cover again and cook on MEDIUM for 15 to 20 minutes, or until the rolls are fork tender. Let stand, covered, for 5 to 10 minutes before serving.

VARIATIONS:

Beef Rolls in Tomato Sauce: Substitute 2 tablespoons tomato paste for the flour. Substitute 1 cup fresh or undrained canned tomatoes, chopped and peeled, for the beef broth. Add 1 tablespoon chopped fresh basil or 1 teaspoon dried, and ¼ teaspoon salt, with the tomatoes.

Beef Rolls with Red Wine: Substitute 2 tablespoons tomato paste for the flour. Substitute ½ cup red wine for half of the beef broth.

Beef Rolls with Ham: Eliminate the sausage and cook the chopped onion on HIGH for 1 minute. Substitute ground ham for the sausage and add to the cooked onion.

Swiss Beef Rolls: Place 8 thin slices of Gruyère or Swiss cheese on top of the meat squares, cutting them to the size of the squares. Top the cheese with 8 thin pieces of boiled ham, also cut to size. Top the ham with 2 dill pickles, cut in quarters lengthwise. Roll and cook as in basic recipe.

Simmered Veal Rolls: Substitute veal round for the beef in the basic recipe or any of the above variations. Substitute Chicken Broth (page 118) for the beef broth and white wine for the red wine.

Lamb, Pork, and Veal Chops Basics:

1. Pork chops may be grilled on the browner, following instructions for a well-done small steak; lamb and veal can be cooked to any doneness. All chops may be breaded or cooked in a sauce.
2. Chops will always be cooked with a cover, unless they are cooked on a browning dish, which retains a very high surface heat. The wax paper or paper towel cover on them, along with a sauce or bread coating, will retain the heat needed to cook them through evenly, but will not make them soggy.
3. Pork chops are first cooked on HIGH power to bring the surface temperature up, and

then cooked on MEDIUM power to develop flavor in a sauce or keep the outer surfaces from overcooking.
4. All chops need to be rearranged and turned over once during cooking so that all areas cook evenly. If cooked in a sauce, the chops should be turned over once, too, so that the hot liquid evenly heats both sides.
5. The standing time for these chops is only a couple of minutes, which is accomplished in the time it takes to bring them to the table. Thus there is no mention of standing time in the recipe.
6. *Doneness:* The meat will be firm but not tough, and when pork is pierced, the thicker portion of meat next to the bone should no longer be pink. Veal and lamb can be cooked until still pink so always start with the shortest cooking time in the recipes.

Underdone: For pork, flesh will still be pink and soft to the touch, with juices running very pink.

Overdone: Chops will be very tough when overdone, but because they are cooked mostly on MEDIUM power, it's hard to overcook them. It could happen for three reasons: The meat was closer to room temperature than refrigerator temperature, in which case the recipe timing would be too long, the amount of meat was less than or thinner than the recipe called for, or the power wasn't turned down from HIGH to MEDIUM. If overcooked, the pork can be shredded and reheated in a sauce or substituted for sliced meat in Flour Tortillas with Sliced Meat (page 273).

✺ BREADED PORK OR VEAL CHOPS

MAKES 4 SERVINGS   BEGIN 20 MINUTES BEFORE SERVING
COOKING TIME: 13 TO 17 MINUTES

With the bread coating, these brown up nicely. A roasting rack is preferred to keep the crust drier, but it is not necessary.

- 1 egg, beaten
- 1 tablespoon water
- ¾ cup fine dry bread crumbs
- 1 tablespoon chopped fresh parsley, or 1 teaspoon dried
- ½ teaspoon paprika
- ¼ teaspoon dry mustard
- ¼ teaspoon salt
- ⅛ teaspoon pepper
- 4 pork or veal chops, ½ to ¾ inch thick (about 1½ pounds) (see Note)

In a shallow bowl or plate combine the egg and water. In a separate bowl or plate combine the remaining ingredients except pork chops.

Dip each chop into the egg mixture and then into crumb mixture, pressing the coating against the surface of the meat. Arrange the chops on a large microwave roasting rack in a 2-quart dish, with the thicker sections to the outside. Cover with a paper towel and cook on HIGH for 4 minutes; rearrange once. Cover again and cook on MEDIUM for 9 to 13 minutes, or until the veal is the desired doneness or the interior of the pork, next to the bone, has lost all its pink color, turning over once.

NOTE: For fewer chops, see the cooking chart on page 63.

VARIATIONS:

Rosemary Breaded Pork or Veal Chops: Add ¼ teaspoon dried rosemary to the breading.

Breaded Pork or Veal Chops with Onion: Top each breaded chop with a thin slice of onion.

Breaded Pork or Veal Chops with Lemon: After turning the chops over, top each one with a thin slice of lemon.

Breaded Pork or Veal Chops with Mushroom Sauce: Prepare Mushroom Sauce (page 172). After the chops are cooked, reheat the sauce on HIGH for 1 to 3 minutes.

Breaded Pork or Veal Chops with Sweet and Sour Apricot Sauce: Prepare Sweet and Sour Apricot Sauce (page 182). After the chops are cooked, reheat the sauce on HIGH for 1 to 3 minutes. Spoon the sauce over the chops before serving, and pass the extra sauce at the table.

Breaded Pork or Veal Chops with Lime and Sour Cream: After turning the chops over, top each one with a thin slice of lime before cooking. While the chops are cooking, combine 1 cup sour cream, 1 teaspoon lime juice, and 1 tablespoon chopped fresh cilantro (coriander). Divide the mixture between chops by spooning it on top. Cover with wax paper and heat on MEDIUM for 1 to 3 minutes.

Breaded Pork or Veal Chops with Orange Slices: Prepare Sweet and Sour Orange Sauce (page 182), if desired. After turning the chops over, top each one with a thin slice of orange before cooking. Reheat the sauce on HIGH for 1 to 3 minutes before serving.

CHOPS WITH FRESH TOMATO SAUCE

MAKES 4 SERVINGS   BEGIN ABOUT 40 MINUTES BEFORE SERVING
COOKING TIME: 24 TO 28 MINUTES

1 tablespoon butter	2 tablespoons chopped fresh parsley, or 2 teaspoons dried
1 garlic clove, minced	1 teaspoon fresh basil, or ½ teaspoon dried
1 medium onion, thinly sliced	½ teaspoon salt
1 cup fresh or undrained canned tomatoes, peeled, seeded, and chopped	¼ teaspoon pepper
2 tablespoons tomato paste	4 chops, ½ to ¾ inch thick (about 1½ pounds)

In a 2-quart rectangular dish combine the butter, garlic, and onion. Cook on HIGH for 2 to 3 minutes, or until the onion is tender. Add the remaining ingredients except the chops, stirring well to mix.

Arrange the chops with the meatiest portions toward the outside of the dish. Cover with wax paper and cook on HIGH for 5 minutes; turn the chops over and rearrange. Cover again and cook on MEDIUM for 17 to 20 minutes, or until the meat is tender and, with pork, no pink remains near the bone. Let stand, covered, for 5 minutes before serving.

VARIATIONS:

Chops with Green Pepper in Tomato Sauce: Add 1 green pepper, sliced and cut into ¼-inch strips, with the tomatoes.

Chops with Green Olives in Tomato Sauce: At the end of cooking, add ½ cup pitted green olives.

Chops with Tomato-Mushroom Sauce: Stir in ½ pound mushrooms, sliced, with the tomatoes.

Chops with Sour Cream: At the end of cooking, transfer the chops to a serving plate and cover. Stir ½ cup sour cream into the sauce. Cook on HIGH for 1 to 2 minutes, or until hot but not boiling. Stir and spoon over the chops.

Mexican Chops: Add 1 jalepeño pepper, seeded and chopped, and ¼ teaspoon crushed cuminseed with the tomatoes. Substitute ½ teaspoon dried oregano for the basil.

CHOPS IN MUSTARD SAUCE

MAKES 4 SERVINGS   BEGIN ABOUT 40 MINUTES BEFORE SERVING
COOKING TIME: 27 TO 32 MINUTES

Serve these chops with Spicy Poached Pears (page 490), if desired.

- 2 tablespoons butter
- 1 garlic clove, minced
- 1 medium onion, chopped
- 2 tablespoons all-purpose flour
- ½ cup Chicken Broth or Stock (page 118)
- ¼ cup dry white wine or vermouth
- 2 tablespoons prepared mustard (preferably Dijon with whole grains)
- 1 teaspoon Worcestershire sauce
- ¼ teaspoon salt
- ⅛ teaspoon pepper
- ¼ cup heavy cream or crème fraîche
- 4 chops, ½ to ¾ inch thick (about 1½ pounds)

In a 2-quart rectangular dish combine the butter, garlic, and onion. Cook on HIGH for 3 minutes, or until the onion is tender. Stir in the flour to blend. Stir in the remaining ingredients except the cream and chops.

Arrange the chops with the meatiest portions toward the outside of the dish. Cover with wax paper and cook on HIGH for 5 minutes;

turn the chops over and rearrange. Cover and cook on MEDIUM for 17 to 20 minutes, or until the meat is tender and, with pork, no pink remains next to the bone. Transfer the chops to a serving platter and cover. Stir the cream into the sauce. Heat on HIGH for 2 to 4 minutes, or until heated through but not boiling, stirring once. Spoon the sauce over the chops.

VARIATIONS:

Chops with Pink Peppercorns: Substitute 2 tablespoons tomato paste for the flour. Add 1 tablespoon pink peppercorns with the cream.

Chops with Green Peppercorns: Add 2 tablespoons drained green peppercorns with the cream.

Stuffed Breast and Butterflied Loin Basics (Veal, Lamb):

1. We found that these pieces of meat were best braised with about 1 cup liquid for 3 to 4 pounds of meat.
2. A flour paste blended with the vegetables and then wine or broth is made before the meat is added. This will help the broth to thicken somewhat into a gravy.
3. The meat is cooked first on HIGH to bring up the surface temperature and then cooked on MEDIUM power. MEDIUM helps these unusually shaped pieces of meat to cook evenly all the way through.
4. Because of their large size, both the breast and butterflied loin need to be turned over once during cooking to ensure that all sides are exposed to the hot liquid in the bottom of the dish.
5. A tight cover, particularly a casserole lid, will retain steam that will help these pieces of meat cook evenly.
6. Standing time is important to let the meat continue cooking until doneness is reached.
7. For doneness, see Less Tender-Cut Roast Basics, page 262.

✺ STUFFED BREAST OF VEAL

MAKES 4 TO 6 SERVINGS BEGIN 1½ TO 2 HOURS BEFORE SERVING
COOKING TIME: 1 HOUR 11 MINUTES TO 1 HOUR 34 MINUTES

Unusual as it may sound, someone at our cooking schools invariably would ask how to cook a stuffed breast of veal. We offer two stuffings but you may have your own favorites. This recipe is dedicated to all those people who asked that question.

½ pound Sage Sausage Patties (page 320) or bulk sausage	1 3- to 4-pound breast of veal, with pocket cut for stuffing
2 tablespoons finely chopped onions	2 tablespoons butter
1 cup fresh bread crumbs	1 carrot, thinly sliced
2 tablespoons chopped fresh parsley, or 1 tablespoon dried	1 celery rib, coarsely chopped
	1 tablespoon all-purpose flour
¼ teaspoon pepper	1 cup white wine or Chicken Broth (page 118)

In a 3- to 4-quart casserole with a lid combine the sausage and onions. Cook on HIGH for 3 to 4 minutes, or until the sausage is cooked, stirring once. Drain off the excess fat. Stir in the bread crumbs, parsley, and pepper. Fill the veal pocket with the mixture. Close with toothpicks or wooden skewers or tie with string. Set aside.

In the same casserole combine the butter, carrot, and celery. Cover tightly and cook on HIGH 3 to 5 minutes, or until the vegetables are tender, stirring once. Blend in the flour until smooth. Pour in the wine and stir to blend. Add the veal. Cover again and cook on HIGH for 15 minutes; turn meat over. Cover again and cook on MEDIUM for 50 to 60 minutes, or until tender, turning over once. Let stand, covered, for 10 minutes.

To serve, slice between the bones. Serve with pan gravy.

VARIATIONS:

Breast of Veal Stuffed with Veal: Substitute ground veal for the sausage, adding ½ teaspoon salt and ¼ teaspoon thyme.

Breast of Veal Stuffed with Ham: Eliminate the sausage. Melt the butter on HIGH for 1 minute in a small microwave bowl. Add 4 ounces ham, chopped, and 2 tablespoons shredded Gruyère cheese to the cooked onion.

Provolone-Stuffed Breast of Veal: Substitute 2 ounces salami, coarsely chopped, and 2 ounces provolone, shredded, for the sausage.

Stuffed Breast of Lamb: Substitute a 3- to 4-pound breast of lamb, with a pocket cut for the stuffing.

BRAISED STUFFED LOIN OF VEAL CORDON BLEU

MAKES 6 TO 8 SERVINGS   BEGIN ABOUT 2 HOURS BEFORE SERVING
COOKING TIME: 1 HOUR 7 MINUTES TO 1 HOUR 20 MINUTES

The rolling of the veal takes a little time, but you'll be pleased with the attractive circular slices that make for a blue-ribbon presentation! Serve with thin cooked noodles, followed by a mixed salad.

- 1 3-pound loin of veal, cut lengthwise and butterflied
- 1 teaspoon chopped fresh thyme, or ¼ teaspoon dried
- ½ teaspoon salt
- ¼ teaspoon pepper
- ¼ pound smoked ham, thinly sliced
- ¼ pound Gruyère cheese, thinly sliced
- 2 tablespoons butter
- 1 medium onion, chopped
- 1 carrot, thinly sliced
- 1 tablespoon all-purpose flour
- ½ cup Chicken Broth or Stock (page 118)
- ½ cup dry white wine

Pound the veal to between ¾ and 1 inch thick, making a 10- × -12-inch rectangle. Sprinkle the veal with the thyme, salt, and pepper. Arrange the ham in a single layer to cover the meat. Top with a single layer of cheese. Roll the meat tightly, beginning from one of the long sides. Tie with string at 1-inch intervals. Set aside.

In a 3-quart casserole with a lid, combine the butter, onion, and carrot. Cover tightly and cook on HIGH for 2 to 5 minutes, or until the vegetables are tender. Stir in the flour to blend. Stir in the broth and wine to blend. Add the veal roll. Cover tightly and cook on HIGH for 15 minutes; turn the meat over and baste. Cover again and cook on MEDIUM for 50 to 60 minutes, or until tender, turning the meat over and basting halfway through cooking. Let stand for 10 minutes.

To serve, slice between the strings and then remove strings. Arrange the slices on a platter and spoon the cooking liquid over the meat. Pass the remaining juices separately.

VARIATIONS:

Chilled Loin of Veal Cordon Bleu: Eliminate the onion and carrot and melt only the butter on HIGH for 1 minute. Chill the veal in its juices after cooking, then remove from the juices and slice and serve chilled with a variety of mustards. Nice for summer entertaining.

Braised Pork Loin Cordon Bleu: Substitute a 3-pound pork loin, butterflied, for the veal. Cook for the time indicated, or until a thermometer inserted in the meatiest section reaches 165°F.

Ribs Basics (Beef, Pork):

1. Ribs are very bony, so estimate about ¾ pound per person for a meal, or ½ pound for appetizers.
2. Rack of pork ribs should be cut into individual ribs to allow for better coating of the ribs with sauce, unless preparing for later barbecuing; in that case, leave whole for easier handling over the coals.
3. Ribs should cook without sauce or liquid during the first half of cooking, because they will exude a lot of fat; the fat is easier to remove before any additions are made.
4. Beef ribs are best cooked with the addition of liquid to help braise and tenderize them. Pork ribs are best when brushed with a sauce. Both these processes should be

done halfway or more through the end of the cooking process, because both liquid and high sugar glaze will attract microwave energy away from the ribs.
5. Pork ribs are covered with wax paper, to keep spatters down and to help them cook through evenly by the retained heat and steam. Beef ribs, which have less fat to tenderize them, are covered tightly to produce the steam that will help tenderize.
6. Ribs are cooked on HIGH for 5 minutes to get the surface hot quickly. Then the beef ribs are cooked on MEDIUM for about 11 to 13 minutes per pound and pork ribs for about 20 minutes per pound.
7. Rearranging ribs partway through cooking is important so that all the areas cook evenly.
8. Standing time is necessary to complete the long slow cooking process.
9. *Doneness:* Before adding the sauce or liquid, pork or beef ribs should be brown on the outside, tender, and just about cooked through. The additional liquid and sauce will slow down the cooking process and only serve to flavor or tenderize even more.

> Warm, moist washcloths are so nice to offer to rib eaters covered with traces from face to fingers.
>
> Take four washcloths and wet them, wringing out the excess moisture. Fold the washcloths in half lengthwise, and roll them up. Place them in a casserole dish and cover. Heat on HIGH for 1 minute. The lucky one to uncover the casserole will get a nice facial. Remove the hot washcloths with tongs and wait for the pleasured sighs of the recipients.

✺ BEEF SHORT RIBS

MAKES 4 SERVINGS   BEGIN ABOUT 1 HOUR BEFORE SERVING
COOKING TIME: 47 TO 56 MINUTES

Serve with boiled potatoes (page 73) or Mashed Potatoes (page 457). Both can be cooked during standing time.

---

3 pounds beef short ribs	1 teaspoon caraway seeds
1 onion, sliced	¼ teaspoon dried thyme
2 tablespoons all-purpose flour	Salt and pepper
1 cup beef broth (see Mock Brown Broth or Stock, page 119)	

Arrange the short ribs in a 2- to 3-quart rectangular dish with the thicker meat sections toward the outside of the dish. Cover tightly and cook on HIGH for 5 minutes, rearranging the less cooked pieces toward the outside. Cover again and cook on MEDIUM for 20 minutes, rearranging the ribs halfway through cooking.

Transfer the ribs to a serving platter. Drain all but 1 tablespoon cooking liquid from the dish. Add the onion to the dish. Cook on HIGH for 1 to 2 minutes, or until slightly tender. Stir in the flour until smooth. Add the beef broth, caraway seeds, thyme, and salt and pepper to taste. Cook, uncovered, on HIGH for 3 to 5 minutes, or until boiling; stir.

Return the ribs to the dish, rearranging the lesser cooked areas toward the outside. Cover tightly and cook on MEDIUM for 18 to 24 minutes, or until tender, rearranging the ribs once during cooking. Let stand, covered, for 5 to 10 minutes.

VARIATIONS:

Italian Ribs with Tomato Sauce: Substitute 1 cup fresh or undrained canned tomatoes, peeled and chopped, for the beef broth. Substitute 2 tablespoons tomato paste for 1 tablespoon flour. Add 1 tablespoon chopped fresh basil or 1 teaspoon dried. Serve with noodles.

Spicy Italian Ribs with Tomato Sauce: Follow the Italian Ribs variation above but add ¼ teaspoon red pepper flakes with basil.

Chili Ribs: Substitute 2 tablespoons tomato paste for the flour. Add 1 tablespoon chili powder with the thyme.

BLAZING PORK SPARERIBS

MAKES 4 SERVINGS   BEGIN ABOUT 1 HOUR BEFORE SERVING
COOKING TIME: 1 HOUR TO 1 HOUR 5 MINUTES

When baked in the oven, these pork ribs can take between 1½ to 2 hours to cook. In the microwave they remain moist and succulent, and a quick 5 minutes under the broiler will give you a crispy exterior if you wish.

For outdoor barbecuing instructions, see the box opposite page.

---

3 pounds pork spareribs
1 cup Blazing Barbecue Sauce (page 181) or prepared barbecue sauce

2 tablespoons honey

Cut the rack of ribs into individual ribs unless precooking for outdoor barbecuing, then leave whole.

Arrange the ribs in a 3-quart rectangular dish, with meaty side down and the thickest section toward the outside of the dish; overlap ribs if you need to. Cover with wax paper and cook on HIGH for 5 minutes; rearrange the less cooked sections to the outside. Cover again and cook on MEDIUM for 45 minutes, turning the ribs over after 20 minutes, rearranging the less cooked sections of the ribs toward the outside.

Meanwhile, in a small bowl combine the barbecue sauce with the honey. Set aside.

Drain the fat from the ribs. Rearrange the ribs again, leaving meaty side up. Brush with barbecue-honey sauce. Cook, uncovered, on

MEDIUM for 10 to 15 minutes, or until cooked through. Let stand for 5 minutes before serving.

VARIATIONS:

Crispy Pork Ribs: Follow the basic recipe, but cook the ribs with the sauce on for 10 minutes. Place the ribs on a metal broiler pan. Broil in a conventional oven for 5 to 10 minutes, until crispy. This is for ribs that crackle when you bite into the skin but are nice and moist inside.

Pork Ribs Glazed with Sweet and Sour Apricot Glaze: Prepare Sweet and Sour Apricot Sauce (page 182) and substitute for barbecue sauce and honey.

Pork Ribs Glazed with Orange: Prepare Orange Glaze (page 313) and substitute for barbecue sauce and honey. Serve with orange segments and rice.

Pork Ribs Glazed with Mustard: Prepare Mustard Glaze (page 310) and substitute for barbecue sauce and honey. Nice and spicy!

BARBECUING PORK AND BEEF

Why mention the microwave and the barbecue in the same breath? The microwave provides the ideal way to cook meat partially before it is transferred to the grill where it is crisped up by dry heat. The double-cooking technique keeps the meat moist and tender, and shaves barbecuing time down to one-third the original.

Barbecuing most often applies to ribs so we have placed this information here, but any pork or less tender beef roast can be cooked in the microwave and then barbecued. We like to use the Blazing Barbecue Sauce (page 181) or Sweet and Sour Apricot Sauce (page 182).

Here are the basic rules:

MEAT	PROCEDURE	TIME
Pork Roasts or Fresh Ham	Add ½ cup broth or water to meat in 3-quart casserole. Cover with lid; turn meat over once. Transfer to preheated grill; baste with sauce.	Cook on HIGH for 5 minutes; then on MEDIUM for 10 minutes per pound, turning over once. Then grill 20 to 25 minutes for roasts, turning over four times; or 10 minutes for ribs, turning over once.
Pork Spare Ribs	Place fat side down in rectangular dish. Cover with wax paper; turn over ribs and rearrange once. Transfer to preheated grill; baste with sauce.	

MUSTARD GLAZE

MAKES 1 CUP

Spicy and slightly sweet at the same time! Brush on ribs during cooking.

- ½ cup prepared mustard (preferably Dijon)
- 2 tablespoons vinegar
- 2 tablespoons brown sugar
- 2 tablespoons honey
- 2 tablespoons catsup
- ½ teaspoon red pepper flakes (optional)

Combine all the ingredients well in a small bowl.

FRUIT GLAZE

MAKES ABOUT ¾ CUP

- ½ cup apricot preserves, orange marmalade, or pineapple preserves
- 2 tablespoons Dijon mustard
- 2 tablespoons brown sugar or honey

Combine all ingredients in a small bowl.

○ ○ ○

Fully Cooked Pork Basics:

1. Fully cooked pork need only be heated through before serving.
2. Ham steaks and smoked chops are heated on MEDIUM power to prevent overdoneness of the thinner edges. Only for a large canned ham and pork butt is the process started on HIGH to bring the surface heat up before cooking later on MEDIUM.
3. The corners of a large ham are shielded with metal foil during the second half of heating to prevent drying out on the outside before the center has had a chance to heat through.
4. To keep the meat juicier, sometimes additional liquid is added, and always a tight cover is used to keep in all the available steam and moisture. The cover, either a lid or plastic wrap turned back slightly, retains the most steam and helps the meat to heat through quicker and more evenly.
5. Because of their larger size and/or surface area, ham steaks, canned ham, and pork butts are turned over halfway through cooking, to heat evenly and through completely.
6. If a ham is to be glazed, it is done in the last 5 to 10 minutes of cooking, and is then cooked uncovered so as to keep the surface dry for the best glazing.
7. Larger pieces of cured ham should stand

5 to 10 minutes so that heat is completely conducted through to the center.

8. *Doneness:* Because precooked pork doesn't need to be cooked but only heated through, the recipe timing is gauged to reach 125°F. The best test for a large ham is to use a temperature probe or insert a conventional thermometer after removal from the oven to register 125°F (both will rise to 130°F upon standing time). If you have neither, you will find that the timing alone is sufficient.

Overdone: The outside casing will begin to get very dark and crusty. The ham will still be moist if you have kept it covered. Cut off the crusty parts and serve the rest.

✸ APRICOT-GLAZED CANNED HAM

HIGH 5 minutes, then MEDIUM 5 to 8 minutes per pound
MAKES 6 SERVINGS   BEGIN ABOUT 40 MINUTES BEFORE SERVING
COOKING TIME: 25 TO 30 MINUTES

Serve with Poached Winter Fruits (page 493).

---

1 3-pound fully cooked canned ham (see Note)
¼ cup water

½ cup Fruit Glaze made with apricot preserves (page 310)

Place the ham in a 2-quart rectangular dish. Add the water. Cover tightly and cook on HIGH for 5 minutes, then on MEDIUM for 5 minutes. Turn the ham over and smoothly cover with foil any areas that appear to be overcooking.

Cover tightly. If using a temperature probe, insert now, through a plastic wrap cover. Cook on MEDIUM for 10 to 15 minutes, or to 125°F. Brush on the glaze. Cook, uncovered, on MEDIUM for 5 minutes. Let stand for 5 to 10 minutes before serving.

NOTE: For a different-size ham, see cooking chart on page 63.

VARIATIONS:

Orange-Glazed Ham: Make Fruit Glaze (page 310) with orange marmalade. While the ham is standing, prepare garnish: Place segments from 2 oranges and 2 tablespoons Grand Marnier in a 4-cup glass measure; cook on HIGH for 2 minutes. Arrange over ham to serve.

Pineapple-Glazed Ham: Make Fruit Glaze (page 310) with pineapple preserves. Serve the ham with Warm Fresh Pineapple Rings (page 495).

Ham with Brandied Glaze: Add 1 tablespoon brandy to any Jelly Glaze (page 313); and substitute 1 teaspoon dry mustard for the prepared mustard. Serve with Brandied Apple Slices (page 494), if desired.

☀ GLAZED HAM STEAK

MAKES 4 SERVINGS   BEGIN 20 MINUTES BEFORE SERVING
COOKING TIME: 14 TO 17 MINUTES

Any glaze will do for this ham steak, but use about ½ cup.

⅓ cup Brown Sugar Glaze (page 314)	2 pounds ham steak (1 or 2 steaks)
1 teaspoon cornstarch	

In a 2-cup glass measure combine the glaze and cornstarch. Cook on HIGH for 1½ to 2 minutes, or until slightly thickened, stirring after 1 minute. Set aside.

Slash fat on the ham to keep it from curling. Place in a shallow heatproof serving dish large enough to hold the steak. Cover tightly and cook on MEDIUM for 10 minutes; drain and turn over. Spoon the hot glaze over the ham. Cook, uncovered, on MEDIUM for 2 to 5 minutes, or until the lid or dish bottom is hot enough to hold your hand on it only 3 Macungie (see page 44).

VARIATIONS:

Flambéed Orange-Glazed Ham Steak: Substitute Fruit Glaze (page 310) made with orange marmalade. At the end of cooking, place orange segments from 1 seedless orange on top of the ham steak. Pour 2 ounces Grand Marnier or other 80-proof brandy or orange-flavored liqueur into a 1-cup glass measure. Heat on HIGH for 15 seconds. Pour over the ham and ignite.

Ham Steak with Cherry Sauce: Eliminate the brown sugar glaze. Combine the juice from 1 12-ounce can pitted Bing cherries with cornstarch in a 4-cup glass measure. Stir in 2 tablespoons brown sugar and 1 tablespoon lemon juice. Cook on HIGH for 2 minutes, or until slightly thickened, stirring once. Add the cherries. Pour the cherry sauce over the ham after it has been turned over. Cover with wax paper and cook on MEDIUM for 5 to 8 minutes to finish cooking. Flambé as in variation above, if desired.

GLAZED PORK BUTT OR CANADIAN BACON

HIGH 5 minutes then MEDIUM 10 to 12 minutes per pound
MAKES 6 SERVINGS   BEGIN ABOUT 1 HOUR BEFORE SERVING
COOKING TIME: 40 TO 42 MINUTES

Surrounded by Poached Winter Fruits (page 493), this dish can be the centerpiece on a holiday brunch table.

- 1 3-pound pork butt or Canadian bacon (see Note)
- ½ cup cranberry juice, apricot juice, or water
- ¼ cup Fruit Glaze (page 310) made with apricot preserves

Remove all wrapping. Place the pork butt in a 9- × -5-inch loaf dish or small casserole. Pour the juice or water over the pork. Cover tightly and cook on HIGH for 5 minutes, then MEDIUM for 20 minutes. Turn pork over. Cover again. If using a temperature probe, insert now through plastic wrap. Cook on MEDIUM for 10 to 12 minutes, or until the temperature probe reaches 125°F. (Add 10 minutes here if cooking in a casserole instead of loaf dish. The loaf dish traps more steam).

Brush with the glaze. Cook, uncovered, on MEDIUM for 5 minutes, or until glazed, spooning the juices over the pork halfway through cooking. Let stand for 5 minutes before serving.

NOTE: For different meat weights, see the cooking chart on pages 62–64.

The following four glazes are suitable for glazing the top of a 5-pound ham or 2 pounds of ham steaks. Double or halve each recipe, depending on the size of the ham.

JELLY GLAZE

MAKES ABOUT ½ CUP
COOKING TIME: 1 TO 2 MINUTES

- ½ cup apple, currant, or grape jelly
- 2 tablespoons prepared Dijon mustard

Place jelly in a 2-cup glass measure. Cook on HIGH for 1 to 2 minutes. Stir in the mustard.

ORANGE GLAZE

MAKES ABOUT ⅓ CUP

- 2 tablespoons frozen orange juice concentrate
- 2 tablespoons brown sugar
- 2 tablespoons Dijon mustard
- ¼ teaspoon powdered ginger

Combine all the ingredients in a small bowl.

BROWN SUGAR GLAZE

MAKES ABOUT ⅓ CUP

- ¼ cup brown sugar
- 2 tablespoons prepared Dijon mustard, or 1 tablespoon orange juice

Combine all the ingredients in a small bowl.

VARIATION:
Honey Glaze: Substitute ¼ cup honey for the brown sugar.

PINEAPPLE GLAZE

MAKES ABOUT ⅓ CUP

- ¼ cup brown sugar
- 2 tablespoons pineapple juice
- 1 tablespoon Dijon mustard

Combine all ingredients in a small bowl.

ORIENTAL HAM AND VEGETABLES OVER RICE

MAKES 4 SERVINGS   BEGIN 50 MINUTES BEFORE SERVING
COOKING TIME: 21 TO 27 MINUTES

Prepare the rice first, and during its standing time complete recipe.

- 1 tablespoon vegetable oil or butter
- 8 scallions, cut into 2-inch pieces
- 1 medium sweet red pepper, cut into ¼-inch strips
- 1 green pepper, cut into ¼-inch strips
- ½ pound snow peas, trimmed
- 1 16-ounce can pineapple chunks packed in their own juice
- 1 tablespoon cornstarch
- 2 tablespoons brown sugar
- 2 tablespoons vinegar
- 2 tablespoons soy sauce
- 2 cups cooked ham cut into ½-inch cubes
- 1 recipe Long-Grain Rice (page 196)

In a 2-quart casserole combine the oil, scallions, peppers, and snow peas. Cover tightly and cook on HIGH for 2 minutes; stir.

Meanwhile, drain the pineapple, reserving juice. In a small bowl combine 2 tablespoons pineapple juice with the cornstarch. Stir into cooked vegetables. Stir in the remaining pineapple juice, brown sugar, vinegar, and soy sauce. Cook, uncovered, on HIGH for 2 to 3 minutes, or until boiling. Stir in the pineapple chunks and ham. Cover tightly and cook on HIGH for 3 to 5 minutes, or until the ham is heated through and the vegetables are tender-crisp, stirring once. Serve over the rice.

HAM A LA KING

MAKES 4 SERVINGS   BEGIN ABOUT 20 MINUTES BEFORE SERVING
COOKING TIME: 8 TO 14 MINUTES

Serve over toast, rice, or noodles.

- 2 tablespoons butter
- 2 tablespoons chopped onion
- 2 tablespoons all-purpose flour
- 1 cup milk
- 1½ cups diced cooked ham
- ½ pound mushrooms, sliced
- 2 tablespoons sherry
- 1 tablespoon chopped pimento
- ¼ teaspoon dry mustard (optional)

In a 2-quart casserole combine the butter and onion. Cook on HIGH for 1 to 2 minutes, or until the onion is tender. Stir in the flour to make a smooth paste. Stir in the milk. Cook on HIGH for 4 to 7 minutes, or until boiling and slightly thickened, stirring after 3 minutes. Stir in the remaining ingredients. Cook on HIGH for 3 to 5 minutes, or until heated through.

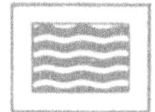

HAM SALAD SPREAD

MAKES 1¼ CUPS

Serve as a sandwich filling or an appetizer spread on small croustades or crackers, topped with a thin pickle slice.

- 1 cup finely chopped cooked ham
- ⅓ cup sweet pickle relish
- 1 teaspoon lemon juice
- 2 to 4 tablespoons Mayonnaise (page 175)

In a bowl combine the ham, pickle relish, and lemon juice. Add enough mayonnaise to bind.

HAM LOAF

MAKES 4 TO 6 SERVINGS   BEGIN 35 TO 40 MINUTES BEFORE SERVING
COOKING TIME: 20 TO 25 MINUTES

A ham loaf with a crispy sweet brown crust, due to the brown sugar that is sprinkled over the bottom of the pan. This loaf is good when sliced cold for sandwiches.

- ¼ cup brown sugar
- 4 cups ground cooked ham
- 2 cups fine dry bread cubes, croutons, or stuffing mix
- ½ cup hot water
- 2 eggs
- 1 medium onion, chopped
- 2 tablespoons chopped fresh parsley
- ½ teaspoon dry mustard
- ¼ teaspoon dried thyme

Sprinkle brown sugar over the bottom of a 9- x -5-inch loaf dish.

In a medium mixing bowl combine the remaining ingredients. Press the mixture evenly into the dish. Cover tightly and cook on MEDIUM for 20 to 25 minutes, or until the center is set and the temperature reaches 160°F, rotating halfway through cooking.

Drain off the excess fat. Let stand, covered, for 5 minutes. Turn out onto a serving platter. Serve hot, at room temperature, or cold.

SAUERKRAUT WITH SMOKED PORK CHOPS

MAKES 4 SERVINGS   BEGIN ABOUT 1 HOUR BEFORE SERVING
COOKING TIME: 28 TO 43 MINUTES

The first batch of sauerkraut was ready at Christmastime and from then on through the winter was a special occasion and still is. Serve with boiled potatoes (page 73) or Mashed Potatoes (page 457), prepared during standing time. Dark pumpernickel or sour rye bread with various mustards is good, too.

- 2 slices of bacon, cut into ½-inch pieces
- 1 medium onion, chopped
- 2 pounds sauerkraut, rinsed
- 1 apple, peeled and coarsely chopped
- ¾ cup Chicken Broth or Stock (page 118) or dry white wine
- 1 teaspoon caraway seeds
- ¼ teaspoon ground black pepper
- 4 fully cooked smoked pork chops (1 to 1½ pounds)

In a 3-quart casserole combine the bacon and onion. Cook on HIGH for 3 to 5 minutes, or until the onion is tender and the bacon partially cooked. Stir in the remaining ingredients except the pork chops. Cover tightly and cook on HIGH for 5 to 8 minutes, or until the liquid is boiling; stir. Cover again and cook on MEDIUM for 10 minutes more.

Remove half of the sauerkraut. Arrange the chops on top of the sauerkraut, with thicker sections facing outward. Cover the chops with the rest of the sauerkraut. Cover tightly and cook on MEDIUM for 10 to 20 minutes, or until the pork is heated enough. Let stand, covered, for 5 to 10 minutes.

VARIATION:

Sauerkraut with Sausage: Substitute 1 to 1½ pounds smoked kielbasa, bratwurst, or frankfurters for the smoked pork chops. Pierce the sausage casings. Cover tightly and cook the kielbasa, bratwurst, or frankfurters on HIGH for 5 to 10 minutes, or until heated through, turning the larger sausages over once.

More Ways to Use Leftover Ham

- *Timbales:* Add to Ham Timbales (page 158)
- *Tomato Sauce over Pasta:* Add 1 cup coarsely chopped ham to Basic "Batch" or Pureed Tomato Sauce (pages 178–79) with tomatoes. Serve over pasta.
- *Hot Ham and Cheese Sandwich:* Toast 2 slices of bread. Lay thin ham slices on top of 1 toast slice. Top with cheese slices. Place on a microwaveproof plate and cook on MEDIUM for 45 seconds to 1 minute, or until the cheese is slightly melted. Top with a tomato or pickle slice. Cover with the second slice of toasted bread. Serve.
- *Ham and Eggs:* Place thinly sliced ham on a microwaveproof plate. Cover with wax paper and cook on MEDIUM for 1 to 3 minutes, or until heated through. Serve with scrambled or poached eggs.
- *Ham Slices with Fruit:* Serve hot or cold sliced ham with pineapple slices, or Sweet and Sour Apricot or Orange Sauce (page 182).

Fully Cooked Sausage Basics:

1. Fully cooked sausages are just heated through to about 125°F, and because they are small and evenly shaped, they can be cooked on HIGH power. Be careful not to overcook them.
2. These types of sausages are most flavorful if steamed or grilled. When steamed, as in this recipe, additional liquid is added. A tight cover or lid, or plastic wrap turned back slightly, is fitted on top to retain the most moisture and steam.
3. Bratwurst or other large sausage, like eggplant, potato, or any food with a membrane, needs to be pierced. If not pierced, steam will build up under the skin and possibly burst it.
4. Because of its shape, a sausage like bratwurst can naturally be arranged in a ring

for the most even cooking.
5. For the most even cooking, sausages like bratwurst should be turned over and frankfurters rearranged halfway through cooking.
6. We prefer fresh sausage that is cooked in its casing to have a crisp exterior. This is achieved on the microwave browning dish following the instructions in the At-a-Glance Cooking Charts on page 62, or by cooking the sausage first in the microwave and then finishing it on the barbecue in the summer (see page 309).
7. Fully cooked sausage is heated through to the point where you can only hold your hand on the top or bottom of the covered dish for *3 Macungie* (see page 44).

✸ SMOKED BRATWURST IN BEER OR WINE SAUCE

MAKES 4 SERVINGS   BEGIN 25 MINUTES BEFORE SERVING
COOKING TIME: 10 TO 16 MINUTES

Bratwurst becomes a mouthwatering dish when thinly sliced and arranged to encircle a heaping mound of German Potato Salad (page 455).

1 tablespoon butter or margarine	½ cup beef broth (see Mock Brown Broth or Stock, page 119)
2 onions, thinly sliced	
1 tablespoon all-purpose flour	1 pound smoked bratwurst (see Note)
½ cup beer or dry white wine	

In a 2-quart casserole or 10-inch pie plate combine the butter and onions. Cook on HIGH for 3 to 5 minutes, or until the onions are tender, stirring once. Stir in the flour until blended. Stir in the beer and broth. Cook on HIGH for 3 to 5 minutes, or until boiling, stirring once.

Pierce the bratwurst on top and bottom to prevent bursting. Arrange the bratwurst around the outer rim of the dish. Cover tightly and cook on HIGH for 4 to 6 minutes, or until the lid or dish bottom is hot enough to hold your hand on it only *3 Macungie* (see page 44), turning over once.

NOTE: For different bratwurst amounts, see the chart on page 62.

VARIATION:

Franks in Beer: Substitute 1 pound frankfurters for the bratwurst. Use beer instead of wine. Instead of arranging the franks in a ring, place them in a dish and rearrange halfway through cooking.

GRILLED FRESH SAUSAGE

Grilled sausages are delicious but it is a delicate process to get the centers cooked through without charring the outsides. It can be accomplished when they are fully cooked in the microwave before final grilling and crisping. We like to serve these with Italian Basil, Peppers, and Onions (page 95) in pita rolls for sandwiches.

Fresh Italian sweet or hot sausage, cut between links

Place in a casserole and cover tightly. Cook on HIGH for 5 minutes per pound, rearranging halfway through cooking. Drain and transfer them to a preheated grill. Grill 2 inches from the coals for 8 minutes, turning once.

Bacon Basics:

1. Bacon can be cooked between paper towels on a microwaveproof plate or on a microwave roasting rack.
2. Cooking between paper towels makes for drier, crisper bacon than cooking on a roasting rack, because the paper towel absorbs much of the fat from the bacon.
3. It is not practical to cook more than 8 pieces of bacon at a time because of the cooking time and rearranging that is necessary. It is best to cook the bacon in batches, for it will keep warm outside of the oven, between paper towels.
4. Bacon should be slightly undercooked from the doneness that you desire, because upon standing time, it will become a little crisper.
5. For cooking time, see the chart on page 61.

FRESH SAUSAGE PATTIES

MAKES ABOUT 1½ POUNDS PORK SAUSAGE MEAT; 8 TO 10 PATTIES   BEGIN ABOUT ½ HOUR BEFORE SERVING
COOKING TIME: 18 TO 29 MINUTES

It is hard to purchase fresh sausage that does not have a lot of preservatives. If you have a meat grinder or food processor at your fingertips, you can make your own sausage in a very short time. It will not only make delicious patties to be served with eggs, but can be used as a stuffing for cabbage or turkey. You can also serve the patties with Cumberland Sauce (page 278) and Colcannon (page 482), or with Sweet and Sour Apricot Sauce (page 182), preparing these before the patties are cooked.

- 1 pound lean boneless pork shoulder or fresh pork butt, cut into 1-inch cubes
- 6 ounces fresh pork fat
- 3 tablespoons water
- 3 tablespoons fresh parsley leaves
- 1 tablespoon chopped scallions
- 1 large garlic clove, minced
- ½ teaspoon dried sage
- ½ teaspoon dried marjoram
- ½ teaspoon salt
- ½ teaspoon pepper
- ¼ teaspoon sugar
- ¼ teaspoon dried thyme
- ⅛ teaspoon grated nutmeg

Combine all the ingredients in a large bowl. Process in a meat grinder or food processor, in 2 batches.

To make patties, measure ¼ cup sausage mixture for each patty. Preheat a microwave browning dish in the oven according to the manufacturer's instructions, on HIGH between 5 and 8 minutes, with the largest-size dish taking longest. Place as many patties as will fit comfortably in the dish, pressing down with a spatula to make the best surface contact. Cook on HIGH for 1½ minutes. Turn the patties over and cook on HIGH for 2½ to 5 minutes more, or until cooked through. Reheat the browning dish for 3 to 5 minutes and repeat the procedure with the remaining patties.

VARIATIONS:

Crumb-Crusted Sausage Patties: After forming the patties, dredge them in ¼ to ½ cup fine dry bread crumbs to lightly coat. Add 1 tablespoon butter to the heated browning dish before cooking the patties. This will add a thin golden crust.

Sage Sausage Patties: Substitute 1 teaspoon fresh sage for the parsley.

Ground Meat Basics:

1. Onion and garlic are always cooked first in oil until tender-crisp, before adding the beef, to release the flavor. This can be covered or uncovered during cooking.
2. Ground beef should be spread out evenly in the dish so that it will cook quickly and with only one stirring during cooking, stirring to break up meat and redistribute chunks on the outside that may be cooked more than those on the inside. Stirring at the end of cooking is important to redistribute heat and finish cooking.
3. For ground-beef dishes, such as chili, for which moistness is important, when remaining ingredients are added they should be cooked with a cover; this will retain moisture for the proper chili consistency and let the flavors develop over a longer cooking time.

    A dish in which a thicker, denser consistency is necessary is cooked uncovered at this point to evaporate moisture.
4. The chili mixture is cooked first on HIGH, to raise the temperature quickly; then the

power is turned down to MEDIUM so that the flavors can develop over a longer period of time (absolutely necessary for a delicious chili).

The other type of ground beef mixture is cooked on HIGH power (which will also serve to evaporate moisture) unless soft cheese is added. In that case the power needs to be lowered so that cheese won't toughen and become hard.

5. Standing time for chili is important because the mixture is very hot when pulled from the oven, and flavors continue to develop for the next 5 to 10 minutes; for the other type of mixture standing time is very short and not worth mentioning.

✸ MOM'S GROUND BEEF CHILI

MAKES 8 TO 10 SERVINGS   BEGIIN ABOUT 1½ HOURS BEFORE SERVING
COOKING TIME: 1 HOUR 3 MINUTES TO 1 HOUR 8 MINUTES

Chili is the most requested recipe in our cooking classes. It is one of those comfort foods, and it's great for informal parties. Although the cooking time may seem long, remember that it would take at least an hour, after the meat is browned and ingredients assembled, just to simmer chili on top of the stove.

Chili, as with any stew, is always best when served the next day after the flavors have blended and become richer. For that reason we like to put it in the oven while we're cleaning up the night's dinner dishes. That way, we're one step ahead of dinner for tomorrow.

- **1 tablespoon vegetable oil**
- **2 garlic cloves, minced**
- **2 large onions, coarsely chopped**
- **2 pounds lean ground beef**
- **4 cups chopped peeled fresh tomatoes, or 2 16-ounce cans stewed tomatoes**
- **4 cups cooked kidney beans (page 71), with cooking liquid, or 2 16-ounce cans**
- **2 green peppers, coarsely chopped**
- **1 6-ounce can tomato paste**
- **3 to 6 tablespoons chili powder**
- **1 tablespoon cuminseed, or 1 teaspoon ground cumin**
- **1 teaspoon dried oregano**
- **1 teaspoon salt**
- **½ teaspoon pepper**

In a 4-quart casserole combine the oil, garlic, and onions. Cook on HIGH for 3 to 5 minutes, or until tender-crisp. Stir in the beef, spreading out evenly over the dish. Cook on HIGH for 10 to 13 minutes, or until just a slight pink color remains, stirring after 5 minutes. Stir at the end of cooking. Drain excess fat, if desired.

Stir in the remaining ingredients. Cover tightly and cook on HIGH for 10 minutes; stir. Cover again and cook on MEDIUM for 40 minutes, stirring once or twice. Let stand 5 to 10 minutes before serving. Serve with one or more of the Toppings or Alongsiders (page 322).

NOTE: *To Halve Recipe:* Cut all the ingredients in half. Cook the onions and garlic on HIGH for 1 to 2 minutes. Cook the meat for 5 minutes, stirring twice. Cook the remaining ingredients with the meat on HIGH for 5 minutes, then on MEDIUM for 25 to 30 minutes.

VARIATIONS:

One-Alarm Chili: Add 1 jalapeño pepper, seeded and chopped.

Two-Alarm Chili: Add 2 jalapeño peppers, seeded and chopped.

Three-Alarm Chili: Add 3 jalapeño peppers, seeded and chopped.

Chili Poblano with Chocolate: Add ½ ounce unsweetened baking chocolate, grated, with the remaining ingredients. Chocolate doesn't add flavor so much, but rather darkens the chili and adds a very rich quality.

Chili with Italian Black Olives: One of our favorite additions. Add 1 cup chopped pitted imported black oil-cured olives with the remaining ingredients. Eliminate the salt.

Toppings
Sour cream
Lime wedges
Salsa Cruda (page 185)
Hot pepper flakes
Grated cheddar or Monterey Jack cheese
Chopped raw onions

Alongsiders
Lettuce wedges
Tortilla chips
Warm flour or corn tortillas
Corn bread or muffins

CINCINNATI-STYLE CHILI

MAKES 6 TO 8 SERVINGS   BEGIN 1 TO 1½ HOURS BEFORE SERVING
COOKING TIME: 41 TO 55 MINUTES

You don't have to be from Cincinnati to love this chili. Even though it has many ingredients, there is little chopping and it's easy to prepare. To quote Jane and Michael Stern, authors of Roadfood, "It [Cincinnati chili] tastes Greek, looks Italian; it is found only in southern Ohio, but it came from Coney Island and has Wisconsin cheese on top." Cincinnati chili is further designated according to the way it is served—on top of spaghetti (two-way), which can be topped first with beans (three-way), then chopped onion (four-way), and finally grated cheese (five-way). The uninitiated may want to start out with a tamer chili on rice and work up from there.

---

1 tablespoon vegetable oil
2 garlic cloves, minced
2 large onions, chopped

2 pounds lean ground beef
2 cups Basic "Batch" Tomato Sauce (page 178), or canned

2 to 4 tablespoons chili powder	½ teaspoon allspice
1 tablespoon unsweetened cocoa powder or grated unsweetened baking chocolate	½ teaspoon ground cardamom
	½ teaspoon ground cinnamon
	¼ teaspoon cilantro (coriander)
1 tablespoon cider vinegar	16 ounces thick spaghetti
1 teaspoon ground cumin	
1 teaspoon paprika	*Toppings:*
1 teaspoon salt	Canned kidney beans, heated
1 teaspoon honey or molasses	1 onion, chopped
½ teaspoon pepper	Grated cheddar cheese

In a 4-quart casserole combine the oil, garlic, and onions. Cook on HIGH for 3 to 5 minutes, or until the onions are tender-crisp. Stir in the ground beef, spreading out to cover the dish. Cook on HIGH for 8 to 10 minutes, or until still slightly pink in the center, stirring after 4 minutes. Stir at the end of cooking. Drain excess fat, if desired.

Stir in the remaining ingredients except the spaghetti and toppings. Cover tightly and cook on HIGH for 10 minutes; stir. Cover again and cook on MEDIUM for 20 to 30 minutes, until the flavors have developed; stir.

Meanwhile cook the spaghetti on top of the stove. Let the chili stand, covered, for 5 to 10 minutes. Serve over the spaghetti with the toppings.

SOUTHWESTERN PIE

MAKES 6 TO 8 SERVINGS   BEGIN ABOUT 1¼ HOURS BEFORE SERVING
COOKING TIME: 34 TO 42 MINUTES

We like to prepare and serve this casserole for guests for casual entertaining, such as watching a sports event. Colorful kerchiefs tied around cold cans of soda and/or beer make an attractive beverage that is easy to hold.

1 recipe Grits (page 193)	1 tablespoon chili powder
1 teaspoon vegetable oil	½ teaspoon salt
1 garlic clove, minced	Dash hot pepper sauce or to taste
1 medium onion, finely chopped	1 egg, beaten
1 pound lean ground beef	4 ounces Monterey Jack cheese, grated
1 large tomato, peeled and seeded, or 1 cup canned peeled plum tomatoes, chopped	*Garnish:*
	Lettuce wedges
2 mild green chilies, coarsely chopped, or 1 green pepper	Sour cream
	Black olives

Let the cooked grits stand in or out of the refrigerator, uncovered, to cool until solid.

In a 2-quart casserole combine the oil, garlic, and onion. Cook on HIGH for 2 to 3 minutes, or until the onion is tender. Stir in the beef, spreading out evenly. Cook on HIGH for 5 to 8 minutes, or until still slightly pink, stirring after 3 minutes. Stir at the end of cooking. Drain excess fat. Stir in the tomatoes. Cook on HIGH for 3 minutes, or until hot and some liquid cooks away. Stir in the chilies, chili powder, salt, and hot pepper sauce. Cook on HIGH for 5 to 6 minutes to develop the flavors and let the moisture cook off, stirring after 2 minutes.

Meanwhile, combine the egg with the cooled grits. Press into a 10-inch pie plate, making a ½-inch crust to cover the sides and bottom. Spoon the hot meat mixture into the crust and smooth evenly with a spatula. Cook on HIGH for 13 to 17 minutes, or until the crust is set and dry around the edges, rotating once during cooking.

Sprinkle the cheese evenly around the outside rim, partially over the meat mixture. Cook on MEDIUM for 3 to 5 minutes, or until the cheese is melted. Let stand for 5 to 15 minutes before serving. Cut into wedges to serve. Serve with the 3 garnishes on the side.

VARIATIONS:

Southwestern Pie with Beans: Spoon 2 cups drained cooked kidney beans into the bottom of the crust. Top with the meat mixture. Proceed with the basic recipe, cooking 2 to 3 minutes longer.

Zippy Southwestern Pie: Substitute 1 or 2 jalapeño peppers, chopped, for the mild chilies.

☀ BEEF-FILLED TACOS OR TOSTADAS

MAKES 6 SERVINGS (10 TACOS OR 6 TOSTADAS)   BEGIN ABOUT 30 MINUTES BEFORE SERVING
COOKING TIME: 15 TO 22 MINUTES

- 1 teaspoon vegetable oil
- 1 garlic clove, minced
- 1 medium onion, chopped
- 1 pound lean ground beef
- 2 medium tomatoes, peeled, seeded and chopped, or 1 8-ounce can California- or Spanish-style tomato sauce
- 1 to 2 tablespoons chili powder
- 1 teaspoon ground cumin
- ½ teaspoon salt
- ¼ teaspoon pepper
- 6 fresh or precooked tostadas or 10 taco shells

Toppings:
- 2 cups shredded lettuce
- 2 large tomatoes, chopped
- 1 red onion, chopped
- 1 cup sour cream
  Chopped fresh or pickled jalapeño peppers
  Salsa Cruda (page 185)

In a 2-quart casserole combine the oil, garlic, and onion. Cook on HIGH for 2 to 4 minutes, or until the onion is tender. Stir in the beef, spreading out evenly in the bottom of the dish. Cook on HIGH for 5 to 8 minutes, or until just a slight pink color remains, stirring once.

Stir at the end of cooking. Drain.

Add the tomatoes, chili powder, cumin, salt, and pepper. Cook on HIGH for 8 to 10 minutes, or until most of the moisture has cooked away and the flavors are developed, stirring after 4 minutes.

To make tostadas or tacos, heat the crisp, precooked flat tostadas or shells on HIGH for 1 to 3 minutes. If the tostadas or tacos are not precooked, but refrigerated, follow the instructions on the package for cooking (this is usually in a frying pan with a small amount of oil). Spoon the filling onto the tostadas or into the taco shells and serve with some or all of the suggested toppings.

VARIATION:

Sloppy Joes: After cooking the ground beef, substitute ½ to ¾ cup Blazing Barbecue Sauce (page 181) or prepared barbecue sauce for the remaining ingredients. Cook as directed and serve over buns.

PICADILLO

MAKES 4 SERVINGS   BEGIN 30 TO 40 MINUTES BEFORE SERVING
COOKING TIME: 16 TO 25 MINUTES

Picadillo is a type of ground beef hash that is made so tasty by using a free hand with various Mexican ingredients. When the cheese is eliminated, it makes a spicy filling for tacos or stuffed peppers. Serve with warm rice or flour tortillas.

- 1 teaspoon vegetable oil
- 1 garlic clove, minced
- 1 medium onion, chopped
- 1 pound lean ground beef
- 2 medium tomatoes, peeled, seeded, and chopped, or 1 cup canned tomato sauce
- 1 tablespoon chili powder
- 1 tablespoon vinegar
- 1 teaspoon sugar
- 1 teaspoon ground cinnamon
- ½ teaspoon salt
- ¼ teaspoon pepper
- 1 cup grated Monterey Jack, Muenster, or mozzarella

In a 2-quart casserole combine the oil, garlic, and onion. Cook on HIGH for 2 to 4 minutes, or until the onion is tender. Stir in the beef, spreading it evenly over the dish. Cook on HIGH for 5 to 8 minutes, or until just a slight pink color remains, stirring once. Stir at the end of cooking. Drain.

Add the remaining ingredients except the cheese. Cook on HIGH for 8 to 10 minutes, or until most of the moisture has cooked away, stirring after 4 minutes. Sprinkle with the grated cheese. Cook on MEDIUM for 1 to 3 minutes, or until the cheese is melted.

VARIATIONS:

Picadillo with Raisins: Add ½ cup raisins with the tomatoes.

Picadillo with Almonds: Add ½ cup chopped almonds with the tomatoes.

Burger Basics:

1. Ground beef, lamb, or veal are tender meats that can be cooked on HIGH power, whether on a roasting rack, plate, or browning dish. The power will be lowered if soft cheese is added, because it is more sensitive to HIGH heat and may become rubbery. The exception to this is when the burgers are cooked on HIGH on the browning dish, with an addition of cheese. The browning dish absorbs some of the cooking energy, and in effect slows down the cooking speed of the cheese.
2. The important thing in cooking burgers is to keep a dry surface, so the end product does not appear, or taste, steamed. This can be accomplished by cooking on a roasting rack, which raises the meat above its juices, and with a cover of paper towel which absorbs juices, or by cooking on the hot surface of the browning dish.
3. Because burgers are cooked so quickly, they don't build up enough heat to turn dark brown. Crusting can be added with the high heat contact of a browning dish, or browning added with a coloring agent painted on.
4. The standing time is very short, and of no particular importance for burgers.
5. *Doneness:* The cooking times given will direct you toward a Medium burger (except for the browning dish method, which includes rare). The best way to test the doneness of all burgers is to first press down on the burgers. The juices that run out should still be pink and the centers of the burgers will still be somewhat soft to the touch and, except for those on the dish, will be pink on the center top. Cutting open one burger will tell you by appearance whether the interior is to your liking.

You may need to rearrange the burgers during cooking on the roasting rack or browning dish so that all are evenly cooked.

✸ BURGERS

Beef, lamb, or veal burgers may be cooked by one of the following three methods. The type of meat mixture and the thickness of the burgers will have some bearing on the cooking time. It is best to make all the burgers as equal in size and shape as possible to gauge the same cooking doneness of all. The cooking times given are for burgers of Medium doneness. A Rare burger is difficult to do on anything other than a browning dish.

ROASTING RACK METHOD:

You will have less fat with this method, which is good for diets where fat is to be reduced. (For more about roasting racks see page 84.)

Quantity (¼ pound each)	First Side	Second Side
1	35 seconds	1 to 1½ minutes
2	1 minute	2 to 3 minutes
4	1½ minutes	2½ to 3 minutes
6	2 minutes	2½ to 4 minutes
8	3 minutes	3½ to 4 minutes

Place the burgers on a microwaveproof roasting rack in a 2-quart dish to keep the meat above the cooking juices. For a browner appearance, brush the burgers with 1 tablespoon of either Worcestershire sauce, Kitchen Bouquet, or a soy sauce–water combination. Cover with wax paper—this prevents spattering but releases excess moisture—and follow the cooking times in the chart above, using HIGH power, turning over after the first side.

PAPER PLATE METHOD:

This method works best if cooking only 1 or 2 burgers, because the plates can't absorb too many cooking juices.

Quantity (¼ pound each)	First Side	Second Side
1	35 seconds	1 to 1½ minutes
2	1 minute	2 to 3 minutes

Line a paper plate with a double layer of paper towels. For a browner appearance, brush the burgers with 1 tablespoon of either Worcestershire sauce, Kitchen Bouquet, or a combination of soy sauce and water. Cover with a paper towel. Follow the cooking times on the above chart, using HIGH power, turning the burgers over after the first side.

BROWNING DISH METHOD:

Because the preheated dish seals in the juices and gives a crisp exterior, this method will come closest to conventional searing in a pan or oven broiling.

Quantity (¼ pound each)	First Side	Second Side (Reduce by ½ minute for Rare)
1 to 2	½ minute	1 minute
4	1 minute	1½ to 2 minutes
6 to 8	3 minutes	3 to 4 minutes

Preheat a browning dish according to the manufacturer's directions on HIGH for 5 to 8 minutes. Place the burgers on the hot dish, pressing down with a metal spatula to make full contact with the surface. Cook, uncovered, following the cooking times in the chart above, using HIGH power, turning the burgers over after the first side.

NOTE: *Reheating:* To reheat 1 room- or refrigerator-temperature burger in a bun, wrap it in a paper towel. Heat on HIGH for 15 seconds to 1 minute, or until warm. (The room-temperature burger will take the least time.)

VARIATIONS:

Cheeseburgers: *Browning dish method:* After cooking the first side, top each patty with a slice of cheese. Continue as directed for the second side. *Roasting rack or paper plate methods:* Add the cheese at the end of cooking. Cook on MEDIUM for 30 seconds, or until melted.

Pizza Burgers: *Browning dish method:* After cooking the first side, spoon 1 tablespoon Basic "Batch" or Pureed Tomato Sauce (page 178 or 179) on each burger. Sprinkle each with 1 tablespoon grated Parmesan cheese and 1 tablespoon grated mozzarella cheese. Continue as directed for the second side. *Roasting rack or paper plate methods:* Add the tomato sauce and cheeses at the end of cooking. Cook on MEDIUM for 1 to 3 minutes, or until the cheese is melted. Serve on toasted burger buns, Italian bread, or in pita pockets.

Bacon Burger: Serve each cooked burger with 2 slices cooked bacon (see page 61) on top.

French Burgers: For each burger, add 1 tablespoon red wine, 1 teaspoon chopped onion, 1 teaspoon chopped fresh parsley or 1 teaspoon dried, salt and pepper to the meat mixture. Follow basic cooking directions. To serve, top with Sautéed Mushrooms (page 439), over crusty French bread.

Mexican Burgers: Top the cooked burgers with 1 tablespoon Warm Jalapeño Salsa (page 187) and 1 tablespoon grated Monterey Jack cheese.

Meatball Basics:

1. It is important to arrange meatballs in a circle or with an open center for the most even cooking.
2. A wax paper cover will keep down the spatters but not make the meatballs soggy. It also helps these dense little balls to cook through quickly.
3. Turning meatballs over once is necessary so that all sides are evenly cooked. If not, the side sitting in the cooking liquid will cook faster because of the heat conduction from that liquid.
4. As with ground meat burgers, meatballs cook well on HIGH power. Even though there is an egg in the meat mixture, it serves as a binding and will not become tough on HIGH.
5. The sauces are made after the meatballs are completely cooked to utilize all of the delicious cooking liquid.

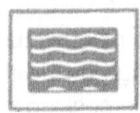

✹ BASIC MEATBALLS

MAKES 16 TO 24 MEATBALLS   BEGIN 15 MINUTES BEFORE SERVING
COOKING TIME: 7 TO 10 MINUTES

Here's a ground meat mixture that can be dressed up or down, depending on the sauce that is served with it. And it's so quick, there's no reason not to treat the family like company.

- 1 pound lean ground beef (or veal, beef, and pork mixture)
- 1 egg, beaten
- 1 medium onion, finely chopped
- 2 tablespoons chopped fresh parsley, or 2 teaspoons dried
- ¼ cup fine dry bread crumbs
- 1½ teaspoons salt
- ¼ teaspoon pepper

Combine all the ingredients in a large bowl. Form 1½-inch meatballs with the mixture. Place them around the outer rim of a 10-inch cake dish or a 2-quart rectangular dish. Cover with wax paper and cook on HIGH for 7 to 10 minutes, or until done, turning the meatballs over and rotating the dish after 4 minutes. If desired, drain excess fat and stir the juices into any of the recommended sauces.

VARIATIONS:

Italian Meatballs: Add 1 garlic clove, minced, 3 tablespoons grated Parmesan cheese, and ½ teaspoon dried oregano to the meat mixture.

Italian Meatballs in Tomato Sauce: Prepare the Italian Meatballs variation above. Add the cooked meatballs to 2 cups tomato sauce. Cover tightly and heat on HIGH for 4 to 6 minutes, or until the sauce and meatballs are heated through. Serve over pasta or on rolls for sandwiches.

Burgundy Beefballs: Add 2 tablespoons red Burgundy wine to mixture. After the meatballs are cooked, make Burgundy Sauce (page 330). Serve as an appetizer with toothpicks, or as a main course over rice, noodles, or mashed potatoes.

Swedish Meatballs: Use ground veal or a mixture of ½ pound ground beef and ½ pound ground veal. Add ¼ teaspoon allspice and ⅛ teaspoon ground cloves to the mixture. Make Sherried Cream Sauce (page 330).

Meatballs with Mushroom Sauce: Make Mushroom Sauce (page 172). Stir the cooked meatballs into the sauce. Heat together on HIGH for 1 to 3 minutes.

Konigsberger Klops: Add ¼ teaspoon grated nutmeg to the meat mixture. Make the Sherried Cream Sauce variation of Burgundy Sauce (page 330). Stir ¼ cup drained and rinsed capers into the cooked sauce. Stir in the cooked meatballs.

Caraway Meatballs: Add 2 teaspoons caraway seeds to the basic meat mixture. Serve with Braised Sweet and Sour Red Cabbage (page 400).

Sweet and Sour Meatballs: Prepare Sweet and Sour Apricot Sauce (page 182). Stir cooked meatballs into the sauce.

Burgundy Sauce

MAKES ABOUT 1⅓ CUPS

Prepare this sauce after removing the meatballs from the casserole. Pour over the meatballs and heat together on HIGH for 2 minutes.

- 2 tablespoons butter
- 2 tablespoons all-purpose flour
- 1 cup beef broth or stock (see Mock Brown Stock or Broth, page 119)
- ¼ cup red Burgundy or other dry red wine

Add the butter to the meatball casserole, stirring to melt. Stir in the flour to make a smooth paste. Stir in ¼ cup beef broth to blend. Stir in the remaining broth and wine. Cook on HIGH for 3 to 5 minutes, or until bubbling and thickened, stirring twice.

Sherried Cream Sauce: Substitute 2 tablespoons dry sherry or vermouth for the wine. Add 2 tablespoons light cream at the end.

Meat Loaf Basics:

1. Shaping the meat loaf with rounded, even ends is important so there are no corners that will overcook.
2. Fine dry bread crumbs work better than fresh bread cubes, which will keep a ground beef mixture too soggy. Lean meat will retain a better shaped meat loaf than fattier meat, which will shrink when the fat cooks out of it, causing the bottom to overcook from the fat.
3. If a meat loaf is made to fit right inside a loaf dish, its sides will have a somewhat steamed appearance. Do not use a loaf dish because not only will it look steamed, but the fat and juices will collect on the bottom to possibly overcook that area.
4. Do not cover a meat loaf during cooking; that will give it a steamed appearance.
5. The tomato cover not only adds flavor but a nice color complement to the top of the loaf.
6. Ground beef, as in meatballs and hamburgers, is cooked on HIGH power. The egg serves to bind the meat with the other ingredients, so that it, too, can cook well on HIGH power—for a reason similar to why scrambled eggs cook on HIGH when stirred well.
7. Standing time is necessary for the heat to be conducted to the center of the meat loaf in completion of cooking.
8. *Doneness:* The sides of the meat loaf, and the top, one-third of the way in from each end, will be dry and firm to the touch, yet the center top of the meat loaf will still be somewhat soft to the touch. If cut open, the inside center will still be pink. If using a thermometer, the center of the loaf should register between 145° and 155°F. If using a pork mixture, cook to 165°F.

Underdone: The top center will be very

soft, almost mushy to the touch. The inside center will still be a deep pink, with juices running very pink. If the outside corners or edges appear to be getting too done for your taste, cover them smoothly with aluminum foil while you continue to cook the meat loaf.

Overdone: Meat loaf will be dry and hard on the outside and the top center will be firm and unresilient to the touch. At this point the meat loaf is still edible but dry. Slice and douse with Basic "Batch" or Pureed Tomato Sauce (pages 178 and 179), Mushroom Sauce (page 172), or another sauce, or reheat the meat loaf slices right in the sauce to make it moist.

✸ MEAT LOAF

MAKES 4 TO 6 SERVINGS BEGIN 25 TO 30 MINUTES BEFORE SERVING
COOKING TIME: 16 TO 20 MINUTES

The complaints we have encountered about meat loaf cooked in the microwave was that it didn't brown enough and it stuck to the sides and bottom of the pan. With all that in mind, we set out to make a loaf that had a nice dry surface and didn't look steamed, yet was moist inside. Here are the results, and we are pleased to say that they are not unlike the old-fashioned meat loaves Mother used to make. Serve with Mushroom Sauce (page 172), Basic "Batch" or Pureed Tomato Sauce (pages 178–79), mustard, or horseradish.

1½ pounds lean ground beef	2 tablespoons chopped fresh parsley, or 2 teaspoons dried
1 medium onion, finely chopped	½ teaspoon salt
½ cup fine dry bread crumbs	¼ teaspoon pepper
1 egg, beaten	1 8-ounce can tomato sauce

In a large bowl combine all the ingredients except half of the canned tomato sauce. Form the mixture into a firm 4- × -6½-inch loaf or 6½-inch-diameter round loaf. If making a rectangle, round the corners and make the top smooth for the most even cooking. Place the rectangular loaf in a 2-quart rectangular baking dish or the round loaf in a 10-inch pie plate. Make sure that the dish is large enough so that the sides of the meat loaf don't touch the sides of the dish. Spread the remaining tomato sauce on top of the meat loaf. Cook on HIGH for 16 to 20 minutes, or until done, rotating after 7 minutes. Let stand for 5 minutes. Transfer to a serving dish.

VARIATIONS:

Dijon Mustard Meat Loaf: Add 2 tablespoons Dijon mustard to the meat mixture.

Zippy Meat Loaf: Add 2 tablespoons prepared horseradish to the meat mixture.

Catsup Meat Loaf: Substitute ¼ cup catsup for the tomato sauce, mixing half into the meat mixture and spreading half on top of the loaf.

Cheese-Topped Meat Loaf: Place ¼ pound cheese, thinly sliced, on top of the cooked meat loaf. Let the cheese melt during standing time. If the cheese is not completely melted, place the meat loaf back in the oven. Cook on MEDIUM for 1 to 2 minutes.

Meat Loaf with Spinach: Cook a 10-ounce package of frozen chopped spinach (page 67); drain well. Substitute the cooked spinach for tomato sauce, adding the entire amount to the meat mixture, along with 1 extra egg and ¼ teaspoon grated nutmeg. Serve with Basic "Batch" Tomato Sauce (page 178) or Mushroom Sauce (page 172).

Veal Loaf: Substitute ground veal for the beef. Add ¼ teaspoon grated nutmeg and 1 teaspoon dried thyme to the meat mixture.

Mixed Meat Loaf: Use 1 pound ground beef, ¼ pound ground veal, and ¼ pound ground pork.

Turkey Meat Loaf: Substitute fresh ground turkey for the beef.

Individual Meat Loaves: Form the mixture into six 6-ounce custard cups, dividing the sauce between them. Place the custard cups in a ring in the oven with about an inch of space between them. Cook on HIGH for 10 to 13 minutes, or until the centers are almost firm, rearranging after 5 minutes and removing any that may appear cooked toward the end. Let stand for 2 minutes. Meanwhile, heat any tomato sauce or Warm Jalapeño Salsa (page 187) on HIGH for 1 to 1½ minutes. Turn out the meat loaves and pour over sauce.

Beef and Calf Liver Basics:

1. Remove the surrounding membrane from the liver to prevent any curling and toughening of the outer edges during cooking.
2. Liver is either cooked on a browning dish or cooked and flavored with a sauce.
3. When cooked on a browning dish, liver is cooked on HIGH power because the dish continues to absorb some of the microwave energy, so the liver won't toughen as it would normally on HIGH. When not cooked with a sauce, liver should be cooked on MEDIUM so as to remain tender.
4. If liver is cooked on a browning dish, it is cooked uncovered, so as not to steam the liver. When cooked with a sauce, the liver is covered with wax paper to speed up cooking and prevent splatters.
5. Liver cooked on MEDIUM power cooks for 7 minutes to 9 minutes per pound.
6. Liver is best when served with a slightly pink interior. Overcooking produces an unpleasant flavor.
7. Liver is salted at the end of cooking time to prevent toughening on the surface.
8. Young beef or calf liver that is sliced into ½-inch strips may be substituted for any of the chicken liver recipes.
9. *Doneness:* Liver is done when the exterior is brown but when cut, the juices still run slightly pink... but not red.

    Underdone: Liver is still red inside and the juices run red. Continue to cook on HIGH for 1 minute at a time.

    Overdone: Liver will become tough and dry if cooked too long on the browning dish or if salted before cooking. At this point there is very little that can be done with it, outside of giving it to the kitties. (There will be less chance of overcooking if the liver is cooked on MEDIUM in a sauce.)

GRILLED LIVER AND BACON

MAKES 4 SERVINGS   BEGIN 15 MINUTES BEFORE SERVING
COOKING TIME: 5 TO 6 MINUTES

---

4 slices of bacon
1 tablespoon butter

1 pound tender or baby beef liver, membranes removed and cut into large slices ½-inch thick
Freshly ground pepper to taste

Place the bacon on a microwave roasting rack in a 2-quart dish, or on a paper towel–lined paper or microwaveproof plate. Cover the bacon with a paper towel and cook on HIGH for 2½ to 3¼ minutes, or until almost crisp. Let stand.

Preheat the microwave browning dish according to the manufacturer's instructions, between 5 and 8 minutes on HIGH. Spread the butter on the dish to melt. Add the liver and press down onto the surface of the hot dish with a metal spatula. Cook on HIGH for 1 minute; turn the liver over and rearrange, pressing down again with the spatula. Cook on HIGH for 1 to 1½ minutes more, or until the juices from the liver are a rose color, indicating a slightly pink interior. Pepper lightly and top with a piece of bacon to serve.

VARIATION:

Liver and Bacon with Burgundy-Onion Sauce: Transfer the grilled liver to a serving platter. Cover to keep warm. To the hot browning dish add ¼ cup beef broth (see Mock Brown Broth or Stock, page 119), ¼ cup red wine, and ½ cup thinly sliced scallions. Cook on HIGH for 2 minutes. Add 2 tablespoons unsalted butter. Cook on HIGH for 1 minute more to melt the butter. Pour over the liver. Sprinkle with chopped fresh parsley.

TYROLIAN LIVER

MAKES 4 SERVINGS   BEGIN 20 MINUTES BEFORE SERVING
COOKING TIME: 11 TO 16 MINUTES

Serve with rice or noodles.

---

1 tablespoon butter
1 medium onion, thinly sliced
1 tablespoon all-purpose flour
1 pound tender or baby beef liver, membranes removed and cut into ½-inch slices

1 cup sour cream
1 tablespoon lemon juice
1 tablespoon drained capers
¼ teaspoon salt
⅛ teaspoon ground pepper

In a 2-quart casserole combine the butter and onion. Cook on HIGH for 2 to 3 minutes, or until the onion is tender. Stir in the flour until smooth. Stir in the liver. Arrange around the outer rim of the dish, leaving the center open. Cover with wax paper and cook on MEDIUM for 7 to 10 minutes, or until only a slightly pink color remains in the center, stirring to push the less cooked areas to the outside of the dish. Add the remaining ingredients. Cover again and cook on MEDIUM for 2 to 3 minutes, or until heated through but not boiling.

TOMATO PASTA SAUCE WITH LIVER

MAKES 4 SERVINGS   BEGIN ABOUT 30 MINUTES BEFORE SERVING
COOKING TIME: 17 TO 20 MINUTES

Serve over pasta.

- 1 tablespoon olive or vegetable oil
- 1 garlic clove, minced
- 1 medium onion, thinly sliced
- 2 tablespoons tomato paste
- 1 cup fresh or undrained canned tomatoes, peeled and chopped
- ½ teaspoon dried basil
- ½ teaspoon salt
- ¼ teaspoon pepper
- 1 pound tender or baby beef liver, membrane removed and cut into ½-inch slices

In a 2-quart casserole combine the oil, garlic, and onion. Cook on HIGH for 2 to 3 minutes, or until the onion is tender. Stir in the tomato paste. Add the tomatoes, basil, salt, and pepper. Cook, on HIGH for 5 minutes, stirring once. Add the liver. Cover with wax paper and cook on MEDIUM for 10 to 12 minutes, or until the liver is tender and done, stirring after 5 minutes.

VARIATIONS:

Tomato Pasta Sauce with Liver and Peppers: Add 1 green pepper, cut into strips, with the tomatoes.

Spicy Pasta Sauce with Liver: Add ¼ teaspoon red pepper flakes with the salt.

Chili-Tomato Sauce with Liver: Add 1 teaspoon chili powder and ⅛ teaspoon cayenne pepper with the salt.

11

POULTRY

"Shoemaker or artist?" As his letters to brother Theo indicate, Vincent van Gogh wrestled with his identity as a painter. Should he apply the colors as he saw them or as he felt them?

As a painter myself, I know that cooking is an art form where the plate is the empty canvas and one builds an edible picture with the colors and textures of food. But in cooking, one has to be both shoemaker and artist, technician and creator. There are certain rules that can't be violated or a recipe just won't work, and therein lies the dilemma. How can one be creative when facing what seems an uninspiring framework of rules?

People who approach microwave cooking as just so many sets of rules will always be disappointed. For what is cooking without creativity? That is why we have tried to make our rules seem less like rules, by starting out the book with a comparison of microwaves to sunlight. Who can get too serious when cooking with sunlight? Even when you have learned how microwaves work, you sometimes have to push that to the back of your mind so that you can feel really free to create.

And that's how, even with all the microwave cooking we've done, we're always surprised by new discoveries. For example, when I pulled the perfect crisp, yet moist duck out of the combined efforts of microwave and conventional cooking, it was a triumph and a delight. Cornish hens that cooked very evenly when boned and then stuffed were perfect for elegant entertaining. Chicken breasts, when arranged around the outside of sliced vegetables on a platter, could be cooked all at once. A turkey that browned *without* Kitchen Bouquet, yet yielded moist and juicy white meat, was our trophy at Thanksgiving.

When we looked for alternative ways to make chicken skin appealing (the microwave alone just doesn't do it) our recipes for breaded boned and skinned chicken breasts were born. If chicken isn't glazed, simmered in a sauce or crisped with the help of conventional heat, we just don't find the skin acceptable. But removing the skin and replacing it with a light breading took care of that, a simple solution that took us a while to discover. Today, these breaded chicken cutlets are some of my favorites because they are so versatile. I find them particularly nice for summer picnics, because they are delicious hot or cold.

Poultry adapts well to a variety of flavors, too. It is hard to imagine a food that can carry off a creamy raspberry vinegar sauce as well as it does one of spicy peanut, but chicken does just that. Other combinations are found in pecan mustard coatings for chicken, honey glazes for turkey and a green peppercorn sauce that sends a crisp duck soaring to culinary heights. If calories seem a bit high, look for the Steamed Chicken Breasts with Herbs and Wine.

Now if you think this sounds like mountains of leftovers in the making, we've got recipes for those, too. A good New American Chicken or Turkey Potpie might just hit the spot.

—Thelma

Buying and Storing Fresh Poultry

- Squeeze the package to make sure that the poultry doesn't crackle with the sound of any ice crystals, front or back. The flesh should be resilient, not spongy. Fresh poultry is sometimes frozen before shipping because it travels better and stores longer, but freezing can cause a loss of natural juices and tenderness. You may in fact see some liquid in the tray. Another indication of freezing is that after poultry is cooked, the bones in the wings and drumstick turn a reddish-black. To prevent buying frozen poultry, look as closely as you can in the store.
- USDA "Grade A" marking on the label tells you that the chicken has met the highest government standards.
- The color of the skin, yellow or white, is an indication of the type of feed the chickens were fed. Whatever the color, it should be uniform and even, which indicates that the top layer hasn't been rubbed off during processing, in removal of the feathers.
- Avoid any bruises or broken skin. This indicates that the bird was treated roughly in processing. Tears in the skin could cause loss of juices and reduce shelf life by admitting bacteria into the meat.
- Plumpness is an indication of more meat in relation to bone weight, or more chicken for your money.
- With whole poultry, look for a full coating of fat in the abdominal cavity, which is the sign of a well-fed bird.

Home Storage

- Place poultry in the coldest part of the refrigerator in its original airtight wrapping for one or two days. Cook or freeze the third day.
- Before preparing poultry, rinse the poultry thoroughly, and if it is a whole poultry, do it inside and out to remove any bacteria. Make sure that hands, knives, and cutting surfaces are washed thoroughly after handling raw poultry.
- Cooked poultry can be refrigerated up to three days, when covered tightly.

Freezing Poultry

- If you're not able to cook fresh poultry within three days, freeze it in the original package wrapped with a second layer of foil. Freezing may cause some loss of juices, but it is preferable to throwing the meat out entirely.
- Fresh poultry can be frozen and stored for up to six months.
- Cooked poultry can be frozen in airtight wrapping and stored for up to two months.

Defrosting Frozen Poultry

Chicken Parts and Boned Breasts, Turkey Legs and Breasts, and Cornish Hens

- Frozen chicken parts and boned breasts, turkey legs and breasts, and Cornish hens thaw on DEFROST power in 6 to 7 minutes per pound.
- A microwaveproof roasting rack placed in a rectangular dish is recommended for defrosting these poultry pieces. Because the rack raises the pieces above any juices that are becoming hot in the bottom of the dish, it prevents overheating on one side. If you don't have a roasting rack, small microwaveproof dishes can be inverted in the cooking dish as a good substitute.
- Unwrap poultry before defrosting, if possible, and remove from the Styrofoam containers. If poultry can't be unwrapped at first, unwrap after the first 3 minutes of defrosting. If left on the entire time, the wrapping will retain too much heat and cook the poultry.
- Boned chicken breasts should be arranged with the thicker portions to the outside of the cooking dish.
- Turkey breasts and Cornish game hens should be placed breast side down, and turned halfway through defrosting.
- Break semifrozen poultry pieces apart after half the defrosting time. Rearrange pieces so that icier ones are toward the outside of the dish.
- If any areas of poultry—breast bones or legs—appear to be cooking, cover these areas smoothly with foil. This will reflect the microwave energy.
- After defrosting, poultry pieces should still be cold to the touch on the meatier portions, with some ice crystals present. The ice crystals will disappear during the standing time.
- After defrosting, rinse the poultry pieces in cold water before letting them stand. Poultry should stand for 5 minutes; Cornish game

hens must stand for 15 minutes before cooking.
- When Cornish game hens are rinsed at the end of defrosting time, the giblets can be pulled out while running cold water into the interior cavity.

Whole Chicken, Turkey, Duck, and Goose

- Whole chicken, turkey, duck, and goose defrost on: HIGH for 1 minute per pound, then MEDIUM for 2 minutes per pound, then DEFROST for 1 minute per pound. This is the fastest way to defrost whole birds.
- A microwaveproof roasting rack placed in a 2-quart rectangular baking dish is recommended for defrosting a whole bird. This will raise it above the juices collecting in the bottom of the dish. These juices should be poured off twice during defrosting.
- Remove any wrappings from the birds before defrosting. If wrappings can't be removed immediately without tearing the skin, remove after HIGH power cooking time.
- Begin defrosting the birds breast side down, and turn over twice during the defrosting process. Turn the birds over after both HIGH cooking time and MEDIUM, to end breast side down.
- Pour off juices when turning over the birds. This will prevent the parts sitting in the juices from overcooking.
- If wing or leg areas appear to be cooking, cover them smoothly with foil. This will reflect microwave energy.
- When removed from the oven, whole birds should have ice crystals inside and between the legs and wings and body when they are removed from the oven. These will dissolve when placed in a cold water bath.
- Place oven-defrosted birds in a bath of cold water. This is to melt any remaining ice crystals. Remove giblets as soon as possible during this time. When you're in a hurry, run hot water into the cavity to remove ice and gizzards quickly.
- After a cold water bath, which melts the ice crystals, let the birds stand—between 30 minutes for smaller birds and 1 hour for turkey—until completely defrosted.

Chicken Livers

- Frozen chicken livers are defrosted on: HIGH for 2 minutes per pound until they can be removed from packaging, then MEDIUM for 2 to 3 minutes per pound, then DEFROST for 4 to 5 minutes per pound.
- After the livers are removed from their packaging, transfer onto a microwaveproof roasting rack in a baking dish or large casserole to defrost. This will raise the livers above their juices, which get hot and may

begin to cook the livers.
- Halfway through the MEDIUM or DEFROST power setting, break up livers, setting icy sections toward the outside of the dish. Pour off any accumulated juices at this point.
- Rinse the livers in cold water to melt any ice crystals.
- Let stand for 5 minutes to thaw completely.
- Pat dry with a paper towel before cooking.

Poultry Defrosting Doneness

Defrosting in the microwave oven will almost, but not quite, eliminate the ice crystals from frozen poultry. This process will be completed when the poultry is rinsed in cold water then stands. If defrosting is carried further in the oven than the ice-crystal stage mentioned above, the poultry will lose its natural juices and become tough and dry upon cooking.

When poultry pieces come from the oven, the pieces should break apart, yet still have ice crystals; the meatiest parts will feel very cold. A whole bird, after defrosting in the oven, will still have ice crystals underneath the thickest part of the legs and wings and the giblets will still be frozen inside. The ice will dissolve in the cold water bath so that the giblets can be removed. The bird will completely defrost upon standing time.

Poached Whole Chicken Basics:

1. Smaller broiler-fryers are generally cooked with ½ cup liquid in the microwave, and covered tightly to help tenderize the meat.
2. Whole chickens that are poached are cooked entirely on HIGH power, because the extra liquid and cover keeps them moist and tender.
3. A large (3-quart) casserole with a tight lid or a plastic-wrap cover is the best utensil for cooking a whole bird.
4. Because of the shape and size of the whole bird, it should be turned over once during cooking for the most even poaching.
5. A 10-minute standing time will complete the cooking.
6. *Doneness:* The flesh should be firm to the touch and the legs should barely wiggle when moved. When pierced between the thickest part of the leg and body, the juices should run clear, not red, before standing time.

Underdone: The indication here will be that the juices don't run clear when pierced as indicated above. The birds should have been completely defrosted before cooking, or that area will take much longer to cook.

Overdone: Tough chicken is sometimes an indication of an old bird. Dryness can come from overcooking. Cut the meat into small pieces and stir together with Rose Sauce (page 178) or into Basic "Batch" Tomato Sauce (page 178) and serve over pasta.

✹ POACHED WHOLE CHICKEN

MAKES 4 TO 6 SERVINGS   BEGIN 45 MINUTES BEFORE SERVING
COOKING TIME: 28 MINUTES

This can be the basis of a classic boiled chicken dinner or the beginning of a chicken salad. If you plan to make chicken salad, let the chicken cool to room temperature in the broth to develop the flavor. By thickening the cooking liquid, the chicken can go on to be served in a variety of ways. If we are serving the chicken hot, we like to use the poaching liquid to cook the vegetables and then make the gravy.

1 3½- to 4-pound broiler-fryer chicken	1 bay leaf, crushed
Salt and pepper	4 sprigs fresh parsley, or 1
2 carrots, coarsely chopped	teaspoon dried
1 garlic clove, crushed	½ cup Chicken Broth or Stock (page 118)
1 onion, quartered	or water

Remove the giblets from the chicken. Lightly salt and pepper the chicken. Place breast side down in a 3-quart casserole. Add the remaining ingredients. Cover tightly and cook on HIGH for 28 minutes, or until done, turning over after 14 minutes. Let stand, covered, for 10 minutes.

VARIATIONS:

Chicken in Broth: Strain the broth. Remove as much fat as possible and correct the seasonings. Cook, uncovered, on HIGH for 5 minutes, until heated. Meanwhile, remove the skin and cut the chicken into serving pieces. Place them in a soup tureen, cover, and set aside. Pour the broth over the chicken and sprinkle with ¼ cup fresh parsley. Serve in soup bowls.

Poached Chicken with Vegetables: Remove the chicken from the broth. Remove the skin from the chicken and discard. Slice the meat, and place in the tureen. Cover and set aside. Add 2 medium potatoes, quartered; 1 cup sliced carrots; and 1 cup thinly sliced leeks or scallions to the broth. (Substitute any vegetables as long as they add up to 3 cups). Cover tightly and cook on HIGH for 7 to 11 minutes, or until tender, stirring after 4 minutes. Spoon the vegetables around the chicken; serve the broth over the chicken. This is the classic way to serve poached chicken, with an accompaniment of vegetables.

Poached Chicken with Hollandaise: Remove the chicken from the broth. Remove the skin and discard; slice the meat. Freeze the broth for later use in soup. Place the chicken on a serving platter. Prepare Hollandaise Sauce (page 174) and serve over the chicken.

Poached Chicken with Garlic: Add 15 to 25 large unpeeled garlic cloves with the broth. Serve the cooked garlic with the chicken, squeezing them from their husks onto slices of crusty French bread as you would butter.

Poached Chicken with Gravy: Remove the cooked chicken from the broth. Remove the skin and discard; slice the meat. Place on a serving platter. Cover and set aside. In a small bowl combine 1 tablespoon all-purpose flour and 2 tablespoons vermouth or cold water until smooth. Stir the flour mixture into the poaching broth. Stir in 1 teaspoon lemon juice and ¼ cup chopped parsley or mixed chopped fresh herbs—parsley, thyme, and tarragon. Cook on HIGH for 3 to 5 minutes, or until thickened, stirring each minute to ensure a smooth sauce. Stir in ¼ cup cream or milk. Correct the seasonings and spoon over the chicken, or pass in a gravy boat.

Poached Chicken with Mustard Gravy: Follow the Poached Chicken with Gravy variation above. Add 2 tablespoons prepared Dijon mustard to the gravy with the herbs.

Poached Chicken with Curried Gravy: Follow the Poached Chicken with Gravy variation above. Add 2 teaspoons curry powder to the gravy with the herbs.

Poached Chicken with Rose Gravy: Follow the Poached Chicken with Gravy variation above. Add 1 tablespoon tomato paste with the herbs.

Poached Chicken with Brandied Gravy: Follow the Poached Chicken with Gravy variation above. Add 2 tablespoons brandy to the gravy with the herbs.

Poached Chicken with Nutmeg-Scented Gravy: Follow the Poached Chicken with Gravy variation above. Add ¼ teaspoon grated nutmeg to the gravy with the herbs.

Roast Chicken and Cornish Game Hen Basics:

1. A larger roasting chicken, 3 pounds and over, is cooked on HIGH first and then finished on MEDIUM to produce a more evenly cooked and tender bird. Any smaller chicken or game hen can be cooked completely on HIGH power.
2. It is important to turn over the whole chicken or game hen during cooking, from breast down to breast up, for the most even cooking. The same is done with quick browning in the conventional oven to expose all surfaces to dry heat.
3. The birds are not cooked on a roasting rack because of the unattractive marks it would place on the breast.
4. Browning occurs in a large roasting chicken because it cooks long enough to build up sufficient surface heat. Glazing compensates for this in smaller Cornish hens. They are also cooked uncovered; covering would keep the surface moist and cool, again inhibiting browning.
5. When trussed, all parts of the birds should cook evenly. If the wings or thin leg areas appear to be overcooking, they can be wrapped smoothly with foil to prevent further cooking (see illustration, page 31).
6. The addition of stuffing to the chicken will not increase the cooking time, because the stuffing is light and porous (not dense) and will become hot from conducted heat from the chicken.
7. Standing time is necessary to completely conduct heat to the interior flesh along the thicker leg areas. The chicken or game hen should be covered with foil at this time, to reflect the heat inward.
8. If a crisp skin is desired, it can only be achieved in a conventional oven, which has dry heat.

9. *Doneness:* See poached whole chicken doneness (page 341). Because roast chicken is cooked uncovered, some parts of it may become tough and dry from overcooking; if so, cut the chicken or game hen into small pieces and stir together with a sauce.

❋ ROAST CHICKEN

For 2- to 6-pound bird: HIGH *6 to 9 minutes per pound*
For 6- to 8-pound bird: HIGH *10 minutes, then* MEDIUM *10 minutes per pound*
MAKES 6 TO 10 SERVINGS   BEGIN 1½ HOURS BEFORE SERVING
COOKING TIME: 1¼ HOURS TO 1 HOUR 25 MINUTES

The advantage of cooking a larger bird over a smaller bird in a microwave oven is that it cooks long enough to brown sufficiently, and yet takes half the time of conventional cooking. For a crisp skin, follow the combination microwave-conventional oven method described in the first variation below. The latter is our favorite method for a moist, flavorful bird.

1 7-pound roasting chicken	**Salt and pepper**

Truss the bird by tying its legs together and the wings to the body. Lightly salt and pepper the bird.

Place the chicken, breast side down, in a 3-quart glass rectangular dish. Cook, uncovered, on HIGH for 10 minutes, then on MEDIUM for 35 minutes. Turn the bird over, breast side up. Cook on MEDIUM for 30 to 35 minutes, or until the bird tests done. Let stand, tented with foil, for 10 minutes before serving.

VARIATIONS:

Crisp Roast Chicken: Preheat a conventional oven to 500°F when you turn the chicken over for final cooking. Transfer the cooked chicken to the preheated oven for 5 or 10 minutes to crisp, before standing time (watch the time carefully). You will have a beautifully crisp yet moist bird, with no spattered conventional oven.

Roast Chicken with Stuffing: Stuff the chicken with 4 cups of your favorite stuffing before trussing. Follow the basic recipe; adding stuffing adds no additional cooking time.

Glazed Roast Chicken: Brush the chicken with Brown Glaze (page 347) before and during cooking.

Honey-Glazed Roast Chicken: Brush the chicken with Honey-Mustard Glaze (page 347) before and during cooking.

Lime-Honey–Glazed Roast Chicken: Brush the chicken with Lime-Honey Glaze (page 348) before and during cooking.

Pineapple-Sherry–Glazed Roast Chicken: Brush the chicken with Pineapple-Sherry Glaze (page 348) before and during cooking.

Apricot-Glazed Roast Chicken: Brush the chicken with Apricot Glaze (page 348) before and during cooking.

Currant-Glazed Roast Chicken: Brush the chicken with Currant Glaze (page 348) before and during cooking.

Chicken with Giblet Gravy: During standing time, prepare Chicken Giblet Gravy (page 380).

Chicken with Pan Drippings Gravy: During standing time, prepare Pan Drippings Gravy (page 173).

✹ GLAZED CORNISH GAME HENS

HIGH *6 to 9 minutes per pound*
MAKES 4 SERVINGS   BEGIN 45 MINUTES BEFORE SERVING, WITHOUT STUFFING
COOKING TIME: 33 TO 39 MINUTES

Because these hens are very small and cook in a short period of time, they won't brown unless basted, glazed, or crisped in the conventional oven. But when treated properly, these very meaty birds are an elegant and easy entertaining selection. A particularly nice way to serve Cornish hens is by boning and stuffing them first, which makes them so much easier to eat.

4 1- to 1½-pound Cornish game hens Salt and pepper 2 cups any stuffing (pages 349–51) (optional)	2 tablespoons butter 1 tablespoon honey 1 tablespoon soy sauce

Remove the giblets and rinse the hens. Pat dry and season inside and out with salt and pepper. Stuff, if desired. Tie the legs together and tie the wings to the body.

Place the hens, breast side down, in a 3-quart rectangular baking dish, with drumsticks toward the center. Set aside.

Place the butter in a 1-cup glass measure. Cook on HIGH for 35 seconds to 1 minute to melt. Stir in the honey and soy sauce. Brush half of the honey-butter mixture over the hens. Cook the hens, uncovered, on HIGH for 16 minutes. Turn over and brush with remaining honey-butter glaze. Cook on HIGH for 16 to 22 minutes, or until the legs move easily and the juices run clear. Let stand, tented with foil, for 5 minutes before serving.

VARIATIONS:

Crisp Cornish Game Hens: Preheat the conventional oven to 500°F during the last half of microwave cooking. Transfer the cooked hens to the preheated oven for 5 minutes to crisp before standing time.

Cornish Game Hens with Waldorf Stuffing: Stuff the hens with 2 cups Waldorf Stuffing (page 350). Glaze with Honey-Mustard Glaze (page 347). Serve with Mustard Pecan Sauce (page 346).

Cornish Game Hens with Cranberry Stuffing: Stuff the hens with 2 cups Cranberry Bread Stuffing (page 349). Glaze with Cranberry Glaze (page 348).

Cornish Game Hens with Corn Bread Stuffing: Stuff the hens with 2 cups Corn Bread Stuffing (page 349). Serve with Mustard Pecan Sauce (page 346). The hens may be boned, if desired, before stuffing and cooking (see opposite page). This version is nice for company.

Cornish Game Hens with Rice, Raisin, and Nut Stuffing: Stuff the hens with 2 cups Rice Stuffing with Nuts and Raisins (page 351). Glaze with Currant Glaze (page 348).

Cornish Game Hens with Giblet Gravy: Prepare Cornish Hen Giblet Gravy (page 380) during standing time.

Veal-Stuffed Cornish Game Hens with Hollandaise Sauce: Bone the hens, following the instructions on the opposite page. Stuff with Veal Stuffing (page 350) and re-form by folding the skins to overlap. Eliminate the glaze. Follow the basic cooking times. During standing time, prepare Hollandaise Sauce (page 174). Pour the hot sauce over the hens and serve.

MUSTARD PECAN SAUCE

MAKES ABOUT 1½ CUPS
COOKING TIME: 4 TO 6 MINUTES

- 1 tablespoon butter
- 2 tablespoons finely chopped onion
- 1 tablespoon all-purpose flour
- 1 cup Chicken Broth or Stock (page 118) or Cornish Game Hen Giblet Stock (page 379)
- 2 tablespoons Dijon mustard
- 1 tablespoon honey
- ⅓ cup coarsely chopped pecans or walnuts

In a 1-quart casserole combine the butter and onion. Cook on HIGH for 1 to 2 minutes, or until the onion is tender. Stir in the flour until dissolved. Stir in the remaining ingredients. Cook on HIGH for 3 to 4 minutes, or until thickened, stirring once.

BONING AND STUFFING CORNISH GAME HENS

1. Placing the hen breast side down on a cutting board, cut through the skin and meat along either side of the backbone with a sharp knife or kitchen shears.
2. Pull out the backbone. Open the back of the hens up and lay flat on the cutting board.
3. With a small pointed knife, cut along one side of the rib bones of the chest cage to the shoulder and center of the rib cage, keeping the knife blade close to the bone. (Push the meat away from the bone with your fingers rather than a knife if this works better.) Cut the shoulder bone at the top of the rib cage at each half of the rib cage. Cut the rib cage in half, down the side of the center soft rib bone. Remove the rib cage.
4. Remove the wishbone at the top of the neck with a knife or your fingers.
5. After stuffing the boned hens, fold back the skins on top of the stuffing to overlap. Gently turn the hens over and tuck the wings akimbo, under the body. Tie the legs and wings to the body with string.

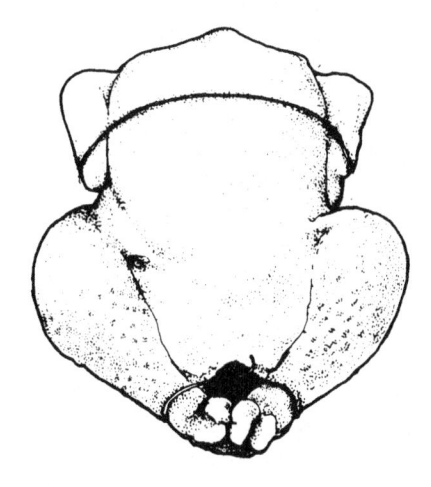

BASIC POULTRY GLAZES

(Enough for 8 pounds)

Double recipe ingredients and cooking times for turkey. These glazes should be brushed on the poultry before and during cooking.

Basic Brown Glaze

Makes about ⅔ cup

- ¼ cup melted butter
- 2 tablespoons Kitchen Bouquet

Combine the ingredients in a small bowl.

Honey-Mustard Glaze

Makes about ⅔ cup

- ½ cup honey
- 2 tablespoons prepared Dijon-style mustard
- 1 tablespoon lemon juice

Combine all the ingredients in a small bowl.

(Continued)

Pineapple-Sherry Glaze
Makes about ⅔ cup
Cooking time: 1 to 2 minutes
- ½ cup pineapple jelly
- 2 tablespoons dry sherry or vermouth

Combine the ingredients in a 2-cup glass measure. Cook on HIGH for 45 seconds to 2 minutes, or until the jelly melts.

NOTE: When using this glaze, stuff the poultry with Pineapple Bread Stuffing (page 349), if desired.

Cranberry Glaze
Makes about ⅔ cup
Cooking time: 1 to 3 minutes
- ½ cup cranberry jelly
- 2 tablespoons dry sherry, orange-flavored liqueur, or orange juice

Combine the ingredients in a 2-cup glass measure. Cook on HIGH for 45 seconds to 3 minutes, or until melted.

NOTE: When using this glaze, stuff the poultry with Cranberry Bread Stuffing (page 349), if desired.

Lime-Honey Glaze
Makes about ⅔ cup
- ½ cup honey
- 1 tablespoon soy sauce
- 1 tablespoon lime juice

Combine all the ingredients in a small bowl.

Apricot Glaze
Makes about ⅔ cup
Cooking time: 1 to 3 minutes
- ½ cup apricot preserves
- 2 tablespoons apricot liqueur or lemon juice

Combine the ingredients into a 2-cup glass measure. Cook on HIGH for 45 seconds to 3 minutes, or until melted.

NOTE: When using this glaze, stuff the poultry with Apricot Bread Stuffing (page 349), if desired.

Currant Glaze
Makes about ⅔ cup
Cooking time: 1 to 3 minutes
- ½ cup currant jelly
- 2 tablespoons sherry, Madeira, or apple juice

Combine the ingredients in a 2-cup glass measure. Cook on HIGH for 45 seconds to 3 minutes, or until melted.

BASIC BREAD STUFFING

MAKES ENOUGH FOR 7 TO 8 POUNDS POULTRY
COOKING TIME: 5 TO 8 MINUTES (BEFORE STUFFING INTO BIRD OR COOKING IN CASSEROLE)

- ¼ cup butter or margarine
- ½ cup finely chopped onion
- 1 cup thinly sliced celery
- 4 cups dry bread cubes
- ¼ cup chopped fresh parsley, or 1 tablespoon dried
- 2 teaspoons chopped fresh sage, or ½ teaspoon crumbled dried
- ½ teaspoon salt
- ¼ teaspoon pepper
- ¼ teaspoon dried oregano
- ¼ teaspoon dried marjoram
- ¼ teaspoon dried thyme
- 1 cup Chicken Broth or Stock (page 118) or water
- 1 egg, lightly beaten (optional)

In a 3-quart casserole combine the butter, onion, and celery. Cover tightly and cook on HIGH for 3 to 5 minutes, or until the vegetables are tender. Stir in the bread cubes and seasonings; stir well.

Pour the broth or water into a 2-cup glass measure. Cook on HIGH for 2 to 3 minutes, or until boiling. Pour into the stuffing mixture and stir well to moisten. Add the beaten egg, if desired; this will make a lighter stuffing.

Use to stuff a small turkey, large chicken, or four Cornish hens, or spoon into a 1½-quart casserole. Cover the casserole with wax paper and cook on HIGH for 5 to 10 minutes, or until heated through. Let stand, covered, for 5 minutes.

NOTES: This stuffing may be prepared a day in advance and refrigerated if desired. Do not stuff the bird until just before cooking.

To Double: Double the ingredients. Cook in a casserole on HIGH for 7½ to 15 minutes, or until heated through.

To Halve: Cut the ingredients in half. Cook in a casserole on HIGH for 2½ to 5 minutes, or until heated through.

VARIATIONS:

Fresh Herb Stuffing: Eliminate the dried herbs. Add to the ¼ cup chopped fresh parsley 1 tablespoon each chopped fresh sage and tarragon

Corn Bread Stuffing: Substitute corn bread for the bread cubes.

Prune Bread Stuffing: Place 1 cup chopped pitted prunes in 1 cup water in a 4-cup glass measure. Cook on HIGH for 3 to 5 minutes, or until the water boils. Let stand. Prepare the stuffing, substituting the liquid drained from the prunes for the broth, if desired. Stir in the drained prunes.

Apricot Bread Stuffing: Place 1 cup chopped dried apricots in 1 cup water in a 4-cup glass measure. Cook on HIGH for 3 to 5 minutes, or until the water boils. Let stand. Prepare the stuffing, substituting the liquid drained from the apricots for the broth, if desired. Stir in the drained apricots.

Cranberry Bread Stuffing: Add 1 cup chopped fresh cranberries with the bread cubes.

Nutty Bread Stuffing: Add 1 cup coarsely chopped nuts with the bread cubes.

Apple Bread Stuffing: Add 1 cup chopped tart apples with the bread cubes.

Mushroom Bread Stuffing: Add 1 cup coarsely chopped fresh mushrooms with the bread cubes.

Pineapple Bread Stuffing: Add 1 cup drained canned pineapple chunks with the bread cubes.

SAUSAGE, VEAL, OR TURKEY STUFFING

MAKES ENOUGH FOR 8 POUNDS POULTRY
COOKING TIME: 4 TO 8 MINUTES

- ½ pound ground sausage, veal, or turkey
- 2 tablespoons butter
- ½ cup finely chopped onion
- 2 teaspoons chopped fresh sage, or ½ teaspoon dried
- ½ teaspoon salt
- ¼ teaspoon pepper
- ¼ teaspoon grated nutmeg
- 2 cups fine dry bread crumbs
- 2 eggs, lightly beaten

Place the meat in a 3-quart casserole. Cook on HIGH for 3 to 5 minutes, or until cooked, stirring after 2 minutes. Drain off any excess fat. Set the meat aside.

In the same casserole combine the butter and onion. Cook on HIGH for 1 to 3 minutes, or until the onion is tender. Stir in the meat and remaining ingredients. Mix well.

WALDORF STUFFING

MAKES ENOUGH FOR 8 POUNDS POULTRY

- ½ cup golden raisins
- 3 tablespoons rum, brandy, or water
- 3 medium Granny Smith or Rome Beauty apples, peeled and chopped
- 1 cup toasted coconut
- ½ cup coarsely chopped walnuts
- ½ cup finely chopped celery
- ½ cup Mayonnaise (page 175)
- 1 tablespoon lemon juice
- 2 tablespoons brown sugar
- 2 tablespoons melted butter

In a small bowl soak the raisins in the rum, brandy, or water.

Meanwhile, in a medium mixing bowl combine the apples, coconut, walnuts, and celery.

In another bowl combine the mayonnaise, lemon juice, brown sugar, and butter; stir to blend. Stir the mayonnaise mixture into the apple mixture. Add the raisins.

RICE DRESSING

MAKES ENOUGH FOR 7 TO 8 POUNDS POULTRY

1 recipe Rice Pilaf (page 201)

At the end of the rice cooking time stir in the mushrooms. Let stand, covered, for 5 minutes.

1 cup coarsely chopped fresh mushrooms

Rice Stuffing with Nuts and Raisins: Substitute ½ cup raisins and ½ cup pine nuts or chopped pecans, almonds, or walnuts for the mushrooms.

BARBECUED CHICKEN

We have been serving moist yet crisply barbecued chicken for years. What is our secret? It is to cook the chicken almost to doneness in the microwave and then finish it off on the grill.

When going boating or camping, we like to cook the chicken in the microwave in this manner and then brush with barbecue sauce before freezing. By the time we have reached our destination, the chicken is defrosted and ready to be grilled in a short time. If desired, marinate the chicken in Sweet and Sour Marinade (page 352) 1 hour before cooking, then drain and baste with Honey-Mustard Glaze (page 347). If not marinating, baste with Blazing Barbecue Sauce (page 181).

Chicken parts

Place chicken skin side down in a rectangular microwave dish. Cover with wax paper and cook on HIGH for 6 minutes per pound. Turn chicken over and rearrange once during cooking. Transfer to preheated grill; baste with sauce. Then grill for 10 minutes, turning over once.

Chicken Parts Basics:

1. If vegetables are cooked with chicken, they are often cooked first or separately to achieve the proper texture before adding the chicken.
2. If the chicken pieces are to be coated, removal of the skin makes for a crispier coating. A paper towel cover will absorb moisture and keep the surfaces dry.
3. Chicken parts must be arranged with the thicker portions to the outside of the cook-

ing dish, so that they cook evenly with the thinner sections. They are turned over once for even cooking with the thicker portions kept to the outside.
4. If the chicken is braised in about 1 cup liquid or in tomatoes and juice, the casserole is covered the entire time. This is to contain all available liquid for flavor and moistness.
5. Chicken parts cook on HIGH power.
6. Standing time is necessary to complete the cooking of the chicken.
7. If a sauce is enriched with cream, it should be done at the end of cooking, once the chicken has been removed.

SWEET AND SOUR MARINADE

MAKES ABOUT ¾ CUP
COOKING TIME: 2 TO 3 MINUTES

This not only flavors the chicken for barbecuing, but can be brushed onto skinned chicken parts before cooking in the microwave.

- ¼ cup soy sauce
- 1½ teaspoons cornstarch
- 2 tablespoons rice or wine vinegar
- 2 tablespoons orange juice
- 1 tablespoon sesame, walnut, or vegetable oil
- 2 teaspoons sugar
- 1 garlic clove, minced

In a 2-cup glass measure combine the soy sauce and cornstarch. Cook on HIGH for 2 to 3 minutes, stirring every minute, until slightly thickened. Stir in the remaining ingredients.

HONEY-MUSTARD SAUCE

MAKES ABOUT ½ CUP
COOKING TIME: 2 TO 3 MINUTES

Brush onto the chicken while barbecuing.

- ¼ cup honey
- 2 tablespoons butter
- 2 tablespoons prepared mustard
- 2 tablespoons lemon, lime, or orange juice
- 1 teaspoon dried tarragon

In a 2-cup glass measure combine all the ingredients. Cook on HIGH for 2 to 3 minutes, or until the butter is melted and the ingredients are blended, stirring every minute.

BRAISED CHICKEN

MAKES 4 TO 6 SERVINGS   BEGIN 45 MINUTES BEFORE SERVING
COOKING TIME: 25 TO 33 MINUTES

Chicken parts are simmered in chicken broth, which is thickened at the end with cream. A hearty chicken-vegetable casserole results—a most satisfying dish to serve in fall and winter.

- 2 tablespoons butter
- 1 garlic clove, minced
- ½ cup coarsely chopped onion
- 1 celery rib, coarsely chopped
- 1 carrot, coarsely chopped
- 2 tablespoons all-purpose flour
- ¼ cup dry vermouth, white wine, or broth
- 2 sprigs fresh thyme, or ½ teaspoon dried
- 2 sprigs fresh parsley, or ½ teaspoon dried, plus ¼ cup chopped fresh parsley
- 1 bay leaf, crushed
- ¾ cup Chicken Broth or Stock (page 118)
- 3 to 3½ pounds chicken parts
- Vegetables (see Note)
- ¼ cup cream, crème fraîche, or sour cream

In a 3-quart casserole combine the butter, garlic, onion, celery, and carrot. Cover tightly and cook on HIGH for 3 to 5 minutes, or until the butter is melted and the vegetables are tender-crisp. Stir the flour into the vegetables until it is dissolved and smooth.

Stir in the vermouth, thyme, parsley sprigs, bay leaf, and chicken broth. Arrange the chicken pieces, skin side down, in the mixture, with the thicker portions toward the outside. Cover tightly and cook on HIGH for 22 to 28 minutes, or until done, turning over and rearranging after 12 minutes, placing the less cooked portions to the outside. Transfer the chicken pieces to a serving platter and cover. Let stand for 10 minutes. Strain the gravy and discard the vegetables. Return the gravy to the casserole. Set aside.

Meanwhile, prepare and cook one of the vegetable dishes suggested in the Note below.

Stir the cream into the gravy. Cook, uncovered, on HIGH for 1 to 3 minutes, until heated through. If the gravy is too thick at this point, add more chicken broth to thin it. Spoon a little gravy over the chicken and serve the rest in a gravy boat. Arrange the cooked vegetables around the chicken on the platter. Sprinkle the chicken with chopped parsley.

NOTE: Choose one of these suggested vegetable recipes and prepare during chicken standing time: Steamed Artichokes with Carrot Topping (page 396), Peas and Snow Peas (page 412), Boiled Potato Slices (page 454), Braised Green Beans (page 413), Sautéed Mushrooms (page 439), Pearl Onions (page 72), Braised Scallions (page 448).

VARIATIONS:

Braised Chicken with Mustard Sauce: Add 2 tablespoons Dijon mustard to the gravy with the cream.

Braised Chicken with Curry Sauce: Add 1 teaspoon curry powder to the gravy with the cream.

Coq au Vin Rouge: Substitute 1 cup dry red wine for the broth and vermouth. Substitute 2 tablespoons tomato paste for the flour. Prepare Mushroom Caps au Naturel (page 439) and Pearl Onions (page 72) as vegetables. If the final gravy seems too thin, make a paste of 1 tablespoon flour stirred into 2 tablespoons red wine. Stir into the gravy. Cook on HIGH for 2 to 5 minutes more to thicken. Onions may tend to thin the gravy.

Hungarian Braised Chicken: Add 2 tablespoons paprika with the flour. Prepare Mushroom Caps au Naturel (page 439) and Pearl Onions (page 72) as the vegetables.

Braised Chicken with Tarragon: Substitute 1 tablespoon fresh or 1 teaspoon dried tarragon for the parsley.

CHICKEN CACCIATORE

MAKES 4 TO 6 SERVINGS   BEGIN 45 MINUTES BEFORE SERVING
COOKING TIME: 25 TO 33 MINUTES

Serve with Polenta (page 194) or rice.

- 1 tablespoon olive oil
- 1 garlic clove, minced
- 1 medium onion, coarsely chopped
- 1 medium green pepper, cut into ¼-inch strips
- 1 carrot, coarsely chopped
- 1 celery rib, coarsely chopped
- ¼ cup tomato paste
- 1 cup fresh or undrained canned tomatoes, peeled and chopped
- ¼ cup dry white wine
- 1 tablespoon chopped fresh basil or oregano, or 1 teaspoon dried
- ½ teaspoon salt
- ¼ teaspoon pepper
- 3 to 3½ pounds chicken parts

In a 3-quart casserole combine the oil, garlic, onion, green pepper, carrot, and celery. Cover tightly and cook on HIGH for 3 to 5 minutes, or until the vegetables are tender-crisp. Stir the tomato paste into the vegetables to dissolve as much as possible.

Stir in the tomatoes, wine, basil, salt, and pepper. Arrange the chicken pieces, skin side down, in the mixture with the thicker portions toward the outside. Cover tightly and cook on HIGH for 22 to 28 minutes, or until done, turning the chicken pieces over and repositioning the less cooked portions to the outside after 12 minutes. Let stand, covered, for 10 minutes.

CHICKEN LEGS WITH MUSTARD-CRUMB COATING

MAKES 4 SERVINGS   BEGIN ABOUT 15 MINUTES BEFORE SERVING
COOKING TIME: 8 TO 11 MINUTES

These tasty legs are a delicious chilled picnic dish, or a spicy snack when dipped warm into Hot Pepper Butter (recipe below).

- 6 chicken legs or parts (1 to 1½ pounds)
- 4 tablespoons butter
- 3 tablespoons dry mustard
- ½ cup fine dry bread crumbs
- ¼ cup toasted sesame seeds (page 609)
- ½ teaspoon salt
- ¼ teaspoon pepper
- 1 teaspoon paprika

Remove the skin from the chicken legs.

Place the butter in a large cereal bowl. Cook on HIGH for 45 seconds to 1 minute to melt. Stir the mustard into the melted butter.

In another bowl combine the remaining ingredients. Dip the chicken legs into the butter-mustard to coat well and then into the crumb mixture to coat.

Arrange the legs in spoke fashion in a 10-inch round pie plate, with thicker sections toward the outside. Cover with a paper towel and cook on HIGH for 7 to 10 minutes, turning over and repositioning if necessary after 4 minutes. Let stand, covered with paper towel, for 3 minutes.

HOT PEPPER BUTTER

MAKES ¼ CUP
COOKING TIME: 1 MINUTE

Serve as dipping sauce for cooked chicken.

- ¼ cup butter
- ½ teaspoon hot pepper sauce or more to taste

Combine the ingredients in a 1-cup glass measure. Cook on HIGH for 45 seconds to 1 minute to melt.

CHICKEN PIECES WITH CIDER AND APPLES

MAKES 4 SERVINGS BEGIN 45 MINUTES BEFORE SERVING
COOKING TIME: 23 TO 30 MINUTES

A delicious blend of flavors. Especially good in the fall when apples and cider are readily available.

2½ to 3 pounds chicken parts	2 tart apples, peeled, cored, and sliced
Salt and pepper	2 tablespoons brown sugar
6 tablespoons butter	1 tablespoon lemon juice
2 tablespoons Dijon mustard	¾ cup apple cider
½ cup fine dry bread crumbs	½ cup heavy cream or crème fraîche
2 tablespoons chopped fresh chives or thinly sliced scallions	

Remove the skin from the chicken pieces. Lightly salt and pepper them.

Place 4 tablespoons butter in a pie plate. Cook on HIGH for 45 seconds to 1 minute. Stir the mustard in the melted butter. Set aside.

In another pie plate combine the bread crumbs and chives or scallions. Set aside.

Place the remaining 2 tablespoons butter, the apple slices, sugar, and lemon juice in a 9-inch pie plate. Cook, uncovered, on HIGH for 4 to 6 minutes, or until the apples are tender, stirring once to coat the apples. Set aside.

Meanwhile, coat the chicken pieces, one at a time, in the mustard-butter and then bread crumbs and chives. Arrange the chicken in a 2-quart rectangular dish, with the meatier portions to the outside. Cover with a paper towel and cook on HIGH for 18 to 23 minutes, or until done, turning over and rearranging the pieces after 10 minutes, placing the less cooked sections toward the outside. Transfer the chicken pieces to a serving platter, reserving the cooking liquid. Cover the chicken with the paper towel. Let stand for 10 minutes.

Meanwhile, stir the cider into the chicken cooking liquid. Cook on HIGH for 6 to 8 minutes, or until boiling and slightly reduced, stirring once. Stir in the cream. Cook on HIGH for 1 to 2 minutes, or until heated through. Spoon the cooked apples over the chicken and pour the sauce on top to serve.

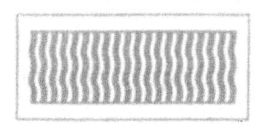

QUICK FRIED CHICKEN

MAKES 4 SERVINGS   BEGIN 35 MINUTES BEFORE SERVING
COOKING TIME: 23 TO 31 MINUTES

Cooking chicken first in the microwave, then frying it quickly in a small amount of oil, not only speeds up the frying process but utilizes less fat. The results are moist chicken inside and a crispy skin outside.

2½ to 3 pounds chicken parts, cut into about 8 serving pieces	½ teaspoon salt
½ cup all-purpose flour	¼ teaspoon pepper
	¼ cup vegetable oil

Wash and dry the chicken well, then place it, skin side up, in a 2-quart rectangular dish with the thicker sections toward the outside. Cover with a paper towel and cook on HIGH for 18 to 21 minutes, or until done, rearranging the chicken pieces after 9 minutes so that the uncooked portions are to the outside.

Heat the oil in a large skillet on top of the stove. Meanwhile, in a small paper bag—not plastic, to avoid melting—combine the flour, salt, and pepper. Drop the warm chicken pieces, one at a time, into the bag. Shake to coat each piece. Place the pieces on a platter until the oil is hot enough for frying. Add the chicken and cook for 5 to 10 minutes, or until golden brown, turning frequently. Remove the chicken pieces from the pan and drain on paper towels. Serve warm or cold.

✸ LOW-CALORIE BUFFALO CHICKEN WINGS

MAKES 4 SERVINGS   BEGIN 25 MINUTES BEFORE SERVING
COOKING TIME: 20 MINUTES

Buffalo chicken wings are that city's spicy deep-fried wings served with a blue cheese dressing and celery sticks. Absolutely delicious, but not kind to the waistline. These low-calorie wings were fashioned with that original idea in mind but with first consideration given to the prevention of just one extra pound.

2 pounds chicken wings	¼ cup chopped fresh herbs, or 1 tablespoon dried
Green or red hot sauce	
1 cup plain yogurt	Celery sticks

Preheat the conventional oven to 500°F.

Cut off the tips from the chicken wings. Cut the wings at the joints. Place the wings in a 2-quart rectangular baking dish. Cook on HIGH for 10 minutes, or until done, turning over once during cooking. Drain. Transfer to the preheated oven. Bake for 10 minutes, or until crisp, turning over once during cooking. Sprinkle with hot sauce at the end of cooking.

Meanwhile, in a small bowl combine the yogurt and herbs. Serve with the cooked wings and pass more hot sauce for sprinkling over. Serve celery sticks alongside.

VARIATION:

Mexican Chicken Wings: Serve the cooked chicken wings with sour cream, limes, and Green Tomato Salsa (page 186).

Chicken Breast Basics:

1. Unless you plan to crisp the skin of the chicken breasts after cooking in the microwave, by frying, grilling, or heating in a conventional oven, it is best to remove and discard the skin. The exception is when it is simmered in a casserole.
2. Chicken breasts are cooked on HIGH power because there are no tough connective fibers, unless cooked with other ingredients in a stew that need flavor development. Because of their compactness, the boneless chicken breasts, especially if pounded, will cook much faster than the breasts with the bone. Pounding actually is for appearance and is not necessary if you want to make cubed chicken, individual diet portions, or chicken salad.
3. Chicken breasts should be arranged with the thicker portions to the outside of the dish and with the center of the dish open. This will cause the chicken to cook evenly, without having to be turned or rearranged during cooking.
4. We call for pie plates for cooking because we prefer the shape for arrangement of the chicken and for attractiveness of serving. Any round dish that holds the chicken will do.
5. Chicken breasts are covered with wax paper to keep some of the moisture in, without causing them to become too watery and lose flavor. Chicken breasts can be covered tightly if they are to be made into chicken salad or some other dish where an ingredient, such as rice, is added that needs rehydration.
6. Standing time is very short because it relates to cooking time and density of the food. It is just enough time to prepare one of the sauces on pages 361–62.

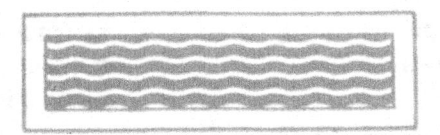

☼ CHICKEN AND RICE CASSEROLE

MAKES 4 SERVINGS   BEGIN ABOUT 1 HOUR BEFORE COOKING
COOKING TIME: 47 TO 53 MINUTES

This is a favorite of our students, because it is simple and the flavors intermingle beautifully. The chicken is cooked with a tight cover because of the addition of rice.

- 1 tablespoon butter
- 1 medium onion, chopped
- 2 tablespoons tomato paste
- 1 cup long-grain rice
- 1¾ cups Chicken Broth or Stock (page 118)
- 2 tablespoons chopped fresh parsley, or 2 teaspoons dried
- 2 whole chicken breasts (2½ to 3 pounds), halved, or 1 whole chicken, cut up
- Paprika

In a 3-quart casserole combine the butter and onion. Cook on HIGH for 2 to 3 minutes, or until the onion is tender. Stir in the tomato paste and rice. Stir in the broth and parsley.

Place the chicken, skin side down, in dish, with the thicker portions toward the outside. Cover tightly, and cook on HIGH for 10 minutes. Move the chicken pieces to one side; stir the rice. Turn the chicken pieces over, placing the lesser cooked area toward the outside of the dish. Sprinkle the chicken lightly with paprika. Cover again and cook on MEDIUM for 35 to 40 minutes, or until most of the liquid is absorbed and the rice in the center is tender. Let stand for 5 minutes before serving.

VARIATIONS:

Chicken with Mushroom Rice: Stir in ¼ pound mushrooms, sliced, with the rice.

Chicken with Rice and Nuts: Stir in ¼ cup slivered almonds or pine nuts with the rice.

Chicken with Tarragon Rice: Stir in 1 tablespoon chopped fresh or 1 teaspoon dried tarragon.

Chicken with Rice in Wine: Substitute ¾ cup dry white wine for ¾ cup chicken broth.

✺ SUCCULENT BONELESS CHICKEN BREASTS

MAKES 4 SERVINGS   BEGIN 15 MINUTES BEFORE SERVING
COOKING TIME: 6 TO 8 MINUTES

Because of their compact and uniform shapes, boneless chicken breasts cook in no time at all—and here are a dozen ways to prepare them. The liquid that remains after cooking can be treated as a chicken broth and the basis for some light and flavorful sauces that follow in the variations.

| 2 whole boneless, skinless chicken breasts (about 1 pound), split | 1 tablespoon lemon juice, dry white wine, or dry vermouth
Salt and pepper |

Place the chicken between 2 pieces of wax paper. Flatten with a meat pounder to about ¼-inch thickness.

Arrange the chicken in a 10-inch pie plate with the thicker portions toward the outside, leaving the center open. Sprinkle with the lemon juice or wine, salt and pepper. Cover with wax paper and cook on HIGH for 6 to 8 minutes, or until done; turn over after 4 minutes. To prepare any of the sauce variations, pour off and reserve accumulated cooking liquid. Re-cover chicken for standing time. Let stand, covered, 2 to 3 minutes.

VARIATIONS:

Boneless Chicken Breasts with Herbs: Sprinkle the chicken with 2 teaspoons fresh chopped herbs or ¼ teaspoon dried herbs along with the salt and pepper.

Boneless Chicken Breasts in Apple Cream Sauce: Prepare Apple Cream Sauce (page 361) during standing time. Pour the sauce over chicken; garnish with apple slices.

Boneless Chicken Breasts with Intoxicating Sauce: Prepare Intoxicating Sauce (page 361) during standing time, then pour over the chicken.

Boneless Chicken Breasts with Mushroom Sauce: Prepare Mushroom Sauce (page 361) during standing time. Garnish chicken with 2 tablespoons chopped fresh parsley.

Boneless Chicken Breasts with Lemon or Lime Cream Sauce: Prepare Lemon or Lime Cream Sauce (page 361) during standing time. With Lime Cream Sauce, place each piece of chicken on ¼ avocado, peeled, sliced, and fanned out on each serving plate. Spoon the sauce over the chicken. Serve with lime wedges.

Boneless Chicken Breasts with Mustard Sauce: Prepare Mustard Sauce (page 361) during standing time, then pour over the chicken.

Boneless Chicken Breasts with Saffron Cream Sauce: Prepare Saffron Cream Sauce (page 361) during standing time, then pour over the chicken.

Boneless Chicken Breasts with Curry Cream Sauce: Prepare Curry Cream Sauce (page 361) during standing time, then pour over the chicken.

Boneless Chicken Breasts with Rose Cream Sauce: Prepare Rose Cream Sauce (page 361) during standing time, then pour over the chicken. Garnish with cherry tomatoes.

Boneless Chicken Breasts with Indian Yogurt Sauce: Prepare Indian Yogurt Sauce (page 362) during standing time. After spooning the sauce over the chicken, sprinkle with ¼ cup thinly sliced scallions and serve with lime wedges.

SINGLE SERVING: Place half the chicken breast, unpounded, into an individual serving dish or ramekin. Sprinkle with 1 teaspoon lemon juice and lightly salt and pepper. Cover with wax paper and cook on HIGH for 2½ to 3½ minutes, or until done, turning over and repositioning after 1 minute.

APPLE CREAM SAUCE

MAKES ABOUT 1¼ CUPS
COOKING TIME: 4 TO 7 MINUTES

This sauce and its variations are made with the accumulated cooking liquid from one of the boneless chicken breast recipes.

- 2 tablespoons butter
- 2 tablespoons finely chopped onion
- 1 tablespoon all-purpose flour
- 2 tablespoons cider or apple juice
- ½ cup heavy or light cream or half and half, or as needed
- About ¼ cup cooking liquid from Boneless Chicken Breasts (page 359) or Steamed Boneless Chicken Breasts with Vegetables (page 362)
- ¼ teaspoon salt
- Dash of pepper

In a 1-quart casserole combine the butter and onion. Cook on HIGH for 1 to 2 minutes, or until the onion is tender. Stir in the flour to blend. Stir in the cider. Cook, on HIGH for 1 minute. Stir in the remaining ingredients. If the cooking liquid doesn't equal ¼ cup, add more cream to make that amount. Cook on HIGH for 2 to 4 minutes, or until bubbling and thickened, stirring after 1 minute.

VARIATIONS:

Intoxicating Sauce: Substitute brandy, scotch, dry vermouth, dry sherry, or champagne for cider.

Mushroom Sauce: After cooking the onion, add ¼ pound mushrooms, sliced. Cook, uncovered, on HIGH for 1 minute. Add the flour. Substitute dry vermouth for the cider. Proceed with the recipe.

Herb Sauce: Add 2 tablespoons coarsely chopped basil or 1 tablespoon freshly chopped tarragon at the end of cooking.

Lemon or Lime Cream Sauce: Add 1 teaspoon grated lemon or lime rind with the cream. Garnish with either lemon or lime wedges.

Mustard Sauce: Add 3 tablespoons prepared Dijon mustard to the sauce with the cream.

Saffron Cream Sauce: Add ⅛ teaspoon saffron threads to the butter and onion before cooking.

Curry Cream Sauce: Add 2 tablespoons curry powder to the butter and onion before cooking.

Rose Cream Sauce: Substitute 1 tablespoon tomato paste for the flour. This will give a unique flavor and coloring.

INDIAN YOGURT SAUCE

MAKES ABOUT 1¼ CUPS
COOKING TIME: 3 TO 6 MINUTES

- 1 teaspoon coriander seeds
- 1 teaspoon cuminseed
- 1 tablespoon butter, margarine, or vegetable oil
- 2 tablespoons finely chopped onion
- 1 tablespoon finely chopped fresh ginger
- 1 teaspoon grated lime rind
- ⅛ teaspoon cayenne pepper
- ¾ cup plain yogurt
  About ¼ cup cooking liquid from Boneless Chicken Breasts (page 359)

In a mortar and pestle, crush the coriander and cumin. In a 1-quart casserole combine the coriander and cumin with the butter or oil, onion, and ginger. Cook on HIGH for 1 to 2 minutes, or until the onion and ginger are tender. Stir in the lime rind, cayenne, yogurt, and cooking liquid. Cook on HIGH for 2 to 4 minutes, or until heated through but not boiling, stirring once.

Boneless Chicken Breast with Vegetables Basics:

1. This recipe employs the Ring Rule, where the denser food (chicken) is placed around the outer edge of the dish while the less dense food (sliced vegetables) is placed in the center. The food placed on the outside absorbs more microwave energy to cook faster and equalize the cooking times of chicken and vegetables.
2. To make this Ring Rule work, the vegetables must be cut into thin strips. Thicker, denser vegetables (such as carrots) are slightly cooked first.
3. Both chicken breasts and vegetables can be cooked on HIGH power.
4. Normally you would want to cover the chicken breasts with wax paper or use no cover at all, in order to prevent too much moisture retention. Since you are cooking vegetables along with the chicken, you now want to hold in as much moisture as possible. A tight cover, probably plastic wrap, will contain the needed moisture.
5. The liquid left after cooking the chicken and vegetables becomes a shortcut chicken stock for making a simple sauce.

✻ STEAMED BONELESS CHICKEN BREASTS WITH VEGETABLES

MAKES 4 SERVINGS   BEGIN 30 MINUTES BEFORE SERVING
COOKING TIME: 12 TO 17 MINUTES

The unique cooking arrangement of boned chicken breasts that encircle sliced vegetables makes it possible to cook chicken and vegetables all at once for a one-dish meal.

- 2 tablespoons butter
- 1 cup carrots, cut into thin 2-inch sticks
- 1 cup zucchini, cut into thin 2-inch sticks
- 1 cup sliced fresh mushrooms
- 1 teaspoon lemon juice
- 2 tablespoons chopped fresh parsley, or 2 teaspoons dried
- 2 tablespoons chopped fresh dill, or 2 teaspoons dried
- 2 whole boneless chicken breasts (about 1 pound), split
- Salt and pepper
- ¼ cup thinly sliced scallions

In a 10-inch pie plate or on a 12-inch platter combine the butter and carrots. Cover tightly with plastic wrap turned back on one side and cook on HIGH for 3 to 5 minutes, or until the carrots are tender-crisp; stir. Pile the zucchini and mushrooms on top of the carrots. Sprinkle the vegetables with lemon juice, parsley, and dill. Push the vegetables to the center of the dish, leaving a 3-inch rim around the outside.

Lightly salt and pepper the chicken pieces. Arrange the chicken around the outer rim of the dish with the thicker portions to the outside. Sprinkle with the scallions. Cover tightly and cook on HIGH for 9 to 12 minutes, or until the chicken is done and the vegetables are tender-crisp. Let stand, covered, for 3 minutes. Serve the chicken and vegetables with the cooking liquid, or drain the cooking liquid to make a sauce, keeping the chicken covered and warm. Draining the cooking liquid is easy when you place a kitchen towel on top of the plastic wrap cover, and drain from the vented side.

VARIATIONS:

Low-Calorie Boneless Chicken Breasts with Vegetables: Substitute 1 tablespoon water or Chicken Broth or Stock (page 118) for the butter.

Boneless Chicken Breasts with Vegetables in Herb Sauce: Prepare Herb Sauce (page 361) during standing time. Pour over chicken and serve.

Boneless Chicken Breasts with Vegetables and Lemon or Lime Cream Sauce: Prepare Lemon or Lime Cream Sauce (page 361) during standing time. Pour over chicken and serve.

Boneless Chicken Breasts with Vegetables and Mustard Sauce: Prepare Mustard Sauce (page 361) during standing time. Pour over chicken and serve.

SINGLE SERVING: Combine 2 teaspoons butter and ¼ cup carrot sticks in a microwaveproof serving dish or ramekin. Cover tightly and cook on HIGH for 2 minutes. Place ¼ cup thinly sliced zucchini and ¼ cup thinly sliced mushrooms on top of the carrots. Sprinkle 1 teaspoon *each* lemon juice, parsley, and dill over the vegetables. Top with ½ boneless chicken breast. Sprinkle with 1 tablespoon sliced scallion. Cover tightly and cook on HIGH for 2 to 4 minutes, or until the chicken is done and the vegetables are tender-crisp.

Breaded Chicken Basics:

1. When chicken pieces are breaded, they need to be coated first with some fat—butter, oil, or mayonnaise. The fat will raise the surface temperature, which is necessary for browning.
2. Because the chicken skin won't crisp without dry heat—and there is no dry heat in the microwave—it is best to remove the skin before breading, because the skin holds too much moisture. To our tastes, the texture of chicken skin, cooked for a short period of time in the microwave, is unappealing.
3. A larger dish is called for so there is no overlapping of chicken pieces, which could keep the surfaces from staying dry.
4. Cover the breaded chicken pieces with a paper towel to absorb excess surface moisture that would cool off the surface and keep the breaded coating from getting hot enough to brown.
5. Breaded chicken pieces should be turned over once during cooking, to release the moisture building up underneath and to allow both sides to become dry on top.

✴ BREADED CHICKEN CUTLETS

MAKES 4 SERVINGS   BEGIN 20 MINUTES BEFORE SERVING
COOKING TIME: 8 TO 11 MINUTES

Conventionally chicken cutlets are pounded, dipped into beaten egg and bread crumbs, then fried in hot oil. It is the combination of heat and starch coating that makes the browning take place. In microwave cooking the cutlets are first dipped into the butter (which when heated raises the temperature) and then the crumbs.

2 whole boneless, skinless chicken breasts (1 to 1½ pounds), split
3 tablespoons butter
1 egg, beaten
¾ cup fine dry bread crumbs
1 tablespoon chopped fresh parsley
½ teaspoon paprika
½ teaspoon dried oregano
¼ teaspoon salt
¼ teaspoon dried basil
⅛ teaspoon pepper
Lemon wedges

Place the chicken between 2 pieces of wax paper and flatten with a meat pounder to about ¼-inch thickness.

Place the butter in a microwaveproof cereal bowl. Cook on HIGH for 45 seconds to 1 minute, or until melted. Let cool slightly, then stir in the egg until blended.

Meanwhile, in a separate bowl combine the remaining ingredients except the lemon wedges. Dip each piece of chicken into the butter-egg mixture, then into the crumb mixture, pressing the coating against the chicken. Arrange the chicken pieces in a 2-quart rectangular dish with the thicker sections toward the outside. Cover with a paper towel and cook on HIGH for 7 to 10 minutes, or until done, turning over and repositioning the chicken pieces after 4 minutes. Let stand for 2 to 5 minutes. Serve with lemon wedges.

VARIATIONS:

Italian Chicken Cutlets: Substitute ¼ cup grated Parmesan cheese for ¼ cup of the bread crumbs. Eliminate the paprika.

Chicken Cutlets Parmigiana: Substitute ¼ cup grated Parmesan cheese for ¼ cup of the bread crumbs. Eliminate the paprika. Cook according to basic recipe. Cut 8 ounces mozzarella cheese into 8 thin slices. Place 1 slice of cheese on top of each cooked chicken cutlet. Pour 2 cups tomato sauce on top of the chicken. Cover with wax paper and cook on MEDIUM for 4 to 8 minutes, or until the sauce is heated through. Top the cutlets with the remaining 4 slices of cheese. Cook, uncovered, on MEDIUM for 1 minute more, or until the cheese is melted.

Sesame-Coated Chicken: Prepare rice and Mixed Wok-Style Vegetables (page 481). During vegetable standing time, prepare breaded chicken according to the basic recipe, substituting ¼ cup toasted sesame seeds (see page 609) for ¼ cup of the bread crumbs. Serve with Oriental Dressing (page 184).

Chicken Cutlets with Pecans: Substitute chopped pecans for the bread crumbs. Eliminate the remaining herbs and seasonings except the salt and pepper. To serve, top each breast with 2 whole pecan halves and a dollop of crème fraîche, if desired.

Chicken Cutlets with Wine Sauce: Substitute ¼ cup grated Parmesan cheese for ¼ cup of the bread crumbs. Eliminate the paprika. After cooking, transfer the cutlets to a serving dish. Add 4 tablespoons butter and ¼ cup thinly sliced scallions to the cooking dish. Cook on HIGH for 1 to 2 minutes, or until the scallions are tender. Stir in ½ cup dry white wine, dry vermouth, or dry sherry. Cook on HIGH for 3 to 5 minutes. Return the chicken to the wine sauce. Cover with wax paper and cook on HIGH for 2 to 5 minutes, or until heated through. Serve with lemon wedges and Rice Pilaf (page 201) that's been made in advance.

☼ CHICKEN CUTLETS COATED WITH PECAN-MUSTARD MAYONNAISE

MAKES 4 SERVINGS   BEGIN 15 TO 20 MINUTES BEFORE SERVING
COOKING TIME: 7 TO 10 MINUTES

The mixture of prepared mustard and mayonnaise in the coating keeps the chicken very moist.

- ½ cup Mayonnaise (page 175)
- 2 tablespoons Dijon mustard
- 1 teaspoon grated lemon rind
- 1½ cups (6 ounces) coarsely ground pecans (see NOTE)
- 2 whole boneless, skinless chicken breasts (about 1 pound), split
- Sour cream or crème fraîche (optional)

In a cereal bowl combine the mayonnaise, mustard, and lemon rind. Place the ground nuts in a separate bowl.

Dip each cutlet into the mayonnaise mixture to coat, then into the ground nuts, pressing the coating against the chicken. Arrange the coated cutlets in a 2-quart rectangular dish with the thicker sections toward the outside. Cover with a paper towel and cook on HIGH for 7 to 10 minutes, or until done, turning over and repositioning after 4 minutes. Serve with a dollop of crème fraîche or sour cream, if desired.

NOTE: You can substitute walnuts or almonds for pecans.

VARIATION:

Pecan Chicken Cutlets with Raspberry Sauce: Prepare Raspberry Sauce (page 367) and set aside. Prepare the basic cutlet recipe. Reheat the sauce on HIGH for 1 to 3 minutes and serve over the cutlets, topping each one with 4 fresh raspberries. A quick but spectacular company dish.

QUICK RASPBERRY VINEGAR

MAKES ¼ TO ⅓ CUP

- **1 10-ounce package frozen raspberries, thawed**
- **2 tablespoons red wine vinegar**

Drain the raspberry juices; set aside the raspberries for other use. In a 1-cup glass measure combine the raspberry juices and vinegar.

RASPBERRY SAUCE

MAKES ABOUT ¾ CUP
COOKING TIME: 5 TO 8 MINUTES

This is delicious with almost any breaded or plain chicken breasts.

- 4 tablespoons raspberry vinegar or Quick Raspberry Vinegar (page 366)
- 3 tablespoons sugar
- ¼ cup Chicken Broth or Stock (page 118)
- ¼ cup heavy cream or crème fraîche
- 1 tablespoon tomato paste
- 12 fresh or frozen raspberries

In a 1-quart casserole combine the vinegar and sugar. Cook on HIGH for 4 to 5 minutes, or until slightly caramelized, stirring once. Stir in the broth, cream, tomato paste, and raspberries. Cook on HIGH for 1 to 3 minutes, or until bubbling and heated through; stir.

☀ BREADED CHICKEN CUTLETS WITH STUFFING

MAKES 4 SERVINGS   BEGIN ABOUT 30 MINUTES BEFORE SERVING
COOKING TIME: 14 TO 22 MINUTES

This is a favorite of our classes. It offers a delicious chicken-and-stuffing dinner for the busy person in just a short period of time.

To complete the meal, a vegetable can be cooked during the standing time of the chicken. If the cooking dish is attractive enough, you may wish to spoon the cooked vegetables into the center of the dish for serving, or, around the holidays, cranberry sauce adds a festive touch.

- 2 whole boneless, skinless chicken breasts (about 1 pound), split
- 7 tablespoons butter
- 1 egg, beaten
- ¾ cup fine dry bread crumbs
- 3 tablespoons chopped fresh parsley
- ½ teaspoon paprika
- ½ teaspoon salt
- ¼ teaspoon dried basil
- Pepper to taste
- 2 tablespoons chopped onion
- 1 cup Chicken Broth or Stock (page 118)
- 4 cups fresh bread cubes, with crusts
- 1 teaspoon chopped fresh sage, or ¼ teaspoon dried

Place the chicken between 2 pieces of wax paper and flatten with a meat pounder to about ¼ inch thickness.

Place 3 tablespoons butter in a large microwaveproof cereal bowl. Cook on HIGH for 45 seconds to 1 minute, or until melted. Let cool slightly, then stir in the egg until blended.

Meanwhile, in a separate bowl combine the bread crumbs, 1 tablespoon parsley, paprika, ½ teaspoon salt, basil, and ⅛ teaspoon pepper. Dip each piece of chicken into the butter-egg mixture, then into the crumb mixture, pressing the coating against the chicken. Set aside.

In a 10-inch pie plate or a 2-quart rectangular baking dish combine the remaining 4 tablespoons butter and the onion. Cook on HIGH for 1 to 3 minutes, or until the onion is tender. Add the broth. Cook on HIGH for 2 to 4 minutes, or until boiling. Stir in the fresh bread cubes, 2 tablespoons parsley, sage, and salt and pepper to taste. Stir to let the bread absorb the liquid. Make 4 mounds of stuffing in the dish, leaving the center open. Place a breaded chicken cutlet on top of each mound of stuffing, positioning each with the thicker portion toward the outside of the dish. Cover with a paper towel and cook on HIGH for 10 to 14 minutes, or until the chicken tests done, rotating a half turn halfway through cooking. Let stand for 5 minutes.

CHICKEN SLIVERS BANDUNG

MAKES 4 SERVINGS   BEGIN 20 MINUTES BEFORE SERVING
COOKING TIME: 9 TO 14 MINUTES

A quick and delicious meal using chicken strips cut from cutlets. Because it has a somewhat Indonesian flair to it, we named it for one of the more pronounceable cities we have visited on the island of Java.

The vegetables are added at the end to attain the proper tender-crisp doneness.

- 2 tablespoons sesame oil or butter
- 1 garlic clove, minced
- 1 large onion, thinly sliced
- 1 pound boneless, skinless chicken breasts, sliced into ¼-inch strips
- 3 tablespoons peanut butter
- 3 tablespoons soy sauce
- 1 tablespoon lemon juice
- ¼ teaspoon red pepper flakes, or a few drops of hot pepper sauce
- 1 sweet red pepper, cut into ¼-inch strips
- 1 green pepper, cut into ¼-inch strips
- ¼ pound bean sprouts, rinsed
- ¼ cup whole unsalted peanuts

In a 10-inch round or 2-quart rectangular dish combine the oil, garlic, and onion. Cook on HIGH for 2 to 4 minutes, or until the onion is tender. Stir in the chicken pieces and move to the outer edge of the dish, leaving the center open. Cover tightly and cook on HIGH for 3 minutes, or until the chicken is partially cooked. Stir in the peanut butter, soy sauce, lemon juice, and pepper flakes until well blended. Stir in the peppers and bean sprouts. Cover again and cook on HIGH for 4 to 7 minutes, or until the chicken is cooked and the vegetables are tender-crisp, stirring after 3 minutes. Sprinkle with peanuts before serving.

VARIATIONS:

Chicken Slivers with Snow Peas: Substitute ¼ pound snow peas, trimmed, or ¼ pound mushrooms, sliced, for the bean sprouts.

Chicken Slivers with Broccoli: Substitute ½ bunch broccoli for the peppers. Cut the broccoli into flowerets, and quarter and slice the stems into ½-inch strips before adding.

Chicken Slivers with Vegetables and Rice or Noodles: Add 1 to 2 cups cooked rice or thin spaghetti after the vegetables have cooked for 3 minutes, just to heat through.

SKEWERED CHICKEN WITH PEANUT SATAY SAUCE

MAKES 4 MAIN COURSE SERVINGS OR 24 APPETIZERS
BEGIN AT LEAST 45 MINUTES BEFORE SERVING   COOKING TIME: 7 TO 13 MINUTES

Satay is an Indonesian or Malaysian dish that can be made with chicken, beef, or pork. When placed on 3-inch toothpicks, satay is a unique appetizer. On long skewers it is an exotic main course over rice. Marinating the chicken first causes it to brown upon cooking; be sure to leave spaces between the pieces of chicken on skewers, to allow for even cooking.

If serving with rice, cook the rice first and then cook the chicken skewers during standing time.

¼ cup soy sauce	1 garlic clove, minced
1 tablespoon brown sugar	1½ pounds boneless, skinless chicken breasts, cut into 1-inch cubes
2 tablespoons orange juice	
1 tablespoon sesame or vegetable oil	1 recipe Peanut Satay Sauce (page 182) (see Note)

In a large deep bowl combine the soy sauce, sugar, juice, oil, and garlic; stir to blend. Stir in the chicken cubes. Let marinate for 30 minutes to 12 hours, stirring occasionally.

Place 2 pieces of marinated chicken on each toothpick, or 5 to 6 chicken pieces on large wooden skewers, with the bigger pieces toward the end keeping the pieces from touching each other. Arrange the skewers in spoke fashion on a 12-inch microwaveproof serving platter. Cook, uncovered, on HIGH for 6 to 10 minutes, or until cooked through, rearranging the skewers if necessary, placing the less cooked ends to the outside.

Reheat the dipping sauce on HIGH for 1 to 3 minutes; stir. Pour some of the sauce over the chicken and pass the remainder at the table or use for dipping.

NOTE: Satay Sauce should be prepared just before cooking the chicken.

VARIATION:

Skewered Satay Chicken with Vegetables: Right before cooking the chicken, cut 1 sweet red pepper and 1 green pepper into 1-inch squares. Clean and trim 24 medium fresh mushrooms. Divide the chicken and vegetables among 12 skewers, placing the chicken on each end, with the peppers next and then mushrooms in the center. Baste the vegetables with the leftover marinade. Cook, uncovered, on HIGH for 8 to 12 minutes, or until the chicken is cooked and the vegetables are tender-crisp.

Potpie Basics:

1. We felt that the best pies were made without a bottom crust because they were prepared faster and the pastry stayed crisper when cooked separately and added at the end just before serving.
2. The ratio for the filling is 4 cups cubed, cooked poultry to 2½ cups vegetables in a sauce of 2 cups broth thickened with 2 tablespoons flour. Just about any vegetables will do—for example, corn may be substituted for peas or extra potatoes for carrots.
3. The poultry-vegetable mixture is all precooked, and just needs to be heated and thickened. That is why it can be cooked on HIGH power, if it is stirred often.
4. In order to thicken the poultry-vegetable mixture, no cover is called for to allow some of the moisture to evaporate.
5. For the large pie, cooking the filling in the same pie plate that it is to be served in keeps cleanup to one dish later.
6. The inclination is to try to prepare these pies in advance and freeze them for when we have less time to cook. The fact of the matter is that they don't take much longer to cook directly from scratch.
7. We have had success with preparing the filling up to 3 days in advance and refrigerating it. If the potatoes have absorbed some of the liquid in that time, you may need to thin the mixture with a small amount of chicken broth. See instructions for reheating pot pies at the end of the recipe.

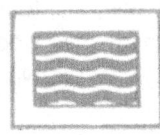

✸ NEW AMERICAN CHICKEN OR TURKEY POTPIE

MAKES 4 SERVINGS   BEGIN ABOUT 1¼ HOURS BEFORE SERVING
COOKING TIME: 24 TO 39 MINUTES

We used to look forward to chicken potpies for dinner the nights the baby-sitter came. Here's the new American potpie—a quick top pastry crust covers a delicious chicken or turkey and vegetable filling.

1 recipe Basic Pastry Dough (page 541)	2 tablespoons butter
1 egg	1 onion, coarsely chopped
2 tablespoons milk	2 tablespoons all-purpose flour
1 celery rib	4 cups cubed cooked chicken (see Note) or turkey
1 medium carrot, cut into ½-inch cubes (about ½ cup)	2 tablespoons sherry, vermouth, or water
1 medium potato, peeled and cut into ½-inch cubes (about 1 cup)	½ teaspoon dried tarragon leaves
2 cups Chicken Broth or Stock (page 118)	¼ teaspoon pepper
1 cup fresh or frozen peas	Salt
	Dash of hot pepper sauce

After the pastry has chilled, roll into a 12-inch circle, which will fit a 10-inch chicken pie. Invert a 10-inch pie plate and place on top of the pastry to measure. With a pastry cutter (for an attractive zigzag edging) or sharp knife, cut a circle the size of the pie plate. Reserve extra pastry dough.

Remove the plate and place the pastry on a double layer of wax paper. With a sharp knife, cut the pastry circle into 4 quarters. In a cup or bowl combine the egg and milk. Brush the mixture on top of the pastry. With a pastry cutter, cut thin decorative strips from the extra pastry. Place on the top outside rim of the pastry quarters to make decorative edging. Brush these with egg also. Prick the dough with a fork every ½ inch. Place the pastry circle on its paper in the oven. Cook, uncovered, on HIGH for 5 to 7 minutes, or until dry and opaque, rotating once.

In a 1½-quart casserole combine the celery, carrot, potato, and ½ cup broth. Cover tightly and cook on HIGH for 4 minutes. Stir in the peas. Cover again and cook on HIGH for 3 to 6 minutes, or until the vegetables are tender.

Combine the butter and onion in a 10-inch pie plate. Cook on HIGH for 2 to 5 minutes, or until the onion is tender. Stir the flour into the butter-onion mixture until dissolved. Add the remaining 1¾ cups broth. Cook on HIGH for 5 to 7 minutes, or until boiling and slightly thickened. Add the cooked vegetables and the remaining ingredients (except pastry). Cover tightly and cook on HIGH for 5 to 10 minutes, or until heated through, stirring once. Place the prepared pastry on top of the pie and serve.

NOTES: Use meat from Poached Whole Chicken (page 342) or from 2 whole chicken breasts, cooked as directed in the chart on page 66.

To Reheat: If made in advance, store the crust separately from the filling to keep the crust from getting soggy. For 1 individual pie, place the refrigerated pie, without crust, in the microwave and cook on HIGH for 2 to 3 minutes, or until hot, stirring each minute. Top with the cooked pastry crust and cook on HIGH for 30 seconds more.

For 2 individual pies, place the 2 refrigerated pies, without crusts, in the microwave and cook on HIGH for 4 to 6 minutes, or until hot, stirring every 2 minutes. Top with the cooked pastry crusts and cook on HIGH for 1 minute more.

VARIATIONS:

Individual Potpies: Roll the chilled pastry into a 12-inch square. Cut 4 individual pastries, the same size as the rims of 4 individual 1½-cup bowls or terrines that you plan to place the filling in. Place the pastries on wax paper. Add trim as indicated in basic recipe, and with a cookie cutter, cut a decorative hole. Brush with the egg mixture and cook as directed. Set aside.

Using a 2-quart casserole follow the basic poultry-vegetable mixture recipe, cooking the onions, then the poultry-vegetable mixture. Divide finished poultry-vegetable mixture between 4 individual dishes and top with cooked pastry rounds. Serve.

Potpies with Grated Cheese: After brushing the pastry with the egg mixture, sprinkle evenly with grated Parmesan cheese. This makes the pastry slightly brown on top.

Potpies with Celery or Sesame Seeds: For a decorative touch, after brushing the pastry with the egg mixture, sprinkle with celery or sesame seeds.

CHICKEN SALAD

AMOUNT: ABOUT 4 CUPS   BEGIN ABOUT 2 HOURS BEFORE SERVING

Chicken salad is a favorite summer main dish. Cooking chicken breasts in the microwave makes quick work of this dish, but for the most flavor, we recommend poaching a whole chicken (page 342) and chilling the chicken in its poaching liquid.

½ cup Mayonnaise (page 175)	¼ cup thinly sliced scallion tops or chives
1 tablespoon lemon juice	Salt and pepper to taste
½ cup thinly sliced celery	4 cups cooked chicken chunks

In a medium bowl toss all the ingredients together.

VARIATIONS:

Chicken Salad with Nuts: Add ½ cup coarsely chopped walnuts, pecans, or cashews.

Chicken Salad with Mayonnaise and Yogurt: Combine ¼ cup plain yogurt and ¼ cup mayonnaise instead of using ½ cup mayonnaise. One of our favorite dressings because of its light, tart flavor.

Chicken Salad with Tarragon Mayonnaise: Add 1 tablespoon chopped fresh tarragon to the mayonnaise, before adding to the salad.

Oriental Chicken Salad: Marinate 2 cups bean sprouts in 2 tablespoons Oriental Dressing (page 184) for 15 minutes. Add ¼ cup thinly sliced water chestnuts and ¼ cup snow peas with the vegetables. Substitute ¼ cup Oriental Dressing for the mayonnaise. After all the ingredients are combined, stir in the marinated bean sprouts. Sprinkle with ¼ cup toasted sesame seeds (page 609). Serve on a bed of watercress.

Chicken Salad with Orange Mayonnaise: Add 1 tablespoon fresh orange juice and 1 tablespoon grated orange rind to the mayonnaise before adding the remaining ingredients. Serve on lettuce, garnishing with orange segments.

Chicken Salad with Cilantro Dressing: Add 1 tablespoon fresh lime juice and 1 tablespoon grated lime rind to the mayonnaise before adding the remaining ingredients. Add 2 tablespoons chopped fresh cilantro (coriander) with the scallions. Serve on lettuce leaves garnished with lime wedges.

Chicken Avocado Salad: Cut half an avocado into ¼-inch slices. Sprinkle with 2 teaspoons lemon or lime juice. Fan the avocado slices out from the center of each of 4 salad plates. Mound salad on top of the wedges in the center of the plate. Sprinkle each serving with 1 tablespoon chopped nuts, if desired.

Chicken Salad with Pineapple: Combine 2 tablespoons pineapple juice with the mayonnaise before adding the remaining ingredients. Fold 1 cup drained canned pineapple chunks into the salad mixture.

LOW-CALORIE CHICKEN SALAD

MAKES ABOUT 4 CUPS   BEGIN ABOUT 2 HOURS BEFORE SERVING

- 4 cups cubed cooked chicken
- 2 celery ribs, thinly sliced
- ¼ cup chopped fresh parsley and tarragon
- 2 tablespoons lemon or lime juice
- Salt and pepper
- Lettuce

In a medium mixing bowl combine all ingredients except lettuce. Serve on a bed of lettuce.

VARIATIONS:

Chicken Salad with Raspberry Vinegar: Substitute 2 tablespoons raspberry vinegar (or see recipe for Quick Raspberry Vinegar on page 366) for lemon juice. Garnish with 1 cup fresh raspberries.

Chicken Salad with Balsamic Vinegar: Substitute 1 tablespoon balsamic vinegar for the lemon juice. Garnish with fresh basil and tomato slices.

Chicken Salad with Blueberry Vinegar: Substitute 2 tablespoons blueberry vinegar for the lemon juice. Garnish with 1 cup fresh blueberries.

Chicken Salad with Cider Vinegar and Apples: Substitute 2 tablespoons cider vinegar for the lemon juice. Add 1 cup tart (Granny Smith) apple chunks to the ingredients.

LOW-CAL CHICKEN BREASTS

A quick and convenient way to watch calories is to cook a chicken breast in this way and serve as is or in one of the low-calorie salads.

Chicken Breasts with Bone

1 whole breast with bone (about 1 pound)
Makes 2 cups cubed chicken

Rub the skin with juice of ½ lemon. Insert 2 sprigs or leaves fresh herbs, or ¼ teaspoon dried between the skin and meat. Place in a small microwaveproof plate. Cover tightly and cook on HIGH for 6 to 8 minutes; turning over once. Remove skin and cube, if desired.

2 whole breasts with bone (about 2 pounds)
Makes 4 cups cubed chicken

Double lemon juice and herbs above. Cover tightly and cook on HIGH for 13 to 17 minutes; turning over and rearranging once.

Boneless Chicken Breast

½ whole breast (about ½ pound)
Makes 1 cup cubed chicken

Place breast on microwave plate and sprinkle with 1 tablespoon lemon juice. Salt and pepper chicken. Cover with wax paper and cook on HIGH for 3 to 4 minutes, turning over after 2 minutes. Substitute white wine or dry vermouth for lemon juice, if desired.

CHICKEN OR TURKEY A LA KING

MAKES 4 SERVINGS   BEGIN 20 TO 30 MINUTES BEFORE SERVING
COOKING TIME: 8 TO 17 MINUTES

Serve on toast or rice. If serving over rice, cook the rice before chicken and keep covered until serving time.

- 3 tablespoons butter
- 2 tablespoons chopped onion
- ½ cup chopped celery
- 2 tablespoons all-purpose flour
- 1 cup Chicken Broth or Stock (page 118)
- ½ cup cream or milk
- 1 tablespoon dry sherry or vermouth (optional)
- ½ teaspoon salt
- ⅛ teaspoon pepper
- 1 cup cubed cooked chicken or turkey
- ½ cup sliced fresh mushrooms

In a 2-quart casserole combine the butter, onion, and celery. Cover tightly and cook on HIGH for 2 to 5 minutes, or until the celery is tender. Stir in the flour until dissolved and smooth. Slowly stir in the broth until blended. Stir in the milk and sherry or vermouth. Add salt and pepper. Cook, uncovered, on HIGH for 4 to 7 minutes, or until boiling and slightly thickened, stirring each minute. Stir in the chicken and mushrooms. Cook, uncovered, for 2 to 5 minutes, or until heated through, stirring once.

VARIATIONS:

Chicken a la King with Pimento: Add ¼ cup chopped pimento with the chicken.

Chicken a la King with Peas: Add 1 cup cooked peas with the chicken.

Chicken a la King with Nuts: Add ¼ cup coarsely chopped nuts with the chicken.

CHICKEN TACOS

MAKES 6 TACOS   BEGIN 10 TO 15 MINUTES BEFORE SERVING
COOKING TIME: 3 TO 4 MINUTES

Top chicken with Warm Jalapeño Salsa or Green Tomato Salsa (page 187 or 186), sliced tomatoes, and sour cream and guacamole, if desired. Garnish with black olive slices.

- 1 teaspoon vegetable oil
- 1 garlic clove, minced
- 2 tablespoons chopped onion
- 1 cup shredded cooked chicken
- ¼ teaspoon salt
- Pinch of pepper
- Pinch of cumin
- 6 taco shells

In a 1-quart casserole combine the oil, garlic, and onion. Cook on HIGH for 1 minute. Add the chicken, salt, pepper, and cumin; mix well. Cook, uncovered, on HIGH for 2 to 3 minutes, or until heated through. Spoon into prepared taco shells.

THAI CHICKEN

MAKES 4 SERVINGS   BEGIN 30 MINUTES BEFORE SERVING
COOKING TIME: 9 TO 15 MINUTES

This recipe was inspired by a recent visit to a Thai restaurant where we tasted a spicy yet light dish with chicken nuggets swathed in something between a soup and a sauce. Here is our rendition of that.

- 1 recipe Long-Grain Rice (page 196)
- 2 tablespoons sugar
- 3 tablespoons red wine vinegar
- 1 tablespoon cornstarch
- 2 cups Chicken Broth or Stock (page 118)
- ⅛ to ¼ teaspoon red pepper flakes
- 1 tablespoon chopped fresh basil leaves, or 1 teaspoon dried
- 2 cups shredded cooked chicken
- Toasted Coconut Strips (page 377)

Set aside prepared rice.

In a 1½-quart casserole combine the sugar and vinegar. Cook on HIGH for 2 minutes; stir. Cook, on HIGH for 2 to 3 minutes more, or until slightly thickened and caramelized. Stir in the cornstarch to dissolve. Stir in the broth, red pepper flakes, and basil. Cook on HIGH for 1 minute; stir. Cook on HIGH for 1 to 4 minutes more, or until slightly thickened and flavors have developed. Cooking uncovered is necessary to thicken the sauce slightly. Stir in the chicken. Cover tightly and cook on HIGH for 3 to 5 minutes, or until heated through, stirring once. Serve over rice and garnish with the toasted coconut strips.

Roast Whole Turkey Basics:

1. We have successfully cooked turkeys of many sizes in the microwave, including a 22-pound bird, but frankly a very large turkey requires a lot of turning over and is more trouble than it's worth. That is why we recommend a 16-pound turkey as the largest, and in your oven there should be at least a 3-inch space between the turkey and the side walls and at least 2 inches between the turkey and the top wall.
2. A turkey, because of its size and uneven shape, needs to be turned over once during cooking so that it can receive the most even penetration of microwave energy.
3. Because the turkey will be cooked breast side down for part of the cooking, it is best not to place it on a microwaveproof roasting rack because of the marks it will make.
4. Browning occurs during cooking because the turkey is large enough to cook long

> ## TOASTED COCONUT STRIPS
>
> MAKES ABOUT 2 CUPS
> COOKING TIME: 5 TO 6 MINUTES
>
> *This is a tasty snack or a garnish for Thai Chicken, fish dishes, or when unsalted, for dessert. Make sure that the paper towel you spread the coconut on for toasting is not the recycled type.*
>
> **1 coconut** **Salt**
>
> Prick holes in 3 soft areas at the top of the coconut shell; pour out the coconut milk. Crack the shell open. Run a small knife between the hard outer shell and the inner meat. Pry the meat from the shell; it isn't necessary to remove the brown skin.
>
> With a vegetable peeler, cut the coconut meat into very thin strips. Place a paper towel on a microwave large roasting rack or microwaveproof plate. Spread one layer of coconut over the paper. Sprinkle with salt. Cook on MEDIUM for 5 to 6 minutes, or until slightly brown, rotating every 2 minutes. Repeat the process until all the coconut is toasted.
>
> NOTE: If you're not using the coconut immediately, line a cookie sheet with a paper towel and let the coconut stand overnight before storing in a jar.

enough to build up sufficient surface heat for browning. The turkey is not covered for that reason, because a cover would keep the surface too moist and reduce browning.

5. Cooking fats are removed with a bulb baster because large amounts of fat can slow down cooking
6. If any areas appear to be overcooking, cover these smoothly with foil as indicated in the illustration on page 31.
7. Because of the size and conformation of a turkey, it requires a 20-minute standing time to completely heat through. The turkey should be tented with foil (see illustration on page 344) to reflect the heat inward.
8. If a crisp skin is desired, the dry heat of a conventional oven is required. Microwave ovens provide no dry heat.
9. *Doneness:* The turkey leg should move freely at the joint and the flesh will feel soft when pressed firmly. The internal temperature of the meatiest part of the thigh will register 180°F after 1 minute. When the breast meat is pierced under the wing, the juices will run clear, and not red, before standing time.

We found that a microwave temperature probe is not always accurate when cooking turkey, because it may touch the bone or fat may run down along the probe and raise the temperature higher than that of the meat. It is better to insert a conventional meat thermometer toward the end of cooking for 1 minute, and then remove it if cooking needs to be continued.

Underdone: If the temperature has reached 180°F, but the juices don't run clear, continue cooking, but cover the wing, upper breast, and leg ends with foil to keep from overcooking, adding 5 minutes at a time.

Overdone: There are certain irregular areas, such as the top leg or breastbone area, that with overcooking could become hard, dry, and stringy. Remove these areas and serve the rest. The rest may be drier than normal, but slice thinly and bathe in juices or serve with gravy. Even this meat won't be any drier than most conventionally cooked turkeys.

✹ ROAST TURKEY

8 to 9 minutes per pound MEDIUM-HIGH or 10 minutes HIGH, then MEDIUM 10 to 12 minutes per pound
MAKES 12 TO 16 SERVINGS   BEGIN 2½ TO 3½ HOURS BEFORE SERVING, WITHOUT STUFFING
COOKING TIME 2 to 3½ HOURS, DEPENDING ON OVEN'S COOKING POWER

A 14- to 16-pound turkey turns out beautifully in the microwave, with a nice brown skin and moist meat. We prefer the MEDIUM-HIGH power setting to accomplish this task, but give you optional power settings if your oven doesn't have MEDIUM-HIGH.

1 16-pound turkey **Double recipe of any stuffing (pages 349–51) (optional)**	¼ cup melted butter.

Stuff the turkey, if desired.

Truss the turkey by tying the legs together and the wings to the body. Don't use metal skewers. Place it breast side down in a 3-quart rectangular baking dish. Brush with the butter. Cook, uncovered, on MEDIUM-HIGH for 60 minutes. (If no MEDIUM-HIGH setting, cook on HIGH for 10 minutes and then MEDIUM for 1½ hours.) Turn the turkey over with the breast side up.

Cook, uncovered, on MEDIUM-HIGH for 60 to 80 minutes, or until done, basting two to three times and draining any fat with a bulb baster. (If no MEDIUM-HIGH setting, cook on MEDIUM for 1 hour 42 minutes.) As you baste, check the wing and leg areas to see if they are done and should be covered with foil to prevent overcooking. Let stand, tented with foil, for 20 minutes. In this time a gravy and vegetables can be cooked.

VARIATIONS:

Crisp-Skin Turkey: Preheat the conventional oven to 500°F during the last part of microwave cooking time. Transfer the cooked turkey to the preheated oven for 5 to 10 minutes to crisp before standing time.

Honey-Glazed Turkey: Double Honey-Mustard Glaze (page 347). Brush the turkey with the glaze before and during cooking.

Cranberry-Glazed Turkey: Double Cranberry Glaze (page 348). Brush the turkey with the glaze before and during cooking.

Apricot-Glazed Turkey: Double Apricot

Glaze (page 348). Brush the turkey with the glaze before and during cooking.

Turkey with Giblet Gravey: During standing time, prepare Turkey Giblet Gravy (page 379).

Turkey with Pan Drippings Gravy: During standing time, prepare Pan Drippings Gravy (page 173).

TURKEY GIBLET STOCK

MAKES 2½ CUPS
COOKING TIME: 38 TO 40 MINUTES

This is a quick way to make an enriched giblet stock that will bring so much more flavor to your gravy. Do this the morning of your turkey feast.

- **Giblets from 1 turkey, chopped (excluding liver)**
- **3 cups Chicken Broth or Stock (page 118)**
- **1 onion, halved**
- **1 carrot, cut into large chunks**
- **1 celery rib, cut into large chunks**
- **3 sprigs parsley, or 1 teaspoon dried**
- **1 bay leaf, broken in half**
- **1 sprig fresh thyme, or ¼ teaspoon dried**

Combine all the ingredients in a 3-quart casserole. Cover tightly and cook on HIGH for 8 to 10 minutes, or until boiling; stir. Cover again and cook on MEDIUM for 30 minutes. Strain and set aside.

Chicken or Cornish Game Hen Stock: Substitute chicken or Cornish game hen giblets for turkey giblets. Use only 2 cups chicken broth. Cover tightly and cook on HIGH for 5 minutes, or until boiling, then on MEDIUM for 20 minutes.

TURKEY GIBLET GRAVY

MAKES 2½ CUPS
COOKING TIME: 9 TO 11 MINUTES

It is simple enough to make the giblet stock the day before, or earlier in the day, and then make this gravy during the standing time of the poultry.

(Continued)

2 to 1½ cups Turkey Giblet Stock (page 379) 3 tablespoons all-purpose flour ¼ cup vermouth or water	Juices from turkey cooking dish, fat removed Salt and pepper

Pour the stock into a 2-quart casserole. In a small bowl combine the flour and vermouth to make a smooth paste. Beat into the stock with a wire whisk until smooth.

Remove as much fat as possible from the juices in the turkey cooking dish. Add the turkey juices to the stock and stir. Cook on HIGH for 9 to 11 minutes, or until boiling and slightly thickened. Salt and pepper to taste. Pour into a gravy boat and serve with the turkey.

NOTE: For thicker gravy thicken with no more than 1 tablespoon flour.

VARIATION:

Chicken or Cornish Game Hen Giblet Gravy: Substitute 1½ cups Chicken or Cornish Game Hen Giblet Stock (page 379) for the turkey stock. Reduce the flour to 1½ tablespoons and the vermouth to 2 tablespoons. Substitute chicken or Cornish hen juices for the turkey juices. Cook on HIGH for 4 to 8 minutes, stirring once.

GLAZED TURKEY BREAST

HIGH 7 minutes per pound, then MEDIUM 8 to 9 minutes per pound
MAKES 6 SERVINGS   BEGIN 1½ HOURS BEFORE SERVING
COOKING TIME: 1¼ HOURS TO 1 HOUR 20 MINUTES

The glazing adds a nice coating to the skin. To determine doneness, the juices that run from the meatiest area of the breast should run clear and not red. The temperature in the meatiest area should reach 170°F before standing time.

5-pound turkey breast	**Choice of glazes (pages 347–48)**

Place the turkey breast, skin side down, in a 2-quart rectangular dish. Brush the entire breast with half of the glaze. Cook, uncovered, on HIGH for 35 minutes. Turn the breast skin side up. Brush with the remaining glaze. Cook on MEDIUM for 40 to 45 minutes, or until done. Let stand, tented with foil, for 10 minutes.

VARIATIONS:

Turkey Breast with Stuffing: Prepare half of any stuffing recipe (pages 349–51). Place 2 cups stuffing under the hollow of the breast, after turning the turkey breast side up. Complete cooking as directed.

Turkey Salad: Don't glaze the turkey breast. Cool and substitute for chicken in Chicken Salad (page 372).

TURKEY DRUMSTICKS

MAKES 3 TO 4 SERVINGS   BEGIN 50 MINUTES BEFORE SERVING
COOKING TIME: 41 TO 46 MINUTES

The wax paper cover helps these large, unusually shaped pieces of poultry to cook evenly by retaining some steam. When the meat cut near the bone is no longer pink and the temperature is about 180°F before standing time, the drumsticks are done.

2 to 3 pounds turkey drumsticks or legs	Choice of glazes (pages 347–48)

Arrange the turkey drumsticks in a 2-quart rectangular dish, with the meatier section toward the outside. Brush with half the glaze. Cover with wax paper and cook on HIGH for 6 minutes, then on MEDIUM for 15 minutes. Turn drumsticks over. Brush with the remaining glaze. Cover again and cook on MEDIUM for 20 to 25 minutes, or until done. Let stand, tented with foil, for 5 minutes.

VARIATION:

Barbecued Turkey Drumsticks: Substitute Blazing Barbecue Sauce (page 181) for the glaze.

Ground Turkey Chili

Substitute 2 pounds uncooked ground or chopped turkey for the ground beef in the recipe for Ground Beef Chili (page 321). This makes a lighter chili.

Turkey Meat Loaf

Substitute 1½ pounds uncooked ground turkey for the beef in the recipe for Meat Loaf (page 331).

TURKEY OR CHICKEN TETRAZZINI

MAKES 4 TO 6 SERVINGS   BEGIN 40 TO 50 MINUTES BEFORE SERVING
COOKING TIME: 23 TO 29 MINUTES

This is a delicious way to serve leftover turkey, and it is a dish that improves with age. When cutting up leftover turkey, why not prepare this dish right away for another occasion? To do that, leave out the cheese and freeze the Tetrazzini when time is short and a turkey casserole seems appealing (see frozen casserole reheating doneness on page 45). Parmesan cheese can be cooked on HIGH because it is a very hard, crumbled cheese and does not become rubbery.

- ½ pound elbow macaroni or ditalini
- 3 tablespoons butter
- 1 garlic clove, minced
- 1 medium onion, chopped
- 2 tablespoons all-purpose flour
- 2 cups hot Chicken Broth or Stock (page 118)
- ½ cup milk, half-and-half, or cream
- 2 tablespoons dry vermouth or sherry (optional)
- ½ pound fresh mushrooms, sliced
- 1 teaspoon lemon juice
- ½ teaspoon salt
- ¼ teaspoon pepper
- 2 cups shredded or diced cooked turkey or chicken
- 1 cup grated Parmesan cheese

On top of the stove, heat water to boiling; cook the macaroni until tender.

Meanwhile, in a 2-quart casserole combine the butter, garlic, and onion. Cook on HIGH for 1 to 3 minutes, or until tender. Stir in the flour until dissolved and smooth. Pour in the hot chicken broth, a little at a time, whisking or stirring to keep the sauce smooth. Pour in the milk or cream and vermouth or sherry. Cook on HIGH for 8 to 10 minutes, or until boiling but only slightly thickened, stirring twice. Stir in the mushrooms, lemon juice, salt, pepper, turkey, and drained macaroni.

Stir ½ cup Parmesan into the mixture. Cover with wax paper and cook on HIGH for 10 minutes, stirring after 5 minutes. Sprinkle the remaining ½ cup cheese on top. Cook, uncovered, on HIGH for 4 to 6 minutes, or until heated through.

VARIATION:

Turkey Tetrazzini with Nuts: Substitute 2 pounds spaghetti or other macaroni for the elbow macaroni. Add ½ cup pine nuts or slivered almonds with the turkey.

Roast Duck and Goose Basics:

1. Removing the fat from the cavity and around the neck of the duck and the cavity of the goose (not as fatty as duck) makes the final product less greasy.
2. It is important to tie the fowl into a compact shape for more even cooking.
3. Pricking the skin and placing the fowl on the roasting rack, and frequent draining of the fat, are essential to removing the fat and producing a moist, nongreasy final dish.
4. No stuffing is suggested for duck because it is so fatty. Because a goose is not as fatty and larger, we suggest a fruit stuffing to help flavor the bird.
5. Both duck and goose are cooked on HIGH power if they are 5 pounds or under. If a goose is over 5 pounds, follow turkey cooking times in the chart (page 66).
6. Turning the fowl over halfway through microwave cooking time allows all parts of the duck to cook evenly. In the conven-

tional oven, they are turned over to expose all surface areas for even browning and crisping.
7. Both duck and goose are cooked completely in the microwave and then crisped in the conventional oven.
8. Standing time will allow heat to conduct to the meatiest parts of the fowl.
9. *Doneness:* When pulled from the microwave oven the meat should feel soft when the skin is pressed and the juices from the thickest part of the thigh, when pricked, should be yellow with a trace of pink.

Underdone: Juices from the pricked thigh will run red or yellow with red. Continue to cook in the microwave, testing after 5 minutes.

Overdone: The areas that may overcook are the tops of the legs and the wings. After crisping the fowl in the oven, just don't serve these parts. The fat in both the goose and duck will keep the remaining meat moist.

✹ CRISPY ROAST DUCK

HIGH *6 to 7 minutes per pound, then 10 minutes at 500°F*
MAKES 4 SERVINGS   BEGIN 1 HOUR BEFORE SERVING (WITHOUT SAUCE)
COOKING TIME: 40 MINUTES

Bar none, this is the best duck that we have ever eaten, especially when it is fresh! The combination of microwave cooking, which renders out the fat but keeps in flavor and moistness, and the crisping by conventional cooking is unbeatable in producing the best results. And with any of the duck sauces in this chapter (see variations below for suggestions), you have a hit meal on your hands.

---

1 5-pound duck

Remove any fat from the body cavity and around the neck. Remove the giblets; reserve if planning to make sauce. (If cooking goose, stuff the body and neck cavity here. Close cavities with long toothpicks or wooden skewers or sew them closed. Don't use metal skewers.) Tie the legs together with string and crisscross over the back to tie the wings to the body. Prick the skin to allow the fat to ooze out. Place the duck, breast side down, on a microwaveproof roasting rack in a 2-quart glass rectangular dish. Cook on HIGH for 15 minutes. Remove from oven and pour off the fat. Turn the duck breast side up. Cook on HIGH for 15 minutes, or until the juices run clear. Meanwhile, preheat the conventional oven to 500°F.

After the duck has cooked, pour off the fat. Place the duck, breast side down, on a metal roasting rack in the same 2-quart dish. Place in the conventional oven for 10 minutes, turning the duck over after 5 minutes. Let stand, tented with foil, for 5 to 15 minutes. Slice the duck to serve.

VARIATIONS:

Crispy Sherried Duck: Prepare Sherried Duck Sauce (page 385) during standing time. Pass the sauce with the duck.

Crispy Duck with Green Peppercorns: Prepare Green Peppercorn Sauce (page 385) during standing time. Pass the sauce with the duck.

Crispy Duck à l'Orange: Prepare Orange Sauce (page 385) during standing time. Garnish the duck with orange segments; pass the sauce.

Crispy Duck with Prune Sauce: Follow the basic recipe, but before cooking the duck, soak the prunes for Prune Sauce (page 385). Complete the sauce during standing time. Pass the sauce with the duck.

Crispy Duck with Drunken Prune Sauce: Follow basic recipe, but before cooking the duck, soak the prunes for Drunken Prune Sauce (page 385). Complete sauce during standing time. Pass the sauce with the duck.

Crispy Fruited Duck: Follow basic recipe, but before cooking the duck, soak the fruits for Dried Fruit Sauce (page 385). Complete the sauce during standing time. Pass the sauce with the duck.

Crispy Duck with Cranberry Sauce: Prepare Cranberry Sauce (page 385) during standing time. Pass the sauce with the duck.

Duck Breast Salad: Remove cooked breast from duck and slice. Serve on a bed of mixed greens. See Breaded Warm Cheese with Salad (page 162) for dressing and presentation, and serve in place of cheese, warm or chilled.

DUCK GIBLET STOCK

MAKES 1 CUP
COOKING TIME: 35 TO 38 MINUTES

Here is a quick stock you can make from your duck giblets to add marvelous flavor to your sauce. You can make the stock as far ahead as the day before; then you'll be ready to whip up your sauce during the duck's standing time.

Duck giblets
2 cups beef broth (see Mock Brown Broth or Stock, page 119)

1 onion, quartered
1 celery rib, coarsely chopped
1 carrot, sliced

In a 4-cup glass measure combine the duck giblets, broth, onion, celery, and carrot. Cover tightly and cook on HIGH for 5 to 8 minutes, or until boiling, then cook on MEDIUM for 30 minutes, or until the broth is reduced to 1 cup, stirring twice (with giblets and vegetables it will measure about 2 cups). Strain the broth, discarding the giblets and vegetables.

Chilled Cream of Tomato-Basil Soup with Sour Cream and Julienned Orange Rind, page 131

New American Pot Pies, page 371

German Potato Salad with Dandelions and Bratwurst, page 455

Seasonal Vegetable Platter, page 478

Ratatouille in Miniature Eggplant Shells, page 421

Grillades and Grits, page 286

Swordfish Steak with Parsley Butter, page 228; Zucchini Timbale, page 158; and Sugar Snap Peas

Chocolate Bread Pudding with Warm Pastry Cream, page 570; Two-Tiered Chocolate Mousse Cake, page 580; Truffle Cake, page 515; and Chocolate-Covered Strawberries and Grapes, page 596

SHERRIED DUCK SAUCE

MAKES ABOUT 1¼ CUPS
COOKING TIME: 11 TO 12 MINUTES

¼ cup red wine vinegar
3 tablespoons sugar

1 recipe Duck Giblet Stock (page 384)
2 tablespoons sherry

Combine the vinegar and sugar in a 1-quart casserole. Cook on HIGH for 3 minutes; stir. Cook on HIGH for 1 to 2 minutes more, or until the mixture begins to brown and thicken, coating a spoon; be careful not to let it burn. Stir the stock into the syrup. Cook on HIGH for 2 minutes, or until boiling. Add the sherry. Cook on HIGH for 5 minutes, or until boiling again and flavors are developed.

VARIATIONS:

Green Peppercorn Sauce: Substitute 2 tablespoons drained waterpacked green peppercorns and 2 tablespoons brandy for the sherry. This sauce is fabulous!

Orange Sauce: Substitute 2 tablespoons orange liqueur for the sherry. Follow basic recipe up to the point where the broth is added to the vinegar-sugar mixture. Slice peels of 2 navel oranges into thin julienne strips. Combine the orange peel strips and 1 tablespoon water in a 1-cup glass measure. Cover tightly and cook on HIGH for 3 minutes, or until tender. Drain. Stir into the broth-syrup along with the orange liqueur. Continue with the recipe.

Apricot Sauce: Cover 1 cup dried apricots with warm water. Let stand for 30 minutes to soften. Drain. Substitute 2 tablespoons apricot-, peach- or orange-flavored liqueur for the sherry. Add drained apricots with the liqueur and cover with wax paper to cook.

Prune Sauce: Cover 1 cup dried pitted prunes with warm water. Let stand for 30 minutes to soften. Drain. Substitute 2 tablespoons brandy for the sherry. Add the drained prunes with the liqueur and cover with wax paper to cook.

Drunken Prune Sauce: Cover 1 cup dried pitted prunes with Armagnac. Let stand for 30 minutes to soften. Drain, reserving 2 tablespoons of the Armagnac as a substitute for the sherry. Add the drained prunes with the liqueur and cover with wax paper to cook.

Dried Fruit Sauce: Cover 1 cup dried mixed fruit with warm water. Let stand for 30 minutes to soften. Drain. Substitute 2 tablespoons brandy for the sherry. Add the drained fruit with the brandy and cover with wax paper to cook.

Cranberry Sauce: Substitute 2 tablespoons orange liqueur for the sherry. Add 1 cup fresh cranberries and 2 tablespoons sugar with the liqueur. Cover with wax paper and cook until the cranberries pop, stirring once.

ROAST GOOSE

MAKES 4 SERVINGS

1 5-pound goose

Follow the instructions for Roast Duck (page 383).

VARIATIONS:

Stuffed Goose: Stuff the goose with 3 to 4 cups any Fruit-Bread Stuffing (page 349). Follow the basic recipe. Because goose is not as fatty, it can be stuffed.

Goose with Apricot Sauce: Follow the recipe for Roast Duck, making Apricot Sauce (page 385).

Goose with Dried Fruit Sauce: Follow the recipe for Roast Duck, making Dried Fruit Sauce (page 385).

Goose with Prune Sauce: Follow the recipe for Roast Duck, making Prune Sauce (page 385).

Chicken Livers Basics:

1. Due to their fat content and air pockets under an outside membrane, chicken livers pop or sputter when cooked on HIGH. Therefore, it is best to cook them on MEDIUM power.
2. Chicken livers are best when arranged in a circle around the outer rim so that they will cook evenly with only one stirring.
3. A 9-inch plate works best for this ring arrangement, but any dish that is large enough to move the chicken livers to the outside, leaving the center open, is fine.
4. Chicken livers are covered with wax paper for more even, quicker cooking, with a minimum of moisture retention. The cover also prevents spatters.
5. Chicken livers are salted at the end of the cooking time because salt draws out moisture and will toughen the livers if added earlier.
6. Standing time is short and not very critical.
7. *Doneness:* Chicken livers should be firm and have no pink color left on the outside.

    Underdone: Pink or red color will remain on the surface. If some pieces appear to be brown and cooked yet others are very pink (possibly a result of not stirring enough), remove the cooked livers. Continue to cook the remaining pink livers until done.

    Overdone: The texture will be very firm and rubbery. Try slicing as thin as possible and putting over toast with a beef gravy or White, Rose, or Mushroom sauce (pages 171–172). Make the Tequila Chicken Livers and serve plenty of tequila at the table.

✹ SAUTÉED CHICKEN LIVERS

MAKES 4 SERVINGS   BEGIN ABOUT 20 MINUTES BEFORE SERVING
COOKING TIME: 10 TO 13 MINUTES

Serve these for a show-stopping breakfast or brunch—say, on buttered toast with scrambled eggs—the eggs can be made in the microwave during standing time. They are even appropriate as an appetizer or in a pasta course. The variations give you an outstanding selection of flavors.

1 pound chicken livers	Salt and pepper
1 tablespoon butter	2 tablespoons chopped fresh
2 tablespoons finely chopped onion	parsley or chives

Rinse the livers in cold water. Pat dry with paper towels and cut in half.

In a 9-inch pie plate combine the butter and onion. Cook on HIGH for 1 to 2 minutes, or until the onion is tender. Add the chicken livers, stirring to coat. Push the livers toward the rim of the dish, leaving the center open. Cover with wax paper and cook on MEDIUM for 9 to 11 minutes, or until the livers have just lost their pink color, stirring to move the cooked pieces to the outside. Salt and pepper to taste. Sprinkle with parsley or chives. Let stand, covered, for 2 to 5 minutes.

VARIATIONS:

Chicken Livers with Mustard: Stir 2 tablespoons prepared mustard into the chicken livers at the end of cooking and before standing time. Serve over toast.

Chicken Livers with Mushrooms: During standing time, cook ½ pound mushrooms, sliced (page 72). Stir into the chicken livers, sprinkling with parsley or chives. Serve on toast.

Gingered Chicken Livers: Add 1 garlic clove, minced, and 1 teaspoon chopped fresh ginger or ¼ teaspoon ground ginger to the onion. Add 1 tablespoon soy sauce, 1 tablespoon dry sherry or vermouth, and 1 teaspoon lemon juice with the chicken livers. Serve over rice or cooked vermicelli.

Chicken Livers in Sour Cream Sauce: At the end of cooking and before standing time, add 1 cup sour cream or crème fraîche and 1 teaspoon lemon juice. Stir to blend. Cover tightly and cook on MEDIUM for 1 to 2 minutes, or until heated through, being careful that the cream doesn't boil. Serve over toast with lemon wedges, and sprinkle with parsley or chives.

Chicken Livers in Sour Cream with Lime and Cilantro: Prepare Chicken Livers in Sour Cream Sauce variation above. Sprinkle with fresh chopped cilantro (coriander) instead of herbs. Serve with lime wedges and flour tortillas.

Chicken Livers with Sour Cream and Mushrooms: At the end of cooking and before standing time, add 1 cup sour cream or crème fraîche and 1 teaspoon lemon juice. Stir to blend. Let stand. Meanwhile, cook ½ pound mushrooms, sliced (page 72). Stir into the chicken livers. Cook on MEDIUM for 2 to 4 minutes, or until heated through, being careful that the cream doesn't boil. Serve on toast, sprinkled with parsley or chives.

Tequila Chicken Livers: Add 2 tablespoons tequila with the chicken livers. Serve with flour tortillas, lime wedges, and Green Tomato Salsa (page 186) or Salsa Cruda (page 185).

Chicken Livers with Tomato Sauce: Prepare Pureed Tomato Sauce (page 179) or have ready a 16-ounce can of tomato sauce. During standing time, reheat or heat the tomato sauce on HIGH for 5 minutes, stirring once. Stir the chicken livers into the tomato sauce. Cover with wax paper and cook on MEDIUM for 3 to 5 minutes, or until heated through. Serve over pasta.

Chicken Livers in Sherry Cream Sauce: During standing time, prepare Intoxicating Sauce with sherry (page 361). Stir the chicken livers into the cream sauce. Cover with wax paper and cook on MEDIUM for 1 to 3 minutes to reheat, if necessary. Serve over toast, pasta, or pastry shells. Garnish with 2 tablespoons chopped fresh parsley, chives, or basil, if desired.

Chicken Livers with Rose Sauce: During standing time, prepare Rose Sauce (page 172). Stir the chicken livers into the sauce. Cover with wax paper and cook on MEDIUM for 1 to 3 minutes to reheat, if necessary. Serve on toast, pasta, or pastry shells.

Chicken Livers with Pink Peppercorn Sauce: During standing time, prepare Rose Sauce (page 172). After cooking the rose sauce, stir in 2 tablespoons pink peppercorns and the cooked chicken livers. Cook, uncovered, on MEDIUM for 1 to 3 minutes to reheat, if necessary. Serve over pasta or in ramekins or custard cups. Serve the ramekins with bread croustades. Our favorite!

12

VEGETABLES

Our family took a two-week vacation every year to New England, where we spent time between Grammy's house on the pond and Uncle George's farm. In that period our world revolved around a new litter of kittens, the unpredictable temperament of the pony, and the crops.

Our first coffee session with relatives would update us on family affairs and the state of the harvest. George would stretch out his gnarled finger to trace a picture of the burgeoning fields on the tablecloth. His soft voice and patient hound-dog eyes made this burly man approachable even to the youngest of us.

Keeping all the relatives straight from year to year was no small task. My system even then was to group them by generations, and then into families. It was so much easier to organize the vegetables for selling at the roadside stand. Each had their own wooden compartment and it seemed so obvious which were the young and old.

The ones that were as youthful as my cousins and I were bright in color and would squeak in our fingers. They were the ears of corn that, when cracked open, sent out a sweet perfume like the smell of my hair when it was washed, and the green beans or baby peas that my aunt snapped firmly when she was displaying their freshness to customers.

The older vegetables were those that were saved for our Thanksgiving visits. They were dustier, muted, the ones that Grandma stored on wooden shelves in the root cellar. They were the potatoes and sweet potatoes that were cooked and whipped to a creamy consistency, a blessing to those relatives whose choppers had fallen out many summers ago. The pumpkin and squash were handsomely turned out in pies that graced the dessert table.

The microwave, which may seem to be the antithesis of all of this, has served to resurrect those old memories and to elevate vegetables to the eminence of those New England farm days. The combination of rapid cooking and minimal cooking liquid is what makes it possible for such vegetables to retain their bright, fresh-picked color and flavor. Microwave cooking has all the advantages of steaming, but in much less time: It has the flavor benefits of braising but without large amounts of water, which can only mean vitamin loss.

Unlike my simple vegetable classifications of those days, we have divided vegetables into twelve families. The purpose is to help you understand why each grouping needs to be treated in different ways. With each division you will find basic teaching recipes and a list of toppings or quick sauces to accompany them. A comprehensive cooking chart for vegetables can be found in Chapter 2, on pages 67–76. A last category will show you how to combine many different vegetables into one dish. Even if you've never spent a summer on a New England farm, here's where you can experience the flavors and imagine what it was like.

—Marcia

ARTICHOKES

Artichokes are edible thistles that should be plucked from the market when firm, unspotted and heavy for their size. The small to medium ones will usually have a better flavor, and when purchased at their peak no vegetable has more class or packs more tender morsels in every bite than the artichoke. In addition to this, artichokes are very hardy and can be refrigerated for up to a week.

Many people have the erroneous impression that artichokes are difficult to cook. On the contrary, they're quite simple, especially when following the basic recipe. In some ways, artichokes are similar to corn. As one or two ears of corn can be cooked in the husk with no water, one or two artichokes can be cooked wrapped in plastic wrap with no additional liquid. For all their elegance, artichokes demand to be eaten with fingers, a process more complicated than the simple approach one takes toward corn.

The exercise is made much easier if the host or hostess has first removed the pinkish inner leaves and hairy choke with a spoon. From there on it is everyone for himself as each dismantles the thistle leaf by leaf in search of the tender heart. Of course each leaf—more precisely called a "scale"—at its base gives a preview of the tender heart to come.

Eating is enhanced when there is a dipping sauce within arm's reach, or better yet, nestled in the hollow of each artichoke. An empty plate or plates should be strategically placed for the discarded leaves that will pile up like shells after a clambake.

Libations are another special consideration. Some experts recommend water as the only drink that won't pale against the choke. We, on the other hand, prefer the dry, crisp flavor of a well-chilled Mâcon Blanc wine.

Artichoke Basics:

1. Trim the top 1 inch of an artichoke. If it is to be stuffed, trim it by 1½ inches.
2. You can prevent discoloration by rubbing the outside of the artichoke with the cut half of a lemon.
3. When cooking 1 or 2 artichokes, it is easiest to encase them in plastic wrap, which causes them to produce their own steam. If cooking 3 or 4, it is easiest to place them in a dish with ¼ cup liquid and a tight cover.

4. When cooking more than 1 artichoke, leave 1 inch of space between them or arrange them in a circle in the dish for more even cooking.
5. If cooking more than 1 artichoke in a dish, rotate the dish once halfway through cooking. This rearrangement will ensure the most even cooking.
6. Letting the artichokes stand, covered, after cooking is important to complete the process, besides which, they are almost too hot to handle at this point anyway.
7. Artichokes must first be cooked according to the basic cooking times (see below) before stuffing is added. Any type of fine-textured cooked meat, vegetable, or breadcrumb stuffing will work here. After stuffing the cooked artichokes, liquid (¼ cup) still needs to be added again for the most even steaming of these vegetables.
8. *Doneness:* To judge the doneness of artichokes, you'll need both hands and eyes. The color is the first indication of doneness and it should be olive green.

When the color appears about right, pick up the artichoke and try pulling at the bottom lower leaves. If they come out with just a little resistance, you've passed one test. Insert a paring knife into the base of one or two artichokes, and if they pierce easily and appear to be tender, they are done—but let standing time complete the cooking process.

Underdone: If you have served the artichokes and perhaps one feels underdone, simply wrap it up again in plastic wrap and place in the microwave oven. Cook on HIGH at 1-minute intervals, until it tests done.

Overdone: This rarely if ever happens with artichokes, but even if the leaves appear very brown and not presentable to serve (which may be the result of an older artichoke and not overcooking), the center heart will be fine. Remove all the leaves and choke and detach the heart intact. Serve it chopped up and warm in a lemon butter over a little cooked pasta as a first course. Or chill the chopped-up artichoke heart and present it on a bed of red-tipped lettuce with a dollop of crabmeat, shrimp, or Hard-Cooked Egg Spread (page 148) on top.

✺ STEAMED ARTICHOKES

Cut off the artichoke stems and cut off about 1 inch from the top. Pull off the few tough bottom leaves, and with scissors, snip off the tips of each of the outer leaves. Rub each artichoke with the cut side of half a lemon to prevent discoloration.

Wrap 1 or 2 artichokes separately and tightly in plastic wrap. If cooking more than 2, pour ¼ cup water into an 8-inch square or round dish and arrange the artichokes in it, base down, leaving the center open if possible. Cover tightly and cook according to the following chart until the low leaves can be pulled out and the base pierced easily, rotating the dish halfway through cooking.

Amount	Cooking Time
1 artichoke, whole	HIGH 4 to 5 minutes
2 artichokes, whole	HIGH 5 to 9 minutes
3 artichokes, whole	HIGH 8 to 12 minutes
4 artichokes, whole	HIGH 9 to 15 minutes

Let stand, covered, for 3 minutes. Drain. Serve hot or chilled on individual plates with a sauce of your choice for dipping (see below).

To eat, pull each leaf out by the tip and dip the fleshy base end into the sauce. To eat the heart, pull out the pointed, rosy-colored center leaves that are clustered together. Scoop out the hairy choke that lies just above the heart. Cut the heart into wedges and dip into the sauce.

VARIATIONS:

Artichokes with Herb Butter: Prepare artichokes as in basic recipe. Place ½ cup butter in custard cup. Cook on HIGH for 2 minutes, or until melted. Add 1 tablespoon chopped fresh rosemary or thyme or ½ teaspoon dried. Dip the fleshy end of the leaves into the butter.

Chilled Artichokes with Oriental Sauce: Cook the artichokes as in basic recipe and chill for at least 1 hour. Prepare Oriental Dressing (page 184) for dipping.

Dips for Artichokes

Dip the cooked leaves from 1 artichoke into any of these mixtures.

Lemon or Lime Juice: 2 tablespoons lemon juice or lime juice.

Lemon Butter: Combine 2 tablespoons butter and 4 teaspoons lemon juice in a small custard cup. Cook on HIGH for 40 seconds to 1 minute to melt.

Lime-Cilantro Butter: Combine 2 tablespoons butter, 4 teaspoons lime juice, and 1 teaspoon chopped fresh cilantro (coriander). Cook on HIGH for 40 seconds to 1 minute to melt.

Hollandaise Sauce: ¼ cup Hollandaise Sauce (page 174).

Béarnaise Sauce: ¼ cup Béarnaise Sauce (page 174).

Herbed Mayonnaise: ¼ cup Herbed Mayonnaise (page 175).

Green Sauce: ¼ cup Green Sauce (page 177).

STUFFED ARTICHOKES WITH PINE NUTS

MAKES 4 SERVINGS   BEGIN ABOUT 50 MINUTES BEFORE SERVING
COOKING TIME: 21 TO 31 MINUTES

4 medium artichokes	1 cup finely chopped fresh mushrooms
½ lemon	½ cup fine dry bread crumbs
¾ cup Vegetable or Chicken Broth or Stock (pages 119 or 118)	¼ cup pine nuts or sunflower seeds
2 tablespoons butter	¼ cup chopped fresh parsley
1 garlic clove, minced	½ teaspoon salt
1 medium onion, chopped	¼ teaspoon pepper
	Lemon wedges or Hollandaise Sauce (page 174) (optional)

Cut off the artichoke stems and about 1½ inches from the tops. Pull off the few tough bottom leaves and, with scissors, snip off the points of the outer leaves. Rub the outsides of the artichokes well with the cut side of the lemon, to prevent discoloration. In an 8-inch round or square dish combine the artichokes and ¼ cup broth. Cover tightly and cook on HIGH for 9 to 15 minutes, or until the bases pierce easily, rotating the dish twice if necessary. Let stand, covered, for 3 minutes. Drain and cool.

After the artichokes have cooled, pull out the rosy pink center leaves. Gently press the green leaves (scales) away from the center of each and, with a small spoon or melon baller, remove the center choke.

In a 2-quart casserole combine the butter, garlic, and onion. Cook on HIGH for 2 to 4 minutes, or until the onion is tender. Stir in the mushrooms. Cook on HIGH for 2 to 4 minutes, or until the mushrooms are tender. Stir in ¼ cup broth, bread crumbs, nuts, parsley, salt, and pepper. Spoon the mixture into the center cavities of the artichokes and between the outer leaves. Pour the remaining ¼ cup broth into the same 2-quart casserole. Place the artichokes in the casserole, stem side down. Cover tightly and cook on HIGH for 8 minutes, or until heated through. Serve the artichokes with lemon wedges or hollandaise sauce.

VARIATION:

Stuffed Artichokes with Rose Sauce: Substitute cooked chopped ham, shrimp, or well-seasoned sausage for the mushrooms. Serve with Rose Sauce (page 172).

STEAMED ARTICHOKES WITH CARROT TOPPING

MAKES 4 SERVINGS   BEGIN 20 TO 30 MINUTES BEFORE SERVING
COOKING TIME: 12 TO 20 MINUTES

These are equally good served warm or chilled. If you use water in place of broth, you may wish to add ½ teaspoon salt to the cooking liquid for seasoning.

4 medium artichokes	1 medium carrot, peeled and chopped
½ lemon	¼ cup Vegetable or Chicken Broth (pages 119 or 118) or water
2 tablespoons butter	
1 garlic clove, minced	2 tablespoons chopped fresh parsley
1 medium onion, chopped	1 tablespoon lemon juice

Cut off the artichoke stems and about ¾ inches of tops. Pull off the few tough bottom leaves and, with scissors, snip off the points of the outer leaves. Rub the outsides of artichokes well with the cut side of the lemon to prevent discoloration.

In a 2-quart casserole combine the butter, garlic, onion, and carrot. Cover tightly and cook on HIGH for 3 to 5 minutes, or until the carrot is tender. Stir in the remaining ingredients except the artichokes.

Position the artichokes, cut side down, on top of the vegetables. Cover again and cook on HIGH for 9 to 15 minutes, or until the bases pierce easily, rotating the dish twice if necessary. Let stand, covered, for 5 minutes. Serve each artichoke with some of the vegetables and cooking liquid on top.

VARIATION:

Sicilian Artichokes with Tomatoes: Substitute 2 large fresh tomatoes, peeled, seeded, and coarsely chopped, or ½ cup undrained canned tomatoes, for the broth or water. Add 1 tablespoon chopped fresh basil or 1 teaspoon dried to the carrots before cooking. Sprinkle with 2 tablespoons chopped black olives right before serving.

CABBAGE FAMILY

The examples of cabbage-type plants are characterized by their distinctive flavors and the sometimes unwelcome aromas created in cooking. The best remedy for the latter is a speedy cooking process, which is just what the microwave provides. Once cooked—in a small amount of liquid, we might add—these vegetables can be taken with a firm hand and led to the table with the boldest of seasonings.

All the cabbage family have a similar crisp texture, but even that varies depending on what part of the plant each represents. The anatomy also dictates the length of time needed to cook.

The cabbage is the leaf of its plant, with savoy having a more tender leaf than the familiar red and green cabbage. Cauliflower and Brussels sprouts are examples of more tightly rolled leaves, thus taking longer to cook.

Broccoli represents both stalk and leaves, but we feel that it cooks most like a "stalk" vegetable and have included it in that section.

Kohlrabi—or "cabbage-turnip," as its German name indicates—looks like a root but is really the dense bulbous stem of this particular cabbage plant. Kohlrabi will take the longest of the group to cook.

CABBAGE FAMILY DONENESS

Cooking doneness is determined by piercing the thickest part of the stalk with a knife, or in the case of shredded cabbage, piercing or biting the leaves. Everyone seems to have their own idea of how done is done. Before standing time, the knife should pierce this area easily but the stalk should still hold its shape well. If you like it crisper than this, the stalk should give more resistance to the knife.

We find that standing time is only necessary for the large whole vegetables (cabbage or cauliflower) or large wedges where heat must continue more to the center. Shredded cabbage doesn't require this.

Underdone: Rearrange or stir the vegetable and make sure that you still have enough liquid. Cover the dish and cook on HIGH for 1-minute intervals, stirring each time if possible. If you find that you can't get your cabbage tender enough, try adding just a bit more water at the beginning of cooking next time.

Overdone: Overcooking is highly unlikely, unless there is not enough cooking liquid, which will produce a dry and smelly vegetable—especially in the case of Brussels sprouts. At this point they are probably good for starting a compost heap.

Toppings for Cabbage Family

Add any of these to 4 servings or 2 cups cooked cabbage or other cabbage-type vegetable (drain if cooked with water).

Nutmeg-Scented White Sauce: Make Nutmeg-Scented Cream Sauce (page 398) with the remaining cooking liquid. Stir into or pour over the vegetable.

Cheese Sauce: Make Nutmeg-Scented Cream Sauce (page 398), eliminating the nutmeg. Stir ¼ cup grated cheddar, American, or Parmesan cheese into the sauce to melt. Stir into or pour over the vegetables. Sprinkle with ¼ cup fine dry bread crumbs.

Cheese-Topped: Sprinkle with ¼ cup grated cheese.

Crunchy: Stir ¼ cup sliced water chestnuts into the cooked vegetable.

Tangy: Add 1 tablespoon vinegar or lemon juice.

Bacon-Topped: Sprinkle with ¼ cup crisp crumbled bacon pieces (see page 61).

(Continued)

Butters: To ¼ cup melted butter, add one of the following; pour over or stir into the cabbage-type vegetables:

- ¼ cup dry bread crumbs
- 2 tablespoons chopped fresh basil, chives, parsley, marjoram, or savory
- 2 tablespoons lemon juice
- 1 tablespoon vinegar
- ¼ cup diced cooked ham
- ¼ cup chopped nuts
- 1 teaspoon caraway seeds
- ½ cup sliced, cooked smoked sausage, franks, kielbasa, or smoky links
- 1 tablespoon curry powder
- ½ cup plain yogurt or sour cream

NUTMEG-SCENTED CREAM SAUCE FOR CABBAGE FAMILY

MAKES ABOUT ½ CUP
COOKING TIME: 2 TO 5 MINUTES

Pour over the cooked vegetable, stirring to coat.

- **1 tablespoon butter**
- **1½ teaspoons all-purpose flour**
- **Cooking liquid from 2 cups cooked cabbage vegetable**
- **Milk**
- **¼ teaspoon grated nutmeg**
- **⅛ teaspoon salt**
- **⅛ teaspoon pepper**

Place the butter in a 2-cup glass measure. Cook on HIGH for 35 seconds to 1 minute, or until melted. Stir in the flour to make a smooth paste. Add the vegetable cooking liquid; then add enough milk to the mixture to measure ½ cup. Add the nutmeg, salt, and pepper. Cook on HIGH for 1½ to 3½ minutes, or until boiling and lightly thickened, stirring after 1 minute. Correct the seasonings.

VARIATION:

Cream Sauce with Onion and Nutmeg: Add 1 garlic clove, minced, and 2 tablespoons chopped onion to the butter. Cook on HIGH for 1 to 2 minutes, or until the onion is tender.

Cauliflower Basics:

1. By removing the core of the cauliflower, you are creating an open center, which forms the doughnut shape or ring that is best for even cooking. The cauliflower will cook more evenly when this dense center is removed.
2. A tight cover is essential to keep in the cauliflower's moisture for steaming; the

cauliflower will provide its own moisture for cooking when it is completely encased with plastic wrap. If you choose not to cover it in this way, place it in a casserole dish with 2 tablespoons water and cover tightly.
3. If salt is to be added, sprinkle on at the end of cooking or dissolve the salt into the cooking liquid first. Salt on vegetable surfaces may cause the surface to become tough and overcooked.
4. During standing time, a sauce or one of the toppings on page 397 can be made.

✻ IMPERIAL CAULIFLOWER

MAKES 6 SERVINGS   BEGIN 15 MINUTES BEFORE SERVING
COOKING TIME: 6 TO 9 MINUTES

Cauliflower makes a majestic entrance when we crown it with a bread crumb topping and bring it to the table on an antique ceramic pedestal. Everyone serves themselves, by cutting the cauliflower into wedges.

- 1 1-pound head of cauliflower, core removed
- 2 tablespoons water (optional)
- ¼ cup butter
- ¼ cup fine dry bread crumbs
- 2 tablespoons chopped fresh parsley
- 1 tablespoon lemon juice

Wrap the cauliflower tightly in plastic wrap and place on a microwaveproof serving plate for ease of handling. Or place cauliflower in a 2-quart casserole with the water, covering tightly. Cook on HIGH for 6 to 9 minutes, or until tender when pierced. Let stand, covered, for 3 minutes.

Meanwhile, combine the remaining ingredients in a 1-cup glass measure. Cook on HIGH for 1 to 2 minutes, or until the butter is melted. Place the whole cauliflower on serving dish and spoon butter on top. Cut into wedges and serve.

MEXICAN CAULIFLOWER OR BROCCOLI SALAD

MAKES 4 TO 6 SERVINGS

- 2 cups cooked cauliflower or broccoli flowerets
- ½ cup Herb Vinaigrette (page 185)
- 2 tablespoons chopped fresh parsley
- ¼ cup sliced black olives

In a medium mixing bowl combine the cauliflower and vinaigrette. Chill for 1 hour. Toss with the parsley and olives before serving.

SAUTÉED SHREDDED CABBAGE

MAKES 4 SERVINGS   BEGIN 25 MINUTES BEFORE SERVING
COOKING TIME: 8 TO 15 MINUTES

- 2 tablespoons butter, margarine, or vegetable oil
- 1 garlic clove, minced (optional)
- 1 medium onion, finely chopped
- 5 cups shredded cabbage (about 1 pound)
- ½ teaspoon salt
- ¼ teaspoon pepper

In a 2-quart casserole combine the butter or oil, garlic, and onion. Cook on HIGH for 1 to 2 minutes, or until the onion is tender. Stir in the remaining ingredients. Cover tightly and cook on HIGH for 7 to 13 minutes, or until tender, stirring once halfway through cooking. Let stand, covered, for 3 minutes.

VARIATIONS:

Sautéed Cabbage with Bacon: Substitute 2 slices of bacon, cut into ½-inch pieces, for the butter.

Sautéed Cabbage with Sparkle: Add 1 tablespoon lemon juice or 2 tablespoons sherry with the cabbage.

Sautéed Cabbage and Apple: Add 1 tart apple, thinly sliced, with the cabbage.

BRAISED SWEET AND SOUR RED CABBAGE

MAKES 8 TO 10 SERVINGS   BEGIN ABOUT 1¼ HOURS BEFORE SERVING
COOKING TIME: 42 TO 53 MINUTES

When we cook this we usually prepare a large amount, because we like it better left over, or we freeze some for eating at a later date. We especially like to serve it with game or smoked sausages. In this recipe, the power changes from HIGH to MEDIUM, to bring up the temperature quickly first, then slow-cook to develop the flavors.

- 2 tablespoons butter, or 2 slices of bacon, cut into ½-inch pieces
- 1 medium onion, chopped
- 1 2-pound head of red cabbage, grated
- 2 medium tart apples, unpeeled, cored, and thinly sliced
- ½ cup dry red wine
- 2 tablespoons red wine vinegar
- 2 tablespoons white or brown sugar
- 1 teaspoon caraway seeds (optional)
- 1 teaspoon salt
- ¼ teaspoon pepper

In a 3-quart casserole combine the butter or bacon and the onion. Cook on HIGH for 2 to 3 minutes, or until the onion is tender. Stir in the remaining ingredients. Cover tightly and cook on HIGH for 10 minutes; stir. Cover again and cook on MEDIUM for 30 to 40 minutes more, or until the cabbage is tender and the flavors are well blended. Let stand for 5 minutes before serving.

Stuffed Cabbage Basics (Whole or Leaves):

1. Blanching the leaves on HIGH in the beginning makes them more supple and easier to remove from the heads (in the case of stuffed cabbage leaves) and mold around stuffing.
2. Any uncooked meat filling may be used because the recipe's cooking time is long enough for the stuffing to cook through. When rice is added, it must be cooked first because not enough liquid can be added in a stuffing to rehydrate it properly.
3. Between ½ and 1 cup liquid is added to the whole stuffed cabbage head or stuffed leaves. The more surface area exposed, the more liquid is added.
4. The stuffed cabbage begins to cook on HIGH power to bring the temperature up quickly, and then on MEDIUM power to slowly develop flavor in the stuffing and cooking liquid for the sauce. MEDIUM power also prevents the outside surfaces from overcooking before the stuffing is finished.
5. A tight cover, lid, or plastic wrap retains steam, which will help both the stuffing and cabbage cook uniformly, even though they are different densities. If the cabbage is cooked in a sauce, however, the sauce is precooked uncovered first to allow some of the moisture to escape so the sauce won't be too watery and flavors will begin to concentrate and cook down.
6. Salt should be added to the cooking liquid or at the end of cooking, to prevent any vegetable surfaces that are salted directly from becoming tough or overcooked.

✹ SAUSAGE-STUFFED CABBAGE

MAKES 4 TO 6 SERVINGS BEGIN 1½ HOURS BEFORE SERVING
COOKING TIME: 57 TO 82 MINUTES

This is an attractive way to serve stuffed cabbage, because it can be cut into wedges. We prefer savoy cabbage because of the attractive curly leaves, but any cabbage will do.

- 1 2-pound head of savoy or other cabbage
- 2 tablespoons water
- 1 pound bulk sausage
- 1 cup fresh bread crumbs
- 1 egg, beaten
- ½ cup Chicken or Mock Brown Broth or Stock (pages 118 or 119)
- 2 tablespoons tomato paste
- ½ teaspoon dried thyme
- ¼ teaspoon freshly ground black pepper

Trim the stem of the cabbage to form a flat bottom; remove any discolored outer leaves. Place the cabbage in a 3-quart casserole with lid and add the water. Cover tightly with the lid and cook on HIGH for 5 to 8 minutes, or until the outer leaves just become supple. Run cold water over the cabbage to cool enough to handle. Gently pull back the outer leaves and spread apart and out flat. Remove the firm heart of the inner leaves from the stem, leaving the outer leaves 2 or 3 layers thick attached.

Chop the inner leaves fine to make about 2 cups. In a medium mixing bowl combine the chopped leaves, sausage, bread crumbs, and egg to form a stuffing. Stuff the mixture into the hollow center of the cabbage, molding the mixture into a ball. Detach 1 or 2 outer leaves and press over the stuffing to cover and keep the stuffing in place. Fold back the remaining outer leaves, giving the cabbage its original shape.

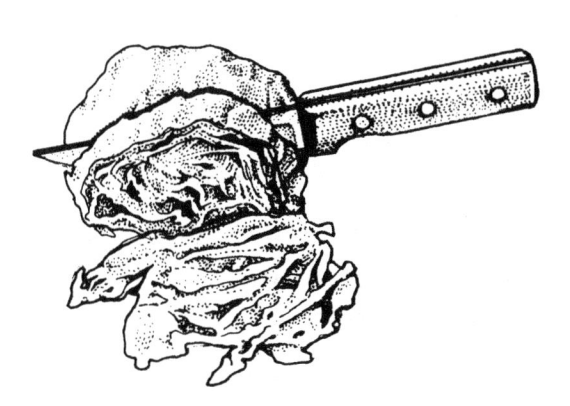

Fasten the top outer leaves together with about 4 toothpicks. Place the cabbage, top side down, in a 3-quart casserole. Add the broth. Cover tightly and cook on HIGH for 10 minutes. Using 2 forks, gently turn the cabbage over. Cover again and cook on MEDIUM for 40 minutes to 1 hour, or until the stuffing is cooked through. Remove from the cooking dish and transfer to a serving platter. Let stand, covered, for 5 to 10 minutes.

Add the tomato paste, thyme, and pepper to the cooking liquid in the casserole; stir. Cook on HIGH for 2 to 4 minutes, or until slightly thickened.

To serve, cut the cabbage into wedges and spoon the sauce over each wedge.

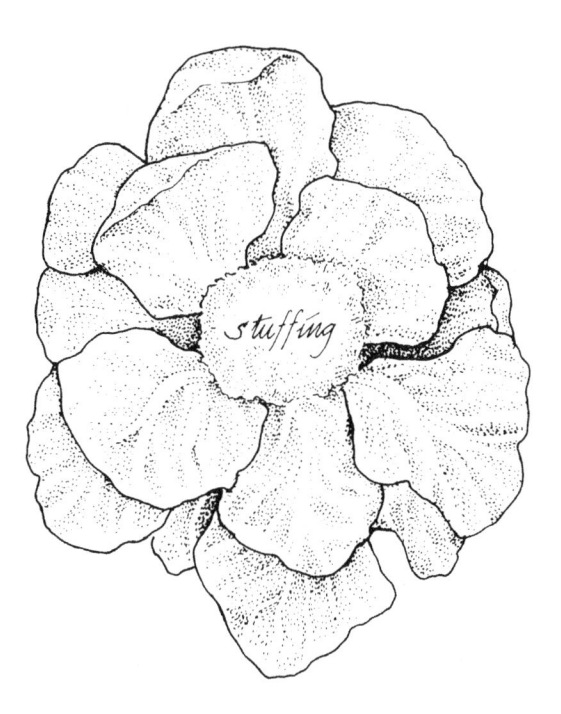

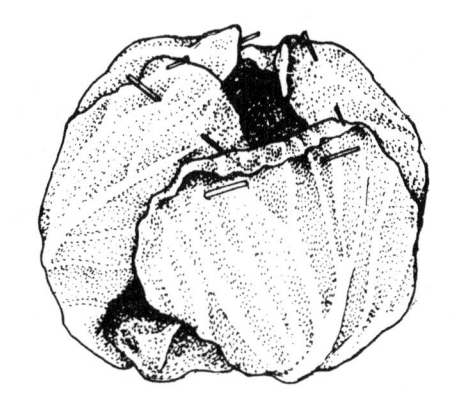

STUFFED CABBAGE LEAVES

MAKES 8 TO 10 SERVINGS   BEGIN 2½ HOURS BEFORE SERVING
COOKING TIME: 1 HOUR 22 MINUTES TO 1 HOUR 46 MINUTES

The cooking time may seem long, but it beats the conventional time by more than half, and many of the steps are simplified by using the microwave. These are very good reheated a few days later, so we always hope for leftovers.

- 1 2-pound head of cabbage
- 2 tablespoons water (optional), plus ½ cup
- ¼ cup uncooked long-grain rice (see Notes)
- 5 slices of bacon, cut into ½-inch pieces
- 2 medium onions, coarsely chopped
- 2 garlic cloves, minced (optional)
- 1½ pounds lean ground beef (see Notes)
- 2 eggs, slightly beaten
- 1 teaspoon salt
- ½ teaspoon pepper
- ¼ cup chopped fresh parsley, or 1 tablespoon dried
- 1 28-ounce can whole tomatoes
- 2 sprigs fresh thyme, or ½ teaspoon dried
- 1 cup beef broth (see Mock Brown Broth or Stock, page 119) or red wine

With a sharp knife, remove about a 2-inch cone containing the core from the cabbage. Cover the cabbage tightly with plastic wrap, or combine with the 2 tablespoons water in a 3-quart casserole, covering tightly. Cook on HIGH for 5 to 8 minutes to blanch the leaves. Plunge the head into cold water. Detach 24 large leaves (2 small ones can be counted as 1), trying not to break any. Set aside. Reserve the center of the cabbage for use in stuffing.

Place the ½ cup water in a 4-cup glass measure. Cover tightly and cook on HIGH for 1½ to 2 minutes, or until boiling. Add the rice, cover again, and cook on MEDIUM for 6 to 8 minutes, or until most of the water has been absorbed. Let stand, covered, for 8 minutes; the remaining water will be absorbed in this time.

In a 3- to 4-quart casserole combine 3 slices of the bacon, 1 chopped onion, and the garlic. Cover tightly and cook on HIGH for 2 to 3 minutes, or until the bacon is partially cooked and the onion is tender.

Meanwhile, finely chop the center of the cabbage. Add to the bacon-onion mixture. Cover again and cook on HIGH for 5 to 8 minutes, or until the cabbage is tender, stirring once. Add the cooked rice, ground beef, eggs, ½ teaspoon salt, and ¼ teaspoon pepper, and parsley. Drain the liquid from the canned tomatoes and add the liquid to the meat-rice mixture. Set the tomatoes aside for later.

Taking the blanched cabbage leaves, cut away the thick central ribs with a sharp knife; this will make rolling easier. Place about ¼ cup stuffing in each leaf. Roll each leaf from the stem and tuck in the sides to make a neat package; secure with a toothpick.

In the same casserole combine the remaining 2 strips of bacon and 1 chopped onion. Cook, uncovered, on HIGH for 2 minutes. Stir in the tomatoes, breaking them up with a fork. Add the remaining ½ teaspoon salt, ¼ teaspoon pepper, and thyme. Cook, uncovered, on HIGH for 5 minutes; stir.

Arrange the cabbage rolls in the casserole, positioning the larger rolls around the outside and the smaller rolls in the center. Pour in the broth or wine. Cover tightly and cook on HIGH for 10 minutes; then cook on MEDIUM for 45 minutes to 1 hour, or until the leaves are tender, pushing the rolls under the sauce if necessary. Let stand, covered, for 10 minutes before serving.

NOTES: Quick-cooking rice can be substituted for long-grain rice, but increase to ½ cup.

Instead of all beef, a mixture of ½ pound *each* beef, pork, and veal can be used.

VARIATIONS:

Sweet and Sour Stuffed Cabbage Leaves: Add 2 tablespoons lemon juice or vinegar and 3 tablespoons brown sugar to the tomatoes in the sauce. A favorite.

Petite Stuffed Cabbages: Place a double thickness of cheesecloth or reusable rayon-fiber cloth about 13 × 12 inches on a plate. Lay 2 drained cabbage leaves on top of one another, rib side down. Spoon about ½ cup stuffing into the center of the leaves. Pull the four corners of the cloth up around the cabbage leaves and twist the cloth tightly until the leaves are formed into a compact cabbage shape. Place the cabbage rolls seam side down into the casserole following basic recipe. Makes 12. Nice for entertaining.

KOHLRABI KÜCHEN REZEPT

MAKES 4 TO 6 SERVINGS   BEGIN 25 MINUTES BEFORE SERVING
COOKING TIME: 9 TO 14 MINUTES

Thelma's European family always served kohlrabi with the traditional Nutmeg-Scented Cream Sauce (page 398), but since we have been experimenting with this vegetable, her family now enjoys this flavorful and quick version in the microwave.

- 2 pounds kohlrabi (see Note)
- 3 tablespoons butter
- 1 garlic clove, minced
- ½ cup plain yogurt or sour cream
- 2 tablespoons chopped fresh parsley
- 1 tablespoon chopped fresh chives or scallions
- ¼ teaspoon salt or to taste
- ⅛ teaspoon pepper
- ⅛ teaspoon grated nutmeg

Peel the kohlrabi and cut in half, then into ⅛-inch slices.

In a 2-quart casserole combine the butter and garlic. Cook on HIGH for 1 to 2 minutes, or until the butter is melted and the garlic is tender. Stir in the sliced kohlrabi. Cover tightly and cook on HIGH for 8 to 12 minutes, or until desired doneness is reached. Stir in the remaining ingredients to coat. Cover again and let stand for 2 to 3 minutes before serving.

NOTE: This recipe can also be made with jicama.

VARIATION:

Jicama in Lime-Sparked Cream Sauce: Substitute jicama for kohlrabi, and peel before slicing. Use plain yogurt and add 1 tablespoon lime juice.

BRUSSELS SPROUTS IN LETTUCE LEAVES

MAKES 4 SERVINGS   BEGIN 15 TO 20 MINUTES BEFORE SERVING
COOKING TIME: 6 TO 10 MINUTES

Here is an edible papillote—lettuce leaves supplant the usual paper wrapping. Be sure not to overcook Brussels sprouts, as the flavor can become overpowering. For best flavor results, the center of the sprout should be tender-crisp; cutting an X in the core will speed cooking.

1 1-pound head of iceberg lettuce	Pepper
1 pound Brussels sprouts	4 lime or lemon wedges
4 tablespoons butter	Pinch of grated nutmeg
Salt	(optional)

Remove the core of the lettuce. Place the lettuce head in a 2-quart casserole. Cover tightly and cook on HIGH for 2 minutes to blanch the outer leaves. Remove 8 outer leaves, trying not to tear them. Place the 4 largest leaves around the outside edge of a 10-inch cooking dish.

Trim the Brussels sprouts; cut an X on the bottom of each. Divide the sprouts into 4 groups and place each group in the hollow of one of the lettuce leaves in the dish. Place 1 tablespoon butter on top of each cluster of sprouts. Sprinkle with salt and pepper. Top with a lime or lemon wedge. Sprinkle with nutmeg.

Place the remaining 4 smaller leaves on top of the sprouts and tuck inside the larger leaves to make a neat package. Cover tightly and cook on HIGH for 4 to 8 minutes or until the sprouts are tender-crisp in the centers; pierce one of the packages with a knife to check. Let stand, covered, for 3 minutes.

To serve, place a packet on each plate. Remove the top lettuce leaf and let everyone squeeze the lime or lemon over the sprouts.

VARIATION:

Brussels Sprouts in Lettuce Leaves with Caraway: Substitute 1 teaspoon caraway seeds for the nutmeg.

CORN, PEAS, GREEN BEANS, LIMA BEANS, AND FAVA (BROAD) BEANS

This category encompasses edible pods and seeds. All the pods and seeds are best when they are eaten as close to harvesting as possible. This is the only insurance that their sugars have not yet turned to starch. If need be, green beans and peas can be refrigerated for up to two days.

Unlike a green bean, the only edible part of a lima or fava bean is its seed. The pods are always discarded. Limas and mature fava beans are higher in starch content than green or wax beans. Their cooking method is closer to that of dry beans where a lower power setting and more water are needed to cook and tenderize the beans after they are brought to a boil. Immature fava beans are small and cooked according to the instructions for peas.

Blanching Fresh Vegetables

Blanching is a partial cooking technique applied to young vegetables, high in cellulose, to preserve their peak flavor, by destroying enzymes that would cause them to become mushy after thawing. It is easy to tell when green vegetables have been blanched sufficiently because their color becomes bright green. Immediately after cooking, they should be plunged into ice water to arrest further cooking. After this they can be dried off and frozen in plastic bags or boxes. When freezing 4 cups vegetables, spread them out on a cookie sheet until frozen before bagging them, to prevent them from sticking together.

Vegetables are blanched in large casseroles with larger than normal quantities of water because they will cook slower, and the doneness can be more easily controlled. The larger casserole is high enough to prevent boilover.

Small amounts of vegetables can be quickly blanched in the microwave in preparation for freezing. We don't recommend larger amounts than suggested here because it is impractical for timing and other reasons, but for picking small amounts at their peak, this process is a real find.

Cook the following vegetables in a 3-quart casserole with 1 cup water, covering tightly. cooked, plunge into ice water.

VEGETABLE	COOKING TIME
2 cups cut-up asparagus	HIGH 3 to 5 minutes; stir once.
4 cups cut-up broccoli	HIGH 4 to 5½ minutes; stir once.
2 to 2½ cups Brussels sprouts	HIGH 4 to 5 minutes; stir once.
2 cups carrots, cut into ⅛- to ¼-inch slices	HIGH 4½ to 6 minutes; stir once.
2 cups cauliflowerets	HIGH 4 to 4½ minutes; stir once.
2 cups green or wax beans, cut into 1½-inch pieces	HIGH 5 to 6 minutes; stir once.
2 cups green peas	HIGH 4 to 5 minutes; stir once.
2 cups lima beans	HIGH 3½ to 5 minutes; stir once.
2 cups sliced zucchini	HIGH 3½ to 4 minutes; stir once.

> **Toppings for Corn, Peas, Green Beans, Lima Beans, and Fava Beans**
>
> Add any of these to 4 servings or 2 cups cooked corn, peas, or beans (drained if cooked with water).
>
> **Buttered Bread Crumbs:** Combine 2 tablespoons melted butter and ¼ cup fine dry bread crumbs. Sprinkle on top.
>
> **Bacon-Topped:** Sprinkle with ¼ cup crisp, crumbled bacon (see page 61).
>
> **Butter-Nut-Topped:** Combine 2 tablespoons melted butter with ¼ cup slivered almonds, whole pine nuts, or chopped cashews. Sprinkle on top.
>
> **Au Citron:** Combine 2 tablespoons melted butter with 1 tablespoon lemon juice. Stir into the vegetable.
>
> **Fines Herbes:** Stir 2 tablespoons chopped fresh basil, summer savory, or tarragon into the vegetable.
>
> **With Mushrooms:** Stir ½ cup fresh mushrooms cooked in 1 tablespoon butter (see page 72) into the vegetable.
>
> **Parmesan:** Sprinkle ¼ cup grated Parmesan cheese on top of the vegetable.
>
> **Mustard Oil:** Combine 1 tablespoon Dijon mustard, 1 tablespoon lemon juice, and ¼ cup olive oil. Stir into the vegetable.
>
> **Herb Butter:** Combine ¼ cup melted butter with 2 to 4 tablespoons chopped fresh chives, rosemary, dill, mint, or thyme. Drizzle on top.

Corn Basics:

1. Corn kernels cook very evenly because of the uniform round shape of the kernels. Stirring once is sufficient to redistribute heat. Cook with added moisture as recommended in each recipe or on the chart to produce tenderizing steam.
2. Frozen corn kernels can be substituted for fresh in recipes if they have been defrosted to remove some of the ice crystals. To do this, cover tightly and cook on HIGH for 1 to 2 minutes, only until the ice is melted, stirring once or twice. Be sure to drain before using.
3. Corn on the cob can be cooked in its natural husk or wrapped in wax paper; no additional liquid is necessary because they produce their own steam. If the corn is removed from the husk, and not individually wrapped, it should be cooked with liquid in a covered dish (see chart, page 69).
4. Salt, if added, should be dissolved into a cooking liquid or sprinkled on at the end to prevent the vegetable surface from toughening.
5. Corn on the cob needs some standing time, unlike individual kernels.
6. *Doneness:* Kernels of corn, when cooked off the cob, are ready to serve when they come from the oven. They will be fork tender but slightly chewy. We don't mention the standing time because it will be about the time it takes to get to the table. Corn on the cob, on the other hand, would be so hot that you could barely hold it. The kernels should be slightly resistant when pressed with the fingers, and these will become more tender during a longer and necessary standing time.

Underdone: If after standing time, the ears of corn are still too firm for your taste, rearrange the ears and re-cover. Cook on HIGH at 30-second intervals.

Overdone or Overmature: Has a dry, crinkly appearance. Make into Corn Pudding Jalapeño with Salsa (recipe below).

CORN PUDDING WITH JALAPEÑO SALSA

MAKES 6 TO 8 SERVINGS   BEGIN 30 MINUTES BEFORE SERVING
COOKING TIME: 7 TO 13 MINUTES

This started out as a recipe for leftover corn and then was elevated into one of our favorite dishes; it makes a great companion to lobster, crab, or any fish, or brunch with sausages. It is, of course, best when made with fresh corn, but canned or frozen corn can also be used. After one stirring, it is cooked on MEDIUM power because of the egg-custard mixture it contains.

We've added cornmeal for extra body so it will come out beautifully in the microwave. Be sure to use a large casserole, to prevent boilover.

½ cup butter	1½ cups cooked corn
2 cups milk	½ teaspoon baking powder
½ cup yellow cornmeal	2 to 4 drops hot pepper sauce
1 tablespoon sugar	1 green or sweet red pepper, cut into ¼-inch squares
½ teaspoon salt	Warm Jalapeño Salsa (page 187) (optional)
¼ teaspoon pepper	
4 eggs, beaten	

Place the butter in a 2-cup glass measure. Cook on HIGH for 1 to 2 minutes to melt. Set aside.

In a 3-quart casserole combine the milk, cornmeal, sugar, salt, and pepper. Cover tightly and cook on HIGH for 4 to 8 minutes, or until the mixture is boiling and the cornmeal has absorbed most of the liquid and it is fairly thick, stirring twice. Let stand for 5 minutes.

Meanwhile, in a small mixing bowl combine the eggs, corn, baking powder, hot pepper sauce and sweet pepper. Fold into the cornmeal mixture. Stir in the melted butter. Pour into a 2-quart casserole. Cook uncovered on HIGH for 6 minutes, stirring halfway through cooking and smoothing the top surface at the end. Cook on MEDIUM for 3 to 5 minutes, or until set and a knife inserted in the center comes out clean. Let stand for 5 minutes before serving.

Serve with the salsa, if desired.

CORN AND PEPPER HASH

MAKES 4 SERVINGS   BEGIN 10 MINUTES BEFORE SERVING
COOKING TIME: 4 TO 7 MINUTES

We like to present this as a summer side dish when company comes—corn on the cob might prove messy.

- 2 tablespoons butter
- 1 medium onion, chopped
- 1 green or sweet red pepper, diced
- 2 cups cooked corn kernels (see Note)
- ¼ teaspoon salt
- ¼ teaspoon pepper

In a 2-quart casserole combine the butter, onion, and green or red pepper. Cover tightly and cook on HIGH for 2 to 4 minutes, or until the onion and pepper are tender. Stir in the remaining ingredients. Cover tightly and cook on HIGH for 2 to 3 minutes, until heated through.

NOTE: Frozen corn kernels may be substituted for cooked fresh corn. See Corn Basics, page 408.

VARIATION:

Southwest Corn and Pepper Hash: Add ¼ teaspoon ground cumin with the salt and pepper. Adds a great taste.

SUCCOTASH

MAKES 4 SERVINGS
COOKING TIME: 2 TO 5 MINUTES

Succotash is just cooked corn and lima beans heated through with some herbs and butter, but it is a colorful way to serve these leftover vegetables.

- 1 cup cooked corn kernels
- 1 cup cooked lima beans
- 1 tablespoon butter
- 2 teaspoons chopped fresh parsley, or ½ teaspoon dried
- Salt and pepper to taste
- Pinch of paprika

In a 1-quart casserole combine all the ingredients. Cover tightly and heat on HIGH for 2 to 5 minutes, or until heated through, stirring once.

Green Peas Basics:

1. Peas should be cooked on HIGH power and covered tightly to retain steam, using a lid or plastic wrap turned back on one corner.
2. Peas cook very evenly because of their uniform round shape. Stirring once is sufficient to redistribute heat.
3. An additional moisture-producing ingredient must be combined with peas to make the tenderizing steam for cooking.
4. Frozen peas can be substituted for fresh in recipes if they have been defrosted to remove some of the ice crystals. To do this, cover tightly and cook on HIGH for 1 to 2 minutes, only until the ice is melted, stirring once or twice. Be sure to drain before using.
5. Peas are often cooked in combination with other vegetables. Carrots, when cut into small pieces, have the same cooking time as peas and can be cooked at the same time. Snow peas have a shorter cooking time, and are therefore added toward the end of cooking.
6. Salt, if added, should be dissolved into a cooking liquid or sprinkled on at the end to prevent the peas from toughening.
7. No more standing time than is necessary to bring peas to the table is required.
8. *Doneness:* Cook until bright green and fork tender from the oven. Stirring during cooking is essential to even cooking.

    Underdone: Try not to mistake overmature green peas (and accompanying toughness) with undercooking. Continue to cook underdone peas on HIGH in 1-minute intervals, stirring each time.

    Overdone: Be careful not to overcook these tender peas. Overcooked peas will become slightly crinkled. Peas will have lost their bright color. They may either become mushy, in which case you can drain and puree with butter or broth, or if they haven't been covered and stirred, peas will get very hard and dry. Add the latter to your compost heap or use as ammunition for your pea shooter.

PEAS DE MENTHE

MAKES 4 SERVINGS   BEGIN 15 MINUTES BEFORE SERVING
COOKING TIME: 5 TO 9 MINUTES

---

2 tablespoons butter
2 tablespoons chopped scallions

2 cups shelled fresh peas or frozen, broken up
1 tablespoon crème de menthe

In a 1½-quart casserole combine the butter and scallions. Cook on HIGH for 1 to 2 minutes, or until tender. Stir in the peas and crème de menthe. Cover tightly and cook on HIGH for 4 to 7 minutes, or until desired doneness is reached, stirring once (or more often if the peas are frozen before cooking).

PEAS AND CARROTS

MAKES 4 SERVINGS BEGIN 15 MINUTES BEFORE SERVING
COOKING TIME: 5 TO 9 MINUTES

We like the idea of combining different flavors, colors, and textures, as in this and the following vegetable combinations.

- 1 tablespoon butter
- 2 tablespoons finely chopped onion or scallion
- 1 cup shelled fresh peas or frozen, broken up
- 1 cup thinly sliced or diced carrots
- 2 tablespoons chopped fresh mint, or 2 teaspoons dried (optional)

In a 1½-quart casserole combine the butter and onion. Cook on HIGH for 1 to 2 minutes, or until the onion is tender. Stir in the peas and carrots. Cover tightly and cook on HIGH for 4 to 7 minutes, or until desired doneness is reached, stirring once. Stir in the mint, if desired.

PEAS AND SNOW PEAS

MAKES 4 SERVINGS BEGIN 15 MINUTES BEFORE SERVING
COOKING TIME: 5 TO 8 MINUTES

- 2 tablespoons butter, margarine, or vegetable oil
- ¼ cup sliced scallions
- 1 cup shelled fresh peas or frozen, broken up
- ¼ pound snow peas, trimmed and cut into 1-inch diagonals

In a 1-quart casserole combine the butter and scallions. Cook on HIGH for 1 to 2 minutes, or until tender. Stir in the peas. Cover tightly and cook on HIGH for 2 minutes. Stir in the snow peas. Cover tightly and cook on HIGH for 2 to 4 minutes, or until the snow peas are tender-crisp.

Green Bean Basics:

1. A pound of green beans are cooked with ½ cup liquid if cut up, or ⅓ cup if just trimmed; these amounts are critical to success. More cooking liquid is needed if more surface area is exposed. The liquid can be either water, broth, or stewed tomatoes. Green beans actually cook better when cut up.
2. Green beans are cooked on HIGH and covered tightly with a lid or plastic wrap turned back on one corner to hold in the steam.
3. Stirring twice is very important for even cooking, to distribute evenly the heat that builds up on the vegetables on the outside of the cooking dish.
4. Make sure to dissolve the salt into a cooking liquid or add it at the end of cooking so that the surfaces don't get tough and overcooked. Salt will attract microwave energy more than the water or beans.
5. Standing will allow the green beans to become even more tender; 3 to 5 minutes, with the cover on is sufficient.
6. *Doneness:* Everyone has their own preference for doneness, but we would suggest that the beans still be slightly resistant to the piercing of a fork before standing time.

   Overdoneness: Make sure that you have enough liquid and a tight cover. Stir often enough and don't try to cook too many beans at once. Beans may toughen if they are old or if they have been salted before cooking.

   Toughening of beans can occur when you try to cook more than 2 pounds. If you divide the beans and cook them in two batches, you will have better results. If you are still having trouble cooking beans to tender, cut them into smaller pieces or julienne them in half, lengthwise, to expose more surface area to the cooking liquid.

BRAISED GREEN BEANS

MAKES 4 SERVINGS   BEGIN 20 TO 25 MINUTES BEFORE SERVING
COOKING TIME: 6 TO 15 MINUTES

Chicken broth is a nice alternative to cooking with water—an easy way to flavor green beans.

- 2 tablespoons butter, margarine, or vegetable oil
- 1 garlic clove, minced (optional)
- 1 medium onion, chopped
- 1 pound green beans, cut into 2-inch pieces
- ½ cup Chicken Broth or Stock (page 118)
- 1 tablespoon chopped fresh parsley, chives, or summer savory, or 1 teaspoon dried
- Salt and pepper

In a 2-quart casserole combine the butter, garlic, and onion. Cook on HIGH for 1 to 2 minutes, or until the onion is tender. Add the beans and broth. Cover tightly and cook on HIGH for 5 to 13 minutes, stirring twice. Sprinkle with herbs, and salt and pepper to taste. Let stand covered, for 3 to 5 minutes.

GREEN BEANS NIÇOISE

MAKES 4 TO 6 SERVINGS BEGIN 25 TO 35 MINUTES BEFORE SERVING
COOKING TIME: 15 TO 21 MINUTES

The colorful combination relies for the necessary liquid on tomatoes, which are first cooked uncovered so that excess moisture is released.

- 2 tablespoons olive or vegetable oil
- 1 garlic clove, minced
- 1 onion, finely chopped
- 1 cup chopped fresh or undrained canned tomatoes
- 1 pound whole green beans, trimmed
- ½ green pepper, chopped
- 2 tablespoons chopped fresh parsley, or 2 teaspoons dried
- 1 tablespoon chopped fresh basil, or 1 teaspoon dried
- ½ teaspoon salt
- ¼ teaspoon pepper

In a 2-quart casserole combine the oil, garlic, and onion. Cook on HIGH for 2 to 3 minutes, or until the onion is tender. Add the tomatoes. Cook on HIGH for 5 minutes. Stir in the beans and green pepper. Cover tightly and cook on HIGH for 8 to 13 minutes, depending on desired doneness, stirring twice. Stir in the remaining ingredients. Let stand, covered, for 3 to 5 minutes.

STIR-SHAKE GREEN BEANS AND BEAN SPROUTS

MAKES 4 SERVINGS BEGIN 20 MINUTES BEFORE SERVING
COOKING TIME: 7 TO 12 MINUTES

For more information about "stir-shake," see page 479.

- 1 tablespoon sesame or vegetable oil
- 1 teaspoon chopped fresh ginger
- 1 garlic clove, minced
- ½ pound green beans, cut into 1-inch pieces
- 1 tablespoon dry sherry
- 1 tablespoon soy sauce
- ½ pound bean sprouts, rinsed

In a 1½-quart casserole combine the oil, ginger, and garlic. Cook on HIGH for 45 seconds to 1½ minutes, or until the garlic is tender. Add the beans and sherry. Cover tightly and cook on HIGH for 4 to 6 minutes, or until the beans are tender-crisp, shaking or stirring the casserole twice. Stir in the remaining ingredients. Cover again and cook on HIGH for 2 to 4 minutes, or until the sprouts are heated through.

Lima and Fava Bean Basics:

1. Two cups of these beans require ½ cup cooking liquid to tenderize them because they are lower in water content than other fresh beans.
2. The beans are first cooked on HIGH power to bring the water to a boil, then simmered on MEDIUM power to tenderize them slowly and prevent overcooking that would occur if they were cooked completely on HIGH.
3. A tight cover is essential for keeping in the steam necessary to tenderize the beans. A casserole lid or a microwaveproof plate are the best choices.
4. By stirring often you will equalize the heat, speed up cooking, and keep the beans on the outer edges from getting dry and overdone.
5. If salt is added, stir it into the liquid or sprinkle it on at the end of cooking to prevent the bean surfaces from toughening.
6. A short standing time completes the cooking as the heat is conducted to the center of the beans.
7. *Doneness:* The beans will hold their shape but are tender to the bite. Check the larger beans for doneness first.

   Underdone: The beans will still be very firm and not at all tender when speared with a fork. Stir and continue cooking on MEDIUM for 2-minute intervals, stirring after each, and adding a little more hot water if the beans don't seem to be getting tender.

   Overdone: The edges on some of the beans will be dry and hard. This could occur if the cover wasn't tight enough, if the beans weren't stirred, or if the power wasn't lowered to MEDIUM. There's no salvation for these beans.... Toss them.

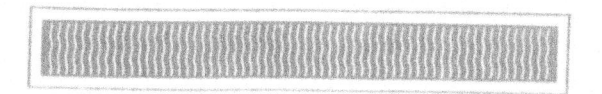

✺ STEAMED LIMA OR FAVA BEANS

MAKES 4 SERVINGS   BEGIN 25 MINUTES BEFORE SERVING
COOKING TIME: 10 TO 17 MINUTES

| 2 pounds lima or fava beans, shelled (about 2 cups) | ½ cup water |

In a 1½-quart casserole combine the beans and water. Cover tightly and cook on HIGH for 5 to 7 minutes, or until boiling; stir. Cover again and cook on MEDIUM for 5 to 10 minutes, or until the beans are tender, stirring once. Let the beans stand, covered, for 2 to 3 minutes. Drain and add any one of the toppings (page 408).

VARIATION:

Lima or Fava Beans in Herb Sauce: During standing time prepare Herb Sauce (page 171). Drain beans and combine with the sauce. Heat on HIGH for 1 to 3 minutes, or until hot, stirring once.

EGGPLANTS, TOMATOES, PEPPERS AND CUCUMBERS

Although served as vegetables, eggplants, tomatoes, peppers, and cucumbers are technically fruits. In fact, the cucumber is thought to be a close relative of the watermelon. All are available in markets year-round but are better when they're grown locally. Tomatoes, peppers, and cucumbers can be eaten raw, but eggplants will have a bitter taste and should be cooked first.

All four are warm-weather plants and respond best to storage in humid conditions at about 50°F. Refrigeration is less than ideal because it is too cool and less humid, but is also sometimes necessary to prevent decay in room temperatures that might be too warm. So for the times when you must chill them, tomatoes and cucumbers can be kept up to five days in the refrigerator, toward the front where they won't get as cold. (Remember that tomatoes won't ripen any more after refrigeration.) Peppers can be refrigerated for up to five days, and eggplants for up to two days. If the vegetables are refrigerated, try to set them out at room temperature before cooking to maximize their flavors and coincide with the cooking times we give in this book. Keep in mind, too, that canned plum tomatoes are an excellent substitute for out-of-season fresh tomatoes in a sauce or casserole.

Recipes may call for parboiled peppers or roasted eggplants. Either can be simulated in the microwave with much less toil and sweat, as shown in the chart on page 70.

Eggplant Slices Basics:

1. Cooking times vary depending on the thickness of the slice.
2. The addition of oil and a tight cover keeps in all the available steam to help soften and flavor the eggplant slices.
3. Cooking one layer at a time is necessary for the most even cooking and the best absorption of oil.
4. Eggplant has to be precooked before adding the toppings, for the most tender product.
5. Add salt at the end of cooking, unless it can be dissolved into a cooking liquid. This will prevent any salted surfaces from becoming tough and overcooked.
6. *Doneness:* Eggplant is finished cooking when its flesh is very soft and tender and can be easily pierced with a fork. Cooking to this doneness will rid the eggplant of any raw flavors, and allow it to absorb the other flavors that surround it. We find that it is a vehicle to carry other flavors to you, and should be cooked to that end.

Underdone: Make sure that there is still enough oil or juices covering the pieces, and stir or turn over the eggplant to coat generously. Continue cooking on HIGH at 1-minute intervals, stirring each time.

✺ EGGPLANT SLICES WITH TOPPINGS

MAKES 4 SERVINGS   BEGIN 15 MINUTES BEFORE SERVING
COOKING TIME: 6 TO 10 MINUTES

---

1 medium (¾ pound) eggplant, cut into 16 ¼-inch slices	**Salt and pepper**
2 tablespoons olive or vegetable oil	**Toppings (page 418)**

Brush both sides of the eggplant slices with the oil. Place 8 slices around the outer edge of a 12-inch round microwaveproof platter or a 2-quart rectangular dish. Cover tightly and cook on HIGH for 3 to 5 minutes, or until tender. Transfer the cooked slices to another dish. Repeat the procedure with the remaining slices.

After cooking the second batch, salt and pepper all the slices to taste. Serve with one of the toppings.

> ### Toppings for Eggplant Slices
>
> **Fines Herbes:** Sprinkle 2 tablespoons of a combination of chopped fresh basil, parsley, and chives onto the cooked eggplant slices.
>
> **Nutty:** Sprinkle ½ cup chopped almonds or pecans, or whole pine nuts, onto the cooked eggplant slices.
>
> **Au Citron:** Sprinkle 1 tablespoon lemon or lime juice over the cooked eggplant slices.
>
> **Tomato Sauce:** Spoon 1 cup heated tomato sauce (canned or Basic "Batch," page 178) over the cooked eggplant slices.
>
> **Quick Creamed:** Spoon ½ cup plain yogurt or sour cream on top of the cooked eggplant slices.
>
> **Bacon- or Ham-Topped:** Sprinkle ½ cup chopped cooked ham or crisp, crumbled bacon (see page 61) on top of the cooked eggplant slices.
>
> **Parmesan Bread Crumbs:** Combine 2 tablespoons melted butter with 3 tablespoons fine dry bread crumbs, 1 tablespoon chopped fresh parsley, and 1 tablespoon grated Parmesan cheese. Spoon over the cooked eggplant slices.

EGGPLANT, MOZZARELLA, AND TOMATO SANDWICHES

MAKES 4 LUNCH OR 8 SIDE-DISH SERVINGS   BEGIN 15 TO 20 MINUTES BEFORE SERVING
COOKING TIME: 8 TO 15 MINUTES

It is important to cut an even number of eggplant slices for these sandwiches. They are cooked uncovered after assembly to prevent them from getting too soggy.

- 1 medium (about ¾ pound) eggplant, cut into 16 ¼-inch slices
- 2 tablespoons olive oil
- 8 ounces mozzarella, cut into 8 slices
- 2 tablespoons chopped fresh basil, or 1 teaspoon dried
- 2 medium to large tomatoes, cut into ¼-inch slices
- Salt and pepper

Brush both sides of the eggplant slices with the oil. Place 8 slices around the outer edge of a 12-inch round or 3-quart rectangular dish. Cover tightly and cook on HIGH for 3 to 5 minutes, or until tender. Transfer to another dish. Repeat the procedure with the remaining slices.

After cooking the second batch, drain and dry the platter. Place half the cooked eggplant slices around the outer edge of the dish, leaving the center open. Top each with a cheese slice, trimming the cheese to fit the eggplant. Sprinkle with basil. Top with a tomato slice. Season lightly with salt and pepper. Top with the remaining eggplant slices. Cover with wax paper and cook on MEDIUM for 2 to 5 minutes, or until the cheese melts slightly.

Caper-Sparked Eggplant Sandwiches: Sprinkle 2 tablespoons capers or pine nuts between the cheese and tomato, dividing evenly between slices. Capers add a tart edge to perk up the tomatoes and eggplant.

CUBED EGGPLANT, TOMATO, AND PEPPERS TOPPED WITH MOZZARELLA

MAKES 4 TO 6 SERVINGS   BEGIN 20 TO 25 MINUTES BEFORE SERVING
COOKING TIME: 12 TO 15 MINUTES

Vegetable combinations that include vegetables having differing cooking times are begun by adding the vegetable with the longest cooking time first to the casserole, and the others in order of cooking time.

- 2 tablespoons olive oil
- 1 garlic clove, minced
- 1 medium onion, chopped
- 1 green pepper, cut into ½-inch squares
- 1 medium (about ¾ pound) eggplant, peeled and cut into ½-inch cubes
- 4 medium tomatoes, peeled and cut into 1-inch cubes
- 2 tablespoons chopped fresh basil, or 2 teaspoons dried
- ¼ teaspoon pepper
- 8 ounces mozzarella cheese, shredded

In a 2-quart casserole combine the oil, garlic, onion, green pepper, and eggplant. Cover tightly and cook on HIGH for 5 minutes; stir. Cover again and cook on HIGH for 2 minutes, or until the eggplant becomes tender, stirring once.

Stir in the tomatoes, basil, and pepper. Cover again and cook on HIGH for 4 to 6 minutes, or until the tomatoes are heated through, stirring once. Stir in the cheese. Cover again and cook on MEDIUM for 1 to 2 minutes, or until the cheese is melted.

VARIATION:

Vegetable-Tofu Casserole: Add 1 tofu square (about 8 ounces), cut into ½-inch cubes, with the tomatoes, using a 3-quart casserole. Follow the recipe cooking times.

Stuffed Eggplant Basics:

1. Before stuffing an eggplant, the filling should be precooked or made with ingredients that just need reheating. It is not necessary, however, to cook the eggplant shell when it is cut ¼ inch thick. Filling ingredients that tend to exude moisture, like ground meat or eggplant itself, should be precooked uncovered to evaporate some of the moisture.
2. Stuffed eggplant is generally cooked on HIGH power, unless there is cheese in the filling, because unlike stuffed peppers or tomatoes, the eggplant shell won't overcook before the filling is heated through.
3. A wax paper cover is necessary to keep some of the steam in for even cooking. If the eggplant is cheese-topped, it is added at the end and the covering is eliminated because the paper will stick to the cheese.
4. Because they can't be stirred, it is important to try to arrange the thicker-shaped part of the eggplants to the outside of the dish, where they will receive the most energy. This will help the irregularly shaped vegetable to cook through evenly.
5. Standing time allows for complete conduction of heat to the center.

STUFFED EGGPLANT IN TOMATO SAUCE

MAKES 4 SERVINGS   BEGIN 30 TO 35 MINUTES BEFORE SERVING
COOKING TIME: 17 TO 24 MINUTES

- 2 small to medium (½ to ¾ pound each) eggplants
- 2 tablespoons olive oil or butter
- 1 garlic clove, minced
- 1 medium onion, chopped
- ½ pound lean ground beef
- ¼ cup fine dry bread crumbs
- 1 tablespoon chopped fresh parsley, or 1 teaspoon dried
- 1 tablespoon chopped fresh basil, or 1 teaspoon dried
- ½ teaspoon salt
- ¼ teaspoon pepper
- 1 cup Basic "Batch" Tomato Sauce (page 178)

Wash the eggplants, remove the stems, and cut in half lengthwise. Scoop out the pulp, leaving ¼ inch of shell. Cut the flesh into ¼-inch cubes.

In a 2-quart rectangular dish combine the oil, garlic, and onion. Cook on HIGH for 1 to 2 minutes, or until the onion is tender. Stir in the eggplant cubes and ground meat. Cook on HIGH for 8 to 10 minutes, or until the meat is cooked and the eggplant is tender, stirring three times. Stir in the bread crumbs, parsley, basil, salt, and pepper; mix well.

Spoon the filling into the eggplant shells. Place the shells, thicker end toward the outside if possible, in the same dish used for the eggplant and meat. Spoon the tomato sauce over the filled eggplant halves. Cover with wax paper and cook on HIGH for 8 to 12 minutes, or until the eggplant is tender, repositioning after 4 minutes. Let stand, covered, for 3 minutes before serving.

VARIATIONS:

Stuffed Nutty Eggplant: Add 2 tablespoons pine nuts or chopped almonds to the filling with the bread crumbs.

Stuffed Eggplant au Gratin: After cooking the eggplant in sauce, top with ½ cup shredded mozzarella cheese at the end of cooking time. Cook, uncovered, on MEDIUM for 2 to 4 minutes, or until the cheese is melted.

Stuffed Eggplant a la Leftovers: Substitute 1½ cups chopped cooked ham or chicken for the ground beef and add to the eggplant and onion after the eggplant has cooked for 5 minutes.

RATATOUILLE

MAKES 4 TO 6 SERVINGS   BEGIN 25 TO 30 MINUTES BEFORE SERVING
COOKING TIME: 12 TO 20 MINUTES

The standing time is important here to allow the vegetables to absorb juices and develop flavor.

- 2 tablespoons olive oil
- 2 garlic cloves, minced
- 1 large onion, coarsely chopped
- 2 medium (½ pound each) eggplants, cut into ½-inch cubes
- 1 green pepper, cut into ½-inch squares
- 2 small zucchini, cut into 1-inch sticks
- 2 tablespoons chopped fresh basil, or 2 teaspoons dried
- 1 pound ripe tomatoes, peeled, seeded, and cut into 1-inch cubes
- ½ teaspoon salt
- ¼ teaspoon pepper
- 2 tablespoons chopped fresh parsley

In a 2-quart casserole combine the oil, garlic, and onion. Cover tightly and cook on HIGH for 3 to 5 minutes, or until the onion is tender. Stir in the eggplant and green pepper. Cover tightly and cook on HIGH for 5 to 7 minutes, or until tender-crisp, stirring after 3 minutes.

Stir in the remaining ingredients. Cover again and cook on HIGH for 4 to 8 minutes, or until the zucchini is tender-crisp, stirring after 3 minutes. Let stand, covered, for 5 minutes.

VARIATIONS:

Ratatouille alla Parmigiana: Right before serving, sprinkle the ratatouille with ¼ cup grated Parmesan cheese.

Eggplants Stuffed with Ratatouille: Before cutting eggplant cubes, cut the eggplants in half lengthwise. Carefully scoop out the flesh, leaving ¼ inch of shell. Proceed with basic recipe. After standing time, divide the mixture between the 4 eggplant shells. Top with 4 ounces Gruyère, Swiss, or mozzarella cheese, thinly sliced, dividing evenly between eggplants. Position around the outside of a 12-inch round microwaveproof plate or 2-quart rectangular dish, leaving the center open. Cook, uncovered, on MEDIUM for 3 to 6 minutes, or until the cheese is melted. This makes a nice appetizer when you substitute 4 small eggplants, about ¼ pound each, for the 2 eggplants called for in the basic recipe.

☼ FRAGRANT WHOLE TOMATOES

MAKES 4 SERVINGS   BEGIN 10 MINUTES BEFORE SERVING
COOKING TIME: 3 TO 6 MINUTES

When fresh ripe tomatoes are available, baked whole tomatoes are always attractive and delicious. Tomatoes have a lot of liquid and a tight cover would make them too watery; the loose cover used here retains some steam for even cooking.

4 medium (about 3-inch diameter) firm ripe tomatoes	¼ cup chopped fresh parsley
Salt and pepper	¼ cup chopped fresh chives or scallion greens
4 teaspoons butter	

Cut ½ inch from the stem end of tomatoes. If desired, remove the seeds by pressing the insides of the tomatoes with your fingers. Salt and pepper lightly. Top each tomato with 1 teaspoon butter. Sprinkle with the remaining ingredients.

Place the tomatoes in a 9-inch pie plate or microwaveproof dinner plate. Cover loosely with paper and cook on HIGH for 2½ to 5½ minutes, or until the plate on the bottom is hot to the touch or 2 Macungie (see page 44), rotating once if necessary.

VARIATIONS:

Brown Sugar 'n' Bacon Tomatoes: After salting each tomato, divide 8 teaspoons brown sugar between them. Top with butter. Eliminate the chives. At the end of cooking, sprinkle the tomatoes with ¼ cup crumbled cooked bacon (see page 61). We love this served with scrambled eggs for brunch. Cook and serve each tomato in its own dish, so that when it is cut you can take advantage of all the wonderful juices.

Mediterranean Tomatoes: Eliminate the butter. Combine ¼ cup each fine dry bread crumbs, chopped fresh basil, and parsley. Divide them between the tomatoes. Eliminate the chives. Sprinkle 4 teaspoons olive oil over the tomatoes. Follow basic cooking instructions.

Onion-Topped Whole Tomatoes: After adding salt and pepper to the tomatoes, top with ¼ cup finely chopped onions, dividing evenly between the tomatoes. Top with butter and eliminate the chives.

Whole Tomatoes Scented with Oregano: Substitute 1 tablespoon chopped fresh oregano, or 1 teaspoon dried, for the parsley.

SINGLE SERVING TOMATO: Remove stem from 1 tomato. Place in custard cup and sprinkle with desired topping. Cover with wax paper and cook on HIGH for 45 seconds for 1 minute.

Toppings for Tomatoes

Add any of these to 4 servings of tomatoes or 4 cooked tomatoes.

Onion-Topped: Combine 2 tablespoons finely chopped onion with 1 teaspoon butter or water in a custard cup. Cook on HIGH for 40 seconds to 1½ minutes, or until the onion is tender. Sprinkle on top of tomatoes.

Celery-Topped: Combine ½ cup finely chopped celery with 1 teaspoon butter or water in a custard cup. Cook on HIGH for 1 to 2 minutes, or until the celery is tender. Sprinkle on top of tomatoes.

Green Pepper–Topped: Combine ¼ cup chopped green pepper and 1 teaspoon butter or water in a custard cup. Cook on HIGH for 40 seconds to 1 minute, or until tender. Sprinkle on top of tomatoes.

Brown Sugared: Stir or sprinkle 1 tablespoon brown sugar into or on top of tomatoes.

Fines Herbes: Sprinkle 1 tablespoon chopped fresh basil, parsley, or oregano, or 1 teaspoon dried, on top of tomatoes.

Bread-Crumbed: Sprinkle ½ cup flavored dry bread crumbs on top of tomatoes.

Garlic Oil: Combine 2 garlic cloves, minced, with 1 teaspoon olive oil in a custard cup. Cook on HIGH for 40 seconds to 1½ minutes, or until the garlic is tender. Stir into tomatoes.

Bacon-Topped: Sprinkle ¼ cup crumbled crisp bacon (see page 61) on top of tomatoes.

Parmesan: Sprinkle 2 tablespoons grated Parmesan cheese on top of tomatoes.

Curried: Stir ⅛ teaspoon curry powder into tomatoes.

Stuffed Tomato and Pepper Basics:

1. The filling should be precooked or made with ingredients that only need reheating before stuffing tomatoes and peppers. Use 2 to 2½ cups of any moist stuffing.
2. Pepper shells need to be partially cooked before stuffing or they will never cook enough to be finished with the stuffing.
3. For the most even cooking, stuffed tomatoes and peppers should be placed in a ring around the outside of a cooking dish.
4. Once tomatoes and peppers are stuffed, they should be cooked on MEDIUM power to allow the flavors to develop without the outer shells overcooking.
5. Because these are vegetables with a very high water content, no additional water need be added during cooking. A wax paper cover will help the vegetables to cook evenly by retaining some steam, but will not cause them to become soggy.
6. Peppers require a short standing time, whereas tomatoes don't.

✺ RICE-STUFFED TOMATOES

MAKES 4 TO 6 SERVINGS   BEGIN 25 MINUTES BEFORE SERVING
COOKING TIME: 10 TO 15 MINUTES

A recipe that is good for leftover rice and meat.

- 4 large or 6 medium tomatoes
- 4 tablespoons butter or olive oil
- 1 small onion, coarsely chopped, or 2 garlic cloves, minced
- 1 cup cooked rice (recipe follows)
- ½ cup chopped cooked ham, poultry, or roast beef
- 2 tablespoons lemon juice
- 2 tablespoons pine nuts or chopped nuts
- 2 tablespoons chopped fresh parsley or basil
- ½ teaspoon salt
- ¼ teaspoon pepper

Cut ½ inch from the stem end of the tomatoes. Scoop out the flesh and seeds, leaving the shell. Turn the tomatoes upside down and let drain for 15 minutes.

Meanwhile, in a 9-inch round pie dish or microwaveproof platter combine 2 tablespoons butter or oil and the onion or garlic. Cook on HIGH for 2 to 3 minutes, or until the onion or garlic is tender. Stir in the remaining ingredients, except the butter. Spoon the mixture into the tomatoes.

Position the tomatoes around the outer edge of the same 9-inch dish, leaving the center open. Top the tomatoes with the remaining 2 tablespoons butter, dividing evenly among them. Cover with wax paper. Cook on MEDIUM for 8 to 12 minutes, or until the bottom of the dish feels hot to the touch or *2 Macungie* (see page 44), rotating once if necessary.

VARIATIONS:

Rice-Raisin Tomatoes: Add ¼ cup raisins.

Sausage-Stuffed Tomatoes: Eliminate all the ingredients but the tomatoes. Stuff with 1½ cups highly seasoned cooked sausage meat. Follow the basic cooking instructions.

Tomatoes Stuffed with Corn and Pepper Hash: Eliminate all the ingredients but the tomatoes. Stuff with Corn and Pepper Hash (page 410). Cover with wax paper and just heat through on MEDIUM for 3 to 5 minutes.

Bacon and Egg Tomatoes: Eliminate all the ingredients but the tomatoes. Prepare 4 Scrambled Eggs (page 150). Fill the tomatoes. Top with ¼ cup crumbled bacon (see page 61). Cover with wax paper and just heat through on MEDIUM for 3 to 5 minutes.

Spinach-Stuffed Tomatoes: Eliminate all the ingredients but the tomatoes. Stuff the tomatoes with 2 cups Creamed Spinach (page 429). Cover with wax paper and just heat through on MEDIUM for 3 to 5 minutes.

COOKED RICE

MAKES 1 CUP
COOKING TIME: 9 TO 13 MINUTES

If you don't have 1 cup leftover rice in your refrigerator for these vegetable recipes, here is a recipe for 1 cup:

⅓ cup long-grain rice

⅔ cup water

In a 2-quart casserole combine the ingredients. Cover tightly and cook on HIGH for 2½ to 5 minutes, or until boiling, then cook on MEDIUM for 6 to 8 minutes, or until most of the water is absorbed. Stir and let stand, covered, for 3 minutes.

BEEF-STUFFED PEPPERS

MAKES 4 SERVINGS   BEGIN 25 TO 30 MINUTES BEFORE SERVING
COOKING TIME: 17 TO 27 MINUTES

4 medium green peppers
2 tablespoons water
1 pound lean ground beef
1 medium onion, finely chopped
1 cup cooked rice (recipe above)
½ teaspoon salt
¼ teaspoon pepper
2 cups canned or Basic "Batch" Tomato Sauce (page 178)

Cut ½ inch from the stem end of the peppers and set the ends aside for later. Remove the ribs and seeds from the peppers. In a 2-quart rectangular dish place the peppers cut side down in the 2 tablespoons water. Cover tightly and cook on HIGH for 2 to 4 minutes, or until tender-crisp. Remove the peppers from the dish and allow to cool and drain while preparing the filling.

Meanwhile, remove the stems from the ends that were set aside. Coarsely chop the small ends of the peppers; set aside for later.

In the dish used to cook the peppers, combine the ground beef, onion, and chopped pepper tops. Cook, uncovered, on HIGH for 5 to 8 minutes, or until the meat is no longer pink, stirring after 3 minutes. Break up the meat with a fork and drain off any excess fat. Stir in the rice, salt, and pepper. Spoon the mixture evenly into the pepper cups and place the filled cups back into the dish.

Spoon 1 cup tomato sauce over the peppers. Cover with wax paper and cook on MEDIUM for 10 to 15 minutes, or until the peppers are tender. Let stand, covered, for 3 minutes.

Meanwhile, place the remaining 1 cup tomato sauce in a 2-cup glass measure. Cook on HIGH for 2 to 3 minutes, or until heated, stirring once. Spoon over the peppers.

VARIATIONS:

Sausage-Stuffed Peppers: Substitute 1 pound bulk sausage for the ground beef. Substitute ½ cup dry bread crumbs for the rice.

Rice-Stuffed Peppers: Using 4 medium green peppers, cooked on HIGH for 2 to 4 minutes, or until tender-crisp, and then drained, follow the recipe for Rice-Stuffed Tomatoes (page 424). Serve with 1 cup heated tomato sauce.

SAUTÉED CUCUMBERS

MAKES 4 SERVINGS   BEGIN 10 MINUTES BEFORE SERVING
COOKING TIME: 3 TO 5 MINUTES

If you have only served cucumbers in a salad, you are in for a treat. Sprinkled with lemon juice and freshly ground pepper, these cooked cucumbers make an ideal low-calorie side dish.

1 tablespoon butter	1 teaspoon lemon juice
2 large cucumbers, peeled, quartered, and cut into ¼-inch slices	¼ teaspoon salt
	Freshly ground black pepper
	1 tablespoon chopped fresh parsley

In a 2-quart casserole combine the butter and cucumbers. Cover tightly and cook on HIGH for 3 to 5 minutes, or until just heated through, stirring after 2 minutes. Stir in the salt and pepper. Sprinkle with parsley.

VARIATIONS:

Dill Sautéed Cucumbers: Substitute 1 tablespoon chopped fresh dill for the parsley.

Yogurt Cucumbers: Fold ½ cup plain yogurt and 2 tablespoons chopped fresh chives or 2 tablespoons fresh dill (2 teaspoons dried) into the cooked cucumbers.

Sautéed Cucumbers with Bacon: Sprinkle ¼ cup crumbled cooked bacon (see page 61) over the cooked cucumbers.

Creamed Cucumbers: Stir 2 tablespoons heavy cream or ¼ cup sour cream into the cooked cucumbers.

Sautéed Lime Cucumbers: Sprinkle 2 teaspoons fresh lime juice onto the cooked cucumbers before serving. Makes thirst-quenching cucumbers even more so.

Low Calorie Sautéed Cucumbers: Eliminate the butter.

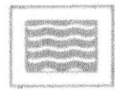

GREENS

Don't let any unpleasant childhood memories cause you to turn your nose up at this section, for there is hardly a category of vegetables that has so many attributes.

First, this group is inexpensive and available all year-round, offering a wide variety of flavors from pungent, full-bodied mustard greens, to the succulent, sweet spinach or sorrel. Even dandelion greens, when picked in the spring before there are any yellow flowers, are young and tender and can be substituted for spinach.

All greens are rich in iron, and are excellent sources of vitamins A and C and fiber. Besides that, nothing can spruce up a drab dinner plate like a cluster of steamed, brilliant greens.

We have divided the greens into "light" greens and "rich" greens, which refer to their texture and flavor. Light greens cook for less time. Rich greens have more "bite" and cook longer, sometimes with more liquid.

Initial quality dictates the final product, so it is important to choose bright green crisp leaves, without yellow spots or visible wilting. However, beet greens will have red tipping, and blue kale has deep green or bluish leaves. Avoid woody stems or wide veins in the leaves, which are a sign of being picked from the field too late.

Washing the leaves well is also important, but only immediately before cooking. Greens should be stored dry and in the coolest part of the refrigerator for only two to three days. In preparation for cooking, it may take two or three separate baths of cold water to remove all the sand and grit. When the sink is clean and free from grit after the final rinse, the greens are ready to be cooked. The water that clings to the greens from the washing will be enough for cooking.

Stalks of Swiss chard can also be used; they are dealt with starting on page 473.

Greens Basics:

1. The liquid that clings to the leaves after washing will be enough for cooking them. If the leaves have been dried before cooking, you should add ¼ cup water.
2. A tight cover, a lid or plastic wrap turned back on the corner, is called for to hold in moisture. By cooking on HIGH with this cover, enough steam will be created and held in to cook and tenderize the greens with just a small amount of water.
3. Even though they will cook down, a large casserole is necessary to hold the uncooked greens and to enable you to stir easily. Stirring well once is necessary for the even cooking of greens.
4. Add salt at the end of cooking to prevent the greens' surfaces from overcooking.
5. No standing time is necessary for greens.
6. *Doneness:* Some of you may like your greens cooked until they are soggy, others may like them still firm to the bite. Your choice will dictate the cooking times. If you like your greens still somewhat firm, slightly undercook them and test them by biting into a leaf. If you prefer an extremely tender leaf, perhaps you should add extra cook-

ing liquid and cook them for the longest time indicated.

Underdone/Overdone: It is hard to overcook greens in the microwave, but you may find that the leaves are not all cooking evenly. You may have to stir more frequently and also check to see that you are using a large enough cooking utensil. This will facilitate the stirring.

Toppings for Greens

Add any of these to 2 cups cooked and drained greens or 4 servings greens.

Italian Oil: Combine 2 tablespoons olive oil and 2 garlic cloves, minced, in a small dish. Cook on HIGH for 1 minute, or until the garlic is tender. Stir into the greens.
Bacon-Topped: Sprinkle with ¼ cup crumbled cooked bacon (see page 61).
Ham-Topped: Sprinkle with ¼ cup chopped thin-sliced ham.
Soya: Stir in 2 tablespoons soy sauce and eliminate the salt.
Cheesy: Stir in ¼ cup grated Gruyère, Swiss, or Parmesan cheese.
Quick Creamed: Stir in ½ cup sour cream or plain yogurt, or ¼ cup half and half or light cream.
With Chicken: Stir in ½ cup chopped cooked chicken.

Retaining Water-Soluble Vitamins

Ascorbic acid, or vitamin C, is a major nutrient found in greens, especially the dark leafy ones. Vitamin C is also unstable in water and easily lost.

The National Dairy Council has some tips on how to preserve this nutrient. Here are the three *R*'s.

- *Reduce* the amount of water in cooking and cover tightly.
- *Reduce* the cooking time.
- *Reduce* the surface area exposed and prepare the vegetables as close to serving time as possible.

By following the preparation tips for greens in this chapter, you will be guarding against vitamin loss.

☀ SAUTÉED LIGHT GREENS
(Chard, Spinach, and Beet Greens)

MAKES 4 SERVINGS   BEGIN 15 TO 20 MINUTES BEFORE SERVING
COOKING TIME: 8 TO 13 MINUTES

A large cooking dish is called for to cook these leaves, which will want to burst over the top when you first put them in. After cooking, they will pack down like leaves in the rain, so you may want to transfer them to a smaller bowl for serving.

Beet greens would go especially well with a dish such as Zesty Julienned Beets (page 462).

2 pounds fresh spinach, chard, or beet greens 2 tablespoons butter	2 tablespoons finely chopped onion ½ teaspoon salt ¼ teaspoon pepper, or to taste

Remove the stems from the leaves, wash the leaves well, and cut into ½-inch strips while still wet. Set aside but don't drain.

Meanwhile, in a 3-quart casserole combine the butter and onion. Cook on HIGH for 1 to 3 minutes, or until the onion is tender. Stir in the chopped leaves. Cover tightly and cook on HIGH for 7 to 10 minutes, or until desired doneness is reached, stirring once. Salt and pepper to taste.

VARIATIONS:

Light Greens au Citron: Add 1 to 2 tablespoons lemon juice or vinegar, depending on taste, to the cooked greens. Adding before cooking will turn the leaves dark.

Light Greens with Garlic: Substitute 2 garlic cloves, minced, for the onion, or add to the onion.

Spinach with Pine Nuts: Substitute 2 tablespoons olive oil for the butter. Add 2 garlic cloves, minced, with the onion. Stir in ¼ cup pine nuts with the salt and pepper.

Soya Sautéed Greens: Stir in 1 tablespoon soy sauce with the salt and pepper.

Lightly Creamed Spinach or Chard: Puree the cooked greens in the blender or food processor. Return to the cooking casserole. Stir in 3 or 4 tablespoons light cream or half and half and a pinch of grated nutmeg. Cook on HIGH for 2 to 4 minutes to heat through.

Creamy-Crunchy Greens: Fold 1 cup sour cream or plain yogurt into the cooked greens. Sprinkle ¼ cup sesame or sunflower seeds on top.

SAUTÉED RICH GREENS
(Collards, Kale, or Mustard)

MAKES 4 SERVINGS BEGIN 20 TO 35 MINUTES BEFORE SERVING
COOKING TIME: 11 TO 22 MINUTES

2 pounds collards, kale, or mustard greens 2 tablespoons vegetable oil, butter, or margarine	2 garlic cloves, minced, and/or 1 small onion, minced Lemon juice or vinegar

Wash the leaves well, discarding any faded leaves; do not drain. Remove the leaves from the stems and remove any tough ribs. Cut the leaves into 1-inch pieces.

In a 3-quart casserole combine the oil or butter and the garlic and/or onion. Cook on HIGH for 1 to 2 minutes, or until the garlic and onion are tender. Add the greens. Cover tightly and cook on HIGH for 10 to 20 minutes, or until tender, stirring after 7 minutes. Serve with lemon juice or vinegar.

VARIATION:

Greens with Bacon: Substitute 2 pieces of bacon, cut into ½-inch pieces, for the oil. Cook with the garlic and onion on HIGH for 3 to 4 minutes, or until the bacon is partially cooked, stirring once. Add the greens and proceed with the basic recipe.

WILTED GREENS SALAD

MAKES 2 TO 4 SERVINGS
COOKING TIME: 2 TO 3 MINUTES

- 12 ounces to 1 pound spinach or romaine leaves, washed and dried
- ¼ cup sesame oil
- 1 medium onion, chopped
- ¼ cup vinegar
- 1 tablespoon soy sauce
- ¼ cup sesame seeds

Tear up the spinach or romaine and place in a salad bowl.

In a 2-cup glass measure combine the oil and onion. Cook on HIGH for 1 to 2 minutes, or until the onion is tender-crisp. Stir in the vinegar, soy sauce, and sesame seeds. Cook on HIGH for 30 seconds to 1 minute, or until heated through. Pour over the greens and toss.

EMERALD ISLE DUMPLINGS

MAKES 4 TO 6 SERVINGS, ABOUT 16 DUMPLINGS   BEGIN ABOUT 30 MINUTES BEFORE SERVING
COOKING TIME: 17 TO 23 MINUTES PER BATCH

These are so comforting on a cold winter night, and would qualify as a meatless meal. Dumplings are steamed gently on MEDIUM power because they contain cheese; a higher power would cause the cheese to toughen and cause the water to weep out.

- 2 pounds spinach, or 1 10-ounce package frozen spinach
- 10 tablespoons butter
- 1 cup ricotta or small-curd cottage cheese
- 1 egg, beaten
- ¼ cup all-purpose flour
- ¼ cup grated Parmesan cheese

Wash the fresh spinach well and remove the stalks. Cut the leaves into 1-inch pieces. Without draining well, place the spinach in a 3-quart casserole. Cover tightly and cook on HIGH for 7 to 10 minutes, or until tender, stirring once. Cook less time for frozen spinach.

Squeeze the liquid out of the spinach by placing in a colander and pressing with a spoon (reserve for a later soup or gravy if you'd like). Puree the drained leaves in a blender or food processor. Return to the cooking casserole. Add 2 tablespoons of the butter. Cook on HIGH for 2 to 3 minutes, stirring once. Stir in the ricotta, egg, and flour.

Spoon 8 separate heaping tablespoonfuls of the mixture onto a 10-inch microwaveproof dinner plate, leaving a 1-inch space between them. Cover tightly and cook on MEDIUM for 8 to 10 minutes, or until the dumplings are set, rotating plate once if necessary. Let stand, covered, for 3 minutes before serving.

Continue with the remaining mixture and cook as before.

Place the remaining 8 tablespoons butter in a 1-cup glass measure. Cook on HIGH for 2 to 3 minutes, or until melted. Pour over the dumplings and sprinkle with Parmesan cheese.

VARIATION:

Spinach Dumplings with Tomato Sauce: Prepare Basic "Batch" Tomato Sauce (page 178) in advance. Heat up and serve with the dumplings.

LEGUMES OR DRIED BEANS

Legumes include all categories of dried peas, lentils, and beans. Legumes are called incomplete proteins because they supply some of the essential amino acids, but not all. Yet when they are combined with corn, rice, pasta, or sesame seeds, they do become complete.

Common among the dried beans are black beans, black-eyed peas, chick-peas (garbanzo beans), Great Northern beans, and kidney, navy, pinto, and dried lima beans. All of these need to be *presoaked* (see page 432).

Split peas and lentils need no presoaking. Once the legumes have been cooked they can be served, hot, with various sauces, or cold, as a salad with a marinade or dressing.

Dried Bean Basics:

1. Beans listed on the speed-soak chart (page 432) should be presoaked before they are cooked.
2. Beans are cooked in a large (3-quart) casserole. This casserole will be twice the height of the beans and water, which will prevent boilovers and will make stirring easier.
3. Beans and water must be brought to a boil first on HIGH, and then simmered slowly on MEDIUM so that the water can be absorbed slowly by the beans. If they were cooked

completely on HIGH, the outsides of the beans would harden before they had a chance to become tender.
4. A tight cover, preferably a lid, or microwaveproof plate, is necessary to keep any liquid from evaporating so that the beans will soak it up. Plastic may split during the long cooking and let out too much moisture. The liquid that remains after cooking will depend on how tight the cover was. There will always be some liquid left, more if the cover was tighter.
5. Stirring once at the end of the HIGH setting, and 15 minutes into the MEDIUM setting, equalizes the heat for faster, more even cooking.
6. Salt can be added before cooking because of the large amount of cooking liquid that will dissolve it.
7. Standing time is important when cooking beans because of the tremendous amount of heat that is generated. In this time they will continue to absorb some liquid.
8. To reheat beans, cover with wax paper or don't cover at all. Plastic wrap will cause the cooked beans to pop from steam buildup. MEDIUM power is the best for reheating.
9. *Doneness:* These vegetables should be cooked to their eating tenderness without regard to a standing time. The standing time will allow them to absorb additional moisture, but not become more tender.

Underdone: If the beans seem tough and underdone, you may have to add ½ to 1 cup more hot liquid. Cook on MEDIUM at 5-minute intervals, checking and stirring after each interval. If the beans continue to be tough, they may not have been presoaked properly and cooking will just take longer.

Overdone: If overcooked, beans will be a little mushier and more of them will have burst. The flavor will be fine and they will work well in any of the recipes here.

Speed Soaking of Dried Beans

It is so nice to be able to prepare and cook with dried beans. They often have a superior texture and more body than the canned variety.

The one drawback in cooking dried beans is that they need to be soaked overnight first—not only does this take time, but one has to think about it in advance. By employing the microwave, however, the whole process can be greatly simplified. Under 10 minutes of cooking is required, with just 1 hour of standing time. Here is how you do it:

Vegetable/Amount	*Cooking Procedure*
1 cup (½ pound, washed) Black, Great Northern, Kidney, Pinto, Navy, Black-eyed Peas, or Chick-peas	Place in a 3-quart casserole with 2 cups water. Cover tightly. Cook HIGH 5 to 10 minutes to boil; stir. Then cook MEDIUM 2 minutes. Let stand, covered, 1 hour.
2 cups (1 pound, washed)	Place in a 3-quart casserole with 3 cups water. Cover tightly. Cook HIGH 7 to 15 minutes to boil; stir. Then cook MEDIUM 2 minutes. Let stand, covered, 1 hour.

✹ BASIC BEANS

MAKES ABOUT 5 CUPS BEGIN 2¼ HOURS BEFORE SERVING, TO PRESOAK BEANS
COOKING TIME: 40 TO 60 MINUTES

Beans no longer signify inexpensive eating; they have become the new trend as we look for ways to cut down on meat. You'll find six tantalizing ways to serve them in this recipe alone. Accompany any of them with cooked rice and you will have a vegetable protein complement that will provide all the essential amino acids your body needs.

2 cups presoaked dried black, kidney, Great Northern, or pinto beans, black-eyed peas or chickpeas (page 432)	3 cups water 1 onion, quartered ½ teaspoon salt Pepper

In a 3-quart casserole with lid combine all the ingredients. Cover tightly and cook on HIGH for 10 to 15 minutes, or until boiling; stir. Cover again and cook on MEDIUM for 30 to 45 minutes, or until the beans are tender, stirring after 15 minutes. Let stand, covered, for 5 minutes. Drain the beans and try one of the variations below.

NOTE: Reserve the cooking liquid for soups or gravies.

VARIATIONS:

Beans with Sautéed Onions and Butter: Combine 1 onion, finely chopped, and 2 tablespoons butter in a small custard cup. Cook on HIGH for 2 to 3 minutes, or until the onion is tender. Stir into the cooked, drained beans.

Great Northern Beans with Garlic and Oil: Combine 2 tablespoons olive oil and 2 garlic cloves, minced, in a custard cup. Cook on HIGH for 40 seconds to 1 minute, or until the garlic is tender. Stir into the cooked, drained beans. Salt and pepper to taste. Stir in 2 tablespoons chopped fresh basil before serving.

Beans with Hot Pepper Flakes and Lime: Combine 2 tablespoons vegetable oil and 1 onion, finely chopped, in a 1-cup glass measure. Cook on HIGH for 2 to 3 minutes, or until the onion is tender. Stir in ½ teaspoon dried thyme, ½ teaspoon red pepper flakes, and 1 tablespoon lime juice into the onion. Stir all into the cooked, drained beans. Garnish with lime wedges, chopped raw onion, and green peppers, if desired.

Curried Beans: Combine 2 tablespoons vegetable oil; 1 garlic clove, minced; 1 onion, finely chopped; and 2 teaspoons curry powder in a small custard cup. Cook on HIGH for 2 to 4 minutes, or until tender. Stir into the cooked, drained beans.

Smoky Beans with Meat: Add 1 ham bone or a 2-pound picnic ham; 1 carrot, chopped; 2 tablespoons chopped fresh parsley; 1 celery rib, chopped; and ½ teaspoon cayenne pepper to the beans before cooking. Follow the basic recipe, turning the ham over halfway through cooking. Serve the sliced ham with beans.

Mexicali Beans: Combine 2 tablespoons vegetable oil; 1 garlic clove, minced; and 1 medium onion, chopped, in a 1-quart casserole. Cook on HIGH for 2 to 4 minutes, or until tender. Stir in 2 cups fresh or undrained canned tomatoes, peeled and chopped; 2 tablespoons chopped fresh cilantro or parsley; 1 jalapeño pepper, thinly sliced; ½ teaspoon salt; and ¼ teaspoon pepper. Cook, uncovered, for 10 minutes, or until the tomatoes cook down and are tender, stirring twice. Stir the mixture into the cooked, drained beans. Sprinkle with chopped onion and grated Monterey Jack cheese. Serve with 4 cups cooked rice or 2 pounds cooked smoked sausage to make a main course.

REFRIED BEANS WITH CHEESE

MAKES ABOUT 5 CUPS   BEGIN 2¼ HOURS BEFORE SERVING
COOKING TIME: 3 TO 6 MINUTES

1 recipe Basic Beans (page 433), drained, reserving ¼ cup cooking liquid	Salt and pepper
1 tablespoon butter	1 cup grated cheddar or Monterey Jack cheese
2 tablespoons chopped onion	Warm Jalapeño Salsa (page 187) (optional)

In a medium-size mixing bowl mash the beans with the cooking liquid. Meanwhile, in a custard cup combine the butter and onion. Cook on HIGH for 2 to 3 minutes, or until the onion is tender. Stir the onion into the mashed beans. Salt and pepper to taste. Turn the beans out into a 10-inch pie plate. Top with the grated cheese. Cook on MEDIUM for 1 to 3 minutes, or until the cheese is melted. Serve with hot salsa, if desired.

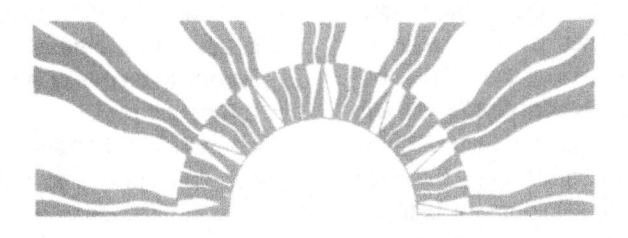

CHILLED SUMMER BEAN SALAD

MAKES ABOUT 5 CUPS   BEGIN 3¼ HOURS BEFORE SERVING

- 1 recipe Basic Beans (page 433)
- ½ cup olive oil
- 1 onion, chopped
- 2 tablespoons vinegar or lemon juice
- 2 tablespoons chopped fresh parsley
- Salt and pepper
- 2 ripe tomatoes, cut into wedges (optional)
- Fresh basil, chopped (optional)

In a large mixing bowl combine the beans, oil, onion, vinegar or lemon juice, parsley, and salt and pepper to taste. Mix well and chill for at least 1 hour. Serve at room temperature, garnished with tomatoes sprinkled with basil, if desired.

LENTIL OR PEA PUREE

MAKES 4 TO 6 SERVINGS   BEGIN 50 TO 70 MINUTES BEFORE SERVING
COOKING TIME: 38 TO 59 MINUTES

Lentils and peas make delicious purees. Our winter holidays are not complete without one of them. Serve with ham, sausage, or wild game.

- 1 cup washed lentils or split peas
- 3 cups water
- 1 onion, chopped
- 1 carrot, chopped
- 1 celery rib, chopped
- ½ teaspoon salt
- Pepper
- Maggi seasoning or soy sauce (optional)

In a 4-quart casserole with lid combine all the ingredients. Cover tightly and cook on HIGH for 8 to 14 minutes, or until boiling; stir. Cover again and cook on MEDIUM for 30 to 45 minutes, or until the beans are tender, stirring after 15 minutes. Let stand, covered, for 5 minutes. Drain, reserving liquid.

Puree the beans, adding the reserved cooking liquid a little at a time if the beans are too thick. Season to taste with additional Maggi (Swiss vegetable seasoning) or soy sauce.

VARIATION:

Lentil or Pea Soup: With any leftover puree, make a delicious soup by adding ¾ cup Brown or Vegetable Broth or Stock (see page 119), to 1 cup puree, heating on HIGH and stirring often. Add leftover sliced smoked sausage or ham, cubed tofu, or croutons to the soup, too.

VEGETARIAN CHILI

MAKES 8 SERVINGS   BEGIN 2¼ HOURS BEFORE SERVING; 3½ HOURS IF PRESOAKING BEANS
COOKING TIME: 1 HOUR 20 MINUTES TO 1 HOUR 48 MINUTES

The addition of bulgur gives this mixture the texture of ground beef. We've upped the seasonings to make a flavorful chili that resembles the original meat version in so many ways.

After all the ingredients are incorporated, the chili is covered tightly to rehydrate the bulgur. The power is reduced for this reason as well, and to develop flavor.

- 1 cup presoaked dried kidney, pinto, or navy beans (page 432), or 2½ cups cooked (page 71), or 1 16-ounce can, undrained
- 2 cups water
- ¼ to ½ cup water, tomato juice, or Vegetable Broth or Stock (page 119)
- 2 tablespoons vegetable oil
- 3 garlic cloves, minced
- 1 large onion, coarsely chopped
- 2 green peppers, coarsely chopped
- 4 cups fresh or undrained canned tomatoes, peeled and chopped
- 1 cup bulgur wheat
- 3 tablespoons chili powder
- 1 tablespoon cuminseed, or 1 teaspoon ground
- 1 tablespoon dried oregano
- 1 teaspoon salt
- ½ teaspoon crushed fresh thyme leaves
- ¼ teaspoon black pepper
- ½ teaspoon red pepper flakes (optional)

Toppings:
- Sour cream or plain yogurt
- Lime wedges
- Grated cheddar or Monterey Jack cheese
- Finely chopped onion
- Sunflower seeds

In a 3-quart casserole with lid, combine the presoaked beans and water. Cover tightly and cook on HIGH for 10 to 15 minutes, or until boiling; stir. Cover again and cook on MEDIUM for 30 to 40 minutes, or until the beans are tender. Drain the beans, reserving the liquid. (If canned or cooked beans are used, eliminate this step and just drain beans.) Add the water, tomato juice, or vegetable broth to the drained liquid to make 2 cups. Set the liquid and beans aside.

In the same casserole combine the oil, garlic, onion, and green peppers. Cover tightly and cook on HIGH for 5 to 8 minutes, or until the vegetables are tender, stirring once during cooking. Stir in the beans, reserved liquid, and remaining ingredients, except the toppings. Cover tightly and cook on HIGH for 10 to 15 minutes, or until boiling; stir. Cover again and cook on MEDIUM for 25 to 30 minutes more, or until the bulgur is tender and the flavors are blended, stirring after 15 minutes. Let stand, covered, for 10 minutes. Correct the seasonings and serve with one or more of the toppings, squeezing lime juice on top.

NOTE: *To Reheat:* To refrigerated chili, add a little extra tomato juice or water. Cover tightly and cook on MEDIUM for 3 to 5 minutes per serving, stirring once.

BAKED BEANS

MAKES 6 SERVINGS   BEGIN 3 HOURS BEFORE SERVING
COOKING TIME: 50 TO 75 MINUTES

4 cups cooked kidney, Great Northern, or pinto beans (page 433)	¼ pound salt pork or bacon, cut into ½-inch pieces
1½ cups reserved cooking liquid from beans, with water added if necessary to make that amount	1 onion, finely chopped
	¼ cup molasses
	¼ cup catsup
	1 teaspoon dry mustard
	½ teaspoon salt

In a water-soaked 3-quart clay pot or casserole with lid, combine all the ingredients. Cover tightly and cook on HIGH for 10 to 15 minutes, or until boiling; stir. Cover again and cook on MEDIUM for 40 to 60 minutes, or until tender, stirring once or twice, adding ¼ cup to ½ cup water if the beans become too dry. Let stand, covered, for 10 minutes.

QUICK BAKED BEANS

MAKES 4 SERVINGS   BEGIN ABOUT 15 MINUTES BEFORE SERVING
COOKING TIME: 8 TO 15 MINUTES

2 slices of bacon, cut into ½-inch pieces	2 tablespoons brown sugar or molasses
1 onion, finely chopped	2 tablespoons catsup
1 16-ounce can baked beans	1 teaspoon prepared mustard

In a 2-quart casserole combine the bacon and onion. Cook on HIGH for 3 to 5 minutes, or until the onion is tender and the bacon partially cooked. Stir in the remaining ingredients. Cover with wax paper; a tight cover would retain too much steam and cause beans to burst. Cook on MEDIUM for 5 to 10 minutes, or until heated through, stirring once.

VARIATION:
Baked Beans and Franks: Add 1 pound frankfurters, cut into ½-inch slices, to the beans, pushing them underneath the surface of the beans. Cover with wax paper and cook on MEDIUM for 7 to 15 minutes, stirring once. This makes a main-dish recipe.

MUSHROOMS

Mushrooms are in a class by themselves. One reason is that they are a fungus and thrive in dark places on dead materials such as straw, vegetable wastes, and others. Who, after tasting a succulent mushroom gently cooked in butter and wine, would ever guess that they come from such inauspicious beginnings?

Many more types of mushrooms have become available to us now that are grown locally or imported. Although each will impart its own distinct flavor, all can be stored in the way field mushrooms are: in the refrigerator, without washing, for up to two days.

Mushroom Basics:

1. One half to 1 pound sliced or whole mushrooms are cooked on HIGH with little or no liquid, because adding liquid will cause them to darken. Two tablespoons butter or wine are added for flavoring only, because the warmed, tender skins of the mushrooms will absorb any liquid that they touch during cooking.
2. During cooking, mushrooms should neither be covered nor salted. Salt will draw out liquid, and covering will retain too much liquid, which will turn them a dark, unappealing color. Liquid is only added for flavor, because the mushrooms are already very moist.
3. Placing whole mushrooms in a ring around the outside of a round dish will cause them to cook more evenly. No rearranging will be necessary and possibly only one rotation of the dish. Sliced mushrooms are stirred once to redistribute heat for even cooking.
4. *Doneness:* Mushrooms hold their shape better and are less likely to darken if just heated through. They are cooked until just heated through or to desired tenderness. They will darken a little naturally in cooking. There is no standing time and overcooking is virtually impossible.

Toppings for Mushrooms

Add any of these to 1 pound cooked or 4 servings mushrooms:

Dijon: Stir 1 tablespoon of Dijon mustard into cooked mushrooms.

Parsleyed: Sprinkle 2 tablespoons chopped fresh parsley over cooked mushrooms.

Quick Creamed Mushrooms: Fold ½ cup plain yogurt or sour cream into cooked mushrooms. Cook, uncovered, on HIGH for 1 to 2 minutes to heat through, stirring once.

Lemon and Oregano: Stir 1 teaspoon lemon juice and ½ teaspoon dried oregano into mushrooms before cooking.

Bread Crumbs: Sprinkle 2 tablespoons toasted fine dry herb bread crumbs over cooked mushrooms.

SAUTÉED MUSHROOMS

MAKES ABOUT 2 CUPS   BEGIN 7 TO 10 MINUTES BEFORE SERVING
COOKING TIME: 3 TO 6 MINUTES

---

1 pound whole mushrooms, wiped clean and cut into ¼-inch slices
1 tablespoon butter

1 teaspoon lemon juice
Freshly ground black pepper

In a 1½-quart casserole combine the mushrooms, butter, and lemon juice. Cook on HIGH for 3 to 6 minutes, until heated through or tender, depending on desired doneness, stirring after 2 minutes. Pepper to taste and serve as is or with any of the suggested toppings (see above).

✺ MUSHROOM CAPS AU NATUREL

MAKES 4 SIDE-DISH SERVINGS; 6 TO 8 APPETIZERS   BEGIN 10 MINUTES BEFORE SERVING
COOKING TIME: 3 TO 6 MINUTES

A simply marvelous appetizer for mushroom lovers. It is so appealing that it makes you think it must be fattening. During cooking the mushroom juice fills the mushroom caps. We find the flavor to be so fresh that even salt and pepper are optional.

---

1 pound fresh mushrooms, stems removed (see Note)

Salt and pepper (optional)

Wipe the mushroom caps clean. Position the caps, hollow side up, around the outer edge of a 12-inch round microwaveproof platter, leaving the center open. Cook on HIGH for 3 to 6 minutes, or until the mushrooms are heated through and tender, but still hold their shape, rotating the plate once. Salt and pepper to taste, if desired.

NOTE: Stems may be made into Carryover Vegetable Stir-Shake (page 480) or Mushroom Pâté (page 98).

VARIATIONS:

Mushroom Caps au Citron: Serve them with fresh lemon juice squeezed on top, or with lemon wedges.

Buttered Mushroom Caps: Divide about 2 tablespoons butter between the mushroom caps before cooking.

STUFFED MUSHROOMS

MAKES 20 TO 36 STUFFED MUSHROOMS   BEGIN 15 TO 20 MINUTES BEFORE SERVING
COOKING TIME: 6 TO 10 MINUTES

Mushroom stems are the main ingredient in the stuffing for the caps. These burnished gems will grace a platter of grilled meats or appetizer plate.

- 1 pound fresh mushrooms
- 4 tablespoons butter
- ¼ cup chopped scallions
- 1 cup fresh bread crumbs
- ½ cup chopped fresh parsley
- 2 tablespoons vermouth, sherry, plain yogurt, or cream
- 1 teaspoon lemon juice
- ¼ teaspoon salt
- ¼ teaspoon grated nutmeg
- ⅛ teaspoon pepper

Wipe the mushrooms clean. Remove the stems and finely chop. Set aside the mushroom caps.

In a 1-quart casserole combine the chopped stems, butter, and scallions. Cook on HIGH for 3 to 5 minutes, or until the butter melts and the scallions and mushrooms are tender, stirring once. Add the remaining ingredients except the mushroom caps; stir to blend.

Place the caps around the outside rim of a 12-inch round microwaveproof platter. Spoon the mushroom–bread crumb mixture into the caps, dividing evenly. Cook on HIGH for 3 to 5 minutes, until the stuffing and caps are heated through.

VARIATIONS:

Crunchy Stuffed Mushrooms: Add ¼ cup sesame seeds or pine nuts to the mushroom stuffing.

Raisin-Studded Mushrooms: Add ¼ cup chopped raisins or whole currants and 1 tablespoon pine nuts to the mushroom stuffing.

Milano Mushrooms with Basil: Substitute fresh basil for the parsley. Substitute olive oil for the butter. When basil is in season, this variation brings sun-kissed Italy to your kitchen.

☼ BREADED MUSHROOMS AND VEGETABLES

MAKES ABOUT 36 BREADED VEGETABLES, OR 6 SIDE-DISH SERVINGS   BEGIN 15 TO 20 MINUTES BEFORE SERVING
COOKING TIME: 3 TO 6 MINUTES

- ¼ cup olive, sesame, or other oil
- ½ cup fine dry bread crumbs
- 2 tablespoons grated Parmesan cheese
- 2 tablespoons toasted sesame seeds
- 1 tablespoon finely chopped fresh parsley, or 1 teaspoon dried
- 12 medium fresh mushroom caps
- 1 large green pepper, seeded and cut into about 12 ¼-inch-thick rings
- 1 small zucchini, cut into 2-inch-long- × -¼-inch-thick fingers

Place the oil in a cereal bowl. In a separate cereal bowl or plastic bag combine the bread crumbs, cheese, sesame seeds, and parsley.

Dip the vegetables, 8 to 12 at a time, into the oil. Dip or shake them in the breading to coat. Place the first 18 pieces of vegetables on a 12-inch roasting rack, or paper towel–lined plate, or paper plate. Cook on HIGH for 1½ to 3 minutes, or until desired doneness is reached. Let stand for 2 minutes.

In the meantime dip, coat, and cook the remaining vegetables, using the same cooking times. Serve plain or with Herbed Mayonnaise (page 175).

VARIATION:

Breaded Mushrooms and Peppers: Eliminate the zucchini. To serve, place a mushroom cap in the center of each pepper ring. Serve with grilled meat.

ONIONS

With each varying flavor, color, size, and function, onions display the diversity of the lily family. For our purposes, they have been divided into dry-skinned onions that have been allowed to mature and onions that are sold fresh.

Dry-skinned onions, the ones with the papery skins, go by the names of Spanish, Bermuda, red-purple, boiling white and pearl onions, shallots, and garlic. They should not be stored in the refrigerator, where they could rot, but instead be put in a dark place at 50°F.

Fresh onions are the leeks, scallions, and chives, the latter being treated more as an herb than a vegetable.

We would never have thought onions could become one of the foods that we crave, but in the form of leeks, they hold a special place in our hearts. There are times when leeks draw us to the produce section like magnets, and the thought of tender leeks bathed in butter and bread crumbs holds more attraction than a chocolate bar.

Onion Basics:

1. Leeks are in their prime in the fall and should have fresh green ends and straight white bases. Leeks need to be washed well before cooking because their many cylindrical layers trap dirt and grit.
2. Both dry-skinned and fresh onions have sufficient moisture in their cells to require only 2 tablespoons of additional liquid per 1 pound onions in a tightly closed casserole. This is important to remember when adding onions to another recipe such as a stew. If many small whole onions are called for in a stew, substituting larger sliced onions will increase the liquid slightly because of the surface area and the liquid exuded.

   When onions are chopped for sautéing to be added to another recipe, covering is optional.
3. If salt is added it should be dissolved into the cooking liquid or sprinkled on at the end of cooking, to prevent the toughening of the onion surfaces.
4. Whole onions should stand, covered, for 3 to 5 minutes to complete cooking.
5. *Doneness: Dry-skinned Onions (whole or quartered)*—These are done when they are fork tender, and if still whole, the inner layers will slip out of one end when slight pressure is applied to the other end.

   Chopped Onion or Garlic—Onions and/or garlic, cooked in oil or butter, are often called for as the first step to any recipe. This is to release their full flavors to the rest of the ingredients. Neither will brown when cooked, but should be tender to the bite with just a slight resilience. When they are the first step in a recipe, cook them until they have just about reached the final eating doneness because they won't become much more tender when other ingredients are added.

   If you are watching your weight, simply eliminate the butter and oil and cook onions alone or with a few drops of water. The onion flavor will be sweeter and less volatile this way.

   Fresh Onions—Leeks and green onions should be cooked to eating tenderness. Some people prefer leeks cooked with more texture and a slight squeakiness, others prefer them to be as tender as boiled onions; it is all a matter of taste that is controlled by cooking time.

   Green onions will tend to turn slightly brown on the ends as the thicker whites cook to the proper tenderness. These can be cut off before serving or garnished with a creamy Lemon Butter (page 247).

   All Onions Underdone and Overdone: If you find that the onions are undercooked, even after standing time, cover again. If you have already drained the cooking liquid, add a little hot tap water. Cook on HIGH at 1-minute intervals, 30 seconds for fresh onions, stirring in between.

   We doubt that you will encounter mushy overcooked onions, because they are cooked in so little liquid for such a short time.

> **Tear-Free Onions**
>
> Before chopping dry-skinned onions, remove the ends but not the papery skin. Place 1 large onion in the microwave oven. Cook on HIGH for 1 minute. This should render all but the most powerful onion powerless to bring tears.

GLAZED ONIONS

MAKES 4 SERVINGS   BEGIN 15 MINUTES BEFORE SERVING
COOKING TIME: 8 TO 10 MINUTES

The onions are steamed covered first to ensure even cooking. They are then uncovered so that the glaze will thicken.

- 1 pound small white onions, peeled
- 1 tablespoon brown sugar
- 1 teaspoon raspberry or plain vinegar
- 1 tablespoon butter

In a 1-quart casserole combine all the ingredients. Cover tightly and cook on HIGH for 5 minutes. Stir well to coat the onions. Cook, uncovered, on HIGH for 3 to 5 minutes, or until the onions are tender and glazed, stirring every minute to coat the onions. Stir and serve.

VARIATIONS:

Honey- or Maple-Glazed Onions: Substitute honey or maple syrup for the brown sugar.

Glazed Onions with Nuts: Sprinkle with 2 teaspoons chopped pecans, almonds, or walnuts before serving.

> **Toppings for Onions**
>
> Add any of the following to 4 servings or 2 cups cooked onions:
>
> *Bacon-Topped:* Sprinkle 2 tablespoons crumbled crisp bacon (see page 61) over onions.
>
> *Parmesan:* Sprinkle 2 tablespoons grated Parmesan cheese over onions.
>
> *Nutmeg:* Sprinkle grated nutmeg over onions.
>
> *Bread Crumbs:* Sprinkle 2 tablespoons toasted dry bread crumbs over onions.
>
> *Nut-Topped:* Sprinkle 1 tablespoon chopped nuts over onions.

CREAMED ONIONS

MAKES 4 SERVINGS BEGIN 15 TO 20 MINUTES BEFORE SERVING
COOKING TIME: 8 TO 11 MINUTES

After the onions and sauce are combined, they are cooked uncovered so the sauce doesn't become too watery.

- 1 pound small white onions, peeled, or larger onions, peeled and quartered
- 2 tablespoons water, dry vermouth, or white wine
- 1 cup White Sauce (page 171)
- Generous dash of nutmeg
- 2 tablespoons fine dry bread crumbs

In a 1½-quart casserole combine the onions and water. Cover tightly and cook on HIGH for 6 to 8 minutes, or until tender, stirring once.

Drain the onions. Fold the white sauce and nutmeg into the onions. Sprinkle with bread crumbs. Cook, uncovered, on HIGH for 2 to 3 minutes, or until heated through. Let stand, covered, for 3 to 5 minutes.

NOTE: To make in advance, prepare the thick white sauce and onions (hold the bread crumbs). When reheated later it will thin out.

To reheat: Cook, uncovered, on HIGH for 3 to 5 minutes, or until the bottom of the dish is very hot or *3 Macungie* (page 44), stirring once.

VARIATIONS:

Onions with Cheese Sauce: Cook the onions, then make the white sauce. Stir in ½ cup grated cheddar cheese. Stir the sauce into the onions and proceed with basic recipe.

Creamed Onions with Bacon: Substitute crumbled crisp bacon (see page 61) for the bread crumbs. Sprinkle with 2 tablespoons chopped fresh parsley right before serving.

Stuffed Onion Basics:

1. Onions are partially cooked on HIGH with a little water first to remove the inner layers more easily and partially cook the outside shell so that it will cook evenly along with the filling.
2. The onion filling must have precooked ingredients so that the stuffing and onion shells just need to be heated through.
3. For the most even cooking, stuffed onions should be placed in a ring around the outside of a cooking dish. No rearranging is necessary.
4. Once onions are stuffed, they should be cooked on MEDIUM power to allow the fla-

vors to develop without the outer onion shells overcooking.
5. Because onions are high in water, no additional water need be added during final cooking. A wax paper cover will help cook the vegetables evenly by retaining some steam, but will not cause them to become soggy.
6. A standing time of 3 to 5 minutes is important to heat the onions through to the center.

✺ STUFFED ONIONS

MAKES 4 SERVINGS   BEGIN 25 TO 30 MINUTES BEFORE SERVING
COOKING TIME: 14 TO 19 MINUTES

Large onions make a delicious and attractive casing for fillings, and we've come up with a number of these that are really tasty. Your task of hollowing out the onions is made easy and tearless, because they are partially cooked first in the microwave. No more scooping, digging, and crying your way through these onions.

- 2 tablespoons water
- 4 large onions, about 3 inches in diameter, unpeeled
- Salt and pepper to taste
- 2 tablespoons butter
- ¼ cup fine dry bread crumbs
- 1 cup chopped fresh mushrooms
- 2 tablespoons chopped fresh parsley, or 2 teaspoons dried
- 1 teaspoon lemon juice
- 1 tablespoon dry vermouth or sherry (optional)

In a 2-quart casserole place the water and position the onions in a circle. Cover tightly and cook on HIGH for 5 to 7 minutes, or until the outer onion layers are tender. Pour cold water over the onions and cool a few minutes, or enough to handle.

Cut off ½ inch from the top of each onion and a thin slice from the bottom, to allow the onions to stand upright. Remove the papery skin and greenish-white layer underneath. From the center of the onions remove all but the 2 outer layers. From the inner part of each onion that was removed, cut a flat square piece, to fit over the bottom opening of the hollowed-out onion. This will prevent the filling from coming out during cooking. Salt and pepper the inside of the onion shells. Finely chop the remaining onion centers. Place the onion shells in a circle around the outer rim of a 9-inch pie plate; set aside.

In the same 2-quart casserole combine the chopped onion and butter. Cook, uncovered, on HIGH for 2 to 3 minutes, until the onion is tender and the butter melted. Stir in the remaining ingredients except the onion shells. Cook on HIGH for 2 minutes.

Spoon the filling into the onions, heaping it about ½ inch above the onion tops. Cover loosely with wax paper and cook on MEDIUM for 5 to 7 minutes, or until heated through. Let stand, covered, 3 to 5 minutes.

VARIATIONS:

Onions with Nut Stuffing: Add ¼ cup chopped nuts with bread crumbs to the filling.

Stuffed Onions with Parmesan: Sprinkle 2 tablespoons grated Parmesan cheese on top of the onions before cooking.

Rice-Stuffed Onions: Substitute cooked rice for the bread crumbs.

Meat-Stuffed Onions: Substitute 1 cup chopped cooked ham, beef, chicken, or sausage for the mushrooms. Season the filling with salt and pepper to taste. Serve the cooked onions with 1 cup heated tomato sauce (canned, "Batch," or Pureed, page 178 or 179), if desired.

Onions Stuffed with Corn and Pepper Hash: Substitute 2 cups cooked Corn and Pepper Hash (page 410) for the filling mixture.

Spinach-Stuffed Onions: Add ¼ cup dry bread crumbs to 2 cups Creamed Spinach (page 429) and substitute for the filling mixture.

Onions Stuffed with Minted Peas: Substitute 2 cups Peas de Menthe (page 411) for the filling mixture.

Onions Stuffed with Candied Carrots: Substitute 2 cups Candied Carrots (page 463) for the filling mixture.

Squash-Stuffed Onions: Substitute 2 cups Pureed Winter Squash (page 466) for the filling mixture.

Onions Stuffed with Peas and Carrots: Substitute 2 cups Peas and Carrots (page 412) for the filling mixture.

Onions Stuffed with Sautéed Mushrooms: Substitute 2 cups Sautéed Mushrooms (page 439) for the filling mixture.

Leek and Scallion Basics:

1. Leeks and scallions must be arranged as the stalk vegetables are, with the thickest portions to the outside.
2. Repositioning the onions is necessary halfway through cooking to move those onions on the inside to the outside, where they will receive more cooking energy and vice versa.
3. One pound leeks or scallions requires 2 tablespoons cooking liquid. A tight cover is needed to retain steam and cook the vegetables.
4. Salt the vegetables after cooking or make sure to stir the salt into the cooking liquid. Salt on the vegetable surface before cooking will draw out cellular water in the vegetable.
5. A 3- to 5-minute standing time is necessary for leeks but not scallions, because leeks are denser.
6. For doneness, see page 442.

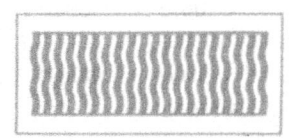

✸ LEEKS AU NATUREL

MAKES 4 SERVINGS AS A SIDE DISH, 2 AS A MAIN DISH TOPPED WITH CHEESE OR YOGURT
BEGIN 15 TO 20 MINUTES BEFORE SERVING
COOKING TIME: 9 TO 15 MINUTES

These sweet onions are delicious warm, topped with cheese or yogurt or a light vinaigrette, or when chilled as a salad.

- 2 pounds (8 to 10) leeks
- 2 tablespoons vegetable oil
- 1 garlic clove, minced
- 1 medium onion, coarsely chopped
- 2 tablespoons Chicken or Vegetable Broth (page 118 or 119) or water
- Salt and pepper to taste

Trim the darker green tops, leaving about 1½ inches green. Cut the leeks in half, crosswise; rinse well to remove any sand.

In a 2-quart rectangular dish combine the oil, garlic, and onion. Cook on HIGH for 2 to 3 minutes, or until softened. Position the leeks in the same dish with the thicker sections toward the outside. Pour the broth or water over the leeks. Cover tightly and cook on HIGH for 7 to 12 minutes, or until fork tender, repositioning the leeks once to move the less cooked ones to the outside. Salt and pepper to taste. Let stand, covered, for 3 to 5 minutes.

Serve warm with their juice spooned on top.

VARIATIONS:

Leeks Parmesan: Sprinkle cooked leeks with ¼ cup grated Parmesan cheese.

Nut-Topped Leeks: Sprinkle cooked leeks with 2 tablespoons chopped nuts or sesame seeds.

Cream-Topped Leeks: Top cooked leeks with sour cream or plain yogurt.

Leeks au Gratin: At the end of cooking, sprinkle the leeks with ¼ cup fine dry bread crumbs and ½ cup shredded Swiss or Gruyère cheese. Cook, uncovered, on MEDIUM for 3 to 5 minutes, or until the cheese is melted. Before serving, sprinkle with 2 tablespoons chopped almonds, if desired.

Mexican-Style Leeks: After cooking, sprinkle the leeks with ½ cup shredded Monterey Jack cheese and 2 tablespoons chopped mild canned chilies. Before serving, sprinkle with pumpkin or sunflower seeds. Serve with Warm Jalapeño Salsa (page 187), if desired.

Leeks with Béchamel Sauce: Prepare White Sauce (page 171). Cook the leeks and drain. Pour the white sauce over the leeks and sprinkle with 2 tablespoons grated cheese. Place under a broiler for 2 to 5 minutes, or until slightly browned.

Chilled Leeks in Vinaigrette: After cooking, cover and chill the leeks in their juice. Stir in ¼ cup Herb Vinaigrette (page 185) or bottled; serve.

Chilled Leeks in Lime: After cooking, cover and chill the leeks in their juice. Pour on 1 to 2 tablespoons lime or lemon juice; stir and serve.

Chilled Leeks with Oriental Dressing: After cooking, cover and chill the leeks in their juice. Stir in ¼ cup Oriental Dressing (page 184); serve.

Chilled Yogurt Leeks: After cooking, cover and chill the leeks in their juice. Combine 1 cup plain yogurt and 1 teaspoon lemon juice. Stir into the leeks and serve.

Chilled Creamed Leeks: After cooking, cover and chill the leeks with their juices. Combine ½ cup plain yogurt, ¼ cup Mayonnaise (page 175), and 2 tablespoons chopped fresh herbs. Stir into the leeks and serve.

✷ BRAISED SCALLIONS

MAKES 4 SERVINGS   BEGIN 10 MINUTES BEFORE SERVING
COOKING TIME: 5 TO 8 MINUTES

Braised scallions are often ignored but they add a very attractive note to any meal.

---

20 scallions (about 3 bunches)	water, or dry vermouth or sherry
2 tablespoons Chicken, Vegetable, or Mock Brown Broth (pages 118–19),	Salt and pepper to taste

---

Cut off the tips and ends of the scallions, then peel the outer layer. Place in a 2-quart rectangular dish. Add the broth, water, vermouth, or sherry. Cover tightly and cook on HIGH for 5 to 8 minutes, or until tender, rearranging the stalks from the outside to the inside after 3 minutes. Salt and pepper to taste. Serve warm or, if serving chilled, cover and chill in the cooking liquid.

VARIATIONS:

Scallions with Lemon Butter: Combine 2 tablespoons melted butter mixed with 1 teaspoon lemon juice or lime juice. Pour over the scallions. Sprinkle with pepper before serving.

Quick Creamed Scallions: Drain the scallions after cooking. Combine 1 cup sour cream or plain yogurt with 1 tablespoon lemon juice. Stir into the warm scallions.

Scallions with Quick Mustard Sauce: Drain the cooked scallions. Combine 1 cup plain yogurt with 2 tablespoons prepared country mustard with seeds. Stir into the warm scallions.

Elegant Scallions with Hollandaise Sauce: Drain cooked scallions. Remove the crusts from 4 slices of bread and toast. Prepare Hollandaise Sauce (page 174). Attractively arrange 5 scallions on each piece of toast. Pour the hollandaise sauce on top.

Scallions au Citron: Drain the cooked scallions. Sprinkle with 1 to 2 tablespoons fresh lemon or lime juice and freshly ground pepper.

Chilled Scallion Salad: After chilling drain and dress with fresh lemon or lime juice and freshly ground black pepper, or ¼ cup Herb Vinaigrette (page 185) or ¼ cup Oriental Dressing (page 184). Sprinkle with 2 tablespoons sesame seeds. Serve on individual plates, garnished with cherry tomatoes or grated raw carrot.

POTATOES

Potatoes are now grown on every continent of the world, but they weren't always this widely accepted. In fact, they weren't introduced to Europe until the mid-sixteenth century from origins in Central and South America, yet today eastern Europe leads all areas in annual potato production.

The American culture has taken a new look at potatoes in recent years. With the realization that potatoes are not in themselves fattening, at only 70 calories for one medium, they have garnered for themselves a treasured place in the American diet.

They have moved from side dish to main dish, a fact especially evident in restaurants and fast-food places, where potatoes have become edible pedestals for all types of protein fillings. Even potato skins, which used to end up on the kitchen floor, are carefully removed and cooked for crispy snacks. Not a bad innovation, because many nutrients lie under the skin of a potato. Potatoes are low in sodium and high in vitamin C, iron, and potassium.

We like to put potatoes into two categories: Baking potatoes (long reddish brown Russets and Idaho potatoes) are thicker skinned, somewhat mealy, and high in starch, low in sugar. They are best when baked alone, without the addition of liquid, because the starch will absorb it and become gummy.

Waxy potatoes (round white, round red, and long white) have thinner skins, shallower eyes, and are higher in sugar and firmer after cooking. They will hold up well when sliced and cooked with liquid, and except for the round red, are good all-purpose potatoes for scalloped, mashed, boiled, or roasted dishes. The round red are not as good for mashing. (New potatoes are young versions of any of these potatoes.) You'll notice that the slices and cubes will take less time to cook than the quarters, because there is more exposed surface area.

All potatoes are optimally stored in a dark place at 50°F. Refrigerator storage will cause the starch to turn to sugar. If stored in sunlight, potatoes may develop green spots, which should be cut out before cooking. If well stored, potatoes can keep up to two months.

The sweet potato is not related in any way to the real potato and should be stored differently. It is thought to have come from Asia, where storage conditions of 55° to 60°F and high humidity are easy to come by. Try putting sweet potatoes in a moistened plastic bag outside of the refrigerator, but don't plan to keep them for more than two weeks.

The sweet potato can substitute for the potato in starch quality and vitamin C and iron, and holds additional vitamin A. It can be treated much the same as the potato in cooking.

Whole Potato Basics:

1. The potato skin should be pierced once on the top and once on the bottom before cooking to release steam that may build up later.

2. All potatoes are cooked on HIGH power.
3. It is best to place potatoes 1 inch apart in the oven, so that the microwave energy can reach all surfaces, and not be blocked by one another. The cooking of potatoes depends on their size and shape. A longer, narrower potato will cook faster than a fat, round potato of the same weight, because there is less thickness to cook through. Pull out any potatoes that feel done.
4. Potatoes are cooked on a paper towel to absorb any excess moisture.
5. Potatoes will continue cooking during standing time, but they should not be covered. Use a terrycloth towel to hold in the heat but keep them from becoming soggy.
6. *Doneness:* White potatoes should be checked while they are cooking because no two potatoes are the same. The smaller ones will obviously cook faster and should be removed when they feel done.

To test for doneness, imagine that you are grabbing the handlebars of your bike to brake. Hold the potato with a cloth or paper towel and firmly press. The cooked potato should give only slightly under your fingers right under the surface; the center will still feel firm. After standing time, the potatoes should feel like a conventionally cooked potato.

Sweet potatoes should be tender all the way through when pierced with a fork, before standing time.

Underdone: Due to varying sizes, a large potato may not be quite done. Turn over and replace it in the oven and cook on HIGH at 45-second intervals until done.

Overdone: In sweet potatoes or pointed white potatoes the ends may become hard and fibrous. These areas should be cut off and discarded.

When a potato bursts or explodes, it is often not because of overcooking, but because of heat and steam buildup under a skin when no holes were pierced. If they should burst, remove from the skins and place in a casserole with one of the suggested toppings (page 451), or make Chili-Stuffed Potatoes (page 452).

Can Potassium Help Lower Blood Pressure?

A diet that is rich in potassium may be an important factor in preventing hypertension, even when sodium intake isn't reduced. This was indicated in a study reported in the *American Journal of Clinical Nutrition*, May 1983.

And for anyone who wants to increase their dietary potassium, here's a cooking tip from a group of Swedish scientists:

To avoid potassium loss in cooking, steam rather than boil vegetables. When doctors at a Swedish hospital tested the two cooking methods with potatoes, a rich source of potassium, they discovered that boiled potatoes lost 10 to 50 percent of their potassium while steamed potatoes lost only 3 to 6 percent. They had similar results with carrots, beans and peas (*Lancet*, January 15, 1983).

Another good reason to cook potassium-rich potatoes and other vegetables in the microwave!

Toppings for Potatoes

Add any of the following to 4 servings sliced or 4 baked potatoes:

For White Potatoes:

Lemon-Buttered: Add ¼ cup Lemon Butter (page 183) to cooked white potatoes.

Sour Cream and Chives: Add ¼ cup sour cream and 2 tablespoons chopped fresh chives to cooked white potatoes.

Yogurt and Chives: Add ¼ cup plain yogurt and 2 tablespoons chopped fresh chives to cooked white potatoes.

Yogurt and Caraway Seeds: Add ¼ cup plain yogurt and 2 tablespoons crushed caraway seeds to cooked white potatoes.

Quick Creamed with Sunflower Seeds: Add ¼ cup sour cream or plain yogurt and 2 tablespoons sunflower seeds to cooked white potatoes.

Bacon-Topped: Sprinkle ¼ cup crumbled crisp bacon (see page 61) over cooked potatoes.

For Sweet Potatoes:

Orange-Buttered: Spoon ¼ cup Orange Butter (page 183) onto baked sweet potatoes.

Lemon-Buttered: Spoon ¼ cup Lemon Butter (page 183) onto baked sweet potatoes.

Lime-Buttered: Spoon ¼ cup Lime Butter (page 183) onto baked sweet potatoes.

Nut-Buttered: Combine ¼ cup melted butter and ¼ cup chopped nuts. Spoon onto baked sweet potatoes.

Sweet-Creamed: Combine 1 cup sour cream and ¼ cup brown sugar. Stir into cooked and mashed sweet potatoes, following initial cooking instructions (page 459).

Stuffed Potato Basics:

1. Potatoes must be cooked completely on HIGH power before stuffing. The skin must be pierced, before cooking, to release steam that will build up inside.
2. Potatoes can be stuffed with any pre-cooked filling, or any filling that needs only reheating.
3. Stuffed potatoes can be heated through on HIGH, unless there is cheese on top, which means that MEDIUM power is in order, to prevent the cheese from becoming rubbery. As with the initial cooking, there is no cover in the final heating to prevent the potatoes from getting too soggy.

☀ CHILI-STUFFED POTATOES

MAKES 4 LUNCHEON SERVINGS   BEGIN ABOUT 40 TO 50 MINUTES BEFORE SERVING
COOKING TIME: 23 TO 30 MINUTES

When there is a collection of leftovers in the refrigerator, we pull out this recipe and make up a few combinations. They also make a nice lunch or breakfast, and are good for carbohydrate cravings late at night. We've included instructions for those solo occasions.

- 4 large baking potatoes
- Salt and pepper
- ½ cup milk, sour cream, or plain yogurt
- 4 tablespoons butter
- 2 cups Ground Beef or Vegetarian Chili (pages 321 and 436)
- ¼ cup grated cheddar or Monterey Jack cheese

Pierce the potato skins. Place in a circle on a paper towel, leaving 1 inch between the potatoes. Cook on HIGH for 15 to 20 minutes, or until tender, turning over once during cooking and removing any that are done after 15 minutes. Let stand for 5 to 10 minutes.

Cut off ½ inch from the long side of each potato. Scoop out the pulp into a bowl, leaving a ¼-inch shell. Salt and pepper the inside of each shell.

In a medium bowl mash the potato pulp well. Stir in the milk, cream, or yogurt, and butter. Fold in the chili. Spoon into the shells, heaping the stuffing into the center. Place on a microwaveproof serving plate. Top with cheese. Cook on MEDIUM for 8 to 10 minutes, or until heated through and the cheese is melted.

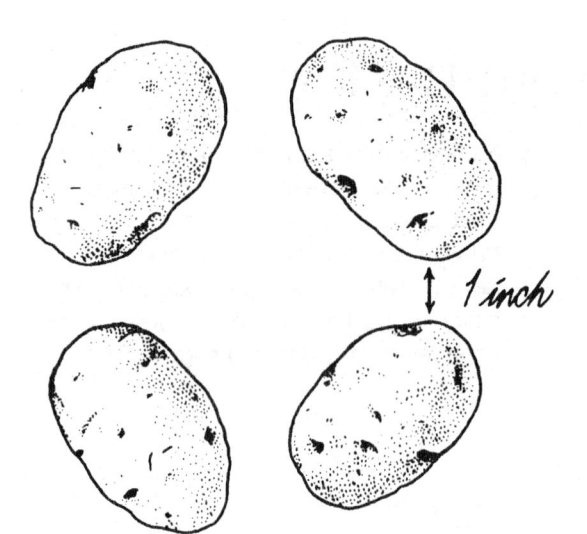

VARIATIONS:

Curry Chicken–Filled Potatoes: Substitute 2 cups Braised Chicken with Curry Sauce (page 354) for the chili. Eliminate the cheese. The stuffed potatoes can be heated on HIGH for 3 to 6 minutes.

Ham-Filled Potatoes: Substitute 2 cups chopped baked ham for the chili; top with ¼ cup grated Swiss, Jarlsberg, or Gruyère cheese.

Crab-Filled Potatoes: Substitute 2 cups Crab Imperial (page 238) for the chili; top with ¼ cup grated Jarlsberg or Swiss cheese.

Shrimp in Mustard–Filled Potatoes: Substitute 2 cups Shrimp in Mustard Sauce (page 236) for the chili. Eliminate the cheese. The stuffed potatoes can be heated on HIGH for 3 to 6 minutes.

Broccoli in Cheese Sauce–Filled Potatoes: Substitute 2 cups cooked broccoli flowerets mixed with 1 cup Mornay Sauce (page 171) for the chili; top with ¼ cup grated cheddar cheese.

Mushroom-Filled Potatoes: Substitute 2 cups Sautéed Mushrooms (page 439) for the chili; top with ¼ cup grated Jarlsberg or Swiss cheese.

Ratatouille-Filled Potatoes: Substitute 2 cups Ratatouille (page 421) for the chili; top with ¼ cup grated Gruyère or Swiss cheese.

Cabbage-Filled Potatoes: Substitute 2 cups Braised Sweet and Sour Red Cabbage (page 400) for the chili; top with ¼ cup grated cheddar cheese.

Mexican-Filled Potatoes: Combine ½ cup chopped mild chilies, ½ cup grated cheddar cheese, and ½ cup sour cream; substitute for the chili. Fill the potatoes and top with ¼ cup grated cheddar cheese. Serve with sour cream and Warm Jalapeño Salsa (page 187).

French Onion-Filled Potatoes: Substitute 2 cups sautéed onions (page 442) for the chili; top with ¼ cup grated Swiss cheese and 2 tablespoons toasted sunflower seeds.

SINGLE SERVING: Cook a potato on HIGH for 5 to 9 minutes. Scoop out the pulp. Add 1 tablespoon butter, 1 tablespoon milk, and ½ cup filling to the pulp. Top with 1 tablespoon grated cheese. Cook on MEDIUM for 3 to 5 minutes.

STUFFED SWEET POTATO BOATS

MAKES 4 SERVINGS   BEGIN 20 TO 30 MINUTES BEFORE SERVING
COOKING TIME: 12 TO 17 MINUTES

---

4 medium sweet potatoes	¼ teaspoon salt
½ cup milk or cream	⅛ teaspoon pepper
2 tablespoons butter	

Pierce the potato skins. Place in a circle on a paper towel, leaving 1 inch between the potatoes. Cook on HIGH for 10 to 13 minutes, or until tender, turning over once during cooking. Let stand for 5 to 10 minutes. Cut a ½-inch slice from the long side of each potato. Scoop out the pulp into a bowl, leaving a ¼-inch shell.

In a medium bowl mash the potato pulp well. Stir in the remaining ingredients. Spoon into the shells, heaping the stuffing into the center. Position on a microwaveproof serving plate. Cook on HIGH for 2 to 4 minutes, or until heated through.

VARIATIONS:

Pineapple Sweet Potato Boats: Fold 1 cup crushed pineapple, drained, into the potatoes with the remaining ingredients.

Orange-Flavored Sweet Potato Boats: Add 2 tablespoons orange-flavored liqueur to the mashed potatoes with the remaining ingredients.

Rum-Pecan Sweet Potato Boats: Add 2 tablespoons rum and ¼ cup chopped pecans to the mashed potatoes with the remaining ingredients.

Boiled Potato Basics:

1. Potatoes must be pierced, peeled, or cut up before being cooked so that steam won't build up underneath the potato skin.
2. One to 1½ cut-up pounds potatoes are cooked with ¼ cup water and covered tightly so that they steam on HIGH power.
3. Potatoes cooked in a casserole dish should be stirred once to redistribute the heat from the outside to the inside of the casserole.
4. If salt is added it should be stirred into the cooking liquid or shaken on at the end of cooking to prevent any surfaces from overcooking.
5. Potatoes must stand for 3 minutes after cooking, with the lid or cover on top to hold in the steam.
6. *Doneness:* Potatoes should be easily pierced with a fork but still remain slightly firm; they should not break apart when pierced.

    Underdone: If still too firm after standing time, cover and return to the oven. Cook on HIGH at 1-minute intervals, stirring after each minute until they test done.

    Overdone: They can still be creamed or topped with grated cheese melted on top.

✸ BOILED POTATO SLICES

MAKES 4 TO 6 SERVINGS   BEGIN 15 MINUTES BEFORE SERVING
COOKING TIME: 8 TO 12 MINUTES

A quick way to make home fries is to cook the potatoes in the microwave first, as described below, and then drain and cook them in a little oil on top of the stove to crisp.

4 medium potatoes (about 1½ pounds), scrubbed but not peeled	**¼ cup water**

Cut the potatoes into ¼-inch slices. In a 2-quart casserole combine the potatoes and water. Cover tightly and cook on HIGH for 8 to 12 minutes, or until tender, stirring once. Let stand, covered, for 2 minutes. Drain. Serve as is or with any potato topping (page 451).

✱ POTATO SALAD

MAKES 4 SERVINGS   BEGIN 1 HOUR BEFORE SERVING
COOKING TIME: 7 TO 10 MINUTES

The secret to a good potato salad is to cook the potatoes in their jackets and marinate them in vinaigrette while still warm. Waxy potatoes hold their shape best and won't become mushy from the dressing.

- 1 pound new or long white potatoes, washed
- ¼ cup water
- ¼ cup vegetable or olive oil
- 2 tablespoons vinegar
- ¼ teaspoon salt
- ¼ teaspoon pepper
- 1 tablespoon finely chopped scallion, chives, or onion
- 1 tablespoon chopped fresh parsley (optional)

Pierce the potatoes. Place them in a 2-quart casserole. Add the water. Cover tightly and cook on HIGH for 7 to 10 minutes, or until tender, turning over and repositioning halfway through cooking. Let stand, covered, for 10 minutes, or until they can be handled.

Drain, then peel and cut the potatoes into ⅛-inch slices, first spearing the potatoes with a fork to keep hands from becoming too warm. Place the potato slices in a serving bowl.

In a small mixing bowl combine the oil, vinegar, salt, and pepper. Pour over the warm potatoes. Let marinate for at least 30 minutes at room temperature. Stir in the remaining ingredients right before serving.

VARIATIONS:

New Potato Salad: Substitute small, red-skinned new potatoes, whole or halved before cooking. Reduce cooking time to 5 to 9 minutes on HIGH. Do not peel.

German Potato Salad: Cook and slice the potatoes as directed. In a 1-quart casserole combine the oil, vinegar, salt, pepper, and ¼ cup beef broth (see Mock Brown Broth or Stock, page 119). Cook on HIGH for 2 minutes. Pour over the potatoes. Let stand for 30 minutes. Fold in ¼ cup crumbled cooked bacon (see page 61) *or* thinly sliced smoked sausage, such as bratwurst or kielbasa, with the scallions and parsley.

In celebration of spring, when the first dandelion plants surface but have yet to blossom, this German potato salad comes to the table, surrounded with a dandelion green salad. Combine 2 cups dandelion greens, 2 tablespoons thinly sliced scallions, and ¼ cup Herb Vinaigrette (page 185).

Sweet Potato Salad: Substitute about 4 sweet potatoes for the potatoes, but cook according to the chart (page 73), without any water.

Sweet Potato Salad Baja: Substitute about 4 sweet potatoes for the potatoes, but cook according to the chart (page 73), without any water. Substitute 2 tablespoons lime juice for the vinegar and cilantro (coriander) for the parsley.

Liberty Steak and Potato Salad: Make New Potato Salad variation. Slice chilled Steak au Poivre (page 280) on the diagonal, making 2 cups. Fold into potato salad. Garnish with salad greens such as arugula, dandelion, or frisia and radishes. A good Fourth of July meal.

Sweet Potato–Pineapple Salad: Substitute about 4 sweet potatoes for the potatoes, but cook according to the chart (page 73), without any water. Substitute 1 cup fresh or canned unsweetened pineapple chunks, drained, for the scallions.

AMERICAN POTATO SALAD

MAKES 4 SERVINGS

BEGIN 1½ HOURS BEFORE SERVING

---

1 recipe Potato Salad, with potatoes cubed instead of sliced (page 455)	½ cup thinly sliced celery pieces
½ cup Mayonnaise (page 175)	2 eggs, hard-cooked (page 55) and sliced
	Paprika

To the chilled salad stir in the mayonnaise and celery. Garnish with hard-cooked eggs and sprinkle with paprika.

VARIATIONS:

Southwestern Potato Salad: Add 2 tablespoons Salsa Cruda (page 185) to the mayonnaise before stirring into the potatoes.

Coastal Potato Salad: Add 1 cup Steamed Clams or Mussels (page 241) with the mayonnaise.

American Potato-Vegetable Salad: Add ½ cup cooked peas, cubed carrots, corn kernels or green beans, or ½ cup peeled, seeded, and chopped raw cucumber in place of the celery pieces.

Tangy American Potato Salad: Substitute ¼ cup mayonnaise and ¼ cup plain yogurt for the ½ cup mayonnaise. We have used this combination often and really like the flavor.

American Potato Salad with Mustard Dressing: Add 1 tablespoon rough country-style mustard to the mayonnaise before stirring into the potatoes.

MASHED POTATOES

MAKES 4 SERVINGS   BEGIN 20 TO 25 MINUTES BEFORE SERVING
COOKING TIME: 10 TO 16 MINUTES

1½ pounds potatoes, peeled and quartered ¼ cup water	2 to 4 tablespoons butter ¼ cup milk Salt and pepper to taste

In a 2-quart casserole combine the potatoes and water. Cover tightly and cook on HIGH for 10 to 16 minutes, or until very tender, stirring once halfway through cooking. Let stand, covered, for 3 minutes.

Mash the potatoes well with a potato masher to remove all the lumps. Stir in the butter. Meanwhile, pour the milk into a 1-cup glass measure. Heat on HIGH for 45 seconds to warm. Add the warm milk and whip until light and fluffy, adding 1 or 2 more tablespoons if necessary. Salt and pepper to taste.

NOTE: *To Reheat:* Cover tightly and cook on MEDIUM-HIGH for 2 to 5 minutes, or until hot, stirring every minute.

NEW BUTTERED POTATOES WITH PARSLEY

MAKES 4 SERVINGS   BEGIN 10 TO 15 MINUTES BEFORE SERVING
COOKING TIME: 6 TO 8 MINUTES

1½ pounds small new potatoes, about 1½ to 2 inches in diameter ¼ cup butter	2 tablespoons chopped fresh parsley Pepper

Scrub the potatoes and peel a single strip around the middle of the potatoes; not only is this decorative, it also eliminates the need to pierce the potatoes. In a 2-quart casserole, combine the potatoes and butter. Cover tightly and cook on HIGH for 6 to 8 minutes, or until tender, stirring once after 3 minutes. Sprinkle with parsley and pepper. Stir to coat well and serve. Let stand, covered, for 3 minutes.

VARIATIONS:

New Buttered Potatoes with Dill: Substitute 2 tablespoons chopped fresh dill for the parsley.

New Buttered Potatoes with Mint: Substitute 1 tablespoon chopped fresh mint and 1 teaspoon grated lemon rind for the parsley.

Steamed New Potatoes: Substitute ¼ cup water for the butter. Drain the potatoes after cooking. Serve with freshly ground pepper, sour cream or plain yogurt, and caraway seeds.

POTATO PIE

MAKES 4 SERVINGS FOR LUNCH, 6 TO 8 AS A SIDE DISH   BEGIN 35 TO 40 MINUTES BEFORE SERVING
COOKING TIME: 21 TO 30 MINUTES

This is good as a luncheon dish, cut in wedges, and dished up with eggs. The version with ham is especially good for brunch. Leaving the skins on the potatoes adds to the nutritive value. After the pie is assembled, it is cooked covered with wax paper. This will keep some steam in for even heating of different vegetables, but will not make the pie soggy, as would a tight cover.

- **4 small to medium potatoes**
- **2 tablespoons butter or margarine**
- **2 cups thinly sliced onions**
- **2 medium green peppers, sliced into thin rings**
- **Salt**
- **¼ teaspoon pepper**
- **8 ounces Cheddar cheese, thinly sliced**
- **1 large tomato, thinly sliced into rounds**

Pierce the potato skins. Place in a circle on a paper towel, leaving 1 inch between the potatoes. Cook on HIGH for 10 to 13 minutes, or until tender, turning over once during cooking. Let stand for 5 to 10 minutes.

Meanwhile, in a 1-quart casserole combine the butter or margarine, onions, and peppers. Cover tightly and cook on HIGH for 3 to 5 minutes, or until the vegetables are tender, stirring once. Cut the potatoes into ¼-inch slices, leaving the skins on, if desired. Spread one-third of the cooked peppers and onions evenly over the bottom of a 10-inch pie plate. Top with one-third of the potato slices. Sprinkle with salt and pepper. Top with one-third of the cheese. Repeat layers two more times. Top with the tomato slices. Cover with wax paper and cook on MEDIUM for 8 to 12 minutes, or until the cheese is melted and the bottom is hot or *3 Macungie* (see page 44).

VARIATIONS:

Ham-and-Muenster-Cheese Potato Pie: Cut ¼ pound thinly sliced baked ham into 1-inch squares. Substitute Muenster cheese for the cheddar. Divide the ham into thirds and layer on top of the cheese. Sprinkle each ham layer with paprika, if desired.

Spicy Potato Bake: Substitute mild green chili pepper for the green peppers. Substitute Monterey Jack for the cheddar cheese. Serve with Warm Jalapeño Salsa (page 187) and/or 1 cup sour cream or plain yogurt.

Bacon-Potato Pie: Add ¼ pound cooked bacon strips (see page 61), cut into quarters. Divide into thirds and layer on top of the cheese.

Swiss Potato Pie: Substitute Swiss cheese for the cheddar cheese. Add ¼ pound smoked sausage, thinly sliced. Divide into thirds and layer on top of the cheese.

Spicy Italian Potato Pie: Substitute mozzarella for the cheddar cheese. Add ¼ pound pepperoni or cooked sweet or hot Italian sausage, thinly sliced. Divide into thirds and layer on top of the cheese.

COMPANY SWEET POTATO PIE

MAKES 6 TO 8 SERVINGS   BEGIN 30 TO 40 MINUTES BEFORE SERVING
COOKING TIME: 18 TO 24 MINUTES

4 sweet potatoes (about 2 pounds)	2 tablespoons brown sugar
¼ cup water	¼ teaspoon grated nutmeg
6 tablespoons butter	¼ cup chopped walnuts
¼ cup heavy cream	2 tablespoons grated orange rind
2 tablespoons orange juice	1 navel orange

Pierce the potato skins. Position the potatoes around the outer rim of a 9-inch pie plate, leaving the center open. Add the water. Cover tightly and cook for 10 to 15 minutes, or until fork tender, repositioning halfway through cooking if necessary. Let stand, covered, for 5 to 10 minutes.

Peel and rice or process the potatoes until smooth. Stir in 4 tablespoons butter, cream, orange juice, brown sugar, and nutmeg. Spoon into a 9-inch pie plate and spread evenly. Sprinkle with the nuts and orange rind.

Peel the orange and remove the segments. Place the orange segments around the outer edge of the dish. Place the remaining 2 tablespoons butter in a 1-cup glass measure. Cook on HIGH for 40 seconds to 1 minute to melt. Drizzle the butter over the pie. Cover with wax paper and cook on HIGH for 7 to 8 minutes, or until heated through.

VARIATIONS:

Sweet Potato Pie with Grand Marnier: Substitute Grand Marnier for the orange juice. Substitute pecans for the walnuts.

Flambéed Sweet Potato Pie: Pour 2 tablespoons 80-proof liqueur into a 1-cup glass measure. Cook on HIGH for 15 seconds. Ignite and pour over the pie. For added drama, turn off the lights.

Sweet Potato Pie with Apples: Combine 2 large tart apples, peeled and sliced, with 2 tablespoons butter, 2 tablespoons brown sugar, and 1 teaspoon lemon juice. Cover with wax paper and cook on HIGH for 3 to 6 minutes, or until the apples are tender, stirring once. Set aside.

Prepare the sweet potato mixture, but eliminate the nuts, orange rind, and orange segments. Spoon the apple-butter mixture on top of the pie. Eliminate the remaining 2 tablespoons butter. Cook as directed.

ROOT VEGETABLES

If there were wise vegetables in the botanical kingdom, they would be the roots. These vegetables hole up in the ground for months while other vegetables are sacrificing their youth. When the blush of summer has passed, these vegetables step forward with a maturity evident in their sweet and mellow flavors. They don't need to be hurried from store to refrigerator, and all but the carrot can be stored up to two months at 50°F. If necessary, they will keep for up to a week at room temperature.

When we were growing up, root vegetables seemed more old-fashioned than wise. It wasn't until we aged a bit ourselves that we grew to like them. But now there is nothing so tasty as carrots cooked in orange juice, or beets with a fine grating of lemon peel. Parsnips make the lightest, creamiest puree for a side dish or pie filling. As you'll see, all the root vegetables are cooked in approximately the same way.

Root Vegetable Basics:

1. Because root vegetables are very thick and dense, they cook most evenly and quickly when diced or cut into thin matchsticks.
2. Root vegetables are cooked on HIGH with about ¼ cup cooking liquid, unless they are to be pureed. If they are to be pureed, ½ cup liquid is called for and a slightly longer cooking time to achieve the most tender vegetable. No more than ½ cup liquid should be added, though, or it will slow down cooking.
3. Root vegetables are covered tightly, with a lid or plastic wrap turned back on one corner. This is to hold in all available steam for quicker and more even cooking.
4. Root vegetables must be stirred once or twice, depending on the length of cooking time, to redistribute heat from the outside to the inside of the casserole.
5. Root vegetables should be salted at the end of cooking, unless the salt is dissolved in the liquid first before adding. Salt on the dry surface of the vegetables will cause the surface to dry out during cooking.
6. Standing time is important to complete the cooking process of root vegetables, especially if they haven't been cut into small pieces.
7. *Doneness:* Root vegetables are particularly sturdy and take longer than most vegetables to cook. They should be cooked until the large pieces can be pierced but remain firm enough to hold their shape. The standing time should make all the pieces tender.

Underdone/Overdone: In the case of underdone, more cooking time is called for on HIGH at 1-minute intervals, stirring in between. The addition of more hot liquid (no more than ½ cup total) might be necessary to soften up the vegetables if time doesn't seem to be doing it.

"Toughness" can be mistaken for underdone or overdone, when really the roots are overmature. If this is the case, finely chop the vegetables in a food processor. Return to the casserole, adding ¼ cup hot water and a cover. Cook until tender and then run through the processor again to puree.

Toppings for Root Vegetables

Add any of the following to 2 cups cooked, drained, or 4 servings root vegetables:

Herb Butter: Melt ¼ cup butter with 2 tablespoons chopped fresh chives, tarragon, or parsley. Pour over cooked, drained root vegetables.

Quick Creamed: Stir ½ cup plain yogurt or sour cream and ½ teaspoon freshly ground pepper into cooked, drained root vegetables.

Quick Herbed Cream: Stir ½ cup plain yogurt or sour cream and 1 tablespoon chopped fresh dill, parsley, or chives into cooked, drained root vegetables.

Quick Mustard Cream: Combine ½ cup plain yogurt or sour cream with 1 tablespoon Dijon or country mustard with seeds. Stir into cooked, drained root vegetables.

Oriental: Stir ½ cup Oriental Dressing (page 184) into cooked, drained root vegetables.

☀ JULIENNED ROOT VEGETABLES

MAKES 4 SERVINGS   BEGIN 20 TO 25 MINUTES BEFORE SERVING
COOKING TIME: 9 TO 12 MINUTES

Any root vegetable can be prepared in this manner and be both attractive and delicious. The time that it takes to cut them into little matchsticks is worth it.

- 2 **tablespoons butter**
- 2 **tablespoons finely chopped scallions**
- 1½ **pounds parsnips, carrots, or other root vegetable, peeled, trimmed, and cut into matchsticks (about 4 cups) (see Note)**
- 1 **teaspoon sugar**
- 1 **tablespoon orange juice**
- ½ **teaspoon salt**
- ¼ **teaspoon pepper**

In a 1-quart casserole combine the butter and scallions. Cook on HIGH for 1 to 2 minutes, or until the scallions are slightly tender. Stir in the remaining ingredients except salt and pepper. Cover tightly and cook on HIGH for 8 to 10 minutes, or until desired doneness is reached, stirring once. Stir in salt and pepper. Let stand, covered, for 2 to 3 minutes.

NOTE: You can also use 2 cups each julienned parsnips and carrots, or 1⅓ cups each julienned parsnips, carrots, and turnips.

VARIATION:

Julienned Root Vegetables with Fresh Herbs: Substitute fresh lemon or lime juice for the orange juice. After cooking, stir in ¼ cup chopped fresh parsley, basil, or dill.

ZESTY JULIENNED BEETS

MAKES 4 SERVINGS   BEGIN 15 TO 20 MINUTES BEFORE SERVING
COOKING TIME: 6 TO 8 MINUTES

Beets should be cooked in their skins, unless you are cooking them this way. Here they are cooked for a short period of time in a small amount of butter, and little or no bleeding takes place; the fact that they are cut into such thin strips accounts for the short cooking time. Serving beets with their greens is one of our favorite vegetables: Serve these in the center of a serving platter ringed with Sautéed Light Greens made with beet greens (page 428).

- 1 pound beets, peeled and cut into ¼-inch matchsticks
- 2 tablespoons butter
- 1 tablespoon lime juice, lemon juice, or vinegar
- ½ teaspoon grated lime or lemon rind
- ¼ teaspoon salt
- ⅛ teaspoon pepper

In a 1½-quart casserole combine the beets and butter. Cover tightly and cook on HIGH for 6 to 8 minutes, or until desired doneness is reached, stirring once. Stir in the remaining ingredients. Cover again and let stand for 2 minutes.

HARVARD OR SWEET AND SOUR BEETS

MAKES 4 SERVINGS   BEGIN 35 MINUTES BEFORE SERVING
COOKING TIME: 5 TO 7 MINUTES

- ¼ cup water
- 2 tablespoons sugar
- ¼ cup vinegar
- 1 tablespoon cornstarch
- 2 tablespoons butter
- ¼ teaspoon salt
- ⅛ teaspoon pepper
- 1 pound beets, cooked and sliced (page 73)

In a 1-cup glass measure combine the water and sugar. In a custard cup blend the vinegar and cornstarch until smooth. Add the vinegar mixture, butter, salt, and pepper to the sugar-water. Cook on HIGH for 3 to 4 minutes, or until thickened and boiling, stirring twice.

Place the beets in a 1½-quart casserole and stir the sauce in to coat them. Cover tightly and cook on HIGH for 2 to 3 minutes, or until heated through.

CANDIED CARROTS

MAKES 4 SERVINGS BEGIN 15 MINUTES BEFORE SERVING
COOKING TIME: 4 TO 8 MINUTES

---

2 cups carrots, cut into ¼-inch slices
1 tablespoon butter

1 tablespoon brown sugar, honey, or maple syrup

In a 1-quart casserole combine all the ingredients. Cover tightly and cook on HIGH for 4 to 8 minutes, or until the desired doneness is reached, stirring every 2 minutes to coat the carrots. Stir and let stand, covered, for 3 minutes.

VARIATIONS:

Gingered Carrots: Add ½ teaspoon of ground ginger.

Cinnamon-Spice Carrots: Add ¼ teaspoon ground cinnamon and ⅛ teaspoon ground cloves.

Brandied Carrots: Add 1 tablespoon of brandy.

Crunchy Candied Carrots: Before serving, stir in 2 tablespoons chopped pecans.

Caraway Candied Carrots: Before serving, stir in ¼ teaspoon crushed caraway seeds.

WINTER CARROT OR BEET SALAD

MAKES 4 SERVINGS

Make the vinaigrette with a fruit-flavored vinegar such as raspberry.

---

2 cups sliced cooked beets or carrots (page 73)
¼ cup chopped onions or scallions

½ cup Herb Vinaigrette (page 185)
Freshly ground pepper
Lettuce leaves

In a medium mixing bowl combine the beets or carrots and onions. Stir in the vinaigrette and pepper to taste. Chill and serve on lettuce leaves.

VARIATION:

Low-Calorie Carrot and Beet Salad: Substitute 1 tablespoon lime or lemon juice for the vinaigrette.

ROOT VEGETABLE PUREE

MAKES 8 SERVINGS   BEGIN 20 TO 25 MINUTES BEFORE SERVING
COOKING TIME: 10 TO 15 MINUTES

Any of the root vegetables lend themselves well to purees. We like to make these warm and soothing vegetable blends in the winter months, and find they go particularly well with game and roasted meats.

- 2 pounds combination root vegetables and potatoes (see Notes), diced
- ½ cup water
- 2 tablespoons white or brown sugar
- ¼ cup butter
- ½ cup cream, crème fraîche, or plain yogurt
- Dash of cayenne pepper

In a 2-quart casserole combine the vegetables and water. Cover tightly and cook on HIGH for 10 to 15 minutes, or until tender, stirring twice. Let stand, covered, for 3 minutes.

Meanwhile, place the butter in a 1-cup glass measure. Cook on HIGH for 1 to 2 minutes, or until melted.

Drain the liquid from the cooked vegetables, and discard the liquid. Puree the vegetables in a food processor or food mill. Stir in the remaining ingredients.

NOTES: Try the following vegetable combinations: carrots and white potatoes, carrots and parsnips, parsnips and white potatoes, parsnips and sweet potatoes, turnips and carrots, turnips and sweet potatoes.

If not serving right away, set the vegetables aside or refrigerate.

To Reheat: Cover tightly and cook on MEDIUM-HIGH for 2 to 5 minutes, or until hot, stirring every minute.

VARIATIONS:

Root Puree with Spice: Add ½ teaspoon grated nutmeg to the melted butter.

Sherried Root Puree: Add 2 tablespoons of sherry, Madeira, or rum to the melted butter.

✺ SAVORY CARROT PUREE

MAKES 4 SERVINGS   BEGIN 15 TO 20 MINUTES BEFORE SERVING
COOKING TIME: 9 TO 12 MINUTES

This delicately herbed side dish is particularly attractive on a dinner plate when served alone, or alongside two other purees, such as lentil and parsnips, to form an orange, green, and white combo. Its versatility extends to filling mushroom caps or small pastry-shell hors d'oeuvres.

1 pound carrots, peeled and cut into 2-inch pieces	1 teaspoon salt
½ cup finely chopped onion	½ teaspoon thyme
½ cup water	2 tablespoons butter

In a 1½-quart casserole combine the carrots, onion, and water. Cover tightly and cook on HIGH for 7 to 10 minutes, or until the vegetables are fork tender, stirring once. Let stand, covered, for 2 minutes. Drain. Puree in a blender or food processor, adding the salt and thyme.

Return to the casserole. Cook, uncovered, for 2 minutes, or until heated through, stirring after 1 minute. Stir in the butter and serve.

SQUASHES

There are two categories of squash. The winter squash are harvested when they are mature and are plentiful from October to February. They have tough skins and seeds, which cannot be eaten, but it's this tough shell that allows them to be stored up to three months in a dry place that is 50°F. That cooked shell also makes the vegetable easy to serve and when uncooked makes a dandy jack-o'-lantern or natural bowl for crisp vegetables or dip.

The summer squash are available from April to August and are harvested when they are immature. Both seeds and skins are edible, but with their thin skins, they will only keep three to four days in the refrigerator. Mild-flavored summer squash are an excellent companion for many other vegetables.

Winter Squash Basics:

1. When winter squash is cooked whole, its thick skin should be pierced to allow the steam to escape. (You'll see this principle exercised with potatoes and eggplants, too.)
2. When cooking the larger whole squashes, it is easier to handle the hot squash when it has been placed on a plate before cooking.
3. The skin on winter squash is particularly tough and hard to cut open when the squash is raw. If, for example, you plan to cut an acorn squash in half and stuff it, the squash can be cooked on HIGH for 2 minutes before halving. These 2 minutes will make your cutting job that much easier.
4. If cooked whole or even cut in half, winter squash needs no additional water for cooking. A squash, cut in half, should be covered tightly to hold in all available moisture. The cooked flesh of the squash can be pureed into a soup or an ingredient for bread.

If winter squash is to be cut up in slices

before cooking and serving, a small amount of liquid is added to a covered dish.
5. If winter squash is cooked whole, it should be turned over during cooking, which will keep steam from building up on the bottom that could soften that bottom part of the skin.
6. Winter squash must stand for at least 5 minutes for the heat to penetrate this dense vegetable.
7. *Doneness:* Take the squash from the oven. If too hot, wrap with a paper towel or dish towel to test. Press as if you were checking the ripeness of a tomato. The flesh should give slightly under the skin when you press it with your fingers. Check several places. After standing, the flesh should collapse easily under the pressure of your fingers.

Underdone: For whole squash or pumpkin, remove any that appear done. Turn over the underdone squash and cook on HIGH at 1-minute intervals. You may even want to cut the larger pumpkin in half and cover the cut ends with plastic wrap to speed the cooking process.

If the squash has been cut up before cooking, stir and continue to cook. Winter squash may need additional liquid (if there is none left in the dish) and cooking at 1-minute intervals on HIGH.

> **Toppings for Winter Squash:**
>
> Add any of the following to 1 serving winter squash (which is ¼ hubbard or butternut squash or ½ acorn squash).
>
> **Melted Butter:** Add 1 tablespoon butter to melt. Salt and pepper to taste.
>
> **Brown Sugar–Buttered:** Add 1 tablespoon brown sugar to 1 tablespoon melted butter. Spoon onto cooked squash.
>
> **Citrus-Buttered:** Add 1½ teaspoons grated lemon or lime rind to 1 tablespoon melted butter. Pour over cooked squash.
>
> **Orange-Buttered:** Add 1 tablespoon Orange Butter (page 183) to cooked squash to melt.
>
> **Honey-Buttered:** Add 1 teaspoon honey to 1 tablespoon melted butter. Spoon onto cooked squash.
>
> **Maple-Buttered:** Add 1 teaspoon maple syrup to 1 tablespoon melted butter. Pour over cooked squash.
>
> **Bacon-Topped:** Sprinkle 1 tablespoon crumbled crisp bacon (see page 61) on top of cooked squash.
>
> **Nut-Buttered:** Stir 1 tablespoon chopped nuts into 1 tablespoon melted butter. Pour over cooked squash.

✹ PUREED WINTER SQUASH

MAKES 4 SERVINGS   BEGIN 20 TO 25 MINUTES BEFORE SERVING
COOKING TIME: 12 TO 18 MINUTES

A delicious way to serve winter squash. When there is an abundance of winter squash, we make a lot and then season it in many different ways.

1 2-pound winter squash	½ teaspoon salt
¼ cup butter	¼ teaspoon pepper

Follow the cooking instructions in the chart on page 75 for the winter squash of your choice.

After standing, remove the seeds and scoop out the squash flesh. Place in a blender or food processor and blend until smooth. Add the remaining ingredients; process to blend.

NOTE: Freeze the puree in 2-cup containers for soups. To make soup, remove the cover from the frozen puree. Heat on HIGH for 2 to 5 minutes, until you can remove and transfer to a 2-quart casserole. Heat on HIGH for 10 to 15 minutes, or until completely defrosted, stirring and breaking up every 5 minutes. When defrosted, add either 2 cups Chicken Broth or Stock (page 118), and 1 cup cream. Season with chopped fresh dill or parsley and a grating of nutmeg or a dash of hot pepper sauce. Cook on HIGH for 6 to 10 minutes, or until hot, stirring occasionally.

VARIATIONS:

Sweet-'n'-Spicy Squash Puree: Add 2 tablespoons brown sugar and ½ teaspoon each grated nutmeg and ground cinnamon with the butter.

Southern-Style Squash Puree: Add 2 tablespoons brown sugar with the butter. Fold in 2 tablespoons chopped cooked bacon (see page 61) before serving.

Vermont Squash Puree: Add 2 tablespoons maple syrup with the butter

Nutty Squash Puree: Fold in ¼ cup chopped nuts or whole pine nuts right before serving.

Squash Puree with Rum: Add 1 tablespoon rum or brandy and 1 tablespoon brown sugar with the butter. Fold in ¼ cup chopped pecans right before serving.

Honey-Orange Squash Puree: Add 1 tablespoon honey and 1 teaspoon grated orange rind with the butter.

Company Squash Puree: Add 1 tablespoon orange-flavored liqueur with the butter. Serve in hollowed-out orange shells garnished with orange rind slivers and chive strips.

CANDIED ACORN SQUASH

MAKES 4 SERVINGS   BEGIN 25 MINUTES BEFORE SERVING
COOKING TIME: 18 MINUTES

The squash is cooked uncovered at the end, to evaporate some of the moisture and to glaze the squash. You may even want to eat the skin on this squash, if it isn't too late in the season when the skin has been coated with paraffin.

- **2 tablespoons butter**
- **¼ cup brown sugar**
- **½ teaspoon ground ginger or cinnamon**

- **2 pounds acorn squash, washed, cut into ½-inch slices, then quartered and seeded**

Place the butter in a 2-quart rectangular dish. Cook on HIGH for 35 seconds to 1 minute to melt. Tilt the dish to coat with the butter. Sprinkle brown sugar and ginger evenly over the butter. Add the squash. Cover tightly and cook on HIGH for 12 minutes, turning the pieces over and repositioning them after 4 minutes. Then cook, uncovered, on HIGH for 5 minutes. Turn the squash pieces over to coat well with the sauce and let stand for 5 minutes, to absorb more of the sauce. Serve, spooning the sauce on top.

Toasted Pumpkin or Squash Seeds

MAKES 1 CUP
COOKING TIME: 10 TO 15 MINUTES

The most asked question when Thelma was answering the New York Cooperative Extension hotline was "How do I toast pumpkin seeds?" These seeds are great for munching alone or with drinks.

- **1 cup pumpkin or squash seeds**
- **1 tablespoon butter**
- **Salt**

Wash, drain, and pat the seeds dry. Place a double layer of nonrecycled paper towels (see Notes) in a 2-quart rectangular dish. Sprinkle the seeds evenly on top. Cook on HIGH for 10 to 15 minutes, or until dried but still white, stirring twice; check frequently the last 5 minutes so as not to overcook. Let stand for 5 minutes, to continue drying.

Place the butter in a 2-cup microwaveproof bowl. Cook on HIGH for 35 seconds to 1 minute to melt. Stir the seeds in to coat. Sprinkle with salt to taste.

NOTES: Butternut squash seeds usually take the longest to toast.

Nonrecycled is particularly important here because this is a drying process and recycled paper toweling may contain metal flecks, which could ignite without any moisture to dampen it.

VARIATION:

Spicy Toasted Seeds: Substitute ½ teaspoon garlic salt for the salt. Add ½ teaspoon curry powder or ⅛ teaspoon cayenne pepper with the garlic salt.

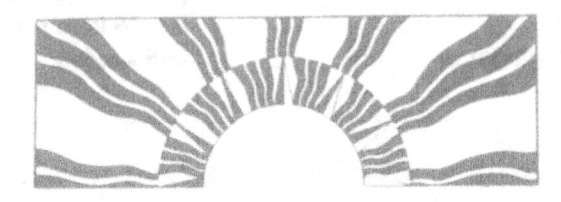

Summer Squash Basics:

1. There is no need to add liquid when cooking this summer squash. Butter or tomatoes are only added for flavoring.
2. Summer squash is cooked on HIGH power covered with wax paper. This will keep some moisture in for uniform cooking, but not enough to make the vegetable soggy.
3. Sliced summer squash is made in a round casserole where it can be easily stirred once during cooking.
4. Salt is sprinkled on at the end of cooking to prevent any drying or overcooking of squash.
5. *Doneness:* Zucchini, straight and crookneck, and pattypan squash should all pierce easily with a fork. Standing time is insignificant. If underdone, continue to cook on HIGH, checking at 30-second intervals.

Toppings for Summer Squash

Add any of these to 4 servings cooked summer squash:

Salt and Pepper: Simple but good.

Fines Herbes: Stir 2 tablespoons chopped fresh basil, chives, parsley, oregano, or sage into squash.

Parmesan: Sprinkle 2 tablespoons grated Parmesan cheese on top of squash.

Nutty: Sprinkle 2 tablespoons chopped nuts on top of squash.

Jalapeño-Sauced: Stir ¼ cup Warm Jalapeño Salsa (page 187) into squash.

Melted Butters: Double any of the butters on page 183.

✸ SAUTÉED SUMMER SQUASH

MAKES 4 SERVINGS   BEGIN 10 MINUTES BEFORE SERVING
COOKING TIME: 5 TO 8 MINUTES

- 1 tablespoon butter, margarine, or vegetable oil
- 2 garlic cloves, minced, or 2 tablespoons chopped scallion
- 3 to 4 medium (1¼ to 1½ pounds) summer squash, cut into ¼-inch slices
- 2 tablespoons chopped fresh herbs (parsley, basil, and chives)
- ½ teaspoon salt
- ¼ teaspoon pepper

In a 2-quart casserole combine the butter or oil and garlic. Cook on HIGH for 1 to 2 minutes, or until tender. Stir in the squash. Cover with wax paper and cook on HIGH for 4 to 6 minutes, or until the squash is tender, stirring after 2 minutes. Stir in the remaining ingredients.

VARIATIONS:

Summer Squash with Parmesan: Sprinkle with 2 tablespoons grated Parmesan cheese right before serving.

Summer Squash with Almonds: Sprinkle with ¼ cup slivered almonds right before serving.

Summer Squash with Tomatoes: Add 1 red ripe tomato, peeled, seeded, and chopped, with the squash.

SUMMER SQUASH PIE

MAKES 6 TO 8 SERVINGS AS A SIDE DISH, 4 AS A MAIN COURSE   BEGIN 35 TO 45 MINUTES BEFORE SERVING
COOKING TIME: 20 TO 30 MINUTES

This qualifies for a vegetarian meal. It is very simple to prepare, and only one cooking dish is required. The pie is cooked uncovered to keep the exterior dry and on MEDIUM *power because this is a sensitive egg mixture.*

2 tablespoons butter or margarine	3 eggs, lightly beaten
1 garlic clove, minced (optional)	½ teaspoon salt
1 medium onion, coarsely chopped	¼ teaspoon pepper
1½ pounds small to medium summer squash, washed, cut into ¼-inch slices	2 tablespoons chopped fresh parsley or 2 teaspoons dried (optional)
1 cup fresh bread crumbs (whole-wheat preferred)	1 tablespoon chopped fresh basil or 1 teaspoon dried (optional)
1 cup grated cheddar, Gruyère, or Swiss cheese	2 tomatoes, cut into ¼-inch slices (optional)
	1 cup plain yogurt or sour cream

In a 10-inch pie plate combine the butter, garlic, and onion. Cook on HIGH for 2 to 3 minutes, or until the onion is tender. Add the squash. Cover with wax paper and cook on HIGH for 8 to 12 minutes, or until tender, stirring twice.

Stir in the remaining ingredients except the tomatoes and yogurt. Spread evenly in the dish. Arrange the tomato slices decoratively around the outer rim of the dish, leaving the center open. Cook on MEDIUM for 10 to 15 minutes, or until a knife inserted 1 inch from the center comes out clean and the center is almost set. Let stand for 5 minutes; the center will set during standing time. Serve with a spoonful of yogurt or sour cream, if desired.

VARIATION:

Mexicali Zucchini Pie: Substitute Monterey Jack cheese for cheddar cheese. Add 2 tablespoons diced canned green chilies with the cheese.

Stuffed Squash Basics:

1. A mature squash is cooked completely first, on HIGH power, before adding any stuffing. It need not be cut in half first because that is much easier to do after it is cooked. Make sure to pierce the skin before cooking so that steam doesn't build up inside the squash.
2. The stuffing is precooked or made of ingredients that need only reheating. When mature squash and filling are cooked again, they are covered with wax paper and just heated through on HIGH power for a few minutes.
3. Pattypan or smaller, immature squash with edible skins are not precooked before stuffing. They are cooked on HIGH—arranged so that no two are touching, so all surfaces are exposed to cooking energy—with a tight cover for a longer time, to cook the squash through and heat the filling.

✺ CRANBERRY-STUFFED SQUASH

MAKES 4 SERVINGS   BEGIN ABOUT 25 MINUTES BEFORE SERVING
COOKING TIME: 13 TO 18 MINUTES

This is appropriate for Thanksgiving or any fall meal, especially good with fowl. Don't throw away the squash seeds, but toast them for snacks (page 468).

- 2 1-pound acorn squash
- ¾ cup fresh or frozen cranberries
- 3 tablespoons orange marmalade, or 2 tablespoons concentrated frozen orange juice
- 3 tablespoons brown sugar
- 2 tablespoons butter
- 1 teaspoon lemon juice

With a fork pierce the whole squash on each side. Place on a paper towel in the oven. Cook on HIGH for 12 to 15 minutes, or until fork-tender, turning over after 5 minutes. Let stand for 5 to 10 minutes.

Meanwhile, in a 1-quart casserole combine the remaining ingredients. Cover with wax paper; a tight cover would cause the berries to boil up and cook over. Cook on HIGH for 3 to 5 minutes, or until all the berries have popped, stirring after 2 minutes.

Cut the squash in half. Remove the seeds and reserve for toasting, if desired. Place cut side up on a 12-inch microwaveproof platter. Spoon the cranberry mixture into the hollowed-out squash. Cover with wax paper and cook on HIGH for 1 to 3 minutes.

NOTES: To prepare in advance, cook and refrigerate the stuffed squash. Cover with wax paper and cook on HIGH for 3 to 5 minutes, or until the bottom of the plate under the squash feels hot to the touch or 2 Macungie (see page 44).

To Double: Since this is a nice holiday dish, you can double all the ingredients and cook the squash on HIGH for 20 to 25 minutes, turning over and rearranging twice. Cook the filling on HIGH for 4 to 8 minutes.

VARIATION:

Apple-Stuffed Acorn Squash: Cook the squash as directed in the basic recipe. Eliminate the cranberries and orange marmalade. For the stuffing, in a 1-quart casserole combine 2 medium apples, peeled, cored, and thinly sliced; 2 tablespoons orange, apple, or lemon juice; and ¼ cup raisins (optional). Cover tightly and cook on HIGH for 3½ to 6 minutes, or until the apples are tender, stirring halfway through cooking. Stir in the butter and brown sugar. Fill the cooked squash halves and proceed with the basic recipe. Top with ¼ cup chopped nuts before serving.

STUFFED PATTYPAN SQUASH

MAKES 4 SERVINGS   BEGIN 25 TO 35 MINUTES BEFORE SERVING
COOKING TIME: 13 TO 21 MINUTES

4 medium mature pattypan squash	¼ cup grated cheese
¼ cup butter	2 tablespoons minced fresh parsley, or 2 teaspoons dried
1 garlic clove, minced	
1 medium onion, coarsely chopped	
¼ cup fresh bread crumbs (whole-wheat preferred)	

Cut the tops from the squash and scoop out the centers, leaving about ¼-inch-thick shells. Discard the stem, stringy pith, and seeds; coarsely chop the flesh.

In a 2-quart casserole combine the butter, garlic, and onion. Cook on HIGH for 2 to 4 minutes, or until the onion is tender. Stir in the squash flesh. Cook on HIGH for 3 to 5 minutes, or until tender, stirring once. Stir in the remaining ingredients. Spoon the mixture into the squash shells.

Arrange the stuffed shells, at least 1 inch apart, on a 10-inch round or 2-quart rectangular dish. Cover tightly and cook on HIGH for 8 to 12 minutes, or until cooked through, rotating the dish once. Let stand, covered, for 5 minutes.

VARIATIONS:

Stuffed Pattypan Squash with Tomato Sauce: Prepare the squash. During standing time, heat 2 cups tomato sauce (see pages 178 and 179) and pour over to serve. Sprinkle with additional grated cheese.

Vegetarian Squash: Add 2 eggs, ½ cup grated cheddar cheese, and ¼ cup toasted sesame seeds or pine nuts to the stuffing with the bread crumbs. Serve with ¼ cup sour cream or plain yogurt. We love this!

STALKS

High in fiber and low in calories are the best descriptive terms for these vegetables. They represent the least expensive (celery) and the most expensive (asparagus) of vegetables, and yet none are so class conscious that they won't take to a delicate cream sauce or a catchall of leftovers with equal appeal. All the stalks are best stored unwashed, in the refrigerator, with asparagus lasting up to three days and celery and fennel up to a week.

Although most can be eaten raw, these vegetables prove much more digestible when they are cooked, which helps to soften the tough cellulose. Because these vegetables are mostly cellulose and water, they are not suitable for vegetable purees, which would only become stringy and watery. But because of their crisp texture, they are excellent for our microwave version of wok cooking, which we call "stir-shake."

When cooked as trimmed stalks, asparagus and celery require special arrangement in a rectangular dish, with the thicker pieces toward the outside. We also have moved broccoli over to this category from the cabbage family because by having both flowers and stalks, its arrangement and cooking are very similar to that of asparagus.

We suggest that the leaves of Swiss chard be cooked separately from the stems (see 427). The chard stalks should be cooked as indicated in this section.

Arranged Stalk Basics:

1. The thicker, longer cooking stalks are positioned toward the outside of the cooking dish, where they will get the most energy. A large enough dish must be used to accommodate the arrangement. This lesson applies to any food that has two different shapes or thicknesses in one piece.
2. Peeling those thicker ends also helps them to cook in the same time as the more porous flower or bud ends.
3. Stalks are cooked on HIGH power with liquid and a tight cover; a lid or plastic wrap turned back at one corner to vent steam provides this. The total effect is the quick cooking and steaming of the stalks.
4. In a rectangular dish the stalks need to be rearranged once for more even cooking. If cooking asparagus in this way, start out by placing the thicker stalks to the outside. If cooked in a large circular dish in wheel-

spoke fashion, no adjustments may be needed. If you find one area cooking more quickly than another, rotate the dish a half-turn.
5. Stalks should be salted at the end of cooking, unless the salt is dissolved in liquid before adding. Salt on the dry surface of the vegetable will cause dry spots.
6. Standing time is fairly short but necessary to complete the cooking process of the thicker stalks.
7. *Doneness:* When taken from the oven, the stalks are done when the point of a paring knife easily pierces the thickest pieces, with a slight firmness remaining.

Underdone: If the stalks are not tender enough after standing time, rearrange the stalks and cover tightly. Cook again on HIGH at 1-minute intervals, making sure that there is some liquid in the dish.

Overdone: Overcooking will only happen if the cooking liquid has boiled away and the ends of the stalks get hard and dried out. Just make sure to cover tightly and add the proper amount of liquid.

If broccoli turns yellow, it may be because it has stood longer than the suggested standing time with the cover on. Uncover if not serving shortly after cooking.

Toppings for Stalks

Add any of these to 2 cups cooked and drained or 4 servings stalks:

Melted Butter: Add 2 tablespoons butter to cooked, drained stalks. Let stand for 1 minute to melt.

Herb Butter: Melt ¼ cup butter with 2 tablespoons chopped fresh chives, parsley, or marjoram. Pour over cooked, drained stalks.

Au Citron: Stir 1 tablespoon lemon juice into cooked, drained stalks.

Nutty: Sprinkle ½ cup chopped almonds or walnuts over cooked, drained stalks.

Soya: Eliminate salt in cooking. Stir 1 tablespoon soy sauce into stalks.

Buttered Bread Crumbs: Combine 2 tablespoons melted butter mixed with ¼ cup fine dry bread crumbs. Sprinkle on top of cooked, drained stalks.

Quick Creamed: Stir ¼ cup plain yogurt or sour cream into cooked, drained stalks.

Fines Herbes: Sprinkle 2 tablespoons chopped fresh tarragon or 2 teaspoons dried over cooked, drained stalks.

Hollandaise: Pour 1 cup Hollandaise Sauce (page 174) over cooked, drained stalks.

Au Jambon: Sprinkle ¼ cup chopped cooked ham over cooked, drained stalks.

Bacon-Topped: Sprinkle ¼ cup crumbled crisp bacon (see page 61) over cooked, drained stalks.

Parmesan: Sprinkle ¼ cup grated Parmesan cheese over cooked, drained stalks.

Chilled Vinaigrette: Pour ½ cup Vinaigrette (page 185) over cooked, drained stalks. Chill 30 minutes and serve.

Fennel au Gratin: Place drained fennel in a serving dish. Top with ½ cup grated Gruyère or Swiss cheese. Cook on MEDIUM for 1 to 2 minutes, or until the cheese is melted.

✺ BROCCOLI WITH LEMON SLICES

MAKES 4 SERVINGS   BEGIN 10 TO 15 MINUTES BEFORE SERVING
COOKING TIME: 6 TO 8 MINUTES

This is a basic teaching recipe for positioning stalk vegetables. We like to cook and serve them on a round 12-inch serving dish with the broccoli arranged in spokes and decoratively topped with thin lemon slices.

---

1 1-pound bunch broccoli (see Note)
1 lemon, thinly sliced

2 tablespoons water

Trim 1 inch from the tough end of the broccoli and slice into long spears; you may wish to peel the skin about 2 inches from the bottom of the spear for better cooking. Position the broccoli in wheel-spoke fashion, with the thicker stalk ends toward the outside of a 2-

quart rectangular dish or a 10-inch round serving dish. Arrange the lemon slices attractively over the stalks. Pour the water on top. Cover tightly and cook on HIGH for 6 to 8 minutes, or until the stalks can be pierced with a fork, rearranging the stalks or rotating the dish halfway through cooking. Let stand, covered, for 3 minutes.

NOTE: You can substitute 1 pound asparagus stalks, trimmed, for the broccoli. Cook on HIGH for 4 to 9 minutes.

SESAME SAUTÉED ASPARAGUS

MAKES 4 SERVINGS   BEGIN ABOUT 10 MINUTES BEFORE SERVING TIME
COOKING TIME: 3 TO 7 MINUTES

- 2 tablespoons sesame or vegetable oil
- 1 pound asparagus, cut diagonally into 1-inch pieces
- 2 tablespoons sesame seeds
- 1 tablespoon soy sauce
- 1 teaspoon lemon juice
- Pepper

In a 1-quart casserole combine the oil and asparagus. Cover tightly and cook on HIGH for 3 to 7 minutes, or until desired doneness is reached, stirring once. Stir in the remaining ingredients. Let stand, covered, for 2 minutes.

SAUTÉED STALKS

MAKES 4 SERVINGS   BEGIN 10 TO 15 MINUTES BEFORE SERVING
COOKING TIME: 3 TO 7 MINUTES

Thelma has family friends from the Black Forest area of Germany that prefer the chard stalks to the leaves. Her mother would give them the stalks grown from the garden while her own family ate the leaves—until they tasted the stalks. Their friends still got the stalks, but not as many. Try them in this basic recipe.

- 1 tablespoon butter, margarine, or vegetable oil
- 1 tablespoon finely chopped onion
- 2 cups stalks (Swiss chard, asparagus, broccoli, or celery), cut into ½-inch lengths
- Salt and pepper, or 1 to 2 teaspoons Maggi Swiss herb seasoning

In a 1-quart casserole combine the butter or oil and the onion. Cook on HIGH for 40 seconds to 2 minutes, or until the onion is softened. Stir in the stalks to coat well. Cover tightly and cook on HIGH for 2 to 5 minutes, or until desired doneness is reached, stirring once. Season to taste.

VARIATIONS:

Bacon-Topped Stalks: Stir in 2 tablespoons cooked bacon (see page 61) that has been cut into ½-inch pieces at the end of cooking.

Soy Stir-'n'-Shake Stalks: Substitute sesame or peanut oil and 1 garlic clove, minced, for the butter and onion. Place in a 2-quart casserole and cook as directed. Stir in 1 tablespoon soy sauce. Add the stalks. Instead of stirring, shake the casserole by holding the lid tightly to the casserole dish with both hands. Shake up as if you were throwing pizza dough and the stalks will stir themselves in the larger casserole. Eliminate salt and pepper.

Sautéed Mustard-Flavored Stalks: Stir in 2 teaspoons Dijon mustard at the end of cooking.

VEGETABLE COMBINATIONS

In developing vegetable recipes, we found that some of our favorites, and those of our students, did not fall neatly into one of our previous vegetable categories. The recipes were not made with predominantly one vegetable, and they seemed to dictate two new principles that we had not previously touched on—ones that arose only when cooking together vegetables that have different textures, densities, and cooking times. In such cases you must either 1) begin cooking the longest-cooking vegetable before the others, or 2) place that longest-cooking vegetable on the outside of the dish, so that it receives more energy.

You'll find these two rules illustrated in some of the following recipes. Once you master them, you'll come up with countless renditions of your own that can be tossed together with confidence, since all the vegetables will be cooked to perfection.

Arranged Vegetable Platter Basics:

1. These vegetable platters need never be stirred if the longer-cooking vegetables are arranged around the outer rim to receive the most microwave energy; a circular platter is best. Onion should always be precooked before being added to a platter.
2. Cooking liquid is added in the form of water or some type of watery cooking sauce.
3. All vegetable platters must be covered tightly with a lid or plastic wrap turned back on one corner. This helps all the vegetables to steam properly.
4. These platters are cooked to tender-crisp and there is no appreciable standing time.

☀ JAPANESE VEGETABLES

MAKES 4 TO 6 SERVINGS   BEGIN 15 MINUTES BEFORE SERVING
COOKING TIME: 3 TO 5 MINUTES

Everyone in our classes loves the sauce on this vegetable platter. We cook the vegetables in the shortest possible time to tender-crisp doneness.

- 1 tablespoon butter
- 1 large Bermuda onion, thinly sliced
- 1 medium zucchini, cut into thin strips
- ¼ pound fresh mushrooms, thinly sliced
- ¼ pound bean sprouts
- ¼ cup soy sauce
- 1 tablespoon orange juice
- 1 teaspoon sherry
- 1 tablespoon grated fresh ginger
- 1 teaspoon prepared mustard
- ¼ cup toasted sesame seeds (page 609)

On a 10- to 12-inch round microwaveproof serving platter combine the butter and onion. Cover with plastic wrap and cook on HIGH for 1 minute. Push the onions to the outer edge of the platter to form a large circle. Place the zucchini in the dish to form a circle inside the onions; place the mushrooms in circular fashion inside the zucchini. Place the bean sprouts in the center of the dish.

In a small bowl combine the soy sauce, orange juice, sherry, ginger, and mustard; stir well to blend. Pour half the soy mixture over the vegetables. Cover with plastic wrap with one corner turned up and cook on HIGH for 2 to 4 minutes, or until the vegetables are tender-crisp. Sprinkle with sesame seeds. Pass the remaining sauce with the vegetables.

✸ SEASONAL VEGETABLE PLATTER WITH HERBED BUTTER

MAKES 10 TO 12 SERVINGS   BEGIN 15 TO 20 MINUTES BEFORE SERVING
COOKING TIME: 5 TO 8 MINUTES

A favorite at our cooking schools for economy, flavor, and appearance, we often use this as the centerpiece of the table. When cutting up the vegetables, save the unused parts for the stir-shake recipe that follows.

The platter is arranged with the denser, longer-cooking vegetables around the outside, and the less-dense, shorter-cooking vegetables in the center. That arrangement means even cooking without stirring, but a delightful by-product is the attractive circular pattern that is formed. Also, because the vegetables are spread out and more surfaces are exposed to the microwave energy than in a deep bowl, less water and cooking time are needed.

- 1 cup broccoli flowerets
- 1 cup white cauliflowerets, plus 2 cups purple cauliflowerets
- 2 large carrots, cut into ¼-inch slices
- 1 medium acorn squash, halved, seeded, and cut into ¼-inch slices
- 2 cups mushroom caps
- 2 tablespoons water
- 2 tablespoons butter or margarine
- 1 tablespoon lemon juice
- 1 tablespoon each finely chopped fresh parsley, dill, and chives

---

Around the outside rim of a 12- to 14-inch circular microwaveproof platter, arrange a single row of broccoli and white cauliflowerets, alternating them with the stalks facing toward the outer rim.

Arrange a single row of sliced carrots, angling against the broccoli and cauliflower stalks.

Arrange the purple cauliflowerets in a single circular row, with the stalks tucked underneath the broccoli and white cauliflower.

Place the acorn squash slices, arching crosswise, over the outside rows. Place the mushroom caps, least dense of all, in the center of the platter.

Sprinkle with the water. Cover with plastic wrap, turning up one corner to vent. Cook on HIGH for 5 to 8 minutes, or until tender-crisp, rotating once after 3 minutes. Remove from the oven and allow to stand a moment, covered.

Meanwhile, place the butter in a 1-cup glass measure or small bowl. Cook on HIGH for 30 seconds to 1 minute, or until melted. Stir in the lemon juice and herbs.

Gently drain most of the water from the vegetables. Pour the melted butter over the platter and serve.

VARIATIONS:

Summer Vegetable Platter: Substitute 1 medium tomato, cut into wedges, or 2 cups thinly sliced zucchini for the mushrooms. Substitute 1 cup string beans, cut into 1-inch pieces, for the broccoli.

Springtime Vegetable Platter: Substitute 8 asparagus spears, arranged in spokes with tips pointing toward the center, for the acorn squash.

Pimento-Studded Vegetable Platter: Before cooking, place pimento strips over the mushrooms, in spokes from the center to look like a flower.

Stir-Shake Vegetable Basics:

1. Stir-shake or wok-style vegetable combinations usually team up vegetables of different cooking times. The vegetables are added in the order of their cooking times, with the longest-cooking (usually denser or larger) vegetables added first. Additional liquid is needed when vegetables are added.

2. Garlic, onion, and oil are always cooked slightly before adding any vegetables. Once the other vegetables and ingredients are added a tight cover is necessary.
3. Meat may be added to the vegetables, but it must be cooked first. It is added in the beginning, after the onion and oil, to heat before adding the remaining vegetables.
4. No standing time is necessary.

☀ CARRYOVER VEGETABLE STIR-SHAKE

MAKES 4 SERVINGS BEGIN 10 MINUTES BEFORE SERVING
COOKING TIME: 3 TO 5 MINUTES

This is the microwave version of Oriental "stir-fry" and is one of our family favorites, because it is fun to stir the vegetables by simply holding the lid tight and shaking the dish upward as if you were throwing pizza dough. This motion causes the vegetables to stir themselves. The soy sauce not only adds the additional liquid necessary, but a pungent flavor too.

1 tablespoon vegetable oil
1 garlic clove, minced
1 teaspoon chopped fresh ginger
1 cup leftover broccoli and/or asparagus stems
½ cup leftover mushroom stems
1 cup bean sprouts
1 teaspoon soy sauce

In a 2-quart casserole combine the oil, garlic, and ginger. Cook on HIGH for 35 seconds to 1 minute, or until the garlic and ginger are tender.

Add the leftover broccoli and/or asparagus. Cover tightly and cook on HIGH for 1 to 3 minutes, stir-shaking after 1 minute.

Add in the remaining ingredients and stir shake. Cover again and cook on HIGH for 1 minute, or until heated through.

VARIATIONS:

Chicken-Vegetable Stir-Shake: For a main dish meal, add 2 cups cubed cooked chicken after cooking the garlic and ginger. Cook on HIGH for 2 minutes. Add the broccoli and/or asparagus and stir shake. Continue with the basic recipe.

Vegetable-Grain Stir-Shake: Add 1 cup cooked rice or pasta with the broccoli and/or asparagus.

MOCK LOBSTER BROCCOLI AND CAULIFLOWER PLATTER

MAKES 6 VEGETABLE SERVINGS, OR 12 APPETIZERS   BEGIN 15 MINUTES BEFORE SERVING
COOKING TIME: 6 TO 9 MINUTES

This dish is unique in that the steam from the melted butter aids in cooking the vegetables that surround it. The flavors in the dipping butter make the vegetables taste surprisingly like lobster.

¼ cup butter	½ head of cauliflower, broken into flowerets
2 tablespoons chopped fresh parsley	
2 tablespoons chopped fresh dill	½ bunch of broccoli, broken into flowerets
1 tablespoon lemon juice	

In an 8-ounce microwaveproof bowl combine the butter, parsley, dill, and lemon juice. Place bowl in the center of a 12-inch microwaveproof platter. Surround the bowl with the cauliflower and broccoli. Cover tightly and cook on HIGH for 6 to 9 minutes, or until the vegetables are tender when pierced. Let stand, covered, for 2 minutes.

MIXED WOK-STYLE VEGETABLES

MAKES 4 SERVINGS   BEGIN 15 MINUTES BEFORE SERVING
COOKING TIME: 6 MINUTES

We call this "wok-style," because the vegetables are added in the order of their cooking times so that all are completed together. Constant stirring is eliminated. Their tender-crisp texture makes them a perfect complement for rice.

Mushrooms are not usually covered in the microwave, but by being cooked such a short time, as they are here, the mushrooms won't darken and the steam will help cook other vegetables. Serve with rice, as a side dish with meats or fish.

1 tablespoon sesame or vegetable oil	8 young corn ears; optional
1 garlic clove, minced	2 tablespoons soy sauce
4 scallions, cut into ¼-inch pieces	¼ pound snow peas, trimmed
4 carrots (about ½ pound), cut into thin 1½-inch sticks, or baby carrots	1 cup thinly sliced fresh mushrooms (see Note)

In a 2-quart casserole combine the oil, garlic, and scallions. Cook on HIGH for 1 minute, or until the scallions are tender. Stir in the carrots, corn ears, and soy sauce, coating well. Cover tightly and cook on HIGH for 2 minutes. Stir in the snowpeas. Cover again and cook on HIGH for 2 minutes. Stir in the mushrooms. Cover again and cook on HIGH for 1 minute, or until just heated through.

NOTE: A variety of mushrooms, such as tree ears or porcini, make a nice addition.

VARIATIONS:

Gingered Wok-Style Vegetables: Add 2 teaspoons chopped fresh ginger with the garlic and scallions.

Italian Mixed Vegetables: Substitute 3 tablespoons olive oil for the sesame oil and soy sauce. Add 2 tablespoons chopped fresh basil or 1 teaspoon dried, ½ teaspoon salt, ¼ teaspoon black pepper, and, if desired, ¼ to ½ teaspoon red pepper flakes with the carrots.

Wok-Style Vegetables over Pasta: Prepare the basic recipe or any variation above. At the end of cooking stir in ¼ cup melted butter. Toss with 1 pound cooked linguine or fettuccine.

COLCANNON

MAKES 6 TO 8 SERVINGS BEGIN 40 TO 50 MINUTES BEFORE SERVING
COOKING TIME: 15 TO 28 MINUTES

The Irish have a wonderful way of serving cabbage and mashed potatoes. Try it with sausage patties, corned beef, pot roast, or sautéed ham slices.

4 medium potatoes, peeled and cubed	1 onion, chopped
¼ cup water	4 cups shredded cabbage
¼ cup milk	½ teaspoon salt
6 tablespoons butter	¼ teaspoon pepper

In a 2-quart casserole combine the potatoes and water. Cover tightly and cook on HIGH for 7 to 13 minutes, or until fork tender, stirring once halfway through cooking. Let stand, covered, for 3 minutes.

Meanwhile, in a 1-quart glass measure combine the milk and 4 tablespoons butter. Cook on HIGH for 1 minute; set aside.

In a 2-quart casserole combine the remaining 2 tablespoons butter and the onion. Cook on HIGH for 1 to 2 minutes, or until the onion is tender. Stir in the shredded cabbage. Cover tightly and cook on HIGH for 7 to 13 minutes, or until the cabbage is tender, stirring once halfway through cooking. Let stand, covered, for 3 minutes.

Meanwhile, mash the potatoes. Blend in the warm milk and butter. Add salt and pepper to taste. Stir in the cooked onion and cabbage. Cover tightly and cook on HIGH for 2 to 3 minutes to heat, if necessary.

VARIATION:

Rumbledethumps: After combining the mashed potatoes and cabbage, place in a 1½ quart casserole. Sprinkle the top with ½ cup grated sharp cheddar cheese. Cook, uncovered, on MEDIUM for 1 to 4 minutes, or until the cheese is melted, rotating once. This is the Scottish version!

ORIENTAL VEGETABLE KABOBS

MAKES 4 SERVINGS   BEGIN 15 MINUTES BEFORE SERVING
COOKING TIME: 4 TO 6 MINUTES

Vegetable kabobs are attractive to serve with grilled meats. The vegetables are placed on a bamboo skewer in the order of their individual cooking times—the longer-cooking vegetables on the two ends and the shorter-cooking vegetables in the center. The vegetables used all have a high moisture content and therefore are cooked uncovered.

- 1 medium red onion, peeled and quartered
- 2 small zucchini or yellow squash, cut into ½-inch slices
- 8 medium whole fresh mushrooms, cleaned
- 1 medium ripe tomato, quartered
- 2 tablespoons Oriental Dressing (page 184), plus more, if desired

Cut each onion quarter in half, crosswise, to make 8 pieces.

Thread the vegetables on each of 4 bamboo skewers in this order: an onion piece, squash, mushroom, tomato, mushroom, squash, and onion, making sure that the skewer pierces all the vegetables securely. Repeat with the remaining vegetables.

Place the skewers on a 10-inch microwave-proof plate and brush them with 1 tablespoon dressing. Cook, uncovered, on HIGH for 2 minutes.

Turn over the kabobs and reposition so that the inside skewers are moved to the outside of the plate. Brush the vegetables with the remaining 1 tablespoon dressing. Cook on HIGH for 2 to 4 minutes, or until the vegetables are tender-crisp. Serve with extra dressing, if desired.

NOTE: *To Double:* Double the ingredients. Place the kabobs on a 12-inch microwave-proof platter. Cook on HIGH for 6 to 10 minutes, turning and rearranging the kabobs every 2 minutes, brushing with 1 tablespoon of marinade each time.

VARIATIONS:

Greek Vegetable Kabobs: In a small bowl combine 2 tablespoons olive oil; 1 teaspoon lemon juice; 1 tablespoon chopped fresh parsley, basil, or chives; and a pinch of salt and pepper. Substitute for the Oriental dressing.

Simple Vegetable Kabobs: Substitute 2 tablespoons of your favorite oil-based bottled dressing for the Oriental dressing.

13

FRUITS, FRUIT SAUCES, JELLIES, AND JAMS

When I was a child, there was a mandatory task that I looked forward to every summer and fall—berry picking. The day would begin early, with mother wrapping up sandwiches for my brother and me. She would plant big brimmed hats on our heads to ward off the sun, and rub our legs and arms with citronella, to ward off the bugs. We smelled like a cheap candle shop.

With buckets slung around our waists, we would arrive at the farm, ready to weasel in among the blueberry bushes. A chorus of musical pinging from berries landing in empty pails would turn into quiet thuds as the morning wore on. Farther down the row, mother would instruct us to "leave the green ones" and "throw out the stems," but we were more concerned with how many ripe ones we could slip into our mouths.

Peach season meant one day's freedom to pick in a neighbor's orchard. That same evening we would stand on stools over the sink and peel peaches with the sticky sweet nectar running down our arms.

Fresh fruit held a special place in our home and was as popular as any cake for dessert. The extras from the summer were "put up" and enjoyed through most of the fall and winter. By Christmas, we had moved on to "poached winter fruits," which were dried fruits and the holiday specialty.

These same childhood treats are still part of my repertoire because the microwave has made them so easy to prepare. Pears, apples, and plums are cooked in a shorter amount of time in reduced cooking liquid, so that they hold their shapes. I love them just plain in their cooking juices, but can be persuaded to spoon them over ice cream, too. I would suggest beginning with Poached Pears with Hot Fudge or Raspberry Sauce, a Piquant Peach Sauce or Berry Sauce for ice cream, and of course Poached Winter Fruits with a touch of Armagnac. You may come to serve fruit as often as I do for dessert.

—Thelma

Poached Fruit Basics:

1. Fruit is cooked in a sugar-liquid syrup with a ratio of 2 to 1, sugar to liquid. It is the high sugar concentration that causes the fruit to become soft while still holding its shape.
2. Depending on the fruit, between 2 tablespoons and ¼ cup liquid or butter is the amount needed to cook 4 servings of fruit. Dried fruit is the exception—it requires less sugar and more liquid for cooking.
3. A round casserole is necessary to arrange whole fruit or to facilitate the stirring or turning over of fruit pieces.
4. A tight cover, preferably a casserole lid, is necessary to keep in all available steam produced by the cooking liquid.
5. Stirring or turning fruit over is necessary to redistribute the heat to all sides and surface areas.
6. Standing time is not important to finish the cooking process of poached fruit. Even whole fruit will cook through to the center, because generally the cores have been removed, causing cooking to take place on an inner surface as well as the outside. Standing time is more important for flavoring the fruits by absorption of the liquid.
7. *Doneness:* A sharp knife should pierce through the fruit as it would room temperature butter, yet the fruit should retain its shape.

   Underdone: Fruit should still be firm when pierced. It is very important that the fruit be ripe but not hard, so let any unripe fruit ripen at room temperature, rather than in the refrigerator. Unripe fruit is not only almost impossible to cook until softened, it will also lack that nice rich, ripe flavor. Flavor can be increased in the cooking liquid, as in Spicy Poached Pears or Poached Brandied Peaches.

   Overdone: If cooked too long, poached fruit will become very soft. You may find one or two fruits that appear overdone. In the case of pears, they will be very soft and won't stand up. This could have happened because the pears were too ripe to begin with or because they weren't turned over during cooking. Stand them up in a thick mound of yogurt, whipped cream, or crème fraîche and spoon over a delicious sauce. They will still taste wonderful.

✺ POACHED PEARS

MAKES 4 SERVINGS   BEGIN 35 MINUTES BEFORE SERVING
COOKING TIME: 14 TO 16 MINUTES

Pears poached in this manner will keep their shape and develop a beautiful sheen. They make a regal presentation with stem arched upward and the pears resting in individual goblets or in a bowl, surrounded by cream, crème fraîche, or a dessert sauce.

4 firm *ripe* pears	¼ cup water
1 lemon, quartered	1 teaspoon vanilla
½ cup sugar	

Keeping the stems intact, core the pears so that they retain their shape by cutting a cone out of the base with a grapefruit knife or other small knife. Peel the pears and rub with the cut lemon to prevent discoloration. Set the pears aside and reserve the lemon quarters.

In a 1½-quart casserole combine the sugar, water, vanilla, and lemon quarters. Cook on HIGH for 2 minutes, or until the sugar is dissolved, stirring once. Place the pears on their sides, positioning the thicker ends toward the outside. Cover tightly and cook on HIGH for 6 minutes. Baste the pears and turn them over. Cover again and cook on HIGH for 6 to 8 minutes more, or until tender. Let the pears cool in their liquid, turning them over occasionally. Pears can be served at room temperature or made ahead and refrigerated up to 2 days.

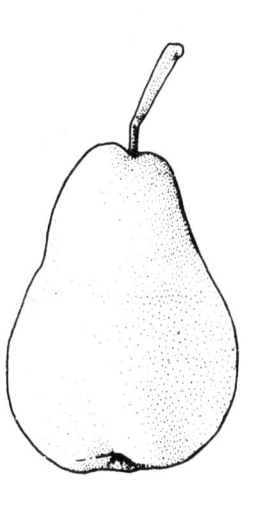

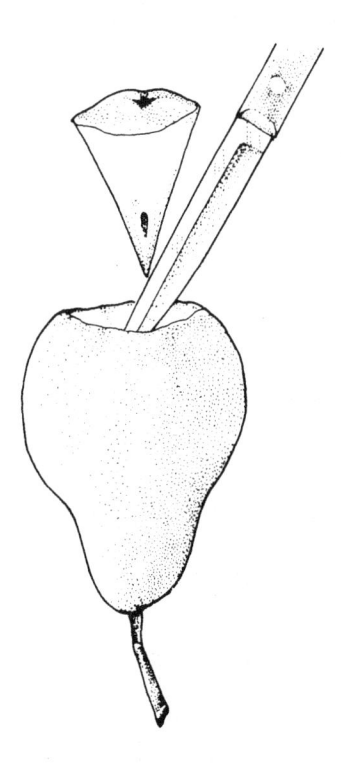

VARIATIONS:

Poached Pears with Hot Fudge Sauce: Prepare Hot Fudge Sauce (page 564). Serve over the pears.

Poached Pears with Cream: Spoon crème fraîche, sour cream, or plain yogurt around the pears in their serving dish.

Poached Pears with Nutmeg Whipped Cream: Whip ½ pint heavy cream. Mix in 2 to 4 tablespoons sugar. Spoon around the pears and sprinkle with fresh grated nutmeg.

Poached Pears with Currant Sauce: Prepare Currant Sauce (page 565) right before serving the pears. Spoon over them.

Poached Pears with Butterscotch Sauce: Prepare Butterscotch Sauce (page 565) right before serving the pears. Spoon around them.

Poached Pears with Raspberry Sauce: Prepare Raspberry Sauce (page 565) right before serving the pears. Spoon over them.

Poached Pears with Orange Segments: Substitute ½ cup wine for the water and add 1 to 2 tablespoons Triple Sec or other orange-flavored liqueur. Decrease the sugar to ¼ cup. Discard the lemon quarters after rubbing the pears. Add the peeled segments of 2 medium oranges with the pears. Follow the basic cooking times. Serve in stemmed glasses surrounded by oranges. Garnish with julienned orange rind.

Spicy Poached Pears: Substitute ½ cup dry white or red wine or cranberry juice for the water. Reduce the sugar to 2 tablespoons. Add 2 whole cloves or ⅛ teaspoon ground and 1 cinnamon stick or ⅛ teaspoon ground cinnamon with the sugar water. Follow the basic recipe cooking times. Serve warm or chilled in liquid. Pears cooked in this way can be served with a main course of roast pork or lamb.

POACHED PEACHES

MAKES 4 SERVINGS   BEGIN 20 MINUTES BEFORE SERVING
COOKING TIME: 3 TO 5 MINUTES

These are always delicious and elegant served in chilled poaching juices or with one of the suggested additions.

---

4 firm ripe peaches (1 to 1½ pounds), peeled (page 497)	1 teaspoon lemon juice
¼ cup dry white wine or water	Whipped cream, plain yogurt, crème fraîche, or Raspberry Sauce (page 565) (all optional)
2 tablespoons sugar	

Cut the peaches in half and remove the pits. In a 2-quart microwave casserole combine the wine or water, sugar, and lemon juice, stirring well. Add the peach halves. Cover tightly and cook on HIGH for 2 minutes; turn the peaches over and rearrange. Cover again and cook on HIGH for 1 to 3 minutes more, or until the peaches are tender. Cool, covered, in the cooking liquid, turning over once to coat. Serve in the cooking liquid, or add whipped cream, yogurt, crème fraîche, or raspberry sauce.

VARIATIONS:

Poached Peaches with Cinnamon: Add ½ cinnamon stick or ¼ teaspoon ground cinnamon with the sugar.

Poached Brandied Peaches: Add 2 tablespoons brandy or bourbon to the wine. Serve with Basic Pastry Cream (page 555), if desired.

POACHED PLUMS

MAKES 4 TO 6 SERVINGS　　BEGIN 15 TO 20 MINUTES BEFORE SERVING
COOKING TIME: 2 TO 4 MINUTES

Serve poached plums with roasted meats in a main dish, or as dessert over yogurt or ice cream, or simply alone in their own poaching liquid.

¼ cup dry white wine, apple juice, or water	1 teaspoon lemon juice
¼ cup sugar	1½ pounds plums, halved and pitted

In a 1½-quart casserole combine the wine, juice, or water; sugar; and lemon juice. Add the plums. Cover tightly and cook on HIGH for 2 to 4 minutes, or until just tender but not overcooked, stirring once (plums lose their shape if overcooked). Serve warm or let cool, covered, in their juices, turning once to coat.

VARIATIONS:

Poached Plums with Port: Substitute port for the wine.

Poached Spiced Plums: Add 1 cinnamon stick or ½ teaspoon ground cinnamon and ¼ teaspoon grated nutmeg with the sugar.

Poached Brandied Plums: Add 2 tablespoons brandy to the wine.

BAKED APPLES

MAKES 4 SERVINGS　　BEGIN 20 MINUTES BEFORE SERVING
COOKING TIME: 6 TO 7 MINUTES

Baked apples are an old-fashioned winter favorite as a dessert or snack, and can be cooked individually or together in a round dish.

4 medium tart baking apples	4 teaspoons orange juice or brandy
4 tablespoons chopped walnuts	1 tablespoon lemon juice
4 tablespoons brown sugar	½ teaspoon ground cinnamon
4 teaspoons butter or margarine	Cream (optional)

Remove the apple cores, but do not cut all the way through to the bottoms. Peel a 1-inch strip around the top of the apple. Halfway down on the apple, cut a ¼-inch-deep slit in the skin around the circumference; this will let steam escape and keep the skin from splitting.

Place the apples in four individual 10-ounce microwave serving dishes or around the outside of a 9-inch round cooking dish. Spoon 1 tablespoon nuts, 1 tablespoon brown sugar, and 1 teaspoon butter into the center of each apple. Pour 1 teaspoon orange juice or brandy over each apple; sprinkle each with lemon juice and cinnamon. Cover tightly and cook on HIGH for 6 to 7 minutes, repositioning the individual dishes or rotating the large dish once, a quarter turn. (If using individual dishes, position them in a circle with a 1-inch space between them.) Serve warm or chilled with cream.

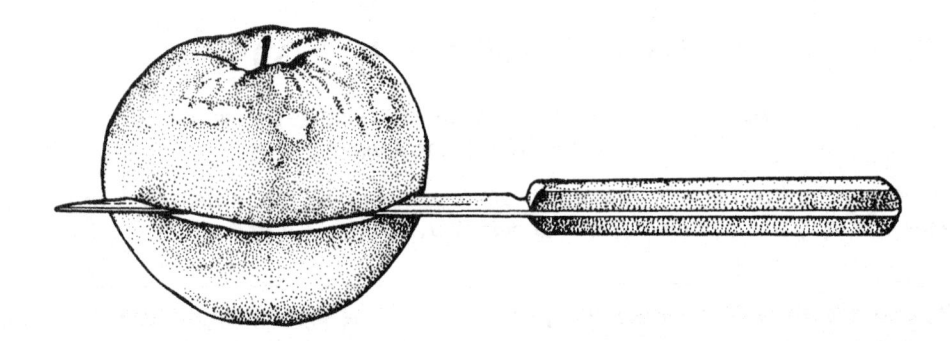

VARIATIONS:

Individual Baked Apples: Cook 1 apple in a small dish, covered with plastic wrap, on HIGH for 2 to 4 minutes. Cook 2 apples in two small dishes, covered with plastic wrap, on HIGH for 3 to 6 minutes.

Baked Apples with Cranberries: Substitute fresh or frozen cranberries for the walnuts.

Baked Apples with Raisins: Substitute raisins for the walnuts.

Baked Apples in Red Wine: Substitute red wine for the orange juice.

Baked Apples with Butterscotch: Serve with warm Butterscotch Sauce (page 565), made before the apples are cooked.

Baked Apples with Preserves: Substitute 4 tablespoons raspberry or apple preserves for brown sugar.

APPLESAUCE

MAKES 2 TO 2½ CUPS   BEGIN 25 MINUTES BEFORE SERVING
COOKING TIME: 10 TO 14 MINUTES

We prefer making applesauce in the microwave because we don't have to worry about the apples burning in the bottom of the pot when we've forgotten to stir. We usually cook apples with their skins on for added flavor and nutrition and the nice pink color they add. Our families love this simple, fresh apple side dish, and for that reason we usually double the recipe. If by chance there is any left over, we'll freeze it for later. The sugar is not added until after cooking to enable the apples to cook down—sugar tends to encourage them to keep their shape.

FRUITS, FRUIT SAUCES, JELLIES, AND JAMS

2 pounds cooking apples, washed and quartered	¼ to ½ cup sugar, or to taste
¼ cup water	1 teaspoon butter
1 tablespoon lemon juice	1 teaspoon ground cinnamon (optional)

In a 2-quart casserole combine the apples, water, and lemon juice. Cover tightly and cook on HIGH for 5 minutes; stir. Cover again and cook on HIGH for 5 to 9 minutes more, or until the apples are tender. Force the apples and their cooking juices through a food mill to puree. Pour the puree into a bowl, then stir in the remaining ingredients.

NOTE: *To Double:* Double all the ingredients. Place in a 4-quart casserole. Cook, covered, on HIGH for 15 to 20 minutes, until tender.

VARIATIONS:
Chunky Applesauce: Core, peel, and slice the apples before cooking. When the apples are tender, stir in the remaining ingredients. Do not puree (nice for a change).
Horseradish-Flavored Applesauce: Add 2 tablespoons prepared horseradish to the pureed applesauce. Great with sliced pork.
Gingered Applesauce: Substitute 1 teaspoon ground ginger for the cinnamon.
Orange-Flavored Applesauce: Substitute ¼ cup orange juice for the water.

POACHED WINTER FRUITS

MAKES 6 SERVINGS   BEGIN 30 TO 45 MINUTES BEFORE SERVING
COOKING TIME: 15 MINUTES

This is a traditional dish at Thelma's Christmas dinners, served along with ham and pease porridge, but is good all winter long with any smoked meat. These fruits may be cooked one to two days in advance and then brought to room temperature before serving.

2 cups dry white wine, apple juice, or water	¼ teaspoon ground ginger
½ cup dark brown sugar	1 cinnamon stick, or ½ teaspoon ground cinnamon
½ teaspoon lemon juice	1 pound mixed dried fruit (prunes, apricots, pears, etc.)
½ teaspoon vanilla	

In a 2-quart casserole combine all the ingredients except fruit, stirring to blend. Stir in the fruit. Cover tightly and cook on HIGH for 15 minutes, or until the fruit has plumped up, stirring halfway through cooking time. Let cool to room temperature.

VARIATIONS:

Armagnac-Poached Winter Fruits: Add 2 tablespoons Armagnac or Cognac before cooking.

Poached Winter Fruits with Nuts: Add ½ cup coarsely chopped walnuts or pecans before cooking.

Poached Dried Apricots with Grand Marnier: Substitute all dried apricots for the mixed fruits and add 2 tablespoons Grand Marnier or other orange liqueur, or apricot brandy.

Poached Dried Apples with Calvados: Substitute all dried apples for the mixed fruits and add 2 tablespoons Calvados before cooking.

Fruit Slices Basics:

1. Fruit slices are cooked in a combination of liquid and water, but the ratio is balanced more by flavor than the need to retain the shape of the slices.
2. Because they are cut up, fruit slices can be cooked in a smaller, flatter dish, which also helps to coat all the cut surfaces with the flavorful cooking liquid.
3. Fruit slices are covered with wax paper, primarily to prevent spattering. If they were covered tightly with a lid or plastic wrap, the sauce would become too watered down and not as flavorful.
4. Stirring, rearranging, or repositioning once during cooking is important to cook and coat evenly all the cut surfaces.
5. Standing time is of little importance with these fruit slices, since they are not very thick or dense and cook for such a short period of time.
6. *Doneness:* Fruit slices will either be cooked until fork tender, as in the case of apples, or until just warm, as with pineapple slices.

✹ BRANDIED APPLE SLICES

MAKES 4 TO 6 SERVINGS   BEGIN 20 MINUTES BEFORE SERVING
COOKING TIME: 4 TO 6 MINUTES

Warm apple slices fare as well with pork as they do as a dessert over ice cream or yogurt. For extra flare, flambé before spooning over ice cream.

- 4 tablespoons butter
- 4 tart cooking apples, peeled, cored, and cut into ¼-inch slices
- ¼ cup brown sugar
- 2 tablespoons brandy
- 1 tablespoon lemon juice
- ½ teaspoon ground cinnamon

In a 9-inch pie dish place the butter. Heat on HIGH for 35 seconds to 1 minute, or until melted. Stir in the remaining ingredients, except apples, to blend. Stir in the apples to coat. Cover with wax paper and cook on HIGH for 4 to 6 minutes, or until the apples are tender, stirring once.

VARIATION:

Flambéed Apple Slices over Ice Cream: Pour 2 ounces brandy or other 80-proof liqueur in a 1-cup glass measure. Heat on HIGH for 10 to 15 seconds. Pour over the apples and ignite. Spoon the fruit over vanilla ice cream.

WARM FRESH PINEAPPLE RINGS

MAKES 4 TO 6 SERVINGS   BEGIN 15 TO 20 MINUTES BEFORE SERVING
COOKING TIME: 4 TO 6 MINUTES

A refreshing summer dessert when served with a scoop of vanilla ice cream, frozen yogurt, or orange sherbet, and garnished with mint.

2 tablespoons butter	¼ cup brown sugar
1 2½- to 3-pound ripe pineapple, peeled, cored, and cut into ½-inch rings	1 tablespoon rum, brandy, or water

Place the butter in a microwave dish (see Note). Cook on HIGH for 35 seconds to 1 minute to melt. Place the pineapple slices in the melted butter, turning over to coat both sides. Sprinkle the top of the slices evenly with brown sugar and rum, brandy, or water. Cover with wax paper and cook on HIGH for 2 minutes. Turn the slices over and reposition. Cover again and cook on HIGH for 1 to 3 minutes, or until heated through. Place the pineapple rings on individual dessert plates and spoon cooking juices over them.

NOTE: If you have 4 pineapple slices, use a 9-inch round cooking dish; for 6 slices use a 2-quart rectangular dish.

STRAWBERRIES IN WINE

MAKES 4 SERVINGS   BEGIN 30 MINUTES BEFORE SERVING
COOKING TIME: 4 TO 6 MINUTES

A light, easy dessert for spring and summer that is impressive when served in wine goblets with a sprig of mint. The cooking method falls between sliced fruits and sauces. Strawberries are cooked just enough to release some of their juices while still retaining their delicate shape.

- ½ cup dry white wine
- ¼ cup sugar
- 1 tablespoon lemon juice
- 1 tablespoon kirsch, framboise, or orange-flavored liqueur (optional)
- 1 pint whole strawberries, washed and hulled
- Mint leaves or Chocolate Triangles (page 594)

In a 1-quart casserole combine the wine and sugar. Cook on HIGH for 3 to 5 minutes, or until the sugar is dissolved. Stir in the lemon juice, kirsch or liqueur, and strawberries. Cook on HIGH for 1 minute. Cover and chill until serving time. Serve chilled in wine goblets. Garnish with a sprig of mint or chocolate triangles, if desired.

☼ PEACH SAUCE FOR ICE CREAM

MAKES 4 TO 6 SERVINGS   BEGIN 15 TO 20 MINUTES BEFORE SERVING
COOKING TIME: 2 TO 4 MINUTES

In high school Thelma worked in an ice cream parlor, where firm peach slices floating in a sweet nectar was her favorite sundae topping. She couldn't wait until August, when peaches were again in season and she could assure customers of superior quality by frequent sampling. Taste this sauce and you'll understand why she enjoyed her work so much.

- ¼ cup water
- ¼ cup sugar
- 1 tablespoon lemon juice
- ½ teaspoon vanilla
- 3 peaches, peeled (see page 497), pitted, and thinly sliced

In a 1-quart casserole combine the water, sugar, lemon juice, and vanilla. Cook on HIGH for 2 to 4 minutes, or until boiling rapidly. Stir in the peaches. Chill. Serve over ice cream.

VARIATION:

Piquant Peach Sauce: Add 1 tablespoon Grand Marnier with the peaches. Even in high school, Thelma knew that the flavor of the peaches could be improved with this secret ingredient.

Peeling Peaches

Pour 4 cups water into a 2-quart casserole. Cover tightly and cook on HIGH for 7 to 10 minutes, or until boiling. Place 3 to 4 peaches in the hot water. Let stand, covered, for 1 to 2 minutes. Remove the peaches and run cold water over them. Peel.

If you're peeling more peaches than this, repeat process.

Berry Sauce Basics:

1. A slightly larger casserole than appears necessary keeps the berries from boiling over during cooking.
2. Using wax paper or no cover at all is best for cooking berries in a sauce. Unlike a tight cover, wax paper keeps down spatters yet without cooking berries too fast and causing a boilover.
3. Stirring halfway through cooking is important to redistribute heat from the outside to the inside.
4. No standing time is necessary on this sauce.

✺ BASIC BERRY DESSERT SAUCE

MAKES 1⅓ CUPS   BEGIN 15 MINUTES BEFORE SERVING
COOKING TIME: 8 TO 12 MINUTES

We like to pick lots of berries in the summer and freeze those we can't eat. In the depths of winter, a little of this sauce goes a long way to reminding us that summer is not far off. Serve with fruit tarts, cakes, puddings, or over ice cream or sherbet.

2 cups fresh or frozen blueberries, raspberries, or strawberries	⅓ cup sugar (see Note) 2 tablespoons lemon juice

In a deep 2-quart casserole combine all the ingredients. Cover with wax paper and cook on HIGH for 4 to 6 minutes, stirring after 3 minutes, until the mixture is boiling and the berries begin to fall apart.

Puree the mixture in a food processor or blender or force through a sieve; the latter is the preferred method if you wish to remove any seeds found in raspberries. Return the puree to the casserole. Cook, uncovered, on HIGH for 4 to 6 minutes, or until slightly thickened. Serve warm or chilled.

NOTE: If you wish a sweeter sauce, add 2 or 3 tablespoons more sugar.

VARIATION:

Whole Berry Sauce: Reserve 1 cup whole blueberries, raspberries, or quartered strawberries until the end of cooking. Stir in the uncooked berries right before serving.

CANDIED RHUBARB SAUCE

MAKES 2 CUPS BEGIN 25 MINUTES BEFORE SERVING
COOKING TIME: 5 TO 9 MINUTES

Rhubarb is a fibrous fruit that must be covered tightly to steam through. This rhubarb sauce is particularly delicious served over vanilla ice cream, plain yogurt, whipped cream, crème fraîche, strawberries, or chocolate cake!

1 pound rhubarb, cut into ½-inch pieces	¾ cup sugar 2 tablespoons orange juice or water

In a 1½-quart casserole combine all the ingredients, stirring well to mix. Cover tightly and cook on HIGH for 3 minutes; stir. Cover again and cook on HIGH for 2 to 6 minutes or until the rhubarb is tender; stir. Chill, covered, until ready to serve.

VARIATION:

Candied Rhubarb Strawberry Sauce: Add 1 pint strawberries, hulled and sliced, to cooked rhubarb. Cover again and cook on HIGH for 1 to 3 minutes, or until the strawberries are heated through, stirring once.

CITRUS SAUCE

MAKES 1 CUP BEGIN 10 MINUTES BEFORE SERVING
COOKING TIME: 3 TO 5 MINUTES

Spoon this over blueberry fruit tarts or pound cake.

A cornstarch-thickened sauce is cooked uncovered, to evaporate liquid, and stirred once to redistribute heat and make smooth. For more about cornstarch sauces, see Sauce or Gravy Basics (page 170).

¼ cup sugar 1 tablespoon cornstarch 1 cup water 1 egg yolk	1½ tablespoons lemon or lime juice, or 3 tablespoons orange juice ½ teaspoon grated lemon, lime, or orange rind

In a 4-cup glass measure combine the sugar and cornstarch. Stir ¼ cup water into the cornstarch mixture to form a smooth paste. Stir in the remaining ¾ cup water. Cook, uncovered, on HIGH for 3 to 5 minutes, or until the mixture boils and is slightly thickened, stirring once.

Place the egg yolk in a small bowl. Pour a little of the thickened hot mixture into the egg yolk, stirring constantly. Pour the egg yolk mixture into a glass measure. Stir in the fruit juice and rind until blended. Serve warm or chilled.

GORGONZOLA WINE DIP WITH FRUIT

MAKES 4 TO 6 SERVINGS   BEGIN 15 TO 20 MINUTES BEFORE SERVING
COOKING TIME: 4 TO 6 MINUTES

This cheese wine dip takes the place of a European cheese and fruit course that follows a meal. It was designed specifically for blue cheese lovers, of which we are two, and it is the kirsch that makes it slightly sweet. Serve it as a fondue with skewers to pierce the fruit for dipping.
For more on cheese dips, see Cheese Melting Basics (page 161).

½ pound Gorgonzola, broken into small pieces	1 tablespoon kirsch or brandy
1 teaspoon cornstarch	2 to 3 pears
¼ cup dry white wine	4 small bunches of seedless grapes

In a 1-quart casserole suitable for serving combine the cheese and cornstarch so that the cornstarch coats the cheese. Stir in the wine and kirsch or brandy. Cook on MEDIUM for 3 minutes; stir. Cook on MEDIUM for 1 to 3 minutes more, or until heated through and well blended; the mixture will be slightly lumpy due to the nature of the cheese.

Meanwhile, slice the pears. Arm each person with a wooden skewer, half a sliced pear, and a bunch of grapes. Dip the fruit pieces into the warm cheese.

VARIATION:

Cheddar Wine Dip with Fruit: Substitute ½ pound sharp natural cheddar cheese, grated, for the Gorgonzola. Serve with apples, pears, and grapes, or spoon over apple pie or Basic Apple Pizza Tart (page 551).

Jam and Jelly Basics:

1. When pectin is called for, we prefer liquid pectin because it is easier to use—the fruit is cooked completely before it is added.
2. Jams and jellies are cooked on HIGH power the way any fruit or fruit slices would be.
3. Stirring where indicated is very important to redistribute heat and to dissolve sugar completely.
4. For home use, we recommend keeping jellies in the refrigerator, tightly covered. This eliminates the need for paraffin, which can't be melted in the microwave because it has no fat, sugar, or water to attract the microwaves to melting. If you want to give your jam or jelly as a gift and would like to seal with paraffin, melt the paraffin in a double boiler and pour over jelly or marmalade that has cooled and set slightly.
5. Jars cannot be sterilized in the microwave by just putting them in the oven and turning it on. Boil them conventionally, or run them through the dishwasher and fill them while they are still hot.
6. *Doneness:* Jams are dense fruit mixtures, with sugar for flavoring and sheen, and pectin to thicken. Jams are finished when they come to a boil and the fruit has cooked down somewhat, but individual pieces are still visible.

   A marmalade is cooked until it sheets from the side of a spoon in one large drop or blob, rather than two separate drips. Just as accurate a test, if you are cooking in the 3-quart casserole, is to watch the level to which the jelly boils when it comes to a boil the second time. When it reaches the top, it is done.

ORANGE MARMALADE

MAKES 2 CUPS
COOKING TIME: 15 TO 19 MINUTES

The key to perfect marmalade is to choose perfect unbruised oranges. (If Seville oranges are available, try them.) This is so beautiful to look at that Thelma once made it for a neighbor's golden wedding anniversary. Marmalade is very nice with pound cake, a combination we first sampled while touring a convent outside Mexico City.

1 cup paper-thin seedless orange slices with skins (about ½ pound oranges)	½ cup water 2 tablespoons lemon juice 2 cups sugar

In a 3-quart casserole combine the oranges, water, and lemon juice. Cover tightly and cook on HIGH for 5 to 7 minutes, or until the orange rinds are tender. Stir in the sugar; mix well. Cook, uncovered, on HIGH for 5 minutes; stir. Cook on HIGH for 5 to 7 minutes more or until the bubbles reach the top of the casserole and the jelly sheets. Pour into sterilized jars; cover. Refrigerate for up to 4 months.

VARIATIONS:

Lemon marmalade: Substitute lemons for the oranges.

Lime Marmalade: Substitute limes for the oranges.

Lemon-Lime Marmalade: Substitute a combination of lemons and limes for the oranges.

To Speed Jelly Making

While preparing the other jam or jelly ingredients, heat 3 cups sugar on HIGH for 5 minutes, stirring once. Warming the sugar first will speed up the cooking process whether you're making preserves conventionally or in the microwave.

✺ RASPBERRY OR STRAWBERRY JAM

MAKES 4 CUPS
COOKING TIME: 11 TO 13 MINUTES

Jams and jellies made in small amounts are hostess gifts with a homemade touch that can be whipped up on very short notice. When it comes to making small batches of jam, the microwave is the most suitable cooking appliance. It eliminates the need for constant stirring and the possibility of scorching. Larger batches should be left to the big kettle on top of the stove.

---

4 cups fresh or unsweetened frozen raspberries or strawberries
3 cups sugar

2 tablespoons lemon juice
2 tablespoons liquid pectin

In a 2-quart casserole combine the berries, sugar, and lemon juice; stir to mix. Cook, uncovered, on HIGH for 5 minutes; stir. Cook on HIGH for 6 to 8 minutes more, or until boiling and the fruit is cooked down somewhat; stir well to dissolve the sugar. Stir in the pectin. Pour into sterilized jars; cover. Store in the refrigerator for up to 4 months.

☀ MULLED WINE JELLY

MAKES 1 TO 1¼ CUPS
COOKING TIME: 4 TO 6 MINUTES

There was, and probably still is, a custom in parts of Italy of dipping bread into red wine for breakfast. That's what this jelly reminds us of. It is also delicious served at dinnertime with pork. If you plan to give this jelly as a gift, place a cinnamon stick in the sterilized jar before pouring in the hot mixture, or insert a stick into a bow on top.

1 cup red wine	¼ teaspoon ground cloves
2 tablespoons brown sugar	½ teaspoon ground cinnamon
1 tablespoon lemon juice	1 tablespoon plain gelatin
2 tablespoons orange juice	3 tablespoons water

In a 4-cup glass measure combine the wine, brown sugar, lemon and orange juices, cloves, and cinnamon. Cook, uncovered, on HIGH for 3 to 5 minutes, or until boiling; stir.

In a 1-cup glass measure combine the gelatin and water. Cook, uncovered, on HIGH for 30 seconds; stir to dissolve. Stir into the wine mixture. Pour into a sterilized jar; cover. Refrigerate for up to 4 months.

14

CAKES, BREADS, AND MUFFINS

Almost every family has a mother or grandmother who had a recipe that was guarded as carefully as a cherished heirloom. In my family, the Linzer torte recipe was a carefully guarded treasure.

When I was a little girl, mother would set aside one afternoon to bake this moist hazelnut cake, layered with jam for Papa's ("Vati's") birthday. The special torte originated in Linz, Austria, and it was Vati's favorite.

I can recall those cool September afternoons when the aroma of nuts, spices, and raspberry preserves would permeate the house. Several hours went into grinding the ingredients and baking the cake. All were labors of love and it was a custom that I wanted to preserve for my family.

But as life filled up with children, carpools, and a part-time job, leisurely afternoons spent preparing Vati's cake were replaced by quick trips to the bakery. A tradition lost, I thought. Who could have guessed that the microwave would salvage that delicious cake from my dusty recipe file? I had already begun to use the microwave for most of my cooking, and I felt that it was time to try desserts.

So with the fragrances of this torte still fresh in my mind, I set about creating a microwave version. My goal was not to lose anything but time. A presentation to Vati and his hearty approval confirmed my success.

That triumph spurred me on to a Walnut Apple Cake with Chocolate Cream Glaze and a cranberry Cape Cod Jewel Cake, and many more. I found to my great pleasure that with the microwave "the more things change, the more they stay the same!"

—THELMA

Cake Basics:

1. Because there is no dry heat in a microwave oven, there will be no traditional hard crust. Yet because there is not a hard crust to restrict the rising cake, it also means that a cake can rise slightly higher and be slightly lighter than a cake of an equal volume made conventionally. (To see how a cake crust can be duplicated in the microwave, see Pound and Bundt Cake Basics on page 522).
2. We have tested these cakes with all-purpose and cake flour and there is little noticeable difference in texture between the two.
3. We found it very easy to soften the butter on DEFROST power, 45 seconds to 1 minute per ½ cup, before creaming it with the sugar.
4. The bottom of the cake dish is lined with two circles of wax paper, instead of one, because the moisture from the cake batter might cause one to stick to the dish. The dabs of shortening placed on the inside of the dish will hold the paper in place when the batter is spooned onto it.
5. An 8½-inch round cake dish works best with this amount of batter, because it has been portioned to fill just half the dish (preventing cook-overs), and this depth of batter will cook most evenly with the cooking times and powers designated. Don't use a larger dish or the cake will be dry.
6. Once it is spooned into the dish, the cake batter is spread evenly on top to prevent any areas from cooking faster than others and thus overcooking, due to the thinner depths of batter.
7. The cake is placed on top of a microwaveproof cereal dish to raise it even closer to the center of the oven, where cakes seem to cook most evenly. This procedure may eliminate rotating, but if not, rotate the cake one-quarter turn, two to three times throughout cooking.
8. A cake is cooked uncovered to give it room to rise and to let moisture evaporate. A cake, covered tightly during cooking, could become very soggy.
9. The cake is cooked first on MEDIUM so that the gas and heated air can expand evenly while the cake structure is forming. Once this has happened, the cake can be safely cooked on HIGH to finish it off quickly.
10. After cooking, a cake should stand directly on a counter top so that heat is reflected back into the cake to cook it. If it were to stand on a cooling rack, the surrounding air would take away much of the heat needed to continue cooking.
11. *Doneness:* Cake is done when a toothpick, inserted in the center, comes out clean. The top may appear slightly moist, but not wet. When this moist area is touched lightly with the finger, it will reveal a finished and completely dry cake below.

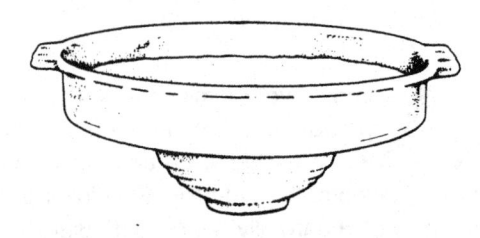

During standing time, the cake is placed on a counter to reflect heat back inside.

This will cause the top of the cake to dry completely and the cake will begin to pull away from the sides.

Underdone: The cake will still be very wet on top and a toothpick inserted in the center will not come out clean. Continue to cook on MEDIUM, 1 minute at a time. The center top should be the last area to finish cooking. If you find there is another spot that is wet, rotate the cake more often during cooking.

Overdone: The cake will be completely dry around the rim and will have begun to pull away from the sides. Either the cake was cooked too long, or perhaps it was cooked on too high a power. Did you begin on MEDIUM power before going to HIGH? Did you use the proper size cake dish? In any of these cases, the cake will be somewhat dry, but can still be delicious if made into Marmalade Cream Cake (page 508) or our Trifle with Strawberries (page 557). The longer it stands to absorb the pastry cream, the moister the cake will become.

NOTE: Large eggs work best in our cake and bread recipes.

✸ BASIC YELLOW CAKE

MAKES 8 TO 10 SERVINGS   BEGIN 30 MINUTES BEFORE SERVING
COOKING TIME: 8 TO 11 MINUTES

Here is a basic yellow cake that is very light and yields itself to so many different frostings, toppings, and ingredient additions.

Shortening	⅓ cup milk
6 tablespoons butter	1 teaspoon vanilla
1 cup cake or all-purpose flour	Confectioners' sugar, Lemon or
1¼ teaspoons baking powder	Orange Frosting (page 509), or
¾ cup sugar	Chocolate Cream Glaze (page 512)
2 eggs	

Cut 2 circles of wax paper to fit the bottom inside of an 8½-inch round cake dish. Put 3 small dabs of shortening on the inside bottom of the dish and place the wax paper circles on top. Set aside.

Place the butter in a large microwaveproof bowl. Heat it on DEFROST for 30 to 40 seconds to soften; do not melt. Meanwhile, sift the flour and baking powder together; set aside. Beat the sugar into the butter until fluffy. Beat in the eggs. Beat in the milk and vanilla. Fold in the flour until well blended.

Spread the batter evenly in the prepared cake dish. Place the dish on top of a microwaveproof cereal bowl in the oven. Cook on MEDIUM for 6 minutes, then on HIGH for 1 to 4 minutes, or until the cake tests done, rotating one-quarter turn once or twice if necessary.

(The cake is done when a toothpick inserted in the center comes out clean, even though the top appears slightly moist.) Let the cake stand directly on the counter for 5 to 10 minutes. Invert the cake onto a serving plate and firmly tap the bottom of the dish to loosen; peel away the wax paper. Let cool completely before sprinkling with confectioners' sugar or spreading with frosting.

NOTE: *To Double:* Double the ingredients. Cook each layer separately. If you plan to use the same dish, turn out onto a cooling rack after standing time is complete. Reline the pan with wax paper and repeat the procedure.

VARIATIONS:

Lemon Cake: Add 1 tablespoon lemon juice and 1 teaspoon grated lemon rind with the vanilla. After the cake cools, spread on Lemon Frosting (page 509). Garnish the sides with grated lemon peel. Chocolate-Coated Strawberries (page 596) also garnish this cake nicely.

Orange Cake: Add 1 tablespoon orange juice and 1 tablespoon grated orange rind with the vanilla. After the cake cools, spread on Orange Frosting (page 509). Garnish the top outer rim with seedless orange slices.

Cocoa-Cinnamon Cake: Add 2 tablespoons unsweetened cocoa powder, 1 teaspoon ground cinnamon, ½ teaspoon grated nutmeg, and ¼ teaspoon allspice to sifted flour mixture.

Marmalade Cream Cake: While the cake is cooling, prepare Basic Pastry Cream (page 555). After the cake has been turned out and cooled, mark the sides into 3 layers with toothpicks. Using the toothpicks as a guide, cut the cake into 3 thin layers. Divide the pastry cream in half, and spread half on top of each of the 2 bottom layers. Reassemble the cake. Place ¼ cup apricot marmalade in a 1-cup glass measure. Heat on HIGH for 1 minute, or until melted. Pour over the cake top and smooth so that it partially runs down the sides. Let cool. Cover the cake with Vanilla Frosting (page 509).

Boston Cream Pie: Prepare Basic Pastry Cream (page 555); chill. Prepare Basic Yellow Cake recipe. Slice the cooled cake in half, horizontally. Spread the bottom layer with pastry cream. Replace the top layer of the cake. Prepare Chocolate Cream Glaze (page 512). Spread on top of the cake and let drip down over the sides.

STRAWBERRY SHORTCAKE

MAKES 8 TO 10 SERVINGS

1 recipe Basic Yellow Cake (page 507) 2 cups heavy cream ¼ cup plus 2 tablespoons sugar	2 cups sliced fresh strawberries, plus 8 whole fresh strawberries for garnish

While the cake is cooling, whip the cream with the ¼ cup sugar. Combine the sliced strawberries with the 2 tablespoons sugar.

Cut the cooled cake in half horizontally. To assemble, place 1 cup sliced strawberries on the bottom cake layer; spread with ½ cup whipped cream. Place the remaining cake layer on top. Cover the cake with the remaining sliced strawberries and whipped cream; garnish with whole strawberries.

VARIATIONS:

Blueberry Shortcake: Substitute 2 cups whole blueberries for the sliced strawberries.

Peach Shortcake: Substitute 8 peaches, peeled and sliced, combined with 1 tablespoon lemon juice and ¼ cup sugar for the sweetened sliced strawberries.

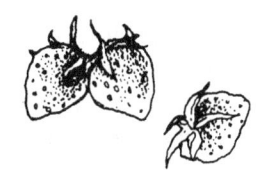

VANILLA FROSTING

MAKES ENOUGH FOR 1 LAYER CAKE
COOKING TIME: 1 MINUTE

3 tablespoons butter
1 cup sifted confectioners' sugar
1 tablespoon light cream
¾ teaspoon vanilla

Place the butter in a medium microwave-proof bowl. Heat on DEFROST for 1 minute to soften; *do not melt*. Beat with sugar and cream until well blended. Stir in the vanilla. Spread over the cake while the frosting is still soft.

VARIATIONS:

Lemon Frosting: Substitute 1 tablespoon lemon juice for the cream. Substitute 1 teaspoon grated lemon rind for the vanilla.

Orange Frosting: Substitute 1 tablespoon orange juice for the cream. Substitute 1 teaspoon grated orange rind for the vanilla.

CRUMB COFFEE CAKE

MAKES 8 SERVINGS   BEGIN 25 MINUTES BEFORE SERVING
COOKING TIME: 8 TO 12 MINUTES

This is the favorite coffee cake at our houses. We like it best warm, right out of the oven, and it usually doesn't last much past breakfast time.

Cake:
- ¼ cup butter
- 1 cup cake or all-purpose flour
- 1 teaspoon baking powder
- ½ cup sugar
- 1 egg
- ½ cup sour cream
- 1 teaspoon vanilla

Crumb Topping:
- ¼ cup butter, softened
- ½ cup cake or all-purpose flour
- ⅓ cup brown sugar
- ½ teaspoon ground cinnamon
- ¼ cup chopped nuts (optional)
- Confectioners' sugar (optional)

To make the cake: Place the butter in a large microwaveproof bowl. Heat it on DEFROST for 30 to 40 seconds to soften; *do not melt.* Meanwhile, sift the flour and baking powder; set aside. Beat the sugar into the butter until fluffy. Beat in the egg. Beat in the sour cream and vanilla. Fold in the flour until well blended. Spread the batter evenly into an 8½-inch round cake dish. Place the cake on a microwaveproof cereal bowl in the oven. Cook on MEDIUM for 6 minutes.

Meanwhile, make the topping by placing the butter in a medium mixing or food processor bowl. With a pastry blender, 2 knives, or processor, cut in the flour, brown sugar, and cinnamon. Stir in the nuts, if desired.

Sprinkle the topping over the cake and cook on HIGH for 2 to 4 minutes, or until the cake tests done, rotating one-quarter turn once or twice if necessary. (The top may appear damp but not wet; a toothpick inserted in the center will come out clean.) Let the cake stand directly on the counter for 5 to 10 minutes. Sprinkle with confectioners' sugar, if desired.

VARIATIONS:

Cinnamon–Brown Sugar Coffee Cake: Eliminate the crumb topping. Substitute ⅓ cup brown sugar and 1 teaspoon ground cinnamon, combined, for the crumb topping. Sprinkle over the cake and follow the basic cooking times.

Coconut-Crumb Coffee Cake: Add ½ cup grated coconut to the crumb topping.

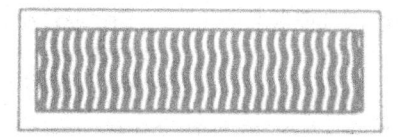

CAKES, BREADS, AND MUFFINS

RICH CHOCOLATE CAKE

MAKES 8 TO 10 SERVINGS BEGIN 45 MINUTES BEFORE SERVING
COOKING TIME: 13 TO 18 MINUTES

A rich chocolate cake that could be called a "brownie cake."

- 2 1-ounce squares of semisweet chocolate
- Shortening
- ¼ cup butter
- 1 cup cake or all-purpose flour
- ½ teaspoon baking powder
- ½ teaspoon baking soda
- ½ cup sugar
- 1 egg
- ½ cup sour cream
- 1 teaspoon vanilla
- 1 recipe Chocolate Cream Glaze (page 512)
- Walnut halves, Chocolate Triangles (page 594), or Chocolate-Covered Strawberries (page 596) (optional)

Open the chocolate square wrappings, leaving the chocolate in the center of the paper. Place the chocolate in the paper in the oven. Heat on MEDIUM for 3 to 5 minutes, or until melted.

Meanwhile, cut 2 circles of wax paper to fit the bottom inside of an 8½-inch round cake dish. Put 3 small dabs of shortening on the inside bottom of the dish and place the wax paper circles on top. Set aside.

Place the butter in a large microwave bowl. Heat on DEFROST for 30 to 40 seconds, or until softened; *do not melt*. Meanwhile, sift the flour, baking powder, and baking soda together; set aside. Beat the sugar into the butter until fluffy. Beat in the egg. Beat in the sour cream, vanilla, and melted chocolate. Fold in the flour until well blended.

Spread the batter evenly in the prepared cake dish. Place the dish on a microwave-proof cereal bowl in the oven. Cook on MEDIUM for 8 minutes, then on HIGH for 1 to 4 minutes, or until the cake tests done, rotating one-quarter turn once or twice if necessary. (The top may appear damp but not wet; a toothpick inserted in the center will come out clean.) Let the cake stand directly on the counter for 5 to 10 minutes. Invert onto a serving plate and firmly tap the bottom of the dish to loosen; peel away wax paper. Let cool completely before covering with chocolate cream glaze. Decorate with walnut halves, chocolate triangles, or chocolate-coated strawberries, if desired.

NOTE: *To Double:* Double the ingredients. Cook each layer separately. If you plan to use the same dish, turn the cake out onto a cooling rack after standing time. Line the dish, again, with wax paper and repeat the procedure.

VARIATIONS:

Rich Chocolate Cake with Nuts: Stir in ½ cup coarsely chopped nuts after the flour.

Chocolate Chocolate Chip Cake: Stir in 1 cup semisweet chocolate pieces after the flour.

CHOCOLATE CREAM GLAZE

MAKES ENOUGH FOR 1 LAYER CAKE
COOKING TIME: 2 TO 4 MINUTES

This is our preferred cake frosting because it covers easily and smoothly without disrupting any cake crumbs. The warm, glossy frosting then cools into a rich, fudge coating: Pour the glaze while still warm over the top of the cake and spread lightly down over sides. Chill the cake until the icing is set.

¼ cup cream
4 ounces semisweet chocolate pieces

1 tablespoon vanilla

In a 2-cup glass measure combine all the ingredients. Cook on HIGH for 2 to 4 minutes, stirring after 1½ minutes and checking every 30 seconds after that to see if the chocolate has become soft and spreadable; it needs to be stirred often to redistribute heat and melt evenly. Remove from the oven and stir for 2 to 4 minutes, just until well blended, thickened, and smooth.

VARIATIONS:

Chocolate Brandy Glaze: Substitute 1 tablespoon brandy for the vanilla.

Mocha Cream Glaze: Add 1 teaspoon dry instant coffee.

Chocolate Cream Frosting: Beat in ½ cup sifted confectioners' sugar when the icing is removed from the oven. Spread while still warm. Here is a more traditional chocolate frosting.

GINGERBREAD

MAKES 8 SERVINGS   BEGIN 25 MINUTES BEFORE SERVING
COOKING TIME: 8 to 11 MINUTES

Pop this into the oven when you sit down to dinner and you'll have warm gingerbread for dessert. And that, gingerbread lovers, is really the best way to eat it.

1 cup cake or all-purpose flour
½ cup dark brown sugar
1 tablespoon unsweetened cocoa
1 teaspoon ground ginger
½ teaspoon baking powder
½ teaspoon baking soda
½ teaspoon ground cinnamon
¼ teaspoon grated nutmeg

⅛ teaspoon ground cloves
¼ cup molasses
1 egg
⅓ cup warm water
Sweetened whipped cream or Butterscotch Sauce (page 565) (optional)

In a medium mixing bowl or food processor combine all the ingredients. Blend at low speed; then blend at medium speed for 2 minutes. Pour the batter evenly into an 8½-inch round cake dish. Place the dish on a microwaveproof cereal bowl in the oven. Cook on MEDIUM for 7 minutes; then on HIGH for 1 to 4 minutes, or until the cake tests done, rotating one-quarter turn once or twice if necessary. (The top will still feel moist while a toothpick inserted in the center comes out clean.) Let stand directly on the counter for 5 to 10 minutes. Serve warm with sweetened whipped cream or butterscotch sauce.

VARIATIONS:

Coffee Gingerbread: Add 1 teaspoon instant coffee granules, or ⅓ cup very strong brewed coffee in place of the water.

Apple Upside-Down Gingerbread: Place 3 tablespoons butter into an 8-inch round microwave dish. Heat on HIGH for 35 seconds to 1 minute. Sprinkle the bottom of the dish evenly with 3 tablespoons brown sugar. Peel and core 2 apples, and cut into ¼-inch slices. Arrange the apples in concentric circles in the bottom of the dish. Pour the gingerbread batter evenly over the apples. Follow the basic recipe cooking directions. After standing time, invert the cake onto a serving plate, tapping the bottom of the dish to release.

PACIFIC CARROT CAKE

MAKES 8 TO 10 SERVINGS   BEGIN 30 MINUTES BEFORE SERVING
COOKING TIME: 10 TO 13 MINUTES

The tropical additions of pineapple and coconut will add a somewhat exotic flair that will please adults and children alike.

Shortening
1 cup cake or all-purpose flour
½ cup granulated sugar
¼ cup brown sugar
½ teaspoon ground cinnamon
¼ teaspoon grated nutmeg
⅛ teaspoon ground cloves
1 teaspoon baking powder
2 eggs, beaten
¼ cup vegetable oil
¼ cup shredded coconut
½ cup drained crushed canned pineapple
½ cup coarsely chopped walnuts
1 recipe Cream Cheese Frosting (recipe follows)
10 walnut halves (optional)

Cut 2 circles of wax paper to fit the bottom of an 8½-inch round cake dish. Put 3 small dabs of shortening in the bottom of the dish and place the wax paper circles on top. Set aside.

Place all the remaining ingredients, except

the cream cheese frosting and walnut halves, into a mixing bowl. Blend at a low speed, then at medium speed for 2 minutes. Spread the batter evenly in the prepared dish. Cook on MEDIUM for 8 minutes, then on HIGH for 2 to 5 minutes, or until the cake tests done, rotating the dish one-quarter turn once or twice if necessary. (The top may appear damp but not wet; a toothpick inserted in the center will come out clean.) Let the cake stand directly on the counter for 5 to 10 minutes. Invert onto a serving plate and firmly tap the bottom of the dish to release; peel away the wax paper. Cool completely and cover with the cream cheese frosting. Garnish with walnut halves, if desired.

CREAM CHEESE FROSTING

MAKES ENOUGH FOR 1 LAYER CAKE
COOKING TIME: 1 MINUTE

- 4 ounces cream cheese
- 2 tablespoons butter
- ¼ cup confectioners' sugar
- ½ teaspoon vanilla

In a small mixing bowl combine the cream cheese and butter. Heat on DEFROST for 35 seconds to 1 minute to soften. Beat in the remaining ingredients until smooth. Spread on cooled cake.

☀ WALNUT-APPLE CAKE WITH CHOCOLATE CREAM GLAZE

MAKES 8 TO 10 SERVINGS   BEGIN 45 MINUTES BEFORE SERVING
COOKING TIME: 12 TO 14 MINUTES

A dense, moist chocolate cake, laced with raspberry jam and studded with apple slices and walnut chunks.

- Shortening
- ½ cup butter
- ½ cup sugar
- 2 large eggs
- ¼ cup raspberry jam
- 1 cup coarsely chopped walnuts
- 1 medium apple, peeled, cored, quartered, and cut into ¼-inch slices
- 1 teaspoon vanilla
- 1 cup fine dry bread crumbs
- 2 tablespoons unsweetened cocoa
- 1 teaspoon baking powder
- 1 recipe Chocolate Cream Glaze (page 512)
- Walnut halves or Chocolate Triangles (page 594) (optional)

Cut 2 circles of wax paper to fit the bottom inside of an 8½-inch round cake dish. Put 3 small dabs of shortening on the inside bottom of the dish and place the wax paper circles on top. Set aside.

In a large mixing bowl cream the butter and sugar together. Add the eggs and jam; beat well. In a separate bowl combine the remaining ingredients except the chocolate cream glaze and walnut halves. Add to the egg mixture, stirring to blend well. (This can all be done in a food processor.)

Spread the batter evenly in the prepared cake dish. Place the cake on a microwave-proof cereal dish in the oven. Cook on MEDIUM for 8 minutes, then on HIGH for 4 to 6 minutes, or until the cake tests done, rotating one-quarter turn once or twice if necessary. (The top may appear damp but not wet; a toothpick inserted in the center will come out clean.) Let the cake stand directly on the counter for 10 minutes before turning out. Cut around the edges with a knife to loosen. Invert onto a serving plate and firmly tap the bottom of the dish to loosen; peel away the wax paper. Let cool before covering with the chocolate cream glaze. Decorate with walnut halves or chocolate triangles, if desired.

VARIATIONS:

Truffle Cake: Substitute coarsely ground hazelnuts for the walnuts. Substitute Chocolate Brandy Glaze (page 512) for the chocolate cream glaze. Decorate the top of the cake with a ring of Chocolate Truffles (page 598).

Chocolate Grand Marnier Cake: Substitute Grand Marnier for the vanilla. Substitute ¼ cup orange marmalade for the raspberry jam. Coat with chocolate glaze as directed. Garnish with seedless orange segments.

LINZER JAM CAKE

MAKES 8 SERVINGS   BEGIN 45 TO 50 MINUTES BEFORE SERVING
COOKING TIME: 9 TO 11 MINUTES

This cake has the mingled scents of almonds, chocolate, and raspberry that went into the Linzer cake mother made for father's birthday. The Old World German tradition has been continued for our family.

—Thelma

Shortening
9 tablespoons butter, softened
1 cup (16 tablespoons) finely ground unblanched almonds
¾ cup sugar
2 large eggs
2 tablespoons kirsch
1 tablespoon grated lemon rind
1 cup fine dry bread crumbs
1 tablespoon unsweetened cocoa powder
1 teaspoon baking powder
½ teaspoon ground cinnamon
¼ teaspoon ground cloves
⅓ cup raspberry jam
2 tablespoons confectioners' sugar

Cut 2 circles of wax paper to fit the bottom inside of an 8½-inch round cake dish. Put 3 small dabs of shortening on the inside bottom of the dish and place the wax paper circles on top.

Grease the sides of the cake dish with 1 tablespoon butter. Sprinkle 2 tablespoons ground almonds onto the buttered sides, pressing with fingers to make them stick.

In a medium mixing bowl cream the remaining 8 tablespoons butter and the sugar together. Add the eggs, kirsch, and lemon rind; beat well. In a separate bowl combine the remaining 14 tablespoons almonds, the bread crumbs, cocoa, baking powder, cinnamon, and cloves. Stir the dry ingredients into the egg mixture to blend well.

Spread the batter evenly in the prepared cake dish. Place the cake on a microwave-proof cereal bowl in the oven. Cook on MEDIUM for 7 minutes, then HIGH for 1 to 3 minutes, or until the cake tests done, rotating one-quarter turn two to three times, if necessary. (The top may appear damp but not wet; a toothpick inserted in the center will come out clean.) Let the cake stand directly on the counter for 10 minutes before turning out. Cut the cake around the edges with a knife to loosen. Invert onto a serving plate and firmly tap the bottom of the dish to release; peel away the wax paper.

Place the jam in a 1-cup glass measure. Cook on HIGH for 40 seconds to 1 minute to melt. Prick the top of the cake about every inch with a metal skewer. Pour the jam evenly over the top of the cake to glaze and sink in. Spread the jam to the edges with a knife or spatula. Let the jam set for 10 to 15 minutes before decorating.

For decoration, place a paper heart doily or paper cut in a heart shape on the top center of the cake. Sift confectioners' sugar over the cake. Remove the paper heart for the finished design.

Cupcake and Muffin Basics:

1. See Cake Basics (page 506). For more specific information, read below.
2. Line custard cups or microwave cupcake or muffin dishes with 2 cupcake liners to keep the surface of the cakes drier.
3. Cupcakes should fill up only one-third of the custard cups, rather than one-half as in larger cakes. Muffins, because they are denser and don't rise as much, should fill halfway.
4. If cupcakes are cooked in custard cups, they are arranged in a circle with at least 1 inch space between them. This simulates the ring shape and a microwave cupcake or muffin dish, and is the best arrangement for the most even cooking.
5. Because muffins are very small, they can be cooked on HIGH power. Microwave penetration is between ¾ and 1½ inches, so that the center of an individual cake cooks more equally with the sides.
6. If any cupcakes appear to be done before the others, remove them and let the others continue to cook. Rearranging or rotating the cupcake dish will help the cupcakes or muffins cook most evenly.
7. Unlike the larger cakes, it is impractical to lift up cupcakes on a cereal bowl, for more

even cooking. That is why repositioning cupcakes and removing those that are finished first makes more sense.
8. Cupcakes in papers should be removed from their dishes right after cooking and cooled on a rack, to prevent them from becoming soggy. During standing time the top will dry.

✹ CHOCOLATE CUPCAKES

MAKES 12 SERVINGS   BEGIN 35 MINUTES BEFORE SERVING
COOKING TIME: 5 TO 8 MINUTES

1 recipe Rich Chocolate Cake batter (page 511)	1 recipe Chocolate Cream Frosting (page 512) or Vanilla Frosting (page 509)

Place 2 cupcake liners into six 5- or 6-ounce custard cups or into a microwave cupcake pan. Fill each cup one-third full with cake batter. If the cakes are made in custard cups, place in a circle in the oven with 1 inch of space between them. Cook on HIGH for 2½ to 4 minutes, or until they test done, repositioning the cups or rotating the dish one-quarter turn once. (The tops may appear damp but not wet; a toothpick inserted in the centers will come out clean.) Remove the cupcakes and papers immediately from the cooking dishes and cool on a cake rack.

Repeat the procedure for the second batch. Frost the cupcakes when cooled.

VARIATION:

Yellow Cupcakes: Substitute Basic Yellow Cake batter (page 507) for the chocolate batter. Frost with any frosting desired.

Cooking Times for Individual Muffins or Cupcakes:

1 muffin or cupcake	HIGH	30 seconds
2 muffins or cupcakes	HIGH	1 minute
4 muffins or cupcakes	HIGH	1½ minutes
6 muffins or cupcakes	HIGH	2½ to 3 minutes

NOTE: Muffin batter can be refrigerated in a tightly covered plastic container for up to a week. Stir before each usage. This way you can have fresh muffins in the morning.

✸ BRAN MUFFINS

MAKES 12 MUFFINS   BEGIN 30 MINUTES BEFORE SERVING
COOKING TIME: 5 TO 8 MINUTES

A topping on the muffins gives them a nice appearance and crunchy texture.

Muffins:
- 1 cup bran flakes
- ⅓ cup vegetable oil
- ⅔ cup buttermilk
- 1 cup whole-wheat flour
- ½ cup packed brown sugar
- 1½ teaspoons baking powder
- ½ teaspoon salt
- 1 egg, beaten
- ¼ cup raisins
- ¼ teaspoon grated nutmeg
- ½ teaspoon ground cinnamon

Topping (optional):
- ¼ cup butter
- ¼ cup finely chopped nuts, or ¼ cup sugar and 1 teaspoon ground cinnamon

---

To make muffins: Combine all the muffin ingredients in a large bowl until just mixed; *do not overmix.*

Place 2 cupcake liners in six 5- or 6-ounce microwave custard cups or a muffin pan. Fill the cups one-half full with batter. Cook on HIGH for 2½ to 4 minutes, or until they test done, repositioning the cups or rotating the dish one-quarter turn once. (The tops may appear damp but not wet; a toothpick inserted in the centers will come out clean.) Remove the muffins and papers immediately from the cups and cool on a cake rack.

Repeat the procedure for the second batch. Moist tops will dry during standing time.

For the topping: Place the butter into a small deep dish. Cook on HIGH for 45 seconds to 1½ minutes to melt. Meanwhile, place the nuts or sugar and cinnamon in a separate small bowl. Dip each cooled muffin into the melted butter first, and then into the nuts or sugar.

Upside-Down Cake Basics:

1. See Cake Basics (page 506). For specifics about upside-down cakes, read below.
2. The batter for upside-down cakes is reduced slightly to accommodate the fruit that is placed in the bottom of the dish.
3. Having fruit on the bottom of the dish takes the place of wax paper and makes the cake easy to turn out. The butter, sugar, and fruit combination also makes a glaze for the cake when cooked.
4. Some fruit, because of its higher water content, will increase the total cooking time.

PLUM UPSIDE-DOWN CAKE

MAKES 6 TO 8 SERVINGS BEGIN 30 MINUTES BEFORE SERVING
COOKING TIME: 12 TO 16 MINUTES

As kids, when plum season arrived, we always looked forward to plum cake. The cake Thelma's mother made always had the plums on the top, but for the microwave we found that it worked better to put the plums on the bottom and flip the cake over.

6 tablespoons butter	1 cup cake or all-purpose flour
10 tablespoons sugar	½ teaspoon baking powder
½ teaspoon ground cinnamon	⅓ cup milk
5 or 6 plums (about 1 pound), cut in eighths	1 tablespoon vanilla, kirsch, or brandy
1 egg, beaten	Sweetened whipped cream or crème fraîche

Place 2 tablespoons butter in an 8½-inch round cake dish. Cook on HIGH for 45 seconds to 1 minute to melt. Tip the dish to coat evenly with the melted butter. Meanwhile, in a cup or small bowl combine 2 tablespoons sugar with the cinnamon. Sprinkle evenly over the buttered dish. Arrange the cut plums, overlapping, in concentric circles inside the buttered dish. Set aside.

In a medium mixing bowl combine the remaining 4 tablespoons butter and remaining 8 tablespoons sugar; cream until light. Beat in the egg. Combine the flour and baking powder. Add the flour alternately with the milk to the creamed butter mixture. Stir in the vanilla.

Spoon the batter evenly over the plums, spreading with a spatula to make a level surface. Place the dish on a microwaveproof cereal bowl in the oven. Cook on MEDIUM for 8 minutes, then on HIGH for 3 to 7 minutes, or until the cake tests done, rotating one-quarter turn two to three times, if necessary. (The top may appear damp but not wet; a toothpick inserted in the center will come out clean.) Let the cake stand directly on the counter for 5 to 10 minutes before turning out. Invert the cake onto a serving plate, firmly tapping the bottom of the dish to release. Serve warm with whipped cream or crème fraîche.

VARIATIONS:

Peach or Nectarine Upside-Down Cake: Substitute 1 pound peaches or nectarines for the plums, slicing into sixteenths.

Apricot Upside-Down Cake: Substitute 1 pound apricots for the plums.

CAPE COD JEWEL CAKE

MAKES 6 TO 8 SERVINGS   BEGIN 40 MINUTES BEFORE SERVING
COOKING TIME: 15 TO 22 MINUTES

We call this upside-down cake Cape Cod Jewel because the top glistens like a crown of garnets. The cranberries given to Thelma to make this cake were truly jewels, picked from a treasured bog annually by her friend Marilyn's father, who picks them in an abandoned cranberry bog in South Dennis, Massachusetts. The bog is believed to be at least 150 years old and one of the first in the area.

A warm butterscotch sauce is an unexpected but perfect complement to the pungent cranberries.

- 6 tablespoons butter
- 2 cups cleaned whole fresh or frozen cranberries
- 2 tablespoons orange juice
- ½ cup brown sugar
- ½ cup granulated sugar
- 1 egg
- 1 cup cake or all-purpose flour
- ½ teaspoon baking powder
- ⅓ cup milk
- 1 teaspoon vanilla
- Sweetened whipped cream or Butterscotch Sauce (page 565) (see Note)

In an 8½-inch round cake dish combine 2 tablespoons butter, the cranberries, orange juice, and brown sugar. Cover with wax paper; this prevents the cranberries from splattering. Cook on HIGH for 4 to 7 minutes, or until the butter and brown sugar are melted and the cranberries partially pop, stirring once. Spread the cranberries evenly over the bottom of the dish. Set aside.

Meanwhile, in a large mixing bowl beat the remaining 4 tablespoons butter and the granulated sugar together until light and fluffy. Beat in the egg. In a separate bowl combine the flour and baking powder. Add the flour mixture alternately with the milk to the creamed butter. Beat in the vanilla.

Spoon the batter evenly over the cranberries in the dish, spreading with a spatula to make a level surface. Place the dish on a microwaveproof cereal dish in the oven. Cook on MEDIUM for 8 minutes, then on HIGH for 3 to 7 minutes, or until the cake is set and tests done, rotating one-quarter turn two to three times, if necessary. (The top may appear damp but not wet; a toothpick inserted in the center will come out clean.) Let the cake stand directly on the counter for 5 to 10 minutes before turning out. Invert the cake onto a serving plate, firmly tapping the bottom of the dish to release. Spoon any berries that cling to the dish onto the cake top. Serve warm with whipped cream or warm butterscotch sauce.

NOTE: If serving with Butterscotch Sauce, make this during standing time.

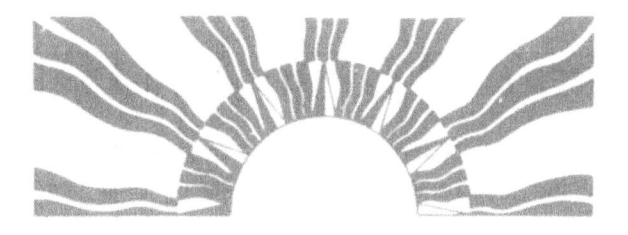

BLUEBERRY UPSIDE-DOWN CAKE

MAKES 6 TO 8 SERVINGS   BEGIN 30 MINUTES BEFORE SERVING
COOKING TIME: 12 TO 16 MINUTES

A pretty and delicious cake that is especially nice when Citrus Sauce is spooned on top. In the recipe, the butter is reduced and some cornstarch added because blueberries have more liquid and need to be thickened slightly.

5 tablespoons butter	1 cup cake or all-purpose flour
2 cups fresh or frozen unsweetened blueberries	½ teaspoon baking powder
	⅓ cup milk
1 teaspoon cornstarch	1 teaspoon vanilla
1 teaspoon grated lemon peel	Whipped cream, crème fraîche, or lemon Citrus Sauce (page 498)
½ cup plus ¼ teaspoon sugar	(see Note)
1 egg	

Place 1 tablespoon butter in an 8½-inch round cake dish. Cook on HIGH for 35 seconds to 1 minute. In a large bowl combine the blueberries, cornstarch, lemon peel, and ¼ teaspoon sugar, stirring to coat the berries. Spoon evenly over the melted butter.

Meanwhile, in another large mixing bowl beat the remaining 4 tablespoons butter and remaining ½ cup sugar together until light. Beat in the egg. In a separate bowl combine the flour and baking powder. Add the flour mixture alternately with the milk to the creamed butter. Beat in the vanilla.

Spoon the batter evenly over the blueberries in the dish, spreading with a spatula to make a level surface. Place the dish on a microwaveproof cereal bowl in the oven. Cook on MEDIUM for 8 minutes, then on HIGH for 3 to 7 minutes, or until the cake tests done, rotating one-quarter turn two to three times, if necessary. (The top may appear damp but not wet; a toothpick inserted in the center will come out clean.) Let the cake stand directly on the counter for 5 to 10 minutes before turning out. Invert the cake onto a serving plate, tapping the bottom of the dish to release. Spoon any berries that cling to the dish onto the cake top. Serve warm with whipped cream or lemon Citrus Sauce.

NOTE: If serving with Citrus Sauce, make this during standing time.

Pound and Bundt Cake Basics:

1. See Cake Basics (page 506). For specifics about Bundt cakes and pound cakes, read below.
2. The loaf or Bundt dish is greased well with shortening or unsalted butter or margarine to coat all crevices completely, so that the cocoa powder or chopped nuts will adhere evenly. (Unsalted fat is preferred so that no flavor is added.) The powder or nuts cook right onto the cake surface, giving it something akin to the dark crust that is found on conventionally baked cakes.
3. Because of the loaf dish shape, the ends of the pound cakes will have to be protected with foil, smoothly wrapped over the dish. Metal will reflect the microwaves during the first part of cooking, after which it is removed.

   Bundt cakes, on the other hand, are made in the ring shape, which will make for the most even cooking. Do not substitute a smaller dish than called for or the batter will cook over.
4. Pound cakes and Bundt cakes, because of their denser batter or larger volume, must be cooked longer than layer cakes. The principle of MEDIUM power first, then HIGH, remains the same.
5. Again, because of the larger, denser batter, Bundt and pound cakes have a longer standing time. After 15 minutes the bottom of the dish should feel just slightly warm to the touch. If the cake is turned out before this, it may stick to the dish, causing part of the top to break off. If this happens, it can be repaired and covered with a frosting or glaze.

✹ HALF POUND CAKE

MAKES 10 TO 12 SERVINGS   BEGIN 45 MINUTES BEFORE SERVING
COOKING TIME: 15 TO 18 MINUTES

A traditional pound cake was once made with a pound of sugar, a pound of butter, and a pound of flour. The formula varies these days, but we've made our version with a half pound sugar, butter, and flour for a dense cake that is especially good toasted. In fact, try the old-fashioned Brown Derby Pound Cake variation.

Let the cake stand, covered, overnight for the best texture.

- 1 tablespoon shortening, unsalted margarine, or butter
- 3 tablespoons Zwieback or plain cookie crumbs
- ½ pound butter
- 1½ cups cake or all-purpose flour
- ½ teaspoon baking powder
- 1 cup granulated sugar
- 4 eggs
- 2 teaspoons vanilla
- Confectioners' sugar

Grease a 9-x-5-inch loaf dish with the shortening. Coat the inside of the dish with the crumbs.

Place the ½ pound butter in a large microwaveproof bowl. Heat on DEFROST for 1½ to 2 minutes, or until softened; *do not melt*. Meanwhile, sift the flour and baking powder together in a bowl; set aside. Beat the granulated sugar into the butter until fluffy. Beat in the eggs, one at a time. Stir in the flour until well blended. Stir in the vanilla. Cover the ends of the loaf dish with 2-inch wide strips of foil to prevent overcooking.

Pour the batter into the prepared dish. Place on a microwaveproof cereal bowl in the oven. Cook on MEDIUM for 10 minutes, remove foil and cook on HIGH for 3 to 6 minutes, or until a skewer inserted in the center all the way to the bottom comes out clean, rotating one-quarter turn, twice, if necessary. (The top may appear damp but not wet; a skewer or broom straw inserted in the center will come out clean. Make sure the skewer goes all the way to the bottom of the dish and comes out clean.) Let the cake stand directly on the counter for 15 minutes. Turn out onto a serving dish and cool completely. Sprinkle with confectioners' sugar.

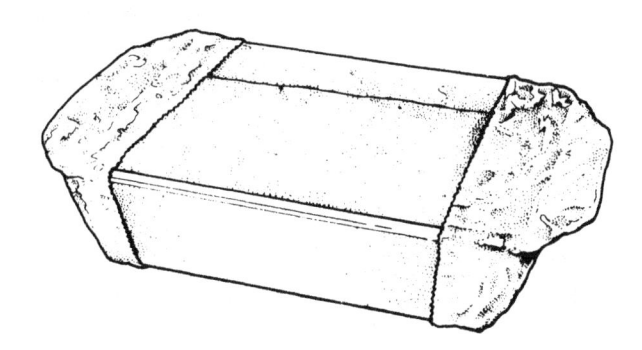

VARIATIONS:

Lemon Pound Cake: Add 2 tablespoons grated lemon rind with the vanilla. Spread Lemon Frosting (page 509) on top of the cooled cake.

Cranberry Pound Cake: Fold in 1 cup fresh cranberries with the vanilla. Serve plain or with Butterscotch Sauce (page 565). The cranberry nuggets look pretty when the cake is sliced, and they add a nice tart flavor.

Fresh Blueberry Pound Cake: Fold in 1 cup fresh blueberries and 2 tablespoons grated lemon rind with the vanilla. Serve with lemon Citrus Sauce (page 498) or blueberry Basic Berry Dessert Sauce (page 496). A nice summer dessert; only fresh blueberries will hold their shape.

Chocolate Chip Pound Cake: Fold in 1 cup chocolate chips with the vanilla. Spread Chocolate Cream Glaze (page 512) or Chocolate Cream Frosting (page 512) on top of the cooled cake.

Brown Derby Pound Cake: Cut the cake into ½-inch slices, depending on the number of servings desired. Toast in the toaster. Meanwhile, prepare Hot Fudge Sauce (page 564). Top each toasted cake with a scoop of vanilla ice cream. Spoon on the fudge sauce and it will look like a derby hat.

CHOCOLATE–CHOCOLATE CHIP BUNDT CAKE

MAKES 24 SERVINGS   BEGIN 45 MINUTES BEFORE SERVING
COOKING TIME: 16 TO 20 MINUTES

Bundt-type cakes cook particularly well in a microwave oven because of their shape. The open center allows microwave penetration through an inner surface area as well as the outside surface. We find a Bundt cake more practical for the microwave than making two separate cake layers. This one in particular is for chocolate lovers.

3 tablespoons shortening, unsalted butter, or margarine	1 cup brown sugar
6 tablespoons unsweetened cocoa powder	3 eggs
	1 teaspoon vanilla
¾ cup butter	1 cup buttermilk
2 cups cake or all-purpose flour	1 12-ounce package (2 cups) semisweet chocolate pieces
1 teaspoon baking powder	1 recipe Chocolate Cream Glaze (page 512)
1 teaspoon baking soda	

Grease a 10- to 12-cup microwaveproof Bundt dish with the shortening, making sure all the crevices are coated. Sprinkle 2 tablespoons cocoa powder into the greased dish, turning the dish to coat all the surfaces very well and very evenly.

Place the butter in a large microwaveproof bowl. Heat on DEFROST for 1½ to 2 minutes, or until softened; *do not melt*. Meanwhile, sift together in a bowl the flour, baking powder, and baking soda; set aside. Beat the sugar into the softened butter until fluffy. Beat in the eggs, one a time. Stir in the vanilla. Add the flour alternately with the buttermilk. Fold in the chocolate pieces.

Pour the batter into the prepared cake dish and spread to make even on top. Place the cake on a microwaveproof cereal dish in the oven. Cook on MEDIUM for 9 minutes; then on HIGH for 5 to 9 minutes, or until the cake tests done, rotating one-quarter turn once or twice if necessary. (The top may appear damp but not wet; a toothpick inserted in the center will come out clean.) Let the cake stand directly on the counter for 15 minutes. Turn out onto a serving plate. Finish cooling and pour the chocolate glaze over the cake.

APPLESAUCE BUNDT CAKE

MAKES 24 SERVINGS   BEGIN 45 MINUTES TO 1 HOUR BEFORE SERVING
COOKING TIME: 19 TO 23 MINUTES

Delicious with or without frosting, this cake stores very well, covered tightly, because the applesauce keeps it moist.

3 tablespoons shortening, unsalted butter, or margarine	2 teaspoons baking soda
4 tablespoons unsweetened cocoa powder	2 cups sugar
	2 eggs
¾ cup butter or margarine	2 cups applesauce
2½ cups cake or all-purpose flour	1 cup raisins
1 teaspoon ground cinnamon	1 cup coarsely chopped walnuts
½ teaspoon allspice	Vanilla Frosting (page 509) (optional)

Grease a 10- to 12-inch microwaveproof Bundt dish with the shortening, making sure all the crevices are coated. Sprinkle 2 tablespoons of the cocoa powder into the greased dish, turning the dish to coat all the surfaces very well and very evenly.

Place the butter or margarine in a large microwaveproof mixing bowl. Heat on DEFROST for 1½ to 2 minutes to soften; *do not melt.* Meanwhile, sift the remaining 2 tablespoons cocoa, flour, cinnamon, allspice, and baking soda in a bowl together; set aside.

Beat the sugar into the softened butter until light and fluffy. Beat in the eggs, one at a time. Beat in the applesauce. Mix ½ cup flour mixture with the raisins and walnuts; this will keep them from falling to the bottom of the mixture. Set aside. Stir the remaining flour mixture into the butter-egg mixture. Fold in the floured raisins and nuts.

Pour the batter into the prepared dish and spread to make even on top. Place the dish on top of a microwaveproof cereal bowl in the oven. Cook on MEDIUM for 9 minutes, then on HIGH for 8 to 12 minutes, or until the cake tests done, rotating one-quarter turn once or twice, if necessary. (The top may appear damp but not wet; a toothpick inserted in the center will come out clean.) Let the cake stand directly on the counter for 15 minutes. Turn out onto a serving plate and let cool completely. Frost, if desired.

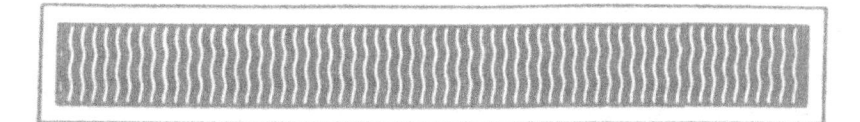

WALNUT-BRANDY BUNDT CAKE

MAKES 24 SERVINGS   BEGIN 45 TO 50 MINUTES BEFORE SERVING
COOKING TIME: 16 TO 20 MINUTES

This cake is great for entertaining because of the large number of people it serves. Don't be afraid to serve it at a family gathering of kids and teetotalers because the brandy adds a light flavor but the alcohol cooks away and evaporates.

3 tablespoons shortening, unsalted butter, or margarine	1 teaspoon baking soda
2½ cups finely chopped walnuts	1½ cups granulated sugar
¾ cup butter	3 eggs
1½ cups cake or all-purpose flour	1 cup plain yogurt
1 tablespoon grated nutmeg	¼ cup brandy
1 teaspoon baking powder	Confectioners' sugar or Walnut-Brandy Sauce (page 564) (optional)

Grease a 10- to 12-cup microwaveproof Bundt dish with the shortening, making sure all the crevices are coated. Sprinkle ½ cup chopped walnuts into the greased dish, turning the dish to coat all the surfaces very well and very evenly.

Place the butter in a large microwaveproof mixing bowl. Heat on DEFROST for 1½ to 2 minutes to soften; *do not melt.* Meanwhile, sift the flour, nutmeg, baking powder, and baking soda together in a bowl; set aside. Beat the sugar into the softened butter until light and fluffy. Beat in the eggs, one at a time. Stir in the yogurt and brandy. Blend in the flour mixture. Fold in the remaining 2 cups nuts.

Pour the batter into the prepared dish and spread to make even on top. Place the cake on a microwaveproof cereal bowl in the oven. Cook on MEDIUM for 9 minutes, then on HIGH for 5 to 9 minutes, or until the cake tests done. (The top may appear damp but not wet; a toothpick inserted in the center will come out clean.) Let the cake stand directly on the counter for 15 minutes. Turn out onto a serving plate and let cool completely. Serve plain or sprinkled with confectioners' sugar, or serve with the walnut-brandy sauce.

BANANA BREAD RING

MAKES 24 SERVINGS   BEGIN 45 TO 50 MINUTES BEFORE SERVING
COOKING TIME: 16 TO 20 MINUTES

The ring Bundt dish makes it easy to cook a large amount of this banana bread, and besides, it looks so pretty!

The Irishman-in-Haiti Cake variation derived its name from the fact that immigrants have always adapted to a foreign land by mixing the local ingredients with a little of their own imported ones. How better would an Irishman adjust to the abundance of bananas in Haiti than with a little Irish whiskey?

- 3 tablespoons shortening or unsalted margarine
- 2½ cups finely chopped walnuts
- ¾ cup butter
- 1½ cups cake or all-purpose flour
- 1 teaspoon baking powder
- 1 teaspoon baking soda
- 1½ cups granulated sugar
- 3 eggs
- 1 cup sour cream
- 2 ripe bananas, mashed (1⅓ cups)
- 1 teaspoon vanilla
- Confectioners' sugar (optional)

Grease a 10- to 12-cup microwaveproof Bundt dish with the shortening, coating all the crevices. Sprinkle with ½ cup chopped walnuts to coat completely and evenly.

Place the butter in a large microwaveproof mixing bowl. Heat on DEFROST for 1½ to 2 minutes to soften; *do not melt.* Meanwhile, sift the flour, baking powder, and baking soda in a bowl together; set aside. Beat the granulated sugar into the softened butter until light and fluffy. Beat in the eggs, one at a time. Stir in the sour cream.

In a small bowl combine the bananas and vanilla. Blend the bananas and flour alternately into the butter. Fold in the remaining 2 cups nuts.

Spoon the batter into the prepared pan. Place the cake on a microwaveproof cereal bowl in the oven. Cook on MEDIUM for 9 minutes, then on HIGH for 5 to 9 minutes, or until the cake tests done, rotating one-quarter turn once or twice. (The top may appear damp but not wet; a toothpick inserted in the center will come out clean.) Let the cake stand directly on the counter for 15 minutes. Turn out onto a serving plate. Let cool and sprinkle with confectioners' sugar, if desired.

VARIATION:

Irishman-in-Haiti Cake: Eliminate 1 banana. Add ¼ cup Irish whiskey to the remaining banana and mash. When the cake is turned out onto the serving plate, with a long skewer pierce every inch on top of the cake. In a 2-cup glass measure combine ¼ cup corn syrup and ¼ cup Irish whiskey. Cook on HIGH for 2 minutes. Pour over the cake, making sure the syrup runs into the holes. Serve. This cake is just lightly scented with the whiskey.

Quick Bread Basics:

1. Because there is no dry heat in a microwave oven, there will be no hard crust on your breads. Yet because there is not a hard crust, it also means that the bread can rise slightly higher, making a lighter-textured product. A crust can be simulated

by precoating the cooking dish with graham cracker crumbs as in Zucchini-Nut Bread.
2. Quick breads are cooked in many different shape dishes. If cooked in a loaf or square dish, the corners of the batter will have to be protected with foil, smoothly wrapped over the dish. (See illustrations, pages 523 and 531.) The foil is removed after MEDIUM power is turned up to HIGH. It is important to smooth the batter evenly across the top of the dish too, so that there is an equal depth of batter in all parts of the dish.
3. Other than this foil protection, quick breads are cooked uncovered, to give them room to rise and to let moisture evaporate. A quick bread, covered tightly during cooking, would retain too much liquid and become more like a steamed bread.
4. The quick bread dish is placed on top of a microwaveproof cereal dish to raise it even closer to the center of the oven, where cakes and breads seem to cook most evenly (see illustration on page 506). This procedure may even help to eliminate rotating, but if not, rotate the cake one-quarter turn two to three times throughout cooking.
5. Quick breads are cooked on MEDIUM power first so that the gas and heated air can expand evenly to form the cake structure. Once this has happened, the bread can be safely cooked on HIGH.
6. After cooking, a bread should stand directly on a counter top so that heat is reflected back into the bread to cook it. If it were to stand on a cooling rack, the surrounding air would take away the heat needed to continue cooking.
7. For doneness, see Cake Basics, page 506.

✹ CORN BREAD

MAKES 16 TWO-INCH-SQUARE PIECES   BEGIN 25 TO 30 MINUTES BEFORE SERVING
COOKING TIME: 9 TO 12 MINUTES

1 cup all-purpose flour	½ teaspoon salt
1 cup cornmeal	1 egg, beaten
¼ cup sugar	4 tablespoons melted butter
2 teaspoons baking powder	⅔ cup buttermilk

Combine all the ingredients in a large bowl, stirring until fairly smooth. Pour into an 8-inch square or 8½-inch round cake dish and smooth the top of the batter. (If using a square pan, cover the corners with foil to prevent overcooking, as in the illustration, page 531.)

Place the dish on top of a microwaveproof cereal bowl. Cook on MEDIUM for 8 minutes; remove the foil corners. Cook on HIGH for 1 to 4 minutes, or until a toothpick inserted in the center comes out clean, rotating one-quarter turn once or twice (The top may appear damp but not wet.) Let stand directly on the counter for 5 to 10 minutes before serving from the dish. Serve warm.

VARIATIONS:

Whole-Kernel Corn Bread: Add ½ cup cooked corn to the batter. A good use for leftover corn.

Cracklin' Corn Bread: Add 2 slices of crisp bacon (see page 61), broken into pieces, to the batter.

Calico Corn Bread: Add ¼ cup chopped green pepper and ½ cup chopped sweet red pepper to the batter.

Cajun Corn Bread: Follow the Calico Corn Bread variation above, but add 1 or 2 jalapeño peppers, chopped, to the batter. Nice and spicy!

✸ ZUCCHINI-NUT BREAD

MAKES 1 LOAF   BEGIN 25 MINUTES BEFORE SERVING
COOKING TIME: 11 TO 14 MINUTES

When stored wrapped in foil, the flavor of this bread improves with time.

- 2 tablespoons shortening
- 3 tablespoons graham cracker, Zwelback, or bread crumbs
- 2 eggs
- ¾ cup dark brown sugar
- ½ cup vegetable oil
- 2 teaspoons vanilla
- 1½ cups all-purpose flour
- 1½ teaspoons ground cinnamon
- ½ teaspoon baking powder
- ½ teaspoon baking soda
- ½ teaspoon salt
- ½ teaspoon grated nutmeg
- ½ teaspoon ground cloves
- 1 cup shredded zucchini, tightly packed (about ¼ pound)
- 1 cup coarsely chopped walnuts

Prepare a 9- × -5 or 8- × -4-inch loaf dish by greasing well with the shortening and coating completely and evenly with the cracker or bread crumbs.

Place the eggs in a large mixing bowl and beat until foamy. Beat in the sugar, oil, and vanilla. In a separate bowl combine the dry ingredients. Gradually add to the egg mixture, stirring until just blended. Fold in the zucchini and nuts.

Pour the batter into the prepared dish, smoothing evenly on top. Cover the ends of the loaf dish with 2-inch-wide strips of foil to prevent overcooking (see illustration on page 523). Place the dish on top of a microwave-proof cereal bowl in the oven. Cook on MEDIUM for 10 minutes; remove the foil corners. Cook on HIGH for 1 to 4 minutes, or until a toothpick inserted in the center comes out clean, rotating one-quarter turn once if necessary. (The top may appear damp but not wet.) Let stand directly on the counter for 5 to 10 minutes, until the dish is warm, not hot, on the bottom. Turn out onto a serving plate and slice. Store tightly wrapped in foil.

VARIATIONS:

Whole-Wheat Zucchini Bread: Substitute whole-wheat flour for the all-purpose flour.

Pumpkin Bread: Substitute 1 cup pumpkin puree for the zucchini. Add 1 teaspoon ground ginger and ½ cup golden raisins, mixing with dry ingredients.

Carrot Bread: Substitute 1½ cups grated carrots for 1 cup zucchini. Add ½ cup raisins, mixing with dry ingredients.

Raising Bread Dough

Testing the Oven Power: It is critical that bread dough be raised on a very low power. Even a slightly higher power will kill the yeast and keep it from rising. We call for WARM power, but since all oven manufacturers gauge their ovens differently, it is best to determine whether this lowest power setting on your oven is satisfactory for this delicate procedure. Follow these instructions:

Place 2 tablespoons refrigerated butter in a custard cup. Heat in the microwave oven on WARM (lowest power setting on oven) for 4 minutes. If the butter has melted completely in 4 minutes, the power is too high and may kill the yeast. If the butter has partially melted, but some chunks of butter still remain, the power will be perfect for raising bread dough.

Raising 1 Loaf Bread Dough: Place yeast bread dough (amount for 1 loaf) in a lightly buttered microwaveproof bowl. Place this bowl in another large bowl holding 2 to 3 cups boiling water. Cover the dough loosely with wax paper. Heat on WARM for 4 minutes. Let stand for 15 minutes. Repeat the process until the dough has doubled in bulk, turning over if the top appears dry.

Defrosting Frozen Bread Dough: Butter the frozen loaf all over and place in a buttered microwaveproof loaf dish. Place the loaf dish in a 2-quart microwaveproof rectangular dish holding 1½ cups boiling water. Cover the bread dough loosely with wax paper and heat on DEFROST for 5 to 10 minutes, or until defrosted, rotating each minute. Turn the dough over. Re-cover and heat on HIGH for 2 minutes, rotating the dish once. Let stand for 10 minutes. Raise the dough following the directions above.

BROWNIES

MAKES 16 TWO-INCH BROWNIES   BEGIN 30 MINUTES BEFORE SERVING
COOKING TIME: 12 TO 16 MINUTES

Brownies are a dense bar cookie that cooks well in the microwave. We prefer them made with the chocolate squares because they are a little chewier, but they can also be made with unsweetened cocoa powder (see variation below).

If you make them in the nontraditional round cake dish you won't need to shield any corners. The wedges are then often nice topped with ice cream and Hot Fudge Sauce (page 564) for dessert. Frost, if desired, with Chocolate Cream Frosting (page 512).

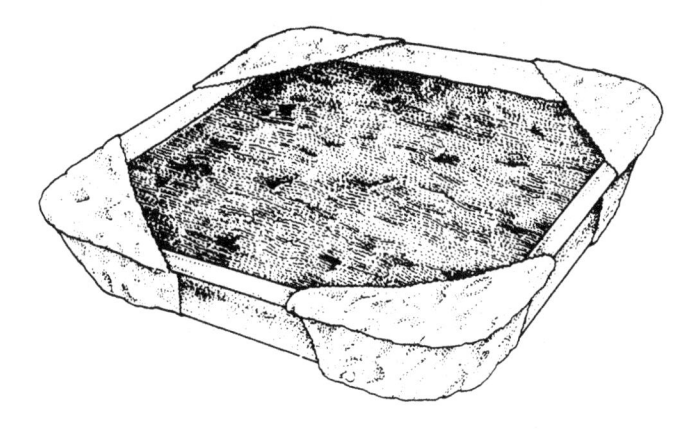

- 2 ounces unsweetened chocolate
- ½ cup butter, cut into 4 pieces
- 1 cup brown or granulated sugar
- 2 large eggs, beaten
- 1 teaspoon vanilla
- ⅔ cup all-purpose flour
- ½ teaspoon baking powder
- ½ cup coarsely chopped walnuts (optional)

In a large microwaveproof mixing bowl combine the chocolate and butter. Cook on MEDIUM for 2½ minutes, stir. Continue to cook for 30-second intervals, or until melted, stirring each time. The chocolate may be melted but still hold its shape, so press down with a spoon to check. Stir the sugar into the melted chocolate until well blended. Beat in the eggs. Stir in the remaining ingredients until well blended.

Spread evenly into an 8½-inch round or 8-inch square cake dish. Place on top of a microwaveproof cereal bowl in the oven. Cook on MEDIUM for 8 minutes, then on HIGH for 1 to 4 minutes, until a toothpick comes out of the center clean, rotating one quarter turn once or twice. (If baking in a square dish, shield the corners with foil while cooking on MEDIUM power. Remove the foil to cook on HIGH power.)

Let stand directly on the counter for 10 to 20 minutes, or until cooled.

VARIATIONS:

Cocoa Brownies: Substitute ¼ cup unsweetened cocoa powder for the chocolate squares. Add the cocoa, with sugar, to the butter, which has been melted on HIGH for 1 to 2 minutes. Proceed with basic recipe.

Whole-Wheat Brownies: Substitute whole-wheat flour for the all-purpose flour. Use brown sugar. Instead of nuts, add sunflower seeds, if desired.

Butterscotch Bars: Eliminate the chocolate. Melt the butter on HIGH for 1 to 2 minutes and add brown sugar. Fold in ¾ cup butterscotch bits with the remaining ingredients.

RASPBERRY-OATMEAL BARS

MAKES 15 OR 16 BARS   BEGIN ABOUT 1¼ HOURS BEFORE SERVING
COOKING TIME: 10 TO 13 MINUTES

These bar cookies are delicious and work very well in the microwave. They are quick and easy and always make a hit—especially when you want to keep the kitchen cool.

¾ cup butter	1½ cups old-fashioned oats
1½ cups all-purpose flour	1 cup dark brown sugar
1 teaspoon baking powder	1 10-ounce jar raspberry preserves

Place the butter in a large microwaveproof bowl. Heat the butter on DEFROST for 1 to 2 minutes, or until softened; *do not melt*. Meanwhile, in a separate bowl combine the flour, baking powder, and oats. Beat the sugar into the butter until fluffy. Stir in the dry ingredients.

Press half the mixture into an 8-inch square cake dish. Spread the top with preserves. Top with the remaining mixture. Cover the corners with foil to prevent overcooking (see illustration on page 531). Cook on MEDIUM for 7 minutes; remove the foil. Cook on HIGH for 2 to 4 minutes, or until the preserves bubble through the top, slightly, in the center; be careful not to overcook, since the cookies will harden upon cooling. Let stand on the counter until cooled, 1 hour, before cutting into squares. Refrigerate them to speed cooling.

Steamed Cakes and Breads Basics:

1. Batter for steamed cake is poured into a buttered mold before being cooked conventionally, but in the microwave, a double layer of wax paper is placed on the bottom of the dish. The bread or cake retains so much moisture that only one piece of wax paper would stick to the mold.
2. The best cake molds to use for steamed cakes and breads have a small base, and sides that are at least two times as high as the diameter of the base.
3. This is the only type of cake or bread that is covered during cooking. Because cake molds don't usually have covers, plastic wrap that is turned back slightly to vent steam works well. The purpose is to keep all available moisture in the batter to form a heavier cake. Cooking the steamed breads right on the bottom oven shelf also helps to hold in heat and moisture.
4. Steamed cakes and breads are cooked entirely on MEDIUM power. This is best considering the denseness of the batter and because of the shape that the batter takes in the taller, thinner molds.

5. As with any cake, it may be necessary to rotate the steamed cakes for more even cooking.
6. Standing time is important for these dense cakes and breads. It is important to let them stand directly on the counter top, rather than on a rack, to reflect all the heat back to the inside. When the dish is warm, not hot, to the touch, it will be easier to unmold.
7. For doneness, see Cake Basics (page 506).

ENGLISH PLUM PUDDING

MAKES 8 TO 10 SERVINGS   BEGIN 40 MINUTES BEFORE SERVING
COOKING TIME: 10 TO 14 MINUTES

Thelma's grandmother studied cooking in England as a young girl and brought back a recipe for a traditional dense cake full of raisins that she called a "pudding." Her German family adopted it with relish but, unfortunately, the recipe was never written down, and it was finally forgotten—until a friend of the family, Mrs. Lily Gillman, shared with us this recipe, one that she garnered from watching her relations make the pudding in an old English kitchen. She cooks it conventionally for 2½ hours in a water bath or in the pressure cooker for 50 minutes. Now we cook our own version in under 15 minutes.

- 1 15-ounce box raisins
- ¼ cup finely ground suet
- 1 ounce (about 2 tablespoons) fresh bread crumbs
- 2 tablespoons all-purpose flour
- 1 ounce (about 2 tablespoons) mixed chopped fruit peel
- 2 tablespoons brown sugar
- 1 tablespoon molasses
- ¼ teaspoon ground cinnamon
- ¼ teaspoon grated nutmeg
- ¼ teaspoon baking powder
- 1 egg, beaten
- ½ cup beer
- 4 tablespoons brandy or whiskey
- 1 recipe Plum Pudding Sauce (page 534) or Hard Sauce (page 535)

In a large bowl combine all the ingredients, except 2 tablespoons of the brandy and the sauce; stir well to blend.

Cut 2 circles of wax paper to fit the bottom inside of a 4-cup porcelain or glass mold. Place the paper in the dish. Spoon the batter into the mold. Cover with plastic wrap and cook on MEDIUM for 10 to 14 minutes, or until a toothpick inserted in the pudding center comes out clean, rotating two to three times if necessary. The top may appear damp but not wet. Let stand directly on the counter for 10 to 15 minutes. Loosen the edges of the pudding from the dish and turn out onto a serving platter.

To serve, pour the remaining 2 tablespoons brandy into a 1-cup glass measure. Cook on HIGH for 15 seconds *only*, and pour over the pudding. Light with a match. Turn off the lights for the full effect. Serve with the sauce.

NOTE: If you don't serve immediately, this pudding can be stored for a long time. *To Reheat:* Cover with plastic wrap and heat on HIGH for 2 to 5 minutes.

VARIATION:

Figgy Pudding: Substitute 1 pound dried figs, chopped, with stems removed, for the raisins.

PLUM PUDDING SAUCE

MAKES 3 CUPS
COOKING TIME: 6 TO 7 MINUTES

Leave it to the British to know the best way to warm your heart on a cold day. Serve this immediately poured over the pudding.

- 2 eggs, separated
- ½ cup half and half
- 2 tablespoons brandy or whiskey
- 1 cup confectioners' sugar
- ¼ cup butter

In a 4-cup glass measure combine the egg yolks, half and half, brandy, and sugar until smooth. Add the butter. Cook on MEDIUM for 6 to 7 minutes, or until the butter has melted and the sauce has slightly thickened, stirring every 2 minutes.

Meanwhile, beat the egg whites until stiff. Gradually pour the warm mixture into the egg whites, stirring constantly.

NOTE: This recipe can be cut in half and cooked for half the time, stirring every minute.

✸ BOSTON BROWN BREAD

MAKES 2 LOAVES   BEGIN 25 TO 30 MINUTES BEFORE SERVING
COOKING TIME: 6 TO 8 MINUTES PER LOAF

In conventional cooking, brown bread in its mold is set into steaming water on the top of the range. It usually takes 3 hours to cook. Cooking the bread in the microwave duplicates these results very well, in just 6 to 8 minutes for each loaf. Cut them into ½-inch slices and serve with softened cream cheese or beans and franks.

- ½ cup whole-wheat flour
- ½ cup cornmeal
- ½ cup all-purpose flour
- ½ teaspoon baking powder
- ½ teaspoon baking soda
- ½ cup molasses
- ⅔ cup buttermilk
- 1 egg
- ½ cup raisins
- ¼ cup chopped nuts

Combine all the ingredients in a large bowl, stirring to mix well. Cut 2 circles of wax paper to fit the bottom inside of a 2-cup glass measure. Spoon in half the batter, which will reach close to the 1⅓-cup mark. Cover with plastic wrap, vented on one side and cook on MEDIUM for 6 to 8 minutes, or until a toothpick comes out clean from the center, rotating a half turn halfway through cooking. Let stand directly on the counter for 5 to 10 minutes.

Meanwhile, repeat the procedure for the second loaf.

With a knife, loosen the cooked loaves from the dish and turn out.

HARD SAUCE

MAKES 2 CUPS
COOKING TIME: 1 MINUTE

When spooned over warm English Plum Pudding, this hard sauce melts over the top, making a delicious winter dessert. Keep a covered container of it in the refrigerator to spread it on toasted brown bread to be served with tea.

- 1 cup unsalted butter
- 1 cup sifted confectioners' sugar
- ¼ cup brandy or rum

Place the butter in a medium microwave-proof bowl. Heat on LOW for 45 seconds to 1 minute, until softened but not melted. Beat in the sugar with a wooden spoon or electric mixer until well blended. Beat in the brandy or rum, a little at a time, until smooth and blended. Cover and chill for at least 1 hour, until stiff.

VARIATION:

Hard Sauce with Nutmeg: Stir in ¼ teaspoon freshly grated nutmeg with the brandy.

15

Pies, Puddings, and Other Desserts

I love desserts. Not in large quantities, but I can think of no better way to end a meal than with a bite of something rich and sweet.

It wasn't always that way. I don't remember dreaming of desserts as a child, and I had a grandmother who knew what dessert dreams were made of. I shunned desserts in college, and even in my early working career they didn't hold much appeal. It was only as I became downwardly mobile as a happy but impoverished traveler/freelance writer that desserts drew me with such magnetism. When a needed haircut would have sapped all my liquid assets, I could console myself with a coffee and a sweet—anywhere in the world. Now I'm hooked.

For the serious dessert lover, I think we have covered all bases, and appealed to all levels of expertise and time availability. For the times when you need or want something sweet in fifteen minutes, Amaretto Sauce, Black Raspberry Sauce, Butterscotch Sauce, and more, can be made to pour over cake, fruit, or dessert. Pastry cream can be whipped up and served in the summer with fresh fruit. When dessert can be planned in advance, the Three-Tiered Chocolate Mousse Cake, Baileys Irish Cream Pie, and Orange Cheesecake will benefit from refrigeration overnight.

Much to the surprise of many "serious cooks," we have had great success with pastry crusts in the microwave. We have been able to make it light and flaky, rolling and cutting it into free-form round and even pear-shaped pastries. The results are some unique desserts, such as the Large Summer Fruit Tart, Apple Pizza Tart, and Pears in Pear-Shaped Tart Shells.

The pastry reminds me so much of my grandmother's pastry, which she took great pains to pull from the oven before it was brown. It seemed odd to me at the time, when everyone else's pastry was so much darker, yet in color and flavor her crusts always married beautifully with their fillings and never overpowered them. Not until years later, when I studied cooking in France (my grandmother's maiden name was Belleville), did I realize that the French were also careful to keep their crusts light. Now in the microwave you will be able to produce that same beautiful, blond crust. I know that you'll enjoy eating from this chapter as much as we did creating it.

—MARCIA

Pastry Dough Basics:

MIXING

1. Solid vegetable shortening makes the pie dough tender; butter makes the dough flaky. A combination of the two in a dough is best.
2. The key to mixing the fat into the flour is to add the vegetable shortening first, then work quickly when adding the butter to keep from melting into the dough. It doesn't even hurt to chill the forks and bowl first. All this adds to flakiness.
3. Liquid (in small amounts) with the flour produces enough gluten to give dough its elasticity and makes it rollable. The liquid can be in the form of water, liqueur, or an egg, the latter of which will make a firmer, cookielike pastry. When adding water, be careful to add it slowly so that you don't end up with too much in the dough. Too much water will cause the starch to gelatinize too much, which will keep the dough from cooking into a dry, flaky pastry.
4. Overmixing can cause the butter to melt, resulting in a tougher pastry. So be careful not to overmix it in the food processor (mix until just before the ball shape), or when gathering the dough into a ball when making by hand, do so quickly so as not to warm dough.
5. Flatten pastry before chilling to make it easier to roll out.
6. Chilling makes a pastry dough that is easier to roll out, and one that shrinks less during cooking.

COOKING

1. The amount of dough in the basic recipe is designed for a 9-inch pie plate. If you use a larger plate you will be forced to roll the dough too thin.
2. Cooking the dough on the outside of an inverted 9-inch dish gives a drier exterior, because no steam will be trapped between the bottom of the crust and the plate. (In conventional cooking, this moisture would be evaporated by the hot air in the oven and the hot dish.) Any steam that builds up on the inside will quickly evaporate once the pastry is removed from the dish.
3. It is important to prick the dough before it is cooked to keep it flat and prevent it from bubbling up and holding that shape. Some bubbling will occur but the steam will eventually escape through the holes.
4. HIGH power will quickly melt the butter and water, to produce the necessary steam to separate the layers of dough, forming the traditional flaky crust.
5. Wax paper, rather than butter, is better for lining the dish for easy removal of the crust after cooking.
6. *Doneness:* When the pastry is dry and opaque and the liquid starts beading up slightly on the crust, the pastry is done. When you open the oven door to check, you may hear a distinct sound that resembles two pieces of sandpaper being lightly rubbed together. In more humid weather, the liquid will be seen bubbling out of the holes made with the fork.

There will be a slight golden color, but no overall browning, because there is no dry heat in the oven. The crust should be watched closely so that it doesn't overcook and darken in spots.

Underdone: There will still be transparent undercooked areas, or if it does appear dry, you won't see the small beads of butter on the surface and hear the sandpaper sound described above. Return to the oven and cook for 30 seconds at a time.

Overdone: Brown spots will appear first in areas where the dough is higher in fat. The crust will be harder and tougher in those areas. If it doesn't look too bad, the crust will still be edible. If there are too many large brown spots, remove the darkened areas and try to cut the good pastry into triangles that will be a nice garnish to ice cream or pudding.

❈ BASIC PASTRY DOUGH

MAKES ENOUGH FOR 1 PIE OR 6 TARTLETS
BEGIN 20 MINUTES TO 1¼ HOURS BEFORE COOKING, DEPENDING ON CHILL TIME

The tenderest and flakiest pie dough is made with a combination of solid vegetable shortening and butter. The shortening should be added first and the butter should be well chilled. You'll find that it's easier to make the dough on a dry, cool day than a hot, humid one, so that the fat won't melt during mixing.

- 1 cup all-purpose flour
- ½ teaspoon salt
- 3 tablespoons solid vegetable shortening
- 3 tablespoons very cold unsalted butter
- 2 to 3 tablespoons ice water

In a large mixing bowl or food processor blend the flour and salt. Cut the butter into 12 pieces. This will blend better into the flour. Working quickly, cut the shortening into the flour with a pastry blender, 2 knives, or a food processor, until the particles are pea-size. Cut in the butter. Add the water, 1 tablespoon at a time, using a tossing motion to incorporate into the dough, until the particles can be gathered lightly into a ball.

Flatten the dough into a pancake approximately 4½ inches in diameter. Cover with plastic wrap and freeze 30 minutes, if in a hurry, or refrigerate for at least 1 hour or up to 3 days (see Notes).

NOTES: The dough can be frozen at this point for up to 1 month.

To Double: Double the ingredients, but mix each ball of dough separately. They will be easier to roll out, eliminating the problem of dividing 1 ball in half evenly.

VARIATIONS:

Amaretto Pastry Dough: Substitute 3 tablespoons amaretto or other nut-flavored liqueur, chilled over ice, for the water. Adds a lightly sweet and nutty flavor!

Rich Egg Pastry Dough: Substitute 1 large egg for the water. This makes a pastry that is more cookielike in texture.

Sweet Lemon Pastry Dough: Substitute 2 tablespoons sugar and ½ teaspoon grated lemon rind for the salt.

Nut-Egg Pastry Dough: Substitute 1 egg for the water. Add ¼ cup finely chopped nuts to the flour. A cookie-type dough.

✺ BASIC PIE SHELL

MAKES ONE 9-INCH PIE SHELL   BEGIN 30 MINUTES TO 1½ HOURS BEFORE SERVING, DEPENDING ON CHILL TIME
COOKING TIME: 6 TO 8 MINUTES

We choose to cook the pastry dough on the back of a pie plate, because it produces a crust so flaky that, in a blind test, no one could tell the difference between it and a conventional crust. Even the light color, because of the absence of dry heat, is reminiscent of the lighter crusts Marcia's grandmother achieved.

After baking, it can be filled with any sort of prepared fruit filling or poached fruit and pastry cream. The crust is fragile, so treat it with care.

---
1 recipe Basic Pastry Dough (page 541)

Cut a 14-inch square of wax paper and trace a 9-inch circle on it, drawing four 2-inch tabs as shown in the illustration below. Cut out and set aside.

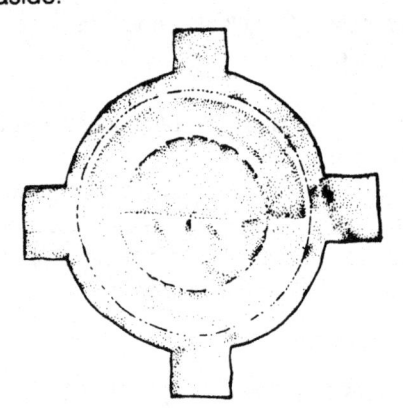

On a lightly floured surface, roll the chilled dough into a 12-inch circle. (A roller stocking on a rolling pin will make this process easier, requiring less additional flour.)

Lay the paper circle over the bottom of the inverted 9-inch pie plate. Place the dough on top of the paper, pressing it against the plate. Trim the dough so that it extends ½ inch over the edge of the pie plate. (Save the dough trimmings, sometimes they come in handy for patching.) Turn the overhanging dough back ½ inch, pressing firmly against the edge of the plate with a fork, moistening the dough with water if necessary. The dough should be folded evenly all the way around. Lightly prick the dough, every inch, with a fork.

Place the inverted pie plate, dough side up, into the microwave. *Even though the crust bubbles up during cooking, don't worry about it and don't push it down, for it flattens out later.* Cook on HIGH for 6 to 8 minutes, or until the pastry is opaque and dry but not brown, rotating a half turn after 3 minutes. Let the pastry cool for 5 minutes on the plate. Invert the pie plate onto a microwaveproof serving plate. Loosen the crust with a sharp knife to gently lift the pie plate, and peel the paper from the crust.

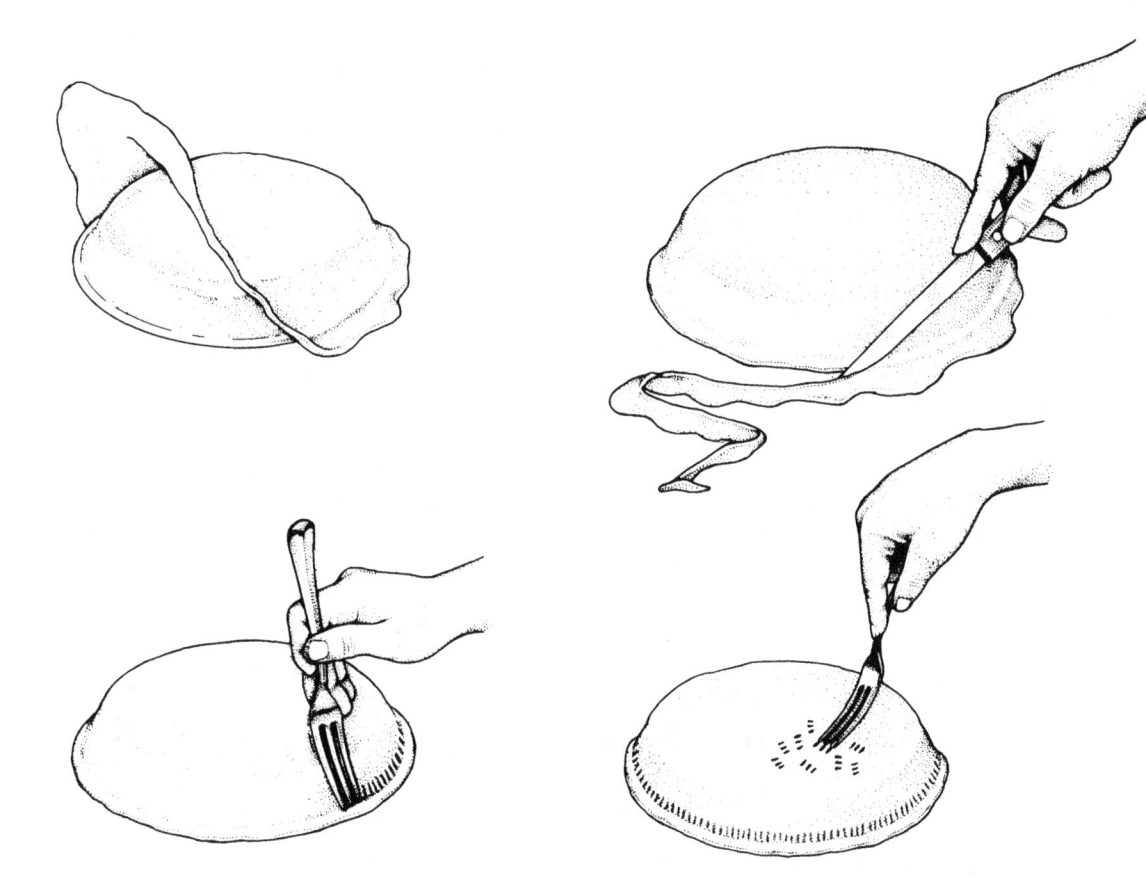

FLAKY SHORTBREAD TRIANGLES

MAKES 12 TRIANGLES   BEGIN 1½ HOURS BEFORE SERVING
COOKING TIME: 5 TO 7 MINUTES

Do you know anyone who prefers the crust over the filling in a pie? Then these buttery pastry triangles are for them, served with tea, or as an attractive addition to ice cream that has been topped with one of the warm sauces.

1 cup all-purpose flour	1 large egg, slightly beaten
2 tablespoons sugar	2 tablespoons water
¼ teaspoon grated nutmeg	1 egg yolk
6 tablespoons cold butter, cut in 24 cubes	Coarse white or colored sugar for topping

In a large mixing or food processor bowl combine the flour, sugar, and nutmeg; mix well. Add the butter with your fingertips, a pastry blender blade, 2 knives, or a processor, and working quickly, cut the butter into the flour until the particles are pea-size.

Lightly stir in egg and form the dough into a ball; do not overwork or the dough will become tough (if the dough is made in a food processor, process only until the dough forms small granules). Flatten the dough ball into a pancake approximately 4 inches in diameter, for easier rolling out later. Cover with plastic wrap and refrigerate for 1 hour or up to 3 days.

Cut two 12-inch squares of wax paper, placing one on top of the other. Lightly flour the top of the wax paper. Roll the chilled dough on wax paper to form an 8-inch circle, about ¼ inch thick. Pinch the dough to flute the outer edges. Lightly prick the dough, every inch, with a fork. Cut the circle into 12 triangles, separating the triangles from each other slightly.

In a custard cup add the water to the egg yolk and beat with a fork. Brush the egg mixture onto the pastry. Sprinkle with coarse or colored sugar. Place the dough on the wax paper into the microwave. Cook on HIGH for 5 to 7 minutes, or until the dough is dry and opaque, rotating one-quarter turn once. Transfer the pastry with the wax paper to a cooling rack. Let cool for 10 minutes; then remove from the wax paper, if possible, to cool completely. Store in a cookie tin.

✸ GRAHAM CRACKER CRUMB CRUST

MAKES ONE 9-INCH PIE CRUST   BEGIN 10 TO 15 MINUTES BEFORE SERVING
COOKING TIME: 3½ TO 4 MINUTES

This crust is quick and easy in the microwave.

5 tablespoons butter or margarine	2 tablespoons sugar
1⅓ cups crushed graham crackers	

Place the butter or margarine in a 9-inch pie plate. Melt on HIGH for 1 to 2 minutes. Stir in the crumbs and sugar. With the back of a spoon, press the dough against the sides and bottom of the dish to form an even crust. Cook on HIGH for 1½ to 2 minutes, or until set. Let cool and fill.

VARIATIONS:

Nut Crumb Crust: Substitute ⅓ cup finely ground nuts for ⅓ cup of the graham cracker crumbs.

Zwieback Crust: We prefer this crust for cheesecakes and fresh fruit pies. Substitute finely ground zwieback crumbs for the graham cracker crumbs.

Zwieback and Nut Crust: Substitute 1 cup zwieback crumbs and ⅓ cup ground nuts for the graham cracker crumbs.

Cookie Crust: Eliminate the sugar. Substitute 1⅓ cups vanilla wafers, chocolate wafers, or gingersnaps for the graham crackers. If using gingersnaps, add 1 teaspoon ground ginger to the crumbs.

10-Inch Piecrust: Increase the butter to 6 tablespoons. Increase the crumbs to 1½ cups and sugar to ¼ cup. Proceed with the basic cooking times. For a 10-inch nut crust, substitute ½ cup ground nuts for ½ cup cracker crumbs.

APPLE CRUMB PIE

MAKES 8 SERVINGS   BEGIN 45 MINUTES TO 2 HOURS BEFORE SERVING
COOKING TIME: 14 TO 18 MINUTES

If you are watching calories, this pie can also be made without a crust. When eliminating the crust, add an extra apple to the filling but keep the cooking time the same.

---

1 recipe Rich Egg Pastry Dough (page 542)	½ cup quick rolled oats
Apples and Crumb Topping:	½ cup chopped nuts
4 tart green apples (preferably Granny Smith), peeled and thinly sliced	¼ cup all-purpose flour
	½ teaspoon ground cinnamon
1 tablespoon lemon juice	¼ cup butter or margarine, cut into 8 pieces
¾ cup brown sugar	Whipped cream, vanilla ice cream, or plain yogurt

---

Cut a 14-inch square of wax paper and trace a 9-inch circle, with four 2-inch tabs (see illustration on page 542).

On a floured surface, roll the chilled dough out into a 12-inch circle. Lay a paper circle over the bottom of an inverted 9-inch pie plate. Trim the dough so that it just meets the end of the dish; it is important to have the proper depth of shell later for the filling. Turn the dough back ½ inch, pressing firmly against the plate with a fork, moistening the dough with water to stick if necessary. The dough fold should be even all around. Lightly prick the dough, every inch, with a fork.

Place the inverted pie plate, dough side up, in the microwave. Cook on HIGH for 6 to 8 minutes, or until the pastry is dry and opaque, but not brown, rotating a half turn after three minutes. Let the pastry cool on the plate for 5 minutes. Invert the pie plate onto a 10-inch or more microwaveproof serving plate. Loosen the crust with a sharp knife and gently lift the pie plate. Peel the paper from the crust.

Arrange the apple slices in the crust. Sprinkle with lemon juice.

In a medium bowl combine the brown sugar, oats, nuts, flour, and cinnamon. Cut in the butter or margarine to make a crumbly mixture. Sprinkle evenly over the apples. Cook on HIGH for 8 to 10 minutes, or until the apples are tender and the juices have bubbled up through the topping, rotating one-quarter turn once or twice.

Serve topped with whipped cream, yogurt, or ice cream.

NOTE: To warm cooled pie, cook on HIGH for 1 to 2 minutes.

VARIATION:

Crustless Apple Crumb Pie: Eliminate the crust. Add 1 extra apple, sliced, to the filling. Follow the basic recipe.

Double-Crust Fruit Pie Basics:

1. It is important to seal the juices of the fruit into the pie, so that the pie crust remains flakier. With a double-crust pie this is done first by cooking the pie in the microwave. The filling, which is high in sugar and water, attracts the microwaves and will cook faster than the crust.
2. Fruit pies are cooked on HIGH to cook the fruit quickly before it seeps into the crust.
3. The fruit pies have a built-in cover in the pastry dough to trap steam to cook the fruit evenly. No additional cover is necessary.
4. It may be necessary to rotate the pie for more even cooking, depending on your oven.
5. *Doneness:* In a double-crust pie, the pie should be cooked in the microwave until the fruit begins to bubble up through the pastry crust. It is then transferred to the conventional oven until the crust is dry and golden brown.

☀ TESTIMONIAL DOUBLE-CRUST APPLE PIE

MAKES 8 TO 10 SERVINGS   BEGIN ABOUT 1½ HOURS BEFORE SERVING
COOKING TIME: 16 TO 24 MINUTES

We made three pairs of double-crust fruit pies, baking one of each pair in the conventional range and the other first in the microwave then in the conventional range to brown the top crust. Now you may ask, why would anyone bother using two ovens for one pie? Well, after six tasters, aged 11 to 83, sampled the pies, with no knowledge of which was which, they were asked to pick the ones they preferred. The microwave-conventional combination pie won hands down because of its flakier crust, fresher-tasting fruit, and brighter-colored fruit. We thought we'd let you in on this secret for the best-tasting fruit pie.

---

2 recipes Basic Pastry Dough (page 541)

Filling:
5 to 6 cups tart apples, peeled, cored, and cut into ¼-inch slices
½ to ¾ cup sugar
1 tablespoon lemon juice
1 tablespoon cornstarch
1 teaspoon ground cinnamon
2 tablespoons butter, cut into pieces

Preheat the conventional oven to 425°F.

On a lightly floured surface roll out one pie dough ball into a 12-inch circle. Place the dough into a 9-inch pie plate to form a bottom crust.

In a large mixing bowl toss together all the filling ingredients, except the butter. Spoon the filling into the bottom crust. Dot the apples with butter.

Roll out the top crust in the same way as the bottom crust. Place over the apples. Cut a few decorative slashes in the upper crust to vent the steam. Tuck the upper crust under the lower crust. Flute the edges or press with a fork. Cook the pie on HIGH for 8 to 12 minutes, or until the juices start to bubble through the slits in the crust, rotating after 4 minutes. Transfer to the preheated oven. Bake for 8 to 12 minutes, or until the crust is golden brown.

VARIATIONS:

Sugar-Glazed Double-Crust Apple Pie: Make egg glaze by combining 1 small egg and 1 tablespoon milk. Brush over the top crust. Combine 1 tablespoon sugar and ½ teaspoon ground cinnamon. Sprinkle the sugar-cinnamon over the glazed pie. This results in a browner crust with a wonderful flavor.

Double-Crust Rhubarb Pie: Substitute the following rhubarb filling for the apple filling: In a large mixing bowl combine 4 cups rhubarb stalks, unpeeled, cut into ½-inch pieces; 1¼ to 1½ cups sugar; 4 tablespoons all-purpose flour; and 1 teaspoon grated orange rind (optional). Place the rhubarb filling into the pie shell. Dot with butter. This is one of our favorites.

Double-Crust Pie with Fresh Berries or Cherries: Substitute the following berry or cherry filling for the apple filling: In a large mixing bowl combine 4 cups berries or pitted cherries and ½ to ⅔ cup sugar. In a small bowl combine 2 tablespoons cornstarch, ¼ cup water or fruit juice–fruit liqueur combination, and 1 tablespoon lemon juice. Stir into the fruit. Place the filling into the pie shell. Dot with *only* 1 tablespoon butter.

Double-Crust Pie with Canned Berries or Cherries: This is when you want to use your own berries that you have preserved, or canned berries from the store. Substitute the following berry filling for the apple filling: Measure out 1 cup fruit juice. In a 1-quart casserole combine 1 tablespoon cornstarch and ¼ cup fruit juice. Stir in the remaining ¾ cup fruit juice, and ½ to ⅔ cups sugar; stir to blend. Cook on HIGH for 3 to 4 minutes, or until boiling and thickened, stirring once. Stir in 2½ cups canned cherries or berries. Place in the pie shell. Dot with *only* 1 tablespoon butter.

Double-Crust Pie with Canned Fruit Pie Filling: Substitute 1 21-ounce can fruit pie filling mixed with 1 tablespoon lemon juice for the apple filling. Spoon into the pie shell. Dot with *only* 1 tablespoon butter.

GRANDMA'S FLUTED WALNUT TARTLETS

MAKES 6 SERVINGS   BEGIN 1¾ HOURS BEFORE SERVING
COOKING TIME: 8 TO 9 MINUTES

These rich walnut tartlets topped with an amaretto pastry crust and dollop of amaretto cream are a very special dessert. The pale, flaky crusts are a perfect foil for the dark, dense walnut filling.

- 1 recipe Amaretto Pastry Dough (page 541)
- ½ cup butter, softened
- ½ cup sugar
- 2 large eggs
- 1⅓ cups coarsely chopped walnuts, plus ¾ cup large walnut pieces, plus 6 walnut halves
- 3 tablespoons amaretto
- ¾ cup whipped cream
- ¼ teaspoon freshly grated nutmeg

Form the dough into a 5-inch square before chilling.

While the dough is chilling, in a food processor or mixing bowl cream the butter and sugar. Add the eggs, chopped walnuts, and amaretto, mixing well. Set aside. The filling should be soft and at room temperature before cooking.

Flatten the chilled dough into a 16- × -11-inch rectangle and cut into six 5-inch circles. Place the circles on the inverted bottoms of 6 custard cups (about 1½-inch diameter) or a microwave muffin pan, pressing the dough about 1½ inches up on the sides. Flute each dough cup with your fingers to make the dough look like a flower. Lightly prick the dough, every inch, with a fork.

Place the inverted cups, dough side up, in the microwave, arranging in a circular pattern with a 1-inch space between them. Cook on HIGH for 5 to 6 minutes, or until dry and opaque, rotating the pan or repositioning the cups after 3 minutes. Let the pastry cool on the cups for 5 minutes. Remove the shells.

Spoon the filling into the pastry shells. Top with a layer of walnut pieces.

Place the tartlets on wax paper or a microwaveproof serving dish in a circular pattern, arranging them with 1-inch space between them. Cook on HIGH for 2½ to 3½ minutes, or until the filling is firm, rotating the tartlets and repositioning them once during cooking.

Cool and garnish with the whipped cream, nutmeg, and walnut halves.

VARIATION:

Fluted Pecan Tartlets: Substitute pecans for the walnuts. Substitute bourbon or brandy for the amaretto.

Flat Pastry Tart Basics:

1. See Pastry Dough Basics, page 540.
2. Unlike a pie shell, a flat tart is rolled out on wax paper and then cooked directly on that in the oven. A double layer of wax paper is sturdier for moving the tart from work surface to oven.
3. On the large tart, nuts can provide a rim to hold the pastry cream as well as an attractive brown color. Fluting provides an edging for the apple tart.
4. A tart crust should be pricked before cooking, because it should cook as flat as possible.
5. Pastry is never covered during cooking, so that it will remain dry and not soggy.
6. HIGH power will quickly melt the fat and water to produce the steam necessary to part the layers of dough into a flaky pastry.
7. In most cases, the flat pastry tarts will need to be rotated (and small tarts rearranged) during cooking.
8. Tarts should be cooled on the paper on a rack to allow for the most air circulation. This will keep pastry dry and crisp. If the large tart cannot be easily removed from the wax paper, leave it and trim the paper to size. You will find small tarts and triangles easier to remove from paper, and these can then cool directly on the rack.

✺ LARGE SUMMER FRUIT TART

MAKES 8 SERVINGS   BEGIN 1½ HOURS BEFORE SERVING
COOKING TIME: 5 TO 8 MINUTES

Through many experimentations we found that the best way to make a flat tart shell was not in a dish, but directly on wax paper. Wax paper retains less moisture and produces a much drier crust. The almonds that grace the outer rim of the tart add decoration and an attractive brown color.

1 recipe Sweet Lemon Pastry Dough (page 542)	1¼ cups blueberries, or 1 pint strawberries, halved, or 4 to 6 peaches, peeled and sliced
2 ounces whole shelled almonds	
1 recipe Basic Pastry Cream (page 555)	¼ cup currant jelly

While the pastry dough is chilling, cut two 12-inch squares of wax paper, placing one on top of the other. Lightly flour the top.

Roll the chilled dough onto the wax paper to form a circle slightly larger than 10 inches in diameter. About ½ inch from the outside rim, place the almonds, slightly overlapping, to form an outer ring. Push the outside dough up about halfway on the almonds to form a rim. Lightly prick the top surface of the pastry with a fork every inch or so.

Place the dough and wax paper in the microwave. Cook on HIGH for 4 to 6 minutes, or until dry and opaque but not brown, rotating one-quarter turn every 2 minutes. With 2 spatulas, gently slide the pastry and paper onto a cooling rack. Let cool for 10 to 15 minutes, then transfer to a flat serving platter. (If the pastry should crack when you transfer it, don't worry. It can be patched together with the pastry cream.) Spread a thin layer of pastry cream inside the nut rim. Arrange the fruit on top, as desired.

Place the currant jelly in a 1-cup glass measure. Cook on HIGH for 45 seconds to 1½ minutes, until melted. With a pastry brush, glaze the fruit.

BASIC APPLE PIZZA TART

MAKES 8 SERVINGS   BEGIN 45 TO 50 MINUTES BEFORE SERVING
COOKING TIME: 15 TO 19 MINUTES

A flat, buttery pastry crust topped with apple slices is a sheer delight to make and eat. Try it topped with the Cheddar Wine Dip.

- 1 recipe Basic Pastry Dough (page 541)
- 3 tart cooking apples (Granny Smith or Rome Beauty)
- 2 teaspoons lemon juice
- ¼ cup sugar
- ½ teaspoon ground cinnamon
- Cheddar Wine Dip (page 499), Butterscotch Sauce (page 565), vanilla ice cream, whipped cream, or plain yogurt

While the pastry dough is chilling, cut two 12-inch squares of wax paper, placing one on top of the other. Lightly flour the top.

Roll the chilled dough on the wax paper to form a 12-inch circle. Turn the outer edges of dough under 1 inch and pinch the edge tightly to flute. Lightly prick the surface of the dough with a fork every inch or so.

Place the dough and wax paper in microwave. Cook on HIGH for 5 to 7 minutes, or until dry and opaque, rotating one-quarter turn every 2 minutes. Gently slide the paper and pastry onto a cooking rack. Let cool for 5 to 10 minutes. Meanwhile, peel, core, and cut the apples into ¼-inch slices.

Place the pastry on a microwave round platter. If the pastry looks like it might break, leave the wax paper attached and trim to size; the juices from the apples will mend the cracks. Arrange the apples on the pastry in slightly overlapping concentric circles. Sprinkle with lemon juice. In a small bowl combine the sugar and cinnamon. Sprinkle over the apples.

Cook the tart on HIGH for 10 to 12 minutes, or until the apples are tender, rotating one-quarter turn once, if necessary. Let stand for 5 minutes. Serve warm with the cheddar wine dip or butterscotch sauce, or vanilla ice cream, whipped cream, or yogurt.

FRESH BERRY TARTS

MAKES TWELVE 3½-INCH TARTS   BEGIN 1¾ HOURS BEFORE SERVING
COOKING TIME: 3 TO 7 MINUTES

These small fruit tarts are beautiful additions to a dessert table, or an afternoon tea.

- 1 recipe Nut-Egg Pastry Dough (page 542)
- ¾ cup heavy cream, whipped
- 3 cups blueberries, or strawberry halves

Before chilling, form the pastry into a 5-inch square, to make rolling easier.

On a lightly floured surface, roll out the chilled dough into an 11½-inch square. With a cookie cutter or custard-cup rim, mark and cut nine 3½-inch rounds of dough. Reserve the remaining dough. Lightly prick with a fork every inch or so.

Place 2 pieces wax paper, about 14 × 12 inches, in the microwave. Place all the 9 pastry rounds on the paper, arranging in a circle with 1 inch between them. Cook on HIGH for 2 to 5 minutes, or until they appear dry and opaque but not brown, repositioning once if necessary. Transfer the pastries and wax paper to a cooling rack. Let cool for 10 minutes, then remove from the wax paper, as soon as possible, to cool directly on the rack to make the bottoms crisp.

Meanwhile, roll out the remaining dough and cut 3 more rounds. Place on wax paper in the oven. Cook on HIGH for 1 to 2 minutes.

Place a few spoons of whipped heavy cream on each cooled pastry round. Top each pastry with 2 tablespoons berries.

VARIATIONS:

Berry Tarts In Lemon Sauce: While the tarts are cooling, prepare lemon Citrus Sauce (page 498). Assemble the tarts as directed. Spoon some lemon sauce on each dessert plate, and spread to cover the surface. Place a tart in the center of the sauce.

Berry Tarts Nouveau: While the tarts are cooling, prepare lemon Citrus Sauce (page 498) and blueberry Basic Berry Dessert Sauce (page 497). Assemble the tarts as directed. Visually, divide each dessert plate in half and spoon lemon sauce on one half and blueberry sauce on the other. Place a tart in the center.

PEARS ON PEAR-SHAPED TART SHELLS

MAKES 6 TARTS   BEGIN 1 HOUR 40 MINUTES BEFORE SERVING
COOKING TIME: 15 TO 18 MINUTES

Free-form flaky pear-shaped pastries are crowned with pastry cream and a poached pear half. The final decoration is a thin ribbon of hot fudge sauce that is drizzled over the glistening pear. Don't be put off by the many steps in this recipe, for they are really very simple, and the tarts are sure to impress. Try them out on Valentine's Day!

1 recipe Basic Pastry Dough (page 541)	2 teaspoons vanilla
3 firm, ripe pears	¾ cup milk
1 lemon, quartered	2 large egg yolks, beaten
¾ cup sugar	2 tablespoons all-purpose flour
¼ cup water	1 recipe Hot Fudge Sauce (page 564)

While the pastry dough is chilling, remove the stems from the pears and core so that they retain their shape by cutting a cone out of the base with a grapefruit knife or other small knife (see illustration, page 489). Peel the pears and rub with the cut lemon to prevent discoloration. Set the pears aside for the moment.

In a 1½-quart microwave casserole combine ½ cup sugar, the water, 1 teaspoon vanilla, and lemon quarters. Cook on HIGH for 2 minutes, or until the sugar is dissolved, stirring once. Place the pears on their sides, positioning the thicker ends toward the outside. Cover tightly and cook on HIGH for 4 minutes. Baste the pears and turn them over. Cover again and cook on HIGH for 5 to 6 minutes more, or until tender. Let the pears cool in their liquid, turning them over occasionally.

Meanwhile, cut two 12-inch squares of wax paper, placing one on top of the other. Lightly flour the top.

Roll the chilled dough onto the wax paper to form a 12-inch circle.

Cut the poached pears in half lengthwise. Using a pear half as a pattern, outline and cut out 6 pear shapes, about ½ inch larger than the pear. Lightly prick the dough with a fork. Fashion leaves with the excess pastry dough. Place them beside the pear cutouts on wax paper and discard the extra dough.

Place the dough and wax paper in the microwave. Cook on HIGH for 4 to 6 minutes, or until dry and opaque, repositioning once if necessary. Gently slide the paper and pastry onto a cooling rack. Let cool for 5 to 10 minutes, removing the pastry from the paper to the rack as soon as possible.

Meanwhile, pour the milk into a 1-cup glass measure. Cook on HIGH for 1 to 2 minutes to steam but not boil. In a 1-quart bowl combine ¼ cup sugar, the egg yolks and flour. Gradually add the warm milk to the egg mixture, beating constantly. Cook on HIGH for 30 seconds; beat. Cook on HIGH for 30 seconds to 1 minute more, or until the cream thickens and almost begins to boil. Stir in 1 teaspoon vanilla. Cool. Rub the top with a little butter or stir occasionally to prevent a skin from forming. The mixture may be put in the freezer at this point for 30 minutes, to speed cooling.

To assemble: Place a pear cutout on each of 6 dessert plates. Place a rounded spoonful of pastry cream in the center of each pastry cutout. Place a drained pear half, cut side down, on top of the pastry cream. Spoon a 1-inch ribbon of hot fudge sauce diagonally over the pear half and pastry cutout. Pass the extra sauce at the table.

VARIATIONS:

Pear Tartlets with Raspberry Sauce: Substitute Raspberry Sauce (page 565) for the hot fudge sauce. Garnish with fresh mint leaves.

Peach Tartlets with Raspberry Sauce: Substitute Poached Peaches (page 490) for the pears. Substitute Raspberry Sauce (page 565) for the hot fudge sauce. Cut the pastry in peach shape, ½ inch larger than peach halves. Depending on the size of peaches, you may be able to make 8 peach tarts.

PUMPKIN PIE IN GINGER CRUST

MAKES 8 SERVINGS   BEGIN 50 MINUTES BEFORE SERVING
COOKING TIME: 17 TO 24 MINUTES

Cook your own pumpkin for this pie.

- 1½ cups pumpkin puree (see Pureed Winter Squash, page 466)
- 3 large eggs
- ½ cup sugar
- ⅓ cup heavy cream
- ½ teaspoon ground ginger
- ¼ teaspoon grated nutmeg
- ¼ teaspoon ground cinnamon
- 1 recipe Cookie Crust (page 545), made with gingersnaps
- Whipped cream
- Candled ginger

In a 4-cup glass measure or bowl combine the pumpkin puree, eggs, sugar, cream, and spices. Stir with a whisk to blend well. Cook on HIGH for 4 minutes, or until heated, stirring halfway through cooking. (This begins the cooking process of such a thick filling.) Pour the filling into the cooled crust. Cook on MEDIUM for 13 to 20 minutes, or until done, rotating one-half turn once.

Chill and garnish with whipped cream and candied ginger.

VARIATIONS:

Pumpkin Pie In Graham Cracker Crust: Substitute Graham Cracker Crumb Crust (page 544) for gingersnap crust.

Pumpkin Pie In Vanilla Crust: Substitute Cookie Crust (page 545) made with vanilla wafers.

☀ APPLE CRUMBLE

MAKES 6 SERVINGS   BEGIN 25 TO 30 MINUTES BEFORE SERVING
COOKING TIME: 12 TO 14 MINUTES

This is a crustless crumb pie that is easy to assemble and best when eaten warm with ice cream, crème fraîche, plain yogurt, or whipped cream. It can be popped into the oven to cook when you sit down to eat your main course. The crumble topping helps to seal in the fruit moisture—an additional cover would make the topping soggy.

- 6 cups cooking apples, peeled, cored, and thinly sliced
- 1 tablespoon lemon juice
- 6 tablespoons butter
- ¾ cup all-purpose flour
- ⅓ cup brown sugar
- ⅓ cup granulated sugar
- ⅔ cup rolled oats

1 teaspoon ground cinnamon	½ cup coarsely chopped walnuts
¼ teaspoon grated nutmeg	

Place the apples in an 8½-inch round or 8-inch square cake dish (the shape of the dish is not as important as it would be for a cake). Stir in the lemon juice and lightly toss. In a medium mixing bowl cut the butter into the flour until it resembles coarse cornmeal. Stir in the remaining ingredients. Sprinkle evenly over the apples. Cook on HIGH for 12 to 14 minutes, or until the fruit is tender, rotating once.

VARIATION:

Peach Crumble: Substitute peaches, thinly sliced, for the apples. Cook on HIGH for 8 to 10 minutes, or until the fruit is tender, rotating once.

Pastry Cream Basics:

1. Warming the milk before adding it to the eggs will warm the eggs gently first before the cooking begins.
2. Even though this sauce contains egg yolks, it can be cooked on HIGH power because the egg is warmed slightly first and because the sauce is stirred frequently.
3. Stirring where indicated is extremely important to producing a lump-free sauce. We prefer a wire whisk for this. Lumping will occur if an egg in one part of the sauce cooks too quickly and coagulates. Stirring redistributes the heat evenly.
4. Cooking uncovered lets the steam evaporate more quickly to thicken the sauce.
5. There is no standing time to speak of, and the pastry cream can be served warm or chilled. Coating the top with butter or placing a piece of plastic wrap directly on the surface will keep the air from forming a skin on the cream as it cools.
6. *Doneness:* The cream will be thick enough to form soft peaks and will become very smooth when stirred. The cream will become very thick if chilled.

If small tiny lumps appear in the cream after it is removed from the oven, beat vigorously and these will disappear into a smooth cream. This cream will be slightly thinner, but will become thick after chilling.

✸ BASIC PASTRY CREAM

MAKES 2 CUPS   BEGIN 15 TO 20 MINUTES BEFORE SERVING
COOKING TIME: 6 TO 7 MINUTES

A luxurious dessert cream becomes a simple feat in the microwave. Because there is no direct heat underneath the cream, as with the conventional stove, there will never be scorching of the cream. Prepare it for Trifle with Strawberries (page 557) or as a filling for cream puffs, or serve it with fruit or fruit sauce.

- 1½ cups milk
- ½ cup sugar
- 4 large egg yolks, beaten
- ¼ cup all-purpose flour
- 1 tablespoon vanilla, sherry, or rum

Pour the milk into a 4-cup glass measure. Cook on HIGH for 3 minutes, or until hot but not boiling.

Meanwhile, in a 2-quart microwave casserole beat the sugar into the egg yolks until well blended. Stir in the flour. Gradually add the heated milk to the egg mixture, beating constantly. Cook on HIGH for 1 minute; beat with a whisk. Cook on HIGH for 2 to 3 minutes more, or until thickened, beating every 30 seconds. Stir in the vanilla, sherry, or rum. Chill until needed. Place a piece of plastic wrap directly on the cream, or dot the top with butter, to prevent a skin from forming.

PASTRY CREAM FOR TARTS

MAKES ¾ CUP   BEGIN 15 MINUTES BEFORE SERVING
COOKING TIME: 2 TO 3 MINUTES

This is the perfect amount of pastry cream for any of the large or individual flat tarts. It is just like the Basic Pastry Cream (page 555), only the recipe makes a smaller amount. For more information, see Pastry Cream Basics (page 555).

- ½ cup milk
- 1 large egg yolk
- 1 tablespoon sugar
- 1 tablespoon all-purpose flour
- ½ teaspoon grated lemon rind or vanilla

Pour the milk into a 1-cup glass measure. Cook on HIGH for 1 minute, or until hot but not boiling.

Meanwhile, in a small microwaveproof bowl blend the egg yolk, sugar, flour, and lemon rind or vanilla. Gradually add the heated milk to the egg mixture, beating constantly. Cook on HIGH for 30 seconds; beat with a wire whisk. Cook on HIGH for 30 seconds to 1 minute more, or until thickened, beating every 30 seconds to keep the mixture smooth. Stir in the lemon rind. Chill until needed. Place a piece of plastic wrap directly on the cream, or dot the top with butter, to prevent a skin from forming.

○ ○ ○

TRIFLE WITH STRAWBERRIES

MAKES 8 SERVINGS   BEGIN 30 MINUTES BEFORE SERVING, 45 MINUTES IF YOU MAKE THE CAKE
COOKING TIME: 1 TO 2 MINUTES

- 2 cups hulled strawberries
- 4 tablespoons sugar
- 1 recipe Basic Yellow Cake (page 507), or 1 layer yellow cake
- 2 tablespoons sherry
- ½ cup raspberry or strawberry preserves
- 2 cups Basic Pastry Cream (page 555), made with sherry
- 1 cup heavy cream
- ¼ cup slivered almonds (optional)

Into a small bowl, slice 1 cup strawberries. Sprinkle with 2 tablespoons sugar and refrigerate.

Cut the cake in half horizontally. Sprinkle each cut side with sherry.

Place the preserves in a 2-cup glass measure. Heat 45 seconds to 1½ minutes to melt; stir. Spread the top of each layer with the preserves. Cut the cake layers into 2-inch squares. Line the sides and bottom of a 1-quart serving bowl with a layer of cake squares, preserve side facing up, filling in all the spaces with other uneven pieces. Spread the sliced and sweetened strawberries on the bottom of the cake-lined dish. Spoon in the pastry cream. Top with the remaining cake pieces, preserve side up.

In a small mixing bowl combine the cream and remaining 2 tablespoons sugar; whip. Spread or pipe on top of the cake. Top with the remaining cup of whole strawberries and the slivered almonds, if desired.

NOTE: If not serving immediately, chill without adding whipped cream. Spoon the whipped cream on top right before serving.

VARIATION:

Trifle with Fruit in Season: Substitute orange segments, sliced peaches, or fresh fruit salad for the strawberries.

Pudding Basics:

1. Pudding is based on a ratio of 3 tablespoons cornstarch to 2 cups milk. Instant tapioca can be substituted for cornstarch in the same proportions.
2. Cornstarch swells to its greatest thickening capacity at the boiling temperature. A pudding is cooked quickly on HIGH power to reach that point. (A 4-cup glass measure or a 2-quart casserole should be large enough to prevent boilovers.)
3. Stirring is critical where indicated to keep the sauce from becoming lumpy.
4. Cook uncovered for the most evaporation of moisture, which will help thickening. It is also easier to stir without a cover to remove.
5. Standing time is only necessary to cool the pudding. If cooling in a casserole, place plastic wrap down onto the surface of the pudding to keep a skin from forming.
6. *Doneness:* Once this mixture comes to a rolling boil, it is done. The pudding will be thick, smooth, and pourable, and will thicken even more upon cooling.

✸ BASIC VANILLA PUDDING

MAKES 2 CUPS OR 4 SERVINGS   BEGIN 15 MINUTES BEFORE SERVING
COOKING TIME: 5 TO 11 MINUTES

Considering that a conventional pudding takes 20 minutes of cooking time and requires continuous stirring, a pudding cooked in the microwave is a busy mother's dream come true. Old-fashioned scratch puddings have become practical again. Serve plain, with fresh fruit, or with Raspberry Sauce (page 565).

3 tablespoons cornstarch	2 cups milk
⅓ cup granulated sugar	1 tablespoon vanilla extract

In a 4-cup glass measure combine the cornstarch and sugar. Stir in the milk and vanilla. Cook on HIGH for 3 minutes; stir. Cook on HIGH for 2 to 8 minutes more, or until boiling and thickened, stirring each minute to keep smooth. Pour the pudding into individual serving dishes or a bowl.

VARIATIONS:

Chocolate Pudding: Add ⅓ cup unsweetened cocoa powder to the sugar and cornstarch. Reduce the vanilla to 1 teaspoon. Serve with Chocolate Triangles (page 594), if desired.

Café au Lait Pudding: Add 1 tablespoon instant espresso crystals with the cornstarch. Pour the hot pudding into espresso cups and chill. Serve with a twist of lemon and grated bitter chocolate. Pour a teaspoon of Sambuca onto each cup before serving, if desired. Makes enough for 8 espresso cups.

Butterscotch Pudding: Eliminate the granulated sugar. Place 2 tablespoons butter and ½ cup brown sugar in a 2-cup glass measure. Cook on HIGH for 1 to 3 minutes, or until the butter and sugar are melted and blended together, stirring every 30 seconds. Stir in the cornstarch and *only* 1 teaspoon vanilla. Stir the milk in slowly to make the mixture as smooth as possible. There will be some lumps, but these will smooth out when cooked.

Butterscotch-Nut Pudding: Follow the Butterscotch Pudding variation above. When the pudding is cooled, stir in 1 cup coarsely chopped pecans.

Tapioca Pudding: Substitute instant tapioca for the cornstarch. Add 1 egg yolk. Reduce the vanilla to 1 teaspoon. Serve with fresh fruit. For a lighter tapioca, after the tapioca is cooked, stir in 1 egg white, beaten.

CHOCOLATE PUDDING PIE

MAKES 6 TO 8 SERVINGS   BEGIN 30 TO 40 MINUTES BEFORE SERVING

Pour a basic pudding mix into a crumb pie crust and voilà—a pudding pie!

PIES, PUDDINGS, AND OTHER DESSERTS

1 recipe Chocolate Pudding (page 558) 1 recipe Cookie Crust (page 545) made with chocolate wafers 2 cups heavy cream	¾ cup confectioners' sugar Chocolate shavings or Chocolate Triangles (page 594)

Pour the pudding into the cooled crust. Lay plastic wrap directly on top of the pudding to prevent a skin from forming and chill the pie. Before serving, in a small mixing bowl combine the cream and sugar. Whip to form stiff peaks. Remove the plastic wrap and spoon the whipped cream on top of the pie. Garnish with chocolate shavings or triangles.

VARIATIONS:

Mocha Cream Pie: Substitute Café au Lait Pudding (page 558) for the chocolate pudding.

Butterscotch Cream Pie: Substitute Nut Crumb Crust (page 545) for the cookie crust. Substitute Butterscotch Pudding (page 558) for the chocolate pudding. Chill the pie and top with whipped cream. Garnish with pecan halves.

Strawberry Cream Pie: Substitute zwieback Crumb Crust (page 545) for the cookie crust. Substitute Basic Vanilla Pudding (page 558) for the chocolate pudding. Eliminate the chocolate shavings. When the pudding is chilled, top with 1 pint hulled strawberries. Place ¼ cup currant jelly into 1-cup glass measure. Cook on HIGH for 35 seconds to 1½ minutes. With a pastry brush, coat the strawberries with melted jelly and let set. Serve with whipped cream, if desired.

Raspberry Cream Pie: Prepare the Strawberry Cream Pie variation above, but substitute raspberries for the strawberries.

BANANA CREAM PIE

MAKES 6 TO 8 SERVINGS   BEGIN 40 MINUTES BEFORE SERVING
COOKING TIME: 5 TO 7 MINUTES

This is a simple pudding that has been enriched with an egg for flavor. The Baileys Irish Cream Pie variation is a nice one to serve guests.

⅓ cup granulated sugar 3 tablespoons cornstarch 2 large egg yolks, beaten 2 cups milk 1 teaspoon vanilla 1 recipe Graham Cracker Crumb Crust (page 544)	3 to 4 ripe bananas, cut into ¼-inch slices 2 cups heavy cream ¾ cup confectioners' sugar

In a 4-cup glass measure combine the sugar, cornstarch, and egg yolks. Stir in milk. Cook on HIGH for 2 minutes; stir. Cook on HIGH for 3 to 5 minutes more, just until it comes to a boil, stirring each minute. Stir in the vanilla. Lay plastic wrap directly on top of the pudding to prevent a skin from forming; let cool. Chill slightly. Spread half of the cream over the bottom of the baked crumb crust. Cover with a layer of sliced bananas. Spoon the remaining pudding on top. Cover with plastic wrap and chill until serving time. Just before serving, whip the cream with the confectioners' sugar and spread on the pie. Garnish with banana slices.

VARIATIONS:

Baileys Irish Cream Pie: Substitute Zweiback Crumb Crusts (page 545) for the graham cracker crumb crust. Eliminate the bananas. Substitute 1/3 cup Baileys Irish cream for 1/3 cup milk. Follow the basic pudding recipe and cool. Pour into the baked shell. Chill until serving time. Before serving time, top with sweetened whipped cream. This pie is for a special occasion, but as Mae West said, "Every day is a holiday."

Kahlúa Cream Pie: Substitute Cookie Crust (page 545) made with chocolate wafers for the graham cracker crumb crust. Eliminate the bananas. Substitute 1/3 cup Kahlúa for 1/3 cup milk. Follow the basic pudding recipe; cool. Spoon all of the pudding into the pie shell. Cover and chill until serving time. Top with sweetened whipped cream.

Coconut Cream Pie: Eliminate the bananas. Fold 1/2 cup shredded coconut into the cooled filling. Pour the pudding into the crust and chill. Top with whipped cream. Garnish with 1/4 cup grated coconut.

COCONUT JOY PIE

MAKES 8 SERVINGS   BEGIN 3¾ HOURS BEFORE SERVING
COOKING TIME: 8 TO 10 MINUTES

Our favorite childhood candy bar was the inspiration for this pie—a chocolate crust filled with creamy coconut–egg custard. We found that this dessert doesn't take any longer to prepare than it used to take us to walk to the candy store. But with a child's impatience, we find the hardest part is waiting for it to chill.

Custard:
- 2 cups milk
- 4 large egg yolks
- 2 tablespoons cornstarch
- 2/3 cup sugar
- 1½ cups grated coconut
- 2 teaspoons coconut flavoring

Crust:
- 5 tablespoons butter
- 5 ounces semisweet chocolate bits
- 1 cup chocolate wafer crumbs
- 2 tablespoons heavy cream

To make the custard: Pour the milk into a 4-cup glass measure. Cook on HIGH for 3 minutes, or until the milk is steaming but not boiling.

Meanwhile, in a medium glass bowl combine the egg yolks, cornstarch, and sugar; blend with a wire whisk. Gradually add the warm milk to the egg mixture, beating constantly. Stir in the grated coconut. Cook on HIGH for 1 minute; stir. Cook on HIGH for 2½ to 5 minutes more, or until thickened, stirring once. Remove the egg-milk mixture from the oven and stir in the coconut flavoring. Cool the mixture in the refrigerator or place in the freezer for 30 minutes to cool quickly.

To make the crust: In a 9-inch pie plate combine 4 tablespoons butter and 3 ounces of the chocolate bits. Cook on HIGH for 1 to 2 minutes, or until the chocolate is melted, stirring into a smooth paste. Stir in the wafer crumbs and cream. With the back of a spoon, press the mixture against the sides to form a crust. Freeze or refrigerate until solid.

Spoon the chilled custard into the chilled chocolate crust. Chill the pie to completely set, about 3 hours.

To garnish, combine the remaining 1 tablespoon butter and 2 ounces chocolate in a glass custard cup. Cook on HIGH for 1 minute, or until melted. Drizzle the chocolate with a spoon over the top of the pie for decoration.

VARIATION:

Coconut Cream Pie: Substitute Basic Pie Shell (page 542) for the chocolate crust. Garnish with ½ cup toasted coconut.

LEMON MERINGUE PIE

MAKES 6 TO 8 SERVINGS   BEGIN 40 MINUTES BEFORE SERVING
COOKING TIME: 11 TO 16 MINUTES

1⅓ cups sugar	1 tablespoon lemon rind
⅓ cup cornstarch	1 tablespoon butter
2 cups water	1 recipe Graham Cracker Crumb Crust (page 544)
3 large eggs, separated	
⅓ cup lemon juice	½ teaspoon cream of tartar

In a 1½-quart casserole combine 1 cup sugar and the cornstarch. Stir the water in gradually to keep the mixture smooth. Cook on HIGH for 6 to 8 minutes, or until thickened and clear, stirring every 2 minutes. Beat the egg yolks and stir a little thickened cornstarch mixture into them. Stir the heated yolks back into the remaining hot mixture. Stir in the lemon juice, lemon rind, and butter. Cool slightly. Spoon into the prepared piecrust.

Meanwhile, beat the egg whites and cream of tartar until soft peaks form. Beat the remaining ⅓ cup sugar into the whites to make a glossy foam. Spread over the pie. Cook on MEDIUM for 3 to 4 minutes, or until the meringue is set, rotating one-half turn halfway through cooking time. Meringue will set but not brown; to brown meringue, place the cooked meringue pie under a preheated broiler in a conventional oven for 2 to 4 minutes.

VARIATION:

Lemon Pie with Whipped Cream: Eliminate meringue made with egg whites. Top instead with 2 cups sweetened whipped cream and garnish with grated lemon rind or thin lemon slices.

IRRESISTIBLE MINCEMEAT ICE CREAM PIE

MAKES 8 TO 10 SERVINGS   BEGIN 2½ HOURS BEFORE SERVING
COOKING TIME: 6 TO 8 MINUTES

Mincemeat pie is a tradition at Thanksgiving, and this unusual frozen version takes just 10 minutes to prepare before it goes into the freezer. The cranberry variation is delicious, too.

Crust:
- 6 tablespoons butter or margarine
- 1½ cups graham cracker crumbs
- ¼ cup sugar
- ½ teaspoon ground cinnamon

Filling:
- ½ gallon vanilla ice cream
- 2 cups prepared mincemeat
- 1 tablespoon rum (optional)

To make the crust: Place the butter or margarine in a 10-inch pie plate. Cook on HIGH for 1½ minutes, or until melted. Stir in the crumbs, sugar, and cinnamon. Press the crumbs evenly and firmly against the bottom and sides of the plate. Cook on HIGH for 2 to 2½ minutes, or until set, rotating one-half turn after 1 minute. Cool.

To make the filling: Place the ice cream container in the microwave. Heat on LOW for 2 to 3 minutes, or on DEFROST for 1 minute, to soften.

Meanwhile, in a medium bowl combine the mincemeat and rum, if desired.

Spoon half of the ice cream into the cooled pie shell and smooth down evenly. Spread 1½ cups mincemeat evenly onto the ice cream. Top with the remaining ice cream and smooth down with a spoon. Spoon the remaining ½ cup mincemeat around the outer circle of the pie for decoration. Freeze for at least 2 hours, or overnight.

VARIATION:

Cranberry Ice Cream Pie: Substitute 1½ cups whole-berry Cranberry Sauce (page 187) for the mincemeat.

☀ AMARETTO ICE CREAM PIE

MAKES 10 SERVINGS   BEGIN 2¼ TO 2½ HOURS BEFORE SERVING
COOKING TIME: 2 TO 4 MINUTES

This pie and the variations that follow are so easy for entertaining a group. A simple crumb crust is filled with softened ice cream that has been swirled through with any number of delectable ingredients, before being frozen again. The warm dessert sauce spooned on at the end makes the pie really special.

Crust:
- 6 tablespoons butter
- 1¼ cups chocolate cookie crumbs
- ¼ cup finely chopped almonds

Filling:
- ½ gallon vanilla ice cream
- ½ cup coarsely chopped almonds
- 2 ounces almond-flavored liqueur
- 1 recipe Amaretto Sauce (recipe below)

To make the crust: Place the butter in a 10-inch pie plate. Cook on HIGH for 1 to 2 minutes, or until melted. Stir in the crumbs and nuts until all are well coated. With a spoon, press evenly against the sides and bottom of the plate to form a crust. Cook on HIGH for 1 to 2 minutes, or until just set; overcooking will make the crust too hard. Let stand until the crust becomes room temperature.

To make the filling: Transfer the ice cream from the carton to a large glass mixing bowl or casserole. Soften the ice cream on DEFROST for 1 to 2 minutes, or until it is still somewhat frozen but can easily be broken up with a spoon. Quickly stir in the nuts and liqueur, just to give it a marbled effect. Spoon into the cooled pie shell and smooth the top. Freeze until serving time, at least 1 hour. Serve with amaretto sauce.

VARIATIONS:

Crème de Menthe Ice Cream Pie: Eliminate the nuts from the crust and add ¼ cup more crumbs. Eliminate the nuts from the filling and swirl in ¼ cup green crème de menthe. Serve with Hot Fudge Sauce (page 564), whipped cream, and nuts, if desired.

Pecan-Bourbon Ice Cream Pie: Substitute chopped pecans for the almonds in the crust. Substitute bourbon for the almond liqueur in the filling, and coarsely chopped pecans for the almonds. Serve with Bourbon Praline Sauce (page 564).

Kahlúa Ice Cream Pie: Substitute coffee-flavored liqueur for the almond flavor in the filling. Serve with Hot Mocha Sauce (page 564).

❈ AMARETTO SAUCE

MAKES ABOUT 1½ CUPS
COOKING TIME: 4 TO 6 MINUTES

This simple sauce has been very well received at catered parties, no less. Serve over pie or ice cream.

- ⅔ cup light brown sugar
- ¼ cup butter
- ¼ cup half and half
- 2 tablespoons light corn syrup
- 2 tablespoons almond-flavored liqueur
- 1 cup coarsely chopped almonds

(Continued)

In a 4-cup glass measure combine the sugar, butter, half and half, and corn syrup. Cook on HIGH for 2 minutes; stir. Cook on HIGH for 1 to 3 minutes more, or until boiling. Stir in the liqueur and nuts. Cook on HIGH for 1 minute.

VARIATIONS:
Walnut-Brandy Sauce: Substitute walnuts for the almonds and brandy for the almond-flavored liqueur.

Bourbon-Praline Sauce: Substitute bourbon for the almond liqueur. Substitute pecans for the almonds. Sprinkle with freshly grated nutmeg.

HOT FUDGE SAUCE

MAKES 1½ CUPS
COOKING TIME: 3 TO 5 MINUTES

6 ounces semisweet chocolate pieces
½ cup half and half
¼ cup light corn syrup
1 teaspoon vanilla

In a 4-cup glass measure combine the chocolate, half and half, and corn syrup. Cook on HIGH for 2 minutes; stir. Cook on HIGH for 1 to 3 minutes more, or until smooth, stirring each minute. (Chocolate can be cooked on HIGH when combined with other ingredients that absorb some of the heat.) Stir in the vanilla.

VARIATION:
Hot Mocha Sauce: At the end of cooking, stir in ¼ cup coffee-flavored liqueur.

FROZEN PISTACHIO CHOCOLATE CUPS

MAKES 4 SERVINGS   BEGIN 1½ HOURS BEFORE SERVING
COOKING TIME: 3 TO 5 MINUTES

Frothy green pistachio ice cream is mounded into chocolate cups as dessert for an elegant, no-fuss dinner party. No more double boilers or nasty pots to clean, because the chocolate is melted in a cereal bowl!

6 ounces semisweet chocolate bits
½ pint pistachio ice cream
2 teaspoons brandy (optional)
½ cup chopped pistachio nuts
4 candied violets (optional)

Arrange the chocolate bits in a cereal bowl, leaving the center free. Cook on MEDIUM for 3 to 5 minutes, or until just soft enough to spread, stirring after 2½ minutes to check doneness.

Divide the chocolate among 4 foil-lined paper baking cups, each about 2½ inches in diameter. Spread the chocolate up along the inside of the cups with a spoon. Freeze for about 30 minutes, or until hardened.

Peel the foil away from the chocolate cups and fill each cup with ice cream. If desired, make a hole in the ice cream with the handle of a wooden spoon and fill each with ½ teaspoon brandy. Smooth the ice cream over the hole and refreeze for about 30 minutes.

Before serving, sprinkle the top of each ice cream cup with pistachio nuts and garnish with a candied violet, if desired.

BUTTERSCOTCH SAUCE

MAKES 1½ CUPS
COOKING TIME: 7 TO 11 MINUTES

This smooth, buttery sauce can be spooned over ice cream or cake. A wooden spoon makes stirring and cleanup easier.

- **1 cup sugar**
- **¼ cup light corn syrup**
- **1 tablespoon hot water**
- **¼ cup butter**
- **½ cup half and half**

In a 4-cup glass measure combine the sugar, corn syrup, and water. Cook on HIGH for 1 minute; stir well, then cook on HIGH for 4 to 7 minutes, or until it reaches a light golden, butterscotch color, stirring once.

Meanwhile, cut the butter into 4 pieces. Add to the warm sugar mixture, stirring until melted.

Stir in the half and half. Cook on MEDIUM for 2 to 3 minutes, until well blended. Let stand for 5 minutes, until it becomes slightly thicker and a deeper gold.

NOTE: *To Reheat:* Heat on MEDIUM for 2 to 3 minutes, stirring once.

RASPBERRY SAUCE FOR FRESH FRUIT OR SHERBET

MAKES 1 CUP
COOKING TIME: 2½ TO 3 MINUTES

It is hard to believe that something as quick and easy as this can taste so luscious. It gives fruit sherbet or ice cream a lovely flavor accent.

(Continued)

1 cup raspberry preserves
2 tablespoons Triple Sec, framboise, or brandy

1 teaspoon vanilla or liquid from poached fruit

In a 4-cup glass measure combine all the ingredients. Cook on HIGH for 2½ to 3 minutes, or until the jam is melted, stirring once.

VARIATIONS:

Apricot Sauce: Substitute apricot preserves for the raspberry preserves. Substitute Grand Marnier, Triple Sec, or brandy for the vanilla.

Black Raspberry Sauce: Substitute black raspberry jam for the raspberry preserves. Substitute Triple Sec, framboise, or brandy for the vanilla.

Currant Sauce: Substitute 1 cup red currant jelly for the raspberry preserves. Substitute 2 tablespoons crème de cassis, Triple Sec, or brandy for the vanilla.

Rice Pudding Basics:

1. In both the Traditional and Custard Rice Puddings, the increased liquid in the form of milk will cause the cooking times to be longer than regular rice cookery. Otherwise, the cooking procedure for rice puddings is very similar. (See also Rice Basics, page 196).
2. Depending on the version of rice pudding you make, the proportion of rice to milk can be ½ cup rice to either 1⅓ cups milk or 2½ cups milk. This is because rice seems to absorb milk differently than it does water, and also for rice pudding, some more milk is needed to make the rice creamy.
3. If the larger amount of milk is called for, as in the traditional pudding, it is heated first. This is to save on total cooking time later once the rice is added. In the custard pudding, the basic rice cooking method is called for as described on page 197.
4. *Doneness*: The Traditional Rice Pudding and Custard Rice Pudding vary in their final appearance after cooking. In both, the rice should always be very tender. In the traditional pudding, less rice is cooked with more milk, which will make it milkier at the end. The Custard Rice Pudding is more like conventionally cooked rice, in other words, dry on the surface but if stirred, some unabsorbed liquid will appear beneath. A custard cream is then stirred into this thicker rice mixture to lighten it up.

We prefer to serve both warm or at room temperature, because when chilled, the rice becomes firmer in texture. Reheat on HIGH power for 1 minute per serving and stir.

TRADITIONAL RICE PUDDING

MAKES 4 SERVINGS   BEGIN 1 HOUR BEFORE SERVING
COOKING TIME: 40 TO 45 MINUTES

There seem to be two schools of thought on rice pudding: One is that it should be a "milky" pudding—like this traditional one, which thickens slightly, to become creamy upon standing. It doesn't save a lot of time, compared to the conventionally cooked ones, but we feel that it is worth it just for the convenience and cleanup. The rice also holds its shape very well and doesn't burst or get starchy.

The second type of rice pudding is creamier and thicker, having a pastry cream folded into it. That follows next, in Custard Rice Pudding.

---

2 tablespoons butter	2 tablespoons sugar
2½ cups milk	½ teaspoon ground cinnamon
½ cup long-grain rice	

Place the butter in a 3-quart casserole. Cook on HIGH for 45 seconds to 1 minute to melt.

Pour the milk into a 4-cup glass measure. Cook on HIGH for 5 minutes, or until hot but not boiling.

Meanwhile, stir the rice into the melted butter to coat the grains well. Stir in the sugar. Pour in the hot milk, stirring to coat the rice evenly. Cover tightly and cook on HIGH for 6 to 8 minutes, or until boiling, then on MEDIUM for 25 minutes. *Do not stir.* The rice pudding will be very milky at this point.

Uncover and sprinkle the pudding with cinnamon. Cook, uncovered, on MEDIUM for 3 to 5 minutes, or until most of the milk is absorbed and the rice is tender. Stir. The rice pudding will not be thick; let stand 10 minutes to become a thicker consistency. Serve warm or at room temperature.

Traditional Rice Pudding with Raisins: Stir in ½ cup raisins with the cinnamon.

CUSTARD RICE PUDDING

MAKES 4 TO 6 SERVINGS   BEGIN 40 MINUTES BEFORE SERVING
COOKING TIME: 19 TO 24 MINUTES

This rice pudding gains its rich yellow color from a pastry cream that is stirred into it. The addition makes it almost elegant, especially when served with Raspberry Sauce.

¾ cup long-grain rice	2 large egg yolks
2 cups milk	¾ cup half and half
¼ cup sugar	1 teaspoon vanilla
1 tablespoon all-purpose flour	Raspberry Sauce (page 565) (optional)

In a 3-quart casserole combine the rice and milk. Cover tightly and cook on HIGH for 7 to 10 minutes, or until boiling, then on MEDIUM for 12 to 14 minutes, or until most of the liquid is absorbed and the rice is tender. *Do not stir.* Let stand for 5 minutes.

Meanwhile, in a 1-quart casserole combine the sugar, flour, and egg yolks; beat together. Stir in the half and half, beating to mix well. Cook, uncovered, on HIGH for 1 minute; beat with a whisk. Cook on HIGH for 1 to 1½ minutes more, or until soft and thickened, beating every 30 seconds. Stir in the vanilla.

Fold the warm sauce into the cooked rice. Serve warm, spooning the raspberry sauce over the finished pudding, if desired.

VARIATION:

Foamy Custard Pudding: Reserve the 2 egg whites from the custard. Chill the cooked pudding. Beat the egg whites until stiff and fold into the pudding.

HAWAIIAN RICE AND CREAM

MAKES 4 TO 6 SERVINGS   BEGIN 1½ HOURS BEFORE SERVING
COOKING TIME: 14 TO 18 MINUTES

This is simple, and the kids' favorite.

---

1 cup long-grain or converted rice
1⅔ cups water
1 cup heavy cream, whipped
2 tablespoons sugar

1 cup crushed or chunk pineapple, fresh or canned in own juices, drained

---

In a 3-quart casserole combine the rice and water. Cover tightly and cook on HIGH for 6 to 8 minutes, or until boiling, then on MEDIUM for 8 to 10 minutes, or until the rice is tender and most of the liquid is absorbed. *Do not stir.* Let stand, covered, for 5 to 10 minutes. Chill the rice, still covered.

Whip the cream with the sugar until stiff. Fold the cream and pineapple into the chilled rice and serve.

VARIATION:

Rice Pudding with Yogurt and Fresh Fruit: After the rice has completed standing time, stir in 2 tablespoons brown sugar until the sugar is melted and coats the rice completely. Chill the rice. Fold 1 cup plain yogurt and 1 cup cut-up fresh fruit into the chilled rice.

Bread Pudding Basics:

1. Bread puddings are cooked in buttered and crumbed bowls so that if you desire to unmold the bread puddings, they will have a brown coated crust on the outside. Any 1-quart bowl, casserole, or mold will do.
2. In the bread cube pudding the milk and eggs are heated together first, to cook the custard partially so that it uniformly coats the bread cubes. In the apple pudding, less milk is required because of the moisture provided in the apples, so this step can be eliminated.
3. The bread cubes are soaked first in the egg custard, for the raisin-nut bread pudding, to moisten and flavor all the cubes evenly. This step is not necessary with the apple pudding because it is made with bread crumbs that absorb liquid more readily in the cooking bowl. Also, there is no cooked egg custard with the apple pudding.
4. Bread puddings are covered with wax paper to speed up cooking and to seal in some of the moisture.
5. The apple pudding is first cooked on HIGH power to start releasing the necessary steam from the apples that will moisten the bread crumbs. The power is then turned down to MEDIUM because it is a type of egg custard that can't be stirred, so MEDIUM allows it to cook evenly all the way through. The raisin-nut bread pudding is cooked entirely on MEDIUM because of the larger amount of egg custard.
6. It may be necessary to rotate the puddings during cooking, as is true with any large cake or large egg custard.
7. Standing time is important to complete the cooking process. The pudding should stand directly on the countertop, rather than on a rack, so that all the heat can be reflected inside rather than dissipated by circulating air.
8. *Doneness:* Bread pudding can be made either with or without an egg custard mixture, and it can be made with bread crumbs or bread cubes. The first bread pudding recipe is made with the egg custard mixture, and thus is tested much like an egg custard. A knife should come out clean when inserted about 1 inch from the center. The center, like any other egg custard, will continue cooking and solidify upon standing.

The apple pudding, on the other hand, has less of an egg custard and most of the moisture from the apples and milk is readily absorbed by the finer bread crumbs. A knife inserted right into the center should come out clean.

✸ RAISIN-NUT BREAD PUDDING

MAKES 4 TO 6 SERVINGS   BEGIN 40 MINUTES BEFORE SERVING WARM
COOKING TIME: 12 TO 16 MINUTES

Bread cubes in a spoonable egg custard make this old-fashioned dessert an inexpensive but delicious favorite.

1½ cups milk	½ cup raisins (optional)
2 large eggs	1 tablespoon butter
¾ cup granulated sugar	¼ cup fine dry bread crumbs
1 teaspoon vanilla	½ teaspoon ground cinnamon
6 slices of bread, ½ inch thick, cut into 1-inch cubes	1 recipe Basic Berry Dessert Sauce with Raspberries or Strawberries (page 497)
½ cup coarsely chopped nuts (optional)	

Pour the milk into a 4-cup glass measure. Cook on HIGH for 2 minutes, or until heated but not boiling.

Meanwhile, in a mixing bowl, beat the eggs and sugar together. Stir in the vanilla. Slowly pour half the warm milk into the egg mixture, stirring constantly. Pour the mixture back into the 4-cup glass measure. Cook on MEDIUM for 2 minutes, stirring once. Stir in the bread cubes, nuts, and raisins, if desired. Let stand for 5 minutes, occasionally pushing the bread cubes down into the sauce.

Meanwhile, butter a 1-quart glass or ceramic bowl with the 1 tablespoon butter to within 1½ inches of the top. Sprinkle with 2 tablespoons bread crumbs. Pour the bread mixture into the prepared casserole. Sprinkle the top with the remaining bread crumbs and cinnamon. Cover with wax paper and cook on MEDIUM for 8 to 12 minutes, or until a knife inserted 1 inch from the center comes out clean, rotating the pudding one-quarter turn twice. Let it stand directly on the counter for 10 minutes. Unmold, if desired.

Serve warm with raspberry or strawberry dessert sauce.

VARIATIONS:

Bread Pudding with Brandy: Substitute 1 tablespoon brandy for the vanilla.

Chocolate Bread Pudding: Add 4 ounces semisweet chocolate bits to the milk in the 4-cup measure. Cook on HIGH for 2½ to 3½ minutes, or until the chocolate melts without boiling milk, stirring twice. Proceed with basic recipe reducing to ½ cup sugar and eliminating the raisins. Serve with a half recipe of Plum Pudding Sauce (page 534) or with Pastry Cream for Tarts (page 556).

Whole-Wheat Bread Pudding: Substitute whole-wheat bread for the white bread. Substitute brown sugar for the granulated sugar. Whole wheat gives a nice brown color—very wholesome in flavor and appearance.

APRICOT-GLAZED APPLE BREAD PUDDING

MAKES 6 TO 8 SERVINGS   BEGIN 30 TO 40 MINUTES BEFORE SERVING
COOKING TIME: 15 TO 23 MINUTES

A bread-crumb pudding flavored with apples and a touch of brandy.

5 tablespoons butter	¼ cup milk
1½ cups fresh bread crumbs	1 tablespoon brandy
1½ pounds cooking apples (about 6), cut into ⅛-inch slices	1 tablespoon lemon juice
	2 tablespoons apricot preserves
¾ cup brown sugar	1 tablespoon apricot-flavored brandy
1 large egg	2 cups warm cream or milk

Rub the inside of a 1-quart glass or ceramic bowl, suitable for serving, with 1 tablespoon butter. Sprinkle with 2 tablespoons bread crumbs.

Place about ½ cup apple slices in the bottom of the prepared bowl. Next, layer one-third of each ingredient: bread crumbs, sugar, remaining 4 tablespoons butter (cut up into small pieces), and remaining apples. Follow this procedure two more times to make 3 layers.

In a small bowl combine the egg, ¼ cup milk, brandy, and lemon juice. Pour over the layers. Cover with wax paper and cook on HIGH for 5 minutes; rotate one-third turn. Cook on MEDIUM for 8 to 15 minutes, or until the apples are tender and a knife inserted in the center comes out clean; rotate the pudding one-third turn after 6 minutes. Remove from the oven and cover with a plate, pressing down slightly to pack the pudding. Let stand for 15 minutes.

Meanwhile, in a 2-cup glass measure combine the preserves and apricot-flavored brandy. Cook on HIGH for 1 minute, or until melted. Remove the plate and wax paper from the pudding. Unmold, if desired. Pour the heated preserves over the pudding.

Place 2 cups cream or milk in a 4-cup glass measure. Heat on HIGH for 2 to 3 minutes, or until warm. Transfer to a serving pitcher and pass with the hot apple pudding.

Sweetened Egg Custard Basics:

See Egg Custard and Timbales Basics, page 156.

☀ SWEETENED EGG CUSTARDS

MAKES 4 SERVINGS   BEGIN 25 TO 20 MINUTES BEFORE SERVING WARM
COOKING TIME: 8 TO 10 MINUTES

There is no easier way to bake egg custard than in the microwave. Forget about setting the custards in a pan of water to cook. The purpose of that in conventional cooking is to keep the custard cooking at no higher than the boiling point. By turning the microwave power down to MEDIUM, *you can accomplish the same regulated slow cooking.*

Serve the plain custard with fresh fruit or raspberry or strawberry Basic Berry Dessert Sauce (page 497), if desired.

1¼ cups milk
2 teaspoons vanilla
4 large eggs, beaten

¼ cup sugar
Freshly grated nutmeg (optional)

In a 4-cup glass measure combine the milk and vanilla. Cook on HIGH for 2 minutes, until hot but not boiling.

Meanwhile, in a medium bowl beat the eggs and sugar together until frothy. Add the heated milk, pouring slowly and stirring constantly. Pour into four 5- or 6-ounce custard cups. Place the cups in the oven with at least a 1-inch space between them. (If you place the custard cups on a large round plate or tray before cooking, they will be easier to rotate and remove.) Cook, uncovered, on MEDIUM for 6 to 8 minutes, or until firm, repositioning the custards once or twice. Serve warm or chilled.

To unmold and serve: Run a small knife around the custard cup rim and invert the custard onto a serving plate.

VARIATIONS:

Tijuana Avocado Egg Creams: Substitute 1 large ripe avocado, peeled and mashed, for ¾ cup milk (avocado will make about ¾ cup puree). Add the avocado puree to the remaining ½ cup milk. Add 2 tablespoons tequila to this. Place the milk-avocado mixture in a 4-cup glass measure. Cook on HIGH for 2 minutes, or until hot but not boiling. Proceed with the basic recipe but cook on MEDIUM for *8 to 10 minutes.* Garnish with lime slices that have been dipped into sugar or salt, and serve as a different dessert or a snack served with a flavorful cinnamon coffee.

Chocolate Pots de Crème: Place 3 ounces semisweet chocolate pieces in a medium microwaveproof bowl. Heat on MEDIUM for 2 minutes; stir. Heat on MEDIUM for 1 minute more, or until melted and smooth, stirring every 30 seconds. Heat the milk as directed. Meanwhile, stir the sugar into the melted chocolate, then beat in the eggs. Pour the heated milk into the chocolate mixture, stirring continuously. Add 2 tablespoons chocolate-flavored liqueur, if desired. Follow the basic cooking instructions. To serve, top with sweetened whipped cream. The kids like these for breakfast, served warm, sans liqueur, of course, instead of hot cocoa and an egg. So do we!

Mexican Pots de Crème: Prepare the Chocolate Pots de Crème variation above. Sprinkle the tops with ground cinnamon.

Mocha Pots de Crème: Prepare the Chocolate Pots de Crème variation above, but add 2 teaspoons instant espresso coffee or 2 tablespoons coffee-flavored liqueur to the milk before heating.

Orange Egg Custards: Add 2 tablespoons orange-flavored liqueur and 2 tablespoons grated orange rind to the milk before heating. To serve, garnish with orange segments that have been marinated in 2 tablespoons orange-flavored liqueur for 1 hour.

Lemon Egg Custards: Add 2 tablespoons grated lemon rind to the eggs and sugar.

Pumpkin Egg Custards: Substitute ¾ cup pumpkin puree for 1 cup milk. Add the puree to the remaining ¼ cup milk. Cook, uncovered, on HIGH for 2 minutes, or until hot. Add ¼ teaspoon grated nutmeg and ½ teaspoon ground ginger to the milk. Follow the basic recipe. Serve with sweetened whipped cream.

Coconut Custards: Substitute ¾ cup (3 ounces) grated coconut plus ½ cup milk for 1¼ cups milk. Cook on HIGH for 2 minutes, or until hot. Proceed with basic recipe. Serve with sweetened whipped cream.

Brown Sugar–Glazed Egg Custards: Prepare the basic recipe and chill. Place ½ cup brown sugar and 2 teaspoons water into a 2-cup glass measure; stir. Cook on HIGH for 1 minute; stir. Cook on HIGH for 1 to 2 minutes more, or until boiling. Divide the sugar syrup evenly among the chilled custards, spooning it on top. Serve at once. These are similar to crème brulée, but technically they can't be because they aren't passed under a broiler or salamander. They are nonetheless delicious and raise the custards onto a higher plane.

INDIAN PUDDING

MAKES 6 SERVINGS   BEGIN 35 TO 45 MINUTES BEFORE SERVING
COOKING TIME: 21 TO 28 MINUTES

These pumpkin-colored custards are one of our favorite New England desserts. Served warm with a scoop of vanilla ice cream, it always makes us feel like we're sitting in an old inn in front of a roaring fire. This is traditionally made in a large casserole, but we find that the pudding cooks more evenly and quickly in the microwave in individual custard cups. Serve with vanilla ice cream or sweetened whipped cream.

- 2 tablespoons butter
- ½ cup molasses
- 2 cups milk
- ¼ cup sugar
- ¼ cup cornmeal
- ¼ teaspoon grated nutmeg
- ¼ teaspoon ground ginger
- 3 large eggs, beaten
- ½ teaspoon vanilla

Place the butter in a medium microwave-proof bowl. Heat on HIGH for 35 seconds to 1 minute, or until melted. Set aside.

In a 3-quart casserole combine the molasses, milk, sugar, cornmeal, nutmeg, and ginger. Cover tightly and cook on HIGH for 5 minutes; stir to blend well. Cover again and cook on HIGH for 5 to 10 minutes more, or until thickened, stirring once.

Meanwhile, beat the eggs into the melted butter. Slowly add the cooked molasses mixture to the eggs, stirring constantly. Stir in the vanilla. Pour into six 5- to 6-ounce microwave custard cups. Place the cups in the oven in a circle with a 1-inch space between them. Cook, uncovered, on MEDIUM for 10 to 12 minutes, or until a knife inserted ½ inch from the center comes out clean; reposition the custards once halfway through cooking. Let stand for 10 minutes. Serve warm or chilled.

VARIATION:

Indian Pudding in Casserole: Pour the mixture into a 2-quart casserole. Cook, uncovered, on MEDIUM for 18 to 22 minutes, or until a knife inserted ½ inch from the center comes out clean, stirring every 5 minutes until almost set. Let stand for 10 minutes.

INDIVIDUAL RICE CUSTARDS

MAKES 4 SERVINGS BEGIN 15 TO 20 MINUTES BEFORE SERVING WARM
COOKING TIME: 10 TO 12 MINUTES

When there is just a cup of rice left over from last night's dinner or the takeout Chinese restaurant, it would be a shame not to make these custards.

If you wish, invert the custards onto serving plates and top with raspberry or strawberry Basic Berry Dessert Sauce (page 497).

- **1 cup cooked rice**
- **¾ cup milk**
- **3 large eggs**
- **2 tablespoons sugar**
- **1 teaspoon vanilla**

In a 2-cup glass measure combine the rice and milk. Cook, uncovered, on HIGH for 2 minutes, until hot but not boiling.

In a separate bowl combine the eggs and sugar; beat lightly. Stir in the vanilla. Pour in the heated milk, stirring constantly. Spoon evenly into four 5- to 6-ounce custard cups.

Arrange the cups in a circle in the oven with a 1-inch space between each one. Cook, uncovered, on MEDIUM for 8 to 10 minutes, or until a knife inserted ½ inch from the center comes out clean; reposition the custards halfway through cooking. Let stand for 5 minutes. Serve warm or chilled.

Cheesecake Basics:

1. The cheese filling is heated through first on HIGH power before being poured into the cake dish. This cheese and egg mixture can be cooked on HIGH, in the bowl, if it is stirred where indicated to redistribute the heat. The preheating is critical in helping the cheesecake cook more quickly and evenly in the dish, by raising the starting temperature evenly throughout the batter.

2. Once it is poured into the dish the cheesecake is cooked on MEDIUM, because it can't be stirred and is also a sensitive cheese and egg mixture.

3. Make sure to smooth the cheesecake out evenly on top so it is of equal thickness all over.

4. We found that a straight-sided cake dish was better for cooking the cheesecake

more evenly than a pie plate; we also liked being able to unmold the cheesecake. In addition, in the pie plate the cheesecake may possibly overcook on the top edges. This batter is designed for an 8½-inch cake dish, and is optimal for microwave cooking. We do not recommend baking larger cheesecakes than this in the microwave.

5. Cheesecakes are cooked uncovered. The filling is completely heated through before it is poured over the crust, so it is not necessary to keep the steam in with a cover, which ordinarily would allow such a dense filling, with its large surface area, to heat more evenly.

6. Just as with cakes, a cheesecake will cook more evenly if it is raised up in the oven on a microwaveproof cereal bowl (see illustration, page 506). Rotating a quarter turn once or twice may still be necessary, depending on your oven.

7. It is important to let this dense cake stand, directly on the counter, for 30 minutes. This not only lets the cake cook through completely, but allows it to cool enough so that it can be turned out.

8. *Doneness:* Touch the cheesecake on top, 1 inch from center. When the top adheres to your finger, the cheesecake underneath should be moist but set, not gooey. The sides should begin to pull away from the dish sides. (See special doneness test for Peanut Butter Cheesecake, page 576, because it is a different consistency.)

Underdone: The cheesecake will be almost set, but will jiggle slightly when shaken. When touched on the surface, 1 inch from the center, the cheesecake that adheres to your finger will reveal a wet and foamy mixture underneath.

Overdone: Edges of the cheesecake begin to get very firm and possibly crack. Did you heat the filling first on HIGH? Did you use an 8½-inch round dish? Did you turn the power down to MEDIUM to cook it in the cake dish?

✸ CREAMY CHEESECAKE

MAKES 8 TO 10 SERVINGS   BEGIN 1 DAY BEFORE SERVING
COOKING TIME: 19 TO 31 MINUTES

This creamy cheesecake is turned out onto its crumb crust, to stand free form and be topped with fruit, or nothing at all! It can be quickly prepared but it requires patience to let it chill thoroughly. The flavors are best after at least 8 hours.

Crust:
- ¼ cup butter
- 1 tablespoon sugar
- ¾ cup zwieback cookie crumbs
- ¼ cup finely ground walnuts
- ¼ teaspoon ground cinnamon

Filling:
- 2 8-ounce packages cream cheese
- 2 tablespoons all-purpose flour
- ¾ cup sugar
- 2 large eggs
- 2 teaspoons vanilla extract
- 1 cup sour cream

To make the crust: Place the butter in a medium microwaveproof bowl. Heat on HIGH for 1 to 2 minutes to melt. Stir in the remaining crust ingredients until well blended. Cut 2 circles of wax paper to fit the bottom inside of an 8½-inch round cake dish. Place the wax paper circles in the bottom of the dish; this will make it easy to remove the cheesecake. Press the crumbs on top of the wax paper to make an even crust. Cook on HIGH for 1 minute to set partially. Set aside; the crust will continue to set and harden.

To make the filling: Place the cream cheese in a large microwaveproof mixing bowl. Heat on DEFROST for 3 to 4 minutes to soften. Beat until creamy. Add the remaining ingredients. Beat with a mixer until well blended and smooth. Place the bowl with the filling in the oven. Cook on HIGH for 6 to 10 minutes, or until it is very warm to the touch in the center, stirring every 2 minutes. The mixture will be a little lumpy at this point, but it will cook into a smooth cake.

Pour the filling into the crust, spreading out evenly on top. Place the crust dish on top of a microwaveproof cereal bowl. Cook on MEDIUM for 8 to 14 minutes, or until almost set in the center, rotating one-quarter turn once or twice. Let stand directly on the counter for 30 minutes.

The cheesecake will come out easily, but you'll have to turn it out and then turn it over. Here's how: Cover the top of the cheesecake with wax paper. Invert a plate on top and flip the cheesecake out onto the plate. Gently peel the wax paper from the crust. Flip the cheesecake, crust side down, onto the serving plate. Chill for 3 hours or overnight before serving.

VARIATIONS:

Fruit-Topped Cheesecake: Top the chilled cheesecake with 1 pint blueberries, cleaned, or strawberries, hulled, or 4 peaches, peeled and cut into ¼-inch slices. Arrange attractively on top. The peaches should be placed in slightly overlapping concentric circles. Melt ¼ cup currant jelly in a 1-cup glass measure on HIGH for 40 seconds to 1 minute. Brush over the fruit to glaze.

Lemon Cheesecake: Substitute 2 teaspoons grated lemon rind for the vanilla in the filling. Garnish the outside rim of the cake with 3 to 4 lemons, sliced paper thin and dipped into sugar.

Orange Cheesecake: Substitute 2 teaspoons grated orange rind and 2 tablespoons orange-flavored liqueur for the vanilla in the filling. Garnish the cake top with seedless orange segments. Heat ¼ cup orange marmalade in a 1-cup glass measure on HIGH for 40 seconds to 1 minute to melt. Strain and brush over the segments to glaze.

Chocolate Cheesecake: Eliminate ¼ cup sugar from the filling. Mix the filling and set aside before heating. Place 6 ounces semisweet chocolate pieces around the outer rim of a microwaveproof cereal bowl. Cook on MEDIUM for 2 minutes; stir. Cook for 30 seconds to 1 minute more, or until melted, stirring every 30 seconds. Beat the chocolate into the filling. Heat the filling, then pour into the crust to cook. Garnish with Chocolate-Covered Strawberries (page 596), if desired.

Peanut Butter Cheesecake: Substitute chocolate wafers for the zwieback cookies. Substitute 1 cup smooth peanut butter for 1 package of cream cheese. To test for doneness: Insert a toothpick into the cake, 1 inch from the center, as you would test a custard (see also page 156).

Mousse Basics:

1. Making a mousse involves first heating or cooking egg yolks, before they can be chilled and other ingredients folded in. Egg yolks can be heated on HIGH power, if they are stirred frequently to redistribute heat; we prefer a wire whisk for this task. Pastry cream (page 555) is another example of this method.
2. In the Luscious Chocolate Mousse, it is the hot melted chocolate that adds heat to the egg yolks which later cools into a thick base.
3. In any mousse, the egg mixture must be cooled sufficiently so that when the beaten whites and cream are folded in, the entire mixture can be lightened into an airy foam. If the egg mixture is too warm, it will form a thick soup.
4. *Doneness:* In the Grapefruit Mousse, the egg yolks, juice, and sugar mixture are cooked until they "form a ribbon" before being chilled. The mixture will be lighter in color than the original yolks, and when drizzled on itself it will stand up in what looks like a thin ribbon.

In the chocolate mousse, the egg yolks and sugar are beaten to incorporate air before the hot chocolate mixture is added. The heat from the chocolate will cause the yolks to thicken slightly, and the chocolate will cool into a thick mixture.

Too Thin: Did you allow the heated egg mixture to cool sufficiently? It should be cool to the touch. If not, it won't become airy when the egg whites and whipped cream are folded in.

✺ GRAPEFRUIT MOUSSE

MAKES 6 SERVINGS   BEGIN 2½ HOURS BEFORE SERVING
COOKING TIME: 3 TO 4 MINUTES

Grapefruit is often served at the beginning of the meal as an appetite stimulant, but there's no reason why an airy grapefruit mousse can't create excitement at the end of the meal. When made at the height of grapefruit season, this dessert is as economical as it is elegant.

3 **small to medium grapefruits, with unblemished shells**	¾ **cup granulated sugar**
⅓ **cup fresh grapefruit juice**	⅛ **teaspoon cream of tartar**
1 **teaspoon grated lemon rind**	¾ **cup heavy cream**
2 **large eggs, separated**	2 **tablespoons confectioners' sugar**
	6 **fresh strawberries**

Insert a sharp-pointed paring knife at the widest part of the grapefruit, angling down, about 1½ inches from the outside skin. Cut the grapefruit in half by cutting "lion's teeth" around the middle of the grapefruit and carefully pulling the 2 halves apart. Remove the pulp so that the shells are clean. Chill the grapefruit shells for individual mousse serving bowls.

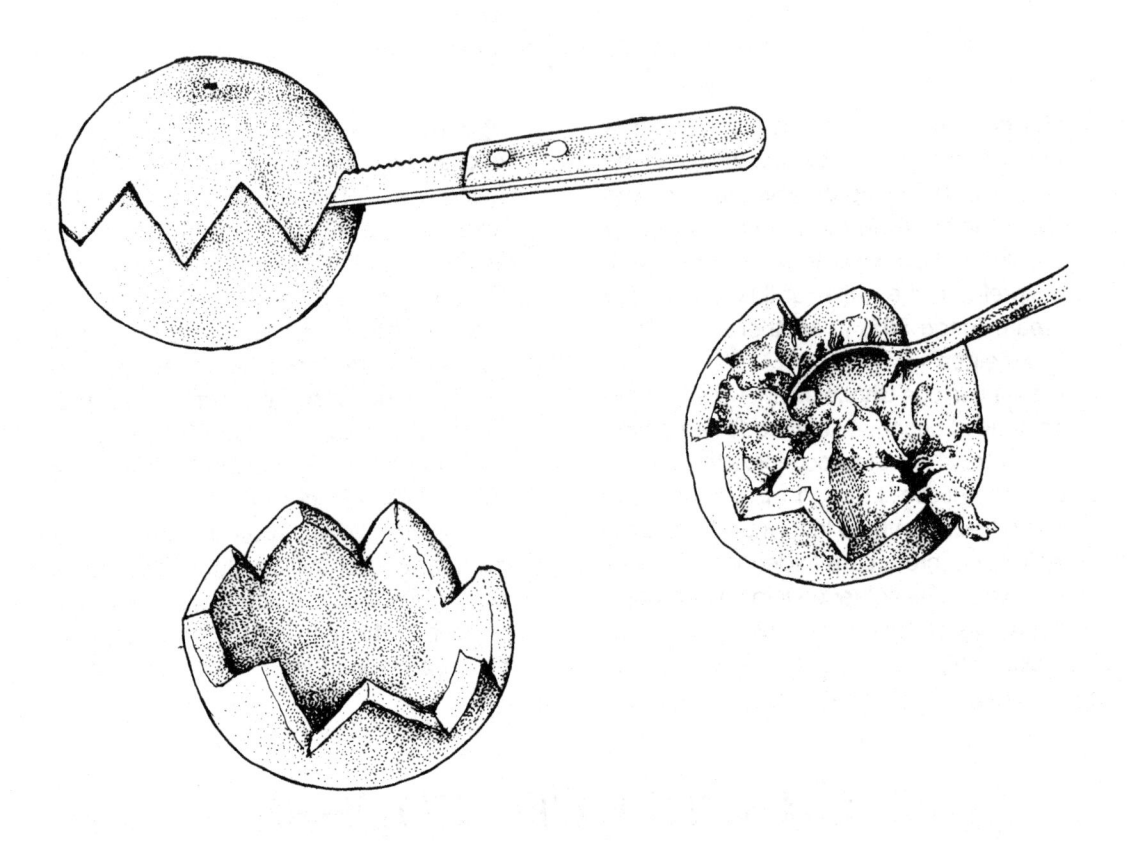

Squeeze the grapefruit pulp to make the ⅓ cup juice, straining the seeds but not pieces of the pulp.

In a 4-cup glass measure combine the grapefruit juice, lemon rind, egg yolks, and granulated sugar; beat with a whisk to blend. Cook on HIGH for 3 to 4 minutes, beating *each* minute until thick enough to form a ribbon. Pour into a large mixing bowl and refrigerate to cool and thicken. It is important that the mixture is thoroughly cooled and thickened. The mixture may be put in the freezer for 20 minutes to speed cooling.

Place the egg whites in a deep bowl. Beat with an electric mixer until frothy; add the cream of tartar and beat until stiff peaks form. Fold the whites into the cooled grapefruit mixture.

Meanwhile, pour the cream into another bowl and beat with an electric mixer until thickened. Add the confectioners' sugar and beat until just blended. Fold the cream into the cooled grapefruit mixture.

Spoon the mousse into the chilled grapefruit shells and place in the freezer for 2 hours, until solid. Before serving, garnish each with a strawberry.

VARIATIONS:

Lime Mousse: Eliminate the grapefruit. Substitute lime juice for the grapefruit juice. Spoon the mousse into dessert or wine glasses; Chill. Garnish with Chocolate Triangles (page 594).

Lemon Mousse: Eliminate the grapefruit. Substitute lemon juice for the grapefruit juice. Spoon the mousse into dessert or wine glasses; chill. Garnish with grated lemon rind and fresh mint.

☀ LUSCIOUS CHOCOLATE MOUSSE

MAKES 6 SERVINGS   BEGIN 1½ HOURS BEFORE SERVING
COOKING TIME: 3 TO 4 MINUTES

- 6 ounces semisweet chocolate pieces
- 2 tablespoons rum or vanilla
- ¼ cup sugar
- 2 large eggs, separated
- 1 cup heavy cream, whipped, plus additional for garnish
- Chocolate-Covered Strawberries (page 596) or Chocolate Curls (page 595)

In a microwaveproof cereal bowl combine the chocolate and rum or vanilla. Cook on MEDIUM for 2 minutes; stir. Cook on MEDIUM for 30 seconds to 2 minutes more, or until melted, stirring every 30 seconds.

Meanwhile, in a large mixing bowl combine the sugar and egg yolks and beat together until foamy. Slowly beat in the melted chocolate, until well blended and smooth. Cool the mixture until thickened.

Whip the heavy cream until thick. In a separate bowl beat the egg whites until stiff but not dry. Fold the whipped cream into cooled chocolate mixture. Fold in the beaten egg whites. Spoon into individual stemmed glasses or cups; chill for at least 1 hour before serving.

To serve, top with a dollop of whipped cream and a chocolate-coated strawberry or chocolate curls.

VARIATIONS:

White Chocolate Mousse: Substitute white chocolate for the semisweet chocolate. If the white chocolate is in a large piece, cut it into small pieces. Reduce the sugar to 2 tablespoons.

Mocha Mousse: Substitute 2 tablespoons coffee-flavored liqueur for the rum or vanilla.

Amaretto Mousse: Substitute 2 tablespoons almond-flavored liqueur for the rum or vanilla. Stir in ¼ cup finely chopped almonds.

Hazelnut Mousse: Substitute 2 tablespoons hazelnut-flavored liqueur for the rum or vanilla. Stir in ¼ cup finely chopped hazelnuts when adding the whipped cream. Garnish with whipped cream and whole hazelnuts.

TWO-TIERED CHOCOLATE MOUSSE CAKE

MAKES 8 TO 12 SERVINGS   BEGIN 1 DAY BEFORE SERVING
COOKING TIME: 3 TO 5 MINUTES

Although there are many steps to this dessert, it is not difficult to make. The best part is the pride you can take when you slice this mousse cake with its white, mocha, and dark chocolate layers encased in hard chocolate. Even the people "who have seen it all" will be impressed!

Firm Chocolate Mousse:
- 6 ounces semisweet chocolate pieces
- 2 tablespoons rum or vanilla
- ¼ cup sugar
- 2 large eggs, separated
- 1 envelope plain gelatin
- ¼ cup water
- 1 cup heavy cream, whipped
- 1 recipe Mocha Mousse without egg whites (page 579)

Firm White Chocolate Mousse:
- 6 ounces white chocolate, broken into pieces
- 2 tablespoons rum or vanilla
- 2 tablespoons sugar
- 2 eggs, separated
- 1 cup heavy cream, whipped
- 1 envelope plain gelatin
- ¼ cup water

Garnish:
Chocolate Rectangles (page 595)
Grated chocolate (optional)

To make the firm chocolate mousse: In a microwaveproof cereal bowl combine the chocolate and rum or vanilla. Cook on MEDIUM for 2 minutes; stir. Cook on MEDIUM for 30 seconds to 2 minutes more, or until the chocolate is melted, stirring every 30 seconds.

In a large mixing bowl combine the sugar and egg yolks and beat together until foamy. Beat in the melted chocolate, until well blended and smooth. Cool the chocolate mixture until thickened.

Meanwhile, in a 1-cup glass measure combine the gelatin and water. Cook on HIGH for 30 seconds or until the gelatin is dissolved.

Whip the heavy cream until thick. In a separate bowl beat the egg whites until stiff but not dry. Fold the heavy cream into the cooled chocolate mixture. Fold in the egg whites. Cut a circle of wax paper to fit the bottom of an 8- or 10-inch cup metal springform pan. Place the circle in the bottom of the pan. Pour the dark chocolate mousse into the pan and spread the top to make smooth. Chill for at least 2 hours.

Spoon half the mocha mousse on top of the dark chocolate mousse; reserve the remainder to frost the cake. Chill the 2 layers of mousse for at least 2 hours.

To make the solid white chocolate mousse: Follow the firm chocolate mousse instructions above. Spoon on top of the mocha mousse. Chill for at least 2 hours.

To assemble the cake: When chilled solidly, loosen the mousse from the pan with a sharp knife and remove the sides from the pan. Remove the bottom and the wax paper. Smooth the remaining mocha mousse on top of the cake. Place the chocolate pieces around the outside rim of the cake, standing up like a picket fence to cover the surface. Sprinkle the top with grated chocolate, if desired. Refrigerate until serving time, at least 1 hour.

BOURBON STREET SOUFFLÉ

MAKES 6 SERVINGS   BEGIN 40 MINUTES BEFORE SERVING
COOKING TIME: 21 TO 27 MINUTES

And they said soufflés wouldn't rise in the microwave! The truth is that it is difficult to make them fall. Once the egg structure has cooked into place, opening the microwave oven door will not disturb it in the same way that hot air released from a conventional oven can cause a soufflé to fall.

To simulate a dry crust on the top, this recipe is topped with pecan pieces after cooking. It's served with a rich Bourbon-Praline Sauce, bringing to mind the flavors found around New Orleans' Bourbon Street restaurants.

For more information, see Soufflé Basics (page 154).

- 2 tablespoons butter
- 2 tablespoons all-purpose flour
- 1 cup light cream
- 1 cup ground pecans
- ½ cup brown sugar
- 2 tablespoons bourbon
- 5 large eggs, separated
- ½ teaspoon grated nutmeg
- 1 teaspoon cream of tartar
- 1 recipe Bourbon-Praline Sauce (page 564)

Place the butter in a 4-cup glass measure. Cook on HIGH for 45 seconds to 1 minute, or until melted. Stir in the flour. Blend the cream in well with a whisk. Cook on HIGH for 1½ to 2 minutes, or until thick and smooth, stirring once. Stir in ¾ cup ground pecans, sugar, and bourbon.

In a small bowl beat the egg yolks slightly. Blend in a small amount of the hot sauce. Pour the heated egg yolk mixture into the remaining sauce, stirring quickly to avoid lumping. Add the nutmeg. Set aside.

In a 2-quart mixing bowl beat the egg whites and cream of tartar until stiff peaks form. Gently fold the egg whites into nut mixture.

Pour the mixture into a 1- to 1½-quart soufflé dish. Sprinkle the top with the remaining ¼ cup pecans. Cut a 26-inch piece of wax paper. Fold the paper in half lengthwise and wrap around the top of the soufflé dish to form a collar. Secure with tape and attach to the dish with the tape. Cook on DEFROST for 18 to 23 minutes, or until the top is dry, rotating once or twice as needed. (The soufflé will rise very high while cooking and will fall just a little when removed from the oven.)

Reheat the bourbon-praline sauce on HIGH for 1 minute; stir. Serve with the soufflé.

16

CANDIES AND CONFECTIONS

To me, saltwater taffy or fudge and the New Jersey shore are inseparable. In the past, my candy samplings had always been as whimsical as a sea breeze, but this particular year I was going to take a more serious approach. I was going to conduct the definitive study on chocolate fudge in my favorite seaside town.

Armed with a map of all the fudge shops in town (there were five), a camera, and a note pad, I set out to locate the best fudge and determine the qualities that made it so. As my study progressed, I found myself determining just by store appearances what shops would probably offer the best fudge. If the inside was so white and clinical that it looked as if a drop of hot fudge had never hit the floor, had it? And did it really make its fudge on the premises? Could any store that touted parrot green pistachio and pink fuschia strawberry fudge really be serious in its endeavors? And would an owner who insisted I buy a whole pound of fudge when all I wanted was a few pieces be more interested in quality or quantity?

At last I stopped at a shop that looked promising from the outset. It was a red brick building that had been there for thirty years. The owner (and candy maker) made only fudge, and supposedly changed his recipe daily to accommodate the humidity and weather. Rumor had it that his lawyers were begging him to pass the recipe on to his children, for there was not a copy written down anywhere.

Those who waited on me were both cordial and related to the owner. They cut pieces of fudge for me from pans right in front of my eyes rather than from pans unseen in a back kitchen. Their most daring flavors were peanut butter and maple, and they never encouraged me to buy more than I wanted. My initial impressions proved true as I sunk my teeth into the densest, richest, smoothest, creamiest, most chocolatey piece of fudge I had ever tasted.

Our intent is not to compete with a candy maker of thirty years, although we think the results compare quite favorably. The treats in this chapter are designed to aid you during those times of the year when you want to bring out candy for a housewarming gift, for the holidays, at a PTA dinner, or when the kids need an activity on a rainy day.

Our fudge recipe is as buttery, or more so, than any homemade recipe you'll find, but you'll be able to produce it in half the time and with one-quarter of the mess. A number of our candies have real "kid appeal," not only in taste but in the ease with which they're made. You don't need to worry about even the youngest when there is no open flame or burner to cook over.

Candy making is not an everyday occurrence, and for that reason some of us might not feel as confident or proficient at it. But for those times when candy is called for, the microwave can make it as effortless an endeavor as if you did it every day.

—MARCIA

Sugar Candy Basics:

1. Candy is cooked in a 3- to 4-quart casserole that should be at least twice as high as the basic mixture to prevent boilover.
2. Candy is cooked uncovered so that moisture will evaporate. Some steam does remain in the dish, which will help melt those crystals on the sides of the dish during cooking.
3. Stirring the mixture well, before cooking, is important to blend well and scrape as many of the sugar crystals from the sides of the dish as possible.
4. Stir only once before the candy reaches the hard-crack stage, and not afterwards, or the sugar crystals will make the candy grainy. Be careful to use a clean spoon (and candy thermometer; see below) so as not to carelessly introduce sugar crystals into the mixture. We recommend a wooden spoon.
5. Sugar–corn syrup mixtures are cooked on HIGH power throughout the recipe.
6. A regular candy thermometer is used outside of the oven, and will take 2 minutes to register accurately. For an accurate reading, don't let the thermometer touch the bottom of the dish. A microwave candy thermometer that can be left in the dish during cooking is fine, if you can find it in the store.
7. Stir in flavorings and other ingredients at the end of cooking, after the bubbling has stopped, to prevent splattering and the possibility of skin burns.
8. *Doneness: Hard-crack:* Candy has reached the hard-crack stage when it is a medium-golden beige, and a small drop of hot candy placed in ice water will separate into threads, which will become brittle and crack when pulled out.

    Measure the temperature at the shortest cooking time given for each recipe, using a conventional candy thermometer, *outside of the oven*. It will register 290°F, which is lower than conventional hard-crack temperatures, but the temperature will continue to rise rapidly even after the 290°F is reached. Only a microwave candy thermometer can be left in the oven during cooking.

    Soft-crack: Candy has reached the soft-crack stage when it is a very light golden color and a few drops of the hot syrup placed into ice water separate into threads which, when removed, will bend and not crack.

    Measure the temperature after the shortest cooking time given for each recipe, using a conventional candy thermometer *outside of the microwave oven*. It will register 270°F, which is lower than conventional soft-crack temperatures, but the temperature will continue to rise rapidly even after 270°F is reached. Only a microwave candy thermometer can be left in the oven during cooking, but they are not always available in the store.

☀ BASIC HARD CANDY

MAKES ABOUT 2 POUNDS   BEGIN ABOUT 1 HOUR BEFORE SERVING
COOKING TIME: 20 TO 27 MINUTES

When Thelma first started teaching home economics, she and her students would make candy apples to raise money for charity. Even a good cause can be sticky business. She often found the last traces of hardened candy on saucepots, range burners, and tops days after the cooking session was over. We recommend this much neater microwave method.

3 cups sugar	1 teaspoon flavoring oil (see Note)
1 cup light corn syrup	Food coloring (optional)
¾ cup warm water	

Lightly butter or grease 1 cookie sheet.

In a 3-quart casserole combine the sugar, corn syrup, and water. (Warm water speeds up cooking and helps to melt the remainder of residue corn syrup from the measuring cup.) Stir well. Cook on HIGH for 8 to 12 minutes, or until boiling; stir. Cook on HIGH for 12 to 15 minutes more, or until the mixture reaches 290°F, almost hard-crack stage; check after 7 minutes into the second cooking stage. Let stand until all bubbling has ceased. Stir in the flavoring and coloring.

Pour onto the buttered cookie sheet. Cool and break into pieces. Store in airtight containers.

NOTE: Flavoring oil is found in candy-making stores or pharmacies and is stronger than the vanilla-types in grocery stores.

VARIATIONS:

Snipped Candy Pieces: Before cooking, place 1 cup confectioners' sugar in a small brown paper bag. Cool the candy enough to handle, and snip into 1-inch pieces. Shake the pieces in the bag with sugar. This is nice for the holidays, when a few flavors are made and packaged in glass containers.

Spiral Candy: Cool the candy enough to handle, and cut into 3- × -1-inch pieces. Work quickly, twisting each piece into a spiral. The kids love to help on this one.

Lollipops: Pour the hot candy into lollipop molds, or make round circles by spooning 2-tablespoon dollops onto 2 buttered or greased baking sheets, with enough space between dollops to insert sticks. Insert sticks into the center of each candy. Another method is to roll the candy into balls when the mixture begins to cool. Insert a stick into the middle of each and let harden.

Candy Apples: While the candy is cooking, wash 15 to 20 medium apples. Remove the stems, dry well, and insert wooden tongue depressor–type sticks into the stem ends, testing to see that they hold securely.

Add red food coloring to the candy mixture with the flavoring. Tilt the bowl with the hot candy and, working quickly, twirl each apple to coat. Place on a buttered cookie sheet until hardened. (If the mixture begins to harden before all are coated, reheat on HIGH for 1 to 2 minutes.) Pour any extra candy mixture onto a buttered sheet and allow to harden. Break into pieces. These special treats at friends' houses always made Halloween so special.

NUT BRITTLE

MAKES ABOUT 2 POUNDS   BEGIN 40 MINUTES BEFORE SERVING
COOKING TIME: 8 TO 12 MINUTES

This basic brittle is so simple to make that it will come in handy if you need a gift in a hurry and don't have time to run out to the store.

- 2 cups sugar
- ½ cup light corn syrup
- 3 tablespoons warm water
- 2 tablespoons unsalted butter
- 1 teaspoon vanilla
- 2 cups roasted peanuts
- 1 teaspoon baking soda

Lightly butter or grease a cookie sheet.

In a 3-quart casserole combine the sugar, corn syrup, and water, stirring well to mix. Cook on HIGH for 4 to 6 minutes, or until boiling; stir. Cook on HIGH for 4 to 6 minutes more, or until the syrup reaches 290°F, or the beginning of the hard-crack stage.

When bubbling stops, stir in butter, vanilla, and nuts; blend well. Stir in the baking soda (this will make a light, airy brittle). Pour immediately onto the lightly greased cookie sheet. Let cool for about 30 minutes and break into pieces. Store in an airtight container.

VARIATION:

Variety Brittle: Substitute pecans, cashews, almonds, walnuts, or sunflower seeds for the peanuts.

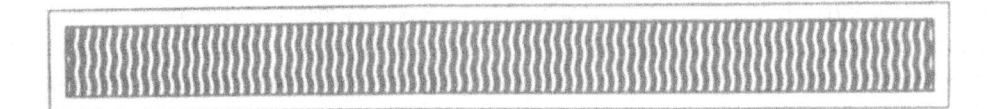

ALMOND CRUNCH

MAKES ABOUT 1 POUND   BEGIN 30 TO 45 MINUTES BEFORE SERVING
COOKING TIME: 7 TO 19 MINUTES

This makes a good ice cream topping if broken up, after hardening, with a food processor or even a wooden rolling pin.

1 cup sugar	½ cup unsalted butter
3 tablespoons warm water	½ cup chopped roasted almonds

Lightly butter or grease a foil-lined 8-inch square pan. Set aside.

In a 3-quart casserole combine the sugar and water; stir well. Add the butter. Cook on HIGH for 3 to 4 minutes, or until boiling; stir. Cook on HIGH for 4 to 5 minutes, or until the mixture almost reaches the hard-crack stage, or 290°F. When bubbling stops, stir in the nuts. Pour into the lightly buttered pan. Cool and break into pieces.

VARIATIONS:

Chocolate-Topped Almond Crunch: After the crunch has been poured into the dish, sprinkle ½ cup semisweet chocolate pieces evenly over the top. Let stand for 5 minutes; in this time the chocolate will soften. Spread the chocolate evenly with a spatula. Sprinkle ¼ cup finely chopped nuts on top, if desired.

Nut Crunch: Substitute chopped walnuts, cashews, pecans, pine nuts, or sunflower seeds for the almonds.

☀ FROSTED NUTS

MAKES ABOUT 1 CUP   BEGIN 10 MINUTES BEFORE SERVING
COOKING TIME: 4 TO 6 MINUTES

These crispy nuts are good to make with a leftover egg white. They are nice served with a fruit and cheese plate, or as a garnish to dessert.

2 tablespoons butter	½ cup sugar
1 egg white	1 cup unsalted nuts

Place the butter in a 2-quart rectangular microwave dish. Cook on HIGH for 30 seconds to 1 minute, or until the butter is melted.

Beat the egg white until stiff. Stir in the sugar. Stir in the nuts to coat evenly. Stir the nut mixture into the melted butter. Cook on HIGH for

3 to 5 minutes, or until the nuts develop a white glaze, stirring once halfway through cooking. Let cool.

Spiced Frosted Nuts: Add ½ teaspoon ground cinnamon or ¼ teaspoon grated nutmeg to the egg white with the sugar.

CARAMEL CORN

MAKES ABOUT 8 CUPS BEGIN 30 MINUTES BEFORE SERVING
COOKING TIME: 6 TO 10 MINUTES

This brings back memories of youthful shopping trips, where caramel corn was sold next to the bus station in Waterbury, Connecticut. The smell of the freshly popped corn and warm candy was always too good to pass up without making a purchase.

6 to 8 cups Popcorn (page 106)
1 cup brown sugar
¼ cup warm water
¼ cup light corn syrup
2 tablespoons unsalted butter
1 teaspoon vanilla

Line a cookie sheet with foil. Pour the popcorn into a large heatproof bowl.

In a 3-quart casserole combine the brown sugar, water, corn syrup, and butter; stir well. Cook on HIGH for 2 to 4 minutes, or until boiling; stir well. Cook on HIGH for 4 to 6 minutes more, until the mixture reaches 270°F, or almost soft-crack stage. When bubbling stops, stir in the vanilla.

Pour the candy mixture over the popcorn quickly, stirring well to coat the corn evenly. Pour out onto the lined cookie sheet, pulling the candied corn apart into bite-size pieces with 2 forks.

VARIATION:

Caramel Corn with Nuts: Stir 2 cups toasted nuts into the popcorn in the bowl.

Fudge Basics:

1. Fudge is cooked in a 3- to 4-quart casserole that should be at least twice as high as the basic mixture to prevent boilover.
2. Fudge is cooked uncovered so that moisture will evaporate. Some steam does remain in the dish, which will help melt those crystals on the sides of the dish during cooking.
3. Stirring the mixture well before cooking is important, to blend well and scrape as many of the sugar crystals from the sides of the dish as possible.

4. Stir only once before the fudge reaches the soft-ball stage, and not afterwards, or the sugar crystals will make the fudge grainy. Be careful to use a clean spoon to prevent careless introduction of sugar crystals into the mixture. We recommend a wooden spoon.
5. Fudge mixtures are first brought to a boil on HIGH and then reduced to MEDIUM to control the consistency and texture.
6. A candy thermometer (also clean) is inserted into the mixture outside of the oven, and will take 2 minutes to register accurately. For an accurate reading, don't let the thermometer touch the bottom of the dish. A microwave candy thermometer that can be left in the dish during cooking is fine, if you can find it in the store.
7. Let the mixture cool to lukewarm (110°F) before adding flavoring; cooling can be speeded by placing the dish in a larger pan of cold water.
8. If the fudge hardens too quickly before you have a chance to spread it in the pan, add 1 to 2 tablespoons cream and continue to beat.
9. *Doneness:* Fudge has reached the soft-ball stage when a drop of the hot mixture in ice-cold water will form a soft ball that does not disintegrate, but flattens under the pressure of your fingers.

Measure the temperature after the shortest cooking time given in the recipes, using a conventional candy thermometer *outside of the oven*. Don't allow the thermometer to touch the bottom of the dish. It should register 234°F, and will continue to rise even after cooking has stopped. Only a microwave candy thermometer can be left in the oven during cooking.

The fudge may appear curdled in appearance at this point, with the butter layer swimming on top of the cream layer below. This will become smooth and creamy upon beating.

Underdone: Taking the temperature will require a good 2 minutes for the mercury to rise. That is why we gauge our temperatures slightly lower than conventional soft-ball stage temperatures, so that you err on the side of undercooking.

If the fudge cools to be too thin for cutting into squares, make the peanut butter variation, or stir in ¼ to ½ cup marshmallow cream, or 2 tablespoons confectioners' sugar, to thicken.

Too Grainy: Make the peanut butter variation, or stir in ½ cup marshmallow cream to mask the graininess.

Overdone: If the temperature has risen too fast, stir in ¼ cup cream to cool down.

✺ CHOCOLATE FUDGE

MAKES ABOUT 1¼ POUNDS   BEGIN ABOUT 1 HOUR BEFORE SERVING
COOKING TIME: 17 TO 23 MINUTES

The secret to a smooth, creamy fudge is to cook the mixture to the proper temperature and then beat it well when it has cooled to lukewarm. After you have made a few batches, it will seem very simple.

2 cups sugar	⅔ cup half and half
½ cup unsweetened cocoa powder (Droste or Hershey's)	¼ pound unsalted butter
	½ cup chopped nuts (optional)

In a 4-quart casserole combine the sugar, cocoa, and half and half, stirring well to blend. Add the butter. Cook on HIGH for 5 to 8 minutes, or until the butter melts and the mixture boils and the bubbles cover the entire surface, stirring well once to dissolve the sugar. (Do not stir after this point, to prevent graininess.) Cook on MEDIUM for 12 to 15 minutes to the soft-ball stage or to 234°F. The light golden mixture will appear curdled at this point, but it will become beautifully smooth during beating.

Let the mixture cool to lukewarm, 110°F, until you can hold the bottom of the dish (after about 10 minutes). Beat by hand or with a mixer until the fudge thickens and loses some of its sheen. Add the nuts. Spread quickly in an 8-inch square pan. If the fudge hardens too quickly before you have a chance to spread it out, add 1 to 2 tablespoons of cream and continue to beat. Cool and cut into squares.

VARIATIONS:

Vanilla Fudge: Eliminate the unsweetened cocoa powder and add 1 tablespoon vanilla after the mixture has cooled before adding the nuts.

Peanut Butter Fudge: Add ½ cup peanut butter and ½ cup marshmallow cream (sold in supermarkets) with the vanilla. The marshmallow cream will help prevent graininess and makes a lighter, fluffier fudge.

Coffee Fudge: Add 2 tablespoons instant coffee with the sugar.

NO-FAIL FUDGE

MAKES ABOUT 1¼ POUNDS   BEGIN 15 TO 30 MINUTES BEFORE SERVING
COOKING TIME: 2 TO 4 MINUTES

This fudge does not compare in flavor and texture to our first fudge, but it has the advantage of being fast and will not become grainy. It is a good first fudge for kids to make.

1 16-ounce box confectioners' sugar (3⅔ cups)	½ cup unsweetened butter or margarine
½ cup unsweetened cocoa powder	1 tablespoon vanilla
¼ cup light cream or milk	

Lightly butter or grease an 8-inch square pan.

Sift the sugar and cocoa together, and place in a 3-quart casserole. Add the cream or milk and butter or margarine. Cook on HIGH for 2 to 4 minutes, or until the butter is melted, stirring once. Add the vanilla; mix well to blend. Spread in the buttered pan. Cool and cut into squares.

VARIATIONS:

No-Fail Peanut Butter–Chocolate Fudge: Add 1 cup chunky peanut butter with the butter or margarine.

No-Fail Chocolate-Nut Fudge: Add ½ cup chopped nuts with the butter or margarine.

No-Fail Chocolate-Marshmallow Fudge: Add 1 cup miniature marshmallows with the butter or margarine.

No-Fail Chocolate-Cream Fudge: Add 1 cup marshmallow cream (sold in supermarkets) with the butter or margarine.

Chocolate Melting Basics:

1. Never use imitation chocolate, which will not melt properly.
2. When possible, chocolate that is melted alone, should be in small pieces and arranged in a ring in a round dish or casserole. This will create an inner surface area for the quickest and most even melting.
3. If chocolate is melted alone, it should be melted on MEDIUM power rather than HIGH, because it is easier to watch and regulate melting so that overcooking doesn't occur. If ingredients such as cream or butter are added to the chocolate as it melts, it can be safely melted on HIGH power. The added ingredients seem to act as a cushion in absorbing some of the heat.
4. Chocolate is melted uncovered, so that no extra moisture is retained, which will cause white streaking. Be careful, also, that your cooking dish is dry so as not to introduce any other moisture.
5. Stirring two to three times during melting not only equalizes between the hotter temperatures on the outside and cooler ones on the inside, but helps you to gauge doneness. If left alone, chocolate will melt without losing its shape, so appearances can be very deceiving.
6. No standing time is necessary.
7. *Doneness:* The only way to test melted chocolate is to stir it and sense the texture. By first appearances, it may look as if the glistening pieces are holding their shape and not melting. Stirring will reveal a completely smooth, shiny paste, and you know you have arrived.

   Underdone: If when stirred there still remain some shiny chocolate pieces that won't form a smooth paste, add 30 seconds more on MEDIUM power and stir.

   Overdone: If when you stir the chocolate you have a smooth paste with some dry, hard, nonshiny pieces of chocolate, you know you have gone too far and scorched some of the chocolate. Throw it out and start over.

CHOCOLATE BARK

MAKES ABOUT 1¼ POUNDS   BEGIN ABOUT 35 MINUTES TO 1 HOUR BEFORE SERVING
COOKING TIME: 3 TO 4 MINUTES

1 cup toasted almonds or other nuts of your choice	1 pound semisweet, milk, or white chocolate pieces

Line a cookie sheet with wax paper. Sprinkle the almonds evenly over the wax paper.

Place the chocolate pieces in a circle in a 1-quart casserole, leaving the center open. Cook on MEDIUM for 2 minutes; stir. Cook on MEDIUM for 1 to 2 minutes more, or until the chocolate is melted, stirring every 30 seconds.

Pour the melted chocolate over the almonds. Spread into a thin layer, making a barklike design. Refrigerate for 1 hour to harden, or freeze 30 minutes, then break into pieces.

VARIATION:

Marbled Chocolate Bark: Use 1 pound semisweet chocolate. After spooning over the nuts, place ½ pound broken white chocolate in the same casserole. Cook on MEDIUM for 1½ minutes; stir. Cook on MEDIUM for 30 seconds to 1½ minutes more, or until melted. Spoon the white chocolate in rows over the dark chocolate. With a knife, cut through the 2 chocolates every inch or so to make a marbled design. Chill to harden.

CHOCOLATE TRIANGLES

MAKES 32   BEGIN 20 TO 25 MINUTES BEFORE SERVING
COOKING TIME: 3 TO 5 MINUTES

These chocolate triangles, or the rectangle variation, may be used for decorating cakes, pies, or ice cream. They are easy to make and impressive to look at.

6 ounces semisweet chocolate pieces

Place a sheet of wax paper on a cookie sheet and, using a cake plate as a guide, take a knife and draw two 8-inch circles.

Arrange the chocolate pieces in a circle around the outer rim of a microwaveproof cereal bowl, leaving the center free. Cook on MEDIUM for 3 to 5 minutes, or until the chocolate is melted and shiny, stirring after 2½ minutes to check doneness.

Pour the chocolate inside the 2 wax paper circles, dividing evenly between them. With a knife, spread the chocolate evenly to the circle outline. (A serrated knife will give an interesting design, if desired.) When the chocolate has started to cool, after 15 minutes, score each circle in half. Then, beginning in the center, score each half in half again, until there are 16 wedges, with the wax paper clearly shown below each score. (Cutting from the center will make the delicate points easier to break apart later, but see Note below.) Let the chocolate harden; this can be speeded up in freezer for 15 minutes. Peel the wax paper from the hardened chocolate and break into wedges. Decorate cakes, pies, and ice cream with the wedges. Store in the freezer in warm weather, or between wax paper in a tin.

NOTE: If the chocolate points break, they can easily be remelted by placing the wax paper in the microwave. Cook on MEDIUM for 2 to 4 minutes, or until softened. Respread the chocolate into a smooth circle with a knife. Cool slightly and cut new wedges. Cool and harden again.

VARIATION:

Chocolate Rectangles: These are called for in decorating the Two-Tiered Chocolate Mousse Cake (page 580). Instead of drawing two 8-inch circles on the wax paper, draw one 6- x -12-inch rectangle. Melt the chocolate and spread inside to fill the rectangle. After standing for 15 minutes, score the rectangle in half lengthwise. In 1-inch intervals, make 12 scores perpendicular to this. You will end up with 24 1- x -3-inch rectangles. Freeze until needed.

CHOCOLATE CURLS

MAKES 16   BEGIN ABOUT 30 MINUTES BEFORE SERVING
COOKING TIME: ABOUT 4 MINUTES

Chocolate curls add a finished professional touch to desserts, and if the chocolate is pliable enough and rolled to 1/16-inch thickness, they aren't that difficult to fashion.

We recommend that you make them on a dry, cool day, because humidity can cause the chocolate to become sticky and difficult to handle. The chocolate curls can be kept indefinitely in the refrigerator or freezer, but will become cloudy after a few hours at room temperature.

3 ounces semisweet chocolate bits or coarsely chopped squares or bars

Arrange the chocolate pieces in a circle around the outside of a microwaveproof cereal bowl. Cook on MEDIUM for 2 minutes; stir. Continue to cook on MEDIUM for 30-second intervals until the chocolate is melted, stirring each time.

Meanwhile, cut two 12-inch pieces of wax paper and place one piece on the counter. Pour the melted chocolate onto the center of the wax paper. Place the second sheet of wax paper on top of the chocolate and, using even pressure with a rolling pin, roll the chocolate to 1/16-inch thickness, making a 10-inch square of chocolate. Place the chocolate and both sheets of wax paper on a cookie sheet and freeze for 10 minutes until hard.

Remove the sheet from the freezer and discard the top sheet of wax paper. Remove the chocolate and bottom paper from the cookie sheet and place the chocolate in the microwave. Heat on DEFROST for 15 seconds.

Trim the chocolate square so that it is even on the sides, and cut it into approximately 1½- × -2-inch strips. Place the handle of a wooden spoon, that is about ⅜ inch in diameter, at the shorter end of each chocolate strip and loosely roll the chocolate around the handle. Don't worry if the curls break a little bit.

Place the curls back on the cookie sheet and freeze them until firm. You will also have some loose chocolate strips that you can scatter around with the curls for decoration. If not using the curls right away, store them in a moistureproof container in the freezer or refrigerator.

☀ CHOCOLATE-COVERED STRAWBERRIES

MAKES ABOUT 24   BEGIN ABOUT 40 MINUTES BEFORE SERVING
COOKING TIME: 3 MINUTES

Serve these strawberries separately as a dessert, or as a garnish on cakes, custards, or puddings.

---

6 ounces semisweet chocolate pieces
2 tablespoons unsalted butter

1 pint strawberries, with hulls intact, washed and dried

Line a cookie sheet with wax paper.

Place the chocolate in a circle in a 1-quart microwaveproof bowl, adding the butter to the center; the butter will make the chocolate shiny. Cook on MEDIUM for 2 minutes; stir. Cook on MEDIUM for 30 seconds to 1 minute more, stirring every 30 seconds until melted and smooth.

Using the hull as a handle, partially dip the strawberries, twirling in chocolate. As much as possible, place hull side down on a wax paper–lined sheet. Refrigerate for 30 minutes to harden.

VARIATIONS:

Chocolate-Covered Cherries and Grapes: Substitute cherries or seedless grapes, with stems, for the strawberries.

Chocolate-Covered Oranges: Substitute orange segments, well dried, from 2 navel oranges for the strawberries, coating half of each segment.

Frozen Chocolate-Covered Banana Pieces: Eliminate the strawberries. Cut 2 to 3 bananas into eighteen to twenty-four 1-inch pieces, and place on a wax paper–lined cookie sheet. Insert a heavy-duty toothpick into each piece. Freeze the bananas for about 1 hour, or until frozen solid. Melt the chocolate and dip the frozen banana pieces in it. You may wish to roll the chocolate-dipped banana pieces in ¼ cup finely chopped nuts. Place the bananas back onto the cookie sheet; refreeze until the chocolate is hardened, about 30 minutes.

Blueberry Chocolate Cups: Eliminate the strawberries. Set out 24 miniature cupcake liners. Spoon the melted chocolate into the cupcake liners and press 4 blueberries into the chocolate cup. Set aside to harden.

Chocolate-Coated Pretzels and Cookies: Eliminate the strawberries. Dip 24 pretzels or cookies in the chocolate to coat partially. Place on a wax paper-lined cookie sheet to harden. Dip the chocolate-coated cookie tips into ¼ cup finely chopped nuts before setting aside to harden.

White or Pastel-Coated Fruits: Substitute white or pastel-colored chocolate pieces for semisweet chocolate. Eliminate butter. Follow basic recipe.

CHOCOLATE CRISPY CLUSTERS

MAKES 24   BEGIN 40 MINUTES BEFORE SERVING
COOKING TIME: 3 TO 4 MINUTES

This is probably one of the easiest candies to make. Depending on your tastes, a variety of additions give these candies an individual touch.

6 ounces semisweet chocolate pieces	2 cups Rice Krispies

Line a cookie sheet with wax paper.

Place the chocolate pieces in a circle in a 1-quart casserole, leaving the center open. Cook on MEDIUM for 2 minutes; stir. Cook on MEDIUM for 30 seconds to 1½ minutes more, stirring every 30 seconds. Stir in the cereal and mix well to coat. Spoon rounded teaspoonfuls onto the wax paper. Refrigerate to harden.

VARIATIONS:

White Chocolate Clusters: Substitute white chocolate for the semisweet chocolate.

Chocolate Crunchy Clusters: Substitute cornflakes or any crunchy cereal for the Rice Krispies.

Chocolate–Peanut Butter Clusters: Stir ½ cup peanut butter into the melted chocolate; stir well to melt. Substitute cornflakes for the Rice Krispies. This was Marcia's grandmother's specialty and we loved it.

Chocolate Noodle Clusters: Substitute crispy Chinese-style noodles for the Rice Krispies.

Chocolate Coconut Clusters: Substitute shredded coconut for the Rice Krispies.

Chocolate Nut Clusters: Substitute coarsely chopped nuts for the Rice Krispies.

Chocolate Raisin Clusters: Substitute raisins for the Rice Krispies or a cereal with raisins in it.

Chocolate Raisin-Nut Clusters: Substitute 1 cup raisins and 1 cup coarsely chopped nuts for the Rice Krispies.

Chocolate Pretzel Clusters: Substitute 2 cups broken pretzel sticks for the Rice Krispies.

☼ CHOCOLATE TRUFFLES

MAKES 24   BEGIN ABOUT 1 HOUR BEFORE SERVING
COOKING TIME: 3 TO 4 MINUTES

The nice thing about truffles is that one little bite makes a heavenly and satisfying dessert.

- 6 ounces semisweet chocolate pieces
- 2 tablespoons heavy cream
- 4 tablespoons butter, cut into 8 pieces
- 2 tablespoons vanilla
- 2 tablespoons sifted unsweetened cocoa powder

Place the chocolate pieces in a circle in a 1-quart microwaveproof bowl, leaving the center open. Pour the cream over the chocolate. Cook on MEDIUM for 2 minutes; stir. Cook on MEDIUM for 30 seconds to 1½ minutes more, or until melted, stirring every 30 seconds. Stir the butter into the chocolate until it melts. Stir in the vanilla. Place the bowl in the refrigerator for about 35 to 45 minutes, or until the mixture is stiff enough to roll into balls.

Line a cookie sheet with wax paper. Place the cocoa powder in a small dish. Take 1 rounded teaspoon of the chocolate mixture at a time and roll into a rough ball. Roll in the cocoa and place on the wax paper. Chill to harden. Store in a tightly sealed container in the refrigerator.

VARIATIONS:

Almond Truffles: Add ½ cup finely chopped almonds to the melted chocolate after the butter has been stirred in. Substitute almond-flavored liqueur or rum for the vanilla. Roll each teaspoon of chocolate mixture around a whole almond, if desired, using the almond to give it an oval shape.

Coffee Truffles: Substitute 2 tablespoons coffee-flavored liqueur for the vanilla. Roll each teaspoon of chocolate mixture around a coffee bean.

Chocolate-Orange Truffles: Substitute 2 tablespoons orange-flavored liqueur for the vanilla.

PEANUT BUTTER–CHOCOLATE SQUARES

MAKES ABOUT 1 POUND   BEGIN 30 MINUTES BEFORE SERVING
COOKING TIME: 4 TO 6 MINUTES

If you are a peanut butter lover, these will hit the spot. A favorite with kids and adults alike.

½ cup brown sugar
5 tablespoons unsalted butter or margarine
1 cup chunky peanut butter
½ cup graham cracker crumbs
6 ounces semisweet chocolate pieces

Lightly butter or grease an 8-inch square dish.

In a 1-quart casserole combine the brown sugar and 4 tablespoons butter or margarine. Cook on HIGH for 1½ to 3 minutes, or until the butter is melted. Stir in the peanut butter and graham cracker crumbs; mix well. Spread the mixture evenly into the greased dish.

In the same 1-quart casserole combine the chocolate pieces and remaining 1 tablespoon butter. Cook on MEDIUM for 2 minutes; stir. Cook on MEDIUM at 30-second intervals, or until the chocolate is melted, stirring each time. Spread the melted chocolate evenly over the peanut butter layer. Chill and cut into squares.

VARIATION:

Double Peanut-Chocolate Squares: Add ½ cup coarsely chopped unsalted nuts with the peanut butter. This is our favorite version.

EASY CARAMEL TURTLES

MAKES ABOUT 24　　BEGIN ABOUT 1¼ HOURS BEFORE SERVING
COOKING TIME: 2 MINUTES

1 cup nut halves (about 48)
½ pound caramels
1 tablespoon heavy cream

Position 2 nut halves end to end on a wax paper–lined cookie sheet. Place the other pairs in the same fashion, 1 inch apart from each other.

In a 1-quart casserole combine the caramels and cream. Cook on HIGH for 1 minute; stir. Cook on HIGH for 30 seconds to 1 minute more, or until the caramels are melted; stir. Let stand for 5 minutes, or until the mixture stiffens a little. Spoon a teaspoonful of the caramel mixture on top of each nut pair. Chill to harden, about 1 hour.

VARIATION:

Chocolate-Covered Turtles: Follow basic recipe before chilling, then place 6 ounces of chocolate pieces in a circle in a microwave-proof cereal bowl, leaving the center open. Cook on MEDIUM for 2 minutes; stir. Cook for 30 seconds to 1½ minutes more, or until the chocolate is melted, stirring once. Spoon on top of the turtles to cover the caramel, leaving the nut "feet" showing. Chill to harden for 1 hour.

CARAMEL APPLES

MAKES 5 OR 6 BEGIN 1¼ HOURS BEFORE SERVING
COOKING TIME: 2 TO 3 MINUTES

5 or 6 medium apples 1 pound light caramels	1 tablespoon water

Wash the apples well and dry. Insert a skewer firmly into the stem end of each apple, checking to see that the apple is secure. Line a cookie sheet with wax paper.

In a 2-quart casserole combine the caramels and water. Cook on HIGH for 1 minute; stir. Cook on HIGH for 1 to 2 minutes more, or until the caramels are melted; stir. Let stand for 1 minute to cool slightly. Tilt the bowl a bit and dip the apples into the caramel, then place on the wax paper–lined sheet. Chill to harden, about 1 hour.

☼ MARSHMALLOW CEREAL SQUARES

MAKES 24 TO 30 BEGIN 15 MINUTES BEFORE SERVING
COOKING TIME: 2 TO 3 MINUTES

¼ cup unsalted butter or margarine 10 ounces (about 40) large marshmallows, or 5 cups miniature	5 cups Rice Krispies or other crunchy cereal

In a 2-quart rectangular baking dish combine the butter or margarine and marshmallows. Cook on HIGH for 1 minute; stir, to prevent any one spot from getting too hot. Cook on HIGH for 1 to 2 minutes more, or until the butter is melted and the marshmallows have puffed evenly all over; stir until smooth.

Stir in the cereal until it is evenly coated with the marshmallow mixture. Press evenly into the dish. Cool until set. Cut into squares.

VARIATIONS:

Marshmallow Raisin Cereal Squares: Stir in 1 cup raisins with the cereal.

Marshmallow Sunflower Cereal Squares: Stir in ½ cup sunflower seeds with the cereal.

Marshmallow Chocolate Chip Cereal Squares: Stir in 1 cup mini-semisweet chocolate pieces with the cereal.

17

MEAL PLANNING

In deciding what foods to cook when, ask yourself these questions:

1. Are you having dessert?
   - Is it something that needs to be chilled or benefits from standing or marinating? Cook that first.
   - Is it something that you want to serve warm? Cook it while you're eating your main course or clearing the table.

2. Are there any vegetables or appetizers to be chilled?
   - Make them earlier in the day.

3. If you are serving a main dish, vegetable, and potato or rice, which has the longest standing time?
   - *In most cases, the recipe having the longest standing time will be cooked first.* While this recipe cooks, you can be chopping or making preparations for the other dishes. If necessary, reheat the first recipe right before serving.
   - If the recipe with the longer standing time has a two-step cooking process (mashed potatoes, stuffed potatoes, or pureed vegetables that are cooked first and then reheated), another recipe can be cooked in between the first cooking step and final reheating.
   - Choose a fish and vegetable, or chicken and vegetable platter, where two foods cook together. If serving rice or potatoes, cook them first, because they have the longer standing time.

4. Do two foods that you are cooking have equally long standing times?
   - Do the recipe that will continue to develop flavor as it stands first. Examples are stews, chilies, soups, or bean dishes. The standing time indicated on the recipe is the time that the food needs to completely cook through. Any additional standing time on these recipes will only serve to blend and meld flavors.

Here are some examples of menus, numbered in the order that they should be cooked:

1
SPICY POACHED PEARS
2
BEEF POT ROAST WITH
3
BOILED POTATO SLICES AND BRAISED GREEN BEANS

1
BROCCOLI WITH CHILLED VINAIGRETTE
2
POACHED WINTER FRUITS
3
SHERRIED ROOT PUREE
4
GLAZED PORK BUTT

1
CUMIN SALSA
2
MOM'S GROUND BEEF CHILI AND
3
LONG-GRAIN RICE

1
BAKED POTATO
2
STEAK AU POIVRE
3
ASPARAGUS WITH FINES HERBS

1
CLAMS CASINO
1
WOK-STYLE VEGETABLES OVER PASTA

1
FRESH HOT TOMATO SOUP
2
BASMATI RICE WITH ALMONDS
3
STEAMED BONELESS CHICKEN BREASTS WITH VEGETABLES

1
PESTO-COATED RICOTTA CHEESE TIMBALES
2
THIN FISH FILLETS AU CITRON
3
SEASONAL VEGETABLE PLATTER WITH HERB BUTTER

1
CRANBERRY SAUCE WITH RASPBERRY VINEGAR
2
TURNIP PUREE (ROOT VEGETABLE PUREE)
3
CRISPY DUCK WITH GREEN PEPPERCORN SAUCE
4
CANDIED ACORN SQUASH

18

TIPS

Here's a collection of thirty-six additional ways to make your life easier and make your microwave indispensable.

Brandy, flamed: Pour ¼ cup 80-proof alcohol in a glass measure. Heat on HIGH for 10 to 15 seconds. Quickly pour into a large metal or glass ladle and ignite. Pour, flaming, over cooked cake or fruit. If no ladle, pour on the food and then ignite, but know that additional liquid in the fruit may dilute the flame.

Bread cubes, dried: Place 4 cups bread cubes in a rectangular dish. Heat on HIGH for 6 to 7 minutes, stirring once.

Brown sugar, softened: Place brown sugar in a glass dish. Add 1 slice of soft white bread or apple wedge. Cover tightly and heat on HIGH for 30 to 40 seconds. Let stand for 30 seconds; stir.

Butter, softened: Place 1 stick (¼ cup) in its non-foil wrapper on a microwaveproof plate. Heat on DEFROST for 30 to 40 seconds.

Cheese, to room temperature: Unwrap ½ pound firm or semisoft refrigerated cheese. Place on a microwaveproof plate and heat on MEDIUM for 45 seconds to 1 minute, or until no longer chilled on the surface.

Chocolate squares, melted: Open up paper wrapping and place on a microwaveproof dish. Heat a 1-ounce square on MEDIUM for 1½ to 2½ minutes; 2 1-ounce squares on MEDIUM for 3 to 5 minutes; and 3 1-ounce squares on MEDIUM for 4 to 6 minutes.

Citrus juice, plus: Get more fresh juice by warming 1 lemon, 1 orange, or 1 lime on HIGH for 30 seconds.

Coconut, dried: Place ½ cup freshly grated coconut on a microwaveproof plate. Cook on HIGH for 2 to 3 minutes, stirring each minute.

Cream cheese, softened: Remove the cheese from the foil wrapper. Heat 8 ounces on DEFROST for 1½ to 2 minutes.

Crystallized honey, made spreadable: Remove lid, or if the jar is over half full, or the jar is plastic, transfer to a glass measure. Heat on HIGH for 2 to 2½ minutes per cup. Let cool slightly.

Dog or cat food, take chill off: Remove from the can. Heat 3 ounces on HIGH for 15 to 20 seconds.

Finger towels, warmed: Wet 4 to 8 washcloths with water that is scented with cologne or lemon juice. Wring out, fold, or roll and place in a wicker basket with no metal staples. Heat on HIGH for 2 to 3 minutes.

Frozen juice concentrate, thawed: Remove the metal lid from a 10-ounce can. Heat on DEFROST for 2 to 4 minutes.

Ice cream, softened: Place a 1-quart carton of ice cream in the oven on DEFROST for 30 to 40 seconds.

Ice cream topping, heated: Remove the lid from the glass jar. If the sauce fills more than half a jar, spoon into a 2-cup glass measure or serving container to prevent boilover. Heat room temperature sauces on HIGH for 30 to 45 seconds to melt. Heat refrigerated sauces on HIGH for 1 to 2 minutes, stirring once.

Instant coffee, heated: Combine 1 cup tap water and 1 teaspoon instant coffee. Heat on HIGH for 1½ minutes.

Jams and jellies, softened: Refrigerated jellies become spreadable without changing color or texture. Remove the jar lid. Heat on HIGH for 1½ to 2 minutes per cup.

Lemon or orange peel, dried: Grate 1 lemon or orange, or peel into thin strips, making about 2 tablespoons of peel. Spread the peel out on an unrecycled paper towel or paper plate. Heat on HIGH for 2 to 3 minutes, or until dried but not dark, rotating the plate after 2 minutes. Cool and store in a plastic container in the freezer. Yields 1 tablespoon dried peel, which is double the strength of fresh amount when cooking.

Marinate, quickly: Place the marinade in a glass bowl. Heat on HIGH for 1 to 2 minutes per each cup marinade, to warm. Add meat, chicken, or vegetables to the warm marinade. Let stand for at least 30 minutes.

Milk shelf life, extended: Milk ordinarily has a refrigeration shelf life of 7 to 10 days, after which the microorganisms that are naturally present bring about off-flavors. The shelf life can be extended another 10 days by heating the milk in the microwave before the expiration date on the carton. Place the milk, in its carton, in the microwave and heat on HIGH until the temperature reaches 160°F (1 cup milk takes about 1½ to 2 minutes). Refrigerate in the carton to chill quickly. (Developed by Dr. Gertrude Armbruster, Cornell University.)

Natural peanut butter, made spreadable: Refrigerated peanut butter can be softened in the jar. Remove the lid and heat on HIGH for 1½ minutes per cup, stirring once if more than 1 cup.

Nuts, toasted: Spread 1 cup nuts evenly on a paper plate or unrecycled paper towel. Cook on HIGH for 2½ to 4 minutes, or until heated through, stirring every 2 minutes.

Overset gelatin, recovered: Bring back overset gelatin. Heat on MEDIUM for 1 to 2 minutes for 6 ounces gelatin dissolved and only slightly set, stirring twice. Stir in additions and refrigerate to set.

Pancakes, reheated: Wrap 4 medium pancakes in an unrecycled paper towel. Heat on HIGH for 35 seconds to 1½ minutes, or until warm to the touch.

Pancake syrup, reheated: Pour 1 to 2 cups into a glass serving pitcher. Heat on HIGH for 1½ to 2 minutes.

Pecans or walnuts, shelled: Place 2 cups nuts and ¼ cup water in a glass casserole.

Cover tightly and cook on HIGH for 1 to 2 minutes. Drain and dry before shelling.

Pie slice, warmed: Place on a microwaveproof plate. Heat on HIGH for 30 seconds. A scoop of ice cream can be added on top of the pie before heating, too, and it will just soften.

Pizza, frozen, reheated: To achieve a crispy, not soggy bottom, frozen pizza can only be reheated on a browning dish that is preheated in the microwave on HIGH for 4 to 5 minutes. Place 1 to 3 pizza slices on the hot dish and heat on HIGH for 2 to 5 minutes, until the crust is crisp and the cheese is bubbly.

Pizza, slice, reheated: Place 1 room-temperature pizza slice on a paper towel or paper plate in the microwave. Reheat on HIGH for 15 to 25 seconds. For 2 slices, reheat on HIGH for 30 to 40 seconds.

Potato chips and pretzels, refreshed: Put 2 to 3 cups on an unrecycled paper towel placed on a plate or basket without metal staples. Heat on HIGH for 15 to 60 seconds, or until warm to the touch. Let stand for 5 minutes to cool and crisp.

Raisins or dried fruit, plumped for cooking: Place 1 cup raisins or dried fruit in a 4-cup glass measure. Add ½ to 1 cup water, brandy, bourbon, sherry, or vermouth. Bring to a boil on HIGH for 3 to 5 minutes. Let stand, covered, for 30 minutes.

Raisins or dried fruit, softened for eating: Combine 1 cup dried fruit and 1 tablespoon water. Cover tightly and heat on HIGH for 45 seconds, or until softened. Let stand, covered, for 1 minute.

Sesame seeds, toasted: Spread 1 cup seeds on an unrecycled paper towel placed on a microwaveproof plate. Heat on HIGH for 2½ to 4 minutes, or until very hot, toasted brown, and crunchy, but not too dark, rotating the plate once, if necessary.

Tacos, heated: Heat 10 to 12 precooked crisp taco shells on HIGH for 1 to 3 minutes, until warm.

Tomato, peeled: Place 1 ripe tomato in the microwave oven. Heat on HIGH for 15 seconds to loosen peel.

Tortillas, reheated: Wrap 6 to 8 flour tortillas in a dampened paper towel. Heat on HIGH for 1 minute.

INDEX

A

acorn squash:
  apple-stuffed, 472
  candied, 467–68
  cooking chart, 75
  cranberry-stuffed, 471–72
aioli, 175–76
almond(s):
  crunch, 589
  filling, fish fillet rolls with, 221
  long-grain rice with, 197
  picadillo with, 325
  soup, sweet Spanish, 135
  summer squash with, 470
  trout amandine, 233
  truffles, 598
Alsatian cheese ryes, 103
amaretto:
  ice cream pie, 562–63
  mousse, 579
  pastry dough, 541–42
  sauce, 563–64
American potato salad, 456
anchovy:
  and chopped liver spread, 95
  pea pods stuffed with cream cheese and, 99
  tomato sauce, 249
  vinaigrette, 185
appetizers and snacks, 89–113
  brandied shrimp, 113
  breaded warm cheese, 163
  cheese nachos, 103–4
  chile con queso, 104
  chilled steamed mussels with herb sauce, 110
  chopped liver spreads, 94–95
  clams casino, 111
  crab-stuffed mushrooms, 112
  dishes for heating and serving, 110
  egg pinwheels, 93–94
  eggplant dip, 100–101
  flavored pita triangles, 97
  granola, 107
  hot crab dip, 112
  Italian basil, peppers, and onions, 95
  Italian sand dollars with cheddar-onion topping, 96–97
  lightly breaded ham and cheese rollups, 105
  lobster nuggets with caviar, 234
  marinated vegetables, 91–92
  meal planning and, 603
  melted cheese and crackers, 102–3
  mushroom pâté, 98
  new potato appetizers, 101
  Oriental chicken wings, 108–9
  pickled ginger, 99
  pita pizzas, 102
  popcorn, 106–7
  reheating or crisping, 93
  sausage with sweet and sour sauce, 108
  scallop, with golden caviar, 240
  spicy nuts, 100
  stuffed snow pea pods, 98–99
  won tons with scallop stuffing in basil butter, 90–91
  yummy golden barbecued ribs, 109
apple(s):
  acorn squash stuffed with, 472
  baked, 491–92
  bread pudding, apricot-glazed, 570–71
  bread stuffing, 349
  candy, 588
  caramel, 600
  chicken pieces with cider and, 356
  cream sauce, 361
  and fish salad, 226–27
  and mussel salad, chilled, 227
  pizza tart, 551
  poached dried, with Calvados, 494
  slices, brandied, 494–95

apple(s) (*cont.*)
  slices, flambéed, over ice cream, 495
  upside-down gingerbread, 513
  walnut cake with chocolate cream glaze, 514–15
apple pies:
  crumb, 545–46
  crumble, 554–55
  sweet potato, 459
  testimonial double-crust, 546–48
applesauce, 492–93
  bundt cake, 525
apricot(s):
  apple bread pudding glazed with, 570–71
  bread stuffing, 349
  canned ham glazed with, 311
  glaze, 348
  poached dried, with Grand Marnier, 494
  sauce, 385, 566
  sweet and sour sauce, 182
  upside-down cake, 519
arborio rice, 195
arcing, 32
Armagnac-poached winter fruits, 494
artichokes, 392–96
  basics, 392–93
  dips for, 394
  Sicilian, with tomatoes, 396
  steamed, 393–94
  steamed, with carrot topping, 396
  stuffed, with pine nuts, 395
asparagus:
  blanching, 407
  cooking chart, 76
  cream of, soup, 128
  poached eggs with Hollandaise and, 145
  risotto with, 203
  sesame sautéed, 476
  timbales, 158
  see also stalks
au gratin dishes:
  fennel, 474
  leeks, 447
Austrian goulash soup, 136–37
avgolemono sauce, 205
avocado:
  chicken salad, 373
  egg creams, Tijuana, 572

B

bacon:
  basics, 319
  browning, 30
  'n' brown sugar tomatoes, 422
  Canadian, cooking chart, 64
  Canadian, glazed, 313
  cooking chart, 61

  creamed cucumbers with, 426
  creamed onions with, 444
  defrosting, 256
  and egg tomatoes, 424
  greens with, 430
  grilled liver and, 333
  melted cheddar snacks, 103
  storing, 256
Baileys Irish cream pie, 560
baked beans, 437–38
banana:
  bread ring, 526–27
  cream pie, 559–60
  frozen pieces, chocolate-covered, 596–97
barbecued dishes:
  chicken, 351
  pork or beef, 309
  ribs, golden, 109
  turkey drumsticks, 381
barbecue sauce, blazing, 181
basil:
  butter, 183
  butter, won tons with scallop stuffing in, 90–91
  fish salad with, 227–28
  Milano mushrooms with, 440
  peppers, and onions, Italian, 95
  shrimp, 113
  tomato cream soup, chilled, 131
  tomato sauce, 179
  vinaigrette, 185
basmati rice, 195, 198
beans, dried, 431–38
  baked, 437–38
  basic recipe, 433–34
  basics, 431–32
  cooking chart, 71–72
  cubed beef chili with tomatoes and, 298
  lentil or pea puree, 435
  refried, with cheese, 434
  salad, chilled summer, 435
  Southwest pie with, 324
  speed soaking, 432
  vegetarian chili, 436–37
beans, green, *see* green beans
béarnaise sauce, 174
beef:
  barbecuing, 309
  boeuf bourguignon, 291–92
  boiled, 265–67
  buying and using, 254–55
  carbonnades a la flamande, 292
  corned, 267–69
  cubed, chili with, 297–98
  defrosting, 256–58
  grillades, 286
  Hungarian goulash, 293
  kabobs, 287–88
  less tender cubes, basics, 289–90

peppers stuffed with, 425–26
pita sandwiches with, 272
ragout, 290–91
ribs, basics, 306–7
rolls, simmered, 299–300
satay, 288–89
shepherd's pie, 274
short ribs, 307–8
sliced, flour tortillas with, 273
stefado, 294
strip and red onion salad, 261
Stroganoff, 285
tender-cut chunks, basics, 286–87
tenderloin, cooking chart, 60
tender strip, basics, 283
teriyaki, 284
beef, ground:
  burgers, 326–27
  chili, Cincinnati-style, 322–23
  chili, Mom's, 321–22
  cooking chart, 59
  defrosting, 256–57
  meatballs, 328–29
  meat loaf, 331–32
  picadillo, 325
  pie, Southwestern, 323–24
  sloppy Joes, 325
  tacos or tostadas filled with, 324–25
beef, pot roast, 262–63
  basics, 262
  marinated, 263–64
  sauerbraten, 264–65
beef, roast, 260–61
  cooking chart, 59
  less tender-cut, basics, 262
  rules of thumb for cooking times, 53
  tender-cut, basics, 258
beef liver:
  basics, 332
  dumpling soup, Münchner, 137–38
  grilled bacon and, 333
  tomato pasta sauce with, 334
  Tyrolian, 333–34
beefsteak:
  au poivre, 280
  cheese sandwich, 281
  chuck, briskly braised, 282–83
  cooking chart, 60
  leftover, 281
  less tender-cut, 282
  and potato salad, liberty, 456
  rules of thumb for cooking time, 53
  tender-cut, 278–80
  teriyaki, 284
beer:
  boiled beef in, 266
  cheddar soup, 134
  cubed beef chili with, 298
  franks in, 318
  sauce, 318
  spicy shrimp in, 236–37
beet(s):
  and carrot salad, low-calorie, 463
  cooking chart for, 73
  Harvard or sweet and sour, 462
  salad, winter, 463
  soup, victory garden, 126–27
  zesty julienned, 462
beet greens:
  cooking chart, 70
  sautéed, 428–29
berry(ies):
  dessert omelet with, 153
  pie, double-crust, 547
  sauces, 497–98
berry tarts:
  with fresh berries, 551–52
  in lemon sauce, 552
  nouveau, 552
black raspberry sauce, 566
blanching fresh vegetables, 407
blazing barbecue sauce, 181
blazing pork spareribs, 308–9
blood pressure, potassium and, 450
blueberry:
  chocolate cups, 597
  pound cake, 523
  shortcake, 509
  upside-down cake, 521
bluefish:
  Oriental, 226
  salad, chilled Japanese, 226
boeuf bourguignon, 291–92
bok choy, cooking chart for, 68
Boston brown bread, 534–35
Boston cream pie, 508
bourbon:
  Kentucky veal stew with, 295
  pecan ice cream pie, 563
  praline sauce, 564
Bourbon Street soufflé, 581–82
brandy:
  apple slices with, 494–95
  bread pudding with, 570
  carrots with, 463
  chocolate glaze, 512
  chopped liver with, 94–95
  dessert omelet with, 153
  flamed, 607
  peach soup with, 138
  poached peaches with, 490
  poached plums with, 491
  sauce, 279–80
  shrimp with, 113
  walnut bundt cake, 526
  walnut sauce, 564

bran muffins, 518
bratwurst, smoked, in beer or wine sauce, 318
Brazilian braised beef with coffee, 291
bread(s), 526–30
    banana, ring, 526–27
    Boston brown, 534–35
    browning, 30
    carrot, 530
    corn, 528–29
    crumbs, buttered, 247, 474
    cubes, dried, 607
    pumpkin, 530
    quick, basics, 527–28
    raising dough for, 530
    reheating doneness, 49–50
    sauce, chilled cilantro, 245
    stuffings, 349
    zucchini-nut, 529–30
    see also steamed cakes and breads
breaded:
    fish fillets, 220
    mushrooms and vegetables, 441
    pork or veal chops, 301–2
    warm cheese with salad, 162–63
bread puddings, 569–71
    apple, apricot-glazed, 570–71
    basics, 569
    with brandy, 570
    chocolate, 570
    raisin-nut, 569–70
    whole-wheat, 570
brittle, nut, 588
broad beans, *see* fava beans
broccoli:
    blanching, 407
    and cauliflower mock lobster platter, 481
    in cheese sauce–filled potatoes, 453
    chicken slivers with, 369
    cooking chart for, 76
    with lemon slices, 475–76
    and pork, Oriental, 275
    salad, Mexican, 399–400
    soup, creamy, 127
    timbales, 158
broths and stocks:
    chicken, 118
    egg drop, 266
    fish, 120
    giblet, 379, 384
    mock brown, 119
    vegetable, 119–20
brown bread, Boston, 534–35
brown broth or stock, mock, 119
brown derby pound cake, 523
brown glaze, basic, 347
brownies, 530–31
browning, 29–30
browning dish cheese sandwich, 166

browning dishes, 30, 32, 85
brown rice, 195, 199
brown sugar:
    'n' bacon tomatoes, 422
    cinnamon coffee cake, 510
    egg custards glazed with, 573
    glaze, 314
    softening, 607
Brussels sprouts:
    blanching, 407
    cooking chart, 68
    in lettuce leaves, 406
buerre Dijonnais, 229
Buffalo chicken wings, low-calorie, 357–58
bundt cakes, 524–27
    applesauce, 525
    banana bread ring, 526–27
    basics, 522
    chocolate chocolate chip, 524
    Irishman-in-Haiti, 527
    walnut-brandy, 526
burgers, 326–28
    basics, 326
    browning dish method, 327
    paper plate method, 327
    reheating, 328
    roasting rack method, 326–27
    rules of thumb for cooking times, 54
Burgundy beefballs, 329
Burgundy sauces, 330
    onion, 333
    scallion, 261
butter(s):
    buerre Dijonnais, 229
    for cabbage family, 397
    cilantro-lime, 229, 394
    herb, 247, 461, 474
    hot pepper, 355
    lemon, 183, 247
    melted, 183, 247
    nut, 247
    softened, 184
    softening, 607
buttered:
    bread crumbs, 247, 474
    mushroom caps, 440
    red wine sauce, 261
butternut squash, cooking chart for, 75
butterscotch:
    bars, 531
    cream pie, 559
    pudding, 558
    red, baked apples with, 492
    sauce, 565
    sauce, poached pears with, 490
buying:
    beef, 254–55
    eggs, 141–42

fish and seafood, 212, 213
lamb and veal, 255
pork and ham, 255–56
poultry, 338

C

cabbage:
  colcannon, 482–83
  cooking chart, 68
  potatoes filled with, 453
  red, braised sweet and sour, 400–401
  rumbledethumps, 483
  sautéed shredded, 400
cabbage, stuffed, 401–5
  basics, 401
  leaves, 404–5
  with sausage, 402–3
cabbage family, 396–406
  cooking chart, 68–69
  doneness, 397
  nutmeg-scented cream sauce for, 398
  toppings for, 397–98
  see also Brussels sprouts; cauliflower
cacciatore, chicken, 354
café au lait pudding, 558
cakes, 506–27
  basics, 506–7
  browning, 30
  cheesecakes, 574–76
  cocoa-cinnamon, 508
  crumb coffee, 510
  cupcakes, 516–17
  gingerbread, 512–13
  lemon, 508
  Linzer jam, 515–16
  marmalade cream, 508
  orange, 508
  Pacific carrot, 513–14
  pound, 522–23
  strawberry shortcake, 509
  trifle with strawberries, 557
  truffle, 515
  walnut-apple, with chocolate cream glaze, 514–515
  yellow, 507–8
  see also bundt cakes; chocolate cakes; steamed cakes and breads; upside-down cakes; frostings
calf liver:
  basics, 332–34
  dumpling soup, Münchner, 137–38
  grilled bacon and, 333
  tomato pasta sauce with, 334
  Tyrolian, 333–34
Canadian bacon:
  cooking chart, 64
  glazed, 313
candied:
  acorn squash, 467–68
  carrots, 463
  carrots, onions stuffed with, 446
  rhubarb sauce, 498
candies and confections, 585–600
  almond crunch, 589
  caramel apples, 600
  caramel corn, 590
  caramel turtles, 599
  frosted nuts, 589–90
  hard candy, 587–88
  marshmallow cereal squares, 600
  nut brittle, 588
  sugar candy basics, 586–87
  truffles, 598
  white- or pastel-coated fruit, 597
  see also chocolate candies and confections; fudge
Cape Cod jewel cake, 520
caper(s):
  beef strip salad with, 261
  eggplant sandwiches sparked with, 419
  sauce, 280
  veal daube with, 295
  vinaigrette, 185
caramel:
  apples, 600
  corn, 590
  turtles, 599
caraway:
  candied carrots, 463
  meatballs, 329
carbonnades a la flamande, 292
carrot(s):
  and beet salad, low-calorie, 463
  blanching, 407
  braised chuck steak with potatoes and, 283
  bread, 530
  cake, Pacific, 513–14
  candied, 463
  candied, onions stuffed with, 446
  cooking chart, 73–74
  marmalade-glazed pork roast with, 271
  onions stuffed with peas and, 446
  peas and, 412
  potato soup, 125
  puree, savory, 464–65
  salad, winter, 463
  soup, orange-flavored, 126
  timbales, shimmering, 157–58
  topping, steamed artichokes with, 396
carryover vegetable stir-shake, 480
casseroles:
  chicken and rice, 359
  cubed eggplant, tomato, and peppers topped with mozzarella, 419

casseroles (cont.)
  grits and cheddar, 194
  reheating doneness, 44–45
  vegetable-tofu, 419
cassis, cranberry sauce with, 188
catch of the day soup, 121
cat food, taking chill off, 607
catsup meat loaf, 331
cauliflower, 398–400
  basics, 398–99
  blanching, 407
  and broccoli mock lobster platter, 481
  cooking chart, 68–69
  imperial, 399
  rules of thumb for cooking times, 51–53
  salad, Mexican, 399–400
  soups, 127
caviar:
  golden, scallop appetizers with, 240
  lobster nuggets with, 234
celery:
  cooking chart, 76
  tomatoes topped with, 423
cereal:
  cooked, basics, 192
  cooking chart, 56
  hot, 192
  marshmallow squares, 600
  soup, wholesome, 122–23
chard:
  lightly creamed, 429
  sautéed, 428–29
cheddar cheese:
  and grits casserole, 194
  melted, and bacon snacks, 103
  onion topping, Italian sand dollars with, 96–97
  soup, 133–34
  wine dip with fruit, 499
cheese:
  breaded warm, with salad, 162–63
  broccoli or cauliflower soup, creamy, 127
  cereal soup with, 123
  chile con queso, 104
  and ham rollups, lightly breaded, 105
  macaroni and, 207
  meat loaf topped with, 332
  melted, and crackers, 102–4
  melting or softening, 161
  nachos, 103–4
  polenta, 195
  raclette, 164
  refried beans with, 434
  scrambled eggs with, 150
  shirred eggs with, 147
  soufflé, New Yankee, 155–56
  steak sandwich, 281
  warming to room temperature, 607
  see also fondues; specific cheeses

cheesecake:
  basics, 574–75
  creamy, 575–76
cheese sandwiches:
  browning dish, 166
  ham and, 165
  open-face toasted, 164–65
  rarebit, 162
cheese sauce, 397
  broccoli in, potatoes filled with, 453
  onions with, 444
  parsley tomato, 179
cherry(ies):
  chocolate-covered, 596
  double-crust pie, 547
  sauce, 312
chicken, 337–76
  a la king, 375
  barbecued, 351
  braised, 353–54
  breaded, basics, 364
  broth or stock, 118
  cacciatore, 354
  cooking chart, 64–66
  curry, potatoes filled with, 452
  defrosting, 339–40, 341
  giblet stock, 379
  legs, with mustard-crumb coating, 355
  meal planning and, 603
  parts, basics, 351–52
  pieces, with cider and apples, 356
  pilaf, 202
  poached whole, 341–43
  potpie, 370–72
  quick fried, 357
  and rice casserole, 359
  roast, 343–45
  salads, 372–74
  skewered, with peanut satay sauce, 369–70
  slivers, Bandung, 368–69
  tacos, 375
  Tetrazzini, 381–82
  Thai, 376
  timbales, 158
  vegetable stir-shake, 480
  see also poultry
chicken breast(s):
  basics, 358
  low-cal, 374
  and rice casserole, 359
chicken breasts, boneless:
  sauces for, 361–62
  succulent, 359–60
  with vegetables, 362–64
chicken cutlets:
  breaded, 364–65
  breaded, with stuffing, 367–68
  coated with pecan-mustard mayonnaise, 366

chicken liver(s), 386–88
  basics, 386
  chopped, with brandy, 94–95
  cooking chart, 67
  defrosting, 340–41
  dumpling soup, 138
  sautéed, 387–88
chicken wings:
  Buffalo, low-calorie, 357–58
  Mexican, 358
  Oriental, 108–9
chile con queso, 104
chili:
  barbecue sauce with, 181
  Cincinnati-style, 322–23
  with cubed beef, 297–98
  green, 298–99
  ground beef, Mom's, 321–22
  ground turkey, 381
  with pork cubes, 298
  potatoes stuffed with, 452
  ribs, 308
  tomato sauce with liver, 334
  vegetarian, 436–37
chilled:
  cilantro bread sauce, 245
  cream of tomato-basil soup, 131
  fillets with herb sauce, 223
  fresh herb sauce, 176
  leeks in vinaigrette, 447
  steamed mussels with herb sauce, 110
  sweet and sour chicken wings, 109
  whole fish, 231
chilled salads:
  Japanese bluefish, 226
  mussel and apple, 227
  scallion, 448
  summer bean, 435
Chinese subgum rice, 205
chive(s):
  butter, 183
  cereal soup with, 123
chocolate:
  bark, 594
  brandy glaze, 512
  bread pudding, 570
  cream frosting, 512
  cream glaze, 512
  melting, 593, 607
  mousse, luscious, 579
  pistachio cups, frozen, 564–65
  pots de crème, 572
  pudding, 558
  pudding pie, 558–59
  white, mousse, 579
chocolate cakes:
  cheesecake, 576
  chocolate chip, 511

chocolate chip bundt, 524
  cupcakes, 517
  Grand Marnier, 515
  mousse, two-tiered, 580–81
  rich, 511
chocolate candies and confections:
  almond crunch topped with chocolate, 589
  bark, 594
  blueberry-chocolate cups, 597
  cherries and grapes covered with chocolate, 596
  clusters, 597
  curls, 595–96
  frozen banana pieces covered with chocolate, 596–97
  fudge, 590–93
  oranges covered with chocolate, 596
  peanut butter–chocolate squares, 598–99
  pretzels and cookies coated with chocolate, 597
  strawberries covered with chocolate, 596–97
  triangles, 594–95
  truffles, 598
  turtles covered with chocolate, 599
chocolate chip(s):
  chocolate bundt cake, 524
  chocolate cake, 511
  granola with, 107
  marshmallow cereal squares, 600
  pound cake, 523
chops:
  rules of thumb for cooking times, 53
  see also lamb chops; pork chops; veal chops
chowder, Manhattan clam, 134–35
chuck steak, briskly braised, 282–83
cilantro:
  bread sauce, chilled, 245
  lime butter, 229, 394
Cincinnati-style chili, 322–23
cinnamon:
  brown sugar coffee cake, 510
  cocoa cake, 508
  granola, 107
  poached peaches with, 490
  spice carrots, 463
citrus juice, extracting, 607
citrus sauce, 498–99
clam(s):
  basics, 241
  casino, 111
  chowder, Manhattan, 134–35
  cooking chart, 59
  steamed, 241–42
coastal potato salad, 456
cocktail sauce, 247
cocoa:
  brownies, 531
  cinnamon cake, 508
coconut:
  chocolate clusters, 597

coconut (*cont.*)
  cream pie, 560, 561
  crumb coffee cake, 510
  custard, 573
  drying, 607
  joy pie, 560–61
  strips, toasted, 377
  veal and lamb curry with, 297
cod, poached, in cream sauce Dijonnais, 224
coffee:
  Brazilian braised beef with, 291
  fudge, 592
  gingerbread, 513
  instant, heating, 608
  truffles, 598
coffee cake, crumb, 510
colcannon, 482–83
collard greens:
  cooking chart, 71
  sautéed, 429–30
confections, *see* candies and confections; chocolate candies and confections
converted rice, 195
cookie crumb crust, 545
cookies, chocolate-coated, 597
cooking charts, 55–76
  cereal, pasta, and rice, 56–57
  dry and fresh vegetables, 68–76
  egg, 55–56
  fish and seafood, 57–59
  frozen or canned vegetables, 67–68
  meat, 59–64
  poultry, 65–67
cooking time:
  cauliflower, 51–53
  doubled recipes, 34
  fish fillets, 54
  halved recipes, 35
  hamburgers and sausage patties, 54
  individual muffins or cupcakes, 517
  potatoes, 51
  roast beef, 53
  rules of thumb, 51–54
  scallops, 54
  shrimps, 54
  steaks and chops, 53
  volume principle, 32–33
coq au vin rouge, 354
corn, 407–10
  basics, 408–9
  bread, 528–29
  bread stuffing, 349
  cooking chart, 69–70
  cream soup, 122
  pudding with jalapeño salsa, 409
  soup, with jalapeño salsa, 121–22
  succotash, 410
  toppings for, 408

see also hash, corn and pepper
corned beef:
  basic boiled dinner, 267–68
  glazed, 268–69
  Reuben sandwiches, 269
  salad, with horseradish dressing, 268
  sandwiches, 269
Cornish game hen(s):
  boning and stuffing, 347
  cooking chart, 66
  defrosting, 339–40
  giblet stock, 379
  glazed, 345–46
  roast, basics, 343–44
cornstarch-thickened sauce or gravy basics, 170–171
cottage cheese mushroom timbales, 160
country potato-leek soup, 125
crab:
  dip, hot, 112
  imperial, 238
  mushrooms stuffed with, 112
  potatoes filled with, 452
  shrimp stuffed with, 237–38
  stuffing for braised whole fish, 232
crab sauce, 244
  fish fillets with, 217
  salmon with, 223–24, 229
cranberry(ies):
  baked apples with, 492
  bread stuffing, 349
  glaze, 348
  ice cream pie, 562
  pound cake, 523
  sauces, 187–88, 385
  squash stuffed with, 471–72
cream:
  chocolate, frosting, 512
  chocolate fudge, no-fail, 593
  Hawaiian rice and, 568
  leeks topped with, 447
  marmalade, cake, 508
  mocha, glaze, 512
  nutmeg whipped, poached pears with, 489
  poached pears with, 489
  see also soups, cream
cream cheese:
  frosting, 514
  pea pods stuffed with, 99
  softening, 607
creamed dishes:
  cucumbers, 426
  goulash, 293
  leeks, chilled, 448
  mushrooms, 439
  onions, 444
  root vegetables, 461
  scallions, 448

spinach or chard, 429
stalks, 474
cream pies:
  Baileys Irish, 560
  banana, 559–60
  Boston, 508
  butterscotch, 559
  chocolate pudding, 558–59
  coconut, 560, 561
  Kahlúa, 560
  mocha, 559
  raspberry, 559
  strawberry, 559
cream sauces:
  apple, 361
  curry, 361
  Dijonnais, 224
  golden, 225
  gravy, 271
  herbed, 461
  horseradish, 273
  lemon or lime, 361
  mustard, 240, 461
  nutmeg-scented, 398
  with onion and nutmeg, 398
  rose, 361
  saffron, 240, 361
  sherry, 171
  whipped herb, 177
creamy:
  cheesecake, 575–76
  crunchy greens, 429
  rice pilaf, 202
  rice salad, 197
  veal daube, 295
  see also soups, creamy
crème de menthe:
  ice cream pie, 563
  peas with, 411
crisping:
  appetizers, 93
  browning techniques, 29–30
crumb coffee cake, 510
crumb-crusted sausage patties, 320
crustless apple crumb pie, 546
cucumber(s), 416
  sauce, chunky, fish fillets with, 218
  sautéed, 426
Cumberland sauce, 278
cumin salsa, 186
cupcakes:
  basics, 516–17
  chocolate, 517
  cooking times for, 517
  yellow, 517
curls, chocolate, 595–96
currant(s):
  glaze, 348
  long-grain rice with almonds and, 197
  sauce, 566
  sauce, poached pears with, 490
curried dishes:
  beans, 433
  chicken-filled potatoes, 452
  cream sauce, 361
  fish, 223
  lemon marinade, 288
  potato-zucchini soup, 124
  sauce, 171, 246
  scrambled eggs, 150
  tomato soup, 130
  veal or lamb, 297
custard:
  rice pudding, 567–68
  see also egg custards, sweetened; timbales

D

dandelion leaves, cooking chart for, 71
Danish cheese rounds, 103
daube, veal, 295–96
defrosting, 50
  bread dough, 530
  chicken livers, 340–41
  chicken parts and boned breasts, 339–40
  Cornish hens, 339–40
  fish and seafood, 213–14
  juice concentrate, 608
  meat, 256–58
  poultry, doneness of, 341
  turkey legs and breasts, 339–40
  whole chickens, turkeys, ducks, or geese, 340
desserts, 505–600
  apple crumble, 554–55
  flaky shortbread triangles, 543–44
  meal planning and, 603
  omelets, 153
  pastry cream, 555–56
  see also bread puddings; bundt cakes; cakes; candies and confections; chocolate cakes; chocolate candies and confections; cream pies; egg custards, sweetened; ice cream; ice cream pies; mousse; pies; puddings; steamed cakes and breads; tartlets; tarts; upside-down cakes
dessert sauces:
  amaretto, 563–64
  apricot, 566
  berry, 497–98
  black raspberry, 566
  bourbon-praline, 564
  butterscotch, 565
  candied rhubarb, 498
  candied rhubarb strawberry, 498
  citrus, 498–99
  currant, 566

dessert sauce(s) (cont.)
  hard, 535
  hot fudge, 564
  hot mocha, 564
  peach, 496
  plum pudding, 534
  raspberry, for fresh fruit or sherbet, 565–66
  walnut-brandy, 564
  whole berry, 498
Deutsch melted cheese and sausage, 103
deviled chopped liver, 94–95
deviled egg spread, 149
Dijon mustard meat loaf, 331
dill:
  butter, 183
  horseradish sauce, chilled, 176
  mustard sauce, chilled, 176
  pumpkin soup, creamy, 128–29
  sautéed cucumbers, 426
  Scandinavian veal stew with, 295
  shrimp, 113
  squash soup, creamy, 129
  tomato soup, 130
dill salsa cruda, 248
  chilled whole fish with, 231
  fish fillets with, 217
  scallops in, 240
dips:
  for artichokes, 394
  cheddar wine, with fruit, 499
  eggplant, 100–101
  Gorgonzola wine, with fruit, 499
  hot crab, 112
dishes, 81–83
  browning, 30, 32, 85
  covers for, 27–28
  depth of, 82
  for heating and serving appetizers, 110
  materials for, 81
  metal, 29, 32
  microwaveproof test for, 85
  rotating, 24
  shape of, 81
  simmerpots, 86
  temperature of, 27
dog food, taking chill off, 607
dressings:
  ginger, 184
  horseradish, 268
  mustard, 184
  Oriental, 184
  rice, 351
  see also vinaigrette
dried fruit:
  granola with, 107
  plumping for cooking, 609
  sauce, 385
  softening for eating, 609

drunken prune sauce, 385
duck:
  cooking chart, 66
  giblet stock, 384
  sauce, sherried, 385
  whole, defrosting, 340
duck, roast:
  basics, 382–83
  crispy, 383–84
  with green peppercorns, 384
dumpling(s):
  beef or calf liver, Münchner soup, 137–38
  chicken liver, soup, 138
  Emerald Isle, 430–31
  spinach, with tomato sauce, 431

E

East Indian rice, 200
egg(s), 141–60
  added to vegetable dishes for complete protein, 147
  buying and storing, 141–42
  cereal soup with, 123
  cooked, emulsion basics, 173–74
  cooking chart, 55–56
  creams, Tijuana avocado, 572
  drop broth, boiled beef with, 266
  hard-cooked, 147–48
  hard-cooked, spreads, 148–49
  huevos rancheros, 145
  new Yankee cheese soufflé, 155–56
  nut pastry dough, 542
  pinwheels, 93–94
  rich, pastry dough, 542
  salad sandwich filling, 149
  scrambled, 149–50
  scrambled, and bacon tomatoes, 424
  shirred, 146–47
  soufflé basics, 154–55
  square, 143
  see also eggs, poached; omelets; timbales
egg custards, sweetened, 571–73
  brown sugar–glazed, 573
  chocolate pots de crème, 572
  coconut, 573
  Indian pudding, 573–74
  individual rice, 574
  lemon, 572
  Mexican pots de crème, 572
  mocha pots de crème, 572
  orange, 572
  pumpkin, 572–73
  Tijuana avocado egg creams, 572
eggplant, 416–22
  appetizer dip, 100–101
  cooking chart, 70

ratatouille, 421–22
stuffed, 420–22
tomato, and peppers topped with mozzarella, 419
vegetable-tofu casserole, 419
eggplant slices, 417–19
  basics, 417
  mozzarella, and tomato sandwiches, 418–19
  with toppings, 417–18
eggs, poached, 142–43
  with asparagus and Hollandaise, 145
  benedict, 143–44
  Mornay, 144
Emerald Isle dumplings, 430–31
English plum pudding, 533–34
equipment, *see* dishes; utensils

F

fats, browning and, 30
fava (broad) beans, 407
  basics, 415
  cooking chart, 69
  in herb sauce, 416
  steamed, 416
  toppings for, 408
fennel:
  au gratin, 474
  cooking chart, 76
feta cheese, stefado with, 294
figgy pudding, 534
finger towels, warming, 608
fish, 211–33
  broth or stock, 120
  browning, 30
  buying, 212
  catch of the day soup, 121
  cooking chart, 57–59
  defrosting, 213–14
  meal planning and, 603
  rules of thumb for cooking times, 54
  sauces for, 244–49
  sauces made from cooking liquid of, 244–46
  storing, 212
  see also shellfish; *specific fish*
fish, whole, 230–33
  basics, 230
  braised, 230–31
  chilled, 231
  cooking chart, 58
  mushroom stuffing for, 232
  poached trout with lemon butter, 232–33
fish fillets, thick, 222–28
  basics, 222–23
  cooking chart, 57
  lean, wrapped in lettuce leaves with golden cream sauce, 225
  Oriental bluefish, 226

poached, 223–24
poached cod in cream sauce Dijonnais, 224
rules of thumb for cooking times, 54
fish fillets, thin, 214–22
  au citron, 216–17
  basics, 214–16
  breaded, 220
  with chunky cucumber sauce, 218
  cooked in paper, 221–22
  cooking chart, 57
  meal planning with, 217
  rolls with almond filling, 221
  rules of thumb for cooking times, 54
  with zucchini in cream sauce, 218–20
fish salad(s):
  apple and, 226–27
  with basil, 227–28
  chilled Japanese bluefish, 226
  chilled mussel and apple, 227
  sandwich, hot open-faced, 228
fish steaks, 228–30
  basics, 228
  cooking chart, 58
  lemony, 228–29
  salmon, with salmon-colored sauce, 229–30
flaky shortbread triangles, 543–44
flambéed:
  apple slices over ice cream, 495
  orange-glazed ham steak, 312
  sweet potato pie, 459
flour-thickened sauce or gravy basics, 170–71
flour tortillas with sliced meat, 273
foamy custard pudding, 568
fondues:
  with blanched vegetables, 162
  Vermont, 161–62
food arrangement, 23
  ring rule, 38–39
fragrant whole tomatoes, 422
franks:
  baked beans and, 438
  in beer, 318
freezing:
  poultry, 339
  see also defrosting
French fondue, 162
French onion-filled potatoes, 453
frosted nuts, 589–90
frostings:
  chocolate cream, 512
  cream cheese, 514
  lemon, 509
  orange, 509
  vanilla, 509
frozen juice concentrate, thawing, 608
frozen pistachio chocolate cups, 564–65
fruit, 487–502
  brown rice salad with, 199

fruit (cont.)
  canned pie filling, double-crust pie with, 548
  cheddar wine dip with, 499
  cheesecake topped with, 576
  glaze, 310
  Gorgonzola wine dip with, 499
  jams and jellies, 500–502
  rice pudding with yogurt and, 568
  sauces, 496–99
  in season, trifle with, 557
  slices, basics, 494
  summer, large tart, 549–50
  white- or pastel-coated, 597
  see also dried fruit; *specific fruits*
fruit, poached:
  basics, 488
  peaches, 490
  pears, 488–90
  plums, 491
  winter, 493–94
fudge, 590–93
  chocolate, 591–92
  coffee, 592
  no-fail, 592–93
  peanut butter, 592
  sauce, hot, 564
  vanilla, 592

G

garlic:
  butter, 183
  mayonnaise (aioli), 175–76
  oil, tomatoes topped with, 423
  shallot butter, 183
gelatin, overset, recovering, 608
German potato salad, 455
giblet:
  gravy, 379–80
  stocks, 379, 384
ginger:
  applesauce, 493
  carrots, 463
  dressing, 184
  pickled, 99
  sauce, squid in, 243–44
  snow pea pods stuffed with, 98–99
  sweet and sour apricot sauce with, 182
gingerbread, 512–13
  apple upside-down, 513
  coffee, 513
glazed:
  boiled beef, 269
  corned beef, 268–69
  ham steak, 312
  marmalade-, pork roast with carrots, 271
  onions, 443

  pork butt or Canadian bacon, 313
glazes:
  apricot, 348
  basic brown, 347
  brown sugar, 314
  chocolate brandy, 512
  chocolate cream, 512
  cranberry, 348
  currant, 348
  fruit, 310
  honey, 314
  honey-mustard, 347
  jelly, 313
  lime-honey, 348
  mocha cream, 512
  mustard, 310
  orange, 313
  pineapple, 314
  pineapple-sherry, 348
  for poultry, 347–48
golden cream sauce, 225
goose:
  cooking chart, 66
  roast, 382–83, 386
  whole, defrosting, 340
Gorgonzola wine dip with fruit, 499
goulash:
  Hungarian, 293
  soup, Austrian, 136–37
graham cracker crumb crust, 544–45
Grand Marnier:
  chocolate cake, 515
  poached dried apricots with, 494
granola, 107
grapefruit mousse, 577–78
grape leaves, stuffed, 203–4
grapes, chocolate-covered, 596
gravies:
  beef-onion, 266–67
  chicken giblet, 380
  for chuck steak, 282–83
  Cornish game hen giblet, 380
  cream, 271
  flour- or cornstarch-thickened, basics, 170–71
  for leg of lamb, 277
  pan drippings, 173
  for pork roast, 271
  for roast beef, 260
  sour cream, 282–83
  Turkey giblet, 379–80
  vermouth, 260
Great Northern beans with garlic and oil, 433
Greek lemon soup, 136
Greek vegetable kabobs, 483–84
green beans, 407, 413–15
  basics, 413
  blanching, 407
  braised, 413–14

cooking chart, 69
  Niçoise, 414
  stir-shake bean sprouts and, 414–15
  toppings for, 408
green chili, 298–99
green peas, see peas, green
green pepper(s):
  goulash with red peppers and, 293
  and red pepper timbales, 158
  tomatoes topped with, 423
green peppercorn sauce, 272, 385
greens, 427–31
  basics, 427–28
  cooking chart, 70–71
  Emerald Isle dumplings, 430–31
  light, sautéed, 428–29
  retaining water-soluble vitamins in, 428
  rich, sautéed, 429–30
  toppings for, 428
  wilted, salad, 430
green sauce, 177
green tomato salsa, 186
grillades, 286
grits, 193–94
  basics, 193
  and cheddar casserole, 194
  cooking chart, 56

H

half pound cake, 522–23
ham:
  a la king, 314
  basics, 270
  beef rolls with, 300
  breast of veal stuffed with, 305
  buying and using, 255–56
  canned, apricot-glazed, 311
  and cheese rollups, 105
  and cheese sandwich, open-face toasted, 165
  cooking chart, 62, 63–64
  fully cooked, 256
  leftover, 317
  loaf, 316
  macaroni and cheese with, 207
  potatoes filled with, 452
  roast, 270–72
  salad spread, 315
  steak, glazed, 312
  timbales, 158
  and vegetables over rice, Oriental, 314
hamburgers, see burgers
hard candy, 587–88
hard sauce, 535
Harvard beets, 462
hash, corn and pepper, 410
  onions stuffed with, 446

Southwest, 410
  tomatoes stuffed with, 424
Hawaiian rice and cream, 568
hazelnut mousse, 579
herb(s):
  cereal soup with, 123
  fresh, stuffing, 349
  lobster tails with, 234
  risotto with, 203
  shrimp with, 113
herb sauce(s), 171, 361
  butter, 247, 461, 474
  chilled fillets with, 223
  chilled steamed mussels with, 110
  cream, whipped, 177
  fresh, chilled, 176
  mayonnaise, 175
  mushroom, 173
  quick cream, 461
  rose, 172
  vinaigrette, 185
  yogurt, 273
Hollandaise sauce, 174
  elegant scallions with, 448
  poached eggs with asparagus and, 145
  trout with, 233
honey:
  crystallized, making spreadable, 607
  mustard sauce, 352
  orange squash puree, 467
honey glaze(s), 314
  lime, 348
  mustard, 347
  onions with, 443
horseradish:
  applesauce flavored with, 493
  cream, 273
  dill sauce, chilled, 176
  dressing, 268
hot crab dip, 112
hot fudge sauce, 564
  poached pears with, 489
hot mocha sauce, 564
hot pepper butter, 355
hot pepper flakes, beans with lime and, 433
hubbard squash, cooking chart for, 75
huevos rancheros, 145

I

ice cream:
  flambéed apple slices over, 495
  heating toppings for, 608
  peach sauce for, 496
  pistachio, in chocolate cups, 564–65
  softening, 608

ice cream pies:
  amaretto, 562–63
  cranberry, 562
  crème de menthe, 563
  irresistible mincemeat, 562
  Kahlúa, 563
  pecan-bourbon, 563
imperial cauliflower, 399
Indian pudding, 573–74
Indian yogurt sauce, 362
intoxicating sauce, 361
Irishman-in-Haiti cake, 527
Italian dishes:
  basil, peppers, and onions, 95
  cheese snacks, 103
  chicken cutlets, 365
  meatballs, 329
  ribs with tomato sauce, 308
  sand dollars with cheddar-onion topping, 96–97
  tomato sauce, 179
  veal stew with peppers, 295–96

J

jalapeño salsa, 248
  corn pudding with, 409
  corn soup with, 121–22
  poached fish fillets with, 223
  warm, 187
jam(s):
  basics, 500
  Linzer, cake, 515–16
  raspberry or strawberry, 501
  softening, 608
Japanese dishes:
  chilled bluefish salad, 226
  vegetables, 478
  vegetables with long-grain rice, 197
jelly(ies):
  basics, 500
  glaze, 313
  mulled wine, 502
  softening, 608
  speeding making of, 501
Jerusalem artichokes, cooking chart for, 74
jicama:
  cooking chart, 74
  in lime-sparked cream sauce, 406
juice:
  citrus, 607
  frozen concentrate, thawing, 608
julienned root vegetables, 461–62

K

kabobs:
  beef or lamb, 287–88
  Greek vegetable, 483–84
Kahlúa:
  cream pie, 560
  ice cream pie, 563
kale:
  cooking chart, 71
  sautéed, 429–30
Kentucky veal stew with bourbon, 295
kohlrabi:
  cooking chart, 69
  küchen rezept, 405–6
Konigsberger klops, 329

L

lamb:
  color of, 255
  cooking chart, 60–61
  curry, 297
  ground, Moghul rice with, 200
  kabobs, 287–88
  less tender cubes, basics, 289–90
  less tender-cut, basics, 262
  pita sandwiches with, 272
  ragout, 296
  roast, basics, 276
  roast leg of, 277
  satay, 288–89
  shanks, braised, 263
  shepherd's pie, 274
  shoulder, marinated, 264
  shoulder, with rosemary, 277
  sliced, flour tortillas with, 273
  stuffed breast and butterflied loin, basics, 304
  stuffed breast of, 305
  tender-cut chunks, basics, 286–87
lamb chops:
  basics, 300–301
  cooking chart, 60
  with fresh tomato sauce, 302–3
  in mustard sauce, 303–4
lasagna, 206–7
leek(s), 446–48
  au naturel, 447–48
  basics, 446
  cooking chart, 72
  fish fillets with zucchini and, in sauce, 220
  potato soup, country, 125
leftovers:
  beefsteak, 281
  ham, 317
  stuffed eggplant a la, 421
legumes, 431–38
  cooking chart, 71–72
  see also beans, dried
lemon:
  butter, 183, 247

cake, 508
cheesecake, 576
cream sauce, 361
curry marinade, 288
egg custards, 572
fish steaks, 228–29
frosting, 509
long-grain rice, 197
marmalade, 501
meringue pie, 561–62
mousse, 579
peel, drying, 608
pie with whipped cream, 562
pound cake, 523
sauce, berry tarts in, 552
soup, Greek, 136
sweet pastry dough, 542
lentil:
  puree, 435
  soup, 435
lettuce leaves:
  Brussels sprouts in, 406
  lean fish fillets wrapped in, with golden cream sauce, 225
liberty steak and potato salad, 456
lightly breaded ham and cheese rollups, 105
lima beans, 407
  basics, 415
  blanching, 407
  cooking chart, 69
  in herb sauce, 416
  steamed, 416
  succotash, 410
  toppings for, 408
lime:
  beans with hot pepper flakes and, 433
  butter, 183
  chilled leeks in, 447
  cilantro butter, 229, 394
  cream sauce, 361
  honey glaze, 348
  marmalade, 501
  mousse, 579
  sautéed cucumbers, 426
  Yucatan fish fillets in paper, 222
Linzer jam cake, 515–16
liver, *see* beef liver; calf liver; chicken liver
lobster tails, 233–34
  basics, 233
  with butter, 234
  cooking chart, 58
  defrosting, 214
lollipops, 587–88
low-calorie dishes:
  boneless chicken breasts with vegetables, 363
  carrot and beet salad, 463
  chicken breasts, 374
  chicken salad, 373–74
  clams on the half shell, 111
  fish steaks, 229
  poached trout, 233
  sautéed cucumbers, 426

M

macaroni:
  and cheese, 207
  cooking chart, 57
Maltaise sauce, 174
Manhattan clam chowder, 134–35
maple-glazed onions, 443
marinades, 30, 608
  lemon-curry, 288
  sweet and sour, 352
  tomato, 288
marinated dishes:
  Oriental beef or lamb kabobs, 287–88
  pork salad, 274–75
  pot roast, 263–64
marinated vegetables, 91–92
  breaded warm cheese with, 163
  brown rice salad with, 199
marmalade(s):
  cream cake, 508
  lemon-lime, 501
  orange, 500
  pork roast and carrots glazed with, 271
marshmallow:
  cereal squares, 600
  chocolate fudge, no-fail, 593
mayonnaise, 175
  garlic (aioli), 175–76
  herbed, 175
  pecan-mustard, chicken cutlets coated with, 366
  separated, 176
meal planning, 603–4
  with fish fillets, 217
meat:
  added to chilled or frozen sauce, 180
  buying and using, 254–55
  cooking chart, 59–64
  defrosting, 256–58
  ground, basics, 320–21
  less tender cubes, basics, 289–90
  meal planning, 603
  onions stuffed with, 446
  pilaf, 202
  refrigerated sliced, reheating doneness, 49
  rice salad with, 197
  rules of thumb for cooking times, 53–54
  scrambled eggs and, 150
  sliced, flour tortillas with, 273
  smoky beans with, 433–34
  tender-cut chunks, basics, 286–87
  tender strips, basics, 283
  tomato sauce, 180–81

meat (*cont.*)
  see also beef; ham; lamb; pork; sausage; veal
meatballs, 328–29
meat loaf, 330–32
Mediterranean tomatoes, 422
melted butters, 183, 247
melted cheese and crackers, 102–4
melting:
  cheese, 161
  chocolate, 593, 607
menus, 604
meringue pie, lemon, 561–62
metal:
  dishes, 29, 32
  as shield, 31
Mexicali beans, 434
Mexicali zucchini pie, 471
Mexican dishes:
  cauliflower or broccoli salad, 399–400
  chicken wings, 358
  filled potatoes, 453
  fish fillets with almond-cilantro sauce, 217
  leeks, 447
  pots de crème, 572
  rice, 202
microwave cooking, 17–39
  browning in, 29–30
  cooking from outside to inside in, 20–22
  covers in, 27–28
  dish temperature in, 27
  energy converted to surface heat in, 22
  food arrangement in, 23, 38–39
  metal as shield in, 31
  metal dishes in, 29, 32
  oven or stove cooking vs., 17–18, 30
  oven's cooking pattern in, 24, 25
  ring rule in, 38–39
  rotating dishes in, 24
  safety in, 37
  sparking and arcing in, 32
  standing time in, 35–36
  starting temperature in, 24–25, 26
  stirring in, 22–23
  sunlight analogy for, 19
  surface area of food in, 26
  turning over food in, 23
  utensils for, 81–86
  volume principle in, 32–33
  wave frequency in, 18, 19
  see also cooking time
Milano mushrooms with basil, 440
milk, extending shelf life of, 608
mincemeat ice cream pie, 562
mint:
  salsa cruda, 248
  sauce, 276
  shepherd's pie with, 274
mixed wok-style vegetables, 481–82

mocha:
  cream glaze, 512
  cream pie, 559
  mousse, 579
  pots de crème, 572
  sauce, hot, 564
mock brown broth or stock, 119
mock lobster broccoli and cauliflower platter, 481
Moghul rice with ground lamb, 200
Mornay sauce, 171
mousse, 577–81
  amaretto, 579
  basics, 577
  cake, two-tiered chocolate, 580–81
  grapefruit, 577–79
  hazelnut, 579
  lemon, 579
  lime, 579
  luscious chocolate, 579
  mocha, 579
  white chocolate, 579
mozzarella:
  cubed eggplant, tomato, and peppers topped with, 419
  eggplant, and tomato sandwiches, 418–19
muffins:
  basics, 516–17
  bran, 518
  cooking times for, 517
mulled wine jelly, 502
Münchner liver dumpling soup, 137–38
mushroom(s), 438–41
  basics, 438
  beef, and tomato kabobs, 288
  braised chuck steak with, 283
  brandied shrimp with, 113
  breaded vegetables and, 441
  bread stuffing, 349
  caps au naturel, 439–40
  cooking chart, 72
  cottage cheese timbales, 160
  crab-stuffed, 112
  creamy, fish fillets with, 220
  daube aux champignons, 295
  goulash with, 293
  long-grain rice with, 197
  pâté, 98
  pita pizzas, 102
  potatoes filled with, 453
  risotto with, 203
  sautéed, 439
  sautéed, onions stuffed with, 446
  shepherd's pie with, 274
  shirred eggs with, 147
  stuffed, 440
  stuffing for braised whole fish, 232
  tomato fish fillets cooked in paper, 222
  toppings for, 439

mushroom sauce, 172-73, 361
  company braised fish with, 231
  meatballs with, 329
  tomato-meat, 181
mushroom soups, 132-33
  basics, 129
  cream, 133
mussel(s):
  and apple salad, chilled, 227
  basics, 241
  chilled steamed, with herb sauce, 110
  cooking chart, 59
  steamed, 241-42
  with tartar sauce, 110
mustard:
  cheddar soup, 134
  Dijon, meat loaf, 331
  dressing, 184
  glaze, 310
  honey glaze, 347
  pecan mayonnaise, chicken cutlets coated with, 366
  and peppercorn coating, leg of lamb with, 277
  pork roast with, 271-72
  sautéed stalks flavored with, 477
  shrimp in, potatoes filled with, 453
mustard greens:
  cooking chart, 71
  sautéed, 429-30
mustard sauce(s), 171, 236, 361
  butter, 183
  chops in, 303-4
  cream, 240, 461
  dill, chilled, 176
  honey, 352
  pecan, 346
  poached eggs with, 144
  quick, 448, 461

N

nachos, cheese, 103-4
Navarin, lamb, 296
nectarine upside-down cake, 519
New England ragout with turnips, 291
New Yankee cheese soufflé, 155-56
noodle(s):
  chicken slivers with vegetables and, 369
  chocolate clusters, 597
  refrigerated, reheating doneness, 49
  see also pasta
nut(s):
  brittle, 588
  butter, 247
  butterscotch pudding, 558
  caramel corn with, 590
  chocolate clusters, 597
  chocolate fudge, no-fail, 593
  chopped liver spread, 94-95
  crumb crust, 545
  crunch, 589
  egg pastry dough, 542
  frosted, 589-90
  glazed onions with, 443
  hard-cooked egg spread, 149
  leeks topped with, 447
  poached winter fruits with, 494
  raisin bread pudding, 569-70
  'n' raisin brown rice salad, 199
  rice pilaf with, 202
  rich chocolate cake with, 511
  spiced frosted, 590
  spicy, 100
  squash puree, 467
  stefado with, 294
  toasting, 608
  zucchini bread, 529
  see also specific nuts
nutmeg:
  cream sauce scented with, 398
  hard sauce with, 535
  whipped cream, poached pears with, 490
  white sauce scented with, 397
nut stuffing(s):
  for braised whole fish, 232
  bread, 349
  onions with, 446

O

oatmeal raspberry bars, 532
olive ham and cheese rolls, 105
omelets:
  basic, 151-52
  dessert, 153
  fillings for, 152
  puffy, 152-53
  puffy ricotta cheese, 154
onion(s), 441-46
  basics, 442
  basil, and peppers, Italian, 95
  Burgundy sauce, 333
  cheddar topping, Italian sand dollars with, 96-97
  with cheese sauce, 444
  cooking chart, 72-73
  creamed, 444
  cream sauce with nutmeg and, 398
  French, potatoes filled with, 453
  glazed, 443
  red, and beef strip salad, 261
  rings, spirited, 281
  sautéed, beans with butter and, 433
  stuffed, 444-46
  tear-free, 443

onion(s) (cont.)
  tomatoes topped with, 422, 423
  toppings for, 443
open-face sandwiches:
  hot fish salad, 228
  toasted cheese, 164–65
orange(s):
  applesauce flavored with, 493
  butter, 183
  cake, 508
  canned ham glazed with, 311
  carrot soup flavored with, 126
  cheesecake, 576
  chocolate-covered, 596
  chocolate truffles, 598
  egg custards, 572
  frosting, 509
  glaze, 313
  honey squash puree, 467
  marmalade, 500–501
  peel, drying, 608
  segments, poached pears with, 490
  sweet potato boats flavored with, 454
orange sauces, 385
  cranberry, 187
  shimmering, 159
  sweet and sour, 182
Oriental dishes:
  bluefish, 226
  brown rice salad, 199
  chicken salad, 373
  chicken wings, 108–9
  dressing, 184
  dressing, chilled leeks with, 448
  fish fillets cooked in paper, 222
  ham and vegetables over rice, 314
  long-grain rice, 197
  marinated beef or lamb kabobs, 287–88
  pork and broccoli, 275
  pork roast, 272
  vegetable kabobs, 483–84
  see also Japanese dishes
ovens, conventional:
  microwave oven vs., 17–18
  when to use, 30

P

Pacific carrot cake, 513–14
pancakes, reheating, 608
pancake syrup, reheating, 608
pan drippings gravy, 173
Parmesan cheese:
  breaded fish fillets, 220
  chicken cutlets Parmigiana, 365
  leeks with, 447
  ratatouille alla Parmigiana, 421
  stuffed onions with, 446
  summer squash with, 470
parsley:
  butter, 183
  cheese tomato sauce, 179
  potato soup, 124
parsnips, cooking chart for, 74
pasta:
  boiled beef with, in broth, 266
  lasagna, 206–7
  macaroni and cheese, 207
  tomato sauce with liver over, 334
  wok-style vegetables over, 482
  see also noodle
pastel-coated fruit, 597
pastry cream, 555–56
  basics, 555
  for tarts, 556
pastry crust, browning, 30
pastry dough, 541–42
  basics, 540–41
  pie shell, 542–43
pâté, mushroom, 98
pattypan squash:
  cooking chart, 75
  stuffed, 472–73
pea(s), split:
  cooking chart, 72
  puree, 435
  soup, 435
peach(es):
  brandy soup, 138
  crumble, 555
  peeling, 497
  poached, 490
  shortcake, 509
  soup with yogurt, 138
  tartlets with raspberry sauce, 553
  upside-down cake, 519
peach sauces:
  for ice cream, 496
  mustard, 346
  piquant, 496
peanut:
  chocolate squares, double, 599
  satay sauce, 182–83
  satay sauce, skewered chicken with, 369–70
peanut butter:
  cheesecake, 576
  chocolate clusters, 597
  chocolate fudge, no-fail, 593
  chocolate squares, 598–99
  fudge, 592
  natural, making spreadable, 608
pear(s):
  on pear-shaped tart shells, 552–53

peas (*continued*)
- poached, 488-90
- tartlets with raspberry sauce, 553

peas, green, 407
- basics, 411
- blanching, 407
- and carrots, 412
- cooking chart, 70
- de menthe, 411
- lamb ragout with snow peas and, 296
- minted, onions stuffed with, 446
- onions stuffed with carrots and, 446
- risotto with snow peas and, 203
- and snow peas, 412
- toppings for, 408

peas, snow, *see* snow peas

peas, sugar snap, cooking chart for, 70

pecan(s):
- bourbon ice cream pie, 563
- cheese Ritz, 103
- chicken cutlets with, 365
- chicken cutlets with raspberry sauce, 366
- mustard mayonnaise, chicken cutlets coated with, 366
- rum sweet potato boats, 454
- shelling, 608-9
- tartlets, fluted, 549

peel, lemon or orange, drying, 608

peeling:
- peaches, 497
- tomatoes, 186, 609

pepper(s), 416
- basil, and onions, Italian, 95
- beef strip salad with, 261
- braised chuck steak with tomatoes and, 283
- cooking chart, 70
- cubed eggplant, and tomato topped with mozzarella, 419
- green, tomatoes topped with, 423
- Italian veal stew with, 295-96
- red and green, goulash with, 293
- red and green, timbales, 158
- stuffed, 423, 425-26
- tomato pasta sauce with liver and, 334
- *see also* hash, corn and pepper

peppercorn:
- green, sauce, 272, 385
- and mustard coating, leg of lamb with, 277

pesto-coated ricotta cheese timbales, 159-60

picadillo, 325

picante grits and cheese casserole, 194

pickled ginger, 99

pies:
- apple crumb, 545-46
- apple crumble, 554-55
- chocolate pudding, 558-59
- coconut joy, 560-61
- graham cracker crust for, 544-45
- lemon, with whipped cream, 562
- lemon meringue, 561
- Mexicali zucchini, 471
- peach crumble, 555
- potato, 458-59
- potpies, 370-72
- pumpkin, 554
- shepherd's, 274
- Southwestern, 323-24
- summer squash, 470-71
- sweet potato, 459
- warming slices of, 609
- *see also* cream pies; ice cream pies

pies, double-crust:
- with canned fruit pie filling, 547, 548
- with fresh berries or cherries, 547
- fruit, basics, 546
- rhubarb, 547
- sugar-glazed apple, 547
- testimonial apple, 546-48

pie shells:
- basic recipe, 542-43
- crumb crusts, 544-45
- pastry dough, 540-42

pilaf:
- basics, 201
- meat, chicken, or seafood, 202
- rice, 201-2

pimiento-studded vegetable platter, 479

pineapple:
- bread stuffing, 349
- canned ham glazed with, 311
- chicken salad with, 373
- cranberry sauce, 187
- glaze, 314
- long-grain rice, 197
- rings, warm fresh, 495
- sherry glaze, 348
- sweet potato boats, 453
- sweet potato salad, 456

pine nuts:
- spinach with, 429
- stuffed artichokes with, 395

piquant peach sauce, 496

pistachio chocolate cups, frozen, 564-65

pita:
- pizzas, 102
- sandwiches with beef, lamb, or pork, 272
- triangles, flavored, 97

pizza(s):
- browning, 30
- frozen, reheating, 609
- pita, 102
- slices, reheating, 609

plum(s):
- poached, 491
- upside-down cake, 519

plum pudding:
  English, 533–34
  sauce, 534
poached dishes:
  cod in cream sauce Dijonnais, 224
  shrimp, 235
  thick fish fillets, 223–24
  whole chicken, 341–43
  whole trout with lemon butter, 232–33
  see also eggs, poached; fruit, poached
polenta, 194–95
  basics, 193
  cheese, 195
polished rice, 195
popcorn, 106–7
pork:
  barbecuing, 309
  and beef ragout, 291
  and broccoli, Oriental, 275
  butt, glazed, 313
  buying and using, 255–56
  cooking chart, 62–64
  cubes, chili with, 298
  fully cooked, basics, 310–11
  green chili, 298–99
  less tender cubes, basics, 289–90
  loin, braised, cordon bleu, 306
  loin, roast, 270–72
  marinated, salad, 274–75
  pita sandwiches with, 272
  ribs, basics, 306–7
  satay, 288–89
  sliced, flour tortillas with, 273
  spareribs, blazing, 308–9
  sweet and sour, 275
  tender-cut chunks, basics, 286–87
  see also bacon; ham; sausage
pork chops:
  basics, 300–301
  breaded, 301–2
  with fresh tomato sauce, 302–3
  in mustard sauce, 303–4
  smoked, sauerkraut with, 316–17
port, poached plums with, 491
potassium, blood pressure and, 450
potato(es), 449–59
  boiled, basics, 454
  braised chuck steak with carrots and, 283
  chips, refreshing, 609
  colcannon, 483
  cooking chart, 73
  lamb ragout with, 296
  mashed, 457
  meal planning and, 603
  pies, 458–59
  rules of thumb for cooking times, 51
  rumbledethumps, 483
  salads, 455–56

  slices, boiled, 454
  soups, 124–25
  stuffed, 451–53
  whole, basics, 449–50
  see also sweet potato
potato(es), new:
  appetizers, 101
  buttered, with parsley, 457–58
  cooking chart, 73
  salad, 455
  steamed, 458
potpies:
  basics, 370
  new American chicken or turkey, 371–72
pots de crème, 572
poultry, 337–88
  browning, 30
  cooking chart, 64–67
  defrosting, 339–41
  freezing, 339
  fresh, buying and storing, 338
  glazes for, 347–48
  stuffings for, 349–51
  see also chicken; chicken liver; Cornish game hen; duck; turkey
pound cakes, 522–23
power, cooking time and, 20–21
praline bourbon sauce, 564
pretzel(s):
  chocolate clusters, 597
  chocolate-coated, 597
  refreshing, 609
Provolone-stuffed breast of veal, 305
prune:
  bread stuffing, 349
  drunken, sauce, 385
  sauce, 385
pudding pie, chocolate, 558–59
puddings, 557–58
  basics, 557
  butterscotch, 558
  butterscotch-nut, 558
  café au lait, 558
  chocolate, 558
  corn, with jalapeño salsa, 409
  English plum, 533–34
  figgy, 534
  Indian, 573–74
  individual rice custards, 574
  rice, 566–68
  tapioca, 558
  vanilla, 558
  see also bread puddings; egg custards, sweetened
puffy omelets, 152–54
  basics, 152–53
  dessert, 153
  ricotta cheese, 154

pumpkin:
    bread, 530
    cooking chart, 75
    egg custards, 572–73
    pie, in ginger crust, 554
    soup, creamy dilled, 128–29
pumpkin seeds, toasted, 468
purees:
    lentil, 435
    pea, 435
    root vegetable, 464
    savory carrot, 464–65
    winter squash, 466–67

R

raclette, cheese, 164
radiation, 17, 18
ragouts:
    beef, 290–91
    lamb, 296
raisin(s):
    baked apples with, 492
    chocolate clusters, 597
    East Indian rice with, 200
    marshmallow cereal squares, 600
    mushrooms studded with, 440
    nut bread pudding, 569–70
    'n' nut brown rice salad, 199
    picadillo with, 325
    plumping, for cooking, 609
    rice tomatoes, 424
    softening, for eating, 609
rarebit sandwiches, 162
raspberry:
    cream pie, 559
    jam, 501
    oatmeal bars, 532
raspberry sauce(s), 367
    black, 566
    for fresh fruit or sherbet, 565–66
    peach tartlets with, 553
    pear tartlets with, 553
    poached pears with, 490
raspberry vinegar:
    cranberry sauce with, 188
    quick, 366
ratatouille, 421–22
    potatoes filled with, 453
recipes:
    converting, 77
    cutting in half, 35
    doubling, 34
red cabbage, braised sweet and sour, 400–401
red onion and beef strip salad, 261
red pepper(s):
    goulash with green peppers and, 293
    and green pepper timbales, 158
red wine:
    baked apples in, 492
    beef rolls with, 300
    chuck steak braised in, 283
    sauce, buttered, 261
    veal daube with, 295
refried beans with cheese, 434
reheating:
    appetizers, 93
    burgers, 328
    frozen pizza, 609
    one serving of soup, 129
    pancakes, 608
    pancake syrup, 608
    pizza slices, 609
    tortillas, 609
reheating doneness, 43–50
    bread, 49–50
    frozen casseroles, 45, 46
    frozen soups and sauces, 47
    miscellaneous, 50
    refrigerated and room temperature soups and sauces, 47
    refrigerated casseroles, 44–45, 46
    refrigerated individual plates, 48
    refrigerated rice and noodles, 49
    refrigerated sliced meats, 49
    room temperature individual plates, 48
Reuben sandwiches, 269
rhubarb:
    double-crust pie, 547
    sauce, candied, 498
ribs, golden barbecued, 109
rice, 195–205
    basics, 196
    basmati, 195, 198
    brown, 195, 199
    and chicken casserole, 359
    chicken slivers with vegetables and, 369
    cooked, 425
    cooking chart, 56–57
    cooking two servings of, 198
    dressing, 351
    East Indian, 200
    glossary of terms for, 195
    grape leaves stuffed with, 203–4
    long-grain, 196–97
    meal planning and, 603
    Moghul, with ground lamb, 200
    onions stuffed with, 446
    Oriental ham and vegetables over, 314
    peppers stuffed with, 426
    pilaf, 201–2
    raisin tomatoes, 424
    refrigerated, reheating doneness, 59
    risotto, 201, 202–3
    salads, 197, 199

rice (cont.)
  stuffing with nuts and raisins, 351
  subgum Chinese, 205
  tomatoes stuffed with, 424
  tomato soup, 130
  vegetarian, single serving, 205
  wild, 195, 199–200
rice puddings, 566–68
  basics, 566
  custard, 567–68, 574
  Hawaiian rice and cream, 568
  traditional, 567
ricotta cheese:
  puffy omelet, 154
  timbales, pesto-coated, 159–60
ring rule, 38–39
risotto, 202–3
  basics, 201
Riviera-style scallops, 239–40
rolls:
  beef, simmered, 299
  fish fillet, with almond filling, 221
  veal, simmered, 300
rollups, lightly breaded ham and cheese, 105
root vegetable(s), 460–65
  basics, 460
  cooking chart, 73–74
  julienned, 461
  puree, 464
  toppings for, 461
  see also beet; carrot
rose sauce(s), 172
  cream, 361
  herb, 172
  mushroom, 173
  puffy ricotta cheese omelet with, 154
rum:
  pecan sweet potato boats, 454
  squash puree with, 467
rumbledethumps, 483
rutabagas, cooking chart, 74

S

safety precautions, 37
saffron:
  cream sauce, 240, 361
  rice pilaf, 202
  risotto with, 203
sage sausage patties, 320
salad(s):
  beef strip and red onion, 261
  breaded warm cheese with, 162–63
  chicken, 372–74
  chilled Japanese bluefish, 226
  chilled mussel and apple, 227
  chilled scallion, 448

chilled summer bean, 435
corned beef, with horseradish dressing, 268
egg, individual sandwich filling, 149
ham, spread, 315
low-calorie carrot and beet, 463
marinated pork, 274–75
Mexican cauliflower or broccoli, 399–400
potato, 455–56
rice, 197, 199
turkey, 380
wilted greens, 430
winter carrot or beet, 463
salmon:
  Coho, chilled individual, with chilled sauces, 231
  with crab sauce, 223–24
  with herb butter, 224
  pea pods stuffed with, 99
  steaks, with salmon-colored sauce, 229–30
salsa(s):
  clams, 111
  cruda, 185
  cumin, 186
  dill, cruda, 248
  green tomato, 186
  jalapeño, 248
  ranchera, 146
  rosa, 220
  warm jalapeño, 187
salsify, cooking chart for, 74
sand dollars:
  Italian, with cheddar-onion topping, 96–97
  with Italian basil, peppers, and onions, 97
sandwiches:
  browning, 30
  caper-sparked eggplant, 419
  cheese steak, 281
  corned beef, 269
  eggplant, mozzarella, and tomato, 418–19
  hot open-face fish salad, 228
  individual egg salad filling for, 149
  pita, with beef, lamb, or pork, 272
  rarebit, 162
  Reuben, 269
  roast beef, 261
  see also cheese sandwiches
satay:
  beef, pork, or lamb, 288–89
  sauce, peanut, 182–83
  sauce, peanut, skewered chicken with, 369–70
sauces:
  aioli, 175–76
  amaretto, 563–64
  apple cream, 361
  apricot, 385, 566
  avgolemono, 205
  barbecue, 181
  béarnaise, 174
  beer, 318

berry, 497–98
black raspberry, 566
bourbon-praline, 564
brandy, 279–80
Burgundy, 330
Burgundy-onion, 333
Burgundy-scallion, 261
buttered red wine, 261
butterscotch, 565
candied rhubarb, 498
candied rhubarb strawberry, 498
caper, 280
cheese, 397
cherry, 312
chilled cilantro bread, 245
chilled fresh herb, 176
chunky cucumber, 218
citrus, 498–99
cocktail, 247
cooked egg emulsion, basics, 173–74
crab, 245
cranberry, 187–88, 385
cream, with onion and nutmeg, 398
Cumberland, 278
currant, 566
curry, 171, 246
curry cream, 361
Dijonnais cream, 224
dried fruit, 385
drunken prune, 385
flour- or cornstarch-thickened, basics, 170–71
fresh ginger, 243–44
frozen, reheating doneness, 47
golden cream, 225
green, 177
green peppercorn, 272, 385
hard, 535
herb, 171, 361
herbed cream, 461
herb yogurt, 273
Hollandaise, 174
honey-mustard, 352
horseradish cream, 273
hot fudge, 564
hot mocha, 564
hot pepper butter, 355
Indian yogurt, 362
intoxicating, 361
lemon or lime cream, 361
Maltaise, 174
mayonnaise, 175, 176
mint, 276
Mornay, 171
mushroom, 172–73, 361
mustard, 171, 236, 361, 448
mustard cream, 240, 461
mustard pecan, 346
nutmeg-scented cream, 398
nutmeg-scented white, 397
orange, 385
peach, for ice cream, 496
peanut satay, 182–83
piquant peach, 496
plum pudding, 534
prune, 385
raspberry, 366, 565–66
refrigerated and room temperature, reheating doneness, 47
rose, 172
rose cream, 361
saffron cream, 240, 361
sherried duck, 385
sherry cream, 171
shimmering orange, 159
sorrel, 244
spinach, 244
sweet and sour apricot, 182
tartar, 246
tips for, 170
walnut-brandy, 564
watercress, 244
whipped herb cream, 177
white, 171
whole berry, 498
wine, 318
see also butter; dressings; glazes; gravies; salsa; tomato sauce; vinaigrette
sauerbraten, 264–65
sauerkraut:
    goulash with, 293
    with sausage, 317
    with smoked pork chops, 316–17
sausage:
    baked beans and franks, 438
    cabbage stuffed with, 402–3
    cooking chart, 61–62
    Deutsch melted cheese and, 103
    franks in beer, 318
    fully cooked, 256, 317–18
    grilled fresh, 319
    patties, fresh, 319–20
    patties, rules of thumb for cooking times, 54
    peppers stuffed with, 426
    pita pizzas, 102
    sauerkraut with, 317
    smoked bratwurst in beer or wine sauce, 318
    stuffing, 350
    with sweet and sour sauce, 108
    tomatoes stuffed with, 424
    tomato sauce, 181
sautéed:
    chicken livers, 387
    cucumbers, 426
    mushrooms, 439
    mushrooms, onions stuffed with, 446
    shredded cabbage, 400

sautéed (cont.)
  stalks, 476–77
  summer squash, 469–70
savory carrot puree, 464–65
scallion(s):
  basics, 446
  braised, 448
  Burgundy sauce, 261
  cooking chart, 73
  potato soup, 124–25
scallop(s), 238–40
  appetizers with golden caviar, 240
  basics, 238–39
  cooking chart, 58
  in mustard cream sauce, 240
  risotto with, 203
  rules of thumb for cooking times, 54
  with sesame seed topping, 239–40
  stuffing, won tons with, in basil butter, 90–91
Scandinavian veal stew with dill, 295
scrambled eggs, 149–50
  and bacon tomatoes, 424
seafood, 211–49
  cooking chart, 57–59
  pilaf, 202
  rules of thumb for cooking times, 54
  see also fish; shellfish; specific seafood
seasonal vegetable platter with herbed butter, 478–479
seeds, pumpkin or squash, toasted, 468
sesame sautéed asparagus, 476
sesame seed(s):
  chicken coated with, 365
  pita triangles topped with, 97
  toasting, 609
  topping, scallops with, 239–40
shallot garlic butter, 183
shellfish, 233–44
  browning, 30
  buying, 213
  defrosting, 213–14
  soup, simple, 121
  storing, 213
  see also clam; crab; lobster tails; mussel; scallop; shrimp; squid
shelling pecans or walnuts, 608–9
shepherd's pie, 274
sherry:
  pineapple glaze, 348
  root puree, 464
  tomato soup, 130
sherry sauces:
  cream, 171
  duck, 385
  mushroom, 173
shimmering carrot timbales, 157–58
shimmering orange sauce, 159
shirred eggs, 146–47

shortbread triangles, flaky, 543–44
shortcake, strawberry, 509
shrimp:
  basics, 234–35
  brandied, 113
  cooking chart, 58–59
  crab-stuffed, 237–38
  defrosting, 214
  in mustard-filled potatoes, 453
  in mustard sauce, 236
  poached, 235
  rules of thumb for cooking times, 54
  spicy, in beer, 236–37
  stuffing for braised whole fish, 232
Sicilian artichokes with tomatoes, 396
simmered:
  beef rolls, 299–300
  veal rolls, 300
simmerpots, 86
skewered dishes:
  chicken with peanut satay sauce, 369–70
  satay chicken with vegetables, 370
  see also kabobs
sloppy Joes, 325
smoked:
  bratwurst, in beer or wine sauce, 318
  pork chops, sauerkraut with, 316–17
  turkey, and cheese rolls, 105
smoky beans with meat, 433–34
snacks, see appetizers and snacks
snow peas:
  chicken slivers with, 369
  cooking chart, 70
  lamb ragout with peas and, 296
  peas and, 412
  risotto with peas and, 203
  stuffed, 98–99
softened butter, 184
softening:
  brown sugar, 607
  butter, 607
  cheese, 161
  cream cheese, 607
  ice cream, 608
  jams and jellies, 608
  raisins or dried fruit, 609
sorrel:
  cooking chart, 71
  potato soup, 125
  sauce, 244
soufflés, 154–56
  basics, 154–55
  Bourbon Street, 581–82
  New Yankee cheese, 155–56
soups, 117–38
  Austrian goulash, 136–37
  best cooked on medium power, basics, 134
  catch of the day, 121

cauliflower, 127
cereal, 122–23
cheddar cheese, 133–34
chicken liver dumpling, 138
corn, with jalapeño salsa, 121–22
frozen, reheating doneness, 47
Greek lemon, 136
lentil, 435
Lida's peach-brandy, 138
Manhattan clam chowder, 134–35
Münchner liver dumpling, 137–38
mushroom, 129, 132–33
orange-flavored carrot, 126
pea, 435
peach, with yogurt, 138
potato, 124–25
refrigerated and room temperature, reheating doneness, 47
reheating one serving of, 129
simple shellfish, 121
sweet Spanish almond, 135
vegetable, 120, 123
victory garden beet, 126–27
see also broths and stocks; tomato soups
soups, cream:
asparagus, 128
broccoli or cauliflower, 127
broccoli or cauliflower cheese, 127
corn, 122
mushroom, 133
tomato, 130–31
tomato-basil, chilled, 131
soups, creamy:
broccoli, 127
broccoli or cauliflower cheese, 127
dilled pumpkin, 128–29
dilled squash, 129
sour cream:
beef ragout with, 291
cereal soup with, 123
gravy, 282–83
lamb ragout with, 296
Southern-style squash puree, 467
Southwestern dishes:
corn and pepper hash, 410
pie, 323–24
potato salad, 456
soy stir-'n'-shake stalks, 477
soya sautéed greens, 429
spaghetti squash, cooking chart, 75
Spanish fish with vegetables in salsa rosa, 220
Spanish sweet almond soup, 135
sparking, 32
spiced:
breaded warm cheese with salad, 163
hot popcorn, 107
Italian ribs with tomato sauce, 308
nuts, 100

pasta sauce with liver, 334
poached pears, 490
poached plums, 491
pureed tomato sauce, 180
shrimp in beer, 236–37
toasted seeds, 468
tomato soup, 130
spinach:
cooking chart, 71
dumplings, Emerald Isle, 430–31
dumplings with tomato sauce, 431
meat loaf with, 332
onions stuffed with, 446
potato soup, 125
sauce, 244
sauce, fish fillets with, 217
sautéed, 428–29
tomatoes stuffed with, 424
spiral candy, 587
spirited onion rings, 281
spreads:
chopped liver, 94–95
ham salad, 315
hard-cooked egg, 148–49
springtime vegetable platter, 479
squash, 465–73
onions stuffed with, 446
stuffed, 471–73
squash, summer, 469–71
with almonds, 470
basics, 469
cooking chart, 74–75
with Parmesan, 470
pie, 470–71
sautéed, 469–70
with tomatoes, 470
toppings for, 469
see also zucchini
squash, winter, 465–68
basics, 465–66
cooking chart, 75
purees, 466–67
toppings for, 466
see also acorn squash
squash seeds, toasted, 468
squid:
basics, 242
defrosting, 214
in fresh ginger sauce, 243–44
in tomato sauce, 243
stalks, 473–77
arranged, basics, 473–74
broccoli, with lemon slices, 475–76
cooking chart, 76
sautéed, 476–77
toppings for, 474
see also asparagus; broccoli
standing time, 35–36

starting temperature, 24–25, 26
steak, *see* beefsteak
steamed:
　clams or mussels, 241–42
　lima or fava beans, 416
　mussels with herb sauce, chilled, 110
　new potatoes, 458
steamed cakes and breads, 532–35
　basics, 532–33
　Boston brown bread, 534–35
　English plum pudding, 533–34
　figgy pudding, 534
stefado, beef on veal, 294
stews:
　beef or veal stefado, 294
　beef ragout, 290–91
　boeuf bourguignon, 291–92
　carbonnades a la flamande, 292
　chili with cubed beef, 297–98
　chili with pork cubes, 298
　doubling recipe, 34
　green chili, 298–99
　Hungarian goulash, 293
　lamb ragout, 296
　simmered beef rolls, 299–300
　simmered veal rolls, 300
　veal daube, 294–95
　veal or lamb curry, 297
stirrer blades, 24
stirring, 22–23
stir-shake, *see* vegetable stir-shake
stocks, *see* broths and stocks
storing:
　eggs, 141
　fish and seafood, 212, 213
　fresh poultry, 338
strawberry(ies):
　chocolate-covered, 596
　cream pie, 559
　jam, 501
　rhubarb sauce, candied, 498
　shortcake, 509
　trifle with, 557
　in wine, 495–96
Stroganoff, beef, 285
stuffed:
　artichokes, 395
　breast of lamb, 305
　breast of veal, 304–5
　cabbage, 401–5
　eggplant, 420–22
　grape leaves, 203–4
　loin of veal cordon bleu, braised, 305–6
　mushrooms, 440
　onions, 444–46
　peppers, 423, 425–26
　potatoes, 451–53
　snow pea pods, 98–99
　squash, 471–73
　sweet potato boats, 453–54
　tomatoes, 423–24
stuffing(s):
　bread, 349
　for braised whole fish, 232
　Cornish game hens, 347
　rice, 351
　sausage, veal, or turkey, 350
　Waldorf, 350
subgum Chinese rice, 205
succotash, 410
sugar:
　browning and, 30
　candy, 586–87
　carrot timbales coated with, 158
　double-crust apple pie glazed with, 547
　see also brown sugar
summer fruit tart, large, 549–50
summer squash, *see* squash, summer
summer vegetable platter, 479
sunflower marshmallow cereal squares, 600
surface area of food, 26
Swedish meatballs, 329
sweet:
　lemon pastry dough, 542
　Spanish almond soup, 135
　spicy squash puree, 467
sweet and sour:
　beets, 462
　braised red cabbage, 400–401
　chilled chicken wings, 109
　marinade, 352
　meatballs, 329
　pork, 275
　sauce, apricot, 182
　sauce, sausage with, 108
　stuffed cabbage leaves, 405
sweet potato(es):
　boats, 453–54
　cooking chart, 73
　pies, 459
　salads, 455
　shepherd's pie with, 274
　toppings for, 451
Swiss beef rolls, 300
Swiss chard, cooking chart for, 71, 76

T

tacos:
　beef-filled, 324–25
　chicken, 375
　heating, 609
tangerine butter, 183
tapioca pudding, 558
tarragon butter, 183

tartar sauce, 246
tartlets:
   fluted pecan, 549
   fluted walnut, 548–49
   peach, with raspberry sauce, 553
   pear, with raspberry sauce, 553
tarts, 549–53
   apple pizza, 551
   flat pastry, basics, 549
   fresh berry, 551–52
   large summer fruit, 549–50
   pastry cream for, 556
   pear, on pear-shaped tart shells, 552–53
temperature:
   of dishes, 27
   probes, 84–85
   starting, 24–25, 26
teriyaki, beef, 284
testimonial double-crust apple pie, 546–48
Tetrazzini, turkey or chicken, 381–82
Thai chicken, 376
Tijuana avocado egg creams, 572
timbales, 156–60
   asparagus, 158
   basics, 156–57
   broccoli, 158
   chicken, 158
   green and red pepper, 158
   ham, 158
   mushroom-cottage cheese, 160
   ricotta cheese, pesto-coated, 159–60
   shimmering carrot, 157
   sugar-coated carrot, 158
   zucchini, 158
toasted:
   coconut strips, 377
   nuts, 608
   pumpkin or squash seeds, 468
   sesame seeds, 609
tofu-vegetable casserole, 419
tomato(es), 416, 422–24
   beef, and mushroom kabobs, 288
   braised chuck steak with peppers and, 283
   brown sugar 'n' bacon, 422
   cheese sandwich, open-face toasted, 165
   cooking chart, 70
   cubed beef chili with, 298
   cubed eggplant, and peppers topped with mozzarella, 419
   eggplant, and mozzarella sandwiches, 418–19
   fragrant whole, 422–23
   green, salsa, 186
   marinade for kabobs, 288
   Mediterranean, 422
   mushroom fish fillets cooked in paper, 222
   peeling, 186, 609
   sauerbraten with, 265
   Sicilian artichokes with, 396
   single serving, 423
   stefado with, 294
   stuffed, 423–24
   summer squash with, 470
   toppings for, 423
   whole, onion-topped, 422
   whole, scented with oregano, 423
tomato sauce(s):
   anchovy, 249
   anchovy, poached fillets with, 223
   basic "batch," 178–79
   basics, 178
   basil, 179
   beef rolls in, 300
   chilled or frozen, adding meat to, 180
   fresh, chops with, 302–3
   Italian, 179
   Italian meatballs in, 329
   Italian ribs with, 308
   meat, 180–81
   meat, with mushrooms, 181
   parsley-cheese, 179
   pasta, with liver, 334
   pureed, 179
   sausage, 181
   spicy pureed, 180
   squid in, 243
   stuffed eggplant in, 420–21
   stuffed grape leaves in, 204
   stuffed pattypan squash with, 473
tomato soups:
   basics, 129
   basil, chilled cream of, 131
   fresh hot, 130–31
   potato, 125
   quick, 132
toppings:
   for corn, peas, green beans, lima beans, and fava beans, 408
   for eggplant slices, 418
   for greens, 428
   for mushrooms, 439
   for onions, 443
   for potatoes, 451
   for root vegetables, 461
   for summer squash, 469
   for tomatoes, 423
   see also butter; dressings; glazes; gravies; salsa; sauces; vinaigrette
tortillas:
   browning, 30
   flour, with sliced meat, 273
   reheating, 609
tostadas, beef-filled, 324–25
triangles:
   chocolate, 594–95
   pita, flavored, 97
trifle with strawberries, 557

trout, poached, 233
truffle cake, 515
truffles (candies), 598
truffles (fungi), mock, and hard-cooked egg spread, 148–49
turkey, 376–82
   a la king, 375
   breast, glazed, 380
   cooking chart, 66
   defrosting, 339–40
   drumsticks, 381
   giblet gravy, 379–80
   giblet stock, 379
   ground, chili, 381
   meat loaf, 332, 381
   potpie, new American, 371–72
   roast, 376–79
   salad, 380
   smoked, and cheese rolls, 105
   stuffing, 350
   Tetrazzini, 381–82
turmeric rice pilaf, 202
turnip greens, cooking chart, 71
turnips:
   cooking chart, 74
   New England ragout with, 291
turtles (candies), 599
two-tiered chocolate mousse cake, 580–81
Tyrolian liver, 333–34

U

upside-down cakes, 518–21
   apple gingerbread, 513
   apricot, 519
   basics, 518
   blueberry, 521
   Cape Cod jewel, 520
   peach or nectarine, 519
   plum, 519
utensils, 81–86
   inventory, 83–84
   special, 84–85
   see also dishes

V

vanilla:
   frosting, 509
   fudge, 592
   pudding, 558
variety brittle, 588
veal:
   braised stuffed loin of, cordon bleu, 305–6
   color of, 255
   curry, 297
   daube, 295–96
   less tender cubes, basics, 289–90
   less tender-cut, basics, 262
   loaf, 332
   pot roast, 263
   roast, marinated, with vegetables, 264
   rolls, simmered, 300
   stefado, 294
   stuffed breast and butterflied loin basics, 304
   stuffed breast of, 304–5
   stuffing, 350
veal chops:
   basics, 300–301
   breaded, 301–2
   with fresh tomato sauce, 302–3
   in mustard sauce, 303–4
vegetable(s), 391–484
   blanched, fondue with, 162
   broth or stock, 119–20
   combinations, 477–84
   dry and fresh, cooking chart, 68–76
   egg added to, for complete protein, 147
   fresh, blanching, 407
   frozen and canned, cooking chart, 67–68
   Japanese, long-grain rice with, 197
   kabobs, 483–84
   meal planning and, 603
   soup, 120
   soup, basics, 123
   tofu casserole, 419
   see also specific vegetables
vegetable platters, arranged, 477–79
   basics, 477
   Japanese, 478
   pimiento-studded, 479
   seasonal, with herbed butter, 478–79
   springtime, 479
   summer, 479
vegetables, marinated, 91–92
   breaded warm cheese with, 163
   brown rice salad with, 199
vegetable stir-shake (wok-style vegetables), 479–82
   basics, 479–80
   brown rice with, 199
   carryover, 480
   green beans and bean sprouts, 414–15
   mixed, 481–82
   mock lobster broccoli and cauliflower platter, 481
   soy stalks, 477
vegetarian dishes:
   chili, 436–37
   rice, single serving, 205
   squash, 473
Vermont fondue, 161–62
Vermont squash puree, 467
vermouth gravy, 260
victory garden beet soup, 126–27

vinaigrette:
   anchovy, 185
   basil, 185
   caper, 185
   chilled leeks in, 447
   herb, 185
   rice salad, 197
vinegar, quick raspberry, 366
vitamins, water-soluble, retaining, 428
volume principle, 32–33

W

Waldorf stuffing, 350
walnut(s):
   apple cake with chocolate cream glaze, 514
   brandy bundt cake, 526
   brandy sauce, 564
   fluted tartlets, 548–49
   shelling, 608–9
washcloths, warm, 307
watercress sauce, 244
wax beans:
   blanching, 407
   cooking chart, 69
whipped cream:
   herb, 177
   nutmeg, poached pears with, 489
white chocolate:
   clusters, 597
   mousse, 579
white-coated fruit, 597
white sauce, 171
whole berry sauce, 498
wholesome cereal soup, 122–23
whole wheat:
   bread pudding, 570
   brownies, 531
   zucchini bread, 529
wild rice, 195, 199–200
wilted greens salad, 430
wine:
   cheddar dip with fruit, 499
   Gorgonzola dip with fruit, 499
   mulled, jelly, 502
   mussels steamed in, 242
   sauce, 318
   sauce, chicken cutlets with, 365
   strawberries in, 495–96
   see also red wine
winter carrot or beet salad, 463
winter squash, *see* squash, winter
wok-style vegetables, *see* vegetable stir-shake
won tons with scallop stuffing in basil butter, 90–91

Y

yellow cake, basic, 507–8
yellow cupcakes, 517
yogurt:
   cereal soup with, 123
   cucumbers, 426
   herb sauce, 273
   Indian sauce, 362
   leeks, chilled, 448
   peach soup with, 138
   rice pudding with fresh fruit and, 568
Yucatan lime fish fillets in paper, 222

Z

zesty julienned beets, 462
zippy meat loaf, 331
zucchini:
   blanching, 407
   cooking chart, 75
   fish fillets with leeks and, in sauce, 220
   and lamb kabobs, 288
   Mexicali pie, 471
   nut bread, 529
   potato soup, curried, 124
   risotto with, 203
   thin fish fillets with, in cream sauce, 218–20
   timbales, 158
   whole-wheat bread, 529
zwieback crust, 545

About the Authors

Thelma Snyder was born in Chicago but grew up in Connecticut. She holds a Master's in Education from Hunter College, New York. Thelma is an award-winning oil painter, who approaches cooking as she would a canvas. She now lives on Long Island with her husband, Dave, and their two children, David and Suzanne.

Marcia Cone was born in Connecticut and grew up in New York and Pennsylvania. She holds a Bachelor of Science (Foods and Nutrition) from Purdue University and a certificate from Le Cordon Bleu in Paris. Travel is an avocation that she has pursued on six continents and it has been a major influence in her food tastes. Marcia resides in Haddonfield, New Jersey.

Thelma and Marcia met in 1976 while working for a microwave manufacturer. In the past few years they have authored *The Microwave French Cookbook* and *The Microwave Italian Cookbook*. They have contributed to articles that have appeared in *Ladies' Home Journal, Redbook,* and *Woman's Day*. Much of their inspiration comes from their food tastings in restaurants and markets in this country and beyond.

CPSIA information can be obtained
at www.ICGtesting.com
Printed in the USA
LVOW03s1601070616
491590LV00007B/309/P

9 781451 667233